Tom Karis

There seem to be no
comfort zones ~~whie~~ for those
who seek to "live among
the truth-tellers".

With deep respect
and appreciation.

SHADES OF
DIFFERENCE

Mac Maharaj

An honor to sign a book for
a person whose scholarship over
decades documents history in a
unique way & is indispensible
who works about South Africa

With great respect
Padraig O'Malley

May. 2007

Also by Padraig O'Malley

Irish Industry: Structure and Performance

The Uncivil Wars: Ireland Today

Biting at the Graves: The Irish Hunger Strikes and the Politics of Despair

Northern Ireland: Questions of Nuance

WORKS EDITED

The AIDS Epidemic: Private Rights and the Public Interest

Uneven Paths: Advancing Democracy in Southern Africa

Southern Africa: The People's Voices

Homelessness: New England and Beyond

WORKS COEDITED

Sticks & Stones: Living with Uncertain Wars

PADRAIG O'MALLEY

SHADES OF DIFFERENCE

MAC MAHARAJ
AND THE STRUGGLE
FOR
SOUTH AFRICA

VIKING

VIKING
Published by the Penguin Group
Penguin Group (USA) Inc., 375 Hudson Street,
New York, New York 10014, U.S.A.
Penguin Group (Canada), 90 Eglinton Avenue East, Suite 700, Toronto,
Ontario, Canada M4P 2Y3 (a division of Pearson Penguin Canada Inc.)
Penguin Books Ltd, 80 Strand, London WC2R 0RL, England
Penguin Ireland, 25 St. Stephen's Green, Dublin 2, Ireland
(a division of Penguin Books Ltd)
Penguin Books Australia Ltd, 250 Camberwell Road, Camberwell,
Victoria 3124, Australia (a division of Pearson Australia Group Pty Ltd)
Penguin Books India Pvt Ltd, 11 Community Centre,
Panchsheel Park, New Delhi – 110 017, India
Penguin Group (NZ), Cnr Airborne and Rosedale Roads, Albany,
Auckland 1310, New Zealand (a division of Pearson New Zealand Ltd)
Penguin Books (South Africa) (Pty) Ltd, 24 Sturdee Avenue,
Rosebank, Johannesburg 2196, South Africa

Penguin Books Ltd, Registered Offices: 80 Strand, London WC2R 0RL, England

First published in 2007 by Viking Penguin, a member of Penguin Group (USA) Inc.

1 3 5 7 9 10 8 6 4 2

Copyright © Padraig O'Malley, 2007
All rights reserved

ISBN 978-0-670-085233-8

Printed in the United States of America
Set in Minion

For Patricia Keefer,
who has accompanied me
on a long journey

Awakening on Friday morning, June 20, 1913, the South African Native found himself, not actually a slave, but a pariah in the land of his birth.

[The Natives' Lands] Act of 1913 decreed, in the name of his Majesty the King, that pending the adoption of a report to be made by a commission, somewhere in the dim and unknown future, it shall be unlawful for Natives to buy or lease land, except in the scheduled Native areas. And under severe pain and penalties they are deprived of the bare human rights of living on the land, except as servants in the employ of whites.

—Sol Plaatje, *Native Life in South Africa*, 1916

Of the heroes we know about, from history or literature, whether it was love they cried forth, or solitude, or vengeance, or the anguish of being or non-being, whether it was humiliation they rose up against, or injustice—of those heroes we do not believe they were ever brought to the point of expressing as their last and only claim an ultimate sense of belonging to the human race.

To say that one felt oneself contested as a man, as a member of the human race—that may look like a feeling discovered in retrospect, an explanation arrived at afterwards. And yet it was that that we felt most constantly and most immediately, and that—exactly that—was what the others wanted. The calling into question of our quality as men provokes an almost biological claim of belonging to the human race. After that it serves to make us think about the limitations of that race, about its distance from "nature" and its relation to "nature"; that is, about a certain solitude that characterizes our race; and finally—above all—to the vision of its indivisible oneness.

—Robert Antelme, *The Human Race*, 1947

CONTENTS

Chronology xiii

FOREWORD BY NELSON MANDELA 1

INTRODUCTION 21

1. CHILDHOOD AND YOUTH 39
Introduction 39   Mac 47

2. DURBAN DAYS 61
Introduction 61   Mac 66

3. LONDON DAYS 76
Introduction 76   Mac 80

4. GDR DAYS 87
Introduction 87   Mac 89

5. GOING HOME 93
Introduction 93   Mac 101

6. DETENTION AND TORTURE 118
Introduction 118   Mac 121

7. LITTLE RIVONIA 137
Introduction 137   Mac 141

8. ROBBEN ISLAND 147
Introduction 147   Mac 158

9. BANNED IN DURBAN 185
Introduction 185   Mac 190

10. LUSAKA AND LONDON 198
Introduction 198   Mac 210

11. VULA: GETTING STARTED 239
Introduction 239   Mac 247

12. HOME AGAIN 260
Introduction 260   Mac 272

13. VULA: CONFLICT IN KWAZULU-NATAL (KZN) 292
Introduction 292   Mac 296

14. MANDELA 300
Introduction 300   Mac 306

15. OUT OF SOUTH AFRICA 314
Introduction 314   Mac 328

16. TRANSITIONS 337
Introduction 337   Mac 346

17. VULA UNRAVELS 365
Introduction 365   Mac 367

18. VULA ON TRIAL 381
Introduction 381   Mac 385

19. INTO THE NEW SOUTH AFRICA 390
Introduction 390   Mac 397

20. BACK IN THE COLD 414
Introduction 414   Mac 439

21. FAMILY: STRUGGLE AND DAMAGE 458
Introduction 458   Mac 467

22. HUSH! APARTHEID THOUGHTS OF A DIFFERENT KIND 469

POSTSCRIPT 493

Acknowledgments 495

Appendix 501

The Web Site 529

Acronyms: Parties and Organizations 531

A Note on Biographies 533

A Note on Interviewees 535

A Note on Mac Maharaj Interviews 537

Notes 541

Bibliography 613

Index 629

CHRONOLOGY

1806   Second British occupation of the Cape.

1807   Britain bans slave trading in the empire.

1834–1838   Slaves emancipated in the Cape.

1843   British annexation of Natal.

1852   British recognition of independent Boer republic (ZAR) in the Transvaal.

1854   British recognition of independent Boer republic (OVS) in the Orange Free State.

1860   Indentured Indian workers begin arriving in Natal.

1867   Diamonds discovered in the confluence of the Vaal and Harts rivers near present-day Kimberley.

1872   Pass laws are introduced to control and manipulate African labor in the diamond mines.

1886   Discovery of gold on the Witwatersrand near present-day Johannesburg.

1899–1902   The South African War (Anglo-Boer War).

1903–1905   A government-appointed labor commission (SANAC) supports the principle of segregation in the workplace.

1904–1907   Chinese workers are imported to work in the gold mines.

1906   Zulu rebellion (led by Chief Bambatha) against poll tax is put down by British troops.

   Gandhi begins passive resistance against discriminatory laws affecting Indians.

1910   The Union of South Africa is formed.

1911   Mines and Works Act reserves certain skilled jobs exclusively for whites.

1912   South African Native National Congress (SANNC) is founded; it is later (1923) renamed the African National Congress (ANC).

1913   Natives' Land Act designates African reserves (7 percent of land is allocated for African people, subsequently increased to

13 percent in 1936). No African can own land outside the reserves.

1914 The National Party is founded.

1920 Native Affairs Act sets up Black Local Authorities (BLAs) on tribal basis.

1921 The Communist Party of South Africa (CPSA) is formed.

1923 Natives (Urban Areas) Act segregates residence in towns.

1927 Native Administration Act sets up a separate Native Affairs Department, later called Bantu Affairs.

1936 White South African women are given the vote.

1941 The African Mine Workers Union (AMWU) is formed.

1944 ANC Youth League (ANCYL) is formed within the ANC.

1946 Massive mine workers' strike is crushed by police.

1948 The National Party wins the whites-only election and becomes the ruling party. D. F. Malan becomes prime minister.

1949 The ANCYL pushes successfully for a Program of Action within the ANC. Prohibition of Mixed Marriages Act is passed.

1950 A rash of apartheid legislation is passed: the Group Areas Act, the Suppression of Communism Act which proscribes the CPSA, the Population Registration Act, the Immorality Act.

1952 The ANC begins its Defiance Campaign. Spearheaded by the ANC, itself pushed by the ANCYL, the Defiance Campaign saw more than 8,500 people courting imprisonment in 1952 for contravening pass laws and curfew regulations, orders segregating whites and nonwhites in railway stations and post offices, and other "petty" apartheid measures. The campaign led to the formation of the Coloured People's Congress, the Congress of Democrats (white), and the Congress Alliance. Nelson Mandela, president of the ANC Youth League, is appointed volunteer in chief of the campaign. See [] general information/documents and reports /[]Defiance Campaign Recalled.

An anti-apartheid Congress Alliance is formed across the race divide.

1953 The Bantu Education Act and the Reservation of Separate Amenities Act are passed. The CPSA is dissolved and reconstituted as the South African Communist Party (SACP), which remains underground.

1955 The Freedom Charter is adopted at the Congress of the People in Kliptown. Forced removals of black people settled in designated "white" residential areas (such as Sophiatown) cause widespread suffering and discontent.

1956   Twenty-thousand women march to the Union Buildings in a mass demonstration against passes.

1956–1961   The Treason Trial begins. The 156 accused are charged with high treason. The trial lasts for five years, during which the charges against all but 34 are put on hold. In 1961 the 34 are acquitted.

1958   Hendrik F. Verwoerd becomes prime minister.

1959   Robert Sobukwe sets up the Pan-Africanist Congress (PAC). The Promotion of Bantu Self-Government Act and the Extension of University Education Act are passed.

1960   On 21 March, 69 people are killed at Sharpeville when police open fire on marchers demonstrating against pass laws. The first state of emergency is declared. More than 11,000 people are detained between 24 August and 31 August. ANC and PAC are banned.

1961   South Africa becomes a republic and leaves the Commonwealth. ANC and PAC go underground, form military wings (MK and Poqo), and set up offices outside the country.

1962   The SACP incorporates colonialism of a special type (CST) into the program it adopts at the 5th Congress held underground in South Africa.

1963–1964   MK high command is arrested in a police swoop at Lilliesleaf Farm in Rivonia. Eight men, including Mandela, are sentenced to life imprisonment.

General Laws Amendment Act empowers police to enforce a 90-day detention term.

1965   Bram Fischer is arrested.

1966   Prime minister Verwoerd is assassinated. He is replaced by B. J. Vorster.

1969   Black Consciousness Movement initiated by Steve Biko gains wide support. He forms the South African Students Organization (SASO).

Bureau of State Security (BOSS) is formed.

1970   The Bantu Homelands Citizens Act is passed, stripping Africans of their South African citizenship by making them automatic citizens of one of the ten "homelands."

1972   State Security Council (SSC) is formed.

1974   Portuguese dictatorship is ousted in a coup.

1975   Mozambique and Angola gain national independence, both under Marxist rule. The South African Defence Force (SADF) invades Angola.

1976 On 16 June, the Soweto uprising begins when police open fire on approximately 10,000 students protesting the use of Afrikaans as a medium of instruction. Resistance spreads nationwide, and during several months there are 575 deaths. Transkei is granted "independence."

1977 KwaZulu is granted self-government; Bophuthatswana is granted "independence."

1977 Biko dies as a result of police brutality. Seventeen resistance organizations are banned. UN enforces an arms embargo. Calls for economic sanctions against South Africa increase.

1978 Vorster resigns after the information scandal and is succeeded by P. W. Botha.

1979 Venda becomes "independent." National Security Management System (NSMS) is implemented. The Security Branch sets up a special unit at Vlakplaas.

1980 Ciskei is granted "independence."

1982 Government agents kill activist Ruth First by sending her a letter bomb.

1983 White referendum approves government tricameral proposals, but the new system is condemned across the board by blacks.

United Democratic Front (UDF) is formed to oppose the newly proposed system.

1984 The new tricameral constitution is implemented. P. W. Botha becomes state president. Widespread unrest. The Vaal uprising sweeps across townships in the Vaal Triangle, followed by wider deployment of SADF in unrest areas.

1985 Disinvestment campaign commences. Widespread attacks on "collaborators." Vigilante groups emerge. As violence escalates, a state of emergency is declared in 36 magisterial districts. Congress of South African Trade Unions (COSATU) is formed.

1986 State of emergency is extended to entire country in June. By the end of the state of emergency, in June 1987, more than 25,000 people will have been detained. SADF makes raids into Botswana, Zambia, and Zimbabwe. The United States passes the Comprehensive Anti-Apartheid Act, which imposes trade and financial sanctions on South Africa.

1987 In the general elections in May, the Conservative Party replaces the Progressive Federal Party (PFP) as the official opposition in Parliament. A group of 62, mainly Afrikaans-speaking whites, meet with an ANC delegation in Dakar, Senegal, in

July. Following massive strike action, the government covertly bombs COSATU headquarters. Govan Mbeki is released.

1988 South Africa signs the New York Accords, agrees to withdraw from Angola, and accepts Resolution 435, paving the way for the independence of Namibia. ANC closes camps in Angola. Operation Vula is launched inside South Africa.

1989 F. W. de Klerk takes over from P. W. Botha as president of the National Party. In August he becomes acting president of South Africa and in September, following the general elections, he becomes state president in his own right. Walter Sisulu and the remaining Rivonia Trialists are released in October.

In Namibia, the South West Africa People's Organization (SWAPO) wins national elections in March.

1990 Berlin Wall falls.

ANC, PAC, SACP, and 31 other political organizations unbanned on 2 February. On 11 February, Mandela is released from prison.

Namibia becomes independent.

Inkatha/ANC conflict in Sebokeng and KwaZulu begins to escalate.

Groote Schuur Minute signed.

Operation Vula is uncovered.

Pretoria Minute is signed. ANC declares a unilateral suspension of armed struggle.

First exiles arrive in South Africa.

1991 UDF disbands; political exiles return. Forty-eighth National Conference of ANC meets: Nelson Mandela is elected president; Walter Sisulu, deputy president; Cyril Ramaphosa, secretary general; and Jacob Zuma, assistant SG. Convention for a Democratic South Africa (CODESA) gets under way

1992 Mass action campaign by ANC and allies begins. Massacres occur at Boipatong in June. CODESA breaks down. Bisho massacre occurs. Record of Understanding between government and ANC is signed in September.

1993 Multi-Party Negotiations Forum (MPNF) gets negotiations restarted; Chris Hani is assassinated in April.

Interim constitution is endorsed in November.

Mandela and De Klerk are joint winners of Nobel Peace Prize.

1994 First democratic election is held in April. ANC forms Government of National Unity (GNU); Nelson Mandela becomes president of South Africa.

The ANC 1994 election manifesto, the Reconstruction and

Development Program (RDP), promises socioeconomic uplift of previously disadvantaged black people. Among other things the RDP undertakes to provide opportunities for earning decent wages, a national security system, and redistribution of land.

Forty-ninth National Conference, ANC: Thabo Mbeki is elected deputy president; Jacob Zuma national chairperson.

1996 Truth and Reconciliation Commission (TRC) begins its hearings.

The Constitutional Assembly ratifies the South African constitution.

The government replaces the RDP with Growth Employment and Redistribution (GEAR). GEAR emphasizes a free-market economy and fiscal and financial prudence as prerequisites for attracting direct foreign investment (DFI). South Africa has to be perceived as market friendly and fiscally prudent, so the emphasis is on promoting financial macroeconomic stability, bringing the rate of inflation under control, and reducing the budget deficit. In short, it must show that the economic "fundamentals" are sound and that the government is responsive to business concerns such as privatization. The emphasis moves from redistributive measures to growth-inducing measures. Alliance partners COSATU and SACP do not feel that they are adequately consulted before GEAR is endorsed and implemented by the government, especially with reference to privatization.

1997 Fiftieth National Conference, ANC: Mandela steps down as president; Thabo Mbeki is elected president; Jacob Zuma deputy president. Cyril Ramaphosa steps down as secretary general; Mac Maharaj finishes fourth in balloting for the National Executive Commitee (NEC).

1999 Mandela retires; Thabo Mbeki becomes president of South Africa following elections in which the ANC obtains more than 66 percent of the vote. Jacob Zuma becomes deputy president.

2001 Fifty-first National Conference, ANC: Thabo Mbeki is re-elected president of the ANC; Jacob Zuma, deputy president.

2002 Relations between the alliance partners worsen when President Mbeki launches bitter attacks on those within the "broad democratic movement" he characterizes as "ultraleftists." By that he means those who, broadly speaking, oppose GEAR.

2005 In June, President Mbeki dismisses Deputy President Zuma after Judge Hillary Squires finds a businessman, Schabir Shaik, guilty of corruption on charges arising out of his relationship with the deputy president. He appoints minister of minerals and energy Phumzile Mlambo-Ngcuka to fill the position.

A new economic strategy is unveiled. The Accelerated Shared Growth Initiative (ASGI) is designed to address the country's shortage of skills, which had been identified as the most important constraint to achieving a high growth rate. The initiative is spearheaded by Deputy President Phumzile Mlambo-Ngcuka. AGSI will address skills shortages, rand volatility, and excessive red tape. ASGI will be underpinned by more than R350 billion of targeted public investment in infrastructure.

In the general elections in April, the ANC increases its majority in parliament to 70 percent.

The National Prosecuting Authority (NPA) charges former deputy president Jacob Zuma with two counts of corruption.

NPA charges Jacob Zuma with rape.

2006 ANC sweeps municipal elections and wins all metros except for Cape Town.

Jacob Zuma is acquitted on the charge of rape.

In September, corruption charges against Zuma are struck from the court rolls, a decision that provides Zuma with a huge political boost and bolsters his argument that there is a conspiracy among elements of the ruling elite that do not want to see him succeed Mbeki as president of South Africa. The decision, however, leaves the NPA with the option to recharge him at some future date. In early November the Supreme Court of Appeals unanimously dismisses Schabir Shaik's appeal against his fraud and corruption convictions, making it more likely that the state will recharge Jacob Zuma. The year ends with the alliance bitterly divided and the ANC engaged in an internal struggle between pro-Mbeki and pro-Zuma factions jousting for advantage in the long runup to the ANC national conference in 2007 at which the president of the ANC will be elected, the winner becoming the person most likely to succeed Mbeki as president of South Africa in 2009.

On 31 October, P. W. Botha dies. President Mbeki is almost effusive in his praise of the role the Old Crocodile played in preparing the way for a negotiated settlement. He along with other state dignitaries attend Botha's funeral, a gesture of reconciliation that reminded South Africans that only as an undivided nation did South Africa have a future.

For more detailed maps of South Africa and Southern Africa, go to [] maharaj/
documents and reports/other [] maps.

SHADES OF DIFFERENCE

FOREWORD

I HAVE WRITTEN the forewords to a number of books since I was released from prison in 1990. Some I did because the author had contributed much to the struggle over the years, and I felt that he or she was deserving of my support, and some because I felt that the authors were truly deserving because of the quality of the books they had written.

Writing the foreword to *Shades of Difference: Mac Maharaj and the Struggle for South Africa* is in a special place of its own. Mac is a longtime friend and a confidant whom I have turned to over the years for advice. I might not always fully take his advice, but I always find it valuable. Mac has a knack for providing you with insights that broaden your understanding of an issue, and you will find that whatever decision you take in some matter is invariably influenced by his insightfulness.

Mac put the struggle for the freedom of South Africa above everything in his life. In the pursuit of that cause he became a legend for the torture he had been subjected to by the apartheid state, the risks he undertook and the activities he engaged in, and his popping up in the most unlikely places in the most unlikely disguises, as well as his uncanny ability to outmaneuver the enemy. Were it not for the selflessness of so many comrades like him, our efforts would not have come to fruition. In every war of liberation the foot soldiers are the generals.

But Mac is someone special. His contributions to the struggle have been multifaceted, spanning an extraordinary range of activities, many of which were extremely dangerous, especially those he carried out within South Africa. Mac willingly put his life on the line, not on many occasions but as each occasion demanded. He did so without ever a thought to what might happen, but always with meticulous preparation. If he was to die, it would not be because of carelessness on his part. He developed a capacity for putting himself in the shoes of the enemy and thinking through a situation from the perspective of the enemy. As secretary of the Internal

Political and Reconstruction Department (IPRD) and a member of the ANC's Revolutionary Council (RC), he taught the underground that it must respect rather than simply hate the enemy. If you hated the enemy, you dismissed him, depersonalized him; and as a result, you would always underestimate his ability to destroy you. On the other hand, if you respected your enemy, you never forgot how formidable he was; therefore, you always had to be on guard. Vigilance was the key to surviving. Whatever your feelings, you had to put them aside and remember that the enemy was a clever fellow, not some stupid Boer. Hatred would kill you, not the enemy.

Mac ran the ANC's underground in South Africa. In the crucial years before I was released, reliable, encrypted communication between the ANC in Lusaka and London and the ANC underground in South Africa, which at this point had managed to infiltrate the government's intelligence apparatus at a number of levels, was indispensable for a critical evaluation of the government's intentions and the strategies it would employ to achieve them. Mac developed and implemented that system, one of the most important achievements of the struggle.

Whether in the design of the negotiating process, astute stewardship as cosecretary of the Secretariat during the Convention for a Democratic South Africa (CODESA), and again of the Planning Committee during the Multi-Party Negotiation Process (MPNP), and participation in the Technical Executive Committee (TEC), Mac's formidable finger was in every pie.

His energy was inexhaustible. He had that rare ability to contextualize an issue, not only in terms of its immediate fixed framework but also in terms of an evolving long-term framework that would depend on both our decisions and the decisions of the government, thereby enabling us to reconsider positions we had hitherto considered to be sacrosanct.

When I visited Lusaka after I was released from prison, I learned that Mac was retiring from politics because, among other reasons, he wanted to spend more time with his family—something he had never had the opportunity to do. Now he had two children—Milou and Joey—at that stage in their young lives when a father's presence becomes an important part of their development. He had been unable to be present for the birth of Milou. Zarina, his wife, had had to bring up the two children with little support from Mac, an extremely difficult task made more difficult after she was involved in a serious car accident in October 1988. While I empathized with Mac completely, I was very unhappy with his decision. The

ANC was then beginning to face new challenges, including setting up its head office and regional and local structures within South Africa, and preparing to enter the "talks about talks" phase of negotiations. I must confess to literally twisting his arm until he agreed to stay on.

At the June 1990 meeting of the National Executive Committee (NEC)—the first NEC meeting on South African soil since we had been driven into exile—Mac again gave notice of his intentions to retire. He said that he would help for another six months and that then he would quit. In December 1990, he did. For seven months Mac was out of the picture, until many comrades persuaded him to reconsider his position, which he did. The stakes in the negotiations had become very high, and I wanted him to be at the center of the action. And Mac came back to the action with a vengeance.

When we became the government of a free South Africa in May 1994, we faced enormous challenges. We had won our freedom, but that was only the beginning. Now we had to build a nation, a nation that was inclusive, that would make every South African proud to be part of it. In addition, we had to put in place policies that would lay the groundwork for the transformation of the social and economic structures of South Africa, address the huge disparities among our people in every sector of society, and create a South Africa that would bind us with a national identity that would acknowledge our diversity yet also recognize that unity would enhance that diversity. And again I called on him to serve, this time as minister of transport, a member of my cabinet, and a trusted adviser whose advice I often sought and always valued.

In putting together the first cabinet of a free South Africa, I sought the advice of Thabo Mbeki, who was to serve as one of the two deputy presidents. I realized that there were many who had been involved in the struggle from exile and that Thabo had firsthand knowledge of them. Thabo's recommendations included Mac for the post of transport minister. I rejected two or three of his suggestions and retained his suggestion with regard to Mac.

Why minister of transport? Ahmed Kathradra (Kathy) likes to tell the story when he takes guests on a tour of Robben Island that when I was going through the list of possible ministerial appointees, I came across Mac's name and said, "What can we do with this chap?" And then, as Kathy tells the story, without waiting a second, I said, "Well, he transported my autobiography out of Robben Island, so I'll make him minister of transport!" But it was an inspired choice, so much so that in 1997, *Infrastructure*

Finance, a leading international infrastructure journal, chose him as one of the eight most innovative ministers worldwide in charge of developing infrastructure in developing countries.

I have known Mac since 1964, when he came to Robben Island to serve a twelve-year sentence after the Little Rivonia trial. He arrived on the island about six months after I had arrived with the other Rivonia Trialists. We were still settling in and setting up means of communications with each other, since we had been consigned to the single-cells section of the prison, away from other prisoners. He was kept in isolation for a few months after he arrived, and then one day he, too, was assigned to our section—about six cells away from me.

From the beginning I could see that Mac would be a bit of a problem. He was tough, would give backchat to the warders, was too quick with the barbed remark, too argumentative, too unwilling to concede a point in debate even when he had won it, too intelligent for his own good. In truth, he reminded me a bit of my younger self, and I cringed! It fell to Walter Sisulu, Kathy, and me to take him under our wings and put sense in his head.

From early on, I realized that it was futile trying to win a debate with Mac, so when some issue arose and he was being his usual self—holding on to an opposite view even though the rest of us had come to a consensus on the matter—I would say to Kathy: "Go and straighten this boy out." Kathy would go, come back, and say: "Madiba, there is nothing I can do with this chap. He has an answer for everything." So then I would turn to Walter and say, "Walter, Kathy can get nowhere with Mac; why don't you go and bring him into line on this matter." And Walter would go, come back, and say, "Nelson, I can get nowhere with him; you'll have to go yourself." And then I would have to go and straighten him out. "No arguments, Mac," I would say when Mac would begin to launch into his barrage of arguments. "Just answer one question. You're a Communist, a member of the leadership. Now when the leadership has reached a consensus on something, and your arguments have been heard but not accepted by your comrades, most of whom think differently, what, Mac, do you do when the leadership makes a decision?" And he would say, "Well, Madiba,* of course, I'd follow it." And I would say, "Thank you, Mac." And that would be the end of the matter. "Go slowly, Neef,"† I would caution, but Mac was never one for going slowly.

---

*Mandela is often addressed as Madiba, which is his clan name, as a mark of respect.
†*Neef* is Afrikaans for nephew.

He had, of course, his own way of retaliating. On one occasion when a number of us had been assigned to work at the lime quarry, he and I were side by side, hacking away with our picks at the walls of lime facing us, when my pick slipped, struck Mac's pick with some force, and injured his thumb. He was expecting a visit from his mother that Saturday, and he went to great lengths to conceal the injury from her. When they met, even through the double-sealed window that separated them both, she noticed that something was wrong with his hand. As he would recount the story, his mother became very agitated. "Put your hand up so that I can see it," she demanded in a strident voice. "Who did this to you? What warder hurt you? Give me his name, and I'll report him!" She would not be fobbed off, her voice more strident still. "I want to know, tell me now!"— the voice more demanding this time. And the warders supervising the visit were laughing because they knew what had happened. And then Mac said, "Mom, the person who did this to me—his name is Mandela." And his mother said, "Well, you can tell that Warder Mandela chap that when I get back to Cape Town, I'm going to call a press conference and tell the world what he has done to you." And when the visit was up and Mac was being led away, he said, "Remember, Mom, it was Mandela."

When he returned to the cells that afternoon, I bumped into Mac and asked him how my girlfriend was doing—that was how I jocularly referred to Mac's mother—and Mac said, "You're in deep trouble, Madiba. Your girlfriend is going to tell the world how Warder Mandela beat me up." And we both laughed because we both knew that when Mac's mother got back to Cape Town, she would tell friends and relatives and they would know it was all a joke.

Mac was a quick learner, and we learned too, in quick time, that in our community on the island, he was one of the brightest. He always challenged the status quo, and he challenged us to be more rigorous in our arguments. He was provocative in discussions, sometimes maddeningly so, but the provocation always had a point to it, leading us to recognize that whatever you thought on an issue, there were always alternative ways of thinking about it.

Sometimes too many. Kathy tells of how he got into a conversation with Mac one morning when they were at work. Mac told Kathy, "I was having a hell of an argument last night, and I went into the two sides of the argument like two people were in a great debate." He went on to give Kathy a blow-by-blow account of the argument, and when he was finished, Kathy said to him, "But Mac, we're locked up in individual cells; who were you arguing with?" And without batting an eyelid, Mac responded, "I was arguing with myself." To this day, I wonder which side of him won!

In the discussions we held on the island, we talked about the shape the struggle should take, and how we could contribute to it, given the position we were in. Our discussions allowed for all points of view to be openly aired. Sometimes there were sharp divisions among the comrades on particular issues, such as the tactics our movement should adopt in the case of the Bantustans (the homelands policy of the government). At times the debates erupted into personal exchanges that were, well, a little "uncomradely"—we, too, were all too human, perhaps even more because of the conditions of our confinement. But these discussions, whether divisive or not on occasions, had a special purpose. Many young comrades knew little of the history of the ANC and the alliances; we had to deepen their breadth of understanding and prepare them for reentry into the struggle once they had completed their sentences. There was no doubt in our minds that we would be victorious against apartheid, that the black majority would be enfranchised, and democracy enshrined in our constitution.

I have heard many comrades say that the period they spent on Robben Island was the best time of their lives. And when I think about it, I know why. In many respects, it was more like a close-knit family and a university than a prison. Outside, the movement had to push the struggle against an implacable state that suppressed our people with a type of social engineering that was not just oppressive but evil. It was based on the belief that blacks were inferior human beings and that they were, therefore, to be confined to their own communities to reinforce their sense of inferiority. Every day they were "exported" to drive the white industrial machine that benefited whites only.

The demands of the struggle left our leaders with little time to consider the shape, structures, institutions, and constitutional alternatives we would have to forge. On the island we all had the time to reflect and dream dreams of freedom. There was, so to speak, a division of labor. On the mainland the struggle was active: armed encounters, mass mobilizations, strikes and propaganda, the infiltration of both MK* and the underground. On the island we had the time to discuss, debate, and analyze the issues we would have to deal with in ending apartheid and building a post-apartheid South Africa.

One manifestation of these indabas is the collection of essays that Mac

---

*Umkhonto we Sizwe, "the Spear of the Nation," the ANC's armed wing.

"commissioned" after my autobiography had been completed and concealed and there was still some time left before he would be released. These essays reflect the views of a number of the senior leaders on the island, from different organizations in the liberation struggle, on the problems we faced in liberating southern Africa. They were written on the eve of the Soweto uprising, an event that would transform both the nature of the struggle and the politics of the struggle. Mac smuggled these essays off the island too.

The collection, for reasons I won't go into here, gathered dust for twenty-five years, but it eventually saw the light of day when it was published in 2001. The book *Reflections in Prison*, which Mac edited, distills the issues we were preoccupied with in the university of the prison. Some of the issues raised are as relevant today as they were when they were written. But I will let Mac speak, since he had to transcribe the essays from the miniaturized form he had reduced them to, and had again to unravel the scripts before editing them. In the introduction, he writes:

> In a certain sense the contributors can be seen as unwittingly debating among and against each other. A careful reading of their views on racism [for example] allows us to detect some of these tensions and discern the different assumptions from which they proceed. . . .
>
> . . . The collection enables us to see the strategic perspectives, tactical considerations, methodologies and the material and psychological conditions that shaped the contributors' thinking, and therefore have to be taken into account as we devise ways and means that will take our country to its desired goal. They bring a much needed perspective to the current debates. . . .
>
> The principled positions, the strategic clarity, the consciousness that drove us to ensure that the just cause of the denied majority would become a national cause in the interest of the entire nation, oppressed and oppressor, permeate these essays. As we debate and shoulder the tasks of building the nation, we need to carry forward the knowledge we have acquired and use it to help us chart the course.*

MANDELA: More than ever we need debate in South Africa today—debate for, against, and among. The right to free expression enshrined in our constitution is not just one of the cornerstones of a democracy, it is part of the

Reflections in Prison (Mac Maharaj, ed.) (Cape Town: Zebra Press and Robben Island Museum, 2001), pp. xv–xvi.

edifice itself. If it were to disappear, it would reduce our constitution to rubble.

I've mentioned in my autobiography, *Long Walk to Freedom*, Mac's role in smuggling it off the island when he was released in December 1976. But I am not doing him justice. After I wrote my fifteen pages of foolscap every night, the pages were passed on to Walter and Kathy and then on to Mac, who reduced them to a quarter of a page or less by miniaturizing his transcription. The original fifteen pages were concealed in one safe spot, and the miniaturized version in another. In all, he reduced a book that would run to more than five hundred pages to sixty foolscap pages. These were concealed in a third separate place. He and Laloo Chiba then had to construct a number of concealed spaces in the file covers containing his personal papers—correspondence course materials and items like that. They slipped his sixty-odd sheets of my miniaturized manuscript into these spaces. When he was released, all his possessions were searched repeatedly, of course, and in the most thorough way, with Mac, nonchalant to the last, watching; but none of the security guards found any of the concealed spaces.

When the story of how the manuscript of my autobiography was smuggled off the island is told, something is usually lost in the telling, namely, what the consequences would have been for Mac if the manuscript had been discovered. Mac undertook the task willingly, knowing full well that if he was caught, he would be charged and find himself back on Robben Island. But none of these considerations deterred him; he was simply himself—performing a task by initiating a plan of action with adequate preparation and getting on with the job. He knew that if you dwelled on the possible consequences of what might happen if things went wrong, you would immobilize yourself and nothing would ever get done.

Later, Oliver Tambo sent him to London to decipher the smuggled text and produce a typed copy of the autobiography. I think that these two episodes—having to miniaturize the manuscript and then bring it back to life, so to speak—gave him a special insight into how my mind works: the way I look at things, what I draw on to analyze a situation, how I reach decisions, and what a stubborn old man I am, much like Mac himself!

But my relationship with Mac transcends the struggle, the negotiations, the transition, and his innumerable contributions to nation building. Among the many I know, he has a place in that special group of people to whom I turn for advice. I know that what he will tell me will always be a candid and honest assessment of the situation I have to deal with, and it's what I have come to expect from him after a friendship that spans forty years. Sometimes what he says is painful to hear, but painful or not, Mac will plow on with little regard for the niceties. He is not seeking favor from me; he is looking out for the protection of my integrity.

And this is what astonished me when I read *Shades of Difference: Mac Maharaj and the Struggle for South Africa*. Here you find two brutal honesties clashing. On the one side, you have Padraig O'Malley, the interviewer, with his piercing, probing, relentless questioning of Mac, sometimes gentle, sometimes brutal, but always with respect for him— eleven years of building up a relationship of trust before he would inch himself into Mac's soul; on the other, you have Mac, the interviewee, with his unflinching replies, his unique ability to counterpunch a question, his anticipation of where a line of questioning is leading, but going there, often knowing that he is revealing things in his life that he had tucked away in the recesses of his heart.

He goes there because of his compulsion to be brutally honest with himself, and O'Malley follows him, revealing in his questions that he, too, has things tucked away in the recesses of his own heart. In the end, it is difficult to know who is the interviewer and who is the interviewee. You hear the tone change from formal and rather stiff in the early years to the shared intimacy of their conversations in the later years. You can feel the trust that has developed between the two. All the barriers are down; for both there is nothing to conceal.

O'Malley's book set me thinking about a number of things that I would like to share with you. The first relates to Operation Vula, the second to the torture Mac endured, and the third to the losses freedom fighters suffer and the damage they do to their families, the matter of unfinished business that haunts us all and that we feel is too difficult to speak about, and sometimes are unable to share.

The Vula project was conceived in Lusaka, and Oliver Tambo, with his unerring ability to pick the right man for the right job, asked Mac to head up the operation, which involved setting up a communications system that would allow the underground in South Africa to stay in touch with Lusaka via London, and to settle senior ANC leadership in the country.

Some commentators on that period have gone to some length to try to debunk Vula and the ANC's underground in South Africa. I think their commentaries are incomplete and do not take into account the fact that Vula must always be viewed through the prism of the infrastructure of a people's war.

The communications system that Mac, along with others, including his wife, Zarina, put in place—after a trial-and-error approach to establish a system that would elude all attempts of the South African intelligence agencies to find and easily decipher—took two years to develop. This communications system extended the boundaries of the struggle, and in doing that transformed the nature of the struggle itself. For the first time ever, the ANC was able to connect the various tentacles of the struggle.

Without Vula, we would not have been able to coordinate the activities of Umkhonto we Sizwe (MK), the ANC underground within South Africa, and the on-the-ground structures, especially the United Democratic Front (UDF), the Congress of South African Trade Unions (COSATU), ANC headquarters in Lusaka, our London office, and the international campaign against apartheid. We were able to ensure that the activities of the overt mass organizations, in South Africa in particular, were operating to further a common set of strategic objectives and in support of other ANC and MK operations at the same time. The communications system also allowed for direct communication between the UDF and the ANC underground structures, and between the underground and MK, creating a synergy among them, allowing each to reinforce the other in a dynamic context, thus advancing the four pillars of the struggle.*

The communications system reached into my quarters at Victor Verster Prison, ensuring that my communications with Lusaka were directed through a more secure and quicker channel. The increasing emphasis we put on mass action and mass mobilization in the late 1980s was a strategic move on our part that was orchestrated through the ANC underground and the UDF and COSATU on the ground. We were involving the people in their own struggle. Once passive spectators to what was happening and what the state was doing to them, they now began to realize the power of their numbers. This feeling of empowerment raised their political consciousness, creating a critical mass of support from which would emerge a highly politicized public. If armed struggle on a more intense level was going to be necessary, we would have an integrated political leadership that would guide the Area Political Committees (APCs) and the mass organizations in place, the routes to bring arms into the country in place, the political underground in place, and a critical support base within the

---

*The four pillars were: mass mobilization and action, building a sustainable political underground, building MK and developing the armed struggle, and international action to isolate apartheid South Africa.

country that would provide cover for the cadres in place. And most important, we had the communications system in place that would enable us to coordinate and oversee the activities of all the other structures and ensure that they were acting in harmony.

Commentators sometimes forget that a revolutionary struggle operates on a number of levels, some antithetical to others, but each taking into account what the others are doing, each having a specific task. At one level we were exploring the route of a negotiated settlement and whether the regime was serious; at another level we were preparing ourselves for a people's war. In our circumstances, the aim of a people's war was not to "win," but gradually through a process of attrition to bring the government to the realization that we could not be defeated and the government could not win. General Magnus Malan, the minister of defense, had bluntly told his government that the situation in South Africa was 80 percent political and 20 percent military. Our task, had it become necessary, would have been to bring the government to the realization that the situation was 100 percent political.

Without Vula, little of this planning would have been possible because you cannot run a revolution from an office in Lusaka. I have heard some say that Vula only managed to bring two members of the NEC into the country, and therefore it was a failure. My answer to those people is simple: you do not understand what the dimensions of Vula were. Vula was designed to address the long view. It was a process that would evolve with time. It was not a series of concrete events. It was uncovered in circumstances that would not have prevailed had I not been released, or the ANC, MK, SACP, PAC, and other organizations unbanned, and had negotiations about negotiations not been underway.

After I was released I met with Mac, who was still deep underground and illegally in the country, and told him to continue with Vula activities. We had many conversations—some while he was still in South Africa illegally and others after he was indemnified and had to leave South Africa illegally in order to return legally—on how we might refocus the work of the underground and the military in the new situation. We envisaged a special role for the underground in ensuring that the masses were not demobilized, so that the pressure on the government to get on with negotiations was maintained. We also discussed how the underground might be used to intervene in a new phenomenon, then depicted as black-on-black violence, before we were in a position to say that the state itself was behind much of the violence, and how we might secure the top leadership, who were obvious candidates for assassination.

These discussions, of course, came to a halt when Mac was arrested on 25 July 1990 in connection with Vula. When Siphiwe Nyanda, now chief of staff of the South African National Defense Force (SANDF),* was arrested on 11 July, Mac told me it would only be a matter of time before he was arrested. We discussed how we might use his arrest for maximum tactical advantage, but before we could put any plan into action, he was nabbed at the home of Valli Moosa, who later served as a minister in my government.

But there is a strange twist to his arrest. On 20 July 1990, the NEC met to discuss the agenda for a forthcoming meeting with the government scheduled for 6 August. We were disappointed with developments after the first meeting at Groote Schuur. The government was stalling. Prisoners were not being released; the granting of indemnity to some of our key people in exile was crawling along, precluding us from putting our organizational and negotiating structures in place; and no formal negotiating process had been set up.

For the ANC, at this NEC meeting, this posed certain tactical challenges. How would we come out of the scheduled August meeting with the government in a position to force the pace of negotiations so that it would begin to reach a formal process, and how would we consolidate the moral high ground in South Africa and the international community? Joe Slovo's proposal that we declare a unilateral suspension of the armed struggle appeared to address both issues. But Joe's proposal was likely to meet with a lot of debate and resistance from some comrades, so I proposed that the NEC set up a committee of four—Thabo Mbeki, now president; Ronnie Kasrils, now minister of intelligence; Joe Slovo, now deceased but prior to his untimely death minister of housing; and Mac—to draw up a formal resolution that would be put to the NEC, debated, and then voted on. That is what happened, and the resolution was passed unanimously.

What did not emerge until later was that the other three had appointed Mac to do the drafting notes of their meeting and that when he was arrested—a few days later—the police found the draft resolution in his handwriting in his briefcase. Since Mac was being held incommunicado, there was no way he could let us know that our August "surprise" would come as no surprise at all to the government. Of course, I didn't learn about this until I was allowed to visit him in Sandton Police Station, the day after our meeting with the government.

Even when we did unilaterally suspend the armed struggle in August

*Nyanda retired as head of SANDF in May 2005.

1990, we did not do so with our eyes closed. We had other alternatives. What we might choose from that range of alternatives would depend on what combination of tools we decided would best advance our strategic objectives at that point in time. As circumstances altered, we would be able to replace one mix of tools with another. Certainly, a few gestures on the part of the government would not create the building blocks for a solid foundation that would enable us to proceed in good faith. And if the government ever thought that by releasing me from prison after twenty-seven years of incarceration, it was somehow doing me a favor for which I should be grateful, it was misreading the situation completely. Our suspension of the armed struggle was unilateral. We did not call on the government to do something specific in return, but we expected the government to respond by stepping up the pace of negotiations.

There is a difference between "a voluntarily suspension" of an armed struggle and "a cessation" of an armed struggle. The former is conditional and involves only those parties that participate in a voluntary action. It makes very clear in its wording that if things do not work out, then that voluntarily suspension may be lifted. Embedded in the meaning of a voluntary suspension of anything is the possibility of returning to what you have volunteered to give up. In the case of an armed struggle, it has nothing to do with your continuing to purchase arms, to bring them into the country, to infiltrate your cadres, to train them, to increase your capacity in every way to wage war if a return to that form of struggle becomes necessary. Not to do all these things, to take these precautions, would be foolhardy and very naive. We certainly didn't believe that the government, on our announcement, would stop building its military capacity.

A cessation of conflict is a different kettle of fish. A cessation of an armed conflict involves all parties to the conflict, without the conditionality of a possible return. It is permanent, and is invariably followed by some agreement on how the arms should be disposed of. We never disposed of our arms or disbanded Umkhonto we Sizwe until we were sitting in the Union Building.

Besides, after our announcement of a voluntary suspension, there were ominous developments. The violence in the Vaal Triangle, south of Johannesburg, which had been simmering for some time, suddenly escalated at a horrifying rate. Inkatha forces, aided and abetted by either rogue elements or "third force" members of the security forces of the state, were attacking our people all across the area. It was apparent that we would have to do something to protect our people, since my pleas to F. W. de Klerk to bring the situation under control and investigate assistance by the security forces to Inkatha had fallen on deaf ears. And we did supply armed and political support for the protection of our communities.

The third matter—if you could call it a matter—is something quite different. It is about torture.

When I read Mac's account of the torture he underwent before he went to trial in 1964, at the Grays Building, which was the headquarters of the Security Branch, I could not bear my own suppressed pain. I could not believe what I read; indeed, if the same account had come out of the mouth of a human being other than Mac, I would not have believed him. On Robben Island I had raised the matter with him on a few occasions. Once, he merely said, "Pretty severely," and shrugged his shoulders as if to tell me that we were all tortured at one stage or another, and his experiences were not much different. And when I pursued the matter after hearing Kathy say that Mac was the most tortured man at that time in South Africa, Mac just gave me that half smile of his—the one with no smile in the eyes that said, if you knew him well enough, "Don't go there." The very casualness of his response hinted at something more, but I had been warned, so I let it stand.

But now that I have heard his words—yes, heard, not read, because you could hear the voice behind every word spelling out in a grim, staccato-like manner, as though the narrator himself were detached from the events he was describing, the frightening details of what he had gone through—I am overwhelmed. And I pride myself on not being easily overwhelmed. No human being could endure such repeated bouts of the torture he described and come out alive. And if you did come out alive, it seemed to me that you would be so crippled psychologically that you would curl up in a corner and whimper for the rest of your days because the unimaginable had become the unspeakable. For all these years I thought I knew him as few people do, and here I was reading the words pulled wrenchingly out of his soul by O'Malley, and I wondered, do I know Mac at all?

Ordinary men do evil, and we forgive them because there is no one among us who can say, with certainty, that he would not commit evil under certain circumstances. But for some crimes, so evil in their commission, forgiveness is hard to find. It is no good saying apartheid made men do bad things; it's men who did the bad things and subsequently found it convenient to hang their consciences on apartheid's broad shoulders.

But Colonel Theunis Swanepoel defies the odds to forgive. He was a man, Mac says, "who took pride in his brutality." But in my eyes he had gone further: he had refined torture into a form of art. Before he went to work on Mac, he questioned him and others extensively—and attentively—learning every little detail of his life, meticulously looking for the fault lines of fear. Once he had determined those fault lines, he customized the torture he would use, homing in on the fears that we reveal only under the extreme stress of round-the-clock interrogation, when sleep deprivation alone has us revealing little intimate things that we hide even from ourselves.

I can hear Swanepoel's baton drop in one swift movement, like a guillotine. The enormity of the pain inflicted, hearing the screams strangled in Mac's throat, his efforts to stop them surrendering inevitably to the uncontrollable. And then the waiting: waiting for Swanepoel's next crack of the raised baton, the false movements in Swanepoel's body as if to forewarn Mac that the baton would fall, but didn't; and the game for Mac's mind would go on. But I won't go on—you have to read it for yourself, and if you do not feel afterward as overwhelmed as I was, then I will be very, very puzzled.

From my conversations with prisoners on Robben Island and on other occasions, I learned that the psychological pain induced by the anticipation of physical pain once experienced is as unbearable as the physical pain you feel when your torturer actually strikes again. They would tell me that they could tell the difference between a "good" torturer and a "bad" one by the way he was able to get to you psychologically. The psychological impact was greater when the torturer knew how to use your waiting for him to strike as a weapon. Allowing your anticipation of the expected to build and always varying the moment, then suddenly striking, was one of the most successful ways of breaking you down.

Perhaps most odd is the respect Mac and Swanepoel developed for each other. On the one hand, Swanepoel was the master torturer facing his biggest challenge: how to break a prisoner who would not break no matter how he tortured him. On the other, Mac, hauled into the torture chamber each day, bloodied and still semiconscious from the previous day's assaults, was aware that he still held the ace card. Swanepoel wanted information; a dead man was of no use to him if he had not broken him first. Swanepoel was driving Mac to the brink, but if he pushed him over, Mac would have won the macabre chess game.

In a twisted way, Mac always held the advantage, which Swanepoel knew—and Mac knew that Swanepoel knew. But when he says he "respected" Swanepoel, he does not mean that he respected anything about Swanepoel's humanity; he respected the skill that resided beneath the man's many layers of brutality. And when other inmates who were tortured by Swanepoel recounted that Swanepoel told them that he had respected Mac, that respect was not a statement about Mac's humanity either, but about Mac's skill at being able to read him and his almost superhuman capacity to absorb physical pain and remain psychologically intact.

Swanepoel could not torture Mac's mind. For a man plying Swanepoel's trade, that was deserving of respect.

Yet Mac's unsparing account of his torture forced me, having heard so many stories of torture in prison and seeing the effects of torture, to relook at this issue and to come to terms once more with what comrades had gone through in our struggle at the hands of their torturers. It brought home to me once more the realities they had to deal with in moments of extreme deprivation, and I realized that we can easily forget the horrendous brutalities our comrades were subjected to in order that I and all other South Africans can enjoy the fruits of their endurance.

For many, the price came high. On Robben Island we did not, of course, have access to the mental relief from these experiences that some form of therapy might have provided. We listened to the stories, though most men were inclined to keep them to themselves unless coaxed, and it was easy to see from the behavior of some that they were in acute mental pain. But other than listening to and watching out for them, our task was to hold the struggle together in the prison, to keep the comrades focused on the struggle and the future, to keep them believing from the depths of their souls that we would prevail, no matter what the odds against us were. We could not, therefore, allow for the situation to develop where the suffering we had already endured at the hands of our oppressors began to become the focus of our communal attention. If that had happened, the results would have been disastrous. We were trapped. The cohesion of the struggle took precedence over everything, which meant that our capacity to deal with the damage our torturers had committed, easily evidenced in many of our comrades, was severely limited.

Some of our comrades broke under torture, and we embraced them with compassion and as comrades. We know that every man's capacity to endure inhuman forms of torture is different. We know that every comrade faced his torturers with courage and fought them to the best of his or her ability. The fact that some could not go beyond the limits of their capacity to endure is no shame. Rather they should wear it as a badge of honor. There is no need to forgive them because there is nothing to forgive. They gave their all, and that is all that you can expect of anyone.

I, who have had the great honor of being elected the first president of a free South Africa, and have had the privilege of serving my people and re-ceiving more honors than any person reasonably deserves, will never for-get that all that has been showered on me was, and continues to be, made possible by the price paid by my comrades in the torture chambers of a renegade state. Were I ever to forget, I would betray the struggle.

Today the freedoms we enjoy are often casually practiced without any thought of the blood they are inscribed in. Neither we nor our leaders who hold positions of great power in our country and on the world stage should ever be allowed to forget that we are who we are because of the men and women huddled in their lonely prison cells, waiting day after day for the jangle of the key in the door before they were marched off to the torture chambers.

And, finally, there is the question that O'Malley raises—and Mac ad-dresses forthrightly and with poignant eloquence—the question each of us raises on occasion when we are alone with our own thoughts: what did we do to the people who loved us, our spouses, children, family? What price had they to pay for the choices we imposed on them?

Many comrades, including Mac and me, were separated from our families for long periods, or we saw them only intermittently because we put the struggle first, above all other considerations. The fact is that in many cases we inflicted irreparable damage on those closest to us. We were selfish. Our vision of a future for our people blinded us to any other view. And perhaps that's the way it has to be.

When freedom came, we tried to make amends, but often the amends were on our terms. We found it difficult to adjust to new family situations, and often we were surprised that our families, having had no other choice, had gotten on with their lives. Our sudden reappearance interfered with the rhythms they danced to. We were unable to dance with them.

The families of comrades who were absentee fathers or mothers, hus-bands or wives, lovers or friends for much of their lives take time to heal. Sometimes the healing is impossible. Even when it is not, there is always unfinished business that leaves us unable to be fully whole, creating an emptiness that no amount of happiness can dilute. It is part of whom we have become.

We try to bridge the gap between the missing years, but what is missing can never be recovered. Like infinity, the quicker we walk to reach the light at the end of the road, the more the light recedes. We are better off walking slower and forgetting about the light. That is what struggle teaches, and what life teaches too.

.   .   .

There are many ways of concluding a foreword, most usually by commending the book to the reader. For *Shades of Difference: Mac Maharaj and the Struggle for South Africa*, that is the easy part. But Mac and O'Malley's book calls for something more. First, in order to know how our country came into being, to understand both the complexities and simplicities of our past, there is a pressing need for the people who played a role in our struggle to have their stories told in their own voices. Second, others should analyze their stories within the context of the larger scenario of unfolding events and the changing nature of the context itself as objectively as possible, so that our understanding of our history is as full as possible.

In these regards, O'Malley's book breaks new ground, and it uses a narrative format that is, I believe, a model for others who want to record our history of struggle and the deeds of the men and women who are our history makers, the foot soldiers and generals of our revolution. New nations in particular must have a memory bank in order to establish a strong sense of collective identity. We deposit our stories into the memory bank and draw on our collective account in moments of uncertainty or crisis, or to remember who we are and how we got to where we are.

There is a need for the foot soldiers to tell their stories too. No one is born a leader or rises to leading positions by birth. It happens in the course of time. Leaders emerge and are shaped through a process that selects them. Circumstances bring certain people to the fore who have the ability to change the circumstances from which they have emerged. Mac, in all that he did, conducted himself with the same sense of responsibility that one requires of a leader as well as with the sense of duty that one requires of a foot soldier. As a result of our close interaction in prison, I knew that he had all the qualities and the commitment to stay the course and shoulder responsibilities. Of course, as we got to know each other, life was not just plain sailing, an upward spiral of the wonderful. The stuff of all revolution is the synergy that develops among different personalities. He and I are personalities in our own right, and although he was troublesome to me on occasion—and I, no doubt, was troublesome to him— we learned how to understand each other, and that understanding has enriched both of our lives. Without contradictions all lives would be mundane.

There is one thing that I learned from Mac that stands out in my mind, and it is of particular relevance to South Africa today. His life illustrates that he never succumbed to a sense of victimhood. Yes, he was born into an oppressive system and was at the receiving end of that system. But that did not stop him from making choices that enabled him to lead a life of dignity. He never flinched from the consequences of the actions he took. The level of risk never deterred him. Indeed, he regarded facing up to those consequences as a test of his integrity even though those consequences might sometimes have been painful, might have meant death as the measure of his own integrity. After the Rivonia arrests, when many activists either headed for the border or went underground, fearing further arrests, he did neither. He stayed and went about the business of the struggle. There was no element of bravado in what he did. His concern was simple: to see that the struggle continued and triumphed.

He is entitled to a sense of fulfillment because he dedicated his whole life to freeing us from the oppression of apartheid and to teaching our country to be inclusive so that the unity of our diversity is a cause for celebration, not conflict. It would be foolish of me to say that he was indispensable to the struggle, but I can say he came close to being this. He never flinched from the consequences of his actions. The level of risk never deterred him. He attempted to commit suicide on two occasions while he was in detention, not out of despair but out of a cold-blooded calculation: dead men don't talk. In the pursuit of the struggle he regarded his own life as a disposable commodity, yet throughout all he maintained his wholeness of self. His humanity was immune to the evil that tried to destroy him.

All of us, including me, are indebted to him. His family, especially his wife and children, should take great pride in the fact that their husband and father was one of South Africa's founding fathers. They and generations to come are the beneficiaries of the generations that have gone before them: they are indebted to those who paid the price for their freedom to go to the school of their choice, to select the education they want with no boundaries to the level of success they can achieve, to go to the college of their choice, to pursue a career of their choice, to marry the person they love, to live where they want, to travel freely throughout the country, to vote for the political party of their choice, to say what they want without fear of reprisal. They must remember the past and treasure it because the sacrifices of the past were made on their behalf and give them the gift to a birthright. Above all, they need to live life to the fullest, to enjoy the present, and to build for the future.

We are also indebted to Mac's wife, Zarina, and their children, Milou and Joey—and to the spouses, children, and families of all comrades—for the contributions they made. Were it not for their selfless support when husbands and fathers were away, often in very uncertain circumstances, for their bearing with the uncertainty, for absorbing the pain of loss and the loneliness of separation, our struggle would never have stayed the course. In our absence they became our surrogates, and the contribution they made to the struggle for freedom is no less than ours.

I respect Mac, and I love him. I call him Ngquphephe, after a one-eyed hero in a Xhosa folktale. O'Malley does my Ngquphephe proud. And I am proud of O'Malley too for the extraordinary book he has written for us. He, like us in the struggle, has persevered, and he, like us, has triumphed.

Nelson R. Mandela
November 2004
Johannesburg

INTRODUCTION

In the late 1980s, the apartheid regime in South Africa lurched uncertainly from one reform to the next, but it could not face the ultimate step: abolishing what it could not reform. Only dismantling the entire apartheid apparatus and enfranchising the black masses would suffice.

States of emergency in 1986 and again in 1987 had failed to stop township violence. Moreover, the external climate was rapidly changing; Mikhail Gorbachev's doctrines of glasnost and perestroika opened the Soviet Union to change, and as the cold war wound down, the utility of the South African government to the West dried up. At one time it could portray itself as the principled ally of the West in the war against Soviet expansionism, which had funded so many anticolonial struggles and postcolonial states. As such, it could count on the covert support of the United States and a tacit tolerance for apartheid; during the cold war, the United States found "constructive engagement" with South Africa more expedient than outright condemnation of apartheid.

When the foundations on which these relationships rested began to crumble, changes in South Africa became necessary—an inevitable outcome of the changing world order. The economy was veering toward bankruptcy, the bite of financial sanctions was viselike, and the prospects of things getting better were remote. South African President F. W. de Klerk bowed to reality. On 2 February 1990, he unbanned the ANC and other political organizations, and on 11 February, he released Nelson Mandela. Thereafter he entered into a negotiations process with the ANC and all other political parties claiming to have a stake in a new dispensation. It was a process of uncertainty; no outcome was guaranteed and none ruled out. All parties committed themselves to nonviolence, yet the process unfolded in a climate of endemic violence.

2

I went to South Africa in 1989 to record and study the impending transition from apartheid to a postapartheid era. I had no idea how it would unfold, how long it would take, or what the outcome would be. And, I would learn, neither did the men and women who became the key players in that process.

I met Mac Maharaj by accident in the early 1990s. I was visiting Cyril Ramaphosa, secretary-general of the African National Congress (ANC) and the party's chief negotiator, at ANC headquarters, on Plein Street in Johannesburg. On the way to Cyril's office on the ninth floor, we passed an Indian man—in his fifties, I would have presumed, silver haired, with a small white goatee. He was working the phone, punching at the keyboard impatiently with his fingers, and furiously smoking a cigarette. I remember, for some reason, that the desk had no papers on it, perhaps because the desks around him were piled high with haphazard stacks of paper. The man on the phone talked vigorously and quickly, with an air of urgency— again in contrast to the rather languid pace of things around him. The calls were short. Each ended the same way: "Thanks, pal." I would become used to the phrase.

"That," said Cyril, "is Mac. He is someone you should talk to. Come, I'll introduce you." We walked over to Mac, who gave me a quick once-over and nodded his head between puffs. We made an appointment to meet on 18 August 1993—as it turned out, three months before the establishment of the November 1993 interim constitution that would pave the way for the first democratic elections in South Africa's history.

I knew who Mac was. Indeed, it would have been hard not to. In July 1990, when talks between the ANC and the South African government were already under way, he had been arrested and jailed, allegedly for trying to overthrow the government by violence. For a couple of months it was a big story—James Bond stuff, men in disguises using false passports, caches of arms being secretly transported into the country, an army being trained in secret locations, underground networks and a computer-generated communications system that emitted encrypted messages, a Communist plot. And then the story simply disappeared. After charges against him were dropped several months later, I had tried to reach Mac but failed to make contact. I knew he was important, but just how important I did not know.

During our first interviews, I confined myself to questions about the current state of negotiations. Since my intent was to gather history in the making, I did not dwell on the past. I adhered to the boundaries I had used with other interviewees in my study of the ongoing transition, so there was a certain formality in my interview style. And Mac was, I believe, "sussing me out." He had been burned on a number of occasions by writers, so he was, not surprisingly, a little wary. But in the course of our conversations, certain things began to emerge: his formidable analytical abilities, his phenomenal memory, his capacity to contextualize events and to view outcomes not in the context of present circumstances but in terms of a continually changing environment.

During Nelson Mandela's presidency (1994–1999), Mac served as his minister of transport. We got closer. The range of our conversations became wider and deeper, and he began to address more fully matters he had hitherto brushed aside. The tone of our conservations also changed. The formality fell away.

When Mandela stepped down as president in 1999, Mac stepped down with him. Thabo Mbeki became president, and Mac entered the private sector. At the age of sixty-seven, he turned his thoughts to earning some money. In late 2000, I told him I wanted to write a book that would draw on his life narrative as a guidebook for understanding the culture of the struggle against apartheid. Mac, as was his democratic way, consulted his family: his wife, Zarina, and his children, Milou and Joey. After a family indaba, the matter was settled and the book was on.

His narrative stretches across six decades, from the 1930s through the first years of this century; from struggle to liberation and from liberation through participation in South Africa's first democratic government. But his engagement in the affairs of South Africa did not end there. The "miracle" of April 1994, when black people went to the polls for the first time, soon lost some of its magic. Which was perhaps inevitable. When too much is expected, the anticipation of more always dilutes the benefits of the present.

And Mac would face his own travails—some, it should be said, of his own making. And he was pushed—or jumped, depending on your point of view—from the pedestal of struggle heroes because he dared to stand up for what he believed was right when his integrity was questioned. But in pursuing things in his own way, he found that in the new South Africa the new ANC had little time for the kind of behavior that had served the ANC so well during the struggle.

In the new South Africa, the ANC was quite willing, in the interests of enforcing the hegemony of the party, to rewrite its own history. Being a loyal and disciplined member of the ANC became an ideology in its own right, perhaps to fill the void that opened when the movement that had been the voice of a people's victimhood became the ruling party, the government, with all the instruments of state power in its possession.

Questioning his integrity is a surefire way to trigger a Pavlovian response in Mac—an explosion of ferocious anger, hard edged and cold with menace. He will repulse you, no matter what the cost to himself or others. You have dared to question his core understanding of himself, and he will not tolerate it.

Certainly, living as he chose to, deceit carefully woven into the fabric of his personality, coexisting with that of a moral being for whom personal integrity was the sine qua non defining his sense of self, created inner tensions that must have sometimes been hard to reconcile. A man who could look death coldly in the eye, yet fearful of revealing personal feelings, largely impervious to the impact of his actions on others. Voluble, engaging, and a raconteur who can command rapturous attention, he is emotionally distant within.

Throughout this book, Mac's sense of his own integrity and his willingness to go to any lengths to vindicate it wage a fierce struggle with each other and often leave him with the debris at his feet—but just as often with triumph. Selflessness and selfishness drink in equal measure from the same cup. His life and the struggle for South Africa ran on parallel courses for five decades.

We had our rules of engagement: I sent Mac the raw transcripts of his interviews and the subsequently edited interviews. Frequently, questions for follow-up interviews had their origins in previous ones, as answers begged further elaboration, clarification, or were at odds with other published accounts of events at that time. And, of course, he received the final versions that I wanted to include in *Shades of Difference* so that he had the opportunity to correct and have a say in what went into it.

Each chapter is also made up of an introduction. This consists of my independent investigation, interviews, and analyses. Mac has had no say in this. Indeed, he had no sight of anything I wrote until the final text had been agreed between my editors at Viking and me. Only then was Mac shown the full manuscript. In this part of the book Mac could only correct facts and spellings.

And we kept to the deal: two parallel paths, one resonating with Mac's voice telling his story, one preceding his, in my voice, my critical assessment of the context in which his life was unfolding at that point in his life.

These two paths converge and crisscross, but remain distinct throughout the book. The end product, I like to think, is both a portrait of Mac and of South Africa, intertwined yet singularly apart.

3

But first the context:

There is not *a* South African history, but rather histories according to different perspectives reflecting its cultural, linguistic, and racial differences and the fact that for most of the history under review, one class of people—whites—was the masters and another class—blacks—the servants, firmly under the boot of their masters. The rulers and the ruled, not surprisingly, see a common history in very different lights.

The San, small groups of hunter-gatherers, inhabited the southern end of Africa, including what is today South Africa, for millennia. About two thousand years ago the pastoralist Khoikhoi, from farther north, moved into the same area. In time the San and the Khoikhoi came into conflict with each other over resources.

The first settlers arrived in 1652, when the Dutch East India Company (VOC)* founded a refreshment station at the Cape of Good Hope. Soon the refreshment station had turned into a permanent, fortified settlement. The VOC expanded its area of control and seized enclosed land for cultivation. The native pastoralists either withdrew or remained as servants for the Dutch, or fought back. But the greatest toll on their number came from the diseases that the Dutch brought with them and against which native immune systems had no defense. With settlement, slavery followed. Within years, thousands of slaves had poured into the new colony—mostly from the Indonesian archipelago, Bengal (part of which is now in Bangladesh), South India, Ceylon (now Sri Lanka), Madagascar, and the East African coast. In 1717, there were about 2,500 slaves in the Cape, almost 17,000 in 1795, and by the time slavery ended in 1834 (under British rule), the number had grown to 36,000.[2] In the second half of the seventeenth century, whites entered the country mainly from the Netherlands and Germany. In 1688, a party of French Huguenots escaping from religious persecution in Europe found refuge at the Cape. Over time, but especially during the late nineteenth century, Xhosa-speaking Africans began to migrate into the Cape Peninsula; but the descendants of

*Verenigde Oost-Indische Compagnie.

the Khoisan,* the slaves, and the progeny of early mixed relationships (Coloureds) outnumbered whites and Africans.

For a century and a half the VOC controlled the Cape. Individual rights were based on one's place in the company's hierarchy of employees; settlers; "mixed" races; and at the bottom, slaves. Some historians argue that "race and status in the course of the 18th century were virtually identical since all the burghers were mainly of European descent and all the slaves were black," that culture, not color, was the issue.[3] Others, and a preponderance of black social and political commentators, argue that the VOC established a legal framework based on a racial hierarchy and that racism was institutionalized in South Africa 250 years before apartheid.

Whatever the view, the "cultural" divisions set in place during the VOC era had developed into racial divisions by the colonial era. As a result, embedded social and economic structures of race permeated the colonies that would be joined together to become South Africa before the rest of Africa was colonized and subjected to racial domination. They remained in place well after the rest of Africa had freed itself from racial subjugation. To South Africa's Africans, the centrality of racism to the country's history for 350 years is what sets it apart from the rest of Africa.

In 1795, to prevent French occupation, the British overran the VOC at the Cape, keeping it until February 1803, when in terms of the Treaty of Amiens it was restored, not to the VOC, which had meantime ceased to exist, but to the Batavian Republic after the Treaty of Amiens. With the resumption of the Napoleonic Wars, the British retook the Cape in early 1806, and their possession was confirmed in 1815, after Napoleon's final defeat at Waterloo.

The carrying of pass books, opposition to which became one of the rallying points for opposition to apartheid in the second half of the twentieth century, dates back to the first years of the nineteenth century. In 1809, the British passed the first in a series of laws to conciliate the descendants of the Dutch colonizers. These had, over a period of 150 years, begun to develop the trappings of a new identity. Now Afrikaners, or Boers, they spoke an indigenized creole of Dutch called Afrikaans (literally, "African"). The 1809 regulations required every Hottentot (or Khoikhoi) to have a "fixed place of abode" and if he wished to move, he had to obtain "a pass from his master or from a local official." In 1854, the British ceded representative government to the Cape, transferring political power from London to the Cape's white minority, although the qualified franchise was

---

*The name used for the San and the Khoikhoi together.

nonracial.* In the 1820s and 1830s, the Mfecane transformed the demographic and political geography of the southern Africa interior. It was a period of radical change and crisis among African people in Natal and Zululand. In the 1820s, the Zulu clan, one of a small number of groups among the northern Nguni, created a large empire under the leadership of Shaka, which stretched across most of what is now the KwaZulu-Natal Province of South Africa. The rise of the Zulu kingdom set in motion a chain of warfare and raiding. Competition among northern Nguni societies for land and resources forced defeated groups to flee Natal and Zululand, go west across the Drakensberg and south into the Transkei, disrupting traditional patterns of settlement and resulting in intense conflict for a number of years. Some parts of the country were depopulated; others saw the rise of new states such as the Ndebele under Mzilikazi and the southern Sotho under Moshoeshoe in what is now Lesotho.[4] Huge numbers of refugees, the Mfengu, flooded into Xhosaland, where they were welcomed; but since they arrived with no property and had no local kin, they had little status in Xhosa society. This made them more susceptible to the ideas and practices of traders and missionaries, which encouraged a propensity to be disloyal to their Xhosa patrons.[5] In nine frontier wars stretching over the better part of a century, first against Trekboers (1779–81, 1789–93) and then the British (1799–1803, 1811–12, 1818–19, 1834–35, 1846–47, 1850–52, 1877–78), the Xhosa resisted efforts to subdue them.[6] In the latter wars, the British eventually prevailed by systematically destroying the Xhosa food supplies.

After conquest and humiliation, a lethal disease, brought from Europe, spread among the Xhosa's cattle, which were systematically decimated. Among some clans, up to 80 percent of the cattle died. The vision of a sixteen-year-old girl, Nongqawuse, promised that their ancestors would return to restore a state of normalcy if all the remaining cattle were slaughtered and all the grain destroyed. The mass slaughter that ensued resulted in the killing of four hundred thousand cattle and death by starvation for thirty thousand Xhosas. In early 1858, another thirty-three thousand moved inside the Cape Colony to become laborers.[7] Colonialism marched on.

In the 1830s, several thousand Cape Boers, later known as Voortrekkers, or pioneers, resentful of British rule, the abolition of slavery,

---

*Slaves had been required to carry pass books to travel since 1709. The Khoikhoi were freed from this requirement, but from the mid-1800s, Africans entering the Cape Colony from the east were required to carry passes.

and local government, and starved for land, began to leave the Cape and move northward. The apparent depopulation of parts of the interior made it easier for the Voortrekkers to claim that the lands they settled were virgin territories. These areas later became the bulwarks of the Boer republics: the Transvaal and the Orange Free State. Their journey became known as the Great Trek. The Voortrekkers came into conflict with African tribes, and they defeated a Zulu army at the Battle of Blood River in 1838. The outnumbered Boers had made a "covenant" with God that if they won, it would mean they had his blessing to hold the land for posterity. The Great Trek and the Battle of Blood River are among the founding myths of Afrikaner nationalism, stimulating the belief that Afrikaners were a chosen people, the instrument of God's will, affirming their special affinity with the land.[8]

And thus the Afrikaner paradigm of history: that in much of what became South Africa, Afrikaners and Africans arrived at roughly the same time.[9] This allowed Afrikaners to claim an equal or superior claim of ownership and was used to justify territorial segregation, one of the main platforms of apartheid.

Bantu groups had been moving down into the African subcontinent since the second century, founding chieftainships and kingdoms such as that of the Mapungubwe in Limpopo, now a province of South Africa, and the Monomatapa in what is now Zimbabwe. In 1843, the British annexed Natal. Britain at first recognized the South African Republic (the Zuid-Afrikaansche Republiek, or ZAR—also known as the Transvaal)* and the Orange Free State, but the discovery of diamonds in Griqualand West in the 1860s and gold in the 1870s/1880s transformed the economy and the strategic importance of southern Africa. Britain annexed Griqualand West in 1871 and incorporated it into the Cape in 1880. When gold was discovered in the Witwatersrand area of the Transvaal inside the ZAR, the British again moved to annex.

The fragmentation of southern Africa into British colonies, Boer republics, and autonomous African societies was disadvantageous to Britain. It embarked on a series of grand imperial moves to establish hegemony over the entire region and federate the territories of southern Africa, annexing the Transvaal in 1877, defeating in 1879 first the Zulus—but not before it had been humiliated by them at Isandhlwana—and then the Pedi. After a revolt in 1880–81, the Boers regained most of their indepen-

---

*After 1994, the Transvaal was divided into several provincees: Gauteng, Limpopo, Mpumalanga, and North West. Guateng is basically what was, loosely, Witwatersrand.

dence. In the 1890s, the British South Africa Company, founded by Cecil John Rhodes, prime minister of the Cape from 1890 to 1895, annexed territories north of the Limpopo, the start of aggressive British expansion into the rest of the continent that by the end of World War I would fulfill Rhodes's dream to "paint the African map red from the Cape to Cairo."

The war now known as the Anglo-Boer South African War (1899–1902) was engineered by the British.[10] The war was long and devastating: British and Cape and Natal colonial troops were at first defeated by the highly mobile mounted forces of the Boers, but a campaign of scorched-earth tactics—some twenty-six thousand Afrikaner women and children died in concentration camps—brought the Boers to their knees, leading to the peace treaty signed at Vereeniging on 31 May 1902. Some fifteen thousand Africans also died in the conflict. While this peace led to the emergence of Boer warriors such as Jan Smuts and Louis Botha as national leaders, and led finally to the unification of South Africa in 1910, the aftermath of the Anglo-Boer War also fed into the Afrikaners' anticolonial feeling and contributed to their strong sense of national identity as a formerly oppressed people.

4

From the birth of the Union of South Africa (stitched together from the colonies of the Cape and Natal and the two Boer republics), racial discrimination was institutionalized, as it had been in both the British colonies of the Cape and Natal and in the Boer republics. Whatever divisions existed between Afrikaners and English-speaking whites—and there were many—the two were united in their determination to ensure that blacks remained in a permanent subordinate position. Underlying all white politics was the imperative to contain the *swart gevaar*, "black threat." In 1911, the Native Labour Regulation Act required all male African workers to carry passes, enabling government to direct African workers and Africans seeking work to where it was needed, thus ensuring a cheap supply of labor.[11] In 1913, the Land Act was passed, limiting African land ownership to 7 percent. The Act of 1936 added 6 percent. It was arguably these land acts that underpinned much later apartheid legislation, such as the homelands policy. The novelty of South African–style segregation was to grant Africans "rights" in their own territories.

In terms of the franchise, each province was allowed to retain its own franchise arrangements, but only whites could stand for election to the National Assembly and the Senate. Indians had no franchise. Africans and

Coloureds had a franchise only in the Cape; but Africans were removed from the common voters' roll in 1936, placed on a separate roll, and entitled to vote for three native representatives to parliament—who had to be white. They lost this representation in 1960. Coloureds were removed from the common voters' roll in 1956 and put on a separate roll, which was abolished in 1968.

Between 1910 and 1948, South Africa was ruled by a succession of governments that slowly gravitated toward right-wing Afrikaner nationalism. The first government, under the South Africa Party (SAP), an umbrella party comprised of the former ruling parties in the Free State and the Transvaal (Boer) and Natal and the Cape (English), worked hard to promote reconciliation between Afrikaners and English-speaking whites. But the more the SAP tried to ameliorate English fears that it would acquiesce to the increasingly strident demands of its Afrikaner nationalist rump, the more it alienated sections of the Afrikaner community. In 1914, nationalists broke away and formed the National Party (NP) to protect their interests in the face of what was perceived as the inordinate control of the civil service and business by English-speaking whites. Afrikaners, especially poor Afrikaners, felt marginalized in the Union, and this sense of alienation contributed enormously to the growth of a distinct Afrikaner national consciousness, which forged an Afrikaner identity based on a distinctive spoken language, a common religious faith, and a shared historical past.[12] The government's decision to enter World War I on the side of Britain further broadened the base of support for the party. The Afrikaner Broederbond, a semisecret Afrikaner organization, was created in 1919 to promote the cause of an Afrikaner republic, gain control of the economy, and spread Afrikaans culture. It also sought to advance the cause of poor Afrikaners.[13]

In 1924, the SAP was defeated by a coalition of the Labour Party and the National Party, which together formed the pact government. In the ensuing years, Afrikaans was made an official language for the first time, and segregation became further entrenched in legislation. In 1934, the NP and SAP entered into a coalition and then fused, forming the United South African National Party, which later became the United Party (UP). Disgruntled Afrikaner nationalists left the National Party and formed the Hervormde or Purified National Party (HNP).[14] The HNP and the Broederbond became intimately intertwined. The outbreak of World War II created new divisions within the United Party when the party voted to enter World War II on the side of Britain. Many Afrikaners who opposed the decision left the party and joined the HNP, which swallowed the remnants of the old National Party and took its name.

In 1948, the NP won the general election on a platform that advocated apartheid, the separation of racial groups. What resentments and grievances Africans might have had were of no consequence to the bulk of both Afrikaners and English-speaking whites. Their threat lay in their numbers. A franchise to Africans would sound the death knell for white domination. English-speaking whites in other African countries had either returned to England after decolonization or stayed put. South Africa's English population would have had that option, but Afrikaners did not; there was no mother country to return to. South Africa was their country.

Apartheid gave a legislative face to existing practice and extended the boundaries of application to every aspect of black life. Between 1948 and 1958, the basic legal infrastructure of apartheid was created; the Prohibition of Mixed Marriages Act, the Group Areas Act, the Population Registration Act, and the Reservation of Separate Amenities Act were passed.[15]

The pass laws were further refined and extended. Blacks had to carry a pass book giving the details of their racial classification, place of legal residence, their current work status, and permisson for them to be in a place other than their legal residence. No African could remain in a white residential area for more than seventy-two hours without the proper work permit. It was a world where the color of your skin determined everything that would happen to you, where life's opportunities were defined at the moment of birth if you were black—and if you were black, whether you were African, Indian, or Coloured.

The policies of successive National Party governments, underpinned in part by an ideology of racial superiority, were developed into a rigorous race-based legal framework that remained in force for much of the life of the old South Africa.[16] Some changes that eventually contributed to undermining apartheid, such as the legalization of black trade unions and abolition of influx control, were instituted in the 1980s.

5

The African National Congress (ANC) was founded in 1912 by mission-educated African intellectuals who wanted to ameliorate the Africans' economic plight and to secure the extension of political rights, especially the voting franchise, to all races.[17] Membership, however, was restricted to Africans. But in the first three decades of its existence, the ANC distanced itself from the African masses, did not throw in its lot with African workers, and was unashamedly middle class. It was vehemently anti-Communist; its focus was on furthering the cause of Africans by winning acceptance from whites, and it shied away from any action that whites might disapprove of. It relied on prayer meetings, petitions, meetings with government officials.

Others did not. In 1913, in the Orange Free State, after a campaign by thousands who chose to go to jail rather than carry pass books, the provincial government was forced temporarily to back down, and in 1918, 19 46 fifteen thousand African mine workers went on strike but were bludgeoned into submission.

The ANC underwent a transformation in the 1940s. It began to remake itself as a mass movement under the influence of the ANC Youth League (ANCYL), which was formed at the University of Fort Hare in 1944.[18] In 1949, the ANC adopted a program of action that included calls for civil disobedience and boycotts.[19] In June 1952, it launched the Defiance Campaign,* along with the South African Indian Congress, to demand changes to legislation dealing with pass laws, livestock limitation, so-called Group Areas, separate representation of voters, and the suppression of communism. Although it ground to a halt in November 1952, ANC membership had swelled from under twenty thousand members to more than one hundred thousand. [20]

In April 1960, the ANC was banned and went underground. In 1961, having satisfied itself that it had exhausted all forms of nonviolent protest, and being unable to wring any concessions from the government and facing the prospect of increasing repression, it turned to armed struggle and formed Umkhonto we Sizwe (MK), or "Spear of the Nation." But ANC leaders, including Nelson Mandela, Walter Sisulu, and Govan Mbeki, were arrested, tried and convicted of treason and sentenced to life in prison on Robben Island. The ANC was driven into exile, and from exile it waged a struggle for national liberation. MK, however, with its camps in Tanzania and later in Angola, both far distant from the borders of South Africa and with the national terrains of other countries intervening, was unable to infiltrate a supply of cadres into South Africa to win any decisive victory over the white government and a deeply militarized white populace. In the

---

*More than 8,500 people courted imprisonment by contravening pass laws and curfew regulations, orders segregating whites and nonwhites in railway stations and post offices, and other "petty" apartheid measures. The campaign led to the formation of the Coloured People's Congress, the Congress of Democrats (white), the South African Council of Trade Unions (SACTU), and then a Congress Alliance which played a crucial role in promoting multiracial resistance to apartheid. Nelson Mandela, president of the ANC Youth League, was appointed volunteer in chief of the campaign. The success of the Defiance Campaign led to his election as the Transvaal president and deputy national president of the ANC in 1952. See [] general information/documents and reports. [] Defiance Campaign.

1980s, indigenous mass movements—the United Democratic Front (UDF) and the Congress of South African Trade Unions (COSATU)— created a new terrain of struggle.

6

During the cold war, Western governments tended to support white South Africa, even if only tacitly, as a bulwark against communism in Africa, while the USSR gave financial and military help to the ANC, as it had to other African liberation movements and postliberation governments. Eventually, however, the ANC's cause, and that of the people of South Africa, came to be seen as just in the international community.

In addition to the collapse of communism, a number of factors forced both the National Party government and the ANC to reappraise their options. For the South African government, financial sanctions had begun to bite hard, with little prospect of alleviation; the increasing unrest within South Africa, including semispontaneous populist uprisings partly inspired by the ANC, had begun to become uncontainable; and most important, perhaps, demographics became a consideration: whites simply lacked the numbers to sustain oppression. A negotiated settlement with the ANC emerged as the most desirable prospect. And for the ANC, a negotiated settlement also became the preferred option. Overtures from the South African government, which it was under international pressure to consider, came to be seen as genuine, despite reservations on the part of some; and with communism collapsing and the Soviet Union imploding, its money sources dried up.

The way was paved for a black majority government in South Africa.

7

I chose to write about Satyandranath Ragunanan Maharaj—Mac— because of the extraordinary range of his experiences during half a century of tumultuous change in South Africa. Those times were in part made tumultuous by the actions of Mac himself.

His life is an expression of the struggle against apartheid and institutionalized oppression, of the triumph of endurance in the face of almost insurmountable odds, of absolute conviction in a cause that became his raison d'être and consumed him to the exclusion of all other considerations and led him repeatedly to put his life at risk.

He lived in a special world, one he had to create in order to survive, a

world of half-truths, outright lies, subterfuge, deception, and the compelling need to trust judiciously, for even trust might be the instrument of
betrayal. Few could measure up to his demanding standards, and few had
the stamina and intellect necessary to keep him from a ruthless, relentless
obsession for translating his vision of South Africa into reality. His iron
discipline and will contrasted with his surrender of self to the movement.
Yet he is also a social being and a raconteur, with a laugh that hangs in the
air when it stops.

Although he could take an incisive, clinical, and dispassionate look at
others and their situations, he rarely looked into the mirror of self. This
was a cultivated disposition, perhaps, to shield himself from a niggling in-
trospection that might cause him to question himself. Nowadays, while
the detachment is never removed, it is always placed within a broader,
more encompassing reflection, that of a man who has given his life to the
pursuit of a singular cause, yet who is wise enough to know that causes
robbed of their human content are meaningless.

Yet in Mac's detachment there is a certain wistfulness—not so much
for the things missed as for the things not learned, such as how to deal
with an ordinary normal life. The causes of peace and a conflict-free world
are great and noble, yet it is the small causes of peace in our homes, of
holding families together, that can be harder to carry out.

It would be false to portray Mac simply as a paragon of virtue. Mac is
arrogant to a fault, convinced of the correctness of his analysis of any subject that crosses his line of view, possessed of a sense of moral righteous-
ness that is overbearing on occasion. He is self-absorbed. He does not
mince words, but he can be evasive. If you confront him with his own contradictions, he tries to rationalize them. Injury is rarely acknowledged, but
one is not so sure that it is easily forgotten.

These are the observations of his friends—who are fiercely loyal to
him. He is a man of few friends, although there are many who feel they are
his friends. He draws people in, yet in the end they appear to know little
about him other than his courage, leadership, drive, ruthlessness—and
charm. Charm is not something he has to work at; he can dole it out in
whatever amount is necessary to achieve the results he wants. The fact that
he allows you to know he is plying his charm only adds to it.

Between 1993 and 2003, I taped more than two hundred hours of interviews with Mac. We talked briefly at times, lengthily at others. Sometimes he spoke spontaneously, sometimes more hesitantly; sometimes
guardedly, sometimes unguardedly. Sometimes he would talk with mild
anger bordering on a dismissiveness of sorts, and sometimes with humor

that also bordered on a dismissiveness of sorts. On occasions he would talk with passion, at others dispassionately, but always with an analytical agility to detach himself from the events of which he was part, as if he were an observer rather than a crucial player. His answers were never direct and always segued into tangentials, which themselves segued in still more directions. Getting from A to B required a couple of runs through the alphabet, perhaps an art form mastered to beguile his interrogators during long hours of interrogation, appearing to be saying something that once transcribed was largely devoid of meaning, or, more likely, a natural predisposition. Either way it meant that we often covered the same ground again and again just to get clarity of expression.

Mac was always warm and friendly, and he went to extreme lengths to accommodate me, often at his own inconvenience. We both knew he was a past master of the art of manipulation; I joked with him that all his kindness and willingness to put things on hold so we could get together would have no influence on what I wrote. Both of us were trying to grapple with the truth, but from different perspectives; both of us realized that neither was sufficient to do justice to the subject itself and the individual who records them—all accounts of the past are partial and incomplete and impaired by the biases of the individual who recalls them.

8

Shades of Difference: Mac Maharaj and the Struggle for South Africa is part political autobiography and part the observer, myself, putting the pieces of Mac's life in the context of their time and the events that shaped his life. Whenever Mac gave me his version of an event or conversation that involved other people, I sought out those persons, if they were still alive, either to verify the accuracy of Mac's memory or to record the other person's recollection, if different. If accounts did not dovetail, I annotated the different versions. If the differences were irreconcilable I dropped the matter, preferring to provide no account of the event or conversation, but again I note that.

Mac once said, only half jokingly, that I would never discover everything about him. I didn't try. His narrative is his, the life he has chosen to reveal. I did not force him into any areas of his life he was unwilling to share, nor did I force him to reveal activities he chose not to disclose. Even though we spent several interviews discussing his time in the German Democratic Republic (GDR), where he was sent by the South African Communist Party (SACP) for military training in 1961–62, he never told me that Tim Naidoo, his first wife, spent two weeks with him there on holiday. When I did find out, I mentioned it to him, and he confirmed it without comment. To me the omission is indicative of the way he compartmentalized his life. There was the struggle and there were other people. The struggle part he was comfortable about dealing with; the other people gave him problems. Besides the great difficulties Mac has dealing with personal relationships, Tim presented special difficulties. He did not want to offend Zarina, his second wife and the mother of his children, by drawing too much attention to Tim and the role she played in his life— and to her contribution to the struggle in her own right: her fierce loyalty, imprisonment and solitary confinement, and absolute commitment to him while he was on Robben Island. These memories evoked inner conflicts he would rather squash, so he consigned memories of her to his subconscious and selectively "recalls" what was necessary to deal with the matter at hand. At least, these are the impressions I was left with.*

Mac's voice flows from the conversations we had during eleven years. These conversations attempt to place him—and in that sense the struggle for freedom in South Africa—in various contexts to get a better understanding of the struggle itself. Some matters are not covered in *Shades of Difference*, not because we didn't talk about them but because of space restrictions, but the record of all our conversations is available to the reader elsewhere.

While I was writing and continuing with my interviews, Mac's world fell apart. In quick succession he found himself the object of allegations that he had received payoffs as transport minister, and he was subsequently investigated by the Scorpions, the elite investigative unit of the National Prosecuting Authority (NPA). He found himself at the center of a political storm when he confirmed allegations that Bulelani Ngcuka, director of the NPA, had been investigated by ANC intelligence in the 1980s for being an apartheid spy.

On the occasion of South Africa's celebration of ten years of democracy, Mac was unemployed, facing possible prosecution, ostracized by the ANC leadership, and not invited by the state to a single official commemorative event. At the time of going to press, he was still under investigation. Much of his fall was of his own making, but all of it is consistent with who he is.

---

*In an interview with Fran Lisa Buntman (1994), Mac addresses the propensity of ex–Robben Island prisoners to suppress aspects of their prison lives they are uncomfortable dealing with. See Fran Lisa Buntman, *Robben Island and Prisoner Resistance to Apartheid* (Cambridge: Cambridge University Press, 2003), pp. 78–79.

For the ANC, the struggle to defeat apartheid was not a freedom struggle in the traditional sense of being a war to reclaim land or establish sovereignty. Rather, it had internalized a larger mission: to destroy a system in which one race of human beings (whites) imposed on another (blacks), depriving them of the right to call themselves human.* Thus, whenever I asked Mac a question that might suggest that the South African government had something other than ulterior, diabolical self-serving motives in the late 1980s and early 1990s when it first made overtures to the ANC and then engaged in negotiations, he reacted incredulously and a little sharply. How ill informed could I be! How naive! His inability to see his enemy in any other way than as an object reflected that in dehumanizing him, they had empowered him to dehumanize them.

9

Mac is a South African Indian, a Hindu. He would say that he is a native-born South African who disengaged from religion when he was five. His insistence on being South African, with only a half genuflection in the general direction of India, is struggle driven. The ANC's insistence on one unified South Africa versus the apartheid state's insistence on dividing South Africa into racial segments is a key to that attitude. He belongs to the smallest minority in South Africa (today less than a million out of a population of forty-six million), the last to arrive on its shores and the first to assert its rights. Indians, although they would not have thought so at the time, were the prime movers in a struggle that would last one hundred years.

In 1894, Mohandas Karamchand Gandhi formed the Natal Indian Congress (NIC) to protect the rights Indians believed they were entitled to as subjects of the British Crown.† At first, the NIC served the interests of rich Indian merchants—"passenger" Indians from western India who paid their own fares in search of jobs and opportunities. In his first years in South Africa, Gandhi's attitude toward Africans was as racist as that of

*See, for example, Kader Asmal et al., Reconciliation Through Truth (Cape Town: David Philip, 1997), pp. 2–3.
†Natal was an autonomous region of the Cape colony until 1856, when it was granted its own legislative council. Free Indians had the right to the franchise, but Indians were barred from voting in 1896, two years after Natal was granted responsible government.

whites.[21] But after World War II, the Indian congresses increasingly aligned themselves with the ANC.

Yet Indians were not always welcome in the ANC. In *Long Walk to Freedom*, Mandela admits:

> I had recently become national president of the [ANC's] Youth League, and in my new role I urged that the campaign [the Defiance Campaign] should be exclusively African. The average African, I said, was still cautious about joint action with Indians and Coloureds. While I had made some progress in terms of my opposition to communism, I still feared the influence of Indians.[22] In addition, many of our grassroots African supporters saw Indians as exploiters of black labor in their role as shopkeepers and merchants.[23]

When the issue was taken up by the National Executive Committee (NEC) and voted down, Mandela persisted, raising the issue yet again at the ANC's national conference in 1951. Only when the delegates emphatically rejected his view did Mandela bow and "fully accept the agreed-upon decision."[24]

The Indian community was largely self-contained. It was cohesive, with a highly inculcated set of values in terms of languages, religion, and the importance of family and education. It associated communism with atheism, yet most leading Indian activists were Communists. The Indian community was more privileged than the African community and fearful of African majority rule. Still, the Indian contribution to the struggle is completely disproportionate to their number. In the new South Africa, that contribution, like the Indian community itself, is becoming marginalized. It does not take much to marginalize a community that comprises less than 2 percent of the population and even less to downplay its role in the liberation of the country. For the moment, it is being swallowed by an inexorable—and to some extent understandable—penchant for Africanization.

In 1971, after there were rumblings in the ranks over the decision at the ANC Consultative Conference at Morogoro in Tanzania, two years earlier, to allow non-Africans to become members of the ANC in exile, the matter was discussed at a meeting of the ANC's National Executive Committee (NEC).[25] It reiterated that the mission of the ANC was to free the African people of South Africa and that, insofar as non-Africans furthered that cause, they were freeing themselves. There are, it seems, hierarchies of freedom.

1. CHILDHOOD AND YOUTH

Introduction

THE SYSTEM OF INDENTURE was created primarily in response to the labor crisis experienced in sugar-producing areas after the abolition of slavery. The history of South Africa's Indians began in the British colony of Natal in 1860. Indigenous Africans shunned work in the sugarcane fields and clung to their subsistence economy. The demand for labor, however, was drastically increasing. The British government arranged with the government of India, also a British colony, to allow Natal to import indentured labor, a practice that dated back to the early 1800s in other parts of Africa.

Laborers were recruited from densely populated areas in India, where smaller land holdings were common and there was a large reservoir of lower-caste Hindus. In general, the supplying districts faced great socioeconomic stress as a result of density and poverty. Under these conditions, recruitment was easy, often on the basis of false promises, and often in the manner of press-ganging by notorious *arkatias,** who used any means to lure recruits. For many, indenture was refurbished slavery.

The workers who went to distant places had no right to a negotiated wage, a choice of employer, or even the category of work. The conditions of employment created by the government of India in collaboration with Natal were as often breached as honored. For the most part, the Natal government left these matters to employers, who adhered to the conditions of contract when it was in their own interest to do so. They did not treat

*Licensed immigrant recruiters in India hired men known as *arkatias* to scour the villages for willing migrants. *Arkatia* refers to a hook because the *arkatias* used unscrupulous ways to trick or press-gang unwilling "recruits" into becoming indentured laborers. The recruiter earned about three pounds for each recruit. An *arkatia* might have earned fifty pounds—a fortune in nineteenth-century India.

indentured labor too badly or work it to exhaustion; that kind of treatment could lessen the value of their investment. From the time they arrived, indentured laborers were disparaged, labeled coolies, which in India was a derogatory term for porters.

The first group of indentured Indians to South Africa arrived in Durban in November 1860. The white population of Natal (now the province of KwaZulu-Natal) at the time was under seven thousand. From the onset, there were differences of opinion among whites—mostly English-speaking and some Afrikaners who had made their way from the Cape—between those who wanted a long-term policy of immigration of permanent settlers and those who thought only in terms of their urgent need of relatively unskilled but dependable labor. The question would resurface in the years to come.

For newly arrived Indians, adjustment to the harsh environment of the cane fields was difficult. Suicide rates were uncommonly high. Workers could not leave the plantation estates without a pass. Floggings were not uncommon. Laws to protect the workers were simply ignored by plantation owners.

The terms of their contracts gave indentured laborers the choice between a free passage home to India, when their contracts expired, or reindenture and then freedom and a small plot of land. They usually chose the latter. In 1886, there were more than twice as many free Indians in Natal than indentured Indians. The promise of land was for many little more than just that—a promise.

In the 1870s, a new class of immigrants arrived. These were passenger Indians—Indians who paid their own way to South Africa. They were mostly Muslim traders from the Gujarat area. Often they were people of some means who set up businesses in Natal, the Transvaal, and the Orange Free State, and competed with white shopkeepers. Whites immediately felt threatened, which led to discrimination.

Passenger Indians usually came alone, looked at the economic opportunities they could take advantage of, established themselves, and then returned to India to bring their families back with them or to marry and bring their new wives back. They maintained more links with India, with the villages they came from and with many of their descendants, especially the Gujaratis; they also retained some contact with their extended families in India. By contrast, indentured Indians' contact with India declined. Few members of succeeding generations could remember the villages their families had come from. But religion remained a constant; festivals and traditional practices were observed. Indian culture subsumed most of their Indian sense of identity.

Among Hindus, caste restrictions still prevailed. Marriages could only take place between persons of the same caste, and brides were brought from India. Today, elements of that caste consciousness still persist, ironically, among upwardly mobile Hindus with indentured backgrounds.[1]

By 1893, Indians in Natal outnumbered whites.[2] Once whites determined that Indians represented a severe threat to their economic and commercial interests, they set about putting in place laws that would reduce the size of the Indian population by repatriation, limiting further Indian immigration, controlling the number of trading licenses Indians could have, and restricting the ownership and occupation of property. When self-government was granted to the colony in 1893, whites mounted a campaign to strike from the roll some four hundred Indians with property who had the vote. In 1894, Indians lost their parliamentary franchise, and the following year the government imposed a tax of three pounds on indentured and ex-indentured laborers and their families. The laws were specifically aimed at discouraging Indians from staying on once their contracts had expired. By the century's end, the British governing authority seemed intent on taking away whatever remaining rights Indians had.

The influx of Indians and their increasing tendency to take up residence at the end of their contracts was also viewed with apprehension by whites in the Orange Free State and the Transvaal. To stem what was, in fact, no more than a dribble, both Boer states, at that point independent republics, passed laws forbidding Indian settlement inside their borders and any movement across borders without a pass. These laws remained in force until the mid-1980s.

2

Into this situation stepped Mohandas Karamchand Gandhi. He came to the Transvaal as a lawyer in 1893 to represent a rich Indian client, and it was there he first experienced racial discrimination. In 1894, in Natal, he founded the Natal Indian Congress (NIC) with the aim of organizing the Indian community to resist the erosion of their rights. In 1903, he founded the Transvaal British Indian Association. When the Transvaal Legislative Council passed the Transvaal Asiatic Ordinance of 1906, a law that required all Indians to register and to carry passes, Gandhi embarked on his own particular form of defiance. At a mass protest meeting on

11 September 1906, the Indian community in the Transvaal took a solemn pledge to defy the law. *Satyagraha,* "firmness in truth" or passive resistance, was born.*

Gandhi mounted his great campaign of passive resistance in 1913 to protest the poll tax on indentured labor, using the provincial pass laws, which prohibited Indians in Natal from working or residing in the Transvaal without a pass, to court mass imprisonment and make the situation unmanageable for the government. Newcastle, which is close to the Transvaal border, has a particular place in this history. At Gandhi's instigation, the coal miners of Newcastle and northern Natal went on strike; strikers and their families gathered in Newcastle, camped out, and then in large numbers set out on foot and crossed the Transvaal border. Gandhi was arrested a number of times and imprisoned. These arrests sparked a general strike—up to thirty thousand workers—among all Indians in Natal and eventually forced the government to back down on the poll tax. Memories of that campaign became part of the identity of the Indians of Newcastle.

Despite the setback on the poll tax, the government continued to pursue policies that were designed to encourage Indians to return to India en masse. White fears that Indians might somehow encroach upon what whites considered to be rightfully theirs—economic success—lingered. Indians were not welcome in South Africa, especially passenger Indians.

After Gandhi left South Africa in 1914, the leadership of the congresses fell to "moderates" who believed that Indian interests were best served by making compromises with the government. The congresses became the voice of the small Indian merchant class.[3] But in 1939, a radical leadership, which believed that the Indian community could defend itself by struggle and sacrifice, emerged. In 1946, when the Asiatic Land Tenure and Indian Representation Act (the "Ghetto Act") severely restricting Indian ownership of land was passed by the United Party government under the leadership of Jan Smuts, the radicals took over both congresses and once again invoked Gandhi's philosophy of political struggle to redress Indian grievances. In India, Gandhi's *satyagraha* was the pivotal force behind India's unstoppable drive for independence. In South Africa, a nationwide passive resistance movement was launched under the leadership of Dr. G. M. "Monty" Naicker in Natal and Dr. Yusuf Dadoo in the Transvaal.

---

*In 1911, a year after the Union of South Africa was established, there were 149,800 Indians in South Africa, of which 133,000 lived in Natal. Of these, 43,000 were indentured, 69,000 were free Indians, and 19,000 were passenger Indians. Altogether, 44 percent of the Indian population was South African born.

The passive resistance movement of 1946 united all sections of the Indian community. The campaign was conducted by the Joint Passive Resistance Council of both the Natal and the Transvaal Indian congresses. It involved defying the Ghetto Act by having Indians willfully court imprisonment by crossing the provincial borders without the required permits. Nearly two thousand men and women were voluntarily imprisoned for noncooperation.

Although the 1946 passive resistance campaign failed to achieve its objectives, it led the Indian congresses to make common cause with the African National Congress (ANC). In 1947, Naicker (NIC), Dadoo (TIC), and Dr. A. B. Xuma, the ANC president general, drew up a tripartite agreement—the Naicker/Xuma/Dadoo Pact—which mandated that the Indian and African organizations work together for the enfranchisement of all, the removal of land restrictions, freedom of movement, the abolition of passes for Africans and interprovincial travel for Indians, and an end to discriminatory legislation.

3

Satyandranath Ragunanan "Mac" Maharaj was born on 22 April 1935 in Newcastle. Newcastle was a small coal-mining town on the border with the Transvaal, and the point of departure for the extension of the railway that linked Durban with Johannesburg.

At the time of Mac's birth, English-speaking whites formed the majority of the white population of Natal. They dominated the business sector; they were the professionals; they ran the council; they lived in a separate area. The Afrikaners were mostly poor whites or farmers in rural areas. About once a week these farmers would come to the town to shop. The English looked down on them.

Newcastle was a village town of about 5,500 people, of whom about 500 were white. Of these, in the town itself, some 100 were Afrikaners. Overall, Africans were in the overwhelming majority, probably in the order of 3,500 or 4,000— Newcastle was Zulu territory. Coloureds, people of mixed race, would have accounted for only a handful of families, and the balance of the population was Indian, probably about 1,000 people. Residential areas, like elsewhere in Natal, were segregated; but in township areas, like the Indian residential location, there was a smattering of Africans and poor whites.

Mac grew up in a township called Lennoxton, which formed part of Newcastle. The Afrikaner section was made up of poor, mostly unemployed people who could not make a living on the farms. There were probably about five of these families. The area was mainly African, but there were large numbers of Indians there too.

In an increasingly segregated country, Mac was sealed into the Indian diaspora community in Lennoxton, with its remembered traditions and rituals, to which he was supposed to subscribe submissively and unquestioningly. Grinding poverty provided little leeway for escape, other than through education. Ambition was rooted in small things: a job at the petrol station, or better still, as a long-distance truck driver. Members of the Indian community married early and were expected to have children immediately. This was provision for the future.

Such was life in Lennoxton until 1948. The National Party government came to power and began to implement apartheid. At first this had little impact on the Indian community in Newcastle. The few poor white families in the area moved out of Lennoxton, and Lennoxton became more Indian, but no one thought much of this. The community was self-contained and isolated. Today it is still an Indian enclave.

The Durban riots in January 1949, sparked by an altercation between an Indian man and a fourteen-year-old African boy, lasted two days. Africans attacked Indians on the streets and looted their homes, confirming to the Indian community that Africans were as great a threat to their well-being as whites.[4] If whites believed that Indians were undercutting them in trade and commerce, Africans believed that Indian traders were exploiting them. For once, Africans and whites were in accord. Newspaper accounts ran reports of whites standing at their office windows on downtown Grey Street cheering on the Africans, urging them on to "get" the coolie, to "give him what he deserved."[5]

In Newcastle, the army arrived in force to ensure no spillover effect.[6] The *Newcastle Advertiser*, a paper widely read in the Indian community, editorialized:

> When we remember that fifty years ago the Zulu was a soldier and not a workman we understand why he does not and perhaps never will make an exemplary servant. How can a warrior caste, the Teutons of Africa, ever sink to the degradation of domestic labour? We see that his love of warfare, a throwback from Chaka's [sic] day still finds expression in the blood spilt in faction fights and now riots. By a study of his history we realise that there is nothing in his code of ethics to forbid slaughtering and plundering his neighbours. To him it is the soldiering.[7]

In a country where racism was ubiquitous, racially oppressed communities of different hues were proficient at denigrating each other.

For Mac, growing up in this insular place, the real world was Boundary Road, the street he grew up on, the shop out of which his family eked their existence. Although he came from a large family (three sisters and five brothers), they seem barely to feature in his recounting of his childhood. In the course of two hundred hours of conversation over a three-year period with me, Mac referred only fleetingly to his childhood, to siblings briefly, but never by name, or anyone else who might have touched his childhood. From his mother he learned a lesson that he would put into practice throughout his life: evasiveness, the expedient omission that averts confrontation. Adroit at appearing to concede to her husband's authority, his mother did what she thought was right.

But his father shaped his character. Mac's rebellion against this authoritarian but physically disabled man was a harbinger of the defiance of authority that would dominate much of his own life. Shanthee, Mac's sister and only surviving sibling, recalls their father vividly: "Very well built, over six feet, he used to wear a cap, special size, shoes a size 10. He had blue eyes. If you saw him in his younger days, you'd never say he was Indian. He had curly hair, blue eyes, was fair in complexion. All the Dutch people around called him Blou Oog [Blue Eye], and they were quite friendly."[8]

Growing up, she says, they all regarded themselves as Indian. Their father maintained contact with relatives in India for some time. There were letters from an uncle who had no children urging their father to pack up, go to India, and look after his affairs. Then came World War II, and contact was lost. Shanthee's recollections of her childhood were richly textured and included striking memories of her maternal grandparents and stories told to her by her grandmother about her paternal grandfather, a successful Newcastle businessman and eccentric of sorts who died rather suddenly after returning from a trip to India. With Mac, such memories did not surface. He and Shanthee might have come from different families.

Mac's attitude toward authority carried over into his school life. He gave his teachers a hard time, but he also achieved first place in his class all the way through—a contrarian. Yet he was conflicted. Uniformity and conformity were encouraged as valuable community assets. Children were socialized into not "sticking out." Mac stood out, and the social pressure he felt compelled him to "correct" the situation. He ascribes his sense of queasiness at finishing first in his class—and trying not to—to these social mechanisms. Mac, however, escaped categorization: he was very good at soccer, and he was prepared to challenge his teachers.

Mac had little sympathy for his father's disabilities or the suffering caused by his resultant isolation. His father was demanding, while his mother did the chores and let Mac play. Watching his father grapple with his powerlessness taught Mac about the niceties of power. Early on, one can detect Mac's fascination with power and authority, a glimmer of an understanding of the intricate relationship between the two, of the fact that having one did not necessarily mean you had the other. Authority without power was an illusion, a predicament the ANC would have to confront; and power without authority was a delusion, a fact the National Party never grasped.

The more Mac and I talked, the more "father" became "Dad"; and Mac realized the harshness of his judgment of his father, and he pulled back, perhaps out of the desire to be fair to his father. One day I asked Mac why his recollections of his father all centered on the raging figure barking out demands. Mac thought for a few minutes, and then began to talk quietly as the images of his father came into sharper focus. He recalled how his father's veranda gatherings were ad hoc discussion groups that had taught him to be interested in ideas and had inculcated in him the need for intellectual rigor and the desire to learn.

Mac was thirteen when the National Party came to power; he was still immersed in the things of growing boys. The arrival of the National Party destroyed the bonds of poverty. People of different races who shared little other than their poverty now shared nothing as the Afrikaner government systematically plucked poor whites out of their destitution, leaving racial pockmarks in their wake. Whereas previously those who were marginal had coexisted, that fragile saving grace was eroded with the implementation of the government's racial policies, especially the Group Areas Act of 1950, which sought to confine each racial group to its own area. Willie Maree, the new National Party MP, ran on a platform of repatriating Indians to India. He was comfortably elected.

Growing up, Mac made up his life according to his own impulses. He confronted the rules of the house and the school. His rebellion was against the symbols of the repression around him; he sees a foreshadowing of a larger rebellion emerging, but he cannot put it in a context that integrates the two. Believing in little, he was ripe for belief in something.

At one point in our conversations, Mac mentioned rather jocularly that the best crooks come from small towns. An environment that smothered ambition was built on layers of authoritarianism, whether those of home, school, family, community, or state. To the thwarted enterprising, there must have seemed only two alternatives: crook or revolutionary. For many, the difference came down to a roll of the dice.

Mac

MY PATERNAL GRANDFATHER came from India to South Africa to work as an indentured laborer in the sugarcane fields. When he finished his term, he joined the workforce building the continuation of the Durban/Pietermaritzburg railway line to Johannesburg. He met and married my grandmother in a compound of Indian workers in Pietermaritzburg. She had come to South Africa as a very young, illiterate girl and, unlike my grandfather, had no memory of where in India she had come from. When the railway line reached Johannesburg, my grandfather returned to Newcastle and set himself up as a businessman, opening a butcher shop, a general store, and a brickyard. He was a self-made man. He died in 1906.

My father was seven years old when his father died. From then on, despite the fact that he came from a Hindu background, he was brought up by a Muslim family: by people called the Shaiks, who had traveled with my grandfather from India to South Africa. The Shaiks also took over the shop from my grandmother because she did not feel she could manage it. When my father came of age, he went to work in a dairy. He married when he was still a youngster of fourteen, in about 1913. It was an arranged marriage, out of which five children—three boys and two girls—were born. In 1932, his wife died in childbirth. My father couldn't afford to bring up the youngest daughter, so he gave her to friends in another town as an adopted child. We didn't meet each other until 1952; by then she was married and living in Springs.

My father married my mother in 1932, and she bore him three children, two boys and a girl. I was born on 22 April 1935, the second son. When I was three years old, my father injured his hip and leg in a hit-and-run accident. The fracture did not set properly, and the fact that he was about six feet two inches and about 250 pounds didn't help matters. The combination of hip and ankle fracture restricted his movement, and gradually he became a cripple and couldn't work. Which meant that it was my mother who brought us up. We lived in Newcastle, in a house of galvanized iron. My mother kept the family going. She looked after the house. She sewed for us. She bought coal in bulk and resold it in small quantities.

The Shop

In 1941, during the war, the Muslim family who ran the shop went bank-rupt and gave the shop back to my father. He sold groceries and other small things. We now moved into the brick-built house attached to the shop. My father sat in the shop all day. Whenever customers came in, he would shout for my mother, who was out at the back doing the house-work. She would rush in and serve the customers, and if they came around the back for coal or firewood, she would shovel the coal or sell them fire-wood. In the meantime, she cooked and cleaned and ran the house. Al-though she was only four feet ten inches tall, she was a lean and powerful woman.

My mother was a very strong influence in my life. She was my great at-tachment. Like my father, she was the descendant of Indian indentured la-borers, but she had no memory of the past. Her parents' families worked for an Afrikaner farmer in the Free State in the 1860s, and that is where they grew up. The Free State Republic was the first to pass laws prohibiting people of Indian origin from living there, and her parents came from the only two Indian families with rights to be in the Free State, which I learned was a reward to my maternal grandfather for having served as a reconnais-sance scout for the Boer forces against the British.

Both families were wiped out in a fire, and the only survivors were my mother's parents: these two little kids, a boy in the one family and a girl in the other. The farmer brought up the two of them. They lived and worked on the farm, learned Afrikaans, and were surrounded by Afrikaans culture and an Afrikaner environment. They were two kids who had no memory of their past because their families were gone, and with no attachment to anything else because there were no other Indians in the Free State. The fire not only destroyed families, it destroyed memories.

The farmer arranged for them to be married in Bethlehem,* and they continued working on the farm. All their children were born there and ac-quired residential rights in the Free State. Sometime in the twenties, my mother's parents moved away from the farm to the Natal side of the bor-der, and with the help of the farmer they bought a small farm and began to farm in their own right. They had thirteen children altogether, among them my mother.

My family made a living from my father's shop, but we were always in fairly dire straits. Even our clothes, our trousers and shirts, were made by

*Bethlehem is a town in eastern Free State founded in 1869.

my mother because we couldn't afford to buy them. She bought what was called German print,* the cheapest cloth available. In fact, I went through high school in short pants. I acquired my first long pants only after I graduated! All the other boys at school wore long trousers, but I don't recall that they made fun of me.

Because my father had inherited the property on which we were living, we paid no rent. Our income came from the land, a two-acre plot. What we produced provided the food for the family: vegetables, corn, chickens. The income from the shop fluctuated. Being shop owners gave us some status, but we were neither better nor worse off than our neighbors. As soon as my three older brothers from my father's first marriage finished primary school, they went to work as bowser† boys handling the pumps at the local petrol station to supplement the family income. They earned about two pounds sterling per month. We were eight children altogether, three girls and five boys—two girls and three boys from my father's first marriage and two boys and a girl from his second. I was the second youngest.

Mom's Rules

In our house my father's needs always came first. As a cripple, my father could not always join us for a meal, and often his meal had to be taken to him; the choicest part of the meal had to be served to him first. After that, my mother would serve the whole troop of us children. She would make sure that food was served out in a way that ensured there was something to give us when we asked for a second helping. She sat back and ate last. She never presented herself as a person with needs.

Because my mother had to care for eight children and for my father, there was really no room for visible affection, so my relationship with my mother is a very complex one. She hardly ever had time to sit down and tell us stories. But we knew she was the central pillar of the family. She would get us children to help her with the work: cleaning the house or cooking or gardening or selling coal or running the shop. I can't recall my mother just sitting and resting. She was always on the move. Her only leisure activity that I can recall was when she attended a wedding or a funeral in the community. But I do recall, most vividly, my father sitting

*Inexpensive cotton cloth, typically printed with floral or geometric designs in white on a dark blue or brown background, first introduced into South Africa by German settlers in the mid-1800s.
†Gasoline pump.

there in that chair, a very well-built person, obviously extremely frustrated by his disability, calling for my mother in a loud voice.

Ours was a patriarchal family where my father was supposed to make the rules. And yet my mother had the power. She never let him know that, although he probably did. She never confronted him openly. When I disagreed or did not like what he was asking me to do, she would pull me aside and say, "This is your father, and you have no right to show him disrespect. You sit quietly. Let him say what he is saying, and if you really disagree, don't tell him but go ahead and do what you want to do." That was modeled on her experience. She never confronted his authority, but she ran the house as she saw fit.

There was much humor between my mom and me. She was very short, and her hair trailed down and touched the ground. She would pull it forward and brush it in strands. She would then plait it into a single braid and curl it up into a bun and pin it down. And while she was doing that, we kids would gather round, "Can I help you to comb your hair, Mum?" It was a wonderful sensation to stand behind her and comb her long hair.

It was a painstaking job, and I used to enjoy it. She wouldn't say a thing; she would behave as though she were unaware of what I was doing. Then I would say, "Right, it's done. Get up, Mum"; and when she got up, I would hold the hair like the reins of a horse. "Here is a horse. Come on, stand up and move," and we would banter with each other. She was so tiny that I could hold her two arms from behind, and she would struggle, seemingly powerless to do anything. But as soon as her voice rose to a higher pitch, Dad's voice would boom, "What's happening?" My mum would say, "Nothing!" And both of us would go quiet, and she would say, "You see, I'll tell your father. You'll be in trouble, so let me go." And I would say, "No problem, you can tell my dad. What can he do? He's crippled. You've got no rescuer. There's no knight on a white charger coming to rescue you. You have to deal with me." It was a joke we often shared.

Father's Rule

I did not have that easy a relationship with my father. He was a chore. He sat there, crippled. He only called when he wanted something. When I wanted to rush off and play, he would call me: "I need a cup of tea" or "where's my walking stick?" He used to take snuff that he either sniffed or put under his tongue. So he would need his spittoon: "Where's my spittoon?" I didn't like having to do this. I tried to keep away from my father. I had a passion for soccer. I wanted to be out in the open, out riding my bicycle into the veld.* I saw my father as a liability.

When I was younger, he'd thwack you one. You'd jump away and you'd yell and he'd say, "Come back! Put your hand out! Bring it nearer!" Thwack! But you could always jump out of the way. You can imagine his frustration. He was tall and powerfully built, but he was a cripple. I think it soured his relationships. He had a sense of a loss of control over himself. My father was loud voiced and authoritarian, and I recall clashes between him and my older brothers. The only entertainment, if you can call it that, for a young man in the village was to drink. My brothers were supposed to put their incomes into the family pool, but as they grew older, they objected to this family system of giving their salaries to my father and being given back a tiny fraction for pocket money, not even enough for a drink with their friends. I can recall times when the clashes between my father and one of my brothers would become violent. These clashes really disturbed me, even though later I would clash with my father myself.

My mother used to say, "Even if your father is verbally abusive, it is wrong for your brother to react with equal verbal abuse or to resort to physical force. That line is wrong." Then when I would say, "But on the substantive issue, my brother is right," she would say, "No, no, no, put that aside. That issue is a separate one that can only be dealt with later. The first thing is that the rules are being violated by the abuse, and you cannot transgress that borderline and simultaneously expect to deal with the substantive issue."

The effects carried over into adult life. My wife and children say that when they get caught up in an argument, I get highly disturbed. When they raise their voices and shout at each other, I become agitated. I can't handle it. I can't stand it, and I say to them individually, "But why this abuse?" And they say, "But we are talking our minds; we are telling each other what we think. Yes, we love each other but stay out of this thing." I say, "But there's abusiveness in this, the way you're talking to each other, and the wounds of this abuse will remain." Just to hear a loud voice in my home, a loud angry voice, causes problems inside myself. I become disquieted by it, although I am not immune to raising my voice myself.

*Uncultivated countryside or grassland; Afrikaans, from the Dutch for field.

Veranda Seminars

My father's shop had a veranda where he and his friends, Indian men and a few African men with whom he had grown up with as a kid, would meet. They would walk or ride their bicycles down the street and sit on the veranda and chat.

To be fair to my dad, even though he only had a Standard 2 education, he could read and write English. He was the one who read the newspaper to his cronies. They would discuss what he read to them. My first knowledge of books was Dale Carnegie's book *How to Win Friends and Influence People*, which my dad had. He also read books on philosophy. He had a collection of probably ten books. Those were the only books in the house, and because I was a keen student, passionate about reading, I read them: Jawaharlal Nehru's *Glimpses of World History* and *The Discovery of India* and the Chinese philosopher Lin Yutang translated into English. As a kid, I used to read the Bulldog Drummond and the Saint books. I used to steal them from the bookshop because I couldn't afford them. I read these adventure books on my own, but I also read my dad's books.

He would call one of us, "Bring me that book by Lin Yutang!" He would read it aloud, and then he'd interpret it for his friends. A debate would begin. They all saw my dad as a fountain of information. They would argue about what was happening in the United States or Britain. They would talk about the Boxer Rebellion, the opium trade. They came there to sit with him for hours, drinking cup after cup of tea, all ordered from my mum: "Lily, tea!"

My father was interested in horse racing. He did a weekly column for the local newspaper, predicting the racing results for the week. Even though he could never go to a horse race, he'd study the forms. He kept notebooks, and we kids had to transcribe the results of each Saturday's racing. I hated that! We had to write up things like the weight of the horse, who the jockey was, his starting position, and the distance of the race. Then Dad would sit down and analyze all this stuff with his cronies and do his column on a Thursday.

Identity

My parents were Hindu. Every night before meals we prayed and thanked God for the meal. While my grandmother was alive—she passed away in 1953—we observed the rituals more often. Once she took me to the temple, but I bunked; that is, I went and played outside with a tennis ball. My parents were upset because I'd disobeyed my grandmother, and my father said I would turn out to be a "scoundrel," but it didn't go further than that. They regarded themselves as Hindu, yet they never imposed their religion on me.

The Indian community in Newcastle was in one sense a tight-knit community; in another, it was divided. The Hindus banded together; the Muslims banded together; the Tamils banded together. There was a commonality, but there was also separateness. I had Muslim friends, but if I visited them, my father would say: "Did you eat there? You must never eat there. They are Muslims. They eat beef." For Hindus, the cow is holy.

The Indian struggle for independence from Britain began heating up in the thirties. Many South African Indians supported it. During the Second World War my father was very passionate about it, and he and the older people in the community would talk about it. They rejoiced—as I did—when independence was won in 1947.

In the turmoil following India's independence, we were aware there was conflict between Hindus and Muslims. But the community in South Africa united in putting the blame on the British. They were mates, the Hindus and Muslims of Newcastle. They grew up together; they struggled together; and they avoided allowing that issue to become a point of division. They blamed the British: "These bloody British—who eat pork, by the way." The common rallying point was: "Those Englishmen—they eat pork!"

Indians and Africans had a schizophrenic relationship. The Indian community envied the whites their privileges and despised them at the same time. It empathized with but feared the Africans. The tension in the working relationship between Africans and Indians arose from a sense that opportunity could be realized only by one at the expense of the other.

One of the results of the 1913 coal miners' strike was a law precluding Indians from working underground in the mines and replacing them with African labor. Up until then, the majority of the underground workforce in Newcastle's mines had been Indian. There was fear that, as after the 1913 strike, Africans would take employment away from Indians. My father took this view, though he had African friends. Indians empathized with the African population because they were also oppressed—but they also feared them.

Many of those involved in the passive resistance campaign of 1946 served their sentences in the Newcastle Prison. I can remember as a kid seeing Indian men in prison garb, working with shovels and picks on the roadside, cleaning the road edges. One of the resisters, J. N. Singh, was related to me. He was a key person in the Indian Congress, a communist, and had been a friend of Nelson Mandela's as a student at Witwatersrand University. Singh died in 1999.[9] Mandela in his autobiography recalls how Flat 13, which Ismail Meer occupied, became the gathering point for Singh, Meer, and himself.* So not only were the prisoners seen by me personally, but they were also known and talked about in the family. We used to try to get food to the prisoners working on the roads. Our parents encouraged us to show sympathy to these prisoners, to the Indian passive resisters.

I also have memories of mass meetings being called in Newcastle by the Indian Congress when Dr. Yusuf Dadoo, Dr. Monty Naicker, Debi Singh, and others would come to mobilize the community. This was when I was in high school. There was a struggle going on in the Indian Congress to replace the moderate leadership of Kajee/Pather with the radical Dadoo/Naicker leadership. I recall going to community meetings in support of Dr. Dadoo and Dr. Naicker. A. I. Kajee and P. R. Pather stood for dialogue and deputations to the government and wanted nothing to do with mass action. Dadoo and Naicker were advocates of mass action and unity with the African people.

While I was in Newcastle, the two approaches were jostling. Passive resistance was being waged in South Africa, and I supported it. But in India's struggle for independence, I was, by instinct, a supporter of the militant Subhash Chandra Bose, who was saying: "Let's fight!" I was also aware of the 1950 May Day strike; how, I don't know. That's when nineteen Africans were shot. In solidarity, the African National Congress (ANC) led the first national stayaway campaign in June 1950.[†] I was in Standard 8 at the time and I bunked school and went off to play and picnic out in the hills. In 1952, I was aware of the Defiance Campaign because the con-

---

*"Flat 13, Kholvad House, four rooms in a residential building in the centre of the city Johannesburg." *Mandela*, 79.

†A national one-day strike called by the Convention for Free Speech in which the CPSA and the Transvaal Indian Congress played leading roles. The strike, known as the Freedom Day strike, called for the abolition of pass laws and all discriminatory legislation. It was bitterly opposed by the ANCYL, including Mandela. The strike went ahead without official ANC support. Up to half of the African workforce on the Witwatersrand stayed away on 1 May 1950. On the evening of the strike nineteen people were killed in police clashes. See *Mandela*, pp. 100–102; *Sisulu*, pp. 84–86. In response the ANC and the CPSA called for a national stay at home on 26 June; the first joint action taken by decision of both organizations, the first step in the formation of the alliance between the two. The stayaway was to protest the nineteen murdered on 1 May and impending legislation that outlawed the CPSA. The language of the legislation drafted, however, provided the "legal" space for the government to ban any organization.

gresses were organizing meetings all over the country, including Newcastle, but I was not yet in a political mode.

I was against racism, but I did not question the sectarianism of religious bigotry in the Indian community, the fact that in our small community there were three soccer teams: Tamil, Hindu, and Muslim. I had not yet seen that this disease of racism manifests itself not just in color intolerance but also in cultural and religious intolerance and chauvinism. Leaving home made me aware of this.

I don't recall my father expressing any anti-Afrikaner sentiment during this period; but after the end of the Second World War and the run-up to the elections in 1948, when the National Party won, there was suddenly tension between the black children and the Afrikaner children living in Lennoxton. By 1948–49, my father was expressing a dislike for the white community as a whole. He would say that the Englishman would stab you in the back while embracing you. The Afrikaner, he said, was transparent about his hatred, and so when you engaged with the Afrikaner, he would punch you in the nose up front.

Until then, the English speakers were the dominant social force in Newcastle. Around the time of the 1948 elections, I became aware for the first time of some white people as Afrikaner, that is, distinct from English. The National Party carried Newcastle in 1948. All the farmers in the outlying areas were mobilized, and one farmer, Willie Maree, won. The elections unleashed tremendous racial tension because before them, discrimination was not so in your face. After 1948, Afrikaners took control of the town council, and whites would elbow you off the pavement in the Newcastle town center.

Childhood

As a child, I was a bit of a loner. My brothers went out to work at the age of thirteen or fourteen. We had only one bicycle for the whole family. It was an adult bicycle, an old Raleigh, and as a kid, I learned to ride that bike; we called it monkey riding. We would hold the handlebars, because we were too small to get up onto the saddle or bar, putting one leg through the triangle to peddle. I loved cycling. With only one bike in the family, my kid brother and I had to negotiate the use of the bike and take turns riding it.

By the time I reached high school—I had friends now, and they could borrow bicycles from their homes—three or four of us would get together and go off cycling. Whoever could get hold of a bicycle would join me, but if they didn't manage to get a bicycle, I would go off on my own. It didn't bother me. I enjoyed that sort of solitude.

I read about Gandhi and Nehru a lot while I was still a high school student. At home there were four photographs—of Gandhi, Nehru, Maulana Kalam Azad, and Subhash Chandra Bose. Nehru, Azad, and Bose were the linchpins of the Indian Youth Congress. They were the young Turks. Bose argued for open warfare against Britain during the Second World War to achieve India's independence. He went so far as to say he would form an alliance with Hitler and Japan if that would help the struggle. He disappeared over the Himalayas, purportedly on a flight to Germany to discuss a pact with Hitler. Bose was a hero to me. I saw Gandhi as a hero, but I was prepared at that age to favor Bose. I was still of the view that the enemy of my enemy is my friend.

I was a voracious reader. When I was about twelve, there was a competition in the local newspaper, the *Newcastle Advertiser*, to spot six errors in that week's edition. I found ten and won the prize: two shillings and sixpence in prize money.

My friends and I stole time to play football with a tennis ball on our way to school. The school was two miles away, and we walked the two miles there and back. On our way we took the cattle to the cattle camp, left them to graze for the day, and collected them on our way home. They would then be milked in the cattle enclosure in the yard. That was the milk for the family. Sometimes if our cow gave more milk than was needed, the milk was sold. When we finished school at two or three, we didn't go home, we played in the cattle camp.

In Lennoxton, everyone—Indians, Coloureds, Africans, and poor whites—used to take their cattle to and from the same cattle-grazing camp. We would all play there. We would part to go to our respective racially divided schools. In 1948, though, the Afrikaners, the whites at the camp, suddenly turned on us and assaulted us. The rest of us fought back. The cattle camp became a battleground, and within a year all the poor whites had moved out of our suburb. They had been unemployed, but now they got jobs on the railways, where they supplanted black labor. The railways provided houses for them, so they moved out of our community. We were no longer friends, yet we had grown up in the same place.

Before 1948, there was no integration, but there was a degree of coexistence among the poor across racial lines. There were already white suburbs at the time, but the poor whites and we poor Indians and Africans and Coloureds all lived in the same area. We fraternized to a degree, and yet we maintained our separate soccer clubs. But when the Nats (National Party) came to power in 1948, they formally moved the whites from the community and made us conscious of our color.

School and Rebellion

The Indian community financed our school, St. Oswald's, which at one point had been a Catholic school. Later on it qualified for government assistance, so it was a government-aided school by the time I went to it. We were proud of our school. Both my parents wanted their children to be educated. I went to school at the age of five, in great awe. I was the youngest; in all my classes I was one year younger than the average age.

During the first year I found it very uncomfortable. But I performed well, always at the top of the class. My dad was always extremely boastful about that, which I found embarrassing to the extent that in Standard 3 I deliberately tried to do badly in my exams! After that, I would be at the top of the class by accident. I would try not to study, but I loved reading, and so I would still come out at the top of the class.

At school there was only one teacher who inspired me: A. C. Francis; I don't remember his first name. While he was studying medicine, his father died and his family's financial circumstances changed dramatically overnight. The only thing he could do was become a teacher. He was an alcoholic, an utterly frustrated man, but a magnificent teacher. By Standard 8, Standard 9, I was going out with him on Friday nights. There were two pubs where Indians could go and drink. When he got drunk, I would take him to his room and put him to bed. In the classroom he was a fantastic orator with a great passion for English literature, especially poetry; as a Latin master, he was a great inspiration. Even in his drunkenness he used to tell me, "You are a very bright student; you can go far in the world; don't become like me."

As a schoolboy, I was a rebel, but I was a clandestine rebel. I would disobey my father, who was always calling for us to do chores for him, and I would hide or disappear on my bicycle. I would sleep out in the bush. My father was opposed to my playing soccer. He wanted me to work, to help out around the house and in the shop. Occasionally we had to load a two-hundred-pound bag of cornmeal onto the handlebars of the bicycle and deliver it. What a job! The bicycle would tip over, and then we'd be stuck. And I wanted to play. I wanted to read. I didn't want to do those chores. But I was also becoming a good soccer player, and the school was now going on soccer tours to play other schools in other towns. We traveled in an open van, and when we got there, I would find ways to link up with other kids because there were always a few hours to socialize after we arrived and a few hours after the match had ended. I started smoking when I was thirteen and drinking beer when I was sixteen. I was becoming very rebellious at school.

I perfected new techniques of defiance. For example, I would sneak out on Saturday nights: I would jump out of the window, disappear, and go out drinking. One time, late at night, I came back to find my mother waiting for me. My dad had discovered I had sneaked out, and the next morning he called for me. "Where were you? What were you doing? You only got home at three o'clock in the morning." I said, in a very calm voice, "Dad, do you want the truth?" He said, "Yes, I want the truth." I said, "OK, I'm going to tell you the truth." And he just shut me off—"Stop, I don't want to hear." I was going to underplay it, but the truth was that I had been out drinking at a *shebeen*.* But it was clear from his tone that he was afraid he had gone too far and that if I told him the truth, we would have crossed a boundary; so he didn't want to hear. That became a very powerful instrument for me in my rebellion. My dad would say, "Have you been smoking?" I'd say, "Do you want the truth?" And he'd say, "I don't want to know."

A Clash of Wills

I was the top performer in my class, so there were expectations. My family would ask me if I was going to become a teacher, but I would say I wanted to become a lawyer, and my father reacted as if he were morally outraged. He expected that the entire family, including my brothers, who were working as petrol attendants, should contribute to help me to train as a teacher. He thought it would be the ultimate achievement if a member of the family became a teacher.

My father said that no son of his was going to become a lawyer because lawyers were by nature liars; he was a very stubborn man, not easily dissuaded. I told him I would leave home, and he said: "Well, if you leave home, you get nothing from me. I will not help you." I dug in my heels, and before I finished my matric,† I applied for places at various universities. As a person of Indian origin, I would have had to get a permit to live outside of the province of Natal, but I applied to the University of Cape Town (UCT) and the University of the Witwatersrand (Wits) in Johannesburg.

---

*From the Gaelic, meaning unlicensed premises that sold alcohol.
†High school diploma.

I finished writing my matric exams in November 1952, and I was not only waiting for my results but also anxiously awaiting a response to my applications to UCT and Wits. In the meantime, my father was talking behind my back with the vice principal of the school, who was a friend of the family. Come January, my results arrived and I'd passed. I was now extremely edgy about what was going to happen to me. I'd heard nothing from UCT or Wits, but I kept inquiring, "Has there been any post for me?" Then one day my kid brother said to me, "You know, I think there were one or two letters for you, but Dad and the vice principal opened them."

I was very angry. I went to my dad and asked him, but instead of answering my question, he told me, "There is an opportunity for you to go and study at the University of Natal, non-European section. The vice principal himself studied at that university, and if you insist on going to university, that is the best route. You could go to Durban, and you could go to the teacher training college at Springfield." I said, "You know I don't want to do that." He said, "Well, you could go to the University of Natal and study for a BA." Now the BA was a necessary part of going on to the LLB.* I said to him, "But I want to know what happened; where are my letters from the University of Cape Town and Wits?" And he said, "We destroyed those letters." I said, "Why?" He said, "Because I've decided you're not going to go to Johannesburg or Cape Town." I knew by the way he responded that I had been accepted at either Wits or UCT, or both. This was now about the end of January, and registration was closing. I was furious and determined to leave home. My mum persuaded me to take the position at Natal University in Durban.

But what really stands out in my mind is that after that last argument with my father, my mother came to my room while I was angrily packing my bag to leave home in defiance of my dad and my brothers, and she said to me, "Look, I don't understand it; I don't understand what you want to do except that I hear you want to study and you don't want to be a teacher. You want to be a lawyer. But I also don't understand why you're quarreling with your father. You don't agree with him. OK. Don't say anything. Don't say you're not going to listen to him. The train leaves at midnight. Go to sleep, then when everybody is asleep, get up and go away quietly. Here's twenty pounds I have saved; your father is not aware of it. And here is a ring. As a mother I would have hoped to be party to selecting the woman you marry. But here is the ring because I don't know when or if I will ever see you again. But you need to know that whomever you choose to settle

*Bachelor of laws.

down with and marry, this is the ring that you should give because it has my approval. So stop quarreling; go to bed; and when everybody is asleep, just leave quietly and go."

Now that's how she had divined for herself the rules of conduct in a family where you had to accord your elders their respect, and it's something that I have never forgotten.

Much later, when I was on Robben Island, my dad and I were reconciled. During one of my mother's early visits, I asked her, "How's Dad?" She said, "He's fine." I said, "Are you sure? How is he taking everything?" I knew the newspapers had written about my being involved in a Communist plot, and my dad disagreed with my communism. She said, "He's very proud of you." I was surprised, but she said that the day we were sentenced, a large number of people in our little town of Newcastle came to the house to visit my parents and told them what a wonderful chap I was. They apologized for the fact that they had thought I was a loafer and a no-gooder, bumming around for jobs. They told Dad they were very sorry. Now they understood that I was in the underground. "He's fantastic, he's a hero." My dad was shocked. "You say my son's a good guy?" "Yes, he's a hero!" After that, my mum told me, anybody who walked into the shop or the house, a white man, a black man, within minutes my dad would be saying, "You know, I have a son who's on Robben Island and he's a Communist." He was proud of me.

2. DURBAN DAYS

Introduction

FOR THE FIRST FIFTY or so years of the ANC's history, after its foundation in 1912, its members were African petite bourgeoisie and traditional chiefs concerned about the availability of land to Africans. Members had, for the most part, a Christian education and espoused corresponding social mores and values, which they had in common with the ruling classes. In keeping with the times, they saw their task as one of convincing the "civilized" British that there was a place in South Africa's governance for "civilized," educated, property-owning Africans. They would settle for a limited franchise.[1] From the beginning, however, the ANC denounced tribalism, stressing that Africans were one people and that if they stood united as one people, their demands would be met. It understood that unity was strength.

Until the late 1950s and early 1960s, the ANC was committed to non-violence and to the use of constitutional means to achieve its goals. Gandhi served as the model. But unlike Gandhi, the ANC eschewed mass mobilization for decades, depending on representations to either the British government or the South African government. Like Gandhi, they appealed initially to the British government on the basis of a shared Britishness, as "loyal British subjects."[2] When it became clear that the British would not interfere and that the South African government was simply ignoring its presentations, the Congress "began a long struggle through a quarter of a century of political frustration and organizational weakness that at times all but overwhelmed it."[3]

It was reactive and accommodative, engaging in routine protests whenever a piece of discriminatory legislation was passed, but eschewing nonconstitutional avenues of protest, anxious to show the government that Africans would make "good" citizens. Its impact was negligible, and it lapsed into a state of semiparalysis. It continued to identify itself with the interests of the governing elites rather than with African workers and the unemployed. It ignored rural Africans. It survived the 1930s as "annual provincial and national gatherings of a few dozen personalities."[4] By 1949, the ANC could claim fewer than 2,800 members.

But change was imminent. In 1946, between fifty thousand and one hundred thousand African mine workers went on strike. The state violently put down the strike. Most of the members of the Central Committee of the Communist Party of South Africa (CPSA) were arrested and charged with instigating the strike.[5] The ANC was at this point less of a problem to the government than organized black labor.

The ANC Youth League (ANCYL),[6] Johannesburg, rescued the ANC from irrelevance, perhaps even oblivion. In the postwar years, and especially after the National Party victory of 1948, the ANCYL's crop of new leaders—Walter Sisulu, Nelson Mandela, and Oliver Tambo—provided the movement with a new sense of direction and urgency. Under their influence, the ANC redefined itself as an African nationalist liberation movement. The ideological orientation was neither socialist nor capitalist. The liberation of the people would constitute the sole focus of the organization; the enemy was the colonial/imperial invader. The Youth League set out its vision in its 1944 Manifesto:[7] "The goal of all our struggles is Africanism"; and "the national liberation of Africans will be achieved by Africans themselves." In 1948, it declared in its basic policy document that "the Congress Youth League holds that the Africans are nationally oppressed, and that they can win their national freedom through a National Liberation Movement led by the Africans themselves."[8]

The ANC adopted the ANCYL's program of action at its annual conference in 1949, and Mandela, Tambo, and Sisulu moved into key leadership positions. The emphasis would be on seeking "national freedom" and "self-determination." It called for the "direct representation in all governing bodies of the country" and "the abolition of all differential institutions or bodies created for Africans." Breaking with the tactics of the past, it called for mass mobilization, boycotts, strikes, civil disobedience, and noncooperation to achieve its demands.[9]

In 1950, the government passed the Suppression of Communism Act, and the CPSA dissolved itself, but it was reconstituted in secret as the South African Communist Party (SACP). The party and the ANC began to work more closely together, and African members of the SACP became influential members of the National Executive Committee of the ANC.

The CPSA had adopted a two-stage strategy of struggle, asserting the primacy of "revolutionary nationalism" over socialism in the first instance. Class struggle was subordinated to the imperative to build a broad nationalist coalition to achieve the primary objective of national liberation, after which the socialist revolution would follow. This view was upheld by the new underground party even until the early 1990s.[10] Among party members, never publicized for political reasons, were Walter Sisulu;[11] Thomas Nkobi, later the ANC's Treasurer; Alfred Nzo, later the secretary-general; and most likely for a brief period, Nelson Mandela, according to old colleagues. *

Two competing nationalisms faced each other in the terrain of struggle: Afrikaner nationalism with its iron grip on the instruments of state power, and African nationalism with its moral authority and readiness to embark on large-scale campaigns of mass mobilization and civil disobedience, albeit with a commitment to nonviolence. In 1952, the ANC embarked on the Defiance Campaign.[12] Although it did not achieve any of its demands, membership of the ANC swelled, and by the end of the year it had some hundred thousand members and could for the first time call itself a mass-based organization.[13]

In 1953, the Congress Alliance was established. It included the ANC, the Congress of Democrats (whites), the South African Coloured Organization (Coloureds), the South African Indian Congress (Indians), the South African Council of Trade Unions (SACTU), and the predominantly white Federation of South African Women (FSAW). At this stage in its history, the ANC had not fully committed to the idea of nonracialism as such. It was still organized along racial lines, as the separate constitutions of the congresses of racial groups indicated. ANC membership was limited to Africans until 1969. Non-Africans could not become members of the National Executive Committee (NEC) until 1985. Indians, Coloureds, and whites found their home in the CPSA, later the SACP, as did many Africans who also belonged to the ANC.

In 1955, the Congress Alliance drew up the Freedom Charter,[14] setting out the goals and aspirations of the liberation movement. With time, the Freedom Charter became the bible of the movement; its provisions were

---

*Hilda Bernstein is quite insistent. "Well, Mandela denies that he was ever a member of the party, but I can tell you that he was a member of the party for a period." [] maharaj/interviewees/[] Hilda Bernstein. Brian Bunting also confirms. Other sources embargoed until 2030.

recited as the writ of liberation expressing the "will of the people." The Freedom Charter was adopted by the ANC as its primary political and economic program.

In 1959, a number of dissenting members of the ANC, who believed that the Congress Alliance undermined the concept of African nationalism, left and formed the Pan-Africanist Congress (PAC), a movement advocating a "pure" African nationalism, under the leadership of Robert Sobukwe.[15]

In 1956, the state arrested 156 people of every race and political disposition and charged them with treason. The Freedom Charter, the government claimed, was a Communist document. Among those charged were ANC luminaries Mandela, Sisulu, and Tambo and ANC unknowns like Henry Tshabalala.*

Despite the arrests and the trial—all of the accused were granted bail—the ANC decided to support the white parliamentary opposition parties in the 1958 all-white elections.[16] It still believed that it could woo white liberal support and that a coalition with white liberal and middle-class parties was possible.

The Treason Trial dragged on for four years and ended with all being acquitted. Yet it provided an occasion for Mandela to showcase his skills and demonstrate his charismatic appeal to the masses. The people had found their Moses.

2

In Newcastle, the Maharaj family, for all practical purposes, lived in a ghetto. The family rarely forayed into Newcastle proper. Within this sealed-off world, there was little sense of being discriminated against, little organized opposition to the political and social order. Few expected much change.

In this world, Mac's family was held in high esteem. The Maharaj name alone was indicative of a high-caste pedigree. The family owned a shop, itself a small thing but one that put the family, no matter how poor, one

*Henry Tshabalala had been active in the ANCYL and within the ANC structures since the Defiance Campaign. He was also the secretary of the Working Committee of the ANC in Sophiatown. I met Henry in 1987. At that point he was working for the Soweto Council. His son Siphiwe had gone into exile at age sixteen to join the MK. Henry was my wise man, teacher, companion; and after he lost his job on the council, he was my driver for some years. He died in 2001 while having a nap before celebrating his seventieth birthday. See [] o'malley interviews/[]Henry Tshabalala.

notch above their neighbors, who were their customers and who, no doubt, sometimes incurred debts. Mac's father, crippled or not, was looked up to by his peers.

Mac's own ambitions extended beyond what Lennoxton had to offer, and his time in Durban and at the University of Natal transformed him. It gave coherence to his innate antiauthoritarianism and provided him with a sharp focus and a political ideology, a way of making sense of the world.

Steve "Nandha" Naidoo was probably Mac's closest friend at the university; he was later his flatmate in London and also, still later, his compatriot in the underground in South Africa. He recalls that "most of the mornings were spent arguing about anything and everything, talking politics, arguing about philosophy, socialism, communism. We didn't know much about these things really, in the sense of having studied them. What we did know was that we were being screwed and that only Karl Marx appeared to have the answer."[17] They were, in short, being students.

For the first time, Mac was faced with the impact of racial discrimination, especially the initial effects of laws passed after 1948. Non-European students (nonwhites) studied at Sastri College at the University of Natal Non-European (UNNE) section, not the University of Natal "proper" at Howard College, which only whites attended. There were restrictions on almost all aspects of life—the courses he could take, the degrees available, the facilities he could use, the places where he could socialize, the activities he could engage in, the ambitions he could aspire to.

Mac and his friends grew increasingly resentful of the university's discriminatory practices and the humiliating injustices they were subjected to. He assailed the university at every turn. The facilities at the nonwhite college were inferior to those at the campus for white students. For him the defining moment of his experience at Unne occurred when he was prohibited from proceeding with his law studies.

Mac was drawn to revolution. By the end of his university career, he was ready to put his money where his all-too-loud mouth was: on the overthrow of the capitalist apartheid government and the establishment of a Communist South African state. Marxism provided him with the moral and conceptual vocabulary to express his hatred of the apartheid state. It was inevitable that Mac would find himself associating with like-minded students. He was tutored by Dawood Seedat—veteran Communist, trade unionist, banned by the government—who was among the first antigovernment activists to spend time in prison for public statements in support of his beliefs. Ismail Meer called Seedat fearless. "Some," he wrote, "described him as careless and foolhardy. I knew him as passionate, honest, generous, and very likeable."[18] Decades later many would describe Mac Maharaj with many of the same words, perhaps, though, with a little less emphasis on the "very likeable."

Mac

I ARRIVED IN DURBAN at the end of January 1953 and enrolled at the University of Natal as a part-time student. I was on the non-European campus at Sastri College, which was some distance away from the white campus. You could register full time and attend day classes or you could register part time, which meant you could work for a wage during the day and attend classes in the evening. Most of the students in the nonwhite section worked during the day, and many were teachers.

I told myself I would find a job, but the only thing I could think of was to get a job as a petrol pump attendant. I saw that based on my matric results, I could apply for a university bursary, which I did. The biggest bursary was for about twenty-two pounds a year and, lo and behold, I got it. The bursary would contribute substantially to my fees, but there was still the cost of boarding and lodging. I found a room with a fellow student, Yusuf Kikia.

A friend and I decided that the best way to make a living was to run a gambling school in the Common Room. Come the month's end, we made a killing. All the teachers had their salary checks and were going to pay their rents and university fees. We opened two tables, one conducted by my friend and one by me.

I lived the whole year by gambling. I paid my fees and I paid my board and lodging. I was rich one day and poor the next. I won a motor car over the gambling table, and three weeks later I lost it.

Near the end of the year the university gave me my bursary check of twenty-two pounds. I took a whole group out for dinner. I blew the twenty-two pounds in one night—a night to remember! And then, some time in 1954, I lost my eye. It was gouged out during a drunken brawl, the causes of which I don't even remember.*

---

*Dr. Freddy Reddy, later a psychiatrist who worked in the ANC camps in Angola and Tanzania, worked as an orderly at the King Edward VIII Hospital, where Mac was being attended to after he lost his eye. He has a vivid recollection of his meeting with Mac: "I only heard about Mac through indirect contact that this guy was a street fighter and he was a dangerous person and so on. Anyway, I went to his bedside and tried to ask him if I could do anything for him, but he was so angry that he didn't even answer my questions, he didn't even say a word. Anyway, I had done what I could and I left him." (Their paths crossed again in London and Lusaka.) Go to [] maharaj/interviewees/[]Reddy.

Protest

I wanted to study law, but you couldn't do that in the non-European section. They said there was no such thing as a BA LLB for black students. The Latin lecturer said, "Latin? You're black; you people won't pass Latin 1."

So I started agitating, and I persuaded others to join me. Already in the first year my rebelliousness was taking hold. I incorporated in my BA as many law subjects as were available. I insisted on registering for Latin 1, though I failed it for three years running and only passed it when I wrote it as a supplementary exam after I had completed all the rest of the courses required for the BA!

In 1953, several things began to affect the way I thought. I was fraternizing with Indian students irrespective of their ethnicity or communal background. I began to fraternize with Coloured students; one of my outstanding friends was a chap called Edward Nicholls. Then there was Raymond Kunene, who became the poet Mazizi. He's now Professor Mazizi Kunene at the University of KwaZulu-Natal.

Every area of my life at the university drove me toward rebellion: from the courses it was providing, the types of students I was meeting, to the freshman/graduate hierarchy. I became a member of the Student Representative Council (SRC), which represented nonwhite students, and the editor, in 1955–56, of *Student Call*, the student newspaper, which we published illegally because the university had banned it. The authorities did not like its confrontational tone.

I was active in student affairs and faced expulsion two or three times. The first time was during my first year. Together with forty other students, I stayed away from a function for nonwhite students only that was to be addressed by a visiting dignitary from abroad. I recall that everything was turmoil in my head. I was afraid for my future, for my desire to study, but on the other hand, I was repelled by the arrogance of the white principal, Dr. E. G. Malherbe, who insisted we should apologize for our actions. In the end, we didn't get expelled. I think that Malherbe balked at the idea of expelling forty-one students in one go.

Getting Mad

Even our social activities taught us about the system. My circle of friends was predominantly Indian, but it included Africans and Coloureds, and the Indians included Christians, Hindus, Tamils, and Muslims. If we had a party, the liquor could only be bought by Indians or Coloureds because the law prohibited Africans from buying liquor. If we wanted to go to a bar for a drink, say on a Saturday afternoon before the 5:15 P.M. cinema show, only Indians and Coloureds were allowed by law to go into a pub specially licensed to serve them. When we went to the cinema, it was licensed to admit Africans but not whites. At times we would smuggle a white student or two into the cinema. After going to the cinema, if we decided to go to a restaurant where blacks were allowed, nothing in the law prevented a white person being in the group, but we could not go with any white student to a restaurant licensed for whites only.

By 1954, my second year, I was into organized student activity, leading the demand for LLB classes. I was now working for a lawyer: J. Kissoon Singh. He was the brother of the chairman of the SRC, D. K. Singh. Kissoon Singh had done his articles with a white lawyer called Julius Gurwitz and was working for him as a partner. In those years you had to do an internship called articles, and you were supposed to be paid a cost of living allowance. But places in law firms were so scarce that a black person who wanted to be an articled clerk had to pay his principal. I had no money to pay, so I went to work for Kissoon Singh.

He never gave me articles. I asked him each year, and he would say, "Next year," because I was cheap labor. I became a specialist in appeals that had to go to the Supreme Court, preparing the documentation, then filing and preparing the case. I had quite a few brushes with him. He developed a sort of big-brother attitude toward me. I used to work there from eight in the morning until three in the afternoon, go off to classes, until eight at night, then back to work until late to continue my work. The office had a Roneo machine (a stencil duplicator) and eight typewriters, so I began to publish the clandestine varsity newspaper from there. I would type it in his office, run it off on his paper, and get my gang of guys in to finish it, and then get the lot out of there.

Reading into Struggle

I was living in Hampson Grove off Old Dutch Road. I rented a room from the brother of the legendary Dawood Seedat. Dawood lived across the road and had been in the Communist Party before it was banned. He had gone to prison in 1941 for opposing the war. He had also been involved with the Indian Congress, was banned, and was sent back to prison for breaking his banning order. Through him I came directly into contact with the Congress Movement, his brothers and sisters, the trade unions, and the publication *New Age*. All of this had an impact on me.

I began to read voraciously. Any book I could get on the left wing; on Marxism/Leninism; any critique of capitalism, colonialism, and imperialism. I also read Adam Smith and John Stuart Mill. Marxism and the Communist Party did not distinguish between its members on the basis of class, color, ethnicity, or race. I found the Communist Party's analysis of the South African situation attractive, especially Marxist analysis, which presented colonialism and imperialism as phases in the world development of capitalism. I was coming into political activity at a time when the Soviet Union had triumphed in World War II. Eastern Europe had gone the people's democracy route. Mao Tse-tung's* guerrillas had triumphed in China in 1949, so I read Edgar Snow's *Red Star over China* and Dr. Norman Bethune about doctors from the West who volunteered to go to China. I read about the volunteers who went from the United States to the Soviet Union, and I listened to the music of Paul Robeson, Ella Fitzgerald, and Louis Armstrong.

I read George Padmore's *Pan Africanism or Communism?* He posed these as alternatives and was very critical of communism. But counterbalancing Padmore, who was from the West Indies, was W. E. B. DuBois of the United States. I was also reading about the struggle for independence in India—the Gandhian approach of nonviolence versus those who advocated armed insurrection.

Everything happening in my life was driving me rapidly toward Marxism. Built into the philosophical and theoretical framework of Marxism was the desire to build an egalitarian society. Dawood Seedat still had a lot of Marxist literature. Through him and other people in his circle, I got to read all the Marxist classics during that period: Marx, Engels, Lenin, Stalin, Trotsky—and William Z. Foster about the Second International. I read the anarchist Mikhail Bakunin because Marx and Engels had developed their ideas by critiquing anarchists and others. I read many of the writers they criticized, as well as writings by Communists in the United Kingdom, the United States, China, India, Indonesia, and the East European countries. I discovered the poetry of the anti-imperialist Turkish poet Nazim Hikmet, and the left-wing Chilean poet Pablo Neruda.

The Final Straw

My group boycotted the graduation ceremony of 1956. We were the first group of black graduates to act collectively in such a boycott. We were

---

*Now spelled Mao Zedong.

opposed to separate graduation ceremonies for white and black students. Although black students attended a separate campus, we felt we were graduates of the same varsity and that the graduation ceremony should be a single integrated event—after all, we had written the same exams and passed. The graduation boycott was very successful, but we failed to persuade the university to hold a single graduation ceremony for all students, irrespective of color.

When I finished my BA, I joined a group of students who petitioned for the opening of a law faculty. The university said, "We can only grant a law faculty for you blacks if you produce five graduate students to do the LLB." I produced five students, including myself, and they opened the faculty. We completed the first year. There were five subjects to complete, but the LLB rules stated that you could only move to second year if you passed all five subjects. I was the only one who passed all five subjects as a part-time student. When I went to register for the second year, they said, "Sorry, we've closed the faculty; we can't run a second-year course for just one student." So I said, "Register me for a BComm then." At the time, I was working for a lawyer as a clerk. But the registrar, a white chap, said, "Don't you get the message? We don't want you back here."

I then applied to Wits University and UCT, and they were prepared to admit me, but I couldn't get a permit because people of Indian origin required a permit to live in either the Transvaal or the Cape Province. So I couldn't go to UCT or Wits. I was mad. Every time I tried to advance myself, I was denied and always for one reason only: the color of my skin. At the same time, I became impatient with the nonviolent strategy of the ANC-led Congress Movement.

New Age

Dawood was involved with the newspaper *New Age*, the only independent left-wing paper in the country, which had taken over from the *Guardian* when it was banned. *New Age* reported on the activities of the ANC and other congresses and the condition of the masses under apartheid. I started distributing it on Sundays, door to door in the block known as the Warwick Avenue Triangle.

The editor of *New Age* was Brian Bunting, from Cape Town. The Johannesburg editor was Ruth First. Wolfie Kodesh was working in the Jo'burg office; M. P. Naicker was managing editor of the Durban office; and Govan Mbeki became the Eastern Cape editor.

It was the voice of the broad left; in fact, it was the creation of members of the Communist Party.

My life increasingly centered on *New Age*. We used to gather at its offices at lunchtime and have impromptu discussions. I used to challenge the comrades about nonviolence. I knew that many of the people I was debating with had been members of the Communist Party before 1950. The discussions would become acrimonious. Billy Nair used to attend those lunch meetings. He would say, "You! You're a bloody ultrarevolutionary! You are reckless! You're an anarchist! No, you're a Trotskyite!" I would say, "How could Communists disband the Communist Party?" They would argue with me, but they couldn't tell me that the party had secretly regrouped, so they were fighting me with their hands tied.

To me, just to support something in theory didn't make you a revolutionary. You had to be active. I wanted to overthrow the capitalist class by whatever means could deliver that result, and I could not be bound to nonviolence. I would accuse Nair and Naicker of being pacifists.

The Communist Party had a difficult but a working relationship with the congresses, particularly the ANC, because the ANC represented the aspirations of nationalism. Our approach was not to oppose nationalism but—patronizingly at that stage, I think—to accept that it was a valid impulse. We believed that by engagement in mass struggle, the narrowness of nationalism would end, and it would become broader. The ANC always said it supported the workers' struggle, but it didn't describe itself as a liberation movement in 1953; it described itself as a nationalist movement. This only changed in 1955, once the ANC had adopted the Freedom Charter,* which stated that South Africa belongs to all who live in it.

I participated as a rank-and-file supporter of the Congress Alliance, but I didn't go to the Freedom Charter conference at Kliptown because, although I was not opposed to it, my mind-set at the time was that the movement was too concerned with nonviolence, whereas I felt that what was needed was action.

In 1954, I became part of a group of students who proposed that the non-European section of Natal University should disaffiliate from the National Union of South African Students (NUSAS) because we were dominated by the white universities. I was heavily criticized by my comrades in the Congress Movement and at *New Age*. I wanted a separate vehicle through which the aspirations of the black students could find free expression and

*For text of Freedom Charter go to [] pre-transition/documents and reports/1955/[].

organizational form. Nevertheless, I was uncomfortable about our political organizations' being structured along racial and ethnic lines. This sounds contradictory—starting a black union to protest racial division—and it was, but I was trying to grapple with the theory of the struggle and the practice and hadn't yet quite managed to get the alignment right.

The racial issue didn't arise at New Age because, to me, the white people there were of a different kind. They were united by their leftism. Second, I saw them doing the same work I was doing. They sold New Age with me in different areas; they worked on the New Age committee; they ran risks with me; and they treated me, I felt, differently from the way the majority of arrogant young white students did.

Funnily enough, just before I became the manager of the New Age office in 1956, around the time of the Treason Trial arrests, there was a New Age committee made up of the editor; the manager for Natal, Naicker, who ended up on trial himself; and a chap called Dr. Kurt Danziger.* This was a big shock for me. Danziger had been my psychology professor at the university in 1955! In class, I would question the validity of what he was saying on social psychology. I would bring in South African oppression, and he would say, "Uh-oh, you're going into politics now." I would say, "There's logic to what you are saying on social psychology that has implications for politics." And he would say, "That's your conclusion, but that's not what I'm saying here." Then I found him on the New Age committee! Quietly, he was politically active.

One evening Danziger invited me to dinner at his home. This was the first time a white lecturer had invited me to his home. I accepted. When I got to his home, I saw he'd also invited a group of psychology students, some from the Non-European Unity Movement (NEUM), which was a Trotskyite group. Over supper Kurt started a discussion and, of course, I took on the NEUM guys. Later, I realized that Kurt had been asked by his colleagues in the Communist Party to assess me, and the supper had been set up for that purpose. People were accusing me of being a Trotskyite and, clearly, Kurt had said to them, "Chaps, he sounds like a Trotskyite, but he's not."

*Dr. Kurt Danziger was born in Germany and came to South Africa when he was eleven. He studied psychology at the University of Cape Town (UCT) and completed his D. Phil at Oxford. After leaving South Africa he taught in Indonesia, Australia, Germany, and Canada. He became a world-renowned psychologist in the field of developmental and social psychology. Before retiring, in 1994, he was awarded the Canadian Psychological Association's first award for Distinguished Contributions to Education and Training. He received an honorary degree from UCT in 2005.

Next I was invited—I didn't realize it was as a result of the dinner—to move from selling the paper to being a reporter on *New Age*. I came into contact with trade unionists such as Billy Nair and Moses Mabhida, the SACTU Natal secretary. By then I was committed to Marxism-Leninism. I took to communism like a fish to water. For an Indian who rejected the nonviolent and multiclass posture of the Indian Congress, there wasn't any other water to swim in. In the debates I began to refine my position by claiming that I didn't disagree with nonviolence as a tactic, but that it should not exclude the need to resort to violence. The issue was never resolved.

I was also active in the Natal Indian Congress (NIC), yet I remained uncomfortable about the political organizations' being separated along racial lines. You had the ANC for Africans and the Indian Congress for Indians. I was seeing huge ferment in the anticolonial world and hearing fierce debates about the tactics to be used. I was asking, "Why don't we do that? Why are we so committed to nonviolence?" It was the era of the Malaysian struggle, the Burmese struggle, the Indo-Chinese struggle against the French, the Chinese revolution. These were living examples that nonviolence as a principle was the wrong approach.

I don't think mine was a profoundly intellectual conclusion. I think it was quite a primitive conclusion. But, of course, I later understood that not all of the people in the ANC believed in nonviolence as a principle. They were defending it because of the legal space it gave. Every time we were faced with repression, there would be a group bringing into question whether nonviolence was efficacious in our situation. And the debate would go back to Gandhi—we had made an exception of Gandhi on the grounds that his strategy had been successful in India because the ruling power, Britain, had been amenable to moral persuasion. But the regime in South Africa was not susceptible to moral persuasion.

Tim

I met Tim, my future wife, in 1953, my first year at the university. She was a member of one of Durban's most prominent politically active families. She was teaching part time while studying at the university. Her parents were deceased. Tim was an activist. We fell in love. But her older brother, M. D. Naidoo, and her older sister's husband, Vish Singh, who was a teacher, didn't think highly of me or my lifestyle. They thought I had no career prospects.

Tim participated in the student world. So did her brother M. J. Naidoo.

He dominated the scene. By 1956, we had formed a congress grouping of African, Indian, and Coloured students, and Tim was a part of that group.

M.D. was a legend from the days of the Communist Party in the forties. He had lobbied the UN in 1949 on behalf of the Indian Congress. After he returned from abroad in 1956, I went to see him about my relationship with Tim. I told him that I was in love with her. He shrewdly said his sister had not mentioned it to him, but I know he did everything possible to get others to take her out.

M.D. and I clashed because, in the wake of the treason arrests, he had become the organizer of the Indian Congress. This would have been in early 1957. He called me one day at the time of the reorganization of the congresses, after the arrests, and asked me to stand for general secretary of the Youth Congress. When he told me I would have to account to the senior congresses, I turned him down. I said I'd account only to the executive. I said the congresses were too passive. I'll never forget what he said to me: "You know, Mac, your problem is you're stubborn. Your stubbornness against the enemy is a good thing, but your stubbornness against your own comrades is a weakness." He dismissed me.

Just before I left the country, Tim and I broke up. She was under pressure from her family, and we agreed that it didn't look as if there were a future for us together. I didn't realize then that she was also planning to get out of Durban and that she had already applied to do a nurse's training course in Aylesbury, in Kent.

The Treason Trials and Getting Out

The Treason Trial arrests took place in December 1956, and M. P. Naicker was among the accused. Together with AKM Dockrat and Ebrahim Seedat, I began to organize the Stand by Our Leaders campaign in support of them. I got a message from the *New Age* head office in Johannesburg asking if I would take over as manager of the Durban office.

I felt honored. I agreed, but I said that the moment I got my passport I would leave the country and wouldn't be able to give them any notice. After Natal University had turned me down for second-year LLB study and I could not get permits to attend Wits or UCT, I decided to find a way to go abroad to study law.

I knew it would be hard to get a passport; because I was manager of *New Age*, the police would be keeping an eye on me. I applied for a passport first in Newcastle, then in Dundee, and then in Pietermaritzburg; and in all of these places my application was turned down. Then my nephew

J. N. Singh—a lawyer in Durban, many of whose clients were black, and some of them black policemen—tipped me off about a person working in the Security Branch in Durban who could help. I had not thought of applying in Durban because they knew me there. I went to see this chap. He said he had the other rejections, but he would put them in his tray as if he had not yet seen them and simply approve the passport. He said, "As soon as you get it, get the hell out!" Only then would he put the other reports into the system.

He was a junior cop. In those days, black people working in the Security Branch would sometimes help activists like me, with a mixture of sympathy and payoff. I did not pay him anything, but perhaps JN did. The Security Branch had not by any means reached the level of secrecy or brutality that it would later. At that time, the police would sit at political meetings and openly take notes. You'd make snide remarks at them, and they would tolerate it.

Most security policemen were white, but blacks did much of the legwork and clerical work. Some black people then working for the police or the prisons later became interested in politics and joined the ANC during the states of emergency.

My passport came through in July 1957. Just afterward the police came looking for me. Luckily, I had been forewarned. Some youngsters on Hampson Grove waylaid me on my way home one evening. They said, "The police were here; they're looking for you." That was enough for me. I was gone. I left Durban that very night. University and other friends collected money for me; my brothers borrowed £50 for me. I managed to get another £70, and I booked a flight on a charter airline for £115. I flew to London and arrived with £5 in my pocket.

3. LONDON DAYS

Introduction

AS THE DUST SETTLED after World War II, it became clear that the order of things had changed. The United States bestrode the world, a benevolent colossus—unless it was crossed. The Marshall Plan pulled a devastated Europe out of the ruins of war. With the Soviet Union having established satellite states in Eastern Europe and a large portion of Germany, the standoff of the cold war became the status quo. Both the United States and the USSR developed nuclear weapons, raising fears of a nuclear holocaust. Nations took sides willingly or were cajoled, coerced, or co-opted into doing so.

The resulting alignment of countries into two blocs had profound and long-lasting effects on the decolonization of Africa. Newly independent countries were courted by the two superpowers. There was little room to maneuver because most African countries were desperate for foreign assistance, and many were prepared to sell their souls—and their countries—to the highest bidder, a task made easier since some of the new African leaders regarded their countries as their personal fiefdoms.

Weakened by the war and concerned with their own internal politics in the wake of the war, European countries began to let go of their colonies. In 1951, Libya became the first colonized country in Africa to achieve independence; in 1956, Morocco, Tunisia, and Sudan followed; in 1957, Dr. Kwame Nkrumah led Ghana to independence, the first sub-Saharan African country to achieve that status. Nkrumah's Pan-Africanism was an African ideology that crossed the artificial boundaries that demarcated colonial states, and it was the torch that lit the way for other African liberation.

In 1960, the breakup of colonial Africa began in earnest: French West Africa, French Equatorial Africa, and other territories created countries including Niger, Chad, Somalia, Congo (Brazzaville), Nigeria, and the Belgian Congo. After the latter rapidly descended into civil war in June 1960, accounts of marauding drunken black soldiers and tens of thousands of white refugees fleeing the country filled South African newspapers.[1] South African whites took note; it was a harbinger, they believed, of what would happen in South Africa in the event of black rule.

The Labour Party and the British Communist Party aligned themselves with independence-seeking movements in the colonies. The Labour Party, even in opposition, was able to put enormous pressure on Conservative Party governments to speed up decolonization, and the Communist Party was a powerful lobby group in the Labour Party and the trade unions.

The British prime minister Harold Macmillan went to South Africa in February 1960. It was a mere two years since Hendrik Verwoerd had become South Africa's prime minister with a plan for grand apartheid—total racial separation.[2] Addressing both houses of Parliament, Macmillan delivered an unmistakable message: "Ever since the breakup of the Roman Empire, one of the constant factors of political life has been the emergence of independent nations. The wind of change is blowing through this continent and, whether we like it or not, this growth of national consciousness is a political act. We must accept this fact and our national policies must take account of it."[3]

2

But apartheid South Africa was not listening. On 21 March, police shot dead sixty-nine Africans protesting the pass laws at Sharpeville. The Sharpeville massacre was probably the definitive turning point in the struggle against apartheid, an event from which all others followed or can be traced to.[4] Overnight, apartheid was catapulted into the international domain, where it would stay until a free and democratic South Africa emerged after a forty-year struggle and violent conflict. In the wake of Sharpeville, the government declared the country's first state of emergency. The ANC and PAC were banned from operating as lawful organizations, their leaders detained.[5]

Verwoerd's answer to the flood of international opprobrium that followed Sharpeville was to rally Afrikaner nationalism. He called a referendum in October 1960 to decide whether South Africa should become a republic and withdraw from the British Commonwealth. The referendum was won by 52 percent in a 90 percent poll, Afrikaners on the republic side throwing off, as it were, the yoke of their imperial oppressor; English-speaking whites on the side of remaining in the Commonwealth clinging to fading memories of a mother country.

In August 1960, Mandela stood in the dock at the Treason Trial and made an offer to the apartheid state:

> We demand universal adult franchise and we are prepared to exert economic pressure to attain our demands, and we will launch defiance campaigns, stay-at-homes, either singly or together, until the Government should say, "Gentlemen, we cannot have this state of affairs, laws being defied, and this whole situation created by stay-at-homes. Let's talk." In my own view I would say, "Yes, let us talk" and the Government would say, "We think that the Europeans at present are not ready for a type of government where there might be domination by non-Europeans. We think we should give you 60 seats. The African population to elect 60 Africans to represent them in Parliament. We will leave the matter over for five years and we will review it at the end of five years." In my view, that would be a victory, my lords; we would have taken a significant step towards the attainment of universal adult suffrage for Africans, and we would then for the five years say, we will suspend civil disobedience; we won't have any stay-at-homes, and we will then devote the intervening period for the purpose of educating the country, the Europeans, to see that these changes can be brought about and that it would bring about better racial understanding, better racial harmony in the country. I'd say we should accept it, but, of course, I would not abandon the demands for the extension of the universal franchise to all Africans.[6]

History would never again afford the apartheid regime such an offer.

After the lifting of the state of emergency in September 1990, blacks regrouped, albeit now under very different circumstances. Meeting in Pietermaritzburg in March 1961, an All-In Africa Conference, with 1,500 delegates representing 145 religious, cultural, and political bodies, called on the government to convene a national convention of elected representatives of all South Africans by 31 May, the date apartheid South Africa was set to proclaim itself a republic, to draw up a nonracial democratic constitution. On 13 May, Mandela, who had been elected by the conference to lead the National Action Council (NAC), the umbrella organization set up to take charge of the anti-Republic campaign, called for a three-day national stayaway, beginning on 29 May. But the strike fizzled. With the state now intensifying repression (341,000 were convicted for

contravening pass laws in 1960),[7] the people were hesitant in their response. The struggle could no longer rely on mass demonstrations when
its leaders were either banned or detained, and the state was responding to
mass action with a ferocity it had not hitherto employed. In a statement to
the press, Mandela, who was about to go underground, portended that the
struggle was about to enter a phase from which there could be no turning
back. "If peaceful protests like these are to be put down by the mobilization of the army and police," he said, "then the people might have to use
other forms of struggle."[8]

3

In London the real education of Mac Maharaj began. Compared with
South Africa, London was the epitome of freedom. The social conditions
were strikingly different from those at home. In London you did not carry
a pass book; no policeman stopped you to ask what you were doing; you
did not need a permit to travel from one place to another; there were no
WHITES ONLY signs. There was still some discrimination, however, and Indians, like other immigrant groups, developed their own enclaves and networks. Mac shared a flat with the Seedat cousins, with others at different
times, and entered the circles around the Communist Party.

He immersed himself in London, where competing ideologies clashed,
providing intellectual stimulus. London was still the hub of the universe in
terms of cultural diversity, political expression, and intellectual debate. It
became the locus of African revolutionary and nationalist organizations
from British colonies. People from Britain's colonies had fought alongside
the Allies against Nazi Germany in defense of Britain's definition of freedom. Now they were demanding the same freedoms for themselves.

It was understandable that Mac would be attracted to communism.
For dispossessed and colonized peoples, communism held a visceral appeal: the promise of a future determined by the people themselves. In the
case of South Africa, the apartheid state was perceived as the stepchild of
capitalism. Hence the appeal of communism for members of non-African
racial groups, unable as yet to find a home in the ANC, which was then for
Africans only. The anger that had consumed him in South Africa was now
channeled into an eclectic series of activities—social, cultural, political,
and academic.

In the British Communist Party (BCP), Mac found his first role model,
Henry Pollitt, general secretary of the BCP, although Mac is the first to admit that he has not always lived up to the man's extraordinary integrity.

When World War II broke out, the BCP opposed it as a war between imperialist powers. When the USSR was attacked by Hitler, the BCP reversed
course. But not Pollitt. He asked to be relieved of his post on the basis of
his principled opposition to the war.

The South African Freedom Association, which Mac and others were
instrumental in founding in 1958,[9] became an adjunct of the Boycott
Committee in 1959,[10] which quickly evolved into the Boycott Movement
and then the Anti-Apartheid Movement (AAM) in April 1960,[11] later the
cornerstone of the ANC's fourth pillar: the mobilization of international
support. In each, Mac's fingerprints were to be found, but he kept moving on.

Vella Pillay was the SACP's contact person in London, a representative
of the Central Committee, and the underground conduit for *New Age*. He
was a founder, first treasurer and subsequently cochairperson of the
AAM.[12] Exiled students from South Africa—Kader Asmal, Steve Naidoo,
Manna Chetty, Essop and Aziz Pahad, Thabo Mbeki—found the Pillay
household a home away from home. Pillay well remembered the young
Mac, who arrived at his doorstep in Muswell Hill: "I found him an extremely impressive man of judgment, both of understanding of the South
African situation and his total dedication to the cause to which I had already committed myself. Subsequently, Mac became one of my closest
friends, a relationship that has lasted the better part of fifty years. On
Robben Island he developed a very close relationship with Nelson Mandela. Nelson Mandela was a very fatherly figure toward him. He'd say to
Mac, 'Go Slowly, Neef. Go slowly, go carefully.' Because Mac is a fire-
brand."[13]

"Go Slowly, Neef"—advice Mac was incapable of absorbing, never
mind heeding.

Mac

I ARRIVED IN LONDON in early August 1957 with five pounds in my
pocket. I slept on a bench at the railway station, and began looking for a
job. I had been told by Harold Strachan and his then wife Jean Middleton,
white colleagues in the Congress of Democrats in South Africa who had
been students in London, that the two places you could get a job easily
were the Lyons Corner House self-service restaurants and Securicor, a
night-guard company. I applied to Securicor, but at Lyons meals were included. Working there meant I got breakfast and lunch and high tea!

A few days later I bumped into Tony Seedat from Newcastle. Now Bhai, as Tony was nicknamed, had been my classmate. His cousin Hassim Seedat had been a student at the medical university in Natal, and they had lived near my place in Durban. They had come to Britain by ship and were in London to study. Shortly after their arrival, Hassim had come down with bronchitis and was in bed. Tony had taken a job at a Lyons Corner House. When he told me that Hassim was ill, I went to visit him. I didn't tell them that I was sleeping on a bench at the railway station. The tiny room they had was partitioned, with a kitchenette and a stove and, in the corner, a small bathtub. One of them said to me, "Look, we've got a proposal. Why don't you come and stay here with us? We've already bought pots and pans and plates, so we are able to cook for ourselves. We are paying £5.10s a week rental. If you join us, we'll split the rental three ways instead of two ways." I agreed.

Now I had a room and a job at Lyons. What I earned I put in for rent. I also began to save money to start at the London School of Economics (LSE). I ate my two meals at Lyons and in the evenings we had baked beans, cooked by Hassim, with bread. I worked at Lyons for two or three months. The Corner House opened at about five in the morning—remember, this is August or September, heading for winter, and it's getting colder and colder, and it's getting dark earlier and earlier. I worked as a garbage porter and window washer. My first job in the morning was to get the ladder and wash the windows.

One morning about five, when I came down the ladder, somebody walking past noticed me. It was an Indian chap from Durban. We were very pleased to see each other. He told me that as a graduate I could get a teaching job: "You're a qualified teacher in Britain if you have an undergraduate degree." He told me to go to the County Council Education Department and get on a panel of supply teachers. So I became a teacher, which was ironic in the light of the fights with my father! I was a temporary teacher being shoved from school to school—different day, different school, wherever on any given day a permanent teacher was absent from duty.

Then I applied for permanent employment and was accepted on the permanent staff as a remedial teacher, teaching problem children: kids with psychiatric problems, disturbed backgrounds, thuggish behavior. I was happy with the job. I came from a society where I was one of the underdogs. These kids were underdogs in the UK, and I felt an instant empathy with them.

Hassim, Tony, and I decided we would pool all our income. We would live frugally and start saving for university classes. As soon as we had enough money to pay for one, we would sponsor him until the others came on stream. Tony, of course, still had to do a General Certificate of Education because he didn't have a matric. Hassim looked after the money.

After a few months we found better accommodation. I was teaching and Tony became a conductor on London Transport and later trained as a bus driver. We were earning more now, and the kitty was beginning to grow. So we got a flat in Tottenham Court. It was one floor up: kitchen, living room, two big bedrooms, and a tiny bedroom for a study. It cost twenty-eight pounds a month, which was a little more than we were paying in Notting Hill Gate for a crummy single room.

In late 1957, Kurt Danziger came to London and somehow traced me to my room in Notting Hill Gate. One evening he introduced me to Vella and Patsy Pillay, which led to my being formally integrated into the South African Communist Party (SACP). Kurt was passing through London on his way to take up an academic post at the People's University in Jakarta, Indonesia. Clearly, he had undertaken the task of getting in touch with Vella to get Vella to reestablish a unit of the SACP in London. The unit consisted of Vella; his wife, Patsy; and me. A few years later Vella became the SACP Central Committee representative based in the UK, and later our unit published *The African Communist* and *International Bulletin*. I became lifelong friends with Patsy and Vella.

In November, Steve Naidoo joined us, and Kader Asmal arrived in early 1958. Our flat became a sort of gathering point for South African students. Kader and Steve enrolled to study for the LLB at the London School of Economics (LSE) for the 1958 term, while Hassim enrolled at Lincoln's Inn to study for the barrister exams. I waited for another year because I had to save money to get my fees. I enrolled at the LSE in 1959.

I started again from scratch. I did the first year and was in my second year, in 1960, when the Sharpeville massacre took place. By that time I was a member of the National Union of Teachers, the Movement for Colonial Freedom,[14] the South African Freedom Association, the *New Age* Support Committee, and the British Communist Party and the Africa Committee of the party, the latter under a pseudonym—John Kuluma. I was completely absorbed in the anticolonialist movement.

I found Britain an exhilarating place. Yes, the empire was collapsing. Ghana had become free; Malaysia and Tanganyika (Tanzania) were getting independence. In London there were people from all over the world, little groupings supporting the liberation struggles in their different countries:

Nigerians, Kenyans, Tanganyikans, Burmese, Indonesians, Sri Lankans, Indians, South Americans, West Indians, Irish. It was a very cosmopolitan environment, and we were bound by a unity we felt when we met one another. There was a commonality in our struggles, so I didn't feel lonely, in spite of the insularity of the British.

At that stage, the BCP supported independence for the colonies. It took the view that the Communist world would help the colonies to get out of the clutches of imperialism, without prescribing that they should then immediately build a socialist society. Socialism would be the outcome of a two-phase process—first, the capitalistic stage, then when circumstances were right, the socialistic phase. It was a model later adopted by the SACP.

In the International Affairs Committee of the party and the Africa Committee, I met and worked with people such as Jack Woddis, Idris Cox, and, the chairman of the International Committee, Palme Dutt. I met Maurice Cornforth, the philosopher; Maurice Dobb, the political economist; John Lewis, the philosopher; and J. D. Bernal, the world's leading marine biologist. These guys were running classes at the Marx Memorial Library, and I studied Marxism under them.

I was active in the Movement for Colonial Freedom under Fenner Brockway. He came from the Independent Labour Party and was in the House of Commons. I met face to face people whose books I had read, like the historian Eric Hobsbawm. I got involved in organizing the Paul Robeson* transatlantic concert that was played over the telephone after Robeson's passport had been taken away by the American authorities. Later I was involved in organizing his concert in London and supporting his trip to the Soviet Union. It was an exhilarating period for me.

London was an eye-opener for me with regard to left-wing politics. I went to Speakers' Corner in Hyde Park, and I read, and I went to meetings, and I realized, "Jesus! There are so many brands of socialists! There are Fabians, there are Scientific Socialists, there's this, there's that!" It was like walking into a cheese shop and seeing 250 brands of cheese. I was like a sponge, just absorbing it all.

---

*Paul Robeson was born in Princeton, New Jersey, in 1898, the son of an ex-slave. He became a world renowned scholar, athlete, actor, and singer. At the height of his career in the 1940s, he turned his attention to civil rights, and his views evoked controvesy and anger in America. In 1947, the House Un-American Activities Committee "named" him, and his passport was revoked until 1958. He died in 1968.

The Anti-Apartheid Movement (AAM)

In April 1958, a three-day national stayaway in South Africa took place.*
An appeal came from South Africa: since the regime was likely to react
very harshly, could we step up the activity of solidarity in Britain to act as
a restraint on them? We were to mobilize support from the Labour Party,
the unions, and the British government, and organize protest and solidarity meetings, which in turn would encourage our people to strike at
home. We would internationalize feeling against the apartheid regime.

That was how the South African Freedom Association (SAFA) got established in London. Solly Sachs, father of Albie,† was appointed secretary,
but after a few months he resigned his post and I was appointed secretary.
Vella and Patsy; Dr. Max Joffe and his wife, Saura; Doris Lessing; Naboth
Mokgatle; Sylvester Stein; Ros Ainslie; Guy and Thelma Routh; Cynthia
and Simon Zukas were at the inaugural meeting. We asked Fenner Brockway, the Labour Party, and the Movement for Colonial Freedom to be part
of the process. We began to demonstrate outside shops that sold South
African goods. We collected various sympathizers with whom we formed
the Boycott Movement to boycott South African goods, and it grew
rapidly.

The Freedom Association was the forerunner of the Anti-Apartheid
Movement, which we set up in March 1960. Without disclosing that we
were Communists, we helped these things grow, but they grew by attracting many different people to the cause of supporting South African freedom. Vella Pillay was the first treasurer; Father Trevor Huddleston played a
leading role. Martin Ennals was the organizer, and Abdul Minty subsequently became the secretary.[15]

---

*A national stay-at-home was called by the Congress Alliance from 14–16 April 1958 in
a bid to force the government to make political concessions and to legislate a minimum
wage of one pound a day. After the first day, the ANC called off the strike. One crucial
reason was the absence of consultation with the SACTU leadership beforehand. See []pre
transition/the struggle/strikes and mass action/[] SACTU and the Congress Alliance.
†Albie Sachs was an ANC activist stationed in Maputo. He lost an arm and was badly
scarred in a car bomb explosion in Maputo in 1982. He played a role in the negotiations and in drawing up the constitution of South Africa. He was appointed to the
Constitutional Court in 1994 by President Mandela. Interview with Sachs at [] o'malley/
interviews/[].

The South African Communist Party (SACP)

In 1960, the underground SACP at home began publishing a discussion journal called *The African Communist*, which covered issues from all over Africa. The first issue was a mimeographed copy; it did not disclose that it was run by the SACP. It received a warm welcome throughout Africa, and we had to find a more viable and stable way to keep it in business.

The SACP contacted Vella and asked the London unit to assist. With the help of the BCP, we organized a cover address in London for those who wished to communicate with the publication. Back home, Michael Harmel took charge as editor, and we arranged for the unit in London to receive the text of all the articles. We would then design the layout, have it printed, and distribute it in all sorts of clandestine ways both within South Africa and in other countries in Africa and abroad.

Later the SACP decided to publish *International Bulletin*, aimed at keeping fraternal parties throughout the world abreast of developments in South Africa. This came after it was formally acknowledged that the SACP had been reconstituted in 1953 as an underground party. Until 1960, there was no inkling that the SACP existed. During the 1960 state of emergency, a decision was taken to announce its existence. Some comrades weren't very happy about this, but the deed was done and we had to live with the fact that the apartheid regime would now hunt us down even more zealously.

Marriage and Gone Again

Tim had arrived in the UK around December 1957. I got a letter saying that she was on her way to study nursing in Aylesbury. We'd meet in London once in a while, and we resumed our relationship. She became active in the Nurses' Association, and she began to come to London once a fortnight for weekends. We'd go together to all the meetings whenever it was possible. She was very supportive of my party activities.

We got married in 1958. Tim was still traveling back and forth from Aylesbury. I got my own flat on Turnpike Lane. Our plans for when she finished at Aylesbury were that she would come to London and train as a midwife at Middlesex Hospital. That course would take eighteen months. In the meantime, I would do my final year toward the LLB at the LSE. That would give me time to work a bit in London while she was finishing her midwifery, and we would save for our fare to go back home. That was the plan.

Tim arrived to settle in London at the end of March 1961, and five days later Vella told me that the party wanted me to go abroad for training.* I was in my second year at the LSE. I asked if going abroad would take me back home eventually. They said yes, so I said, "I'm game." They asked, "Don't you want to know what training?" I said, "It doesn't matter as long as I'm full time in the struggle." I thought that it would take a year before I was sent for training, but three days later Vella turned up and said, "Here's your ticket; you're flying tomorrow."

So I left Tim in London and headed for the German Democratic Republic (GDR), or East Germany. It would be the story of my marriage. I was either gone or going somewhere.

---

*After Sharpeville, the movement in the direction of armed struggle was inexorable. What had been discussed in small groups before, often in isolation and without the knowledge of others, now found a broader forum. Vella Pillay was among a delegation attending a meeting of the Communist and Working Parties in Moscow in July 1960, when Joe Matthews, one of the delegates, recalled putting forward a policy of armed struggle and asking for the support of the Communist parties. See South African Democracy Education Trust, *Road to Democracy* (Cape Town: Zebra Press, 2004), p. 83.

4. GDR DAYS

Introduction

ESTABLISHED IN 1949, the German Democratic Republic (GDR) enclosed the area of Germany occupied by the Soviet Union following World War II. East Berlin became the capital of the new country, led by a Communist regime sponsored by the Soviet Union. West Berlin remained part of the Federal Republic of Germany (FRG).

"The construction of socialism" was the state mantra that resonated throughout the GDR after the war. For a period, the GDR's socialism was more rigid than that of the USSR. Giant organizations firmly under party control dominated the socioeconomic structure of the state.[1]

But despite the efforts of the GDR to create the trappings of a utopian egalitarian society, the country lost more than 15 percent of its population between 1948 and 1960—2.7 million people fled to the capitalist West.[2] In August 1961, the Berlin wall was erected to close the chief point of escape.

Increasingly, the internal politics of the GDR began to resemble those of the repressive USSR of the Stalinist era. For a period in the 1950s, there were more than fifty thousand political prisoners, almost one for every two hundred adults.[3] The party itself indulged in periodic "purges" of dissidents or suspected dissidents. Roughly half a million Soviet troops were permanently stationed in the GDR. In 1951, the state established the infamous Ministerium für Staatssicherheit—the Stasi—a secret police with both external and internal operations. At its peak in the late 1980s, the Stasi had roughly one informant for every fifty people.[4]

After the Suez Canal crisis of 1956, East German involvement in Africa became more pronounced.[5] Support for national liberation movements, including hospital treatment for wounded freedom fighters, training for their armies, and financial aid to some, including the South African Communist Party (SACP) and Umkhonto we Sizwe (MK)—the Spear of the

Nation, became official policy. The GDR severed trade relations with South Africa, supported all UN resolutions condemning apartheid, and was at the forefront of countries calling for sanctions to cripple the apartheid regime. For the ANC, the GDR was an ally that could be relied on to come through no matter what, an ally delivered to the ANC by the ANC's alliance with the SACP.

2

In South Africa in March 1960, following the Sharpeville massacre, the National Party government banned the ANC and other organizations and declared a state of emergency. Decades of nonviolent appeal and protest had fallen on deaf ears. The SACP took the first step toward an armed struggle in 1961, when it organized armed units and carried out sporadic acts of sabotage. The ANC, after an intense and sometimes tearful debate, followed.[6] The two parties amalgamated their respective units and founded MK, which would become the military arm of the ANC. Its aim was either to overthrow the government of South Africa through armed struggle or to bring it to the negotiating table through this added pressure. Nelson Mandela, Walter Sisulu, and Joe Slovo formed the High Command, with Mandela as chairman.[7] At first, MK confined its operations to acts of sabotage: forays against military installations, power plants, transportation links, and telephone lines. Sabotage was chosen because initially MK was not equipped to engage in other forms of violence and because such activities did not involve loss of life. The need for trained cadres was acute and limited the scale and type of operation MK cadres could carry out. Nevertheless, during its first year of operations, the MK managed about 130 acts of sabotage, all minor, but inculcating among whites the exaggerated fears of a people living with unconscious forebodings of the dread of things to come.[8]

MK turned to the Soviet Union and its satellites for military hardware, financial assistance, and training. East Germany was among the first countries visited by Slovo, a prime mover in MK. His reception was warm, and the East Germans promised to help in any way they could. In the end, it proved to be almost as generous as that of the USSR.

3

Mac's immediate response to Vella Pillay was that he would go abroad for training only if it led to his return to South Africa to engage full time in the struggle. Typical Mac. No queries about what type of training he would receive or where he would be sent, no "well, let me discuss it with Tim." He left Tim, with her blessing. This, after all, was what she had married into. The law degree Mac had escaped from Durban to pursue was jettisoned.

His acceptance of communism and the demands of the struggle were unconditional. The 1956 uprising in Hungary was the work of capitalist counterrevolutionaries posing as Hungarian nationalists. Nikita Khrushchev's revelations of Stalin's insatiable appetite to liquidate his own people were brushed aside as the aberration of an individual, not the nature of the Communist regime itself. Whatever the East Germans told him was uncritically accepted. He had come to listen, not to question. Whatever the Soviet Union said had the stamp of the Communist equivalent of papal infallibility. All this made him, in the early 1960s, the quintessential Communist intellectual, someone whose ideals defined a classless, poverty-free world in which the proletariat ruled. The revolution would elevate humanity to a higher plane, and its excesses were ignored.

His experiences in the GDR reinforced his beliefs. His brief sketch of Bischofswerda, the small town about one hundred miles outside Dresden, where he underwent a printing apprenticeship, is almost idyllic. It did not occur to him that perhaps he was being spied on—his communiqués to London read, his hosts informants. What mattered to Mac in the GDR was simply how he was treated. For the first time in his life, his color was not an issue, at least not overtly. He discovered his dignity as a human being.

Mac

I WENT TO THE GDR on the basis that I would not mix with anybody from South Africa or from the British colonies. The Germans gave me a student pass under the name of Das Gupta, purporting that I was an Indian from India studying printing. They put me in a village called Bischof-swerda, about twenty miles from Dresden, where nobody spoke English and they had never seen a black man in the flesh. That's where I did my printing course. My hosts wanted to put me up in the party hotel in Bischofswerda, but Walter Wemme, the foreman of the factory where I would be doing my training, said I could stay with him and his wife if I liked—they had a spare room—so I decided I would stay with them, which was a much more enriching experience.

Vella; my wife, Tim; Vella's wife, Patsy; Dr. Dadoo, and obviously some people in South Africa on the Central Committee knew where I was. If Tim wanted to write to me, she had to get in touch with Vella, and Vella would forward her letters to me. The official story to friends in London was that I had left London to return to South Africa.

I was in the middle of training when I learned that the SACP had decided to engage in sabotage against the South African regime. I got hold of them, through Vella, to say that since I was in the GDR, didn't they think it would be a wise idea for me to also train in sabotage? The Central Committee agreed. In the end, I trained for eleven months: six months in all aspects of printing and five months in sabotage—how to use dynamite, blow up pylons, cut railway lines, and manufacture homemade explosives. Then in May 1962 I returned to South Africa via London. I was the first person to undergo training outside the country after the decision to turn to organized violence as a means of struggle.

GDR: Life as a Comrade

My experiences in Germany were favorable and complemented my theoretical commitment to Marxism. For example, it was the first country where I did not feel that I was being discriminated against because I was a black man—unlike London, where I had gone to look for accommodation advertised in the newspapers and been turned away. The Seedats got the room we lived in after they answered an advertisement that said, "For Coloureds Only." In that three-floor building there were ninety-six occupants, all black. I was never refused accommodation in the GDR because I was black or looked at askance in a restaurant. Nor was I ever insulted in the streets.

There was, however, some curiosity about me. In Bischofswerda one day, I was walking from my workplace to my accommodation. Some children gathered behind this strange phenomenon of a Coloured man—they were saying words like *negre* to one another. I was really angry: were they calling me a nigger? They followed me all the way to my flat. When I got there, I opened a dictionary. I found that the word for black was *schwarze* or *negre*. I felt it was necessary to show those kids something, so the family I was staying with invited a group of the children over. One little girl sat on my lap and then suddenly smacked me in the face and said, *"Schmutzig."* I saw in the dictionary that *schmutzig* meant dirty. I took these kids into the bathroom and gave them a nail brush, soap, and hot water and said, "Here, wash me." They scrubbed and scrubbed and scrubbed and, when they couldn't remove my color, we went into the living room, and I said to our host, in my broken German, "Now explain to them that this is not dirt; it's the color of my skin."

The first time I walked into a pub, there was total silence. Everybody was waiting to see: does he speak German? I had looked up in my dictionary how to order a beer, so I said to the waiter, *"Bitte, ein bier,"* and the buzz started. When I finished my beer, I saw the waiter coming over with another beer. I hadn't ordered it. I gestured no, but the waiter indicated that somebody had sent me a free beer. I finished that beer and another beer appeared. I must have drunk a whole barrel that night!

In 1961, the GDR was on the march. Reconstruction of the economy was taking place side by side with social and medical services, and free education for everybody. Unlike London, where if you couldn't afford it, you were left behind. Industry was developing; unemployment did not exist. There was a confidence among the people, and you could sense their optimism about the future. Or so it seemed to me then. There was no sign in 1961 at the level of ordinary people's lives that the state was a repressive force; there was no sign of a secret police spying on people. To the extent that it existed or was noticed, it was seen as a benign defensive force.

The Cold War

The historical memory of Nazism was openly talked about. It was part of the school curriculum to preach against National Socialism and Hitlerism. They pointed to the socialist struggle of the thirties against Hitler as the only force in German political life that opposed Nazism.

I visited Buchenwald and was shown where Ernst Thälmann, the Communist leader of the thirties, had been imprisoned and where he was killed by the Nazis. I was shown the different sections where the Jews had been confined and where the Communists had been kept—and the chambers where they were killed. What had happened in the concentration camps made a great impression on me. I felt that the denunciation of Hitler and Nazism in the Western countries was somewhat hollow when they defended and gave support to Verwoerd and apartheid. After all, apartheid was an autocratic system based on the concept that the whites were the master race.

When I visited Dresden, the party leadership arranged to take me around. I was shown the Oder River and the fantastic buildings that had been bombed, still dilapidated and crumbling. I was told, "When the West

broadcast that Dresden was going to be under aerial bombardment, people gathered near the Oder River for safety, and then the bombers came
and strafed the Oder River civilians."*

I woke up one morning to hear that the Berlin wall had gone up during
the night. It was justified by the GDR state with all sorts of data and economics in the context of the cold war. It was justified to me as the actions
of the progressive forces in the world, and I bought into that. In East Germany it was portrayed as necessary because the West was trying to subvert
the Communist order, and undoubtedly it was.

The environment I was in reinforced my commitment to the Communist cause and, yes, I would have been looking at it through a prism that
refracted my beliefs. To me the West was synonymous with imperialism.
The West was the enemy and the hypocrite. South Africa had fought on
the side of the Allies, but it was enslaving us.

*The Allies' air forces dropped 3,900 tons of bombs on Dresden on 14 and 15 February
1945. The resulting firestorm reduced the city to ashes; between 25,000 to 35,000 civilians were killed.

5. GOING HOME

Introduction

THE SOUTH AFRICA Mac returned to in 1962 was very different from the South Africa he had fled. The newly empowered Security Branch was testing its powers and refining its techniques, and MK's campaign of sabotage, although primitive by most standards, was, nevertheless, beginning to unnerve whites, whose fears were stoked by the government's propagandizing against the ANC and the SACP. The ANC, under Oliver Tambo, established an external mission in Dar es Salaam, Tanzania, later relocated to Morogoro and finally to Lusaka in Zambia.

Apartheid itself had been revamped. Grand Apartheid was the creation of Hendrik Verwoerd, who became prime minister of South Africa in 1958. Verwoerd provided apartheid with an intellectual veneer and moral coherence, as well as its most thoroughgoing and totalitarian form. His policy of separate development, also called Grand Apartheid, aimed for total racial separation, except where blacks served whites.[1]

Separate development preceded independence in sub–Saharan Africa, and it was aimed at preempting black-majority rule in South Africa. By denationalizing the majority of South Africa's inhabitants, separate development would rid the areas designated for whites (87 percent of the country) of Africans. The underlying theory was simple: South Africa was not a single country consisting of African and white people. On the contrary, it comprised a number of ethnic and cultural minorities, separate nations who would find their homes in separate enclaves.

The 1936 Land Act had set aside what remained of traditional African land (about 13 percent of South Africa), and subdivided that land into homelands, nine in all, by ethnic background, though in some cases that was fudged too.[2] These would, according to the plan, provide for the different African nations to realize their own political aspirations.

According to the grand plan, as each homeland (some made up of noncontiguous territories) eventually became independent, its citizens would lose their South African citizenship. The "independent" homeland states would have their own institutions of governance, but in reality they were simply labor reservoirs for white South Africa.* Africans would have citizenship in their own Bantustan, as the homelands were derogatorily nicknamed, and get temporary residence permits to work in all-white South Africa. Wives and children and adults who did not have permits to work in white South Africa remained in the Bantustans.

Implementing this vision was a decades-long process that entailed large population removals as part of an elaborate social and geographical engineering exercise. More than 3.5 million South Africans were forcibly moved between 1960 and 1982.[3] Tens of thousands of other people lived for many years under constant threat of losing their homes.

By 1962, the South African government had weathered the storm of international rebuke and condemnation that followed Sharpeville. Foreign investment was again flowing into the country; the economy was growing at 7 percent.[4]

The SACP adopted a new program, the Road to South African Freedom,[5] which remained the centerpiece of its ideological perspective until the 1980s. Calling apartheid Colonialism of a Special Type (CST), the SACP argued that black South Africa was a colony of white South Africa. The immediate task of the party, therefore, was to support the ANC in the fight for the liberation of the "colonized" as a "national democratic revolution," which would be followed by a socialist revolution, or a further movement toward it.[6]

In October 1962, the ANC held its first annual conference, at Lobatse, in Bechuanaland (now Botswana). The conference linked the ANC with the armed struggle for the first time.[†] There would be no turning back.

---

*The Transkei became the first homeland to receive its independence in 1976, followed by Bophuthatswana in the western Transvaal, the Ciskei in the eastern Cape, and Venda in the northern Transvaal. The African populations of these independent states lost their South African citizenship. Two of the homelands, KwaZulu and Lebowa (in the Transvaal), had self-government but their leaders, Mangosuthu Buthelezi and Cedric Phatudi, refused to claim what they considered bogus "independence." None of the independent homelands received international recognition. The independent states were corrupt, antidemocratic, and incompetent. In the run up to the 1994 elections the independent states were incorporated into South Africa.

†The decisions of the Lobatse Conference were not published, but in a statement issued in April 1963, following the conference, the ANC said: "In the changed South African conditions of struggle, we have the mass political wing, spearheaded by the ANC on the

The following year the government passed the Sabotage Act, which provided for detention without trial for 90 days, subsequently amended to 180 days. This gave the security apparatus carte blanche. Since the law defined sabotage as almost any illegal action furthering political change, it effectively banned all opposition to the government outside the whites-only Parliament. Indeed, John Vorster, then minister of justice, opined in Parliament that he merely had to be satisfied that someone might further the aims of communism for detention to be extended "until this side of eternity." The International Commission of Jurists (ICJ) in Geneva, representing forty thousand lawyers and judges in more than sixty countries, condemned this law.[7]

The banning of the ANC meant that it was harder for it to be a mass organization. MK had to operate in secrecy. The ANC in exile had difficulty establishing viable underground structures and had to turn to the SACP, which had a history of clandestine organization. Initially at least, MK's sabotage operations were not intended as an end in themselves but as a way of driving the apartheid state to compromise. But this did not stand in the way of plans being drawn up—Operation Mayibuye, in particular—that envisaged the overthrow of the government by revolutionary means. [8]

2

Mandela had been arrested in August 1962 and charged with inciting African workers to strike* and leaving the country without valid travel documents. He was convicted in November and sentenced to five years in prison. In July 1963, the upper echelon of the ANC was arrested at Lilliesleaf, a farm in Rivonia about fifteen miles from downtown Johannesburg, that was being used by the ANC as a base for the MK leadership.[†]

---

one hand, and the specialized military wing, represented by Umkhonto, on the other. . . . The political front gives substance to military operations." Vladimir Shubin, *The View from Moscow* (Cape Town: Mayibuye, 1999), p. 50. In *Long Walk to Freedom*, Mandela states the relationship more directly: "The conference was a milestone, for it explicitly linked the ANC and MK. Although the National Executive Committee stated, 'Our emphasis will remain mass political action,' Umkhonto was referred to as the 'military wing of our struggle' " (pp. 294–95). An interesting formulation by Mandela, since part of the defense at the Rivonia Trial was that the ANC and MK were separate organizations.

*As head of the National Action Council, coordinating the anti-Republic campaign, Mandela called for a three-day national stayaway, 29–31 May 1961.

†Those arrested were Walter Sisulu, Govan Mbeki, Raymond Mhlaba, Rusty Bernstein, Ahmed Kathrada, Denis Goldberg, Bob Hepple, and Arthur Goldreich.

Whether out of foolhardiness or foolishness, the ANC underground had continued to use the farm as a safe house after the ANC was banned. Only elementary security precautions had been put in place. When it was raided, the security police captured large quantities of documentary evidence, much of it in the defendants' own handwriting, all of it subsequently used against them.

In October, after ninety days of detention in solitary confinement, the accused—Mandela's name had now been added as accused number one—were charged with 202 acts of sabotage allegedly carried out under their direction as senior members of MK. A conviction could carry the death sentence.

The centerpiece of the prosecution's case was Operation Mayibuye, a detailed outline of a plan using Fidel Castro's model of insurgency to launch guerrilla warfare in South Africa as a precursor to a mass uprising and the overthrow of the state. At his own trial, Bram Fischer, the lawyer who led the defense team for the Rivonia Trialists (and a member of the SACP Central Committee), described the plan as "an entirely unrealistic brainchild of some youthful and adventurous imagination . . . if there was ever a plan a Marxist could not approve in the then prevailing circumstances, this was such a one . . . if any part of it at all could be put into operation, it could achieve nothing but disaster. . . ."[9]

The defendants made little or no effort to deny most of the charges. Their defense rested not only on political grounds, but on moral certitude. They had decided that they would use the trial to indict the government, to highlight the travesties of justice perpetrated by the regime and its merciless oppression of people of color. The prosecutor played to the judge, the defendants to their constituency and international opinion. They would let their people know that the ANC, in spite of being banned, had not abandoned them, that it was fighting back. The defendants successfully turned the accusations against them into a charge of guilt against the state. To the despair of their lawyers, they said that if they were sentenced to the gallows, they would not appeal their sentences.

The trial lasted eleven months. There was drama outside the court as well: among the defendants there was a divergence of views that could have made the difference between a life sentence and a death sentence. Govan Mbeki, who had drafted the Mayibuye plan with Joe Slovo and Arthur Goldreich, maintained that the ANC NEC had adopted Operation Mayibuye as ANC policy. The others did not. Sisulu took the stand to testify that Operation Mayibuye had been drawn up, but no decision regarding its use had been reached at the time of the arrests. The core issue was the use of violence. Had Operation Mayibuye been approved, the range of potential targets would include human beings, especially members of the security forces. The issue festered long after the trial and triggered an acrimonious dispute between Mbeki and Sisulu that strained their relationship for the rest of their lives.

Except for Bernstein, the Rivonia defendants were found guilty, sentenced to life imprisonment, and bundled off to Robben Island. But in his findings, the judge agreed with the defense that MK and the ANC were separate organizations, a finding that had important ramifications for other members of the ANC who would face trial later. Had the judge found otherwise (that MK was the military arm of the ANC and hence subject to its jurisdiction), all ANC Trialists could face the death sentence.

3

The Indian community in Johannesburg was extremely tight knit. In politically active families, becoming involved in politics was a rite of passage for young people. Demonstrations, meetings, leafletting, protesting, assembling—these were all part of the social tapestry. Among the most active families were the Josephs—brothers Paul, Dasu, and Peter—and the Naidoos.

The Naidoos can trace their political involvement in South Africa back one hundred years.[10] Indres Naidoo, a longtime member of the SACP, one-time member of MK, and presently an ANC MP, recalls Mac's stay in the Naidoo household after his return to South Africa. "My three brothers, my two sisters, and I were actively involved. We used to attend demonstrations; we used to go to meetings. Almost every week there was some demonstration or other. Mac would talk about these demonstrations; he would talk about everything but never attended any of these damn things. So we got quite annoyed with this bugger. . . . Kathy [Ahmed Kathrada] was quite worried by this situation and [had to do] everything in his power to prevent us from beating him up. . . . Obviously Kathy knew more than we did about Mac's involvement."[11]

Mac thrived on creating his own legend. Whereas the Naidoos looked down on Mac as some kind of sellout, the Josephs knew he was involved in underground work but inquired no further. He was unable to say anything.

For twenty-six turbulent months, from April 1962 until July 1964, Mac was the struggle's publisher and bomb maker, a member of MK, post-Rivonia consultant to the ad hoc high command, a member of the SACP's Central Committee, and travel agent for MK recruits selected for training abroad. For twenty-six months he worked feverishly—sometimes recklessly—a lonely existence. Mac worked with a small circle of friends, mostly Communists, whom he knew and trusted.

When the struggle within South Africa was in danger of collapsing, Mac and a few others kept it together for months. The struggle probably would have come unglued had it not been for the SACP and its underground networks. They let the masses know that even with the removal of the leadership, there were others who had stepped into the breach.

4

It is easy to make harsh judgments in retrospect about the manner in which the ANC went about its business after it was banned and especially after the decision to resort to armed struggle. It was careless, seemingly oblivious to the fact that the government might be monitoring its activities, and foolhardy in allowing friends and fellow activists to visit the Rivonia farm without a thought to security and no effort to vary travel patterns. These judgments are not meant to damn but rather to put the struggle in the context of its time. The ANC had half a decade of history to draw on. But having never experienced draconian crackdowns by government, it had little by way of practice in such circumstances to draw on.

This was, it must be understood, a revolution of amateurs.* With the exception of a few "founding" members who had some military experience as a result of their being veterans of World War II, most of the regional commands consisted of military illiterates.† When the movement moved to endorse an armed struggle, it had little understanding of the possible consequences of its decision, not in military terms but in the ways it would transform the social order itself. Nothing would ever be the same once the government responded to the meager threat confronting it with a calculated fury that throttled all protest.

---

*In *Slovo: An Unfinished Autobiography*, Joe Slovo says as much: "Theory apart, this venture into a new area of struggle found us ill equipped at many levels. Among the lot of us we did not have a single pistol. No one we knew had ever engaged in urban sabotage with homemade explosives. Some of us had been in the army but for all practical purposes, our knowledge of the techniques required for this early phase of the struggle was extremely rudimentary. (See page 153.)

†Jack Hodgon had fought in the South African army in World War II and was familiar with explosives. Arthur Goldreich had some training; Harold Strachan trained others. Most operations, sporadic at best, were low-intensity acts of sabotage. (See *The Road to Democracy*, pages 90–132.)

In the early years, MK was little more than a motley collection of would-be revolutionaries. Rudimentary training in any type of military activity qualified anyone for immediate promotion to the higher echelons. A little knowledge of weaponry, familiarity with explosives, and the basics of chemistry were enough to elevate someone to be the tutor of others. Theoretical application counted for as much as actual experience.

The plan to overthrow the government, Operation Mayibuye, was phantasmagorical creative writing rather than a hard-nosed assessment of the difficulties facing the movement in a revolutionary war with the government. There was no assessment of the government's military capacity (huge) or the movement's armed revolutionary capacity (none). Yet it boldly asserted: "Armed to the teeth [the government] has presented the people with only one choice and that is its overthrow by force and violence. It can now truly be said that very little, if any, scope exists for the smashing of white supremacy other than by means of mass revolutionary action, the main content of which is armed resistance leading to victory by military means." As in Cuba, the general uprising would be "sparked off by organized and well prepared guerrilla operations during the course of which the masses of the people will be drawn in and armed."[12]

Probably the only factual statement here was that the government was armed to the teeth. Operation Mayibuye called for MK cadres to invade the country: "the simultaneous landing of four groups of 30 based on our present resources whether by ship or air—armed and properly equipped in such a way as to be self-sufficient in every respect for at least a month." And "simultaneously with the landing of the groups of 30 and thereafter, there should be a supply of arms and other war matériel to arm the local population which become integrated with the guerrilla units." On arrival, "there should be at least 7,000 men in the four main areas ready to join in the initial onslaught."[13] Wilton Mkwayi, who became head of MK after the Rivonia arrests, by virtue of his having received training in guerrilla warfare in China, describes the training of the first batch of MK cadres that were sent abroad: "It was just a short duration because we were not actually trained extensively. We were trained in indigenous methods. Ours was to come back and teach others because we knew that getting arms would be difficult, so we would have to resort to indigenous methods—to make, for instance, pipe bombs, use bottles, Molotov cocktails—and those were the small things we learned to do; and melting the iron to make grenades—those were the small things that we received training in."[14]

To make matters worse, the training was in rural guerrilla warfare. MK at this point—and for the greater part of its operational life—had units dispersed for the most part in urban areas. There was a belief that the revolution of the proletariat was a universal phenomenon that followed universally defined rules of implementation.

Initially, six men were sent to China for training in 1962. Of the six, who were supposed to form the command corps of MK on their return, at least four were members of the SACP. In the disruptions that followed Rivonia, the SACP became the stabilizing force, issuing instructions on what should and should not be done, reconstituting underground networks, reallocating resources, giving directions to MK. The SACP's connections in the USSR, Eastern Europe, and China led to training for cadres there. Recruitment was haphazard; there was fuzziness about what it entailed. There was a touching belief that the government would crumble under the weight of the political upheaval that armed revolution would ignite. Most of the would-be revolutionaries found themselves either in prison serving long sentences or seeking the haven of exile.

Some of the first cadres—not that they ever thought of themselves as such—had no training at all. Paul Joseph says: "We had various things to read; we went on some exercises. The little training we got came from chaps who had served in the Second World War, but the training was pretty shabby and it proved a disaster later on, especially the making of the bombs—very primitive."[15] Laloo Chiba says: "When MK was launched on 16 December 1961, I was part of the original units that carried out actual sabotage. So I was there right from the beginning. I had no training whatsoever. People who were used to the idea of making bombs showed us what needed to be done. And that's how we started off. Our first bombs were made in plastic bottles with charcoal and sulphuric acid and things of that nature."[16] Dasu Joseph says: "I didn't have any formal training, but I would say that the training came as a result of my experience in the political movement. Our first act as a member of MK was to go and publicly announce the launching of MK, and that was in 1962."[17]

When the government's security machinery went into action, the Josephs and their families had to flee the country, in 1963. Today they live in London and complain that the new state will not recognize them as MK veterans because they were not formally integrated into MK. They are disappointed and puzzled that their contribution is not recognized, and they feel cheated out of a legacy they hoped to bequeath to their grandchildren. Laloo Chiba, on the other hand, found himself on Robben Island for fifteen years. He retired as a member of Parliament in 2001, two years after Indres Naidoo, also an MP, had called it a day.

At a time that counted most in their lives, Mac had that indefinable combination of personal attributes that allows a special few to rise to such an occasion. He had an abundance of chutzpah and arrogance, mental toughness and physical stamina, conviction and a cheeky charm designed to disarm but, more important, to manipulate. Often abnormal societies require leaders who are themselves abnormal in some way. What, after all, can be said of someone who can blithely claim that he found the experience of laying pipe bombs in the dark on railway tracks "very normal"? "Mac was the kind of bloke who gave the feeling," Dasu Joseph says, "that he was a very warm guy. He never revealed himself. Till today he never reveals himself."[18]

And Tim? Having scraped together the money, she joined Mac in April 1963, nine months after his return. She stayed with him in his home in Doornfontein and for a while she, too, became an extension of the printing operation before she left for Durban to do a nursing refresher course. She saw Mac again for three days in 1964 before she and Mac were arrested. Almost thirteen years would pass before they were reunited.

Mac

I ARRIVED BACK in London in March 1962. Tim was still there. Vella started making arrangements with the SACP at home for my return. The plan was that I would go to my parents in Newcastle for about three weeks, and during that time Jo'burg would make contact with me.

I flew from London on 1 May and arrived in Johannesburg on the morning of 2 May 1962. There was a problem at Jo'burg Airport. I had prepared a story, a legend, that I was living in London and was coming to South Africa to visit my father and mother because my father was not well. I thought that story would get me in. I was traveling on a South African passport, but I had no cash on me except for about thirty or thirty-five dollars in U.S. currency that Vella had given me at the last minute.

Airport security wanted to know where I would be staying. I gave my brother-in-law's address in Durban. They told me to report to the Security Branch offices there. Of course, I had no intention of going to my brother-in-law's. I just wanted to get out of their hands so I could get back to Newcastle until the underground contacted me. The security people kept me at the airport for the entire day, but they had nothing definite on me. Then, at about four o'clock that afternoon, they gave me a document requiring me to be out of the province within twenty-four hours—Indians were not allowed to be in the Transvaal without a permit. I had to go directly to Park Station and catch the train to Durban at six o'clock that evening.

The train reached Newcastle at midnight. I was the only person who got off, and the station was deserted. I went to a call box and called a friend who ran a taxi and lived near my parents' home. He came over in his pajamas, picked me up, and dropped me at my home.

I told my parents that I was on my way to Basutoland (later Lesotho), where I had applied for a teaching job. I knew that would make my father happy, and there would be no questions in the community. My father was very pleased that I was going to be teaching.

I avoided interacting with people aside from a very few close friends of the family. I used my U.S. dollars in the first week to give presents to all my nieces and nephews. I also bought fruit and vegetables for my mum. The three weeks passed—and still I was not contacted. I had no money left. I was not supposed to write to London or post a letter, for the sake of security. I couldn't afford to phone London, so there I was, stranded.

Getting Active

One Friday evening after six weeks had passed, Kathy (Ahmed Kathrada) arrived at night at our door in a Volkswagen car. He was banned and had been restricted to Johannesburg, but he had broken his banning order and driven to Newcastle. I had met him in Jo'burg in the fifties when he was part of the Treason Trial, but only fleetingly. Once we were alone, I told him that I was flat broke. He said, "Sorry about all the mishaps, but we need to see you in Johannesburg. When can you be in Johannesburg?" I was so anxious about having overstayed in Newcastle that I said I would hitchhike and get to Jo'burg the following day. It was too risky to go back with him in case he was stopped and caught breaking his banning order. So we made the arrangements; he gave me some money and left.

I hitchhiked to Jo'burg. When I got there, I made contact with Kathy, and he arranged board and lodging for me at the home of Indres Naidoo, who was living in Doornfontein. The Naidoos were a poor family. Indres's mother, his sisters, and his brothers had legal permits to stay in the Transvaal. His father was deceased. He had been very active in the Indian congresses and his mother had gone to prison during the passive resistance campaign. And it was awkward because I was not supposed to reveal that I was a political activist.

Indres's mother, Amah, kept it all together. I slept upstairs, but the bathroom was downstairs, through the kitchen. One morning she saw me coming down the stairs and heading for the bathroom with an eye patch on my eye, and she said, "What's wrong with your eye?" I said, "I have an artificial eye." And she said, "But you've stayed here before. I remember you." And I had, from time to time during the Treason Trial in 1956. I said to her, "Amah"—the Tamil word for mother—"Amah, yes, I have stayed here before." And she said, "Are you politically active?" I said, "No, not interested in politics." But she had put two and two together.

Indres, of course, was very active at that time. He was working as a clerk for a firm called Frank and Hirsch, and he and his sister Shanthie were the breadwinners in the family. Indres was very, very critical of me. He recognized me from when I had stayed at their house in the midfifties; he was trying to encourage me to become politically involved, but I was refusing! He and his cronies in the Youth League accused me of being a sellout. I was saying nothing.

Joining the Underground

Arrangements were now made for me to meet contacts near Park Station. Two white men arrived in a black Chevrolet, which stopped at the roadside where I was standing. I jumped into the backseat. The two white men were Rusty Bernstein and Joe Slovo, both of whom I recognized. We drove around—Rusty was driving—and they interviewed me. They asked me about my training in Germany. Joe was clearly interested in me from MK side because, when I told him that I'd done sabotage training, he tested my knowledge of that. Then, before we parted, he asked me to write down all the formulas for bombs and the use of dynamite. I said I could do that easily. Rusty said we should go through my printing training—they needed to get a clandestine printing establishment going.

On the basis of that interview, I received a message that integrated me into a unit of the underground Communist Party, a unit led by Kathy that was for my normal clandestine political activity. Then I was put into a technical committee with three other people and asked to find a place where I could set up two or three lithograph machines that had arrived in South Africa but that nobody knew how to use. The machines had been smuggled into the country in 1958 or 1959 and were rusting away in a warehouse.

My job was to house these machines someplace, and see if I could get them working, and to train others how to use them. That was my first assignment. I was later taken to Rivonia because I had to attend to the machines in use there which is where the Security Branch (SB) later found my fingerprints. The different structures were kept apart. I would be with different people in different structures, and no one in any of the structures would know that I belonged to another one. The printing was done clandestinely.

Kathy led my party unit. The other members were Abdulhay Jassat, who later escaped along with Harold Wolpe from the Marshall Square police station in 1963; a chap called Ibrahim Moolla, Mosie Moolla's brother; and a chap called Solly Esakjee. Solly dropped out in 1963 when the ninety-day law came into operation. He feared that he would not be able to cope with a ninety-day detention, so we dropped him but remained friends.

The next question was what my cover would be. What would my legend be? What was I doing in Jo'burg? Large numbers of people were living there illegally, breaking the provincial permit laws. Strictly speaking, an Indian was supposed to carry a little sheet of paper, a permit stating how long he or she was allowed to be in the Transvaal, but I had nothing like that. The police had started looking for me in Durban and Newcastle. I had not reported to the Security Police in Durban. My parents, of course, simply said, "Yes, he came here; he visited us and he has gone to Basutoland." "What's he doing there?" "Oh, he said he was getting a teaching job there." In those days, the Security Police were pretty lax. They would simply say, "Here's a telephone number. Next time he comes, please contact us," and then they would go away.

So I was living in Jo'burg, and I was now in the underground. What was I to say I was doing there to anybody I met? At the time, we were expecting *New Age* to be banned. Every time they had banned the newspaper—it was a weekly newspaper—we had come out with the same paper under another name. It had started off in the thirties as *The Guardian*; and when that was banned in the fifties, it became *The Searchlight*; and when that was banned, it changed to another name and was banned again and became *New Age*. We didn't know what form the clampdown would take this time, but the regime had passed a new press law that required owners of newspapers to put down a deposit of twenty thousand rand (ten thousand U.S. dollars) as security for a newspaper's registration. If it contravened any law, that money would be confiscated.

So the movement began to make preparations for a potential banning. Through the underground, the movement sponsored and registered a variety of titles before the law became effective. One of these was a sports newspaper called *Sports Parade*, which was run by and officially owned by a white comrade named Mannie Brown. Mannie was running various publications like *Amateur Photography*, that sort of thing.

I was interviewed by Mannie in the presence of Rusty. After the interview, Mannie employed me as editor, advertising agent, and salesman for *Sports Parade*, which came out once a fortnight. It was necessary to keep this paper functioning so that, if the bans came, we could reappear under the name of *Sports Parade*. The person who wrote the editorials in the beginning was Dennis Brutus, but not under his real name. I took over the newspaper. I now had a cover job.

Underground with the SACP: Printer and Publisher

I was the sole staff member of *Sports Parade*. I attended to the writing, printing, layout, and selling—everything. This gave me a cover to go around to all the printing establishments in Johannesburg asking for prices and so forth. I got to know the terrain. I bought a linotype machine. These are huge machines, but I bought one in a scrapyard in Pretoria and housed it in premises in Ophirton, one of Jo'burg's industrial areas, in a very old, run-down building. I began quietly to repair the machine, removing the rust and getting it working. Once I got it working, I went around touting for linotype setting work to cover the rent of the place. I had now got to know all the small and big print shops. When Indres Naidoo and family asked me what I was doing, I said I was editing *Sports Parade*. Indres still had no idea what I was doing.

Through my party cell I was also introduced to Dasu Joseph and his brothers Peter and Paul. Peter had picked up two of the escapees from Marshall Square; Dasu and Paul were also active in MK. The Josephs were a very important resource. We became very close.

Dasu was living in Ophirton. I frequented his house a lot, and in a place at the back of his house, I initially started one of the printing facilities. It was through his and Paul's contacts that I rented a commercial building where I located the linotype machine. It was also through the two brothers that I got access to another family who were running flower stalls in an open area off Rissik Street (one of the main streets in central Jo'burg).

Dasu also helped me get a new set of identity papers. He found a Coloured lady living in Kimberley who was prepared, for a small sum of money, maybe twenty-pounds (thirty-five dollars) to sign an affidavit to say I was her illegitimate child, that she had not disclosed my birth because she had been married at the time in Jo'burg, and I was the product of an affair; that she gave birth to me in Kimberley and got friends there to bring me up, but now her husband was dead and we had been reunited. I used that affidavit to get an identity card as Solly Matthews, the name under which I was later arrested.

It was at the flower stalls that I first met Piet Beyleveld. He was a well-known public figure, the president of the Congress of Democrats, and— but not known to me at the time—a member of the Central Committee of the SACP. The flower stall people also had lots of networks. They introduced me to the Brill brothers, who owned a printing company in Fordsburg, where they used the latest offset technology. The brothers were staunch supporters of the National Party (NP). One of my covers was that I was doing typesetting on a job-lot basis—I'd set leaflets for printers. I cultivated a relationship with the Brill brothers and convinced them that I'd like to learn how the photographic technique was used in litho printing. They gave me access. When I had time, they would allow me to go there and let one of their staff teach me. In that way I got to worm my way in. I made a duplicate key for the factory so that I could steal in at night and use the presses. So by day they were printing for the Nats, and by night, unbeknownst to them, their equipment was being used on behalf of the Communist Party and the underground!

Paul introduced me to a Frenchman, whose name I cannot recall, who had a printing establishment in Jeppe, a Jo'burg neighborhood. I approached him too as this meek, down-and-out Indian, and I did some setting for him now and again for a meager payment. I got friendly with him, and he was prepared to help this poor Indian. He said he would teach me how to use the machines.

The other machines I housed in two adjacent rooms I rented in Buxton Street, Doornfontein. I got them repaired and got them functioning. I printed for everybody, for both the ANC and the Communist Party.

The Indian congresses* were not banned, so they could print openly in Ferreirastown at Royal Printers. I had the keys to that establishment too. I

*The Natal Indian Congress (NIC) and the Transvaal India Congress (TIC). See []maharaj/glossary/[].

would tell Essopbhai Bukharia, the owner, "This weekend when you knock off at one o'clock, clean your workshop and deliver the keys to me at two o'clock. Don't come back till Monday morning at eight o'clock." Some comrades and I would use his machines over the weekend, then clear up so that there were no traces when Essopbhai and his staff came back to work on Monday.

In 1962, when Madiba was sentenced for illegally leaving the country, and he delivered his famous speech from the dock,[19] we printed that speech as a pamphlet—a huge run. It took us about five days and nights of printing on those machines. But I didn't have enough people to collate and staple the pamphlets on time, so it was arranged for the Naidoo household and the house next door to them (they were semidetached cottages) to keep their doors closed from about seven or half past seven in the evening, and for nobody to go out to the front veranda. They were to allow a period of time in which anonymous people would deliver suitcases full of pamphlets. It was then the Naidoos's job to take them in and collate them and staple them—without leaving fingerprints. Now as you know, I was a boarder at the Naidoo house, and I was the one who delivered those suitcases of stuff and then disappeared!

The Naidoo family and their friends collected them, took them to a neighbor's house, and started collating. About an hour later I arrived home. Because the houses were semidetached, I could hear through the wall, and they obviously realized I was home. Shanthie came over and said, "What are you doing?" I said I was just relaxing. "Why don't you come and help? We've got a big job." I said, "Help with what?" "Oh, a clandestine pamphlet of Madiba's speech—we've printed it, and we are busy collating it." I said, "No, cut me out! I don't want to be involved in these things. I am not a political animal." "Oh come on! What's wrong with you? We're making sure there are no fingerprints or anything."

She was persistent, so reluctantly I went into the next house and saw them sitting at the table collating. Together we got the Madiba pamphlet done. It was properly stapled, with a photograph of Madiba on the front page—the famous one with him wearing his T-shirt and his beard—with the quotation "I Accuse," which I had borrowed from the Dreyfus trial. We put the pamphlets back into the suitcases and left them on the veranda late that night, and by morning the suitcases had disappeared. They were taken to another place and distributed by the underground structures; various people had to collect one suitcase each.

The pamphlet was a big hit. The authorities wanted to know who had printed it and who had distributed it. They didn't get anywhere, but it caused great excitement in the movement because it meant we had the clandestine capacity to print pamphlets or leaflets properly: it had been linotype set, a professional job. Everybody was impressed. The Communist Party gave me a budget to set up further facilities, and they put me on the propaganda committee.

The Propaganda Committee

The propaganda committee was made up of Ruth First; Duma Nokwe, then assistant secretary-general of the ANC; and Dan Tloome, whom I subsequently met in exile. Tloome was a member of the Central Committee. He fled to Botswana just before my detention. Rusty Bernstein didn't attend meetings because he was under house arrest. Rusty was the head of the unit, and Ruth First took over from him.

The propaganda committee was my core function at the time; the printing was a specialized function within the committee. Later, after the Rivonia arrests, I had increased contact with Bram Fischer; Rusty's wife, Hilda; Michael Dingake (he was on the District Committee of the party and in the ANC Secretariat); Dave Kitson; and Piet Beyleveld. My contact with Laloo Chiba began to develop.

The other person I worked closely with was Ameen Cajee. Kathy and the others used to call him Doha, which means "old man" in Gujarati. He was a veteran. We could never work out his age, though we knew that he had been involved in the struggle with Dr. Dadoo as far back as 1936.

Contact with MK

I knew two of a group of six people who had undergone military training in China while I was training in the GDR. They were Wilton Mkwayi, who had evaded detention during the final phase of the treason trial,[20] secretly returning to the country after escaping arrest, and my old friend Steve Naidoo. Steve had gone to China and trained in radio communications. After that, he went back to London to complete his bar exams before returning to South Africa.

Ruth came to me and told me Mkwayi wanted to see me. I knew he was fully involved in the MK; he would, from time to time, drop in at my cottage at night. I was now living in servants' quarters on Pearce Street,

Doornfontein. It was a bit of a gray area,* filled with gangsters and fraud-sters and criminals. In that kind of area, if you're seen walking around at eleven o'clock at night looking as if you're drunk, nobody worries. I was pretending to be part of that community. I was living there because I didn't stick out. Nobody asked me why I was suddenly driving a car—it was a station wagon—yet I lived in servants' quarters. Nobody asked me why I disappeared for three days, and then for another five days I lolled around apparently doing nothing.

Tim had arrived back in South Africa around Easter 1963. She stayed with me in Jo'burg for a while, first in Mayfair, then on Pearce Street. We integrated her into the printing unit, but she felt she couldn't sit at home and do nothing for days on end; and because she was illegally in the Trans-vaal, she couldn't get work there. She decided to register as a nurse in Na-tal. Then we discovered that because she had interrupted her nursing studies for so long a period, the Nursing Council wouldn't register her un-less she did a refresher course at St. Aidan's Hospital in Durban. So a few months later she went off to Durban.

In the meantime, though, Mkwayi and Ruth asked me to go to Natal to make contact with Steve, which I did. I brought him to Jo'burg, and he met with MK. At my home on Pearce Street, he met with someone I later learned was Lionel Gay, who used to teach physics at Wits. Lionel and Steve discussed Steve's radio communications training. Ruth told me we had to come up with a cover for Steve. The best thing to do was to get him articled to a lawyer, so I went to Durban and asked J. N. Singh to employ Steve. He agreed and Steve went to work for him in Durban.

Ruth First

Ruth was in the Central Committee of the party. She was someone I had great empathy with. My *Sports Parade* salary—my underground salary that was paid through *Sports Parade*—was fifteen pounds a month. My rent for those servants' quarters was thirteen pounds a month, so I was left with two pounds for both Tim's and my needs. Ruth had obviously heard from some comrade, possibly Paul Joseph, that I was living on a shoe-string. One day she said to me, "When do I visit your home and meet Tim?" I said, "It's very risky." She said, "Yes, it is risky, but I will take pre-cautions. I want to visit your home." So she came. She walked into those

*Where races would mix and live in proximity, usually run-down, crime-infested areas.

servants' quarters, and what she saw was a wooden crate in the kitchen, on which was standing a two-plate hot plate. The kitchen had no sink, nothing. In the so-called living room, a tiny room, there was just a set of wooden boxes, tomato crates, over which Tim had put a cloth so that it looked like a coffee table. We sat on wooden crates we had picked up at grocers' shops.

Ruth had tea and we chatted. She didn't say anything to me, but afterward she went to Paul Joseph, who had a job at Ruth's father's furniture factory. She gave Paul a beautiful imbuia coffee table and told him to give it to me. But she must have discussed my situation with Paul, and he must have told her I would reject charity. She told him to tell me that she had won the table in a raffle and had no need of it, so I could buy it from her for five shillings—the price of a raffle ticket. So I bought it for a mere five shillings! I thought that incident had an element of empathy and style behind it.

After the Rivonia arrests, Ruth took steps to integrate me formally into MK. I was rendering assistance to MK without belonging to an MK unit. It started off one day when Mkwayi came to me. Steve Naidoo was in town and was staying at my cottage when one evening Mkwayi turned up. Obviously, he knew that Steve was in Johannesburg because he was in the MK High Command. Mkwayi produced a pistol in a brown paper bag. He said, "Mac, I'm in trouble. I've got a brand-new pistol. I am not familiar with it: It is a Spanish Astra." I'd never seen one before. He said, "I was running a course teaching a group about the structure of the pistol and how to assemble and disassemble and clean and maintain it. I dismantled this pistol very nicely in front of the class, but when I came to assemble it, I couldn't do it. I'm really embarrassed! Can you help out?"

He put the pieces on the table. Steve, who had trained with Mkwayi, was first to tackle it but failed. I said, "Let's work out the function of each of these loose parts." It took us some time, but finally we worked out that there was a part missing. But Mkwayi said there wasn't a missing part. We tumbled to the fact that he hadn't disassembled one part—there were two pieces still attached to each other. We disassembled that part and now, when we started reassembling it, everything fit perfectly. Mkwayi said, "Mac, you're a genius!"* He said he was getting hold of a lot of weapons but didn't know whether they were functional. "Can I bring them to you to check out?" he asked. So I did things like that.

---

*When I met with Mkwayi, I asked him about the gun incident and repeated the words Mac had attributed to him. Mkwayi laughed and repeated the words: "Mac's a genius!"

On another occasion Mkwayi came to me and said, "Pipe bomb ingredients—we can't get them because the regime has found out what ingredients we are using; and when we go to the shops, we can't buy them." I said, "What are you missing?" He said, "Charcoal we can make. My problem is sulfuric acid and permanganate of potash for the ignition, and saltpeter." I said, "What's your problem with saltpeter?" "You can't go into any of the shops and buy saltpeter now. There's been a police alert to all suppliers of saltpeter to note who is coming in to buy, so you can't buy it in quantities." I said, "There must be a way."

I thought about the problem and read up a bit, and I found that saltpeter is used as a fertilizer for roses. It was right there in the encyclopedia on gardening. I put on a gardener's overall and went around inquiring at flower shops as discreetly as possible. I was able to buy stocks of it from shops selling gardening fertilizers. I would go there as a very expert gardener on roses, engage in discussion with the shop owners, and display my so-called knowledge about rose gardening. The chap would be very impressed and say, "You know a lot about roses." We'd get around to talking about various fertilizers, and I would reject some and say, "That one I know; it doesn't really work so well; it really depends on the soil." Then he would say at some point, "And saltpeter is something that you might consider using." I also found a contact Doha had for sulfuric acid. I don't remember where it had been stolen from, but Doha had made the contact. So I would do those things for Wilton Mkwayi.

In the meantime, Steve, on one of his visits to Johannesburg, came and told me that he had described to Mkwayi and Lionel Gay how he could make a homemade oscillator. That's the gadget on which you transmit in Morse code that would be very useful for training people how to actually transmit. Back in Durban, he constructed an oscillator that he sent to me so that I could get it to MK. I gave it to Lionel.

At that point, the SACP underground was still saying, "Mac, just concentrate on the printing side. It's a big job: you've got the Propaganda Committee, the printing, and overtly you're running *Sports Parade*. That's quite a handful. Don't get involved in anything else." Then came the Rivonia arrests in July 1963; the trial; and Nelson Mandela, Walter Sisulu, and others were sentenced to life imprisonment.

The Rivonia Arrests

When I first got news of the Rivonia arrests on 11 July 1963, I was in a café run by Solly Esakjee. His café/takeout was diagonally across the street from where I had the linotype machine printing works. When I walked in, he was sitting there in a stupor, speechless, immobile. He had heard the news on the radio. My first reaction was shock, but I realized I would calmly have to go back to my linotype shop and clear away anything incriminating.

I had to decide on whom to contact. I had an appointment with Ruth First within a day or two, and I needed to decide how to keep that appointment. She had not yet been arrested. Kathy had been arrested, and that meant most of my contacts were gone. With whom was I going to be in touch at the highest levels? They had all been arrested. Ruth was my lifeline. Unless I made contact with her, I would have a very hard job finding other people. Where would they find me? So we had to make contact. I was handling all the funds for my work and for many other people. If I didn't get any money, I would be completely stuck. I couldn't pay the rent for the three clandestine printing works. If the rent wasn't paid, the landlords might check up and discover what we were up to.

So I went to meet Ruth in disguise. She drove up and down the street, and then she stopped and picked me up. She said, "I thought you'd be crazy enough to turn up." We didn't have much time to speak. It was too early for her to know how much damage had been done by the arrests. We had to keep it as brief as possible. We couldn't afford to be seen or picked up. We just had to try to get some arrangements in place and stick it out. Within two or three minutes, she had dropped me off again.

Mkwayi and I tried to deal with some of the problems with regrouping MK, checking which units were still intact, and so on. The printing side was still relatively intact, but the Propaganda Committee was virtually kaput because Duma Nokwe and Dan Tloome had left the country, and Rusty had been arrested. Only Ruth and I were left, though Bram Fischer was still around.

Joining the Central Committee

The party sent me a message about a meeting, giving me the time and place. The Rivonia trial was underway, and I had to disguise myself to get to this meeting. I dressed up as a person delivering laundry. I stacked up my station wagon with things on coat hangers that looked like laundry, and I dressed up in a delivery man's jacket and put on a pair of glasses. I arrived at a building in a white area somewhere in Berea or Hillbrow, and I used the tradesman's entrance and the tradesman's lift. I took a big stack of what looked like dry cleaning and went up to a flat on about the fifth floor. I was there at the precise time. I knocked on the door. Somebody opened it, and suddenly there was consternation inside—they didn't recognize me! They thought the police had arrived!*

Bram Fischer, Hilda Bernstein, and a couple of others were there. Hilda told me that they were regrouping the Central Committee and that I was required to serve on it. A short while later, Ruth was detained for 117 days, then she left the country.[21]

I met regularly with Beyleveld as representative of the Central Committee. He gave me a list of the names of all the party members, which later became a big issue for me when I was in detention and being tortured to reveal such names. Beyleveld also became a conduit through whom money for the MK operatives would come to me, and I would pass it along through other comrades to the respective operatives.

There was a long period during which everything was on hold. We had a discussion in the Central Committee, and it recommended that the MK should cease carrying out sabotage for a while. We didn't know what the implications of sabotage would be for those on trial. We maintained that moratorium until the day the verdict was announced eleven months later.

But our immediate response had created a problem for ourselves. Within days of the Rivonia arrests, I received the written text of a leaflet from Ruth First. Because there was no Propaganda Committee to look at it, we simply issued the leaflet. We printed in different places, on different machines, and distributed it very effectively. But the leaflet caused a problem for the defense at the trial because, even though it was issued after the arrests, the state introduced it as evidence. We'd said something like "We'll strike back—an eye for an eye and a tooth for a tooth." We'd said that the people's wrath would deal with the informers. The state introduced this into the Rivonia trial to show that MK was not committed to preventing the loss of life.

But that was our first reaction: brave shouting from the rooftop, threatening to rain down fire and brimstone. As the trial continued, we issued underground leaflets and stickers that we plastered all over Jo'burg and Pretoria. We said, "The world is watching the trial. We are not alone. Stand by our leaders," and so on. When the trial reached its later stages, we began to prepare MK, saying, "Get ready! Whatever the verdict, we must be ready for a burst of activity immediately after it's announced."

The verdict was handed down on 11 June 1964.[22] The judge pronounced all of them, except Rusty Bernstein, guilty. He adjourned the

*Hilda Bernstein confirmed the manner of Mac's dramatic appearance. Go to []maharaj/interviewees/[]Hilda Bernstein/[].

hearing to a subsequent date when he would hand down the sentence and the defense would put up pleas in mitigation of sentence. That took place on June 12. We planned a radio transmission for June 26. Lionel Gay built the portable transmitter. The broadcast was prerecorded. A team selected a suitable site for the transmission and rigged the aerial on a tree to enable the broadcast to be sent over the airwaves on a predetermined frequency. My job was to post a transcript of the text to the newspapers after the broadcast, but when the broadcast failed to transmit because of technical problems, I burned the envelopes.

After the verdict was handed down, Rusty was immediately rearrested. Later, his lawyers applied for and got bail for him, but he was placed under house arrest. Rusty and Hilda escaped from South Africa a few months later, while I was in detention.

By now *Sports Parade* was done for. The order banning *New Age* was sweeping—it banned virtually every one of our journalists from having anything to do with writing for publication or being involved in publication.

Moving Up: MK Commissar and the Business of Bomb Making

Originally, MK command began with Mandela; then after his arrest, Sisulu worked as head of the High Command for a short period. When Raymond Mhlaba got back from China, he took over, but then he had to go on a mission to Algeria. Either Walter or Mkwayi filled in until Raymond got back. Then the Rivonia arrests took place, and Mkwayi was entrusted with the job of regrouping the High Command.

Joe Slovo was on MK High Command as well as in the SACP Central Committee. He was abroad when the Rivonia arrests took place and couldn't come back. He and J. B. Marks had left the country to discuss the draft plans for Mayibuye and solicit support from the external mission. Mayibuye was still under discussion, but during the Rivonia trial Slovo featured prominently as one of the accomplices, so he couldn't even think of coming back. So besides Mkwayi, after the Rivonia arrests, Kitson, Gay, and Chiba were in the ad hoc MK central command. I helped with setting up a new radio transmitter after one had been captured at Rivonia, and I helped with the manufacture of pipe bombs.

Mkwayi visited me one night and said I was needed to serve in MK High Command in the capacity of commissar. Traditionally the commissar also became the deputy commander. I told Mkwayi that instead, I felt I should have some direct experience in being a member of an ordinary squad carrying out sabotage activity, because unless one has gone through that experience, one cannot be expected to motivate others and ensure that the units function properly. We agreed that I would follow that course.*

I was involved in laying only about three pipe bombs. I found the experience very normal—nothing more in terms of adrenaline or sense of danger than what I was doing in printing. In printing I was transporting things by tons and stealing paper by van loads. I would sit at the linotype machine with my back to the open door. That way it looked as if a very normal activity were taking place whenever anybody walked past the open door.

Buying the saltpeter was more nerve-wracking than setting a pipe bomb in the dark. With the pipe bomb you were cautious, you selected your site, and you selected a moment when there was no activity. Our pipe bombs were rudimentary. A railway line is covered with ballast, and it's got sleepers. If you wanted to blow it up, you removed as much of the ballast as you could, pushed the pipe in underneath the rail and wedged it between the ground and the sleeper, and left the pipe bomb there to explode. We used a gelatin capsule as an igniter. At the last minute, you'd put in a few drops of sulfuric acid with an eyedropper and seal the capsule. We selected bomb sites according to what would have the most impact and still allow a getaway.

So Wilton and I made bombs, sacks of them. Wilton would distribute them to all the units that needed them. The heavy work was doing the threading; that was hard physical work. The threader had big levers and was hand operated, not powered. Wilton and I probably filled three sacks over a night or two.

Many bombs did not go off because the operation depended crucially on putting the sulfuric acid into that gelatin capsule, putting that capsule into the pipe, then quickly sealing and positioning it. You were working in the dark, and if you splashed sulfuric acid onto your hand, it burned you. It was a tiny capsule and you were using an eyedropper; you might think you'd filled it and pressed it, but it could actually be empty. And you couldn't be shining torches or anything. It wasn't rocket science; even hand grenades and mortar bombs don't always go off. (You find them years later, still dangerous.)

Railway tracks became the easiest targets in the immediate post-Rivonia period. The amount of damage depended on how well you'd put the bomb together and how well you'd positioned it. On the other hand,

---

*In my interview with Wilton Mkwayi, he insisted that Mac had been adviser to the High Command, not commissar.

the enemy rapidly developed the capacity to repair bombed rail tracks as quickly as possible, so they could claim there had been minimal damage. But it was an effective tool in our propaganda efforts and for training our cadres to cope with working in dangerous situations, getting them used to dealing with fear and working as a team.[23]

Doha

I went to Doha and said, "I want you at my home, in my kitchen on Pearce Street"—which was near the police station—"and we will manufacture the gunpowder." So we made gunpowder, which has to dry slowly. I couldn't afford to leave this stuff sitting around for days, so I said, "Let's speed it up; let's heat it a little more, just a little more," to take the moisture out—and then it blew up. The whole floor was littered; Doha got showered with the stuff—all over him! He was burning alive. He had to get treatment right away. I had to call a doctor. I knew the MK doctor. He was in the District Committee of the Communist Party with me—Abdullabhai Jassat's brother, Dr. Essop Jassat. I had a code name and a coded arrangement with him. I had an emergency number.

I went to a public call box and called Essop. I didn't mention my name; he didn't mention his name. I said, "Doc, I need your services urgently." He said, "How urgent?" I said, "Very urgent, there's been an accident." I didn't tell him anything else. He knew I was asking him to come to my home, and he rushed over. He guessed it must have been a blast injury, so he arrived with all the equipment, including a full burn kit. I had Doha lying down; I'd plastered him with an antiburn liquid called Acriflavin, which I used in printing. I always used to carry this with me because when you're printing—working with lead—you can get burned easily, and I had once been burned. I had simply plastered his face, his hands, and wherever else I could see burns, with Acriflavin, and then concentrated on cleaning up the kitchen in case the police arrived.

Doha was banned, and Essop realized this injury was the result of a gunpowder explosion. He said, "You've done very well; you've put on Acriflavin." He lanced all the blisters on Doha's face, treated it, and bandaged him. I then took Doha to his flat on Market Street at Kholvad House— Kathy's old flat.* I took him there, and we prepared a cover story. He

---

*Doha looked after Kathy's flat for the twenty-seven years Kathy was in prison. As recently as January 2003, the telephone for the apartment was listed in the Johannesburg telephone directory under Kathy's name.

would say that he had been assaulted, because he was all bandaged up, face and hands and all, and he would have to stay in bed.

One day I got an urgent message from him: "You've got to come and visit me; I'm stuck with all this stuff." I had to take a chance and go. His wife Ayesha let me in, and I went to Doha's bedroom.

There he was lying in bed, all bandaged up. Ayesha left the room, and he said, "I've got forty ounces of sulfuric acid here." The person who had stolen this sulfuric acid in a forty-ounce bottle—a one-and-a-half-liter bottle—had delivered it to his flat. Because the police had been checking on him, he had put the bottle of acid next to him under the blankets. He said, "I'm sleeping with it in my bed. What else can I do?" That was Doha!

I used to do carpentry as a relief from the stress—I would sit for days doing nothing and then I'd have five days and five nights of clandestine activity, without sleep. If I couldn't sleep at three o'clock in the morning, I would get up, go to the kitchen—which was also my carpentry room—and plane something. There is a certain quality about wood. A calming quality. The rhythms of the hands emptied the mind.

Luck Runs Out

I left Jo'burg for Durban on the morning of 27 June 1964 to collect Tim, who had now finished her refresher course there. On the way back to Johannesburg, I suggested we stop in Newcastle. Life in the underground was getting rough, and I said to Tim, "I don't know when we're going to see Mum and Dad again." We decided to spend a few days there.

We arrived on Saturday, 3 July. My parents were very happy to see us. The next morning we got up and went out and bought the Sunday papers—and there I read that Bram, Beyleveld, Kitson, and others had been arrested in Johannesburg. I had a frank realization: "Oh shit, my links are cut." But we had anticipated the arrests, and it was my job to reconnect with people who had survived and get the work going again. I said to Tim, "We've got to leave; we've got to get back to Jo'burg immediately. There's a lot of work to do." We got back that evening.

The next day, Monday, 6 July, we were both detained.

6. DETENTION AND TORTURE

Introduction

FOLLOWING THE GENERAL FAILURE of the Security Branch to conclude investigations in sabotage cases in the early 1960s, a special sabotage squad was formed.* This was part of a more extensive restructuring of legal provisions relating to detentions and police structures introduced by the new minister of justice, police and prisons, John Vorster.[1]

The state began to send security force members who showed an aptitude for extracting confessions to France and Portugal during the first half of the 1960s. The French had developed successful torture techniques in Indo-China and had perfected them in Algeria; the Portuguese, old colonial masters in their own right, were trying to crush insurgencies in Angola and Mozambique. Among the South Africans sent for such training were T. J. "Rooi Rus" Swanepoel and Lieutenant Willem van der Merwe, both of whom, but especially the former, would figure prominently in Mac's interrogation and torture.

The government used torture primarily as a way to gather information

---

*A part of the South African Police (SAP), the SB spearheaded the internal war against the liberation. Besides training in France, selected SB personnel were beneficiaries as a result of joint cooperation agreements between South Africa, Argentina, Chile, and Taiwan in the early 1980s of further training opportunities and an exchange of ideas and experience. Close links with Argentina existed even before this. "Alfredo Astiz, a notorious torturer, was one of four torture experts attached to the Argentinian embassy in Pretoria in 1979. During his stay, there were several seminars at which South African security police and the Argentines exchanged ideas regarding methods of interrogation." See [] maharaj/TRC/report of the truth and reconciliation commission/Vol 1/Chapter 3 [] par 126. The SB, like other government intelligence agencies, successfully infiltrated all tentacles of the liberation movements. It also engaged in abductions, assassinations, disinformation, and torture of detainees. The SB was supplemented in 1969 by the Bureau of State Security (BOSS), a high-budget intelligence service that was replaced in 1978 by the National Intelligence Service (NIS).

about either the activities of the movement or the whereabouts of individuals, and to turn detainees into state witnesses. It was employed by every element of the pervasive security apparatus. Most torturers saw themselves as professionals doing an essential job to break the web of Communist-inspired terror threatening to engulf South Africa. They saw themselves as moral men, Christians.

The 90-day law came into effect on 1 May 1963, the 180-day detention and redetention law on 10 January 1965.[2] They authorized any commissioned officer to detain without a warrant any person suspected of political activities and to hold them in solitary confinement, without access to a lawyer. Vorster said the intention was to detain uncooperative persons "until this side of eternity." This, of course, enabled the state to use torture with impunity.

Still harsher legislation, authorizing indefinite detention without trial on the authority of a policeman of or above the rank of lieutenant colonel was introduced in 1967. The definition of the suspected crime—terrorism—was very broad. Detention could be continued until detainees had satisfactorily replied to all questions.

Between 1960 and 1990, the systematic and extensive use of detention without trial became commonplace. During that period approximately eighty thousand people were detained, of whom about ten thousand were women and fifteen thousand were children and youths under the age of eighteen.[3] Detention without trial was the primary strategy of the security forces.[4] When it began to fail, the state began to murder its political opponents.

2

The torture took many forms. To "warm up" detainees for the real thing, teams of interrogators would work them over. They received the "rugby" treatment: they were beaten, tossed from one interrogator to another, flung across the cell, used as a scrimmage ball—all the while the questions kept coming until the victim became completely disoriented and had been beaten to a pulp. The security police also used a combination of solitary confinement, sleep deprivation, and forced body-position routines—forcing the detainee to stand on a piece of foolscap paper for hours or days, balance on a brick or sit in an imaginary chair for hours on end, or hold an object above her/his head. In the "helicopter" technique, the detainee's hands were manacled above his or her head and the detainee was hung upside down for lengthy periods. Sometimes detainees were handcuffed across an iron bar ten feet off the ground and allowed to dangle for hours.

Sexual torture included forcing detainees (both male and female) to undress; the deliberate targeting of genitals or breasts during torture; the threat of and, in some instances, actual rape of detainees (male and female); the insertion of objects such as batons or pistols into bodily orifices; and placing detainees overnight in cells with common-law prisoners known to rape newcomers. (During the Truth and Reconciliation Commission [TRC] process, some torture victims who spoke openly about other forms of torture would not speak about sexual torture at all.)

Detainees were suspended by their feet outside the windows of buildings of several stories. (Sometimes they were accidentally or deliberately dropped, becoming in either case a "suicide.") From the later 1960s on, the security police used electric shock torture (usually to the genitals) and/or suffocation, in addition to the other methods mentioned above. Often psychological torture, which had the advantage of leaving no physical mark, was used, or it formed an adjunct to physical torture. Solitary confinement was its own torture, especially when detainees were held in isolation in a small cell for an extended period without access to anyone else, and without any idea about how long they would be held. As one detainee put it, after such treatment "I was damaged, a part of my soul was eaten away as if by maggots . . . and I will never get it back again."[5]

Some detainees committed suicide, either driven to it by the torture (wanting to make it end) or because they had broken and were shattered by their own sense of having betrayed their comrades.[6]

3

Swanepoel's name crops up again and again in interviews with activists who were detained at one time or another. His name is scattered throughout the report of the TRC, yet he remains elusive, his name an eponym for torture, but the man himself is present only by virtue of the name's iteration. He was a policeman for all seasons. He makes a brief appearance as one of the "keepers" of the Rivonia Trialists during the Rivonia Trial, "a burly red-faced fellow," according to Mandela, the butt of their practical jokes.[7] In the early 1960s he was sent to France and Algeria for special training in torture and for an "advanced" course to the former in the late 1960s.[8] In March 1965, then a major, he was dispatched to the Caprivi Strip in northern South West Africa (Namibia) to set up an SAP security camp, under the guise of its being an engineering firm, to monitor South West Africa

People's Organization (SWAPO) activity.[9] Sixteen months later SAP forces attacked SWAPO's first military base inside SWA/Namibia, marking the beginning of SA's armed intervention in the region.[10] He was a member of the sabotage squad, a select number of police chosen from outside the ranks of the Security Branch to interrogate sabotage suspects.[11] He was sent into Soweto in June 1976 to command a riot unit, a unit responsible for a high number of civilian casualties. Later he regretted that he had not used more force. "You can only stop violence," he said "by using a greater amount of violence."[12]

By all accounts, he was a pathological sadist, but a very calculating one. He would boast to others of his ability to get even the most recalcitrant detainee to crack. He regarded each detainee under his jurisdiction as a challenge; he studied each one individually, looking for his or her psychological weak points. In prison, prisoners swapped stories about him. "Swanepoel was squat, bullfrog-like." Ruth First wrote. "His face glowed a fiery red that seemed to point to the bottle, but he swore that he never drank so it must have been his temper burning through, for Swanepoel's stock-in-trade was his bullying."[13] Swanepoel was feared; he knew it and used that knowledge to psychologically debilitate detainees facing torture who knew he would be waiting for them in the interrogation chambers.

These feelings enveloped Mac but never engulfed him. He won his "war" with Swanepoel—but at a cost to himself and others that would only manifest itself much later. When I pressed him on the torture he had undergone his usually animated voice dropped to a monotone. In his accounts he put distance between himself and the retelling, as if determined not to remember what he was telling me. Not so surprising, then, that when I later reminded him that he had forgotten to tell me that he had been hung out a window on the seventh floor of the Grays, suspended by his ankles, first two, and then one, nothing but empty space between him and the street below, he was taken aback. Only when I began to fill in the circumstances did his memory begin to arouse itself. But it was a reluctant memory and I didn't disturb it further.[14]

Mac

AFTER TIM AND I were arrested, we were taken to Marshall Square and separated. I insisted I was Solly Matthews, and I produced my ID book to prove it; I said Tim was my string-along girlfriend. Both of us had our stories straight on this point, so I knew she would be saying the same thing. I was housed in a wing consisting of three fairly big cells. In the corridor there were grilles separating these three cells from the rest. I was in the middle cell. They were police cells, not prison cells.

They began to interrogate me immediately. The interrogation was almost continual, broken only by a week or two here and there to allow me to recover sufficiently so that they could start over again—or to allow my expectation of torture to build up in the hope that that, in itself, would induce a new fear in me.

I was tortured for about sixty days. Electric shocks. Beatings—and then more beatings. I ended up with a damaged neck and a paralyzed arm. My chief interrogator was Major Theunis "Rooi Rus" Swanepoel, but the day-to-day torturers were Willem van der Merwe; Johannes Jacobus Viktor; and a warrant officer, Gerrit Erasmus.* Van der Merwe broke his baton on my skull. You can still feel the bump on the back of my head. Erasmus was quite sadistic. I jokingly used to call him my savior because he was small of build relative to the other cops, and he had a complex about his build. They used to rag him about it. I isolated him as a man who could easily be provoked. I was being given this slow and continual torture, but I said to myself, "Maybe if I provoke him, he will assault me." And he obliged. I spat into his face in front of the others, and within seconds he had punched me into unconsciousness. After that, it was a cinch. I'd insult him, and within a minute I'd be unconscious—I used to jokingly call it my "rest period." Swanepoel was in command, and he would intervene at what he saw as strategic moments.

I was taken every day from Marshall Square to the Grays, the Security Branch headquarters nearby. That's where I was interrogated. Then I was brought back at night, thrown into my cell—often semiconscious—and the next morning I was taken back to the Grays.

The Red Russian

Swanepoel was the most brutal of the torturers. He had been given the Afrikaans nickname Rooi Rus, or Red Russian. He was a short, stocky man with a short neck and a very pockmarked, brutal face. He wore his hair

---

*Willem van der Merwe simply disappeared. Erasmus was police commissioner of the Witwatersrand, an area roughly comprising the metro region of Johannesburg, in the early 1990s. He received amnesty from the TRC. He says that Mac is mistaking him for someone else. Viktor, who was head of the Ciskei police when the Bisho massacre occurred in 1992, also disappeared.

close cropped and gave the impression of a commandant of a Nazi concentration camp. He took pride in his brutality. Many lawyers who defended us said words to the effect that they wanted to get Swanepoel in the box to grill him, interrogate him, and crush him. It never happened because Swanepoel always managed to evade going into the witness box.

Paradoxically, he was one of the Security Branch men whom I came to respect. This is not a statement about his humanity. It's about his skill. And he told other detainees that he respected me.[15] He would say, "That one ran circles around us." He would talk about Piet Beyleveld in a derogatory way because Beyleveld had cracked within five hours without a finger being laid on him. Piet was a well-built man, a white man, a comrade who had been a soldier in World War II.

Two months into my detention, after a week of no interrogation, I was suddenly taken to the Grays and put into a room. Three of the walls were lined with Security Branch officers in plain clothes. The whole group was involved in the assault. They gave me the rugby treatment. I tried to absorb the questions as they threw me around, to try to work out what they knew. I realized they had suddenly acquired an enormous store of information about the underground. I was trying to work out who had been their source.

Then Swanepoel walked into the room. That was his style. He would walk into the room in the middle of an interrogation and the torture would stop. There would be a great sense of drama around his entry and, usually, if you had not met him before, he would walk up to you, look you in your face, and ask: "Do you know who I am? I am Swanepoel. Do you know now who I am? Do you know what to expect from me?" When his eyes were locked with yours, you could see a fanaticism that reveled in the possession of unlimited naked power based on brutality.

That day, he pushed me up against the wall and said, "Now you'd better talk. No more games from you because if I come back into this room and you have not started talking, I will personally take over your interrogation." And then he marched out. A little later he came back, put me up against the wall, took out a pistol, put it to my forehead, and said, "You talk." But that was the wrong psychological move as far as I was concerned because I just said to myself, "If you're going to shoot, it's perfectly fine by me. You desperately need me to talk; you kill me, you've lost." You can't get a dead man to talk.

Anyway, he pulled the trigger. Of course I thought there would be a live bullet in it. Now I'd gone through one death, and nothing had happened. He expected me to collapse in panic, and when he looked at me and realized that panic had not set in, he lost a bit of his control. He pistol-whipped me over the head and marched out. Now I was saying to myself, "Ah, I've won a battle."

The next time he came back that day, he pulled a trick that did actually make me panic. He had obviously been thinking about what to do and had focused on the fact that I had only one eye. He took out a box of matches and lit a match next to my good eye. That was a frightening experience for me because I thought the eye would burn in its socket and I would go blind. I was definitely afraid. But it was not enough to make me talk.

Then he resorted to a different tactic. I was escorted to his office and told to strip naked. Told to put my penis on his desk. Then he took a policeman's baton and started to stroke it, without ever taking his eyes off me, and then he raised the baton and brought it whacking down on my penis. After that he paused; he threw questions at me, then left me in agony. When he saw my agony subsiding, he made me stand against that desk and put my penis there again. But this time he did not hit it immediately. He picked up his baton, raised it, and waited for the expectation of pain to capture me before he hit. And then a step further. When my penis was on the table and his baton was raised, he moved his arm, little jerking movements in slight flickers as though it was going to come smashing down, but it didn't. He watched me flinch; I cringed with the pain that was as real as if his baton had struck. And so it went on, a slight movement of his arm as if to strike, but no strike, driving me to a point where I was almost begging him to do it, to get it over with. But he could see that coming too.

Sometimes he would just tell the guards to take me back to Marshall Square, and sometimes he just struck. He did this several times. I had to learn how to internalize the certainty of the unexpected, to counteract his penchant for the random attack. I would fix my eye on something beyond his arm so that the baton was not in my line of sight and I was less conscious of his body movements. I started to place odds to myself on whether he would actually strike or withhold. I started devising mathematical systems to predict the unpredictable—arguing to myself that even unpredictability had logic to it—anything that would distract me, because as long as I could focus on something other than what he might do, the pain of what he did was somewhat diminished, or at least the mental pain was.

It reached a stage where all he had to do was strip me naked and put my penis on the table for the terror to begin. The first time this happened to me, I felt as if there were blood pouring out of my nose. I had to look to see what was falling, and it was just perspiration. Later, he went further. One night, having beaten my penis with the baton and achieved no results, he took a piece of wood and, in front of me, hammered rusty nails through it so that they stuck out. Then he took the plank and put it over my penis with the nails sticking into it and began to press, but never to the point that it pressed through. He would press it so that I could feel the nails and think, "Good Lord, the nails are sinking into my penis!"

I knew what Swanepoel was trying to do. The physical torture was supposed to put you in a state of mind where, before the next session, you began to relive the pain mentally. It was the expectation of the pain that would make you break down.

On the day he lit the match next to my eye, he failed to get me to talk and left the room again. He didn't storm out of the room; he just left with the threat "If you don't talk, I'm coming back." The other guys were all still in the room, and they continued beating me. The next time Swanepoel came back, he pushed me against the wall and barked out questions, "Are you going to talk?" "No," was my answer.

He left the others to assault me for a bit, then he picked me up from the floor, put me against the wall again, and I saw, disoriented as I was, that he had a sword in his hand. A sword! He put the point right against my Adam's apple. Now I really was in a state. But as I was trying to conquer my fear and pain, it suddenly dawned on me that he had handed me a gift. The gift was there in that sharp point on my throat. All I had to do was to dive on it, and I would be dead—and then he would have to explain my death.

Just as that thought went through my head and I was preparing for that final act, in that flash of an instant, we were looking at each other, eyeball to eyeball. Then he panicked and withdrew the sword and stormed out. I saw what had happened. I had lost the moment. What was wrong with me? I should have dived earlier. And then I thought: "Wait a minute. The bastard saw in my eyes what I was planning to do. That was *his* panic." That was the moment I began to have some respect for him. He had read my mind by looking into my eye. It was not even a second—it was an instant in which I had seen a solution and he had understood it and withdrawn the sword. I thought, "Hey, don't underestimate this interrogator. He is studying me. He is not like the others who are just beating the hell out of me. This man goes back and thinks and asks, 'What type of man am I dealing with?'"

After the incident with the sword, Swanepoel no longer played a prominent part in my torture. He was around; he would question and supervise, but he was never as violent with me as the others were. He was never able to throw me into a panic again. My dream was that one day I'd capture Swanepoel, and I believed I would be able to make him talk without physical torture. But of course that never happened; he died some years ago.

Doha (Again)

About a week or more into my detention and torture, I became afraid that I might break and reveal the names of the whole network of people with whom I had contact. Rather than put all their lives in jeopardy, and the lives of others with whom they had networks, I was prepared to kill myself. I made a couple of suicide attempts during this time. My interrogators were accusing me of having the names of all the full-time people in the underground in the entire Transvaal, all the paid officers of MK, and the entire membership of the Communist Party as well. They said I was the paymaster—which was true. I had all the names in my head. This left me with very little space for maneuver. I was becoming afraid that I would break down. I would rather have died than betray the movement. I collected cotton threads and pieces of wire in a desperate attempt to equip myself with some way of escaping, but failing that, I thought the only way out was to commit suicide.

One night I tore up my blankets and tied the strips together. I had a little stone that I had smuggled in from the exercise yard, and I tied it to one of the blanket strips and tried to throw it over the radiator pipe, trying to make a noose from which I planned to hang myself. But there was too small a gap behind the pipe, and the stone kept bouncing off the wall.

But the noise had alerted the chap next door, who started tapping on the wall. The cells on either side of me had been empty when I was first brought in, but later they brought in another prisoner. I didn't know who he was at that point. Now, when he started tapping, I realized that it was my comrade Doha because, when he used to come to my place late at night, he always knocked in a particular way. He was a banned person, but the Security Police didn't know he had been working with me.

Now, in jail, Doha and I started looking for ways to communicate with each other. A set of iron rails protruded from each side of the wall shared by adjacent cells. On these were mounted two wooden benches—one in each cell. They were very long benches that could have seated about eight people. Doha and I had been tapping on the wall, but we didn't know

Morse code. I also didn't want to knock loudly enough for the guards to hear us, so I looked under the bench and saw a piece of protruding steel and realized that if I tapped on it, the sound would be transmitted more easily. And lo and behold! Ameen realized the same thing. So we lay on the floor and began knocking on this piece of steel.

Suddenly I heard a faint voice: "Can you hear me?" I could hear his voice fairly distinctly. He said, "Look, there's a little hole next to this steel bar; can you see it?" The cell was dark, but there was a light in the passage that provided a bit of light. The hole was just pin-sized, but the voice was carrying. I said, "Yes, I can hear you." He said, "Listen, we've got to get to work on widening this hole."

The next evening I approached the hole. Doha told me he had picked up a piece of wire in the exercise yard and was busy widening the hole. That evening we broke through the hole under the bench, made a slightly bigger hole, and chatted virtually the whole night. In effect, he counseled me. I told him they were not providing me with food. I had gone for several days without food, in addition to the interrogation and torture. He said he was getting food from his family, and he wrapped some in a little tube of tinfoil and pushed it through the hole.

I was able now, through Doha, to smuggle some important messages out of jail. For instance, I sent a note to Bram Fischer. I was still pretending to be Solly Matthews, and nobody could demand to visit me or bring me food because they would have been asked, "How do you know him?" But Doha's wife, Ayesha, was there every day, knocking at the police's door, demanding that she be allowed to bring him food and a change of clothes. So Doha was allowed these things, though they would be searched. Despite that, a needle had been smuggled in with his things, and he would sew messages written on toilet paper into the folds of his clothing. He would undo the collar and sew it in there, or in the lapel or the trousers, or into the pajama string. In this way I sent a message to Bram advising him that certain sites should be cleared in case I had to talk.

I gave him addresses that nobody knew. For instance, I had hired two rooms that housed the printing presses we had smuggled in from the GDR in 1958 as well as a library for the party. Now I said, "Whoever clears the rooms must remove all the fingerprints." I said I needed confirmation that the rooms had been cleared so that after confirmation I could point to that address in my interrogation. I also warned that certain comrades should get out of the country, in particular Dan Tloome, who was on the Central Committee.

My strategy was to dole out bits of information to my torturers if I had to. I had to absorb the interrogation to find out what they knew. I only confessed to certain things when I was satisfied that my story was water-tight and my confessions could do no harm.

At that stage in the interrogation, the police said my fingerprints had been found at the Rivonia farm, so they started beating the hell out of me. Initially I was sure that whenever I had visited Rivonia, I had taken ex-treme precautions and never left a fingerprint. I used to go to the Rivonia farm to attend to the printing equipment and duplicators. But I then real-ized, after days of this torture, that they did have my fingerprints. I re-membered that even though I had used gloves when servicing the duplicating machine—we called it a Roneo machine in those days—at some point a part had fallen through inside the machine and I had tried to retrieve it, and I recalled having taken off my gloves to do that. I realized that that was the only place they could have found my fingerprints.

I knew I would have to prepare a fallback story in case I cracked. How could I explain it in a nonincriminatory way? The fingerprints would be proof that I had been there, that I was part of the Rivonia group, and the consequences of that, if I cracked up, would be uncontrollable. I had to fend that off in the torture, see if there was a way out of it.

Doha had been part of my printing group, so I explained the problem to him. I told him that the only way out that I could see was for me to commit suicide. He said, "No, I don't accept that." So we worked on a story. The police had no reason to know that he and I were in touch. The plan was that although I had not answered any questions yet, I would now begin to answer certain of them. The story was that I used to buy and sell stolen goods, and I was a petty criminal caught up in this big web. "Ah! I remember selling to a chap on Market Street." "Who?" "I don't know." "Description?" One to fit Doha. "But I had tried to sell it to him earlier. He refused to take it. Weeks later I offered to sell him an electric Roneo ma-chine, and he said, 'Oh, somebody wants it.' "

If the police came to interrogate him, Doha wasn't to deny his involve-ment. I had said, "Proclaim openly that you have been a member of the Congress Movement from the 1930s, and say, 'Yes, I am totally committed to the struggle against apartheid,' but don't admit you're in the under-ground." He said it was good advice. And if they questioned him about me, he would only answer if they showed him a photograph—"Oh, that one I recognize." Then he was to say, "I don't know his name. I met him in the bloody street. He pestered me. He's a bloody backdoor dealer. He pestered and pestered me, so I bought a cyclostyling machine from him." "What did you do with it?" "Oh, I gave it to Kathrada."

The cover story we developed gave me life for a while. Now I could withstand the torture because I had a plan of action. I said, "You couldn't have found my fingerprints at Rivonia; I was never there." They wouldn't admit that, and they didn't want to tell me because they wanted me to crack. Eventually, in exasperation, one of them said the prints were on "something big." I said, "Big what? You can't expect me to answer your questions if I don't know what they are about. I'm telling you, I was never at Rivonia." They said, "You're talking nonsense." I said, "Were the finger-prints on a movable thing? Could they have been on a chair or a table I made as carpenter, which somehow or other, unbeknownst to me, ended up at Rivonia?" And that moment one of the officers said, "Listen, that's bullshit; they were not on a table." So another obstacle was removed, nar-rowing down the field and bringing them closer to telling me.

My intention was to come out with the information as if I'd dug it up from the recesses of my mind. And, indeed, it worked like a charm because eventually one of the officers said, "Aren't you the bloody government printer for the movement?" I said, "Government printer?" The guy said, "I know you; you fucking expect to become the government printer when you take over." I said, "What shit is this? Me? I have nothing to do with these people, and you say I'm going to be the government printer."

They moved off the subject and went on beating me. Then one day it popped up again, and I said, "You know, it's been worrying me. You say 'government printer'—what makes you say that?" One of the interrogators said, "We know that you know about printing machines." "What do I know about printing machines? I have told you people I'm a backdoor dealer—any stolen goods, radios, tape recorders, whatever—anything I get hold of." Eventually I said, "Oh, you're talking about a duplicating ma-chine?" They said yes. I said, "Oh, that was a time when I made quite a bit of money." And on I went, spinning out my story. So that explained how my fingerprints were found on the machine at Rivonia.

The plan almost went wrong, though. Doha told me through the hole in the wall about the first time they took him for interrogation. I asked if he'd confirmed the story, and he said no. I said, "Why not?" He said, "Shit, they beat me up. Once they gave me the first slap, I decided I'm not to talk." I said, "But you haven't backed up my story." He said, "Oh, sorry about that, but, you know, they annoyed me. Next time they call me for questioning, I'll back you up."

In the end, they bought the story about my being a backdoor dealer and dropped the subject.

Alibi

It also helped that Rusty and Hilda Bernstein had escaped from detention, because then I could point to them without giving them away. The police had information, from Beyleveld, about the printing machines. I was unable to map a way forward and relieve the pressure because any explanation I gave would reveal too much.

But one day, after I'd been brought back to the cells after interrogation, an African warder I had befriended told me Bernstein had escaped and left the country. He produced a newspaper with a photograph taken at Ndola Airport (in Northern Rhodesia, now Zambia) of Rusty and his wife, Hilda, just disembarked from a plane from Botswana. It said that Rusty had evaded arrest, jumped bail, and that he and Hilda had slipped out of the country. That was in August or September 1964.

This meant that I had a way out of some of the interrogation because I could say, "Oh, I did this with Rusty, or I did this with Hilda." They could not probe that any further. But I did agonize over that information— could they have deliberately printed a dummy newspaper so that I would walk into a trap? Could the warder have duped me? But I worked my way through all those issues and, eventually, decided that there was nobody around who could contradict my story.

I gave a semblance of cooperating with my interrogators. I simulated a breakdown with the so-called softie, Lieutenant Nic van Rensburg. He was the good guy in the bad guy/good guy duet, although when Ruth First was in jail, he played the toughie.[16]

One day I was taken into his office. It was late in the evening. He said he was opposed to my being tortured. "Oh, I don't like to see this happen to you," he said, "but I'm powerless. You need to give me something that I can use, and that something is talk."

By now I had prepared myself, and had my explanation sorted out in my mind. He sat me down across the desk from him, trying his best to win my confidence, saying, "Talk. Talk to me, and I can save you from being tortured."

I then got up from my chair and began to simulate a state of extreme agitation, how I thought a person who was breaking down would act. I had read articles about comrades who had been detained, who had been in isolation, describing their delusional, semipsychotic states—they thought they were sleeping on the ceiling, or the floor was the ceiling and the ceiling was the floor. And, of course, I had majored in psychology. So I got up and started pacing, pretending I was very agitated, muttering to myself, "Ja," and then "No."

Then I turned to Van Rensburg in a dramatic way and said, "I can't do it." He got up from his chair and said, "Listen, speak; I'll protect you. Come on, come on." I said to him, "I can betray a man but not a woman." This made him excited: "I'll handle it; I'll protect you," he said. I told him it wasn't a protection problem, it was about conscience—how could I put a woman in trouble? Now he was urging me to speak. This went on for quite some time. "Do you want a cigarette?" "No." "Would you like a cup of coffee?" "No."

I got up and started pacing again. "My conscience! My conscience! Betraying a woman!" He said nobody would know, but I said, "No, no, that's not the important thing. How will I live with myself?" Just when I thought he was going to give up, when I was failing to keep him interested, I dropped in the next thing: "And what's more, you've got her in detention. I can't do this. I can't expose her to the torture that you've been subjecting me to."

This went on for the whole evening. Finally I told him I had collected the printing machines from a garage attached to a house. He wanted to know where this house was. I said, "I don't know, I was taken at night to a white suburb. I don't know this white suburb. I got there and this woman met me. She told me where to drive my car in. I reversed it into a yard, and there was this garage in the back. The garage doors were open, and I had to load these machines."

Van Rensburg wanted to know who this white woman was. Finally, acting very reluctantly and hesitantly, I said, "Hilda Bernstein—and you've got her in detention. I am feeling terrible." He couldn't tell me she had escaped, that she was not in detention. I was not supposed to know that. But now I had a respite because it looked as if I had spoken.

Suicide

Do you see the faint scar here, running right through here, right around there? That is the result of my attempt to cut my wrists with eggshells. From time to time we had boiled eggs for breakfast, and I saved the shells. While I was being tortured by Swanepoel and company, I was able to work out that there was a crisis around Beyleveld. I realized they had information they could only have gotten from him, and I was becoming afraid I would break down.

I wrote a note that was smuggled out before I started attempting suicide. I wrote a will on toilet paper, and I smuggled it out to Bram via Doha. The will said, "This is my last will and testament, and although I'm going to commit suicide, I want the world to know that this is not suicide; it is murder. This is the result of the torture I have been undergoing. These are my torturers." I wanted to let the world know that these people had, in effect, murdered me. I said I was going to commit suicide because the state had closed in on me in the interrogation room. They were saying I had the list of all the full-time MK and Communist Party cadres. That piece of information had allowed me to deduce who was talking in detention, so I wanted to let them know who was in danger and who should get out of the way.

I went on to outline how I'd been conducting myself in interrogation, what information I had extracted that I had not yet smuggled out to Bram. And then I said in the will to my wife that this was the way it had to end. I told her that I had no property, nothing to bequeath to her. All I had was my love for her, and she must never think of my death as a suicide. She must realize that it was murder and that I had taken this action because of my love for her and my love for my country. I said she must not live with any shame. She must live with pride and know that this is the price we have to pay.

I also said things like "I've been a Communist and I'm going to die a Communist. I have my firm beliefs, and I'm taking my life to protect the struggle. I know we will win one day."

When I tried to cut my vein with eggshells, I stretched it with a tourniquet in order to cut it. I used some clothing, a shirt or something, to make the tourniquet. It was very painful cutting with pieces of shell because what I was really doing was cutting by abrasion. The pain was so bad that when I thought I'd managed to get to a vein, I let it go and thought, right, now I'm going to bleed to death, so let me just jump under my blankets and next morning they will find me dead. Instead, what happened was that when I released the tourniquet, the skin just closed up and covered the cuts, stanched the bleeding, and an hour later I was still very conscious.

Having failed in that attempt, I began demanding to see Tim—"my girlfriend" as I continued to call her—who was also in detention. I decided that if they let me see her, I would find a way to let her see the coagulated blood on my wrist, and she would find a way to communicate it outside. They refused to let me see her, of course.

I began accusing them of torturing her as they were torturing me. They denied it. They said, "She's talking." I began to imply that if they allowed me to see her, and I could satisfy myself that she had not been beaten up, they might get me to talk. I was hoping that in the absence of any evidence against her, her conditions would become a little bit easier.

Finally they agreed. It was organized by Van Rensburg. They took me to his office. He was alone in the office, sitting on the side of the desk. He offered me coffee and a cigarette, but I refused. I demanded to see Tim.

Tim

Suddenly she's brought in. We embrace, but it's very tense. I am aware that I must not say anything that is going to compromise her. She's tense because she must not say anything to compromise me. We sit down. I hold her hand. Van Rensburg is sitting at the desk watching us. I am asking how she is; have they assaulted her? She says yes. So I say to him, "There you are." Now he pretends he's innocent. "Who did that to you? I'll take it up." She says some guy called Erasmus has been abusive and slapped her around.*

In the course of this conversation, I maneuver her hand under my sleeve, to where the scars are. I am trying to signal to her that I am trying to commit suicide. She, as it happened, drew the wrong conclusion, that the visible scars were a part of my torture. Anyway, that visit ended.

Tim had been part of the printing process, but if she broke down, it could only lead to small bits of information. One was that, indeed, I was in the underground. That had been independently confirmed for the police by another detainee. They knew she was my girlfriend, but even if she broke or they forced her to appear as a witness, I knew from my knowledge of the law—remember, I was married in Britain—that producing proof that I was married to her would disqualify her from giving evidence against me.

Who else could she finger? Only Doha and a chap called Freddie, and she didn't know his surname. She didn't know where he stayed. I was worried about how she was being treated, but it was a relatively small factor in the face of the other problems I would have to handle.

On another occasion I intercepted her at the Marshall Square cells, where we were housed. She had gone out to the washroom from the women's section, and I was going to the exercise yard in the men's section. I spotted her collecting some water—the women were allowed to get

---

*Tim Naidoo is unsure whether it was Erasmus.

warm water to wash. I broke away from my warder and went to her. I just whispered to her, "Stay strong." They separated us, threatened us.

Those were the two times that I saw her while I was in detention. Then I saw her again when I was awaiting trial and she had been released.

Identity Uncovered

During the time I was in detention, there was a wave of arrests of Indian people. One of them was Steve (Nandha) Naidoo. I discovered he was in jail because he was in a neighboring cell, and he was using Morse code to try to communicate. I thought it might be Steve. I heard the Morse code clicking away. Above my door there was an iron grille, and late at night, when everything was silent, I shouted from there: "Steve, is that you?" After some time, he replied, "Yes—that you, Mac?" I said yes. He said they had questioned him about me. "Under what name?" I asked. He said, "They put a photograph to me." I asked what he had said, and he said, "I told them your name." I said, "You fucking bastard! Will you shut up now and stop talking? Do you realize that identifying me has led to my extra torture?"

I couldn't work out why at times the interrogations had become so urgent. Now I knew who had given them my real name. To be fair to Steve, from that day on he never again gave away information. But there was no longer any point in carrying on with the Solly Matthews pretense.

Murder on the Seventh Floor

In September/October 1964, the Security Branch got information from a detainee that a short Indian man who was banned was responsible for taking people out of the country. Various people, including Arthur Goldreich, Harold Wolpe, Abdulhay Jassat, and Mosie Moola, had escaped from Marshall Square. So they arrested every banned short Indian chap they could find in Johannesburg! I was moved to make space for this huge round of detentions. They arrested Essop Jassat. They also arrested Babla Saloojee, another short Indian, and they killed him. They threw him out of the window of the seventh floor at the Grays.

Nobody was fingered for the death of Saloojee. The inquest found that the cause of death was unknown. Babla was the second or third death in detention, and it obviously sent a tremor through society. There was a huge outcry, with lawyers demanding to see the body, to have their own surgeon at the inquest, and so on.

After Saloojee's death, my interrogation suddenly came to an end.* The security police now had this problem of unexplainable deaths, so they changed their strategy. It became a matter of "charge them, try them, and sentence the bastards." They kept us in detention for another month or so.

Aftermath

I do still feel affected by the experience of detention and torture. Even re-calling it overwhelms me, but I think it's a problem society has to grapple with. At the launch of the book I edited, *Reflections*, Ahmed Kathrada told the story of how I had tried to commit suicide with eggshells.

Kathy told the guests, "This chap was under torture and refused to talk. People don't know this, but he tried to commit suicide." And then he de-scribed how I had taken eggshells from boiled eggs and tried to cut my wrists. He had preceded this with some jocular remarks, and when he came to this part, some members of the audience laughed. But as he was telling it, I had to walk away from the stage because I was afraid I might break, that I might show an emotional reaction. So I left the stage and went to a little platform on the side, and lit a cigarette to try to contain my emotions. I was rescued from that emotional state by the audience's laughter—it just shifted the pressure.

Torture brutalizes both the tortured and the torturers. I think that's part of the reason why there is such an element of brutality in South African society, even in Hyde Park, the posh suburb where I'm living now, which used to be exclusively white. Behind those closed doors and behind those walls, I believe there is a lot of wife beating and child abuse. For the same reason, I believe that nightmares visited those who carried out those brutalities. I don't think you can torture someone without finding yourself changing, leading the split life of being a supposedly caring parent and husband and also a brutal torturer. That would begin to rub off in the form of brutality toward the family, or become trauma inside the person.

Many white parents I met when I was in the underground told me how their sons had changed as a result of doing army service—"He has come back with an authoritarian streak." I believe that that authoritarian streak is a manifestation of brutalization. Power has many dimensions; physical force is just one of them. If a person grows up to understand power only as

---

*Confirmation that Mac didn't break comes from the security police's "super spy" Craig Williamson. See [] maharaj/documents and reports/security files/[] Karl Edwards: The Internal Reconstruction and Development Department [sic].

physical force, as did many young black people during apartheid, then that person is brutalized. Whether it is possible to treat such a person is another question.

When I came out of prison in 1977, I admitted in a BBC radio broadcast interview that I felt brutalized. The interviewer asked me, "What do you mean, brutalized?" I said that I used to think I could kill someone only in anger, but I said I realized now that I could kill someone in a calculated, cold-blooded way. It was with a sense of pain that I recognized that in the pursuit of the struggle and in doing what I still believe was necessary and right to do, I had become brutalized. It had also removed all fear of my personal self and the result is that I went to Robben Island in a fighting mood.

The memories remain. I've seen it in fellow prisoners who were subjected to torture. One man who was in our section on Robben Island used to get up in his sleep, and you would hear the grille door rattling because he was trying to climb out of his cell. He was reliving his tortures, but during the day he was unaware of what he had done at night.

Torture can cripple you. It can cripple your family. The only way to make sense of it is to cling to the recognition that it happened to you while you served your people and your country. Hopefully, you find a way to assuage the pain by taking pride in the fact that you were part of the process of bringing that country to where it is today. That pride becomes, in a sense, the crutch with which you can carry on walking.

7. LITTLE RIVONIA

Introduction

THE TRIAL OF Mac Maharaj and four others* in 1964 on charges of sabotage and treason was dubbed the Little Rivonia Trial, a mopping up of the remnants of MK that had escaped the Rivonia net. Like the earlier trial, this would again put the judiciary to the test.

At that time, the judiciary, like every other state institution in South Africa, both directly and indirectly abetted apartheid.† In 1998, the Truth and Reconciliation Commission (TRC), after exhaustive investigation of judicial processes and practices during the apartheid years, came down hard on the judiciary.[1] The argument that the function of the judiciary is to interpret and apply laws made by the legislative branch of government loses its moral authority when the laws are patently unjust.

The courts meted out severe punishments to opponents of apartheid, and many judges were racists. One judge in particular—Justice H.H.W. de Villiers—is deserving of mention because he personified the typical white support for apartheid. The judge, who retired in 1961, wrote a book on the Rivonia trial,[2] in which he characterized the African population as follows: "The primitive Bantu is still a killer. The Zulu war cry 'Bulala!' can still stir them into a frenzy of uncontrolled aggression and murder. They can so easily be persuaded to kill. One must always remember we have to deal with a primitive people; even higher education does not eradicate their superstitious beliefs in a generation or two."[3]

---

*The four were: Wilton Mkwayi (accused number one), Dave Kitson (accused number two), Laloo Chiba (accused number three), and John Matthews (accused number four). Mac was accused number five.
†There were some nonstate bodies that were at the vanguard of opposition to apartheid: among them the South African Council of Churches (SACC), Black Sash, and the South African Institute of Race Relations (SAIRR).

South Africa had one of the highest rates of judicial execution in the world. Between 1960 and 1990, more than 2,500 people were hanged—1,154 between 1976 and 1985. More than 95 percent of all people executed were African, and the death penalty was far more likely to be imposed if the victim of a capital offense was white and the perpetrator black.[4]

Although the vast majority of executions were for criminal offenses, capital punishment was also used against those found guilty of political offenses, in defiance of the Geneva Convention. South Africa was a signatory to the 1949 convention but declined to sign the 1977 addendum extending the definition of prisoner of war to captured guerrilla fighters.

2

Given the limited damage MK was able to wreak in the two years after Rivonia, the Little Rivonia Trialists enjoyed notoriety out of proportion to their importance. Yet it suited the state to exaggerate the threat—it fueled white paranoia.

The memories of the Trialists differ somewhat. John Matthews died in 1986 and Wilton Mkwayi in 2004, a year after I talked with him. Laloo Chiba is retired, and Dave Kitson lives in a retirement home in Johannesburg. The lawyers who represented them—Joel Joffe and George Bizos, respectively—are still alive.

According to Mac, Lionel Gay, who turned state's evidence in exchange for the charges against him being dropped, tried to put the noose around their necks. He offered information beyond what was asked of him in court, and especially dangerous was his allegation that MK was now willing to kill people. The defense, in fact, curtailed their cross-examination of Gay because of the damage he was doing, with the consent of a biased judge.

Laloo Chiba concurs: "He was vicious in the evidence he gave. Mac is right when he says that when Gay was being cross-examined by George Bizos, he would blurt out things like 'Oh, that brings me to another incident where we set up an execution squad.' We were [indeed] thinking of setting up an execution squad. We wanted to set up an execution squad, and that matter was discussed in one of the meetings of the National High Command. But it was never set up."[5]

Wilton Mkwayi, on the other hand, said, "We expected him [Gay] to divulge some things, but he did not. . . . He could have divulged much more than he actually did. I still see him. He comes and stays with me."[6]

Joffe, who prepared the case for the defense: "Gay was so frightened that he actually exaggerated the facts so as to really tighten the noose around the necks of the accused. Of course, he's a highly intelligent man, and he was in a state of distress—and he was one of the most dangerous witnesses I'd ever seen."[7]

But he is forgiving: "He didn't turn in the sense that he ever lost his commitment to the freedom struggle, and when he did come to England, he really was determined to get back and join the liberation movement and do something active. . . . He wasn't one of those who switched sides. But he was in a state at this trial, and he gave evidence which was so damaging to the accused that it could have led to death sentences. . . . When he got out, he behaved quite differently. . . .

"I never felt that people who break down under torture, and for a time behave in a way which is totally at odds with what they believe simply because they're totally terrified, should be condemned and persecuted. Personally, I have no doubt that if I was tortured the way they were, I would very soon have collapsed."[8]

Reading Gay's testimony under cross-examination suggests that rather than being frightened to death, he was very contained and lucid, and his intelligence is obvious. But he did have a propensity to give responses that went far beyond the remit of the questions asked.

3

Gay, a scientist with a wife and two children, had joined MK in 1961 at Ronnie Kasrils's invitation, to serve on the local technical committee in Durban. He knew little of its history. There was no formal selection procedure, no background check.

Gay worked on technical problems: radio communications, developing explosives, ignition devices, and timers. He was heavily involved in the preparations for the radio broadcast of 26 June 1963, when Walter Sisulu went on the air to rally the masses and raise the cry for freedom. Subsequently, he became a member of the logistics committee that met at the cottage Arthur Goldreich occupied at Lilliesleaf Farm in Rivonia.

After the Rivonia arrests, Kitson told Gay that a new National High Command (NHC) had been established for MK, and he was a member along with Mkwayi and Chiba. All meetings of the new NHC, which met about once every two weeks, took place at Gay's home.[9]

On some points during the Little Rivonia Trial, Gay was adamant. He testified that a decision had been made to execute informers, in particular to "eliminate" a certain Indian informer. Then a decision came from the political leadership that no such action should be taken "lest the chances of the Rivonia accused be prejudiced." Gay was also adamant that the NHC took a decision that all MK units should be "self-sufficient": "They were to be in a position to manufacture their own explosives devices, and they were also expected to choose their own targets and to execute sabotage at a time which they considered favorable." He did not know whether this decision was ever communicated to MK units.

MK, he concluded, "was directly under the control of the Communist Party," and the leadership "would not admit" people other than Communists to MK because it was believed the ANC should be kept in the dark about this. He believed that he was basically "working for the Communist Party."

He stuck to this testimony during cross-examination. Reading this testimony, one feels that when he became expansive, he was doing so to give added credibility to what he had said, not necessarily to endanger the lives of the accused. In some things, as George Bizos observed of Gay, he had a remarkable memory; in others he had little memory to speak of. He had read only one issue of the "The Freedom Fighter."* He insisted that the 26 June statement urged the people to continue with sabotage when it had not.† He was unaware of the fact that when the ANC was still a legal organization, it had let it be publicly known that it had no problems associating with "known" Communists. He was unclear about the relative autonomy of MK in relation to the political leadership.

Lionel Gay was no revolutionary. He had technical skills MK required but little knowledge of the ANC. His path from the Congress of Democrats to the High Command of MK was haphazard and improbable. What he did confirm, however—and no defense advocate tried to refute—was that in the wake of the Rivonia convictions, the SACP held the struggle together and the new High Command was composed of Communists only and it reported to the Central Committee.

His testimony was coherent. He withstood cross-examination and comes across as intelligent, articulate, and not easily addled by the defense. Yet in the unfolding of his testimony, one detects an underlying absence of

---

*A hand-typed paper written by Hilda Bernstein and run off on a mimeograph machine. See copies of the small number of issues she produced at [] maharaj/ documents and reports/ Little Rivonia Trial/[] Freedom Fighter.
†This is the Walter Sisulu broadcast (prerecorded) on Radio Freedom on 26 June 1963. For the full text of the broadcast go to [] maharaj/documents and reports/ANC/ 1963/ [] Broadcast on ANC Radio by W. M. Sisulu.

self-esteem. Perhaps he himself provided the best assessment of his place in the debacle when, in response to a question regarding his appointment to the High Command, he said: "I said to Mr. Kitson that if I had to serve on this body, surely it was an indication that things had reached a level at which we should take stock. Mr. Kitson's remark was, 'I'm afraid we are scraping the bottom of the barrel.' "

Mac

ON 18 NOVEMBER 1964 we were brought to trial: Wilton Mkwayi, Laloo Chiba, Dave Kitson, John Matthews, and I. For a month before the trial we weren't tortured; I suspect that the respite was to allow us to recover physically so that our appearance would not cause a stir. By then, Tim had been released from detention. The police had very little against her, except that she was my wife, which they determined at some point after my meeting with her in the presence of Van Rensburg.

I was being held in Pretoria Central Prison. The first morning of the trial I was taken out of my cell to the reception area of the prison, and there I found Wilton and Laloo. We were put in the prison van. Then they brought Dave and John, the two whites, and put them in the same van. That was the first time we had been together. We were driven off to Jo'burg Supreme Court and put in the basement cells.

Our lawyers had been constantly badgering the Security Police, trying to ascertain where each of us was being kept and when we were to come up for trial. When we appeared on trial, the lawyers were there in the cells of the Supreme Court. It was the first time we had seen them. We didn't even know who they were. We were visited by Joel Joffe (he was the lawyer for all of us) and by George Bizos, the advocate for three of us—Wilton, John, and me.* Dave and Laloo had their own advocates. The day Joel came to see us, he was surprised. He said to me, "I thought I would be meeting somebody older, but you're bloody young. How old are you?" I said, "I'm twenty-nine." He said, "Look, I was on my way out of the country after the Rivonia Trial, but Bram Fischer pleaded with me to stay behind and wait until you and Wilton came up for trial so I could defend you."

Joel told us we would be taken to the courtroom but not asked to plead. The prosecutor would ask for the case to be remanded to a later

*The lawyer prepared the case; the advocate argued the case in court.

date. I said, "But I've been tortured." I said I thought I should tell the court about my torture. He said, "You are not expected or allowed to say anything." I said, "Can't I force my way in and say something?" He said, "You can take a chance, but then you must speak very rapidly. The judge is going to try to stop you, and you must be prepared to be strong and keep talking even if he tells the orderlies to come and stop you from talking." I said, "Great, great."

We went into the courtroom and were ushered into the dock, a wooden enclosure facing the judge. On the right-hand side of the courtroom, the tiered seats were packed with about forty Security Branch men and policemen. Behind us, I remember, was the public gallery, which was divided by an aisle. On the one side were the whites and on the other were the blacks. I saw my wife, Tim, and friends, including the Naidoo family. The public gallery was packed, and on the white side I recall seeing Bram Fischer's daughter, Ilse. I asked Joel, who subsequently became my lifelong friend, when I could see my wife. He said he would try to arrange it.

Suddenly the orderly demanded that everybody rise. We stood, and the prosecutor got up and, in a low mechanical tone, said that he was asking for the case to be remanded. I then interrupted.[10] I said to the judge, "I seek the court's protection!" I didn't wait for him to answer. I said, "I have been tortured. My torturers are here. They are sitting in the courtroom." I started recounting some of my tortures. The judge tried to stop me, but I continued. I was, of course, very nervous because now I knew I was taking on the cops and I was still going to be in prison. In my nervousness, I paused, not sure how to go on. As soon as I paused, the judge grabbed the gavel and said, "A copy of this record will be sent to the police to investigate. You are now an awaiting-trial prisoner. The court is adjourned."

I remember George Bizos coming over to me and saying, "That was fantastic, but you missed one thing." "What?" He said, "You named the guys, but you should have pointed at them. They were sitting there in the gallery, and you should have said, 'That one there is Swanepoel, that one there is so-and-so, that one there is so-and-so.' " I said, "Shit, guys, I fucked it up." They said, "No, you didn't fuck it up."

Then we were taken to the Number 4 Prison, part of the fort in Hillbrow, Johannesburg—today the site of the Constitutional Court. We were separated—whites to one section of the prison; Laloo, Wilton, and I to the single cells, those steel boxes. We were subjected to a strip search—inside your anus and your mouth and all. The police and warders were very abusive, both verbally and physically, during strip searches. We were stripped in the courtyard every time we came in. If we went out to the other section of the prison to consult with the lawyers, they would search us when we were brought back, although it was in the same complex. Then they would interfere with our visitors: they could cancel our visits. One day they wanted to fingerprint us and took us one by one. Laloo resisted, and they forcibly fingerprinted him.

We were now housed in Number 4 for the duration of the trial. Officially we were allowed a visit once a week, but relatives were allowed to bring us food every day. We had to go down from our cells to the visiting area to collect our food.

Tim was able to visit me, but it was not a private visit. There was a wire mesh barrier, and all the prisoners stood on one side with the visitors on the other, in a row—all shouting at one another and talking. Tim's presence there was really moral support and the sharing of confidences; we told each other that we would stand together, we would fight, that she was behind me. She was never able to tell me what she had gone through at Marshall Square, where she was assaulted. Nor afterward. An opportunity never arose.

Trial

Our trial was short—about a month. We were sentenced in December of 1964. The charges: sabotage, in contravention of Section 21 (1) of Act No. 76 of 1962, two counts; contravening Section 11 (a), read with Sections 1 and 12, of Act No. 44 of 1950, as amended; and contravening Section 3 (1) (b), read with Section 2, of Act No. 8 of 1953, as amended. In other words, sabotage, sabotage, sabotage, and sabotage!

The judge was Justice W. G. Boshoff. He was an interesting guy. He had been an advocate in the 1940s and was arrested during World War II for storing dynamite in his chambers on behalf of the Ossewa Brandwag, a right-wing pro-Nazi sabotage group. So we knew from the beginning that we had an uphill battle on our hands. Boshoff was a partisan in defense of apartheid, and he used the courtroom and his privileged position not only to judge us by his own lights, but also to intervene in the evidence from time to time to protect state witnesses when they were saying untenable things, and to reprimand and curtail our defense panel when they cross-examined.*

---

*I asked Mac how he had ascertained that Boshoff had been a member of Ossewa Brandwag. Through Bizos or one of the other lawyers, he thought. But Bizos couldn't confirm that Boshoff was in Ossewa Brandwag. Because prisoners appearing before

In the Rivonia judgment, the court had accepted the argument that our campaign of sabotage was not directed at human life. Mandela and company had gotten away with life sentences. Had they found us guilty of directing activities against human life, it is possible that we and also future Trialists could have received the death sentence.

In the South African judicial system at that time, you had one or two opportunities as an accused in a trial. You could choose to go into the witness box and be cross-examined, or you could forgo that and make a statement from the dock without being subjected to cross-examination. In our case, the prosecution was keenly disappointed when they got wind that we were not going to go into the box.

Lionel Gay

Lionel Gay broke in detention, and at the trial he gave evidence for the state. He was an amazing witness. This man had a remarkable ability to withstand cross-examination by our lawyers and to virtually silence them. While I have no grudge against him for being a state witness, there's something I can't put aside. He had a bag of tricks that he used, not just to co-operate with the regime, but to try to put the rope around our necks. He literally tried to get us sentenced to death. He did this in a very sophisticated way. It was not part of his main evidence. Strictly speaking, you're supposed to cross-examine on the main evidence, but the judge allowed him to make additional statements under cross-examination.

At the Rivonia Trial, the substantive defense point was that MK was carrying out sabotage but avoiding the loss of life. In our trial, if it could be established that we were not avoiding loss of life, we could get the death sentence. Gay alleged that we had changed our policy and taken steps to set up execution squads to deal with turncoats and informers.

South African judges on terrorism and sedition charges believed, with good reason, that the judiciary collectively comprised "hanging judges" who would condemn them to the gallows on the flimsiest of evidence, the fact that they would perceive them as having been pro-Nazi sympathizers is not especially surprising. Boshoff, however, does occupy a little niche in South African history. In January 1985, when he was judge president of the Transvaal Supreme Court, he found that there was prima facie evidence of improper or disgraceful behavior on the part of Drs. Lang and Tucker, the two doctors involved in decisions relating to the circumstances of Steve Biko's death in 1976 (they had provided certificates saying there was nothing seriously wrong with Biko when they signed off on his being transported in the back of a police van from Port Elizabeth to Pretoria). He ordered the South African Medical and Dental Council to open an inquiry. Tucker was subsequently struck from the medical roll.

After the trial, Gay was released. Then he turned to the movement to help him get out of the country in secret. He was due to give evidence in the trial of Steve Naidoo, so our underground helped him escape to Botswana and he got to London. As a result, when Steve was charged, the case against him fell apart. I would have done the same with Gay—gotten him out of the country. Later, MK execution squads caught up with others who had betrayed the struggle, but not with Gay.

After the 1994 elections, Gay visited me at my offices in Cape Town. He apologized for what he had done. I said, "Forget about these bygones." He then said he wanted to help with educational projects in the building of the country, and I said to him, "Well, go to the minister of education, go to the NGO sector." He wanted to know if I could vouch for him, and I said I couldn't. I couldn't stop him, but I would not give him a recommendation. That was the last time I saw him.

Piet Beyleveld

Piet Beyleveld had also turned state's evidence and given evidence in our trial. He later gave evidence against Bram Fischer too. He kept protesting that he had tried to minimize the damage, but that was not good enough. The prosecution kept using him as a state witness until about 1967. He died a lonely death from natural causes, isolated from the struggle.

Piet was not as bad as Gay. He identified me as a member of the Central Committee of the Communist Party, but Gay had insisted that the Central Committee made all the key decisions, even about the sabotage campaign—not the ANC, not the congresses, not MK. "All decisions," he said, "are made by the Central Committee." When Bizos cross-examined Beyleveld, however, and put it to him that the Central Committee did not make all the key decisions, Beyleveld said, "That's true; it did not. The Central Committee made decisions on political questions. It did not make decisions about what MK should do."

The evidence against me was pretty heavy because of my membership in the party and the Central Committee. Bizos was trying to draw a distinction between membership in the Communist Party and membership in MK. The judge intervened. He said, "Mr. Bizos, you and I know the Communists, they don't allow"—and he made this dismissive gesture with his hand from the bench—"they don't allow the left hand to know what the right hand is doing." So poor Bizos had to shut up on that line of questioning!

We didn't go into the box to give evidence. We merely made a statement from the dock when it came to mitigation of sentence. We wanted to go into the box and make impassioned statements calling on the masses to rise up and overthrow their oppressors. We wanted to say that if we were to die, the people would avenge us.

But Bram, who was out on bail, got wind of what we were planning to do and conveyed a message: "Tell the comrades that this is not the time for heroics. It's important for the movement that you be quiet: less fanfare, no drama. Try to minimize your sentences. Your job is to survive and get out of prison as quickly as you can. It's going to be a long struggle, and you'll be needed back in the fight. It's enough for you all to say you're a part of the struggle. Our leaders in the Rivonia Trial have made the political statement; you don't have to repeat it."

So Wilton opened up by saying, "My Lord, I am a professional agitator." Kitson, accused number two, got up and said, "My Lord, I am a Communist." And we all followed suit. When it came to my turn I said:

> I, My Lord, am a reasonably well-educated person. I am eager to work to earn a living, to study in my spare time and be a law-abiding citizen, yet in the country of my birth the universities are closed to me, I have no vote, I cannot go where I like or buy property where I like. There is no way of protest open to me other than sabotage. Whatever punishment Your Lordship metes out to me cannot convince me that I have acted wrongly. I cannot see how morally it can be wrong to fight for one's freedom and the freedom of one's people.[11]

Toward the end of the trial, and because of the evidence Beyleveld had given fingering me as a Central Committee member, Bizos and Joel came to me and said, "Mac, it's going very badly for you. You'd better prepare yourself for the death sentence." I said, "So what? If that's the way it's going to fall, that's the way it falls." I had a simple acceptance that death was part of the price we would have to pay for freedom.

In the end, I got the shortest sentence. I got twelve years whereas Mkwayi got life. Afterward, the joke was that when the lawyers came and said, "Do you guys want to appeal?" I said, "The others can appeal. I'm quite happy with twelve years. I don't want to go back and get twenty!" I was indifferent about the length of my sentence, and so were the others.

8. ROBBEN ISLAND

Introduction

ROBBEN ISLAND, cut off from the mainland by seven miles of daunting sea, is visible from Cape Town, but it is a world away, an unthreatening shape on the horizon almost lost in the great span of intervening water, a place of incarceration from the time of the Dutch for opponents of the colonial state, such as Makana in the 1800s and opponents of apartheid from the 1960s to the 1990s. It was more than a prison; it was a statement of the power of the Afrikaner state. The prison administration created a contained world in which warders played capricious gods.

The first political prisoners arrived on Robben Island in 1962, mostly members of the Pan-Africanist Congress (PAC) and its armed wing, Poqo. From the beginning the conditions were harsh. Initially there were some Coloured prison warders on the island, but they were withdrawn, and for almost forty years white warders policed black inmates. In the early years, warders were given almost free rein, perhaps to break the spirits of the prisoners. Brutality was rampant.

In June 1964, the convicted Rivonia treason Trialists—Nelson Mandela, Govan Mbeki, Walter Sisulu, Raymond Mhlaba, Ahmed Kathrada (Kathy), Andrew Mlangeni, and Elias Motsoaledi—were incarcerated in a newly constructed section of the prison, which was set apart from the communal prison. Here they were confined to single cells and were isolated from other prisoners. It was intended that they would spend the rest of their lives there. In time, they were joined by a number of prisoners from their own organizations as well as others who were considered too dangerous to mingle with the thousand-plus prisoners in the communal section.

In the early years, vicious nonpolitical prisoners, usually members of gangs, were incarcerated in the communal section and, rewarded with privileges, were used to reinforce the brutality of the warders. They were encouraged to assault, often savagely, the political prisoners.[1]

In the 1960s prisoners had to perform the *tauza:* they had to strip naked and then jump around to dislodge from their orifices anything they might be concealing.[2] The purpose was not so much to find anything as to degrade and humiliate, to emasculate a prisoner's sense of self.[3] Gang members were removed from the island in 1965, and matters improved somewhat. Former political prisoners believe that the common-law criminals were removed because the political prisoners had begun to politicize them; they were also a source of news for the political prisoners, and in the end, prisoners of whatever ilk have more in common with one another than with their jailers.

Conditions got worse again in the early 1970s with the arrival of a new commanding officer, Colonel Piet Badenhorst, who instituted a regime of extreme severity. Some prisoners would later describe it as a reign of terror.[4] Badenhorst was selected to smash the emerging psychological emancipation political prisoners were beginning to create for themselves. When he left in December 1972, conditions once again began to improve.

Over time, the tenacity of the prisoners and their assertiveness in demanding rights paid dividends, and with the passage of years, conditions improved markedly. For the prisoners Robben Island was one more terrain of struggle.

Conditions in the single cells (the isolation section) and the main section (the communal prisoners) were determined by apartheid logic. Diet varied according to race. White prisoners convicted of political offenses served their sentences at Pretoria Central. They were fed four ounces of mealie meal or mealie rice per day. Black prisoners served their sentences on Robben Island. There, Coloureds and Indians were fed fourteen ounces of mealie meal per day and Africans twelve. On the other hand, white prisoners were given seven ounces of fish or meat per day, while Coloureds, Indians, and Africans were only allowed four helpings of meat or fish per week—six ounces for Coloureds and Indians, five for Africans. Whites received sixteen ounces of vegetables per day, all others eight ounces. Puzamandla* was prescribed exclusively for Africans, milk exclusively for whites. Dietary standards, prison authorities would explain, were based on the "traditional" diets to which each "culture" ascribed.[5]

---

*A mealie meal–based powder that was mixed with cold water and supplied in prison as a lunch drink to African prisoners.

Food was a political tool, and thus the hunger strike became a weapon of political prisoners. It was used as a weapon of last resort but was usually effective. The hunger strike that marked the first major resistance to the prison regime took place in 1966 as a protest against abysmal conditions. The strike lasted a week, and former islanders tell stories of their being harassed by the warders to work harder at the quarry, of prisoners collapsing and being pushed in wheelbarrows back to the communal cells at day's end.

But improvements followed, including a dining hall for the main section. (Previously, prisoners had squatted in the open to have their food after they returned from work before being herded into the communal cells.) And a soccer ground, or what approximated one, was made available, which meant that prisoners were no longer locked up for twenty-four hours on weekend days.

The hunger strike idea was catching. Shortly after the prisoners ended theirs, the warders embarked on one of their own, demanding an improvement in the quality and quantity of their food rations. Improvements were almost instantaneously granted.[6]

But the success of a hunger strike could not be measured in the material improvements in prison conditions. Its real achievement was psychological: the empowering of prisoners by collective action.

Apartheid logic also applied to clothing. African prisoners were given sandals, short pants, and a canvas jacket, but they were not allowed to wear socks or underwear. These clothing provisions applied to winter as well as summer. Indian and Coloured prisoners were allowed shoes, socks, long trousers, jerseys, and underwear. In 1970, discrimination in clothing was done away with.

In the isolation section, egalitarianism prevailed in every activity. Whether in matters such as the washing of toilets, the disposal of waste, or sweeping the floors, Mandela, Sisulu, Mbeki, and Mhlaba had to do their share. Such shared experiences bred a sense of camaraderie that prisoners had rarely experienced in life off the island.

No communication was allowed with the prisoners in the communal cells. The single-cell prisoners exercised in a small quad, built so that they could see nothing beyond the patch of sky above them. Single-cell prisoners were walked to the lime quarry after breakfast on a route devised to prevent their crossing the path of the communal-cell prisoners, on their way to the stone quarry. At day's end, a similar routine was followed. At all times the warders guarding them carried automatic weapons—more for purposes of intimidation, since even in the unlikely event of a mass uprising and the overpowering of warders, the prisoners would still be on the island.

Warders could punish prisoners for any perceived breach of regulations. Prisoners could appeal the charges or bring complaints, especially with regard to mistreatment by warders, before an administrative court, presided over by the resident commanding officer. During the "court" proceedings, they were given the opportunity to cross-examine the warder against whom they had lodged the complaint or whose charge they were appealing. While they rarely won, they did so occasionally. The sense of vindication, however, came from befuddling the warders. These were exhilarating mental workouts for the more verbally dexterous prisoners, but the warders could all too easily exact a greater revenge. Initially the authorities only allowed prisoners to air grievances on their own behalf. Speaking on behalf of other prisoners was forbidden. But this, too, was fought, and the argument was won. Prisoners formed a committee in which grievances were discussed. When consensus was reached, it was forwarded to Mandela, who would take the matter up with the authorities.

Prisoners were assigned different categories, ranked from A to D, the A category being the highest on the ladder, and the D category the lowest. On arrival, all prisoners were categorized as D. They weren't eligible for an "upgrade" until they had served one quarter of their sentence. Most never made it further than C—they could send and receive one letter every three months. An A category prisoner was allowed most privileges; at the low end, D prisoners were allowed the least—one visitor and one letter to send and receive every six months.

Visits were another occasion for invasion of privacy. Until 1966, prisoners were allowed one letter every three months. From 1966 and into the early 1970s, visits were limited to one per month for thirty minutes. Visits were noncontact: prisoner on one side of a Plexiglas partition, visitor on the other. Each visit required the attendance of two warders, one on the prisoner's side, to monitor what he was saying, and one on the visitor's side, to perform a similar function. When conversation by intercom was introduced, a warder listened in on the telephone. Conversation was strictly controlled.

Mention of another prisoner's name or that of nonrelatives, the relaying of messages, or anything to do with the island and, of course, politics— none of these were allowed. Prisoners could talk about themselves, what they were studying, money they might need for tuition fees, some queries about family members. Visitors could talk about themselves and other family members, but only in the most mundane way. Any conversation that appeared to convey other information could result in an immediate termination of the visit, entirely at the warders' discretion.

When Jimmy Kruger became minister of justice and prisons in 1966, he introduced a further restriction: visitors had to be "first-degree" relatives, a relationship contrary to African forms of kinship. Kruger's concession: anyone wanting to have a visit by other relatives or friends could apply for such visits provided they supplied the prison authorities with particulars of the persons they wished to see or of persons wishing to see them. The information, of course, would have gone directly to the security police, so the prisoners turned the concession down.

The island's authorities raised the censorship of mail to a sadistic art. It was not uncommon for prisoners to receive mail that began with "Dear————," followed by several blacked-out pages, and ending with "Yours lovingly." But since blacked-out pages might on occasion be somehow partially deciphered, the censors resorted to clipping out the undesirable lines and if the writer used the back of a page to continue a letter, the content on that side would also disappear. The most severe form of censorship: warders could inform prisoners that they had received mail but that it was being withheld. Prisoners had no recourse.

Outgoing mail was subjected to word-by-word scrutiny. Anything suspicious was marked and returned to the writer for correction or deletion. The letter had to be rewritten, even if only a single word had met with the censor's red ink. The word *we*, no matter its context, was forbidden. It suggested that the prisoner might be speaking for others too. Many times a single letter had to be rewritten several times before it was given the stamp of approval.

On occasion, the prison authorities would belatedly see where the unintended consequences of their own actions might lead. Thus, at the end of the 1960s, study privileges were suddenly curtailed. Postgraduate study was stopped. Whoever was doing a postgraduate degree at the time was given until February 1970 to finish, irrespective of when he was supposed to complete the degree. Soon after, prisoners were prohibited from taking courses or even pursuing undergraduate degrees in history, law, or political science.[7]

Other restrictions were introduced for the sole purpose of making study more difficult. It became apparent that the government had noticed that many prisoners left the island far better educated than when they had begun their sentences. Thus they were likely to be more sophisticated enemies if they resumed their places in the struggle.

A prison student could not lend his books to a nonstudent; prison students could not exchange books with each other (even if they were both enrolled in the same course). Any violation of such rules could lead to the suspension of study privileges, often for years at a time.

Studying itself was very difficult, at least in the beginning. A prisoner had no stool, bench, or desk. He had to study, take notes, and write while standing. There was a dim light in the cell but hardly enough to read by. In winter the temperature was freezing. But even if prisoners were allowed study privileges, they were forbidden to dabble in creative writing. A few lines of poetry found in one's possession could be sufficient to have study privileges revoked.

Rights and privileges were always matters of contention. The prison authorities would classify prisoners according to their behavior, and reward or punish them by giving or rescinding privileges. But the constant list of demands with which the prisoners confronted the authorities had a dual purpose: what one commanding officer would dismiss out of hand might be granted by the next. Long-term prisoners developed an institutional memory that incoming commanding officers lacked and thus could cite past practice as precedent. Questioning every regulation invariably led to the amelioration of some, and what for the authorities might represent a small concession would be perceived by the prisoners in a very different light.

The alleviation of harsh conditions of confinement and work, or an end to the arbitrary behavior of warders, was perhaps the least of what the prisoners were trying to achieve. But with the accumulation of small and at first seemingly insignificant changes, the power relations between the authorities and the prisoners began to change.

The presence of the Rivonia Trialists, segregated as they were from the prisoners in the main section, was beneficial for prisoners in general. International attention followed. The Anti-Apartheid Movement drew attention not only to apartheid but to the plight of the prisoners on Robben Island. The International Committee of the Red Cross (ICRC) intervened and made its first visit to the island in 1964. The United Nations took up the prisoners' cause. "Release Mandela" became the call that rallied opposition to apartheid across the globe.

Often overlooked in the literature on the struggle to end apartheid is the fact that after 1960, when the liberation organizations were banned, the prisoners on Robben Island were the only faces of their respective movements in South Africa. Although imprisoned, Mandela, as spokesman for the prisoners, met regularly with prison authorities, officials from the mainland, and even with the then minister of justice Jimmy Kruger.

The prisoners, a majority of whom were associated with the ANC, were the living presence of the movement in South Africa. Their struggle for dignity was a symbol of the larger struggle, the one conducted outside the prison.

2

As with criminals, long years of incarceration usually turn fledgling revolutionaries into hardened ones. ANC prisoners, under the leadership of the High Organ—Mandela, Govan Mbeki, Mhlaba, and Sisulu—set up within the prison an administration of their own, one with clear lines of command, assignment of responsibilities, adherence to discipline, and, of course, a communications system.

Perfecting this communications system was a challenge to ingenuity, and it was Mac's forte. Laloo Chiba worked with Mac, "Mac was innovative; he was absolutely brilliant."

> There was a matchbox. In the matchbox he'd built a false bottom and smuggled a written message into that false bottom. . . . Then there was the tennis ball. . . . At some point—much later on—they allowed us to play tennis. We punched a little hole in it, . . . put in the written message and threw it over the wall on to the communal side. Then the shoe— what Mac really came up [with] was absolutely brilliant. . . . There [would be] a slit here on the right-hand side. You take out all these stitches, the thing opens up. So we used to write a message, seal it in here, restitch [it], send the shoe for repairs. . . . When it reached the other side, they used to always look whether this was tampered with, and if it had [been], they would then retrieve the message.
>
> Later he devised another thing. We were allowed to keep photographs in our cells; we were allowed to receive photographs. . . . We were allowed to buy stationery, so we often used to buy board. Now that board, you take one cover and you take another cover and in between the two covers you seal your message and you paste it. Right? On top of it you put your photographs. So when people were released from prison, they were told, "Take this, give it to so-and-so in Lusaka or London."[8]

Says Michael Dingake, another member of the Communications Committee:

> He had a way with a warder. If you saw Mac talking to a warder, you knew something was up. He wasn't exchanging pleasantries; it was a

business . . . , you knew something was up. He would be persuading or trying to suggest to the warder how he could co-operate with him and perhaps smuggle things into prison. He just used to amaze us. He could get banned books into prison and of course not everybody would know that he had done that, only the few trusted ones like myself and of course people like Madiba and Walter, Govan and all those people. He was just fantastic, absolutely fabulous.[9]

Mac and Kathy began to experiment with codes so that letters they sent from the prison would seem innocuous to the censor. Dasu Joseph was Mac's main conduit to the SACP in London. When Dasu received letters from Mac that made no sense to him, he simply turned them over to Vella Pillay, who was able to decipher the codes and pass the letters on to Yusuf Dadoo, the party's representative in London.

3

There was another Robben Island, a place one doesn't hear much about. Loyalty to the ANC has meant that significant differences over a number of important issues have been played down, although the wounds of these disagreements festered for years.

Govan Mbeki, in particular, was the source of bad blood among the principals of the High Organ; Mbeki challenged Mandela's leadership. Sisulu and Mbeki disagreed over whether Operation Mayibuye had been officially approved by the NEC, or whether it was still under discussion at the time of the Rivonia arrests.* When a proposal was put forward that the self-education curriculum should include Operation Mayibuye, Mbeki,

---

*It is a matter of inquiry as to when Govan Mbeki became a member of the ANC. In his diaries, which he kept during his imprisonment, Mandela has a note referring to Mbeki's membership: "G. became active in the ANC when he left teaching in 1955 and became 'New Age' reporter. He became speaker [i.e., chairman at the annual conference] in 1958 when the hard core of the ANC leadership were unavailable by bans and the Treason Trial." [] maharaj/documents and reports/other/[] Mandela diary extracts. Of some puzzlement, too, is the fact that Mbeki was not among persons proscribed under the Suppression of Communism Act, was only banned in 1962; was not himself among then treason Trialists, and was arrested for the first time in 1962. Thus from the 1940s or earlier the first time came to the attention of the security agencies was in late 1962, when he was served with a five-year house arrest order while he was visiting Johannesburg. Ahmed Kathrada says that Govan was only elected to the Central Committee of the Communist Party at the Central Committee meeting immediately preceding their arrest at Rivonia. (*Memoirs*, p. 296)

one of the authors of Mayibuye, strenuously objected and discussion of Mayibuye was forbidden in history classes.

Thus the hundreds of young prisoners coming to Robben Island and being thoroughly educated about the ANC, while in the same jail as the revered Rivonia Trialists, never learned why the Rivonia Trialists were convicted of treason or what Operation Mayibuye was.

Mandela and Mbeki had their first run-in over the question of the purpose of the Communications Committee. Kathrada and Mac argued that the committee should devise ways of communicating with the communal cells and with the outside. They were opposed by the other two members of the committee, Joe Gqabi and Andrew Masondo. The matter went to the High Organ; Mandela and Sisulu arguing in favor of communications with both, while Mbeki and Mhlaba argued that communications should be confined to the communal cells.

Mbeki and Mhlaba won the argument then, but within a brief period of time, the decision was more honored in the breach. Harry Gwala, who was in the communal cells at the time, had set up his own communications system with the outside; and Mac, with the approval of the High Organ, soon followed suit. Mbeki and Gwala also argued that the ANC and the SACP were one and the same; Mandela insisted that they were not. After acrimonious exchanges, the matter was deferred to the ANC in Lusaka, which came down on Mandela's side.[10] Thereafter, the principle of the separateness of the two parties having been established, the ANC represented all the prisoners within the single-cell section.

More tensions followed. Discussion groups of four were conducted under each member of the High Organ. Mandela, in one session on guerrilla warfare, clashed with Gqabi; Gqabi apparently felt the cutting edge of Mandela's tongue. Dingake still has vivid memories of the clashes: "Joe didn't quite like it, and he reported it to Govan—he was very close to Govan."[11] The matter was raised in the High Organ, and Mbeki and Masondo sided with Gqabi. Relations between Mandela and Gqabi deteriorated further.*

Each tension built on the last. The issue of how the ANC should deal with the Bantustans was perhaps the defining issue. Should the ANC

---

*Regarding Joe Gqabi, Mandela wrote in his diary: "Joe is able and articulate, only wish that even at this late moment he can learn the value of team work, of concealing our internal differences from outsiders and of being less offensive to his own colleagues." [] general information/documents and reports/[] Mandela diary extracts.

oppose them entirely, giving them no legitimacy at all, or should it or its surrogates support strategic participation and consider forming opposition parties to contest elections in those states?

Mbeki, Mhlaba, Gqabi, and Masondo took the former view; Mandela and Sisulu took the latter. The feud boiled over when Mbeki demanded that Indians and Coloureds be excluded from internal ANC matters.[12] The High Organ rejected his demand. The debate over the Bantustans was never resolved. Ahmed Kathrada, in his *Memoirs*, presents the differences over the Bantustans as one of the contrasting positions of "communists" versus "nationalists,"[13] perhaps a too sympathetic simplification, since many hard-nosed Communists, like Mac, supported a policy of destroying the Bantustans by infiltrating their structures from within.

The issue might be better understood as a clash of two modes of thinking, ingrained attributes of two self-willed personalities. For Mbeki, the matter was not an issue of discussion because the ANC Lobatse conference in 1962 had passed a resolution that called for a boycott of apartheid institutions. The matter was closed. For Mandela, no policy was given the benediction of holy writ. Times changed. Strategy had to adapt to changing circumstances; therefore, the matter should be one for discussion. For Govan, with his rigid adherence to Marxist ideology, policy was sometimes an end in itself; for Mandela, policy was a means to an end, and while the end remained fixed and firm, policies were the product of the particular circumstances that prevailed at a point in time. There was, therefore, a need to revisit them to gauge whether they required modification as circumstances changed. Mandela, for example, was prepared to question the efficacy of the armed struggle as a tactic;[14] for Mbeki, even entertaining the thought of such a discussion was a nonstarter.

However, not to recognize that the deep disagreements between the two—often pursued by their proxies, fiercely protective of their respective allegiances—were not also a manifestation of a power struggle, or rather an attempt on Mbeki's part to diminish the aura of authority and hence the leadership that Mandela had brought to the struggle since his involvement with the ANCYL in the mid 1940s, would be naive. Gqabi and Masondo were Mbeki acolytes from the Eastern Cape, from his days in Port Elizabeth; Mbeki himself was a relative newcomer to the ANC leadership. Mandela and Sisulu were joined at the hip. Perhaps it should be remembered, too, that Mandela did not for a moment ever think of himself as other than *primus inter pares*. In *Long Walk to Freedom*, he simply dispatches the issue with the unambiguous assertion, "I served as head of the High Organ."[15] Royalty exercises instinctive prerogatives.

Mbeki, supported by Mhlaba, argued that the leadership was collective, and no individual occupied a special position.* Accordingly, Mandela had no claim on being the only spokesperson for the prisoners. Sisulu argued that Mandela was one of the deputy presidents of the ANC, ranking him at the very least as *primus inter pares.*[16]

The ANC prisoners debated the question over a four-day weekend: Easter 1974. Members of other political parties agreed to leave the ANC to its own doings, giving over the new dining room so that the ANC could fight it out. Finally, Sisulu, as secretary-general of the ANC at the time of his arrest, moved a resolution that called for acknowledgment of Mandela's position as leader of the ANC on Robben Island; Kathrada seconded, and the motion easily carried. Mandela was first among equals.

Differences continued to simmer, and the single-cell prisoners, tired of the bickering among their leaders, decided to dismiss the lot and elect a new High Organ.[17] But this proved no more satisfactory, and after a brief period the original High Organ was reappointed with a rotating fifth person; M. D. Naidoo, Tim's brother, was the first nominee.

Both Masondo and Gqabi were released before Mac; Masondo made his way to Lusaka and was co-opted to the NEC. Not surprising, perhaps, that when Mac finally made his way to Lusaka after his release, his accounts of Mandela's actions in prison were met with skepticism by some senior cadres who were more susceptible to rumors of Mandela having sold out.

---

*A memorandum on the ANC "discord" was smuggled out of Robben Island around 1975. Its author(s) remains anonymous. Its accuracy cannot be vouched for. Whether it made its way to Lusaka is unknown. But Karis and Gerhart observe that "[it] is extraordinary for the severity of its criticism of the four leaders. It describes a recomposition of the High Organ in 1973 and 1974, power struggles, challenges to the status of Mandela as leader and a resolution of the conflict that reinstated the original members of the High Organ and reaffirmed Mandela's leadership." From *Protest to Challenge*, pp. 32–33. Go to [] pre transition/documents and reports/1975/[] for text of memorandum.

In his memoirs, Kathrada alludes to tensions between Mandela and Mbeki, mostly to downplay the clash between the two while conceding that the debate (on the Bantustans) was "certainly tense and heated many times." Walter Sisulu, as one would expect, didn't give Elinor Sisulu much material to work with. She writes, "While he concedes that there was a personality clash between Mandela and Mbeki, Walter argues that the whole affair was greatly exaggerated." Raymond Mhlaba in his memoir, *Personal Memories*, is also evasive, but he does say, "We had many . . . disagreements. Even though our disagreements were acrimonious, we did our best to control the tensions" (p. 140). *The Road to Democracy* also avoids all controversy with only a brief mention of the High Organ as the "leading ANC body on the Island which was comprised of Nelson Mandela, Walter Sisulu, Govan Mbeki, and [Raymond Mhlaba, Ahmed Kathrada, and Wilton Mkwayi were rotating members of this body]," p. 405.

4

Whatever the place of Robben Island in the history of the ANC, Mac's island has a special place in his story. His years there presented boundless opportunities for outwitting prison officials; it was a place where his ingenuity flourished, where he was taken under the guidance of Mandela and Sisulu. They took the elemental destructiveness of Mac's "tough kid" attitude out of him by making him understand that prisoners did not exist as individuals but as part of a collective, that the actions of each had repercussions for all. They integrated him ever more fully into the leadership of the ANC.

Mac

WE WERE SENTENCED in Johannesburg and taken to Number 4 Prison, where we had been awaiting trial. I was twenty-nine years old. We were moved by van to Leeukop Prison, not far outside Johannesburg, while our white colleagues were taken to Pretoria Central. At Leeukop we were put into individual cells. We were given a fairly rough time there—we were assaulted during the exercise periods. In fact, when our attorney, Joel Joffe, came to visit us about ten days later, he hardly recognized us. At the conclusion of his visit, he called the head of the prison and said, "I have brought a copy of the prison regulations. The prisoners are entitled to them, and I'm giving them a copy. Do you have a problem?" He said, "No, no problem; give it to them." But as soon as Joel had left, he took the regulations away and told us to go to hell.

At the beginning of January, Laloo Chiba and I were moved by road to Cape Town. Wilton Mkwayi was left behind. We slept one night in the Port Elizabeth jail, where they picked up other prisoners, including Andrew Masondo. When we got to Robben Island, I was put in isolation in a cell overlooking the quadrangle where the prisoners worked. I was kept there on my own for a few weeks. I was not allowed to go out to work, but I could see the others working in the quadrangle. I could even whisper to some of them. I was able to see Madiba and the others breaking stones, and I was able to see how the comrades were conducting themselves. This was a great, great boon and very useful to me because I had never experienced this kind of imprisonment.

Then I was sent to the single cells—the isolation section. I don't know why they put me in a single cell, but I was very fortunate that they did. Of course I was saying to myself, "I'm not going to accept the treatment they are meting out." It was brutality founded on racism and a deep hatred of our political activities. I had to learn how to behave from the example of others. Learning how to behave was a way of surviving. I quickly learned that getting yourself into trouble usually meant getting others into trouble too.

You inevitably looked to see whom you could identify with—those you knew personally or from the newspapers or the record of the struggle, those like Walter Sisulu, Mandela, Govan Mbeki, Kathrada, and Billy Nair. That anchored me because I was able to look at my own circumstances but not drown in them. You got a sense that you were with people who would help to shape how you would deal with problems. Of course I knew Kathy, and he told them who I was.

There were perhaps thirty of us in the single-cell section. The most senior were the Rivonia Trialists: Madiba, Mbeki, Sisulu, and Raymond Mhlaba. They constituted the High Organ and set policy for the rest of us.

I was living in a concrete cell that was seven feet by seven feet and about nine feet high. It was lit by one forty-watt bulb. It had no furnishings except for a bedroll and a mat—no bench, no table, nothing. We had communal toilets, to which we had no access except when the cells were opened, and we were confined in our cells for an average of fifteen hours on weekdays and seventeen on weekends. During the day, we were sent to break rocks in the quadrangle.

As the years went by, Robben Island changed from being a very harsh to a more relaxed place, largely as a result of our demands. Periodically things would relax, then tighten up again, then relax again. A lot depended on the commanding officer. But we kept demanding improvements and went on hunger strike when necessary, and that improved things as well as strengthened our resolve and our morale.

The food improved over the years, and they gave some prisoners beds. We got desks, then benches, and they allowed us to make our own bookshelves with cardboard. They allowed us to make a homemade draughts board; then they allowed us to buy a chess set. Then they allowed us to hold a concert during Christmastime, then during Easter weekend. We were allowed to mingle more, being left in the quadrangle till later in the day.

Somewhere around 1973 or 1974, Madiba became ill, and he was granted a bed for the first time. And as a result of his back trouble, he was given a chair instead of a bench.

In 1973, we were finally given hot water for our showers. Until then, we had only had cold water, and sometimes it was seawater. But typical of the island administration, we found that these facilities, which we began to enjoy, were then used as forms of punishment. In midwinter, while we were engaged in some struggle against the authorities, suddenly there would be no hot water—and that would go on for weeks and weeks. The same thing would happen with the taped music they were playing for us. Just as we'd gotten used to it, it was taken away, as a form of punishment. Of course, they did not say it was punishment, but suddenly it was out of order for six months or a year.

During our first hunger strike, they made us go to work. And when we got back in the evening, we found that they had put a beautiful plate of food into the cell, and we were locked in there with it. Usually our food was cold, but on those occasions it was warm. And it was better prepared. So all through the night we'd have to smell it but steel ourselves not to touch it.

At first we were made to break rocks in the quadrangle. Later we were put to work in the lime quarry. Still later, around 1973–74, we began to collect seaweed on the shore. We demanded that they give us proper clothing; they provided gum boots but nothing for our hands. We worked with our bare hands, and the seaweed and the cold would rub our fingers raw.

The prison authorities promised the Red Cross that the work in the lime quarry would stop. We were demanding more productive and meaningful work. But they took a long time to stop it—not until about 1975 or 1976.

With the stone breaking as well as the lime quarry work, there was a quota we had to fill. Common-law prisoners—criminals, murderers, and rapists—delivered the larger stones to us where we were seated. We had to break the stones into pebbles, and at the end of the day the warders would come and measure what we had done.

We could only get up with the express permission of the warder, say, to go to the toilet or for lunch. We could get up, but we couldn't walk around. None of us were fulfilling our quotas, and they were threatening punishment. Madiba told us, "Look, don't be terrorized by these demands. Yes, work away, but work at your pace."

Later, at the lime quarry, they couldn't measure individual work, so they told us that we had so many truckloads of lime to dig up. This was better than stone breaking; for one thing, we could communicate more easily. We could talk in little clusters as we were working, and at lunchtime, when we dispersed to sit in the shed and eat, we were able to talk in a larger body.

We organized study clusters according to subjects, and we had particular people who would teach certain subjects. Those who were doing the teaching would get together beforehand and agree on a "curriculum." We had many heated debates and discussions, then and later, about everything from politics to strategy to issues of food and clothing. Over the years we studied the struggle in every form.

At an earlier point, when we were having discussion groups in the lime quarry, we got so involved that eventually we reached a point where we were just not working at all. Things came to a standstill. We would just go there and stick our spades into the ground and use them as a seat to lean on and start having classes—history, isiXhosa, English. The warders would try to push us to work, and we would stop talking, take up a pick and dig once or twice, and then stop.

Things got so bad that on one occasion the commanding officer, Colonel Van Aarde, called Mandela into his office. He said, "Mandela, it's unacceptable. My warders and I have lost control. You people are prisoners, but you're totally ignoring our authority."

Madiba said, "Well, I will go and inform my fellow prisoners of what you've said, and I will see what they have to say and where it goes from there." Cleverly, by saying that, he legitimized a meeting of prisoners. Madiba posed this problem to us, and of course we went for Madiba: "Ag, you come back bringing the message of this bloody colonel! You want us to become warders over ourselves?" But after we discussed the issue, we said, "OK, OK, the colonel has got a point. Chaps, can we make it a rule that when the colonel arrives for inspection, we at least make a show of doing a bit of work?"

The colonel had no choice but to recognize Mandela's authority.

It was a game of cat and mouse with the authorities in terms of what we could refuse to do and how they would react. We needed to find ways to refuse that were valid, and we tried to negotiate collectively. We felt we had something to do. We wanted to have our demands met. Our central issues were unconditional release, treatment while in prison as political prisoners, and the removal of all racial discrimination among prisoners. We knew the last, on its own, was a program we could not win altogether, since it was dependent on the wider struggle. But it gave us something to fight for. The fact that we had come to prison as political fighters and were kept together gave us an opportunity to act as a collective.

But we knew that our freedom wouldn't come from negotiation with the enemy. We saw that it was related directly to the struggle outside. Our morale and spirit were helped by the fact that even with all the repression and intimidation, our operations had continued to survive underground. The struggle had carried on despite the blunders and the casualties. That the jails were being filled with more and more people testified to the presence of the organization, to the fact that it continued to live, continued to fight. Then there was the mood of the people themselves: the evidence from the 1970s of a mounting mass of campaigns from our people, a rising tide of anger culminating in the explosions of Soweto and post-Soweto.[18] All these events were evidence to us that the conditions were there for our victory. That we believed.

Mentors

I developed a very close relationship with Mandela and with Walter. It took time to get close to Madiba. I think the way he was brought up in the Xhosa royal household gave him the ability to be friendly and appear to be open with everybody but at the same time keep a distance.

Madiba is very shrewd. He took an interest in every prisoner, and at work he would quietly question you—your background, your family, everything. He would find a special way of addressing you. Take Billy Nair. His family came from South India, so he would speak Tamil or Telugu. Mandela somehow found out surreptitiously what the words were in Telugu for big brother and small brother, younger and elder: *thumbi* for younger brother and *anné* for elder brother, a respectful term. Then Mandela began to call Billy Thumbi, and Billy unobtrusively slipped into calling him Anné.

He used to call me Neef. That means nephew in Afrikaans, but traditionally it is also an affectionate term of address. Of course I was pleased, and I began to respond with Oom, Uncle. Looking back, I can see it was also a way of wrapping us into a relationship in which we had to maintain a certain respect.

When Mandela was worried about something, he did not come out with it easily. His eldest son, Thembi, and his own mother, Nosekeni Fanny, died while I was in prison with him—both deaths were severe blows to him.[19] When he returned from hearing the news, he just stayed in his cell and kept out of the way. Walter noticed this and went to his cell, and he stayed with him a long time, talking to him. By the next morning, Mandela was his usual self. He never complained about personal problems to other prisoners. But when taking complaints to prison authorities, he would show tremendous persistence and stubbornness. So on the one hand, he was kind, gentle, and warm, but he had also toughened himself.

When he acted, it was in a cool and analytical way, and then he followed through with tremendous perseverance.

His views on many matters changed; his understanding of the struggle deepened through the exchange of ideas with other comrades in prison. But he always gave unqualified support to the leadership of the ANC inside the country and abroad. He was completely opposed to any collaboration with the regime. In the early 1950s, his stance had been one of narrow nationalism, almost with racial undertones vis-à-vis other population groups. He was also anti-Communist. But his analysis of the situation in the country in later years led him to modify his views.

In many ways, like all of us, Madiba changed over the years. I think that in prison his anger and hatred of the system increased, but the manifestations of that anger became less visible. They were subdued, tempered. He became cold and analytical in focusing on the evils of the system. Madiba was meticulous in examining issues. Once he had arrived at a position, he was extremely stubborn, almost unshakable. At the same time, he was very dignified and extremely ruthless in debate. He prepared well, and he would pin you with questions; he would be relentless.

Walter, on the other hand, never came across as holding unshakable positions. He had his views, he was a very good listener, but he would probe you very gently. I have always said that he inspired us to think outside the box because he never tried to crush us in debate.

There was something very, very special about Walter. He did not have that sense of inferiority that many people living under oppression acquire, or the countering overassertiveness such people often take on. There was no issue that I couldn't take to Walter. I was never met with a dismissal. I would go to Walter with crazy ideas, but he wouldn't say they were crazy. Instead, he would inspire me to investigate those ideas further, and in that way he would often bring me back to a sober position. He was a great encouragement.

Walter interacted as an equal with those who had a superior education. It's a remarkable ability. Oliver Tambo, who was a mathematician, and Anton Lembede, a philosopher with an MA, a lawyer—they were among those who used to gather at Walter's home in the early 1940s for intellectual discussion. Walter was like a magnet drawing them all to him.

Walter and Madiba had the greatest regard for each other's perceptions of strategy and tactics. Nelson had the determination to grapple with ideas, even to the point of stubbornness, but I think he understood that what Walter brought to the debate was a deep understanding of the human psyche.

I went to prison at the age of twenty-nine and came out when I was forty-one. These are very important years in anybody's life, your thirties. You are at the peak of your mental and physical abilities, and prison can be a very debilitating place. I went through all that personal agony. But against that, I had the privilege of living with people of a very high caliber. We interacted closely, debating vigorously and often acrimoniously. But in the end, the presence of Walter, the presence of Madiba, and seeing how they conducted themselves were major influences in my life.

Whither the SACP?

Wilton Mkwayi and I were among some of the comrades who said we needed to create not just the ANC but also the Communist Party inside prison, but Madiba opposed that. In our debates Madiba challenged us, those of us who were saying re-create the party. Madiba said, "We are living here in prison. Any political organization that we create is illegal. What are the tasks we need to perform here? First and foremost, we need to hold ourselves together as a single force. Do you need two organizations to do that? We need to educate ourselves politically and keep ourselves alive. Do we need two organizations for that?" When I said to him, "What about Marxism?" he said, "In the political education we carry out, we will have space for the members to study Marxism as well. Now what's your objection?" I said, "Well, there's a special discipline to the party." He said, "How special is that discipline in the conditions in which you are living—how different from the discipline that will be brought to you by the ANC? Do you need two parallel organizations? Won't that create more problems for us than it resolves?" I had to concede that he was right. We had to interact with our comrades and persuade them that such division was not productive, and that we should be united within the ANC group.

The debate on this was inside the party, but because we were living cheek by jowl, it inevitably flowed beyond party boundaries. It's not possible, sitting in prison in an isolation cell, to have a debate and think that your disagreements would not become known to others. It happened in the main section of the prison. Certain comrades, including Harry Gwala, a longtime hard-line Communist, formed a group called Mpabanga, which means "we the poor." Harry gave lectures on things like "the labor theory of value." That became a cover for some comrades to organize themselves into a Communist cell. The result was divisions in our ranks. Some comrades were excluded from these lectures when they tried to attend, and they were upset. I didn't know it at the time, but I was to have many run-ins with Harry in later years, and all involved issues where he was being a divisive influence.

So I suppose you could say that Mandela opened us to membership in the ANC before the Morogoro conference opened membership to alliance partners in 1969. The irony for me was that Mandela himself had originally opposed the alliance with the Natal Indian Congress (NIC) back in the early fifties.

The Daily Round

The daily routine on Robben Island varied over the years. Toward the end of my imprisonment, when conditions had improved somewhat, it went something like this: We were wakened at 5:00 A.M. in summer, 6:00 A.M. in the winter. We then went out through the corridor into a section where there were communal baths and toilets. Half an hour was allotted for everyone to wash and to clean their sanitary pails. There were about four sinks for all thirty of us. It was mandatory that we shave as well as clean our sanitary pails. If we wanted to have a bath, we had to have it within that half hour.

Then we collected our food. The food was brought into the section in drums, and we then dished it out ourselves, organized into teams for this purpose. We had our breakfast, and within an hour after the opening of the doors, we were supposed to fall in unless, of course, the warders were late. We then went out to work. We were not allowed to talk at work. In the early years we were allowed the luxury of walking to our workplace, which enabled us to see something of the island, but later they moved us by truck to prevent us from coming across any other prisoners. At work, say, collecting seaweed, we did it until lunchtime, an hour's break. Again, the food was brought in drums; we dished it out, sat down on the ground, and ate. We knocked off work at any time between 3:30 and 4:00 P.M., the timing determined by the fact that we had to be back in the prison with about half an hour for all the prisoners to have a bath before supper, which was dished out and cleared by the prisoners before we were locked up at 4:30 or 4:45 P.M. so the warders could sign off by 5:00 P.M. and the next shift of warders could come on.

From five o'clock, if we did not have study privileges, we were allowed to be up and about in our cells until eight o'clock, when we were supposed to go to bed. Those who had study privileges were allowed to study at the level of matriculation until ten o'clock at night, those at the university level until eleven. When we were supposed to go to sleep, the lights

remained on, but we were not allowed to read. If a warder found you reading after those hours, he could have you punished. In the early 1970s, they
introduced a canned-music broadcast. This was played from about six to
eight o'clock. On no account were you allowed to sing or whistle, either
individually or communally.

That was the typical day.

On Saturdays and Sundays we were locked up for longer periods. Our
cells were opened up later and closed earlier. At lunchtime on weekends
and public holidays, we did not have access to our fellow prisoners; we
were locked up in our cells. Otherwise, the days were the same. In one way
it was monotonous, but in another sense every day was different because
we were able to talk with one another, despite the warders and the regulations, and develop friendships and comradeship and find that we had new
things to talk about.

Attempting to Escape

From the first day of my detention, I began trying to escape. I almost escaped from Marshall Square. On the island I consulted Walter and
Madiba. Walter said that although the idea of my escaping was acceptable
in principle, he would like me to abide by the condition that if it came to
it, I would escape with either Madiba or himself—not both, but one of
them. He stressed that I should make sure one of them was with me because after that, the doors would be closed even more tightly.

An opportunity arose when Wilton, Madiba, and I were taken together
to the dentist in Cape Town. I had been taken to the dentist before, alone,
and had seen how this could be a potential opportunity to escape. When I
was taken there alone, in 1973, I was shackled and handcuffed. I arrived at
the dental surgery escorted by two warders; the surgery was upstairs on
the second floor.

They had obviously cleared the place of all other patients. I was still
shackled and handcuffed, and one of the warders accompanied me when I
went into the surgery. I was put in the dental chair. The dentist and I
greeted each other, and then I took a chance. I said, "Doctor, I find it unacceptable that I should be treated while I'm shackled and handcuffed. I
don't think that's right." I was surprised when he supported me. He turned
to the warder and said, "I cannot treat this man unless you take off the
shackles and handcuffs." The warder obeyed the dentist.

Having succeeded with that, I went further. I said, "I also find it unacceptable that you should treat me with another person who's not an assis-

tant sitting in the room." And, surprise, the dentist said to the warder, "Will you please leave the room. You can stand outside the closed door." So the warder left. As the dentist was examining me, he told me his brother-in-law was a chap called Cyril Jones, a white comrade who had been detained around the time we were arrested and sentenced to two years' imprisonment for possession of Marxist literature.

This interaction with the dentist got me thinking about the possibility of escape. I told Madiba and Walter, and a few months later we all put our names down for dental treatment. We had no elaborate plans; we would improvise. We knew a comrade, Tofi Bardien, who ran a taxi on the Grand Parade in Cape Town. We planned to get from the surgery to the parade, and we knew various people in Cape Town.

On the day we went to the dentist, we were taken from our cells at 5:00 A.M. and handcuffed, shackled, and taken to the boat. We were put in the hold. Madiba said to the warder, "It's against maritime law that we should be transported on the high seas with shackles and handcuffs." So the warders came back and released us from our shackles and handcuffs for the trip to Cape Town. We got to the docks, and there was a prison van there. When we got off the ship, they handcuffed us again and pushed us into the van and locked it.

It was a closed prison van. I began to search it and found a knife in a crevice. I showed it to the others, and we all became excited because we had been wondering how to overwhelm the warders. I hid the knife in my pocket. We were very tense, and I had a great sense of alertness. I was looking for every possibility, the gap when it would be the moment to overpower the warders. When I found the knife, I was elated.

We got to the dentist, and the waiting room was empty. We were trying to decide when we should pounce on the warders. Madiba said to the warders, "You'd better take off the handcuffs." They protested, but they took them off. I was standing near the window overlooking the street, and I noticed a lack of activity: no pedestrians moving, no vehicles moving. I said, "This is a trap. It's all working too smoothly." I called Madiba to the window, and I whispered to him, "Look." So he looked down and said, "What is it?" I said, "There's no movement, no pedestrians, no cars in the street. They took off our shackles, and they've taken off our handcuffs." Madiba instantly saw the problem and said, "You're right, it's off."

We had our dental treatment, and then we were put in the van. But we were not taken back to the docks. We were taken to Roeland Street Prison and put in a big communal cell, just the three of us. I suspected they had put us in a bugged cell. They wanted to find out why we had not tried to escape. I had a little piece of lead pencil, and I wrote on some toilet paper: "No talking—only innocent conversation."

They held us there for about an hour or two, and then we were taken back to the docks and returned to Robben Island, where we reviewed the matter briefly. Madiba and I were convinced that, somehow or other, perhaps by bugging our cells, the authorities had realized that we were planning an escape. They had set it up in such a way that we would attempt the escape, and Madiba would be killed. I said, "Guys, I've spent ten years here. I can last another two years."[20]

The authorities must have planted the knife. There must have been someone trying to anticipate how we were thinking. We made no further attempts to escape because they had got wind of our plans, and we suspected they were determined to kill Madiba, using the attempted escape as an excuse. The lives of Madiba and Walter, even separately, were too important to the struggle for us to risk them. When Eddie Daniels was released after serving a fifteen-year sentence, he put together a proposal for how we could snatch Madiba out of jail from the outside. Madiba went along with the proposal, provided OR (Oliver Tambo) agreed.[21] The proposal reached Tambo, but it was never acted on. Perhaps he also felt it was too great a risk to take with Madiba's life.

Making Demands

We demanded to hear radio news, but this request was turned down outright. So we began to ask for music from the radio to be played to us. They also turned down this one, but they began to tape music and play it over the intercom. Then we asked to be allowed to buy, through the authorities, with money our families and friends sent some of us, certain music records that would meet our tastes. For a while they agreed and allowed it. We listened to the songs of Louis Armstrong, Ella Fitzgerald, and even Joan Baez! We also got records by many local artists. A record by Margaret Singana was very popular.

Often the authorities were unaware of what they had allowed in. After some time they realized we were using our privilege for making written requests about which records they should select to play each evening as a way of communicating between the different sections of the prison. So they stopped the taped music. We had the same situation with books. Books we ordered from the state library for our studies were sometimes censored.

There were other changes to our working conditions and recreation.

First they had us breaking stones with a hammer. Then we were stuck in the quarry till the 1970s. Then they stopped taking the prisoners out to work. First we were allowed to play quoits,* and then we built the volley-ball court in the quadrangle. Later they allowed us to play soccer in the veld, on a Saturday. Then they stopped that. It kept changing, but the work regimen became easier over time. There was also a steady improvement in our diet, and there was a bit of relaxation. But with the loosening of one shackle, another would be tightened. If they relaxed the overt physical brutality, they would increase the psychological brutality. It was a constant battle of wits.

But overall I would have to say that things did change. In the early years we had not only psychological forms of pressure but also open bru-tality. In this sense we in the single cells were better off than prisoners in the main sections. A number of us were assaulted and beaten up, but it was not as common as it was in the main sections, where assaults were communal in character—what the prison staff called a carry on, when they used not just batons but even pickax handles. In our section there was more restraint because the world was watching what was happening to Mandela and others. And as the Anti-Apartheid Movement grew, the fo-cus on Mandela and prison conditions became more intense.

Interestingly, open brutality was not used in 1976 after the Soweto up-rising† but the pressure was intense. There was a desperate effort by the authorities to cut us off from any news sources. There was a drive to work out how we were smuggling out news and to sever those links. There was a month or two of total isolation.

There was also the campaign outside—in and outside South Africa—for the release of political prisoners, for better treatment of them. I only became fully aware of the extent of this campaign after I was released, but in prison we could see evidence of it. We had visits from the Red Cross and prominent people came to the island to meet Mandela.

As I have said, we saw ourselves as political hostages, and our treat-ment fluctuated. We believed our conditions embodied the basic aims of

---

*The game was called tenniquoits. It was played with a ring made of plastic or rubber. Teams were two on a side that served and played, much like tennis, across a net that was perhaps the height of a volleyball net.
†On 16 June 1976, about fifteen thousand students, organized by the Soweto Student Representative Council (SRC), gathered to demonstrate against the compulsory use of Afrikaans as the medium of instruction in African schools. After failing to disperse them with tear gas, the police opened fire, killing at least three students and injuring many others, sparking the Soweto uprising. See Chapter 9, pages 189 and 190.

prison authorities. Whatever techniques they used were designed for one purpose: to demoralize us both as human beings and as freedom fighters. To the extent that improvements took place, the regime was responding to pressure, and whenever it was forced to give in, it would tighten up in some other way.

International pressure helped to keep up our morale. You can adapt to the worst of conditions if you feel you are not alone, if you feel you have support, and if you feel you are there for a just cause, one that will triumph. International opinion did not manage to make any significant or fundamental change, but it helped us to survive our imprisonment. Our treatment was also related to the general development of the struggle in southern Africa.

Long Journey from D to A

The Prison Board would sit once a year and, among other things, look at a prisoner's conduct and establish his classification on the A to D scale. Mandela eventually became an A-group prisoner, but only, I think, after I left prison.

We were D for years, all of us. Eventually, sometime in the 1970s, we were moved up to C until some got promoted to the B group. A few even made it to the A group. The A group was allowed one letter and one or two visits per month. The category determined how much paper we got to write letters and whether we could buy groceries like tea or coffee. We had to buy them from the prison authorities with money from our families. I moved up to B group around 1975 and was promptly demoted back to C or D group because I tried to bribe a warder to supply me with newspapers.

We considered it a right to pursue our studies, but the authorities considered it a privilege they could use to make us toe the line. All courses were of course by correspondence. For matric, prisoners studied through Rapid Results College and all university courses were completed through the University of South Africa (UNISA). Any trouble and your study rights were taken away.

I applied for study permission. They didn't grant it until 1966. Later they restricted us to doing undergraduate degrees. That restriction was in force until 1968, when I graduated with a bachelor of administration degree and applied for permission to do honors. I was turned down, even though Govan Mbeki and Neville Alexander were granted permission the same year. No reasons were given. The following year they introduced a blanket ban: no postgraduate degrees at all. They also tried to restrict what we could study. In 1969, I applied for permission to study Afrikaans at the Standard 6 level plus shorthand and art at the matric level. I wanted to do shorthand and typing, but they refused the typing. They gave me permission to study shorthand and art.

My reason for choosing shorthand arose out of an interesting debate with Madiba about whether the authorities would allow a prisoner to have a watch in his possession. I said that if I got permission to do shorthand, I would also have to get permission to have a watch to time myself. So when I was granted permission to do shorthand, I registered, paid the fees, and then I demanded the watch. As soon as I got it, Madiba was in the queue demanding a watch for himself on the grounds that it could not be dangerous for a prisoner to have a watch to better organize his studies, etc.

They allowed us textbooks, and we used this as a way to smuggle in other titles. The university courses also had a list of recommended reading, so we subscribed to the state library, the only library they allowed us to join. Then we began to smuggle books in through the state library and by other means. Now and then we got caught.

While we were classified as D prisoners, we were allowed to receive one letter of five hundred words every six months and to send one of five hundred words. They tried to restrict them to our relatives and to avoid anybody who was politically connected. They monitored conversations, such as one I had with my nephew, and later quoted me, saying, "He expressed views which say he will never change."[22] The letters were heavily censored.

I was a member of the Communications Committee, which was created to establish clandestine communications with the prisoners in the communal section. Part of my work was also to get hold of news from the outside. One warder was an older man, a Seventh-Day Adventist or Jehovah's Witness. One night when he was on duty, he went along to Kathy with a quiz or crossword competition in an Afrikaans paper and asked Kathy to help. Kathy is more competent in Afrikaans than I am, but he sent this warder to me, perhaps because he saw an opportunity. The warder came; I did the quiz and gave it back to him.

A few weeks later the old man turned up and told me he had won the competition and what would I like as thanks? Something to eat? I said no thanks, but perhaps a packet of cigarettes? He agreed and the next day he brought me a packet.

When the others heard this, they laughed, "Trust you to want cigarettes." I said, "No, no, no. I wanted the cigarettes because to give them to me, he had to touch the packet, and so his fingerprints are on it. I don't intend to smoke them, and my next move is to get newspapers. If he doesn't want to cooperate, I'll let him know I've got his fingerprints on this packet of cigarettes, which we are not supposed to have." Walter said, "That's immoral. That's blackmail." I said, "I need the threat."

Anyway, the warder came back the following week to say he was now short-listed for another round of the competition. I said, "OK, bring it here." He brought me the page, and I said to him, "No, bring the whole newspaper." He said, "I'll get into trouble." I said, "Give it to me, and I'll give it back to you." So he gave me the newspaper, I did the quiz, and I gave it back.

Eventually I persuaded him to bring me newspapers regularly, which I would read and transcribe parts of, writing very fast. Then I would give the newspapers back to him, but we had the news and could circulate it among ourselves.

Walter loved to get the news. He would come to me privately for it, and I had to repeat it two, three times. He wanted to hear it—it was so rich. I had become proficient at translating very rapidly, and I began to tell the warder which newspapers I wanted. I would say, "Here's some money; go and buy the foreign newspapers."

I wanted to get money from abroad, and with the permission of the Communications Committee and Madiba and Walter, I set up communications with London. I wanted to do all sorts of smuggling, and I needed cash to bribe warders to enable these communications and also for the possibility of escape.

They asked how I would get this money. I said, "I'm going to send a letter to London." I remembered a London address I had used after the Rivonia arrests to stay in touch with Vella Pillay and Dr. Yusuf Dadoo. It was for Elizabeth Edwards, at an address in Kentish Town. I told them, "If the same occupant is still there, they will know to take this letter to Vella." They said, "OK, but what about the contents?" I said I would use milk as invisible ink.

I wrote the letter, leaving reasonable spaces between the lines, in which I wrote a message in milk. I couldn't sign it with my own name in case the authorities found it. But how could I let Vella know it was from me? I remembered that his wife, Patsy, when she was in the Young Communists League, once shared a flat with Ruth First in Twist Street, Hillbrow. So in the overt content of the letter to "Dear Elizabeth," I wrote a very casual, chatty letter, mentioning in passing that I had been thinking of old times when P used to share this flat. I wrote, "Those memories reminded me of you, Elizabeth."

In the invisible part I asked for a hundred pounds to be sent to a particular address. And I wrote, "Don't treat any further communications as authentic unless the overt portion refers to incidents similar to what I've mentioned today. I will always refer to a unique incident between us, a very small thing, like going to that party where we had an argument with Barbara Castle. There's no way anyone who was not there could know about this."

Again the warder helped me. I gave the letter to him, and he posted it. And it worked! The warder designated the address to which a response should be sent. Some months later he came to me with a hundred pounds in small notes. Years later, Vella told me this letter caused a furious argument between him, Dr. Dadoo, and Joe Slovo: Was it a trap? Was it authentic? Would it get him into serious trouble, and how had I managed to get it off Robben Island? Finally one of them said, "But what do we have to lose? Suppose it *is* Mac—let's take a chance and send it." And that's how I got the hundred pounds.[23]

Visitation Rights

The best category, the A group, had one or two visits a month. In D category you were allowed one visit every six months. In twelve years I must have had at least twenty-four visits because I was allowed one every six months. The warders and the Security Branch kept lists of who visited me and when.

My Mum visited me, and my brothers. My sisters did not. I don't think they could afford it. Once, a nephew visited me. Once or twice someone not related to me managed by some subterfuge to visit me. You could get access to lawyers by permission of the prison authorities; you had to justify why the lawyer had to see you, but these were not regarded as visits.

Indian visitors had to get several permits: one to come from Natal to Cape Town, one to drive through the Free State, and one from Robben Island, as well as permission from the Security Branch (SB). It could take up to six months to organize. It was an ordeal. Visitors would have to send their ID cards and all their particulars. The Security Branch in their hometowns would call on them to question them.

Tim left the country for London in 1973, on an exit permit. She couldn't take the harassment anymore; the constant SB surveillance made it difficult for her to keep a job. She had trouble wherever she went. She visited me before she left, but they wouldn't allow a contact visit. After that, the visits became fewer. Visits were very unsatisfying. My mother visited me about six times. She was constrained by the expense and by needing somebody to accompany her. She had to travel from Newcastle to Jo'burg and then to Cape Town, two separate train journeys. If she drove with a relative, it was a good twenty- to twenty-four hour drive. They could make no stopovers along the way because there were no hotels for blacks, so they had to take food and blankets with them.

Dodging the Rules

Any system overburdened with rules becomes capricious, and so it creates a set of openings. But you have to have a certain kind of mind-set to identify the openings and exploit them. We were not allowed anything in our cells. We were not allowed to smoke. Where do you hide tobacco in your cell when it is always being searched? They had given us large plastic water bottles with a small manufacturer's label gummed on. So after I had managed to smuggle in a bit of tobacco, I rolled it up in tissue paper; then I took that small gummed label and cut it into narrow strips and pasted the rolled-up tobacco under the bottom edge of the door. The warders never thought to look there.

We collected things for later use—a piece of wire from work, a piece of rusty metal. We never knew when even the most useless-looking object might come in handy. We used a small fragment of a hacksaw blade to make keys. We also made false compartments in shoes.

When they gave us benches, in 1971 or so, I made a concealed compartment in mine. At first I used it to stash communications, but later we were able to smuggle in a transistor radio, and we also hid it in that compartment. We got the radio through George Naicker. He was part of a group of people in the communal cells who had managed to get a warder to get them a radio. Then they smuggled it to our single cells, to me—a battery-operated transistor radio.

The bench was just a stool, really—two flat pieces of wood for legs and a flat top as the seat, with side panels to give it stability. The side panels were just four-inch planks screwed on at the top of each side. Laloo Chiba and I took these side panels and unscrewed them. On the inside of the leg sections we cut a groove, and using any pieces of wood we could find, like tomato boxes, installed another layer below the seat, making a compartment there, about an inch and a half deep. But the workmanship wasn't the best. Because I worked on the paint team, I had access to paint; so we painted the stool to make it look better. Then we painted the seats in every cell so that they all looked the same.

We got an earphone for the radio, and we would listen to the news at night when we were locked up. We smuggled batteries through the communal section or through a warden. I was secretly writing a novel. I think I was on chapter six or seven, but that was abuse of study privilege, so I used to hide it in there with the radio. This continued through 1971.

The Raid

On 28 May 1971, a Friday night, we were raided and assaulted by the warders, who burst in on us unexpectedly at about eight o'clock in the evening. We were on a hunger strike in solidarity with the SWAPO prisoners. It was bitterly cold, and many of us were already asleep.

Suddenly the doors opened and a large group of warders came in, many of them drunk. They had just come from the criminal prison, where they had beaten up many of the prisoners. They made us strip, all of us, and they made us stand against the wall with our hands up for a very long time with our backs facing them. I don't know how long we stood that way while they searched the cells. (It was during this raid that Govan Mbeki collapsed with what seemed to be a mild heart attack.)

The bench with the radio was in Laloo's cell that night. The warders literally tore the cells apart—they even opened the toilet rolls to see if we had written on them and rerolled them. During the search, one warder actually picked up the bench and put it down again. But they found nothing.

After the raid, Madiba checked with me to see if the radio was safe. Then Walter came to me and said, "Instructions: destroy the radio." He said that if it had been found, it would have meant collective punishment for the whole section. I said, "But, old man, do you know how long we struggled to smuggle in this radio?" He said, "I know, but destroy it." I said, "Well, don't ever ask me to smuggle in a radio again." Then he said to me, "And that novel you are writing—destroy that." I said, "What? No, no, you can't do this to me." He said, "When you get out of prison, you can write the novel."

A few weeks after the raid, Walter came to see us, the communications team: "Chaps, what are you doing about news?" I said, "Don't come to me with that nonsense."

The Keys to . . .

But that didn't stop us from finding other ways to get around the rules. We made copies of the keys to the single cells. First we made a master key, over the Easter weekend in 1971 or 1972. Jafta Masemola and two others in the communal section were caught with keys. Jafta was transferred to our section. I told Kathy that, even though Jafta was in the PAC, I thought I could persuade him to bring his technical knowledge to bear on how to make a key. We agreed on the project. I had collected a piece of rusted metal, a little piece of a hacksaw blade, and a small triangular file—all of which I kept hidden away.

I approached Jafta, and he agreed to help me make the key. We had to file the piece of iron on both sides until it was shiny and smooth. We smeared it with lard from our breakfast bread, then put it into the keyhole, turned it, then pulled it out gently to see where the obstruction was. Then we filed it bit by bit.

So that Easter weekend I lined up Kathy and Laloo Chiba and, I think, Michael Dingake to help. Chiba, Jafta, and I were in the cell working on the key while Kathy and Michael patrolled the corridor to warn us, not only if a warder came past, but also if any prisoner came near. Nobody else was to suspect what we were doing.

It worked. We made a single key that would serve as the key for the grille but also do the master locking. We found that by making the master key we could open the door sealing off the corridor, and we could open the door on the ramp. The master key worked for all locks. We could have walked into the sunshine outside the prison, but we had nowhere to go. But the knowledge that we had come that far, right under the noses of our jailers, allowed us to believe that anything was possible. Now we had to make a second key, the key for the outer wooden door of our cells in front of the steel grille.

The wooden door, unlike the steel grille, had no keyhole on the prisoner's side. This key was kept by the warder, at that time a chap named Van Zyl, who had an extremely volatile temper. We used to call him Rooibos.

So one day when the rest went out to work I got hold of Laloo Chiba and said, "Make some excuse, don't go to work today." During the morning I said to him, "Now here's a piece of soap, I want you to make an imprint of this particular key from the warder's bunch of keys. I am going to go and provoke Rooibos and make him come out of his office, leaving the bunch of keys on the desk."

I studied the dictionary for ways to insult Rooibos and provoke him in

Afrikaans and then I walked into his office and he asked me what I wanted. "Oh, I've come to have a chat with you, *meneer.*" I start a polite conversation, we're talking about something whether it's sports or whatever, just chatting away. And then I insult him and he insults me and he tells me that he will kill me. I throw in all these insulting Afrikaans words now and he gets furious and he jumps up to assault me and I run out into the quadrangle and while he's chasing me Laloo has nipped in, made an imprint on the soap, and we've got the imprint of the key. So now we can start finding the piece of metal to shape it to that key imprint and we've got the key.

The keys were in our possession for about four years. We hid them in the secret bench compartments. There were about eighty cells in our section but only thirty of us. Since we had access to all the cells, we were able to use the empty ones to store all kinds of stuff, secure in the knowledge that the warders would never search them. After some time, Madiba and Walter sent a message to say that the keys were too dangerous and had to be hidden outside or destroyed. It was nearing my release time, so I gave them to the others to hide; I didn't want to know where. They buried them in the quarry. But later the authorities bulldozed the quarry, so we couldn't find them.

Mandela's Autobiography

Kathy originally had the idea that Madiba should write an autobiography, and that it should coincide with my departure. Until then we had never smuggled out anything elaborate. Kathy felt that with my release coming up in about a year's time, I would be the ideal person to smuggle out the manuscript because I was always coming up with new ideas about how to smuggle things.

We were preoccupied in 1975; the struggle was still moving very slowly. Madiba's sixtieth birthday was coming up in 1978, and we thought it would be a good idea if he wrote his autobiography. I would smuggle it out, and maybe it could be published to coincide with his birthday, both as a record of and an inspiration to the struggle. So that's how Kathy came up with the idea. Walter agreed. Madiba agreed, and we worked on it. As Madiba drafted the pages, he gave them to me. For security reasons, he would write at night, and first thing each morning he would give me what he had written the night before.

My job was to transcribe it and prepare it for concealment, for smuggling. Every evening I would set about miniaturizing the text. I used a ball-point pen and pieces of A4 paper, full pages, both sides. I wrote out the text, leaving a one-centimeter margin around the lines so I could cut it into strips for concealment. I could reduce probably eight, ten pages onto one side. My writing was very small. But while I was transcribing, I was also writing down questions. After I'd done that, I would take Madiba's original and pass it on to Kathy. I would conceal the copy I had made so that if the prison authorities stumbled onto what Madiba was writing, I had a copy. Kathy would read it and note his own queries. Then he would give it to Walter, who added more questions.

In the meantime, I was discussing what Madiba had written the previous day, raising my queries with him. If it was a question of interpretation, or a factual issue, corrections had to be made as we passed it along between us. But remember, I'd written a copy and concealed it, so the next night I would enter additional cryptic notes. In the meantime, I would be on to the next set of pages.

There was no chance to give it back to Madiba to correct. Madiba would just say, "Take that into account when you finalize it, but in the meantime, note it in the material." When Kathy was finished, he was responsible for hiding the original in Madiba's handwriting so it would not be found during any raids by prison authorities. I had a great opportunity to familiarize myself with the details while I was doing the transcribing. Later I had a second chance in London while I was working on the typed version. The miniaturized copy ran to about 60 sheets. That's 120 pages.

We were aware of the dangers we faced and took steps to avoid being caught. Since Kathy was taking care of the original in Madiba's handwriting, we agreed I shouldn't know where these pages were hidden. We had to ensure that one version survived even if I was caught smuggling out the copy. We also had to guard against my talking under torture if I was caught.

Laloo and I worked out how we would smuggle out the miniature version. I had registered with UNISA for my second-year BSc course. I wanted to ensure that when I was removed from Robben Island, I could demand to take along my boxes of study materials and books. We concealed some messages in the covers of hardcover notebooks. We did this by splitting the cover carefully, inserting a page and resealing the cover. This was a very effective method, but each notebook could only accommodate a few sheets.

After we completed the Mandela autobiography, I initiated the essay project. I got the go-ahead from Mandela to ask each of the eight senior comrades to write an essay on the main issues the struggle was facing.[24] These also had to be miniaturized, but they took up a large number of sheets. So Laloo and I came up with a different idea. We decided to use a large clip file because its cover was double the size of a A4 sheet. In it I would store my set of maps from the South African Bureau of Statistics, material that was germane to studies for my economics major in the bachelor of administration degree. This allowed us to make two A4-size spaces in each cover of the file, a total of four spaces. It also allowed us to conceal both sets of manuscript—at least the bulk of them—in that one file. Other material was hidden in the hard covers of A4-size notebooks and inside the covers of hardback textbooks.

In the meantime, Kathy put the originals into several tins that were carefully sealed and then buried underground in the strip of a garden we had been allowed to make in the quadrangle. Sometime in 1978, after the arrival of the Black Consciousness (BC) prisoners, the authorities decided to construct a wall to separate from our single-cells section a usually empty wing, in which some of the BC members were to be housed. During the construction of the wall they dug up the garden and accidentally found some of the tins.

The authorities were excited by their find, but Madiba, Kathy, and others—I think Laloo and Eddie Daniels—went into action to save as many of the buried tins as possible. The texts found by the authorities were clearly in Madiba's handwriting. The margins had notes in the handwriting of Walter and Kathy. The authorities wanted as little fuss as possible because they did not want the public to know Madiba had been busy writing his autobiography. They punished the three of them—Mandela, Walter, and Kathy—by depriving them of study privileges for a few years. They didn't realize the text had already escaped!

Three Wise Men

I taught classes as well. One of my groups consisted of three old men from the Transkei. They had not come in as political activists. They had killed a headman in the Transkei in 1963 in the ferment over cattle culling and fencing. They had led the rebellion and killed the headman, so they were serving life imprisonment. These three ended up in our section: Baba Mvulane, Baba Batane, and the third one, whose name was Tausand. We used to call him Tausand Dollars.

They were really illiterate—not just in English but even in Xhosa. I was teaching English, the ABCs. We convinced them that they had to become literate. For their literacy class and the basic subjects, we designed a course equivalent to what was going on in the schools in social studies. We talked about the universe, about natural phenomena, and about society and how it functions. That class was assigned to me. I used to conduct the class by outlining a field or subject, giving them a talk on it, and then engaging them in questions and answers.

One day I was teaching them about the universe, about the sun and the planetary system. I was thinking of the basic things I had learned in school: that the sun appears to go around the earth, but in fact the earth is going around the sun, and so on. But when I said it was time for questions and clarification, they were silent. There was absolutely no communication. No matter what I asked them, they wouldn't answer me, and when I invited them to question me, they wouldn't put a question. I realized that something had gone wrong. So in the end, in frustration, I adjourned the class.

I went off to the next group, but I saw the three old men walking over to Mandela. He had to stop what he was doing, and I saw him and the three old men in discussion. A little later Mandela called me and said, "Mac, the old men have come to complain. They are saying to me that they are not prepared to demean themselves. They are elders, and you, Mac, are teaching them patent nonsense. Their own observation shows that what you're teaching them is false. They say, 'We can see the sun traveling, but this boy is telling us, no, it's the earth that's traveling around the sun.' They say, 'We're not prepared to demean ourselves with this young boy or even debate the issue. He's telling us a lie.' "

There were other incidents with the old men. For example, Baba Mvulane asked Walter Sisulu, "Tchobo, you're the general secretary of the ANC?" Walter said, "Yes." "Now how many wives have you got?" Walter said, "One wife, Albertina." "How many girlfriends have you got?" Poor Walter was embarrassed and said, "There are no girlfriends." Mvulane said, "General secretary of the ANC, only one wife, no girlfriend! No, you can't be the general secretary and be like that. You must have more than one wife, and you should have several girlfriends; otherwise we can't respect you as a general secretary."

And yet they had a simple justice, those three old men. Years later they taught me a huge lesson in politics. As the years went by, we began to engage in political discussions with them, and I was part of the group devising the syllabus and running political classes. I thought this was a wonderful opportunity to discuss the land issue—African people had been confined to 13 percent of the land surface of South Africa. In our politics classes we used to ask, "How do we solve the agrarian problem?"

So I engaged the old men in discussion. But they denied there were problems. They said, "We just go to the headman in our community and ask for access to land, and we get it. We have communal pastures for grazing our cattle and our sheep." I said that the headman had all these powers, but they said that they had a village meeting to solve any grievances. I was looking for where the shoe was pinching, and theoretically the shoe has to pinch, but they were saying there was no pinching.

I say it was a huge lesson for me because it taught me that I could not take my theoretical understanding of a macro issue and expect it to find an immediate or direct resonance at the micro level. There is no way you can organize the people from that theoretical and macro position. You've got to see where in their practical lives the shoe pinches the foot. And if you're dealing with issues that don't pinch the foot, don't expect them to agree with you on the macro problems. These old men made that clear to me.

Yet these same three men had killed their headman because he had imposed fences on them. They did not translate that problem as a problem of land possession, but as a headman abusing his power. They perceived the problem as the behavior of the individual headman whom they had killed, not as a problem of the system. They argued that this headman was not operating the system the way it should be—a different level of grievance.

Today in democratic South Africa there are perceptions—right or wrong—that government is out of touch with reality. That means that it has become detached from understanding how people are living on the ground and what problems they are experiencing. That's a connection that every democracy must address because democracy is supposed to be "government of the people, by the people." It means that experiences on the ground must be vented and addressed, but it does not mean that experiences as people articulate them are a correct reflection of the problem. The point is that they must be able to express them, discuss them, and come to understand the real problem and what can be done about it so that democracy becomes governance by consent.

Free at Last!

One afternoon late in October 1976, I was called to the prison office and told I would not be allowed to return to the single cells because I was being removed from Robben Island. So I left the island without the chance of saying good-bye to comrades with whom I had lived, worked, and played for the past twelve years. Warders had gone to my cell and packed my few possessions, including the folders and books with Madiba's manuscript concealed in their covers. For the next three months I was kept in total isolation in six different prisons, ending up in Durban Central Prison.

I was always put into isolation in a single cell. My worst experience was in Kroonstad. I didn't see the prison during the daytime because I arrived late at night. I was driven in a prison van into the complex to what appeared in the dark to be a one- or two-room bungalow. In the entrance was a stairway going down to the basement. They took me down the stairs and locked me in a fairly big cell. Instead of a door, the entire wall was a grille of steel bars, so the cell looked out into a passage. There were no windows, and because it was in the basement, the electric light was on twenty-four hours a day. They locked me in there and disappeared. There was a deathly silence. It's a huge complex with no roads nearby. No traffic sounds. Just silence.

I did as I used to do in most of these prisons. Once I was alone, I'd shout out to try to make contact with any other prisoner nearby—I'd shout *Amandla!** At Kroonstad I shouted, but there was only an echo. Nobody was in that building. No warder. The only time anything happened was when my meals were delivered. They would slip the food through a little space under the bars. I tried to greet them, to get into a conversation with them, but they wouldn't talk. I would say to the warder, "I want to see the officer," but he wouldn't reply. I came to the conclusion that this was part of an attempt to disorient me in case I was smuggling any messages.

I had no idea whether it was day or night. I had no idea of time—no watch. The only mechanism I had for judging the time was when the food arrived, but I'd get confused. I'd say to myself, "Wake up, it must be daytime. Breakfast should be coming just now." Then I'd find myself waiting for what seemed like hours, and I'd say to myself, "Good God, I must have got up at two o'clock in the morning!"

I had already been in prison for twelve years. I had lived in isolation. I knew, number one, you had to keep engaging the authorities. Number two, make sure you do physical exercises. Intersperse these with mental exercises. Number three, keep focused. Keep demanding to see the authorities. Keep challenging them, and keep reminding them that you're on your way out of prison, so they have to be careful about what they do to you.

But at Kroonstad there was nobody to engage. No officer came to see

---

*"Power" in Zulu.

me. I kept asking the warder, threatening to sue, but nobody came. Eventually some warders came, opened the grille door, and said, "Right, come." When I got to the ground floor, I could see it was nighttime. Instead of letting me see the office, though, they put me in a van and drove me to Leeukop Prison, between Johannesburg and Pretoria, and then from Leeukop I was taken across the country to Durban Central Prison. Again I was confined to a single cell, alone—same lousy food. I demanded changes, demanded my study materials, which they wouldn't give to me.

Shortly after 11:00 A.M. on December 17 I was escorted to the office, to a separate room where there were two or three Security Branch officers in plain clothes. I didn't know them. They immediately served me with a house-arrest order, and they read out the terms and conditions. I was prohibited from going into certain suburbs, from attending meetings, from publishing, from writing. They told me to sign, and I did. The whole thing took about thirty or forty minutes. Then they released me. It was 11:45 A.M., fifteen minutes before the deadline.

Across the road a small group of well-wishers was there to greet me. I raised a clenched fist and walked over to my brother's car. We drove to his flat in Merebank, south of Durban. We were excited, chatting. He had an old Toyota, and once we got onto the freeway—built while I was inside—I asked him to let me drive. He was reluctant because I hadn't driven for twelve years. But I insisted. I started driving, and I said, "Now I can feel alive!"[25]

Looking Back

Some things stick in my mind. First, I suppose there was a deepened understanding that social change is not something that can happen spontaneously and automatically, that it needs an organized force to lead the process. That force I saw as the ANC. Second, I left with a deeper conviction that the cause we were fighting for was just and that the success of that cause was long overdue. South Africa was way out of sync with the rest of the world. It was living in an age that belonged to the past. The world—and Africa—had moved on. Third, I left with a deeper conviction that victory would only come if the people were behind us, part of us. That might sound trite, but it wasn't. For me it was fundamental.

In my experience of prison there were, naturally, moments of great pain: Tim being rearrested in 1967, my father passing away, Tim leaving the country in 1973. But now, when I look back on prison, I see it as a period of privilege. What I went through has left me with an enormous asset that nobody who has not been through similar difficult circumstances can claim.* I could readily pick five people, friends to whom I could entrust my life, knowing that they would give their lives to protect me. I can say that with certainty because we passed through those times together. It was a privilege to be with people like Madiba and Walter, to debate with them and watch their conduct and learn from that. It was a very great privilege.

*In an interview with Fran Lisa Buntman (1994) for *Robben Island and Prisoner Resistance to Apartheid* (page 78), Mac was revealing about the physical impact of prolonged imprisonment. When he went to prison he was twenty-nine years of age. He was forty-one when he was released. The prime years of his adult life were spent in incarceration. "I know I hit a period of approximately two years where I was completely listless, very self-pitying, seized with a mental ennui—and in a single cell. Somehow one managed to pull oneself out of it. But I can imagine how others would break under that. Your intellectual capacity is at a premium and you are unable to stretch it. Your capacity to do work is denied. You are at the prime of your physical life. You are totally deprived. It's almost an incomprehensive frustration. . . . That comprehensive blockage of all space for you to express yourself in any way meant that every level of frustration was condensed and if we have come out of it looking like very normal human beings, beneath that normalcy I cannot believe there isn't a level of suppression or repression . . . I have unconsciously learnt to distill from the experience all the good aspects and hang onto them . . . but in a certain way I don't want to confront [the reality of it]. I don't even want to speak of it. . . ."

9. BANNED IN DURBAN

Introduction

THE APARTHEID DREAM STATE lasted from 1964 to 1972—six years of sustained economic growth of 7 percent per annum, high capital inflows, a passive African population that appeared to have acquiesced in its own powerlessness, secure borders, reliable allies in the West (who used its vehement anti-Communist propaganda for its own purposes), and growing rapprochement between Afrikaners and English-speaking whites.

Ironically, the apartheid system itself was the instrument of its undoing. It was as rigid as a Communist or East Bloc economy, with much state control of labor and the market. As the economy grew, imports grew even more rapidly, creating the need for more foreign exchange to close an increasing trade deficit. [1]

For foreign exchange, the country relied on the export of primary resources, principally gold and other minerals. This left the flow of foreign exchange largely out of the country's control. The scale and pace of industrial production were dependent on the inflow of foreign exchange. During the 1960s, inward investment flows were more than sufficient to finance increasing trade deficits, but that would change.[2]

Capital imported for a shift to manufacturing contributed to the trade deficit. Rapid industrialization came with a shift from labor-intensive to capital-intensive production. For black labor this had two consequences: on the one hand, the demand for semiskilled African labor increased; on the other, even larger numbers of unskilled African became increasingly redundant. Thus the need for migrant workers decreased dramatically, and the size of a stable, urban-based, semiskilled labor force increased. Contract labor pushed out migrant labor.

The number of unemployed Africans increased from 582,000 in 1962 to 750,000 in 1966 to 1 million in 1970. The economic cycle turned sharply downward in 1974, capital inflows dried up, and the boom was over. The number of unemployed Africans soared, and the prospects of somehow dumping them back in the Bantustans became an illusion.

Under influx control, these unemployed workers were supposed to be removed from the urban centers in which they had been employed and re-settled in the homeland of their ethnic designation. But the sheer scale of the numbers involved made relocations impossible. The period of sus-tained economic growth had accelerated the rate of black urbanization. Meanwhile, job reservation for whites in semiskilled jobs created labor shortages.[3] An excess of labor at one point in the production process and a shortage at another created an untenable situation. When African trade unions became legal in the late seventies, they revolutionized the African worker's relationship to the workplace and the workplace's relationship to apartheid.[4]

2

The years of Mac's incarceration were years during which the ANC in exile grappled with huge problems, relocating its headquarters from Dar es Salaam to Morogoro to Lusaka, clarifying its identity, establishing the po-litical space in which to articulate its cause, and facing down rising inter-nal dissent in the camps in Tanzania—where increasingly impatient exiles had waited for years for the opportunity to return to South Africa and fight.

Following the unraveling of the MK campaign (the Wankie campaign) in Rhodesia (Zimbabwe) and two years in jail in Botswana, Chris Hani* made his way back to the ANC camps in Tanzania in 1969. Bitter and disap-pointed, he became a lead signatory to a memorandum. The memorandum referred to "the frightening depth reached by the rot in the ANC and disin-tegration of MK accompanying this rot"; it spoke of the leadership being

---

*Hani was the political commissar of the MK's Luthuli Detachment, which crossed the Zambezi River from Zambia into Rhodesia (Zimbabwe) in August 1967 as part of a mili-tary alliance with ZAPU (Zimbabwe African People's Union) to overthrow Ian Smith's Rhodesian government. The combined operation was crushed in the Wankie Game Park. Hani and others who survived the debacle tried to make their way back to Tanzania through Botswana, but they were arrested and incarcerated in Botswana. After their re-lease in late 1968, Hani and the others (about thirty in all) made their way back to ANC camps in Tanzania and Zambia. Some, among them Hani, were disillusioned with the way the ANC was conducting itself and were ready to make waves about it. For Hani's ac-count of the Wankie campaign, the first real armed campaign embarked on by the ANC, go to [] pre transition/the struggle/MK/ [] Wankie Campaign. See also Shubin, pp. 77–83.

"divorced from the situation in South Africa . . . not in a position to give an account of the functioning branches inside the country"; and noted that there had "never been an attempt to send leadership inside since the Rivonia arrests." It berated "the careerism of the ANC leadership who have, in every sense, become professional politicians rather than professional revolutionaries." The memorandum demanded that the leadership be "committed to the resolution and programme of going home to lead the struggle there."

The memorandum also said "the ANC has lost control of MK"; it referred to "secret trials" and "extremely reactionary methods of punishment," criticized the lifestyles of some leaders, and condemned nepotism and the fact that "virtually all the sons and daughters of the leaders had been sent to universities in Europe"—a sign that "these people are being groomed for leadership positions after MK cadres have overthrown the fascists." It warned against the "fossilization of leadership."[5]

The ANC leadership reacted with fury. Hani and his cosignatories were hauled before a tribunal. They were saved from a death sentence by one vote.[6] After a period of suspension they were reinstated in their positions. Nevertheless, the memorandum had a chilling effect on the expression of dissent. It was often hard to draw a line between the legitimate expression of grievances and fomenting dissent—that is, being an enemy agent.

At the ANC's first National Consultative Conference at Morogoro, Tanzania, in 1969* the document adopted by the ANC, "Strategy and Tactics," was a clear expression of the ANC's plans to intensify the armed struggle in the form of guerrilla warfare, which, it had concluded, was the only way to bring the regime to its knees. It clearly stated, however, that the military struggle would be subordinate to political control.[7]

The document is an eloquent exposition of revolutionary guerrilla warfare, and it provides a clear articulation of the relationship between the military and political components. But the ANC made little attempt to turn its theoretical discourses into practice or to examine the obstacles that deterred implementation. There was no clear communication of

---

*In a lecture to the South African Institute of Race Relations (SAIRR) in June 1985, Professor Tom Lodge, South Africa's preeminent commentator pre-1994 on black South African politics, referred to the Morogoro, Tanzania, consultative conference as "an occasion which marked a crisis in the organisation: mutinies in the camps arising from the boredom and frustration of soldiers with no prospect of action, ideological dissent in some sections of the leadership, and a pervading feeling of futility with the exile diplomacy which had had to serve as a substitute for significant political activity." See "The ANC since Nkomati" at [] general information/ organizations/ANC/[].

policy or strategy to MK commanders and through them to the rank and file.

The ANC resolved few of the questions the Hani memorandum raised. In the late 1970s, the armed struggle was being run by military leaders who had yet to set a foot in South Africa. Their operational intelligence was extremely limited. MK operatives involved in hit-and-run missions worked in a political void.

3

Within South Africa discontent simmered, but it did not find an outlet for its expression until the Soweto uprising that began on 16 June 1976, when Soweto exploded, with much of black South Africa following. The event that ignited the spontaneous combustion of defiance was the boycott of schools organized by the Soweto Student Representative Council (SRC) to protest the compulsory teaching of subjects in Afrikaans in African schools. But this was only the spark that lit the fire.

Revolutions are the product of the accumulation of small grievances. Among Africans there were many grievances, but the awareness of those grievances and the right to empower themselves to address them were instilled by the Black Consciousness Movement (BCM), a movement irrevocably associated with Bantu Steve Biko.*

Black consciousness was a philosophy of being, a call for the assertion of self-esteem, of pride in blackness, which had roots in the black power movement that emerged in the United States in the mid-1960s, the writings of Malcolm X and Frantz Fanon, Julius Nyere and Kwame Nkrumah. Blacks were psychologically disempowered, entrapped in a sense of inferiority imposed on them not only by whites but also by their own accep-

---

*"Black consciousness is in essence the realisation by the black man of the need to rally together with his brothers around the cause of their oppression—the blackness of their skin—and to operate as a group in order to rid themselves of the shackles that bind them to perpetual servitude. It seeks to demonstrate the lie that black is an aberration from the 'normal' which is white . . . It seeks to infuse the black community with a new-found pride in themselves, their efforts, their value systems, their culture, their religion and their outlook to life.

"The interrelationship between the consciousness of self and the emancipatory programme is of paramount importance. Blacks no longer seek to reform the system because so doing implies acceptance of the major points around which the system revolves.

"Blacks are out to completely transform the system and to make of it whatever they wish." Steve Biko, *I Write What I Like*, ed. Aelred Stubbs (Johannesburg: Picador Africa 2006), p. 53.

tance of this imposition. They had embraced victimhood. Black consciousness took direct aim at these deeply inculcated beliefs and was determined to smash them. Thus the state's Bantu education system, which was seen to socialize black children into an identity of inferiority, became a target.[8]

The 16 June march was organized by the Soweto SRC, a black student group. About 15,000 students gathered to demonstrate. After failing to disperse them with tear gas, the police opened fire, killing at least 3 students and injuring many others.[9] In the immediate aftermath, 174 Africans and 2 whites were killed.[10]

The photograph of thirteen-year-old Hector Pieterson being carried through Soweto, mortally wounded, was flashed around the world. Within days, the UN Security Council had condemned South Africa and demanded an end to apartheid. The shootings triggered large-scale rioting across the country as students and others vented their anger. The police responded with bullets. Such shootings were followed by funerals, which were followed by rioting, followed by more shootings. Before the uprising was suppressed, at least sixty people, most of them teenagers, had been shot dead and thousands of young people had fled the country to join the liberation struggle. Jimmy Kruger, then minister of justice, wryly summed things up: "Natives had to be made tame to the gun."[11]

The Soweto uprising was a turning point in the war against apartheid.* Ironically, the ANC, isolated in Lusaka, was still pondering questions of how to ferment armed revolution. It had little to do with what happened in Soweto or with the spontaneous upsurge that followed. The people were giving direction to their leaders.

The uprising caught the ANC by surprise but ensured that nothing in South Africa would ever be the same. Between six hundred and seven hundred people died in the ensuing violence during the following year. Among the victims was Biko himself, arrested in August 1977, tortured in Port Elizabeth, and transported naked and unconscious by road to Pretoria, where he died in his cell. Prime Minister John Vorster responded with

---

*The government seemed impervious to the consequences of what it was doing. A cabinet note reads: "10.8.76. Unrest in Soweto still continues. The children of Soweto are well-trained. The pupils/students have established student councils. The basic danger is a growing black consciousness, and the inability to prevent incidents, what with the military precision with which they act. The Minister proposes that this movement must be broken and thinks that police should perhaps act a bit more drastically and heavy-handedly which will entail more deaths. Approved." Quoted in an executive summary of an ANC submission to the TRC at [] post transition/TRC/ submissions/[] ANC/ August 1996.

more arrests, more detentions, and the National Party was reelected to government with an increased majority.

African youth poured across the borders into Botswana, Lesotho, and Swaziland in the thousands, eager to join MK and return to South Africa to overthrow the apartheid regime. Unfortunately, most would languish in camps in Tanzania and Angola, soldiers with nowhere to go. Only a few would make the trip back to South Africa. Fewer would complete their missions; even fewer would return alive.

The Soweto uprising initially only hardened the intransigence of the apartheid state. Spending on both internal and external security increased massively. In 1978, security spending accounted for 21 percent of the government's budget and more than 5 percent of GNP.[12] Every male over the age of eighteen underwent two years of compulsory military service. The South African Defense Force (SADF) consisted of almost 17,000 personnel, of whom about 5,000 were black, and a separate contingent of 38,000 white conscripts. There were also 255,000 white citizen reserve military personnel.[13] In addition, there was the South African Police (SAP) with 37,000 members (55 percent white),[14] better trained to handle mass protests; 31,000 reservists; a sophisticated Security Branch (SB)[15] with a network of informers; and BOSS (Bureau of State Security),[16] the civilian intelligence agency. The few MK networks the ANC had managed to establish had been decimated in countrywide arrests.[17] Underground structures were gutted, leaving a vacuum of leadership and extensive disarray.

Mac

I WAS RESTLESS. I needed to do something to feel that I was in control of my life, so I concentrated on what to do next. I was under house arrest, and I'd been banned. I needed to get out of the country, but I had asked Madiba and Walter to let me stay for six months to get the feel of things. Much had changed in the country since I'd gone to jail. When I got to Zambia and met Oliver Tambo, I wanted to be able to give him my impressions.

I was also thinking about how to maneuver around my banning order's restrictions in order to find out what was going on. I wanted to meet politically active people. Then I had to work out how I was going to escape from the country after the six months. I had to get the files with the hidden material to the UK, where there were reliable people in a stable environment. So I had many issues to think about. I had to find employment that would allow me movement, that would force the regime to give me permission to move outside the suburbs I was confined to.

There had been no mass ferment when we went to prison at the end of 1964—repression had successfully created a climate of fear in the mass mind. But in 1976, the Soweto uprising had exploded that mentality of fear, and people were flexing their muscles. I saw potential there. The seeds of resistance had germinated, but they were starved for water and for the fertilizer that would nurture them, which would turn rebellion into successful revolution.

The potential came through the youth, through the revival of the Indian Congress, through the ferment against the Bantustans, through the trade unions which had reemerged since 1973.* At last one could sense that the masses were being remobilized. Conditions were improving for our cadres to take part in armed struggle.

My brother and his wife had a one-bedroom flat in Merebank, and in the sitting room, beside the sofa and the TV, they put in a bed for me.

The Security Branch (SB) would sometimes come twice a day, hoping that somebody would walk in accidentally to visit me when I already had a visitor, because then I'd be breaking the law. I was allowed one visitor at a time, but not after 6:00 P.M. I had to be in the flat by 6:00 P.M., and I could not leave it before 6:00 A.M. on the five working days. On weekends I was confined to the flat from Friday night at 6:00 P.M. to Monday morning, 6:00 A.M. I had to report to the Wentworth Police Station once a day, between 6:00 A.M. and 6:00 P.M. I was allowed into the white suburbs of Durban, but not the African, Indian, and Coloured suburbs. I could go into

---

*On 9 January 1973, two thousand mostly hostel-dwelling African workers went on strike in Durban at a brick-and-tile company, demanding higher wages. Within two months more than sixty thousand workers in 146 establishments in the Durban area went on strike, the largest strike action in South Africa since the miners strike in 1946. South Africa had never witnessed a wave of strikes involving so many plants over such an extended period. The strike actions were spontaneous. There were no "leaders." In their aftermath, there emerged an environment that eventually opened the way for the Wiehahn Commission, which recommended, in 1979, the legalization of black trade unions. The strikes were also instrumental in rekindling hope among the masses and activists alike after the crackdowns following the Rivonia and Little Rivonia trials. Most of the strikers won wage increases. The people still had the power to act—and win. See Karis and Gerhart, *From Protest to Challenge*, pp. 202–17; SAIRR annual survey 1973 at []general information/ SAIRR/[] 1973.

downtown Durban, but I could not cross Grey Street.* I was not allowed to attend gatherings, and any group of more than two people was a gathering in terms of the law. Some people were exempted: my brother and sister-in-law, for instance, who lived in the flat. The SB was also watching who was visiting me.

I gave the file cover with Madiba's autobiography to my attorney Phyllis Naidoo and asked her to send it, through secure means, to Rusty Bernstein in London. I independently sent word to Rusty to keep the file safe. I also got to know Zak Yacoob, a lawyer. I needed him in case I got into trouble. We got on like a house on fire from the first meeting. Even though Zak was African, he had offices in the white part of Durban, in Fenton House, on the Esplanade, because he was an advocate, and advocates had to have offices close to the courts.†

I began to look for a job. I wanted something in an area of Durban that would require the minister of justice, Jimmy Kruger, to give me permission to move around a bit. With Phyllis's and Zak's help, we got Rabbi Bhagwandeen to employ me as a clerk at a hotel he owned in Reservoir Hills, an Indian suburb about twenty kilometers from downtown Durban. He had been a member of the African Congress, and was a student with me at Natal University in 1956/57. To take this job, I would have had to travel from Merebank into the center of Durban, then travel though various other suburbs—Coloured, Indian suburbs—to get to Reservoir Hills. I applied to Kruger, but the application was turned down. So my lawyers told the newspapers I had been refused permission to take up employment. I was out of prison and had no income.

I spent most of my days in Zak's office, and I tried to live as normal a life as I could. My brother did not have a phone, so I used Zak's. I tried to avoid letting the cops know whom I was contacting. I knew the phones at Zak's offices were bugged, so I was very careful to use his phone in a judicious way. I occasionally phoned my wife in London and had normal conversations with her. Of course, that caused problems because she wanted to know what was going to happen next, and I couldn't tell her. She urged me to join her outside the country, but I had to pretend I wasn't going to leave, or it would have tipped off the police. I knew she didn't understand

---

*Between Victoria and West streets, the right-hand side of Grey Street was the boundary of the Indian community. On this side of the street, the business and commercial premises were Indian; the opposite side (left, coming from Victoria) defined the boundary of the white community. All business and commercial premises were white.
†Zak Yacoob was appointed to the constitutional court in 1998. For interviews with him, go to []omalley/interviews/[].

my fake reasons and was hurt because I didn't seem to want to be with her after all those years. But there was nothing I could do.

I had started meeting people again. I had met Pravin Gordhan for the first time when he and Ketso Gordhan, his nephew, came to visit me at my brother's flat—two visitors at the same time, despite the banning order. They were both politically active and seeking advice. I arranged to meet them on a fairly regular basis. I would visit Pravin every few days at the King Edward Hospital, where he was a pharmacist. It was a huge hospital complex, and Pravin knew all the rooms, so we were able to find a secure place to meet. I'd walk into the hospital, and he'd tell me to go to such-and-such a storeroom. There we would meet and chat for an hour at a time. Pravin was officially involved with the Indian Congress and community work. As students, he and Ketso had been involved in boycotts and the like. He was interested in everything from theory to teaching to tactical questions. I was learning from them, and from others, what was happening on the ground. I had people come from Jo'burg and Cape Town to see me. I met people quietly.

I got a job repairing and painting a house in a very posh white suburb. The house was owned by a woman who was a supporter of the Black Sash, Mrs. Rautenbach. Phyllis raised the matter with her. In terms of my banning order, this was not a job that needed permission—it was in a white suburb of Durban, house repair and maintenance was not prohibited work, and I was the sole worker on the premises.

The house was empty. I had to do small repairs, touch up the painting, fix the roof, and so on. I found this very convenient because the house was near the university. I set up contacts and saw people at the house. I saw the late Joshua Zulu there. As it turned out, the house was being repaired for occupation by Ashley Wills, of the U.S. embassy. Ashley and his wife, Gina, moved in while I was still doing repairs there. That's how we got to know one another. Mrs. Rautenbach had told them I was the handyman, but not my history. Gina used to be at home all day, and we'd talk. A while later, however, somebody from the U.S. consulate must have realized who I was. So one day Ashley asked me, "Aren't you Mac Maharaj?" I said I was. I told him this was the only job I could get, and he said he was comfortable with it.

I avoided political discussion with Ashley.* The ANC saw the U.S. government as hostile, though at that time Jimmy Carter was giving a high

---

*Ashley Wills, the U.S. State Department official newly appointed to the U.S. consulate in Durban in 1977, has a different recollection. He has vivid memories of Mac.

profile to human rights. We believed our struggle was against apartheid colonialism, and in much of the ANC's literature we opposed its association with human rights issues elsewhere. Not because we opposed human rights per se, but when Carter proposed that our problem was one of human rights, we believed the South African anti-apartheid struggle would drown in the larger struggle for human rights. This could reverse the advances we had made against apartheid as institutionalized racism. We feared the pressure for action against South Africa would be relieved by the argument that the UN and the world could not act against South Africa without also acting against all other instances of human rights violations. So Carter's attempt to shift the paradigm from anticolonialism to the promotion of human rights was rejected.

Escape

In the meantime, I was planning my escape. I made contact with a former Robben Islander named Judson Kuzwayo.* He had been a prisoner in the communal cells, had been released, was banned, and was working in the Research Division of the University of Natal. It was through him that I set up my escape.

I sent a message to Oliver Tambo (OR) via couriers to say that I was out of prison and I was going abroad on a mission Madiba and Walter had entrusted to me. I had sensed an uneasiness about who in the movement was working with the regime and who was reliable. So I said I would make my own way out of the country, probably via Maputo. I asked OR to make arrangements for me to get to him in Lusaka whenever I surfaced. Through Judson, I began to set this up.

Phyllis lent me her old Volkswagen. I needed to check whether the car had been bugged, so one day I picked up a friend and drove off to Wentworth, the suburb I was allowed into. Wentworth has a secluded beach. We had to take a remote road over a hill to get to the beach. I picked up a

---

"Mac," he says, "actually didn't work for us as a gardener! He spent a lot of time educating my wife and me about the history of South Africa. I remember long conversations over coffee in the kitchen when he was supposed to be in the garden as he recounted experiences from his own life and his association with Mandela. We found this highly educational, and we became good friends. Calling him a gardener is a joke! That was his nominal title. One morning we woke up and read a newspaper story that Mac Maharaj had fled South Africa." Go to []maharaj/interviewees/[] Ashley Wills.

*Judson Kuzwayo became the ANC chief representative in Harare shortly after Zimbabwean independence. He died in a car crash while traveling from Harare to Zambia.

female friend from the congresses and drove off. I wanted to know whether I was under surveillance and whether the car had a device planted in it. As I drove, I could see a long distance back on this remote road, but there was no sign of anybody following us. We got to the beach and parked the car. We were sitting chatting in the car and—lo and behold!—five or ten minutes later a car appeared and parked next to us: four Indians in plain clothes. I realized they were cops. I knew I wasn't breaking any law, but I thought this meant that the car was bugged. I decided to use the car as a decoy for my escape.

I made arrangements with Judson and two friends of his: another former Robben Islander, Shadrack Mapumulo,* and a chap called Nzima.† I bought a set of clothes and stored them. I bought a leather coat, pants, a shirt, and a pair of spectacles that made me look different because I would need to disguise myself once I left Durban. The border is about 500 or 600 kilometers (350 miles) away, so if I was intercepted on the way, I would already be guilty of committing a crime.

The last thing I did was to visit the offices of the lawyer I had worked for in 1955–56, J. Kissoon Singh. He had a chief clerk called Sewlall, with whom I had become friendly. I visited the lawyer's office and had a chat with the staff. The chief clerk was happy to see me. When we were alone, I said to him, "Listen, mate, I need a spare key to the offices." He asked why. I said, "Because I'm banned, I'm restricted and I don't have places where I can work, write, maybe meet people." He said, "I don't know what you are up to; I don't want to know, but here's a spare key."

I planned to use the offices early in the morning on the day I disappeared. I would change into my disguise and cross over into the neighboring Indian area to meet Shadrack. He would lead me to the vehicle that would get me to the Swazi border. I had a disguise I could take off easily if I needed to. I didn't tell anybody I was going. My brother and sister-in-law hadn't seen the clothes or the spectacles. I had made it a practice to leave the flat at exactly 6:00 A.M., the hour I was allowed out. Every morning I would drive into Durban's center in the bugged car, park it in the white area, then walk to Zak's offices or other offices in the white area. Every evening at 5:00 P.M., I would fetch the car, drive to Wentworth, go to the police station to report, and get back to the flat at five to six.

---

*Shadrack Mapumulo was killed by a hit squad in Manzini, Swaziland.
†Nzima and his wife were killed in Manzini, Swaziland. A bomb was in their car. As soon as they got into the car and started the engine the bomb went off, killing both of them.

That was my daily routine, so anybody observing me saw an unvaried pattern.

On 1 July, the morning of my escape, I left the house as usual at six o'clock. My leather jacket, pants, and spectacles were already in the car. I had been given some money by friends. I drove to town as usual, parked, put the parking ticket in an envelope addressed to Phyllis Naidoo, and dropped it into a mailbox. Then I went to the offices where I'd made the arrangement with the chief clerk. The office wasn't open; work didn't begin until eight o'clock. I let myself in, making sure I hadn't been followed, and went into the chief clerk's office. There I put on my disguise and put what I had been wearing into a plastic bag and hid it behind the filing cabinets. Then, taking the fire escape, I left the building and crossed into the Indian area to meet Shadrack.

But Shadrack wasn't there. There I was, standing on the corner, with no one to meet me. The area was getting busy; I was afraid somebody might recognize me. What could I do, I wondered? I'd have to get back to the office, revert to my normal clothes, and find out what had gone wrong. But just then Shadrack suddenly walked up to me and said, "Follow me."

We walked through a maze of arcades until we reached one of those cheap fast-food restaurants they had in those days, selling chai (tea) and Indian food. Then Shadrack said: "Things have gone horribly wrong. The car has broken down." I said, "Oh, God! Shadrack, you can't do this to me." He said he had been delayed coming to meet me because he'd been trying to repair it. I said, "Listen, friend, I'm going to get arrested and that's not on. Can't we get another car?" He said, "Hold on, sit here, I'll come back."

When he came back, he said, "Look, I can get you a taxi (a van that carries sixteen passengers), and you can travel with the guide who is going to escort you across the border." The guide was Nzima. I didn't know Nzima at that stage. Nzima and I would get one taxi to Tongaat, then catch another to Stanger, where we'd take yet another to the border. Nzima would do the hiring. I said, "Fine, let's go." Nzima, a short, tubby guy, was already sitting in the first taxi. We didn't talk. Around midday we got to Stanger; we were making good time. Nzima went into the Kentucky Fried Chicken to buy a bucket of chicken. I'd never eaten KFC before. I didn't know you could buy it in a bucket!

Now we were on the longest leg, from Stanger to the border. About five kilometers from the village of Golela, on the border with Swaziland, Nzima asked the taxi driver to stop. We jumped out. I didn't know what was happening. He paid the driver, said good-bye, and thanked him. We walked into the bush along the riverbank, toward the border bridge.

Nzima walked ahead, found a clump of trees to hide among, and sat down. "Sit," he said. "What's happening?" I asked. He said, "We're too early, so we're going to hide here." I wanted to know what would happen next. He explained: "As soon as it gets dark, I will be leaving you. I'm going through the border gate officially. I have documents. You'll walk in that direction, you'll come to a fence, you'll cross that fence. Then you will be in no-man's-land. You'll come to another fence, you'll cross that fence, and then you'll go to the village you will see in the distance on the Swazi side. You won't mistake it. It's called Lavumisa. You must find a house with green painted walls. By the time you get to the house with the green walls, I will already be there waiting for you."

It was getting dark. Nzima got up and said, "In half an hour, it will be fairly dark and you can set off. Wait for half an hour, then you move." After he left, the thought hit me: "Jesus, how will I recognize a green wall in the fucking dark?" I can't shout for Nzima because we're in enemy territory, so I run to try to catch up with him, but he's gone.

I wait half an hour. I head for the fence. I find it and cross. I have no sense of direction at all. That's one of my worst faults. But I cross the two fences and go into this village. There are hardly any street lamps, and I am looking for this bloody house with a green wall. Everything looks the same bloody color, and suddenly, when I'm exasperated in the dark, I hear somebody whisper, "Come, come." It's Nzima!

Nzima took me to a house where I met comrades serving in ANC structures. From there, Comrade Henry Ciliza* took me on foot over the border into Mozambique, where I was collected by comrades based in Maputo.

So that's how I got away.

---

*Today Ciliza is a member of the South Africa Department of Foreign Affairs.

10. LUSAKA AND LONDON

Introduction

BY 1978, THE cordon sanitaire that had made South Africa practically immune to attack from MK was disintegrating. In Rhodesia (Zimbabwe), white rule was crumbling. In Mozambique and Angola, Marxist governments had assumed power following Portuguese withdrawal after the Lisbon coup in 1974. In Mozambique, the Frelimo (Liberation Front of Mozambique) government gave sanctuary to the ANC, enabling it to create infiltration routes from Mozambique into South Africa through Swaziland. In retaliation, the South African Defense Force (SADF) clandestinely supported the Renamo (Mozambique Resistance Movement) insurgency against the Frelimo government.[1]

Angola presented more complex problems. Heretofore it had been a buffer zone between South Africa–ruled Namibia and countries under African rule to the north. The MPLA (Popular Movement for the Liberation of Angola) government supported both Swapo (South West Africa People's Organization) and the ANC, allowing the former to use southern Angola to launch forays into Namibia and the latter to establish MK camps in the north and central areas of the country. In October 1975, the SADF intervened, moving deep into Angola. But it was forced to pull out in August 1976.[2] However, when P. W. Botha took over as prime minister from John Vorster in September 1978, the war in Angola became a priority. Incursions quickly escalated into full-scale war.[3] Many of the youth who fled South Africa post-Soweto ended up in ANC camps in Angola and some fought on the side of the MPLA, supported by Swapo and a formidable Cuban military presence against Jonas Savimbi's Unita (National Union for Total Independece of Angola), supported by South Africa. In the shadows the Soviet Union and the United States played covert roles. A cold war proxy war.

For apartheid South Africa, the unraveling of the colonial states beyond its borders posed a major threat to its security. More than ever, whites embraced their sense of siege—from within from a hostile and oppressed majority simmering with discontent and incipient rebellion, from without from unseen threats in need of an ideology with which they could be articulated.

Botha moved to fill the ideological void. "The resolution of the conflict in the times in which we now live," he wrote, "demands inter-dependent and coordinated action in all fields: military, psychological, economic, political, sociological, technological, diplomatic, ideological, cultural, etcetera. We are today involved in a war whether we like it or not. It is therefore essential that a total national strategy [is] formulated at the highest level."[4]

The state's response to "total onslaught" was "total strategy." Apartheid South Africa came to see itself as a vital part of the global ideological struggle between the West and Soviet expansionism. Whites were propagandized to believe that in conducting their struggle against the ANC, they were playing a pivotal role in the West's global resistance to the expansion of Soviet communism. By redefining the security interests of the South African state, Botha gave it a coherence and unity of purpose that it had not had before—hence the rapid militarization of the state and white populace, and the growth of ever more security apparatuses and more violent repression. The National Security Management System (NSMS) was instituted in 1979 as the instrument to coordinate all state actions.[5]

The NSMS became fully functional in the mid-1980s as the government took steps to curb the activities of the mass movements. As the crisis deepened, the intelligence services, particularly military intelligence, increasingly assumed political influence and even executive control over this shadow bureaucracy, which in some respects duplicated the existing administration and displaced its decision-making structures. The State Security Council (SSC), although technically a committee of the cabinet, usurped many of the cabinet's executive functions. The SSC effectively ran the country as a supercabinet without any statutory power, giving credence to the notion that a creeping military coup was taking place in South Africa.[6] The "securocrats" had a role, often not ostensible, in every aspect of government.

The new strategy set the counterrevolutionary agenda: law and order would have to be restored before reforms (which the state grudgingly conceded were necessary) could be introduced. But political reform would be forthcoming only when security interests had been addressed.

2

In the early 1980s, the government implemented a program of reform, "managed change," in response to mounting domestic discontent and international pressure. A new tricameral constitution was introduced in 1983.[7] It provided for three houses of parliament, one each for whites, Indians, and Coloureds, each house to be elected by its own register of voters. The Indian and Coloured houses had authority over Indian and Coloured affairs only. Power, however, remained firmly in the hands of the white parliament and a state president, a position that now replaced that of prime minister.* The new constitutional arrangements were approved by about 66 percent of voters in a whites-only referendum. Africans, Coloureds, and Indians, who comprised 85 percent of the population, were not consulted, while Africans were excluded from any participation in the central government. The theory was that they had their own political structures in the homelands (Bantustans), into which the state poured ever more money.

The elections to the newly created House of Representatives, for Coloureds, and to the House of Delegates, for Indians, were widely boycotted by both—only 18 percent of eligible voters went to the polls. The government also introduced a new Black Authorities Act, whereby African community councils were replaced by Black Local Authorities (BLAs), giving the appearance of Africans having greater powers in local government. When the first elections to the town councils were held in late 1983, political groups opposed to the new constitution exhorted Africans to boycott the elections. Turnout averaged about 20 percent in most townships. In Soweto, the largest township, it was less than 11 percent.[8]

Botha's reforms precipitated widespread resistance. The promise of reforms created expectations, but the actual "reforms" were regarded as trivial, insulting, or irrelevant. To right-wing whites, however, it became equally clear that these kinds of concessions were a form of surrender to eventual majority rule. Reform, no matter how cosmetic, was regarded as selling out, and a segment of the National Party broke away and formed the Conservative Party (CP) in 1982, with an absolute commitment to separate development.[9]

The opposition to the tricameral parliament led to the creation in 1983 of the anti-apartheid United Democratic Front (UDF), a broad, non-

---

*Until this time, the role of state president had been almost entirely ceremonial, with the prime minister playing an executive role. Now the two offices were combined, and the powers of the state president vastly expanded.

racial grouping of about 650 affiliates with a total membership of more than 2.5 million who collectively put the emphasis on mass mobilization and protest politics.[10] In many communities residents turned on the BLAs, destroying their premises, murdering councillors as apartheid stooges, or burning them out of their homes. Special police—"auxiliaries" or "special constables," Africans recruited from the communities they would police— in keeping with the strategies of countermobilization, were dealt with in the same summary form. The Vaal uprising in 1984–85 foreshadowed the longest and most pervasive period of black protest against white rule in the country's history.[11] When Oliver Tambo called on blacks to make South Africa ungovernable in January 1985, much of black South Africa was already ungovernable.

Botha shifted tack. In March 1984, he signed an agreement—the Nkomati Accord*—with Samora Machel, president of Mozambique, under which both countries agreed not to allow their territories to be used as springboards by guerrilla armies for attack on each other. The South Africa regime was largely, but not entirely, successful in removing the overt ANC presence in Mozambique. But the premise that led Botha to sign the agreement—that if the ANC was denied external bases in the region, its capacity to promote its agenda in South Africa would be undermined— was faulty. The ANC's capacity to advance its agenda was a function of its domestic support base and not its regional base capacity. The government was forced to rethink, once again, the basic premises of its political policies in South Africa itself.

3

In KwaZulu-Natal, Inkatha was founded in 1975 by Chief Mangosuthu Buthelezi, chief minister to Zulu king Goodwill Zwelithini, with the sanction of the ANC.[12] The ANC had seen Inkatha as its surrogate in the region, but within a few years relations between the ANC and Buthelezi had

---

*On March 16, 1984, a formal nonaggression pact was signed by the South African government and the government of Mozambique at Komatipoort. Under the Nkomati Accord, as the agreement came to be called, both governments undertook not to interfere in each other's internal affairs to avoid recourse to force, sabotage, or violation of borders. They also agreed that they would not permit organizations that planned violence or terrorism against the other to establish bases, training centers, arms depots, or transit facilities. This was a devasting blow to the ANC, as no forward area was as developed as the structures in Mozambique, which included Joe Slovo and Jacob Zuma. For expanded footnote go to []maharaj/ footnotes/[]201.

deteriorated. Increasingly, Buthelezi adopted an independent posture. He opposed the armed struggle, opposed sanctions, and began to emerge as a political power in his own right. In London in June 1979, a meeting between Buthelezi and Tambo to thrash out the differences between Inkatha and the ANC failed to resolve their discord,[13] and from that point on they descended rapidly into animosity.

The ANC accused Buthelezi of being an apartheid stooge, a homeland leader who kowtowed to Pretoria's wishes (despite the fact that Buthelezi had refused full "independence" for KwaZulu). Buthelezi accused the ANC of trying to destroy him. When the UDF tried to recruit support in KwaZulu, Buthelezi regarded it as an attempt to destroy his political support base. Violence was the result. The ANC accused the government of supporting Inkatha and of fomenting violence between itself and Inkatha. The violence escalated, pitting Zulu against Zulu. By the mid-1980s, a civil war was raging in KwaZulu-Natal.[14]

Meanwhile, the ANC had become addicted to the idea of armed struggle. The more it failed, the more the ANC pinned its hopes on guerrilla warfare and armed insurrection. The ANC's armed struggle failed by almost every yardstick,* but it did succeed as "armed propaganda": armed

*Probably the most comprehensive analysis of MK done to date is Howard Barrell's D. Phil. thesis, "Conscripts to Their Age: African National Congress Operational Strategy 1976–1986" (Oxford University) at [] general information/ Howard Barrell: [] Conscripts to their age/ []. His conclusions: "Even a superficial examination of the ANC's operational activities as a revolutionary movement over the three decades between 1960 and 1990, particularly consideration of its armed struggle, shows that the ANC seldom achieved what it set out to in its operations against the state" (p. 4). ". . . monitoring mechanisms and operational management in the ANC were abysmal. There was no ANC leadership presence on the ground inside South Africa. Key officials often failed to attend meetings of the Revolutionary Council (RC), and of its successor, the Politico-Military Council (PMC)" (p. 451). "Personality and inter-departmental rivalries undermined decisions that were taken from time to time to improve information flows between sections. Furthermore, long and poor lines of communication into and out of South Africa, as well as between ANC machineries in different countries . . . was often out of date by the time it reached ANC decision-makers in Lusaka or Maputo" (p. 451). "ANC operations suffered a high rate of failure" (p. 452). "Often the failure was of the most basic kind: the ANC's failure to implement what it had decided upon, or failure to change what it had resolved to change" and "failure to achieve stated operational objectives when new strategies or tactics were decided upon" (p. 452). ". . . MK did not develop its armed activity beyond the sporadic, symbolic endeavour it was when the ANC first resumed attacks inside South Africa in 1976, despite numerous decisions and attempts to do so" (p. 452). "On average, slightly more than two ANC guerrillas were killed or captured by security forces for every three of the 634 guerrilla attacks between 1976 and 1986" (p. 452). "Until 1984, the largest single form of attack was sabotage and the largest single target category consisted of economic installations (of which railway lines,

struggle achieved a mythical status among the masses, especially the youth, for whom it provided hope of directly overthrowing the apartheid state.[15]

The sheer persistence of the ANC against formidable odds gave it a legitimacy that other, more fragmented liberation organizations, like the PAC or Azapo, could never claim. It linked the history of struggle— Rivonia, Mandela, and Sisulu, and the other prisoners on Robben Island— to the actions of the present. Every comrade who fell while attempting to strike against a regime everyone hated became one more deposit in the memory bank of the people—a bank the ANC would one day draw on.

Another irony was that while the armed struggle was notably unsuccessful as revolution or insurrection, it managed nevertheless to paralyze whites into believing the state's *swart gevaar* (black danger) and *rooi gevaar* (red danger) ideology. The fact that such sporadic attacks[16]—few of which were directed at white civilians—could elicit such hysterical coverage in the white media suggests that something more was going on beneath the surface of white reactions: that they, too, understood the inevitability of black rule.[17] The state, despite the vast military arsenal at its disposal, could only postpone the inevitable.

4

The Revolutionary Council (RC) was established at the ANC's Morogoro conference in 1969 to oversee the prosecution of the war on the home front. Unlike the NEC, RC membership, which was appointed by the NEC, was open to non-Africans and new appointees were co-opted as the RC saw fit. The RC created nine line-function departments, including the Internal Political and Reconstruction Department (IPRD), which was responsible for establishing a political underground within South Africa.

All structures of the ANC between the 1960s and 1985 were replications of each other; Africans on the NEC formed the backbone of the RC. With time, the same narrow pool was assigned other roles as members of senior organs, of politico-military councils, as leadership in the so-called "frontline states,"* commissars, and what have you. In addition, those who were members of the SACP also carried out their assigned responsibilities as party members. Because most members of the NEC were members of

---

electricity transformers and power stations . . .") (p. 453). "There is no evidence to suggest that ANC armed activity ever achieved any significant degree of self-reliance within South Africa" (p. 458).

*Botswana, Zimbabwe, Mozambique, Zambia, Lesotho, Swaziland.

the SACP, it was, in this sense, the repository of the most information and was the most strategically positioned group.

Within the ANC in exile, like all organizations in which career prospects depended on one's not having made a mistake, inertia was the preferred modus operandi—thus the endless rounds of meetings, committees and subcommittees, conferences to be addressed, position papers to be written, consultations made within and among departments, paper pushing, buck passing, and other stratagems of bureaucratic infighting.

The post-1963 generation grew comfortable in exile. With no secure base from which to launch attacks on South Africa or to infiltrate operatives, getting MK cadres into the country was a disheartening process. There was no existing political underground in South Africa with which the exiled ANC could easily communicate. One estimate put the number of formal structures inside the country at fifty, the number of members at two hundred[18]—hardly the makings of an adequate network.

Joe Modise was commander of MK from the midsixties until MK was disbanded in 1994. No one within the NEC questioned his strategic sense or tactical abilities. He never saw any need for a change in strategy; the armed struggle would eventually prevail, all the political "stuff" was mere trimming.[19] No one would take him on. Tambo let him be.*

No voice in Lusaka was raised when the thrust of "Strategy and Tactics,"[20] the policy document adopted at Morogoro, was ignored by the leadership that had commissioned this "new" thinking. In the manifesto that launched MK, Mandela made it clear that the resort to violence was not to overthrow the state, but to bring it to the negotiating table.[21] Morogoro changed the emphasis. Henceforth, the object of armed struggle was to overthrow the state on the model of Algeria, China, and Cuba. The fact that the historical circumstances were different in each case seemed to be beside the point.

Mac's account of this time conceals as much as it illuminates. It is clear that at this point the ANC was bureaucracy driven. The ANC in exile had become increasingly preoccupied with its own internal concerns and increasingly out of touch with events on the ground in South Africa. New members of the NEC of the ANC were chosen by fellow members, not elected. All were Africans until the Kabwe conference in 1985.

Thus, the organizational structure of the ANC promoted a climate in which members of the leadership did not criticize one another. A place

---

*According to Mac, Tambo was never inclined to take on Modise, who more or less ran MK as he saw fit, brooking little criticism.

on the NEC depended on the degree of esteem in which you were held by fellow members and the extent to which you supported its policies and decisions.

Paradoxically, the structures to drive change were in place. The IPRD had a mandate to create a political underground in South Africa, to give MK units a secure base from which to operate, and to interact with the local political infrastructure. But the IPRD was treated like an illegitimate political child. The committee itself lacked coherence, and most members believed that a political underground in South Africa should facilitate the military and not the other way around. The military lobby simply swamped the opposition, of which there was little. In short, having laid out a strategy with a clear definition of purpose, the ANC proceeded to ignore it completely. No one asked why.

5

Mac's appointment to the IPRD, effective December 1977, brought a questioning voice to the proceedings, but not one that others wanted to listen to. The overriding concern within the ANC itself was to ensure there were no splits. The organization could not withstand another trauma such as that which culminated in the expulsion of the Gang of Eight in 1975.*

Mac created waves. He was the new boy on the block, back from prison. He had access to Tambo, was known to be close to Mandela, and came with a reputation—some might say a reputation for being too big for his boots. He had thought through the problems before he came to Lusaka. The empty file Mac inherited when he became secretary of the IPRD was emblematic of the inertia he was up against. Besides, the RC paid scant attention to the IPRD's activities, and when its less-than-dynamic chairman, John Motsabi, made his periodic reports to the RC, he took Mac along to explain what was going on, leading to Mac's appointment to the RC.

The RC itself was disorganized. It met about every two weeks; attendance wasn't mandatory, and frequently scant. It did not have the

---

*A number of prominent ANC leaders, led by Tennyson Makiwane, were highly critical of the ANC's decision at Morogoro to admit non-Africans to the ANC and of what they perceived as the SACP's undue influence within the ANC. The dissident group, calling themselves African nationalists, launched scathing attacks on the "non-African and communist controlled leadership" of the ANC. The ANC leadership responded swiftly, expelling eight dissidents, who became known as the Gang of Eight, the analogy being with China's Gang of Four. See Shubin, *A View from Moscow*, pp. 130–36.

administrative capacity to organize itself and was incapable of monitoring the activities of the seven departments in its jurisdiction. Senior organs, another set of structures in the frontline states, were virtually private fiefdoms. Within each, the political committee and the military committee acted independently of each other; between different fiefdoms there was minimal contact.*

On the ideological level, the ANC embraced the mass mobilization of the people as a prerequisite for the success of the armed struggle. But it was not clear which grew from which; the two were thought of in a state of "parallelism."

6

Even when a trip to Vietnam and an examination of its revolutionary success resulted in the "Report of the Politico-Military Strategy Commission" (the Green Book) in 1979/80,[22] which laid out the political mobilization of the people as the necessary condition of a "people's war," and argued that the armed struggle was subordinate to political development,[23] the ANC still couldn't turn policy into practice.[24]

Ironically, the Green Book carefully catalogued the inadequacy of ANC structures to carry out its far-reaching recommendations. In an unusual bout of robust self-critique, it stated: "The paucity of information on a number of important questions stood in the way of the Commission being able to develop its proposals more fully. This is, in itself, a reflection of the movement's poor style of work in many important areas."[25]

The commission articulated the dilemma of "parallelism." "The armed struggle," it stated, "must be based on, and grow out of, mass political support and it must eventually involve our whole people." At the same time, "All military activities must at every stage be guided and determined by the need to generate political mobilization." And to boot, "The concrete politi-

---

*In his report to the ANC declaring his intention to resign from the ANC, Mathabatha Peter Sexwale catalogues the enormous stresses the ANC in Lesotho was under because of personal differences between Chris Hani and Lehlohonolo Moloi. "As a result," he writes, "conflicts in the region remained almost perpetual and since there was no forum for them to raise their protest, the matter was left to rot. The discrepancies caused by the two leading men were causing disunity in the region. Comrades grouped themselves in a Lehlohonolo's faction and a Chris's faction. Very disturbing. These conflicts were even registered inside the country [South Africa] where people would only take directives from the one they supported, ignored or jeopardized the other." See [ ] maharaj/documents and reports/other/[ ] Mathabatha Peter Sexwale letter of resignation from the ANC.

cal realities must determine whether at any given stage and in any given region the main emphasis should be on political or on military action."[26]

The concept of "people's war" began to replace that of the old armed
struggle as infiltration and guerrilla war. In mid-1983, the ANC produced
a discussion document, "Planning for People's War,"[27] in which "people's
war" was defined as "war in which a liberation army becomes rooted
among the people who progressively participate actively in the armed
struggle both politically and militarily, including the possibility of engaging in partial or general uprising."[28]

The report concluded that "the ANC should continue carrying out and
even escalating those actions which had played an important role in stimulating political activity, mass resistance and mass organization" but that
"there should be more concentration on destroying enemy personnel."[29] In
its 8 January 1985 statement, the NEC said: "We must all take it as a priority task to build up the popular armed forces, to transform the armed
actions we have thus far carried out into a people's war, by helping to root
Umkhonto we Sizwe firmly among the people and actively drawing the
masses into the prosecution of a people's war."[30]

7

At the Kabwe conference in Zambia in June 1985, the mood had become
decidedly more militant. "From the reports given," the ANC publication
Sechaba noted, "it became clear that the ANC has not only had contacts
with the developments and organizations at home, but has been part of
those developments, and has grown with the struggle—at times giving
guidance and advice, but at all times leading the masses in the right direction."[31] Thus the ANC inserted itself into the "people's war" that had already begun. It may in part have inspired that popular unrest, but it by no
means generated it.

By 1985, however, the ANC had been able to step up MK actions
within South Africa. In that year there were 137 incidents of guerrilla activity, either by township militants acting on their own or by MK, up from
45 in 1984. The number of attacks rose to 230 in 1986, 235 in 1987, and
282 in 1988.[32] But two incidents—the bombing of a Wimpy Bar in a sea-
side town, in which five civilians were killed and more than sixty injured
in December 1985,* and the bombing of Magoo's bar on 14 June 1986, in

---

*In the mid-1980s, there was a spate of bombings of Wimpy Bars by the MK. There were
also attacks on restaurants, supermarkets, shopping malls, and night clubs involving

which three civilians were killed and sixty-nine injured*—were seized on by the government to further reinforce whites' belief that blacks were intent on murdering whites simply because they were white.

In 1986, in a statement celebrating the twenty-fifth anniversary of the founding of MK, the NEC exulted:

> Through centuries of white domination our people have learnt how to die for a future. Today, even our eight-year-old children in the townships defiantly pit their strength against the might of the racist soldiers and police. It is only in this framework that we who know how to die for the future can understand the majesty of our young lions who have taken to war and side by side with Umkhonto we Sizwe moved our masses to make People's War a reality.[33]

"People's war" was the ANC's rallying cry. Yet the objective conditions for a people's war in the Vietnamese sense did not exist.[34] Still, as unrest within South Africa grew, the ANC was dragged into the fray, responding to what was happening rather than fomenting or controlling it. The people were not going to wait for a hand-me-down revolution. The people moved, took matters into their own hands, and began to organize their own revolution. In the end, the ANC was astute enough to grab its coattails and eventually claim ownership of the coat itself.

9

And what of Tim? Like other wives of men sentenced to long stretches on Robben Island she was left to fend for herself, to fight her own wars to survive, and to try to get on with her life. After Mac's trial, Tim was "deported" from the Transvaal (for violation of the provicial permits laws). She

---

grenades, bombs, and limpet mines. Civilians were injured and on occasion killed. In its submission to the TRC, the ANC accepted responsibility for some of the attacks but also maintained that others were carried out by counterinsurgency agencies in the state security apparatus, trying to discredit the ANC. Go to www.omalley.co.za and search *Wimpy*. For a list of MK operations go to [] pre transition/MK []. See also Oliver Tambo's press conference on 9 January 1986. []maharaj/ documents and reports/ ANC/1986/[] Oliver Tambo press conference on civilian casualties of the armed struggle.

*Robert McBride was convicted of the killings and sentenced to death three times for the bombing. His sentence was later commuted to life imprisonment. In 1992, Mandela made his release a condition of going forward with the Record of Understanding. See pages 396–98, Chapter 19. In 2003, McBride was appointed head of the Ekhuruleni Metropolitan Police.

returned to Durban and worked in hospitals there. There was no support network to draw on. Some of her own people were more likely to ostracize her than to offer a helping hand. She was perceived as trouble, someone attracting the attention of the Security Branch, and therefore more prudent to avoid than to greet since overt friendliness might cause watching eyes to take note. For years she was shadowed by an Indian named Nayager from the Security Branch. To be closer to Mac, she moved to Cape Town and found work there. She could visit him once every three months for about an hour. All were noncontact visits. Then the SB caught up with her—Indians had no residential or working rights in the Cape—and she had to go back to Natal, where she had great difficulty in getting a job. The SB watched her comings and goings, harassed her, made life unbearable. Getting to see Mac was difficult and costly: the red tape, delays, inquiries, badgering, a month's salary to fly from Durban to Cape Town. Her visits to him were always demands on his part for things he wanted, fees for university, books, everything. Meeting his demands and only being able to make ends meet were life's staples.

"Whatever I did was wrong. Invariably I was wrong because his study money wasn't there; I didn't do this on time; I didn't give that message— and it was always I who was wrong. OK, I was wrong sometimes, but he was never prepared to believe that his friends would be wrong or delay or do nothing. It was always I, and he became very African in his thinking. That's the only way I can say it. I can't explain what I mean."

By 1973 she had had enough. She went to London, over Mac's objections, to start a new life in the hope that he could join her after his release. In London, Tim stayed with her sister, Suria, and reentered the émigré community: ANC meetings, the Women's League and the AAM, the incestuous group of South Africans tied to one another by their relationship to the struggle. She didn't fit. "The ANC elite in London lived off the money received from charities." When Mac eventually returned to London in August 1977, there was a strangeness between them:

"Mac was a changed person. He expected me to have a house. He didn't understand why I hadn't earned more money, saved more money, and bought a house. He looked around my one-room flat and said, 'For God's sake, how can I bring my friends and entertain them here. It's just not acceptable.' And I said, 'Mac, where have all your Communist values gone?' To me, at that point, they were skin deep and rather shallow.

"Every story he told me about Robben Island was all 'I, I, I,'—he was the person who came up with the best plans, with the best ideas, with the best of everything. He never made a mistake. He was extremely vain and arrogant.

"He never once inquired about how life had been for me during the twelve years he had been in jail. All he was concerned about was himself, and in jail all he was concerned about was himself: Would his books be there on time? Would this be there on time? Would that be there on time? He took no consideration of the cost or the effort it involved to get to Robben Island to see him.

"The man who went to prison was my husband. The man who came out was an egotistical, selfish, thoughtless person—someone I didn't know. That's the gist of it. The change. I could see the change there, but I thought I'd wait and see what happened. And what happened happened. It was inevitable."

And it was divorce.

Time and again Tim returns to one theme: she hadn't lived up to Mac's expectations—not on her own behalf but what she should have done for him. Instead, he was disparaging about everything she had done. When he left for Lusaka, she spent months paying off his debts. His telephone bill alone was "astronomical."

She bears no grudges, she says, no grudges against anyone. She admires Mac for what he did for the country, but for the person he became she hasn't much time. She doesn't count. It's Mac's story. Going over the past upsets her. "It stays with me for days," she says. They had made a pact: she'd work and Mac would do the struggle. He broke it.

Mac

THE ANC OFFICE provided me with a travel document, flew me from Maputo to Dar es Salaam, and then to Lusaka in early August 1977. In Lusaka there was somebody at the airport to pick me up. He told me, "The National Executive is meeting at Makeni Farm. My instructions are to take you straight there."

I got to the farmhouse and, after a short wait, was ushered into a room where the National Executive was meeting. Tambo was chairing. I was welcomed, and Tambo asked me to participate in the debate about what was happening at home. I didn't ask on what basis I was participating. When the lunch break came, I asked how long the meeting would be and was told, "Two days." "Where do I sleep?" "Oh, don't worry, comrade, there are beds here. You can sleep here."

Briefing Oliver (OR) Tambo*

I saw OR Tambo privately after the NEC meeting. There were two tasks I had to attend to. There was the issue of Mandela's autobiography. I told OR about it, that it was safe in London, and that it had to be transcribed and typed out. I needed a good typist and a place to work for about six months. He said it would be best if I went to London. I said that was fine because I wanted to see my wife too. I told him I was not to reveal to anyone else that Madiba had written an autobiography because the ultimate decision about whether to publish it would rest with OR.

The second batch of instructions related to the state of debate on Robben Island and the way we saw problems in the country, with a sharp caveat that our assessment should not be prescriptive of what the movement should do. For that reason, I was only to provide a verbal briefing to OR on the state of thinking in prison around strategic issues.

One of these was what our tactics and strategy should be vis-à-vis the Bantustans. I relayed to OR, as I had been asked to do by Mandela and Sisulu, their assessment of the strategic issues, which he could factor into his own assessment. I also gave him a broad overview of the debate on the Bantustans, including Govan's vehement opposition to our having anything to do with them.

I told him that in my assessment of the pulse of the people as I had experienced it, the ANC's presence in the country needed to be rapidly reestablished. I told him there were hopeful signs; that my biggest thrill had been to receive a clandestine copy of *Inkululeko*, the illegal publication of the Communist Party, through the post within weeks of my release. It made me feel that the Communist Party was present. The ANC needed to assert itself; it had to make itself felt on the ground. That did not require dramatic acts; it needed small but systematic efforts.

I went into prison in 1964, I said, and all we heard was that there was a reign of terror; then Soweto exploded and Soweto was suppressed. Coming out of prison and being put under house arrest, I had assumed that the fear that had invaded the masses in 1965 would still be there. But in the six months I was in Durban, I could feel that despite the fear, there was a resurgence of courage and faith.

I gave OR my reading of the mood in the country. We were still grappling with the aftermath of Soweto. The idea of using mass organizations—including the Release Mandela campaign, the release of political prisoners

*Tambo's full name was Oliver Reginald Tambo, hence the "OR" appellation.

campaign, and the antirepublic campaign that was being mooted*—was widely endorsed.

Tim

I arrived in London on 8 August 1977, Women's Day in the ANC. Tim met me at the airport, and we were whisked to an ANC Women's Day meeting, at which I had been asked to speak. Everybody wanted to know about Madiba.

Tim and I tried to patch up our lives. Tim was living with her sister, Suria, and there was no space there. Given that I was going to be in the UK for six months, Tim took a flat and we lived together there for the rest of my stay in London. We hardly saw each other. She was doing two jobs, as both a day nurse and a night nurse, because I had no income; we could only afford the flat if she took both jobs. I was busy transcribing Madiba's autobiography. We saw each other only on her days off.

We tried to rebuild our lives. We had been married for twenty years. She asked me: "What happens now?" I said, "Well, you know my situation. I'm a member of MK, and I have to go wherever they say." She said, "Will you go back home illegally?" I said, "Yes, if they say so. They are likely to say I must go back home." The next day when we discussed the matter she produced an exercise book and said, "You're going to leave again. You're heading for Zambia; you're heading for home. What happens to our life together? We've been married now for twenty years, and I've calculated every day that we've seen each other. Here are the dates: we've seen each other for a day or a weekend or a week here and there. It totals eighteen months out of twenty years."

Tim applied to work in an ANC clinic at the Solomon Mahlangu College in Mazimbu, outside Dar es Salaam in the north of Tanzania, hoping that she and I could be together. I agreed to this, but while she was making these preparations, I was called to Lusaka and told I was to be based there. I could only go to Tanzania if the organization sent me there. My area of operation covered Mozambique, Swaziland, and Botswana. In London one evening, Tim and I sat down and the discussion was not about when she was going to Tanzania. It was about her and me. What was going to

---

*In 1981, white South Africa celebrated the twentieth anniversary of South Africa's declaring itself a republic and taking itself out of the Commonwealth; it was also the twentieth anniversary of the National Action Council's antirepublic campaign, headed by Nelson Mandela, which ended with the three-day national stayaway 29–31 May 1961.

happen to us? Again she asked, "Are you going home?" I said, "I'm secretary of the ANC underground; I expect it's part of the logic of my work that I should go home. How can I be the secretary sending people home and not go home myself?" And she said, "I can't handle this." I suddenly said to her, "Tim, I think we'd better divorce." She just went silent, looked at me, and then she said, "I think so too." That was it. We divorced in 1978.

The chemistry between us was gone. We were no longer on the same wavelength in our passion for the arts, the theater, or even our passion for the struggle. Maybe in a very callous way what was uppermost in my mind was how I could get back into the struggle and steep myself in it. The struggle was my life. Tim was still a supporter of the struggle, still in the ANC, but she asked, "Why is it that so-and-so, who has been in prison, is now able to live in London? Why can't you come and live in London and still be in the ANC?" I said, "For me, to be in the struggle you must give everything of yourself, and the thing that is needed is for us to get home and fight." She said, "But why you? You've done your bit. You've been in prison. Why don't you ask them to let you stay in London and work for the ANC here? Then we can be together."

I was insensitive to her needs. I expected her to be as she was in the sixties, when she still shared the commitment with me. Now I wanted to get back into the fight, but she wanted us to have a life together. I think she remained very much in love with me and wanted to find a way for us to be together. I think she must feel bitterness about our split—and there is legitimacy to her bitterness because shortly after I split with her, I developed a relationship with Zarina, my present wife.

Mandela's Autobiography

I went to visit all the comrades. I went to the ANC office, and they all welcomed me. I went to see Dr. Yusuf Dadoo, chairman of the Communist Party, at the party office. He said he'd heard I needed a good typist and recommended Sue Rabkin. He said he would also provide me with a typewriter, a dictaphone, a magnifying glass, and paper.

Sue had just come out of prison in South Africa. Her husband was still in jail. She said she would prefer to work from home because she had two small children. I used a magnifying glass to read the text. Originally, I had thought I would dictate into the machine, but we found it simpler for me to read it aloud and for her to type as I read. The advantage was that if she had a query, she could make it while I was dictating. With Sue's help I added the observations Walter and Kathy had made and did a limited amount of fact checking, noting matters that needed to be followed up.

Unfortunately, the copy I brought out from prison has disappeared. We tried to trace it around 1990–91, when I gave Madiba the disk version, but without luck. We made three copies of the typed version: one for OR, one for Dr. Dadoo, and one for myself. I don't know what happened to the copies OR and Doc were given, but a few years later, when computers became available, I had my copy transcribed and saved on floppy disks. I gave the disks to Madiba when he was released from prison, and he used that version as a basis to write *Long Walk to Freedom*.

I remember parts of that version that are not in the published book. I've asked Madiba what we should do with the original text. I suggested we give it to a library. He agreed, but I then said, "Wait a minute, old man, are you aware of things that are in the original text that are not in this version?" I said scholars would be studying the text, and there might be things he didn't want to get out. One was a section that dealt with a number of us individually and how he saw us. I think some of the judgments are a little too harsh, and I think they would make some waves. I don't think it's fair while these people are still living.

None of this explains why the book was not published until four years after Madiba's release. Dr. Dadoo and Joe Slovo looked at the manuscript. They did not think it would make a significant impact. Slovo felt it did not go far enough in explaining how MK came into existence. In particular, it made no reference to his role. Ruth First in Maputo made similar observations. Besides, I soon discovered that there were many suspicions and rumors about Mandela in movement circles abroad. This, too, may have played a part in the antipathy to his autobiography.

But I have to accept primary responsibility for our failure to publish the autobiography in 1978. In assigning the task to me, Madiba and Walter had impressed on me how busy OR was and that I should constantly raise the matter with him until the task was done. It was assumed that I would be involved in, if not do, the actual editing. But the ANC work to which I was assigned, after I had finished getting the manuscript typed, got in the way; and although I raised the matter with OR from time to time, I could no longer drive the process of getting the book into print.

Appointment to IPRD

The World Conference for Action against Apartheid was held in Lagos from 22 to 26 August 1977. The conference was organized by the UN in cooperation with the Organization of African Unity (OAU) and the Federal Republic of Nigeria. I was told to attend as a member of the ANC delegation, which also included OR; Johnny Makatini, our UN representative; Thabo Mbeki, Govan Mbeki's son; Duma Nokwe; and quite a few others. In October 1977, the London office of the ANC told me I was needed to speak at a special session of the UN Special Committee Against Apartheid, in New York.

Back in London, Dr. Dadoo called to see me. He said it had been decided I would be made secretary of the ANC's IPRD. The IPRD was charged with establishing a political underground in South Africa. It reported directly to the Revolutionary Council (RC). Dr. Dadoo said I would be based in Lusaka. "From there," he said, "I don't know what happens." I was to attend the first meeting of the IPRD in Lusaka on 5 December 1977 and then come back to London to continue my work.

Until I came out of prison, I could not actually belong to the ANC. But at Morogoro in 1969 the ANC had decided that non-Africans could be members of the ANC in exile. This was a momentous decision—the ANC's decision to work with the Indian congresses had been the catalyst that had led some comrades in 1958 to break away and form the PAC. Although non-Africans could not become members of the NEC until 1985, they could serve in other positions of leadership. When I came out, I was integrated into the ANC straightaway and also into the Communist Party.

Back in Lusaka, I went to the ANC office before the meeting of the IPRD and met with Alfred Nzo, secretary-general of the ANC, and Thabo Mbeki. He and Nzo took me off in a little Fiat 127, the only car the ANC had in Lusaka. You had to push it to make it start. In the car, Nzo said, "We thought we should use this opportunity, before the meeting starts, to brief you on the restructuring that's going on in the ANC." Thabo then outlined the new structures and the mandate of the IPRD. He gave a very clear briefing. The organization chart he used were in his own handwriting. He was very clear, very succinct; it was also clear he was speaking with Nzo's blessing.

The committee members were spread all over: Lusaka, Botswana, Mozambique. Thabo told me the chairperson would be John Motsabi, a member of the NEC, and also attending the meeting would be Henry Makgothi, another member of the NEC and a former prisoner based in Botswana. Indres Naidoo was coming from Maputo; John Nkadimeng, a member of the NEC, from Swaziland; and also Gertrude Shope and Florence Maphosho, who were members of the Women's League. He told me that Ray Alexander, a member of the Executive Committee of SACTU

(South African Council of Trade Unions) based in Lusaka, and Reg September, the ANC's chief representative in London, would also be part of the IPRD's first committee.

At our first meeting, during an adjournment, I wrote a leaflet to be distributed at home. I ended with the slogan Release Nelson Mandela: release all political prisoners. Then two of my committee comrades, Florence Mposho and John Motsabi, told me to remove the words *Release Nelson Mandela*. They said, "We don't want to feature an individual." I said, "Why?" They said because there were uncomfortable rumors that Madiba was selling out. I was appointed to the IPRD in December and then went back to London to wind up.

Release Mandela: Opposition

Less than two weeks later, on the morning of MK Day, December 16, OR's driver arrived where I was staying. No prearrangement. He said, "The chief has sent me to collect you." We went to a suburb called Lilanda, a very depressed area, where we had a house for accommodating cadres. In the backyard there were rows of benches seating about fifty cadres. OR was there. He said, "We're having a small meeting in celebration of MK Day. I thought it would be a good thing if you were present." Great. These were the cadres of the 1962 generation who had left to join MK, stalwarts.

OR gave a short address in which he ambushed me. He mentioned MK Day, exhorted the cadres, emphasized unity, and then he said, "Now comrades, there is one matter I want to address. There have been rumors, from the time of the Lusaka Manifesto in 1969* that Madiba is selling out. The rumors went so far as to say that Madiba had been brought clandestinely to the state house of President Kaunda and had engaged in secret meetings with John Vorster, the prime minister of South Africa." He said, "All of us have been concerned about the rumors. Is Madiba selling out? Now here today we have Comrade Mac—he comes from that section of Robben Island. He has spent twelve years there and was released on 17 December

*In April 1969, the fifth conference of the heads of state of fourteen East and Central African countries, under the chairmanship of Zambian president Kenneth Kaunda, issued a joint statement called the Lusaka Manifesto on Southern Africa, which called for the liberation of blacks in the south but through negotiated settlements rather than through the use of violence. The manifesto was later endorsed by the OAU and adopted by the UN General Assembly. The South African government rejected the manifesto. See Davenport, p. 460.

1976 and then house arrested. We would like to welcome him, and I call upon him to address you."

The message was clear: deal with this question. I dealt with it very simply. I said, "Comrades, I've stayed in that section from 5 January 1965 to October 1976. I lived in it cheek by jowl, in separate cells. Nobody could move away from those sections without my being aware. So I'm surprised to hear this rumor that Madiba was in Zambia. There is no way he could have disappeared, come to Lusaka and met with John Vorster in the state house here, even for a day, without our noticing it."

When I finished, and the event was over, OR walked with me back to the car. He said, "You dealt with these questions very well. I have never been in a position to deal with this question. The way you've put it, nobody can doubt it anymore. Now do you realize why they were saying don't put the words *Release Nelson Mandela* on our propaganda literature?"

So in December 1977, I found—and OR had confirmed it—that among the leaders and veterans of 1962 there were doubts, insecurities about what people like Mandela were doing. These rumors persisted over the years. The leadership was clearly pushing the armed struggle, but even after the Soweto revolt, these rumor mills were churning among the veteran corps. They were debilitating, exacerbated by the fact that no one had any viable plans for how to get us home to fight.

The IPRD: A Work in Progress

I returned to Lusaka in mid-January 1978 and got accommodation with a German couple, Almut Heilscher and Henning Hintze, through Indres Naidoo. The IPRD committee had dispersed. Things were disorganized, to say the least. Some comrades on the IPRD were not of the highest caliber. They all had good intentions—this will sound arrogant and harsh—but they had no clue about what they were trying to do. The reality is that I was stuck with an IPRD that had no idea about how to establish a political underground in South Africa.

I asked for the IPRD files. I was handed an empty folder. There were no records at all about previous activities. It appeared little had been done about political mobilization within South Africa, and for what had been done, there were no records. I was given a task in what was recognized to be a neglected area and told it was a big challenge—please attend to it.

The IPRD and its predecessors had done nothing to implement anything; it was completely different from Central Operations, which had jurisdiction over the activities of MK and Special Operations and saw itself as part of running our camps, organizing the recruitment and training of cadres, and the deployment of trained cadres. In Central Operations were Joe Modise, Joe Slovo, Keith Mokoape, and Paul Dikeledi— it had both a thinking thrust and an activist thrust.

Over the years, work among the masses had been neglected inside the country. There was no political underground. The struggle was being pursued almost exclusively in armed terms, whether armed propaganda or sabotage or clashes with enemy forces. The de facto position now was that *only* the armed struggle was the way forward. We would still talk about the "all-around struggle," but it was theoretical talk. In practice, the Revolutionary Council had tilted the balance between the military and political pillars of struggle in favor of the military.

I remember Thabo saying at the joint NEC and RC meeting in Angola in December 1978, "I don't understand. When I was in Swaziland, I did such and such but nothing happened." Meaning we had contacted people in South Africa and initiated certain political activity, but nothing had come of it. I said to the meeting, "Comrade Thabo says we did all these things, but there was no follow-up."

During the tea break I went over to Thabo, and I said, "Where are those records?" Thabo said, "Mac, I made records of all the work we did from Swaziland. I used to make notes even of the content of my discussions with people. It's all stored there. It was put in a tin trunk when I left Swaziland, and it was entrusted to Comrade Stanley Mabizela." Stanley was then deputy chief representative in Swaziland.

When I later got to Swaziland, I saw Stanley and asked for the trunk of records. He didn't produce it. Later, on another trip, I asked him again. He said, "Comrade Mac, I can't release it to you without permission from Thabo. It's very sensitive stuff, and he entrusted it to my care." I said, "Will you release it if you get a message from Thabo?" He agreed. Now, I couldn't simply pick up the phone and call Thabo, who was usually traveling. I had to wait until I saw him again. When I did, I raised the matter with him. He said he would call Stanley. Whether he did, I don't know. I do know that I never received the trunk. Why, I do not know.

There had to be great sensitivity about the work being done at home, in particular about the safety and security of the comrades you worked with. Often, the slightest whiff of what might be going on could land a comrade at home in trouble with the police. Many efforts had ended up in arrests and imprisonment, torture in detention, even death. In 1974–75, there were many arrests in the Pietermaritzburg/Durban region, in Port

Elizabeth, in Cape Town, and in Jo'burg.* Many were comrades who had recently come out of Robben Island. These were great setbacks. Some of the comrades involved evaded arrest and got out of the country—Jacob Zuma, John Nkadimeng—while others who were acquitted went into exile, like Joe Gqabi. Most likely, people destroyed records before the arrests were made.

The Worms Within

We had neither the means nor the personnel to deal with the deluge of youth crossing the borders after Soweto, and it took some years before we were equipped to do so. This meant that a lot of apartheid agents also slipped through our security net before we got our house in order. Our security problem was huge: as OR himself admitted, some of our best people worked for the enemy.[35]

By 1977–78, our security department had established a procedure. As soon as people arrived, they were interviewed. A member of the security department would help them to write an autobiographical account, or curriculum vitae (CV), which we then checked for inconsistencies. While the refugee was sent on a flight to Maputo or Lusaka, the written CV was sent to our security department. In the meantime, at the next stop the refugee was interviewed again and asked to write another CV. Depending on whether the person was to be sent to Tanzania for studies or Angola for military training, once there, he or she was yet again asked to write a CV. The security department compared these three versions, cross-checked them with other information, and if needed, conducted further investigation, or confronted the individual about substantive inconsistencies. At a rudimentary level of screening, this became our first mechanism to detect agents sent to infiltrate us.

But in reality, the regime's network of informers was extensive. It had penetrated every aspect of our work, often making it difficult for comrades to work together because of the need for secrecy. This often frustrated

*On New Year's Eve 1976, police arrested Joe Gqabi (released earlier in the year from Robben Island), Super Moloi, Murphy Morobe, and then Billy Masethla. Other arrests quickly followed, including Tokyo Sexwale and Tsiki—twelve in all, the Pretoria 12. In Durban/Pietermaritzburg, Harry Gwala and four others received life sentences and another five long sentences. For Gwala, this was the second time around on Robben Island. ANC structures were smashed. Jacob Zuma narrowly escaped arrest. In the Pretoria 12 trial, Joe Gqabi was acquitted and made his way to Lusaka. The others all received long sentences. Karis and Gerhart, pp. 280–81.

efforts to build internal underground structures because we always had to assume that somewhere in the networks we were dealing with enemy agents. We were never able to build relationships based on confidential exchanges unless we were absolutely sure of a comrade's credentials—and sometimes even this was not enough. The fact that a comrade had spent time on Robben Island, had been tortured by the regime, or had an exemplary record of struggle service, was no guarantee that the enemy might not somehow have gotten to him. Often they threatened his family back in South Africa or threatened to expose some indiscretion, or they offered money. Sometimes it was impossible to know what happened. But happen it did.

As a result, we had to build firewalls between people in the frontline states and the head office in Lusaka. The enemy could penetrate the head office or raid its offices. In Lusaka, the RC did not work from the same office as the ANC, but from clandestine places. Not even everybody on the NEC was aware of all the locations of safe houses. It was not just a question of trustworthiness. Loose talk could unwittingly convey valuable information to the enemy.*

The Revolutionary Council (RC)

The Revolutionary Council had its own secretariat to regulate its functions, but as a coordinating supervisory body, it delegated functions to other divisions within it. The IPRD was one such division. In 1978, I was asked to join the RC, which included in its membership military people from the head office, including Joe Modise and Joe Slovo.

In a certain sense, the armed struggle had been elevated from a tactic to a principle. Of the ten departments in the RC, nine were there to support the military struggle. Only the IPRD was concerned with building a

---

*In April 1969, the ANC established the Department of National Security and Intelligence (NAT) to oversee vetting of recruits and members of the ANC and MK to weed out informants or potential informants. Among the most conspicuous detainees of NAT was Pallo Jordan, detained in 1985. Jordan was a member of the NEC. According to Zarina Maharaj, Jordan "was locked up for six weeks in Lusaka in a corrugated iron hut and nearly died of dehydration." Jordan was released and went on to become ANC spokesperson after the ANC was unbanned. In Mandela's government Jordan served as minister for posts, telecommunications, and broadcasting, and after a cabinet reshuffle he became minister for environmental affairs and tourism in May 1996. In Mbeki's government he has served as minister for arts and culture since 1999. Jordan will not discuss the question of his detention and treatment. For a history of NAT and its activities, go to [] general information/organizations/ MK/[] Operations Report: Department of Intelligence and Security.

political underground in South Africa. Besides, the RC over a period of time had been stripped of certain functions: propaganda (not armed, just propaganda) had been shifted away from the RC and assigned to the NEC.

The best formulation of the difference between orthodox forms of political action and armed struggle I know of was written by Walter Sisulu while he was on Robben Island.[36] Walter argued that the armed struggle was not automatically the dominant form of struggle, but simply one of many tactics a movement exploits as part of its arsenal. And even if a particular form of struggle emerges as dominant, it doesn't mean other forms don't coexist, but these are subsidiary and complement the dominant one. It's a pity Walter's thinking was not available to us—it might have persuaded the more militarily inclined to have second thoughts.

The imbalance between military and political considerations was reflected in different ways in Lusaka. The military side, whenever it heard that the political people had groomed some promising recruits, would promptly poach them for MK, and then deny it had done so. The RC was almost harassing me to provide them with the names of comrades I had recruited to be members of the internal underground, but I wouldn't give the names. I wanted to transfer comrades only after the underground in a particular area of the country had developed the capacity to sustain itself.

No real practical consideration was being given to the creation of a political infrastructure in South Africa that would sustain an internal armed struggle. At best, units were sent to carry out single or a small number of operations and then pulled out. On the other hand, maintaining the political focus in our work meant having comrades within the country who could survive and function as the ANC political underground. They could not deliver immediate results, yet the pressure post-Soweto was to deliver tangible results—and that pressure kept tilting the balance in favor of armed activity, hit-and-run style.

The pressure from young people who left after Soweto contributed to the emphasis on armed activity. All of them wanted to join MK because that was what their blood was telling them. "Show me how to use a gun. I want to go back and fight the enemy." So when you said, "Now, comrade, I need you for political work," that seemed a far less glamorous option.

Luckily, there were comrades in Botswana who had come out of South Africa before 1976. They included struggle stalwarts such as Henry "Squire" Makgothi, Joe Gqabi, Marius Schoon and his wife, Jenny Curtis. John Nkadimeng and Jacob Zuma had taken refuge in Swaziland, and comrades like Indres Naidoo had settled in Mozambique. All of them knew people in the country we could work with.

Rebuilding the IPRD

Being secretary provided me with the leeway I needed to get things done without comrades looking over my shoulder. I contacted comrades in the frontline states and found ways to travel to Botswana, Lesotho, Swaziland, and Mozambique.

We faced a conundrum in establishing a viable political underground in South Africa. I knew of reliable comrades who were still in the country. Some had never been arrested, but were under house arrest or banned—Albertina Sisulu, Winnie Mandela. But if you contacted one of them, you were contacting a person the enemy was watching with a hawk's eyes, so you were walking into danger. Yet if you avoided them and approached new, unfamiliar people—unknown to the enemy but without any track record—there was a question mark over their reliability. How to proceed? My instincts were to go with the unknowns—it would at least minimize the risk of their being known to the security police.

My attitude toward building the IPRD was that it was not my job to meet people from home. My strategy was to build the committees in the frontline states—Botswana, Swaziland, Lesotho, and Mozambique after it opened up—so they would be capable of handling people from home. Whenever I met people from home, I would ensure that members of the forward area committee were drawn in. I had to give on-the-job training and guidance to the committees.

Some of the people working in these committees found ways to reside legitimately in Botswana, Lesotho, and Swaziland, but the work had to be totally clandestine. In Botswana, for example, Marius Schoon worked as a teacher; Henry Makgothi looked after refugees coming out of South Africa. In Swaziland, John Nkadimeng was doing the same. Maputo became convenient because we had ease of access to Mozambique and therefore to Swaziland. Lesotho presented greater problems because we either had to cross through South Africa on foot or use a tenuous air link between Mozambique and Lesotho. The South African regime had intelligence agents in all these areas.

The Green Book

After the delegation led by Tambo returned from Vietnam in October 1978, Joe Slovo wrote a report, about five pages long, saying we had been working ass backward: we'd been applying armed struggle as the major means to reconstruct a political base, but this was incorrect and we should build political organization by political means. The Vietnamese had made military struggle subject to political imperatives. But within a short period, Joe had reverted in practice to form, full throttle on the armed struggle.

At a meeting of the RC and the NEC in Luanda at the end of 1978, we discussed Slovo's report and elected a commission—the Politico-Military Strategy Commission (PMSC), chaired by OR, and made up of Thabo Mbeki, Joe Slovo, Moses Mabhida, Joe Gqabi, and Joe Modise. I attended a number of the commission's sessions in Maputo and participated in discussions on the Bantustans.

"The Report of the Politico-Military Strategy Commission," aka the Green Book, was presented to a meeting of the NEC in Dar es Salaam in August 1979.[37] The Green Book stressed the primacy of political mobilization. The strategic line was to be the waging of an all-around people's war in order to effect the seizure of power. The key question was how to get the masses of the people to act against the Bantustans. In this context, we agreed it was legitimate to attack the Bantustans from within and without.

Among the recommendations was a suggestion to set up a Central Organ. It would be small, full time, and hands on—a headquarters for the home front. It would have executive authority, as a subsidiary of the NEC, which would review it every six months. But this idea rubbed the NEC the wrong way. It saw this organ as potentially more powerful than the NEC.

John Motsabi, Tom Nkobi, and several other members of the NEC successfully opposed its creation. Instead, the NEC opted for regional senior organs of the RC, which, it said, would satisfy the need for "integrated leadership." There was no change at the RC level, and I retained my position as IPRD secretary and as a member of the RC. Our strategic line was agreed upon in theory, but in practice nothing ever reached the stage of real implementation.

The senior organs were drawn from political committees and military structures in neighboring territories. The senior organ in Maputo supervised operations in South Africa through Swaziland. On it were Joe Slovo, Jacob Zuma, and Ronnie Kasrils. On its political committee were Jacob Zuma, Ronnie Kasrils, Ebrahim Ebrahim, Sue Rabkin, and Indres Naidoo, among others. Comrades in Swaziland included Archie Abrahams, John Nkadimeng, Moses Mabhida, Ivan Pillay, Siphiwe Nyanda (Gebuza), and Paul Dikeledi.

We did the same in Botswana and in Lesotho.

The Anti-Republic Day Campaign

Things changed during the anti-Republic Day campaign in 1981, when white South Africa celebrated its twentieth anniversary of leaving the Commonwealth and declaring itself a Republic. And the regime did us a favor by stretching its celebrations over a month.

Remarkably, the enemy was not on guard. Activists within the country embarked on concerted political action. Sabotage activity increased, with leaflet bombs and the like, in the months preceding the Republic Day celebrations on 30 May. Media reports picked up on these; analysts noted a buildup of ANC activity. The media presented our activities as a unified force: that military activity inside South Africa was complementing political action and vice versa. Every bomb blast throughout that month was reported as though some massive concerted effort at overthrowing the regime were under way—and that helped to popularize us. There was a sense of excitement. Although it was not planned, there was a convergence of politico-military work. Each component was reinforcing the other. The sense that the two had to work in an integrated way was strong.

This campaign made it clear that mass mobilization couldn't be left to spontaneous forces but required structural arrangements. In my opinion, the anti-Republic Day campaign laid the groundwork for the UDF. Creating it was one of the best moments in our history. At the same time, the idea of united mass action for a people's war had solidified within the NEC.

But then we missed the opportunity. The ANC's response was not always unified. People had differing views. The military and the political groupings remained independent of one another, even though the leadership paid much lip service to the idea of integration. And then there were a few, Joe Modise most prominently, who thought that things should stay the way they were. They didn't stop to consider whether the masses of the people also saw armed activity, underground political activity, and mass mobilization as complementary, part of one struggle that would create favorable conditions for a people's war.

We had to find ways, bearing in mind the conditions underground, inside South Africa, inside the enemy's *laager*.* We needed to compartmentalize our activities to enable us to coordinate and integrate our efforts to mobilize the masses with everything we were already doing outside the country. A whole set of dynamics favorable to the development

---

*Afrikaans best translated as a "defensive enclosure."

of a people's war was being unleashed, which many people—including myself—didn't see clearly at the time.

Looking back, I think there was a reluctance on the military side based on the fear that the progress they made within the country would be at risk if their work were to be integrated with underground political work. I also think that because of the persistence and zeal with which we raised the need for integration, some of us on the political side, including myself, left others feeling we merely wanted access to the greater human and material resources that were available to the military structures. The political side lost. We simply duped ourselves into believing that we did not consciously have to work at integrating the political and the military, that when the right circumstances arose, it would simply happen.

People's War

After the anti-Republic Day campaign, in September 1981, an RC meeting formulated the idea of Area Political Committees (APCs), which would integrate political and military leadership in defined areas of the country. But the APCs didn't take root. A year later, when the RC reviewed the APCs, some of us* believed we had failed because we had not sent in senior cadres to provide the level of leadership necessary to get them off the ground. The Swaziland/Maputo structures had more success, and they sent a number of senior cadres into the Natal and Transvaal. But even this was not done on a long-term basis.

A wide range of organizations had come together to support the anti-Republic Day campaign. Our military action should have become armed propaganda to reinforce and generate political action by community and mass organizations. But implementation of strategy devolved to the military arena, and the idea of a people's war, with the participation of the people themselves, became little more than a slogan. When Joe Slovo wrote of a people's war, he saw it as mass mobilization, underground political work, and armed activity escalating into classic guerrilla war. In the early period, after Rivonia, the Chinese model was favored. Guerrillas based in rural areas went on to take over towns and cities, but this proved

---

*Mac: "This would be the view of Chris Hani, but I cannot be sure that he was at this meeting because he was based in Lesotho and may not have been present; also, many comrades based in the forward areas would have held this view, but I cannot be sure who was at the meeting."

to be very difficult in South Africa. Comrades like Slovo began to argue in favor of starting in the urban areas and spreading from there.

All along, I argued for integration. The overall command had to come from a *political* structure. MK units had a political commissar, but in reality, this officer had no relationship with the political underground. The military defined the commissar's role as a conduit for relaying information between the internal underground and MK. I argued that this was tantamount to reducing commissars to welfare officers delivering political lectures and that it had nothing to do with the need for the armed activity of units to be guided by the political problems of an area.

In Vietnam, armed units went into villages and addressed the people, but they left someone behind to do political work. This was my approach: armed propaganda was the detonator. There had to be a hands-on political leadership to which the military was subordinate, not vice versa. Senior leadership was needed in the country to give order and direction to integrated structures on the ground. The Vaal uprising in 1984, for example, took place in a power vacuum. We were not yet ready or able to exploit fully the potential unleashed by these uprisings.

Zarina

I met Zarina in Mozambique. We fell in love. She moved to Lusaka in 1979, and we got married in 1981. She was the family's breadwinner. We used to see each other about one weekend every month.

Zarina came from a strangely mixed background, a complicating factor in apartheid South Africa. She was born Zarina Carim in Fordsburg, Johannesburg, in 1944, the first daughter of a pukka Indian Muslim father and a Cape Coloured Christian mother. Her father was black as the ace of spades, her mother lily white, and their family of six—four boys older than Zarina and her younger sister, Shirene—ranged across the color spectrum from pale enough to pass as white and dark enough to be a South Indian Tamil. She was raised Muslim. The community was Indian and Coloured, and her family was the object of discrimination by both for being half caste. When she was sixteen, the Group Areas Act earmarked the area she lived in for whites, so Zarina's mother took five of the children to London. If they had stayed, they would have had to relocate to the Indian ghetto, Lenasia, which was adjacent to the African ghetto, Soweto.

Zarina first married a South African Hindu, Chips Chiba, brother of Laloo Chiba. She moved to Derby, where he worked at Rolls-Royce as an aeronautical engineer. She completed a degree in philosophy and mathematics at Leicester University and then did her masters in mathematics under Alan Rose, one of the pioneers who developed the computer, at Nottingham University. After Zarina graduated, she got a job at General Electric as a research mathematician, in digital communications. She helped to develop algebraic codes for detecting and correcting distortions in digital signals. She later worked at Xerox as part of a team of systems engineers developing the "communicating photocopier"—the precursor of the fax machine.

In London she became politically active, getting involved in ANC Youth meetings where she met activists like the Pahad brothers, Essop and Aziz; Johnny Matshikiza; Ronnie Kasrils; Billy Nunan; Pallo Jordan; Bongi Dhlomo; Barry Feinberg; and Thabo Mbeki. For a while in the early 1970s, she helped to produce ANC weekly news briefings and then joined Mayibuye, the cultural unit of the ANC. She occasionally toured Europe with the troupe during this period.

Zarina became disillusioned with life in London. Her mother's death in 1974 devastated her. Her marriage collapsed. She was dissatisfied with her job. She was offered a job at the University of Algiers but decided instead to go to Mozambique to be a "barefoot teacher" in the bush! But the Mozambique government insisted she teach at the University of Maputo, where she became friends with Ruth First, Albie Sachs, and Alpheus Mangezi, and worked with them to assist South African refugee students.

When her contract expired in Mozambique at the end of 1979, she joined me in Lusaka. She had British citizenship and was offered a job at the University of Zambia in the capacity of a British technical cooperation officer. Her job was to "Zambianize" the computer-based administration and processing of the British General Certificate of Education—the GCE O-level exams—part of the Zambian national education system.

Our son was born in 1982. For the last six months of Zarina's pregnancy, I didn't see my wife. I was in Swaziland overseeing Operation Green Vegetables. She flew to London to have the child because the medical facilities for a woman her age weren't available in Lusaka. So our son was born in London, and we named him Amilcar, after Amilcar Cabral, the Cape Verdean leader who was assassinated after the PAIGC,* the organization

*Partido Africano da Independencia da Guine e Cabo Verde. The party was founded in what was then Portuguese Guinea by the Marxist Amilcar Cabral in 1956, with the aim of achieving independence for Cape Verde and Portuguese Guinea. In the 1950s, Portuguese Guinea was the poorest and least developed Portuguese colony in Africa, though it was prized for its strategic position as it acted as a stepping-stone from Portugal to her colonies in Mozambique and Angola.

that led his country's struggle against Portuguese rule, came to power. It's also similar to Hamilcar, the father of Hannibal, the Carthaginian who crossed the Alps.

Our daughter was born on 14 August 1984, in a hospital in Harare after Zimbabwe's independence, again because of medical facilities. I was present at her birth. We named her Sekai, which is the Shona name for smile. We call her Joey, Sekai-Jo. Her name helped me a lot when I traveled from Zambia to Zimbabwe because whenever they searched my car at the border post for illegal stuff and weapons, I would just walk out and show my daughter's passport. When they read the name Sekai, born in Harare, they would say, "Oh? Is she Shona?" And I would say, "Yes."

Operation Green Vegetables

In December 1980, the ANC signed the Geneva Protocol—the first time a liberation movement had formally associated itself with the Geneva Convention.[38] It was a good tactical move because it emphasized again the rules by which we were fighting. We were saying that we would treat the soldiers of the South African regime as combatants when we captured them and that the South African regime should likewise commit itself to treating captured MK comrades as combatants.

We did this for two reasons: to take the moral highground and to try to reduce support for the South African government in some Western countries. But there was a more significant reason, something I had always argued for: we were driven by a sense of morality. Yet, in reality, the rules of the game were constantly being changed by the apartheid regime. We had to ask ourselves whether continuing to operate as we had done for years was good enough. The apartheid state was thumbing its nose at the world and saying "to hell with the rules." Other assassinations and bombings quickly followed: in 1981, Joe Gqabi was murdered in Harare in July; Griffith Mxenge*

---

*Mxenge was an outspoken human rights lawyer murdered by a Vlakplaas death squad under the direction of Dirk Coetzee on 19 November 1981. His wife, Victoria, an executive member of the UDF, was murdered on 1 August 1985. Her funeral was attended by about 10,000. Victoria Mxenge's murder was followed by widescale violence at Umlazi, where she'd lived. The serious ramifications of her murder were underlined in a State Security Council document compiled in March 1989. It described the killing of Victoria Mxenge as the turning point in the conflict in Natal and KwaZulu. Her killers applied for amnesty before the Truth and Reconciliation Commission. The Mxenge family expressed grave misgivings about the TRC process and maintained that justice had not been done. (Source: www.sahistory.org.za.)

was killed in Umlazi in November. Some of us, including me, believed we had to go further.

On the one hand, the ANC was committed to a set of humanitarian values. The apartheid state and its security forces were acting outside of any moral rules. Its only rule was preservation of white power. In pursuit of that, everything else was fair game. By signing the UN protocol—and emphasizing that it had been signed by both the ANC *and* the MK—we had affirmed our humanitarian values. But if the apartheid state changed the rules, what rules should we adopt? How could we ensure that the international community would not simply ignore the way our enemy contravened international accords?

Cadres and leaders asked, "Is it enough that we just go on hitting these targets, buildings, installations?" They also asked how we could strike back when the enemy executed our people. We considered the question of compulsory conscription in the South African army. Was it legitimate to attack conscripts? The End Conscription Campaign (ECC)[39] was already under way and gaining momentum among white people. Attacking conscripts might alienate potential supporters, yet the regime regarded our own kids, trained or untrained, as legitimate targets.

Within this framework, the RC reached a decision: "OK, Mac, take charge of this. Just go ahead quietly and find a way." I suggested we should attack one of their most vulnerable points by taking out a trainload of conscripts, greenhorns, on their way to a training camp, which the RC endorsed. Greenhorns became Green Vegetables. Operation Green Vegetables fudged the lines between our own distinctions of what a permissible operation was.

OR was part of the decision, but the NEC was kept in the dark. I said to him, "Chief, if we're going to carry out this operation, I have to hit them by surprise and I have to avoid a stand-up fight." OR said, "Phew, so that's the way you're thinking!" We agreed we'd have to think carefully about repercussions and reprisals; Pretoria would be furious.

Part of the plan was to derail the train into a ravine. I discussed this with both OR and Joe Slovo. Slovo said it had to be done outside of the regular machinery without creating another structure. He said I'd have to find a new way. There was much secrecy around this—people were very nervous. And there was a lot of debate. People were unsure whether this was the right kind of target. Besides Slovo, OR may have discussed it with Joe Modise, the overall commander. I did not report to any others; I was authorized by the RC to report directly to OR.

I asked around, picked brains on equipment and so forth. Rashid,* who was either deputy commander or commissar of Special Operations at the time, was my technical consultant because he understood the different types of explosives in our armory. We worked out which explosives were best. I would have to train a special group. I selected a comrade whose code name was Castro, from Mpumalanga, as my key guy. He knew the terrain, and I knew he was a very skilled operator. I got Castro to select two other guys.

We began to collect information about the routes conscript trains took. We knew when they reported and where they were moved. I sent Castro and his guys on a reconnaissance mission to find suitable spots for derailment. We settled on a train from Jo'burg that would pass through the Eastern Transvaal on its way to a training camp near Hoedspruit, through Middelburg and Waterval Boven. Along this route are many sheer drops where, if we hit the train at a bend, it would go straight over the edge of a cliff—a drop no one could survive. There were several suitable spots, particularly between Waterval Boven and Waterval Onder, very mountainous terrain. We had to monitor this train all the way to ensure we hit the right one, and not a passenger or goods train.

I saw OR in Maputo and told him what I was doing. He asked, "How many people will be on that train?" I said several hundred at the very least. He said, "Mac, this is going to have terrible repercussions. These guys will go berserk. Let's think about the political implications." But he told me to carry on. When I sent a message saying "Chief, I'm reaching D-day," he replied, "Call it off; we're not ready." I responded: "In what respect are we not ready? Are we not ready from the political side, or are we not ready for reprisals?" He replied, "Both." But in my first message I'd said, "I can't stop. As an operation like this gains momentum, it reaches a point of no return. Can't stop." I wanted to put pressure on him to let me go ahead.

But several other things were going on in my own life. During the final run-up to the train attack, my hands became covered with festering sores. I had to heed OR's orders, so I retreated from Swaziland to Mozambique, where I called a meeting of the Political Department to discuss the political work at home, and asked Indres to call London, where Zarina was about to give birth to our first child.

In the middle of the meeting on 9 July 1982 a call came through: Zarina had just given birth to my son Milou. I stopped the meeting. I went to Thomas Nkobi and said I wanted a ticket to London. He refused, "No,

*In 1983, Aboobaker Ismail (Rashid) was appointed as commander of Special Operations of MK and in 1987 as chief of ordnance on the military High Command of MK.

that's not work; you can't just get a ticket like that." I said I would go to Lusaka, report to the Revolutionary Council, and then go to London. That was a Friday night. I took the Saturday flight to Lusaka, then the Sunday evening flight to London.

When I got to London, I couldn't even touch the baby's napkin, because my hands were so bad. I saw a doctor and he was intrigued. Finally he came to the conclusion that I was living under such tension that it had triggered the sores.

What was that tension? I did not want to acknowledge to myself that I had doubts about whether the train was the correct target to hit. And yet I couldn't stop. When I told OR it had a momentum of its own, deep down I was appealing to him to rescue me, to tell me to stop. I also couldn't tell the cadres involved what we were planning to do, but they also started to show signs of nervousness. In Swaziland we were under intense pressure from the Swazi army and police—comrades were being captured and thrown out of the country or put in jail. Some members of Rashid's Special Ops unit were captured by the Swazi defense forces on their way from Mozambique to South Africa.* That whole operation was destroyed by the Swazis.

As we learned later, Swaziland had quietly signed an Nkomati-type accord with the South African regime. This laid the basis for intense hunting of our cadres by the Swazi authorities, aided and guided by South African security forces. Mozambique was also under intense pressure, eventually signing the Nkomati Accord. They ordered most of our comrades out of the country. Special Operations was still active but also facing setbacks. Military plans to settle MK command structures in South Africa fizzled out.

After that, the possibility of an attack on the scale of Green Vegetables was not raised again. There was relief among those in the RC who had been uncertain about its repercussions. It was as if everyone didn't really want it to happen, including me. There was never any discussion; nobody wanted to talk about it. I did not submit a report nor, until now, have I ever explained to anybody what happened to me.

---

*Rashid's unit was part of Operation Blackout, a plan to attack South Africa's power grid. The unit was making its way from Mozambique to South Africa through Swaziland when it came under attack by Swazi forces backed up by the SADF. (Conversation with Aboobaker Ismail on 24 July 2006.)

Render the Country Ungovernable!

In the meantime, mass mobilization inside South Africa was making some of the biggest advances: the UDF was launched in Cape Town in 1983. In many parts of the country the people were resisting. The Vaal triangle erupted. Within the country, conditions rapidly matured into an almost permanent standoff between the oppressed people and the regime. In the frontline states we had to operate under difficult and tenuous conditions. The apartheid regime was doing everything possible to weaken the link between the masses in the country and the movement in exile.

On January 8, 1985, the ANC made the call: "Make apartheid unworkable; render the country ungovernable!" "Render the country ungovernable" took a leaf out of the copybook of the Vietnamese struggle. Under Ho Chi Minh, the Vietnamese came to realize that it was necessary to destroy the administrative structures of the colonial power and its collaborators, to break its capacity to govern, and thus make space for the resistance's own structures. "Ungovernability" meant the development of grassroots structures called people's organs—rudimentary people's organs of power.

Although the ANC never articulated it clearly, the idea behind ungovernability rested on the premise that to stay in power, an oppressive minority tends to maintain control over the majority by creating a collaborating elite within that majority. With his policy of separate development, Verwoerd deliberately set out to co-opt some African, Indian, and Coloured people through the Bantustans, the Black Urban Councils, the Indian House of Delegates, the Coloured House of Representatives, and the management committees for Coloureds and Asians at the local government level. In these structures they were not given full power but only played an administrative role.

We realized that the epicenter of the revolt would be in the urban areas and that the instruments lay in the urban councils and their adjuncts: civil servants, the police, and so on. Apartheid had even begun to use black police as its frontline shock troops. This was the context in which ungovernability arose. We would make it impossible for the regime to use any of its usual instruments, even indirect ones, to maintain control. The ANC had to find ways to attack the institutions of apartheid both from within apartheid's institutions and without.

The next step was to set up rudimentary structures among the people themselves. That's how the Committee of Ten, which included Dr. Nthato Motlana, came about in Soweto. It would show people how to run their own lives and regulate their activities. That is why people began to talk of Soweto as a "liberated" zone.

It was not all deliberate; you didn't say, "Let the garbage accumulate," but the idea was that while you made an area ungovernable for the apartheid administration, you began to make it governable for your own community. Unfortunately, it didn't always work out that way. In some cases, young comrades took over townships, set up people's courts, enforced boycotts, instilled fear into the local population, and held their communities as virtual hostages. Bad things began to happen, like "necklacing."* Apartheid provocateurs were also at work. The enemy itself took what we were doing and tried to use it against us. It suited them. And sometimes the comrades drastically misread the situation.

The masses were ahead of the ANC, but that did not mean the ANC had no strategy or that our strategy was wrong. Sometimes things on the ground ran ahead; sometimes Lusaka ran ahead. People on the ground fleshed it out in their own way, sometimes so fast you didn't know how to catch up with them. At times we sent out conflicting signals.

Being so far away was a huge problem. If you advised comrades at home to desist from a particular path, they tended to ignore this if it did not answer the real problems they faced. This was a dangerous moment for us as a political movement. And the underground was still too weak at this stage. We needed to persuade the internal leaders to follow our lead; in some cases, even to change their own stance.

Kabwe

Before the ANC's Second National Consultative Conference at Kabwe, Zambia, from 16 to 22 June 1985, the leadership assumed that the ongoing dissatisfaction of the cadres in the camps was the primary issue.† But in

---

*In 1985, there were more than 60 necklacings (a tire is put over a person's head, doused with petrol, and set on fire). Necklacings peaked at 306 in 1986 and declined thereafter. Clark and Worger, pp. 92, 96.

†See [] general information/organizations/MK/[] Inside Quatro (misspelled on site). See also the report of the Stuart Commission at the same location on the site. The commission was set up by the ANC's National Working Committee (NWC) in March 1984 to investigate the root cause of "the disturbances that erupted in the camps in 1983; nature and genuineness of the grievances; outside or enemy involvement and ring leaders and their motives." The report is a damning indictment of the conditions in the camps. See too: [] general information/organizations/ANC/[] Skweyiya commission report and [] general organizations /organizations/MK/ [] TRC report Holding the ANC Accountable, paras 63 to 74.

the wake of the uprisings at home and the attacks by South African forces into neighboring territories, their thinking changed. At Kabwe, delegates raised concerns about how to intensify the struggle at home. Kabwe brought together cadres from the camps and from the front line and some people from inside the country. We had canvassed opinion within South Africa and in the underground. These views were fed into the conference to help us determine what was holding back the struggle and to define how we should go about escalating it.

Kabwe was a watershed: at last there was a formal acknowledgment of the primacy of the political in the balance between the politico-military components of the struggle. It was the culmination of a long process, and it finally articulated the position that to move forward, we had to change drastically. Yet the strategy document to guide our discussions was vague on most issues.[40] It didn't deal with insurrection; it didn't deal with a people's war, except as a slogan. And it didn't address the issue of negotiations. There was dissatisfaction with it.

And, unfortunately, once again we resorted to a piecemeal approach. The conference endorsed Joe Nhlanhla's proposal for a Politico-Military Council (PMC) to replace the RC, but it didn't elaborate on the different levels that would be done by the PMC together with the NEC. The PMC was established, its name recognizing the direct and critical relationship between the two forms of struggle: the political, both overt and covert, and the military. Many people in the Revolutionary Council were also on the PMC. If you looked at the personalities involved, you'd say, "What's changed?" But the name change—*Politico*-Military—implied that our struggle was not just based on armed activity. Kabwe endorsed the idea of integrated leadership.

But this response was mechanistic. It didn't examine the problem. Structures were set up that grew out of different people's theoretical conceptions rather than growing organically and on the basis of strategy. There were boxes within boxes.

Politico-Military Council (PMC)

Central to the PMC's mandate was the development of a co-coordinated politico-military struggle inside South Africa that would evolve into a people's war. But then the PMC papered over the problems it was supposed to solve by setting up regional politico-military committees (RPMCs). The military felt constrained by the intended integration of the military and the political. They were not happy that events would be driven by political considerations. There were gray areas: How do you run your chains of command? These were legitimate concerns.

To further complicate matters, the Nkomati Accord made it imperative for us to develop a front in Zimbabwe. But Zimbabwe's promise of support was predicated on our being structured like a formal army. Their assistance was so important that we had to agree to their demand. The Maseru massacre tipped the balance in favor of setting up a proper military headquarters.* This shifted the focus of the PMC. The military worried about how to create traditional military structures and chains of command to every frontline area, while discussions within the PMC got sidetracked by the need to create these structures.

Zimbabwe's assistance never materialized. The South African government started putting the screws on the Zimbabwean government. It began to bomb Harare and carry out counterintelligence work. Under ZANU-PF (Zimbabwe African National Union-Patriotic Front), Zimbabwe was unable to overcome the historical legacy that the ANC had aligned with ZAPU (Zimbabwe African People's Union), while ZANU favored the PAC.

We were drowning in structures. Before Kabwe, we had the NEC. Under the NEC was Central Operations (the military side) and the IPRD (the political side), both reporting to the RC, which in turn reported to the NEC. After Kabwe, the RC was gone, replaced by the PMC, and Central Operations was gone, replaced by military HQ. A new Political Committee (PC) replaced the IPRD. Josiah Jele was appointed chairperson of the Political Committee, and I was the secretary. I also served on the PMC. New structures, but mostly the same names were juggled around.

The three key leaders of MK were in three different countries. The commander, Joe Modise, was mostly in Lusaka; the deputy commander and commissar—first Chris Hani, then Steve Tshwete—were in Angola; and the chief of staff—first Slovo, then Hani—were mostly in Angola and Maputo. Who then would carry out the work of military headquarters? Joe Modise, Jacqueline Molefe, Cassius Make, Ronnie Kasrils. But the two central pins, Slovo and Hani, who had the experience and the capacity to

---

*There were two Maseru massacres. The first was carried out by SADF commandos on 9 December 1982. The attack targeted a number of houses and a block of apartments, and resulted in the deaths of forty-two people. Of these, thirty were South African and twelve were Basotho citizens. Four SADF attackers were wounded. Among the South African casualties was the ANC's chief representative in Lesotho, Zola Nqini. Three years later on 19 December 1985, a seventeen-strong team of Vlakplaas operatives led by Eugene de Kock attacked two houses in Maseru and killed six South Africans and three Basotho citizens.

think things through, were not there. This doesn't imply that Ronnie and others couldn't think, but they were not in the same category as Chris and Joe Slovo. The setup at military HQ made no sense and certainly was no way to run an army. Much of the time it seemed that half of them were not in dynamic contact with the other half. They were not exchanging ideas, grappling together with problems.

Nothing was happening. We would agree on things at a meeting, but after we left, each of us did his or her own thing. So in practice, in the transformation from RC to PMC, I cannot pinpoint any substantial changes in either theory or practice. Although the phrase *people's war* appeared more often in our jargon, it was all theory. Mass mobilization had to become our imperative.

Soft Targets

At Kabwe, a demand was made to escalate the struggle inside the country, a very powerful demand.[41] For a while, the issue of soft targets was unclear to some comrades, so operations like attacks on Wimpy Bars continued. Inside the country and under pressure, cadres sometimes forgot the rules of engagement and hit easy targets—to bomb a Wimpy, all you did was put a limpet mine in a dustbin and disappear.

We had to end this type of operation; it could slip over into the conscious targeting of civilians. When MK was formed, we decided to eschew the terrorist route. Our revolutionary warfare would not embrace Algerian-style terrorism, but under exceptional circumstances, exceptions might have to be made. For example, if cornered, could you take civilians as hostages? Yes, to extricate yourself. Civilians could be caught in crossfire. There were many such questions: Were reservists civilians or members of the armed forces? Were farmers in the commando system also part of the armed forces? After 1985, I was among those who believed that these people were part of the security forces, and not civilians.

Breaks in the Chain of Command

This was a crucial problem: how to define the enemy. Along South Africa's borders, all the farmers had been mobilized as part of the age-old commando system,* with radio communication between farms and to army

---

*Local citizen units consisting of part-time soldiers in the SADF were called commandos. In border areas they were linked by radio transmission to provide a policing of MK crossings. There were approximately 30,000 commandos in 1994.

command—a front line of defense. This was the way the National Security Management Structure worked. Not only the farmers were involved; the rest of the white population was also encouraged to arm themselves. We had to ask, "Are they civilians or are they an adjunct of the regime?" A number of us argued—I certainly did—that the rules of this war were changing.*

Because of the confusion about "soft targets," OR called a meeting. He was upset by the indiscriminate bombing of civilians in the Wimpy Bar. But he was a diplomat. He had learned not only how to build the organization but also how to hold it together. He didn't blame anyone. Some units were clearly acting on their own. The meeting agreed with him: these bombings had to stop. So the PMC decided that senior people would have to visit our front lines with the message: no more indiscriminate bombing of civilians. Soft targets had to be part of the state's military apparatus, commandos, for instance.

Cassius Make,† who used to be deputy secretary of the RC, and I were delegated to be the messengers. Our mandate was to find ways to persuade the cadres to obey the instruction. But even our best endeavors didn't always work. Gaps in the chain of communication resulted in distortions in the interpretation of instructions as they moved down the chain of command. The people in Lusaka and the frontline areas were supposed to identify targets, but by the time their decisions reached cadres deep inside the country, the messages were often garbled. This often made our ground forces

---

*At the time, Oliver Tambo said: "I will summarize the position taken by the Conference in these terms: that the struggle must be intensified at all costs. Over the past nine to ten months at least—at the very least—there have been many soft targets hit by the enemy. Nearly five hundred people have now died in that period . . . massacred, shot down, killed secretly. All those were very, very soft targets. They belong to the sphere of the intensification of the struggle. What we have seen in places like the Eastern Cape is what escalation means for everybody. The distinction between 'hard' and 'soft' targets is going to disappear in an intensified conflict, in an escalating conflict.

"I am not saying that our Conference used the words 'soft targets.' I am saying that the Conference recognized that we are in it. It is happening every day. It happened two days before we started our Conference—a massacre in Gaborone. We did not complain that soft targets were being hit, because they have been hitting them, as I say, all the time. What we did was to recommit ourselves to intensify the armed struggle . . . until the system which makes massacres and conflicts necessary, is abolished. . . ." Go to [] maharaj/documents and reports/ANC/1986? [] Oliver Tambo: press conference on civilian casualties. See response of the ANC to Truth and Reconciliation (TRC) questions at [] post-transition/ TRC/submissions/ANC/[] further submission 12 May 1997/2.2 Armed operations and civilian casualties/armed actions and civilian casualties.

†On 9 July 1987, Cassius Make, ANC NEC member and senior MK commander; Paul Dikeledi, another senior MK operative; and Augusto Elizah Tsinini, a Mozambican national and ANC supporter, were killed in an ambush at Lobamba, Swaziland.

uncertain about what they were supposed to do, and in turn, could sow doubt among cadres about the leadership capacity of their unit commanders.*

Ultimately, everything was stymied because we did not have senior leadership inside South Africa. All the reports were second- and third-hand. But the frequent capture of cadres entering the country slowly stifled the enthusiasm of the leadership for going in.

Whenever I raised the question of sending senior people into the country, everyone readily agreed. But invariably they would say the time wasn't ripe, that the security of senior personnel could not be guaranteed. It was a stalemate.

*The TRC finding: "[After Kabwe] the ANC hardened its stance on civilians. . . .The risk of civilians being caught in the crossfire when such [MK] operations took place could no longer be allowed to prevent the urgently needed, all round intensification of the armed struggle. The focus of the armed operations had to shift towards striking directly at enemy personnel and the struggle had to move out of the townships to the white areas." While the TRC acknowledged the grave concerns of the NEC, and Tambo in particular, at the rising number of civilian casualties, "it is equally clear," it said, "that action was rarely taken against operatives or units who were responsible for these breaches of humanitarian law." See [] general information/organizations/MK/[] holding the ANC accountable, paras 43 to 47.

11. VULA: GETTING STARTED

Introduction

IN AUGUST 1985, state president P. W. Botha delivered his self-proclaimed Rubicon speech.[1] The South African state was under enormous pressure from within and without, and there were signs that Botha was ready to make some concessions. The international community was convinced that Botha would announce the release of Nelson Mandela, possible negotiations with the ANC, and the steps his government would take to dismantle apartheid.[*2] But in his speech, the concessions and reforms offered were so minor that his insistence that South Africa was now "crossing the Rubicon" to a new dispensation was castigated out of hand. Instead of announcing significant reform initiatives, Botha fulminated at South Africa's perceived enemies, castigated the West for trying to tell him what to do, and was by turn truculent, combative, and nonconciliatory. Some say Botha changed the speech at the last minute, in a fit of pique against the reformists who had drafted it.[3] Whatever the case, the lack of movement on real reform in South Africa after the Rubicon speech simply made matters worse, and on June 12, 1986, a national state of emergency had to be declared to contain internal unrest.

But the speech, in effect, sounded the death knell for apartheid. A

*Pik Botha says that his department submitted a draft speech to Botha's office that included proposals to dismantle apartheid and release Mandela, and that the speech concluded with the words "We are crossing the Rubicon"—the only words in his draft that were included in Botha's speech. [] o'malley interviews/2006/[] Pik Botha. For a further account of the shenanigans surrounding the preparation of the Botha speech and Botha's reactions to what he perceived as an attempt by some of his ministers, especially foreign minister Pik Botha, to put words in his mouth, see Waldmeir, *Anatomy of a Miracle*, pp. 53–57. See, too, interviews with Stoffel van der Merwe [] o'malley interviews/1999/[].

media looking for grand gestures missed the more prosaic ones. "Should any of the Black National States prefer not to accept independence," Botha had intoned, "such states or communities will remain part of the South African nation, are South African citizens, and should be accommodated within political institutions within the boundaries of South Africa."[4] In September 1985, he went a step further: the National Party, he announced, was "committed to the principle of an undivided South Africa, one citizenship and universal franchise, *but within structures of South Africa's own choosing*" (my italics).[5] In February 1986, he repeated the promise.[6] Few believed him.*[7] But within the NP, younger, more worldly-wise MPs, not inhibited by what they regarded as old-fashioned notions of blind loyalty to the *volk*, were growing restless. In particular, the class of 1987 MPs came to parliament impatient with the old order and open to change that challenged the very orthodoxies that were at the core of NP dogma.[†]

Botha's pugnacious Rubicon speech was instrumental in the imposition of financial sanctions: first Chase Manhattan and then other banks refused to roll over South Africa's short-term debts. Financial sanctions would succeed where trade sanctions had failed. By cutting off the country's lifeline to international credit and withholding agreement on the rescheduling of debt, the international community slowly choked off the oxygen of capital inflows into South Africa; without them, the economy could no longer breathe.[8] Between August 1987 and October 1988, South Africa spent almost half of its foreign exchange reserves just to service existing loans.[9]

By the mid-1980s, African townships were hotbeds of militant resistance, most of it unorchestrated, uncoordinated, and unfocused. Successive states of emergency in 1985 and 1986 harnessed the resources of the state to smash new forms of popular resistance. More than thirty-five thousand troops were deployed in the townships. Anti-apartheid activists and organizations were increasingly subjected to new terror tactics: vigilante groups sought out and murdered activists or launched mass attacks on communities with the tacit or overt support of the police.[10] The police themselves murdered in stealth. In 1985 alone nearly two thousand blacks were killed.[11]

---

*Dr. Frederik van Zyl Slabbert, leader of the white, liberal official opposition, the Progressive Federal Party (PFP), denounced Botha and resigned from parliament. He was joined by the party's deputy leader, Alex Boraine, who later became deputy chairperson of the TRC.

†Roelf Meyer, Chris Fismer, Piet Coetsee, Dawie de Villiers, Stoffel van der Merwe, Tertius Delport, Gerrit Viljoen. For interviews with, go to [] o'malley interviews/[].

By mid-1986, the National Security Management System (NSMS) was at the apex of state power. Local national security management committees coordinated security structures. The NSMS was almost a separate arm of government.[12] The security forces, which now came under its jurisdiction, embarked on a campaign to win the hearts and minds (WHAM) of the people.[13] But nothing worked.[14]

The NSMS established a national network that reached into every part of the country, identifying anti-apartheid activities, formulating a continuous national security profile, and making decisions on action at national and local levels that could then be implemented by the formal law enforcement structures backed by legislation—or by other structures acting covertly.

The state of emergency in 1986, under which thirty-six thousand people were detained, slowed but did not halt mass demonstrations. The focus of defiance simply moved from the streets to the workplace. Nine million workdays were lost in 1987, a sixfold increase over the record high of 1986.[15]

2

In November 1985, a new political actor emerged. COSATU (Congress of South African Trade Unions) brought together most of the country's black trade unions, representing more than seven hundred thousand workers, under one organizing umbrella. It immediately endorsed the Freedom Charter. The immense power it would wield became apparent when the struggle entered a new phase—the economic arena. COSATU gave a new direction to protest, taking it off the streets and onto the factory floor. The economy became a new theater of war; business could no longer pretend to be above politics. Internal investment, which had steadily contracted throughout the 1980s, dried up.

In August 1987, NUM (National Union of Mineworkers) took on the all-powerful Chamber of Mines. Some 250,000 black miners embarked on a nationwide strike that lasted for three weeks. The strike crippled South Africa's gold mines and closed down a quarter of its coal pits—a direct assault on a pivotal sector of South Africa's economy. (Gold and coal accounted for more than half of South Africa's total foreign earnings.) Nine mine workers were killed and close to a thousand were injured or arrested. Losses to the mines were estimated from $125 million to $225 million.

NUM called off the strike when forty thousand mine workers were summarily dismissed, but it had accomplished its larger mission. Dismissed miners were reinstated and concessions made. Cyril Ramaphosa, the head of NUM, called it a dress rehearsal. The unions and the UDF synchronized their activities, and this synergy was the catalyst for the emergence of the broad-based Mass Democratic Movement (MDM). Whites, perhaps for the first time, were jerked into a new reality: black trade unions could hold the country hostage to their demands. The strike was a shot across the bow.

3

The generals told the government that the solution to the crisis of the state was political.[16] And the National Party finally admitted that their home-lands policy had failed and that some formula for incorporating the black population into South Africa would have to be found.

In 1986, Botha's Special Cabinet Committee, of which F. W. de Klerk was a member, reported to the cabinet that there would have to be a "180-degree turn in NP policy, forever away from apartheid, separate develop-ment and racial discrimination."[17] The new policy framework "accepted the fundamental principles of one united South Africa; one person, one vote; the eradication of racial discrimination; and the effective protection of minorities against domination."[18] Fine words, but they had no apparent impact. Botha, still immersed in cold war politics, conflated the ANC with communism.*

The NP campaigned on the new policy in the 1987 national elections, albeit with some ambiguity. It won, but with a decreased majority because the Conservative Party had cut into its support. Clearly, there were many South Africans who remained determined not to yield an inch to black de-mands. The split among whites deepened.

During the election campaign, the NP went to extreme lengths to make a distinction between one person, one vote and black majority rule—the latter was anathema to all but the most liberal whites, and would, once negotiations got under way, become the key issue, the impact of which the NP desperately tried to subvert with a plethora of proposals all incorporating an implicit veto for the white minority.

---

*In 1986, sixteen leading theologians in the Dutch Reformed Church, the Afrikaner church, signed a confession of guilt denouncing the church's support for apartheid, and the church's Western Cape branch, reversing a theological position it had adhered to for forty years, declared that there was no biblical justification for apartheid. The church opened its doors to members of all races.

In July 1987, Frederick van Zyl Slabbert led a group of leading Afrikaner opinion makers and businesspeople to Dakar, Senegal, to meet with the ANC leadership, despite P. W. Botha's dire warnings of the repercussions they would face. In Dakar, the two sides found themselves agreeing that "there is an urgent necessity to realize the goals of a non-racial democracy."

On their return, Van Zyl Slabbert and those who had traveled with him spread the word in elite circles: the ANC leaders were people the government could do business with. They were not a gang of zealous Communists hell-bent on overthrowing the South African government and establishing a Communist hegemony. Rather, the ANC leadership comprised reasonable and articulate men and women intent on establishing a democratic franchise in South Africa. Publicly, Botha kept quiet. But the ice had been broken. A new breed of Afrikaner leaders was appearing.

These events, however, took place against a background of increasing violence. The war for South Africa was fought on many different tracks, both overt and covert. Although a consensus was slowly building that a negotiated settlement would ultimately emerge, the securocrats wanted to negotiate from a position of strength. They set out to undermine the ANC to the degree that the regime could dictate the terms of the negotiations.

Thus the State Security Council (SCC), especially in 1986–87, was party to the setting up of death squads.[19] Activists in South Africa became the targets of state security agents or hired killers. The death squads based at Vlakplaas believed they had been given a license to kill.[20] And in KwaZulu-Natal, Inkatha, which was backed by the South African security apparatus, tried to wipe out the UDF. In 1985, the Inkatha Central Committee decided that "the whole of KwaZulu and Natal must be turned into a so-called 'no go area' for the UDF regardless of the consequences."[21] The UDF had other ideas.

Meanwhile, unbeknownst to all but a few, Kobie Coetsee, the minister of justice, had opened informal talks with Mandela in prison. In 1986, a team of senior government officials, headed by Niel Barnard, head of the National Intelligence Service (NIS), joined the talks. Between 1986 and Mandela's release in February 1990, at least forty-eight such meetings were held.

4

In the 1980s, it became increasingly apparent that there was a need for an ANC leadership within the country. Activists would leave South Africa and make their way to Lusaka to ask for guidance. Yet often Lusaka was not in a position to provide any because it did not have enough hands-on knowledge of situations on the ground in South Africa. The struggle paradigm had shifted: those who made the pilgrimage to Lusaka seeking guidance often ended up providing both knowledge and counseling to the struggle's elders.[22]

Vula was an ambitious project aiming to locate senior leaders, including members of the NEC and PMC, within South Africa to take overall charge of the struggle. Vula was under the direct command of Oliver Tambo (OR), assisted by Joe Slovo (JS). But the Vula mandate, hammered out by Tambo and Slovo with Mac, involved multiple tasks. It was to provide local all-around leadership, working with the internal leadership in Natal and the Witwatersrand, in order to bring about effective coordination of underground political work, mass mobilization, and military activity. It was to set up the infrastructure for a people's war, including on-the-spot military recruitment and training, and the importation and caching of arms. It had to establish political structures to ensure that all areas of activity, including military activity, were conducted under the overall political guidance of the ANC.

The operation underwent almost two years of planning. Multiple disguises, passports, and ID cards were prepared; labyrinthine travel routes and sophisticated communications were developed; sleepers were recruited. Finally, Mac, who headed the operation, and his deputy Siphiwe Nyanda (who went under the nom de guerre Gebuza) were ready to cross the border from Swaziland into South Africa.

When the resolution authorizing Tambo to do whatever he saw fit to send NEC members into South Africa was passed, most NEC members probably felt relieved—the long debate on the issue was over. In theory, all agreed that the NEC had to establish a presence in the country. Most, however, also felt that the conditions had to be right: for instance, that the probability of an NEC member being captured by the enemy should be minimal. Such a capture would be a severe drawback for the movement, demoralizing for the masses, and a propaganda coup for the enemy. So NEC members wanted to go but only under safe conditions, and then only for a short period.

Since the demise of apartheid, the proclivity to rewrite the history of the apartheid era has given rise to "struggle" history with its recurring emphasis on the daunting odds facing ANC cadres in their war against an implacable enemy. The truth, of course, is a little more complex. Mac's account of NEC meetings—the same ground being covered again and again, members groping their way to the same inconclusive positions—is telling for what he is too loyal to say in uncompromising terms: the leadership of black South Africa's struggle for freedom convinced itself that it could better serve the cause by absenting itself from South Africa. It was an armchair revolution.

Tambo said he may have pointed his finger at NEC members to order any one of them to return to South Africa at any time, but it is fair to assume that no one, least of all Tambo himself, took this dramatic gesture too seriously. Once the NEC gave Tambo a blank check to deal with the issue, it absolved itself of any further interest in the matter, so much so that when Vula unraveled in 1990, some members who had enthusiastically handed Tambo the blank check in 1986 had forgotten all about it.

By 1987, the first glimmers of a negotiated settlement were beginning to emerge through the fog of obfuscation and denial that are a ritualistic part of conflict-resolution foreplay. Agreeing to disappear from Lusaka into the underground in South Africa removed one from the intrigues of the Lusaka court: the constant maneuvering for position where ambitious men and women began to sniff the sweet odor of power in the political breezes wafting from Pretoria. Consciously putting oneself out of the loop at such a critical time carried with it the risk of becoming irrelevant. Because the cause was just did not mean the politics were less cruel. In short, the ambitious were more likely to be found at the embassy parties in Lusaka than in the undergrowth on the Highveld.

It was no great surprise that Tambo and Slovo told Mac that he had been chosen to lead the operation taking NEC members back into South Africa. Mac, after all, had been the persistent nagging voice on the RC, the PMC, and every other structure he was part of—he would not let the matter drop. Once given the task, he went about it with his usual ferocious determination, but he was largely left to his own ingenuity. He had to raise his own seed money and develop the elaborate preparations. He had to choose his team, a largely Indian group with whom he had developed relations over the years, a tight-knit "cabal" (later a word used in the ANC to label conspiracies of one kind or another, including accusations of an "Indian cabal").[23] He made use of the organizational and managerial skills that were the hallmark of the SACP at its best.

Yet Vula was not the work of a single individual. Translating the idea from concept to implementation was the work of many, mostly working alone, many unaware of the involvement of others, and none, other than a close few, aware of what the purpose of the operation was. Firewalls were built; Vula was an exercise in absolute compartmentalization. All communications went through a single channel, which distributed information to Vula-related cadres.

The operation's most spectacular achievement—the creation of the communications system that linked Vula in South Africa with Lusaka via London in real time—was a team effort with the bulk of the credit due to Tim Jenkin and his partnership with Ronnie Press, both in London, and the technical expertise of Zarina Maharaj in Lusaka. That three-way collaboration produced a system of communications that eluded the best of the state's tracking devices.

5

Ivan Pillay, who was in charge of Vula at the Lusaka end, says he was redeployed by Tambo and Slovo to work on Vula, but he was to be seen in Lusaka primarily as a party apparatchik, further distancing Vula activities from the ANC—the party was the cover. Pillay said: "The party had a certain mystique about it in those days. It was held in very high esteem by Indian people and also by careerists who wanted to get ahead. I had been a member of the party since 1981, but there were very few people who were known to be in the party, and it was decided that I would be known to be a full-time member on the staff of the party."[24]

Pillay stayed in the party house, drove a party car, did party work, and became a member of the Central Committee. He spent 10 percent of his time on party work and the rest on Vula. He set up a small Vula infrastructure, which stretched from London to Holland to Lusaka. In Lusaka there was secret Vula housing for three Dutch people* brought in specifically for the purpose of providing Vula with an infrastructure that could not be connected to a known ANC or party infrastructure. The communications systems were set up in the houses they rented.

But Pillay brings a critical eye to the ANC's actions on Vula. While the NEC dithered, the struggle in South Africa was forging ahead, without the ANC's direct guidance—it was, you might say, only a distant inspiration. "By the time we got that leadership inside the country, it was actually a little bit too late," says Pillay. The goalposts had moved: "The fact of the mat-

*Lucia Raadschelders and a couple, Ineke and Links Vos.

ter is that the situation had managed very well without us." That, he emphasizes, is only his "historical opinion."[25]

His observation is not a popular one, but given Pillay's credentials, it cannot be dismissed. The ANC in exile snatched victory from the jaws of the internal mass movements. The Mass Democratic Movement's (MDM) broad reach and inclusiveness made it noncohesive. The UDF had close to seven hundred affiliates, with representation from every walk of life in South Africa, but it began to wither without central direction. It dissipated its energies, lacked dynamic leadership, and was riven with petty rivalries.[26] Nevertheless, as a vehicle to mobilize the masses, whether for consumer boycotts, rent withholding, stayaways, or strikes, the UDF was unstoppable. Unless the ANC got its act together, the revolutionary express would whiz by as it stood motionless on an empty platform reading the timetable.

By the time the ANC managed to get one member of the NEC inside the country, the struggle had developed its own momentum. Lusaka had become reactive. The mass movements were creating a mass revolution. Lusaka was trying to gain a foothold, parade its pedigree, invoke Mandela— Madiba went down far better with the masses than with the NEC. In a sense, Vula was subversive. It infiltrated the MDM, used the political underground it harnessed to seduce MDM leaders and hijack its revolution-in-the-making. Although the MDM did not know it, the ANC in exile needed the MDM far more than the MDM needed the ANC. Perhaps, when the real history of the period is written, Vula's greatest contribution will be seen to have been its contribution to the ease with which the ANC returned from exile and simply appropriated the machinery of the mass movements. It could do so because Vula had done its homework.

Mac

OPERATION VULA was the only logical conclusion to a discussion we had been having ever since I had been assigned to Lusaka. The struggle had reached a point where the different pillars of struggle—mass struggle, armed struggle, underground political struggle, and international pressure—needed to work more in sync with one another. For security reasons, these activities were isolated from one another so that enemy penetration on the armed side did not lead to destruction of the political or the mass side, or vice versa. But while that separation was needed, we also needed more effective synchronization.

We couldn't talk about making a township like KwaMashu ungovernable—that's mass action—and in the meantime, our armed formations or the political underground were not there to support the creation of people's committees. First, repression directed at the masses needed to be countered by MK. Second, the rudimentary organs of people's power created by communities needed to be defended. So MK actions had to be tuned to what was happening on the ground. Support also had to be forthcoming from the political underground—our propaganda had to be in tune with these developments; we had to speak to the masses in a way that was meaningful to them. We needed to remind ourselves that the call from the ANC was not simply for "ungovernability"—it was to make the apartheid state unworkable.

We needed to send in people with the authority to provide overall leadership and with the status to interact with the command structures on all levels, including the military side.

We had been using less senior cadres to try to create a leadership inside the country. When they bumped into an MK unit on the ground, they were unable to assert their authority. Sometimes an MK unit would try to tell the political side what to do, but also fail to assert its authority. Neither side would bow to the other.

Vula's rationale was that authority could be asserted only if people from the NEC and the PMC came in and worked with the leadership within the country on every other level. Which is why, at the mass level, one of the primary thrusts of Vula was *not* to sit on the committees of the MDM but to interact directly with key comrades in their leadership.

At Kabwe it was agreed that the NEC would have to address the question of getting the leadership into the country. At the first few meetings of the NEC after Kabwe, the same presentation was made by the internal political wing and the military, the gist of it being progress, but no real progress. It became a bore to have that item on the agenda because all that happened was more discussion along the lines of well, you'd better pull up your socks because something's got to be done, and by the next meeting there must be progress. But no real suggestion was put forward about how to move forward.

The First Stirrings

We were now into 1986. The uprisings were petering out. At the first meeting of the NEC that year, once again we ended up saying that we needed to raise the caliber of our political/military leadership inside the country. At the tea break I suggested to Slovo, Zuma, and Hani that we propose a motion for the president to set up a smaller group to deal with this issue. He would not have to disclose details to the NEC because security would have to be very tight to ensure that the enemy did not get even a whiff of what was being planned or done. Hani proposed the motion in the meeting, and it was accepted—the NEC gave Tambo a blank check.

Immediately after that meeting Tambo and Slovo came to my house. They said, "Mac, we want you to put the concept on paper for the two of us." We wanted to bring leadership people into the country, but they had to integrate with the leadership that had already emerged in the MDM. The leadership that was sent in would not dictate to the mass organizations but would get into a proper dialogue with them so that we could strategize together.[27]

I prepared a two-page report and we debated it; then I was asked to refine it; more debate, more refining. I applied it to a couple of regions—Natal and, roughly, the Witwatersrand. By looking at a specific region, I was able to say, "This is how we will do it. The approach should be tailored to the realities of each area."

My idea was to divide South Africa into regions. Each region would have its own operation, and each would be in communication with Lusaka. We didn't get to the point of discussing how the regions should relate to one another because the core problem at this stage was about survival within the country. It would have been premature to start discussing how to link up cadres across provinces.

I set down a number of basic requirements that I thought would have to be met before we even contemplated sending anyone into a region. The structure required a means of communicating with Lusaka in place; the people who went in should each, separately, find accommodation and safe houses for themselves. The key issues were, first, how to create a structure and insulate the different units and substructures and, second, how to relate to the mass organizations.

We also had to look at improving our communications, which were slow. I reminded them of the Zimbabwe experience, where the enemy captured the couriers, quickly got them to talk, and then sent them back as if everything were working fine, and also of Zarina's experience as a systems analyst for Xerox, so I suggested they authorize me to look into the problem. They agreed. Zarina and I decided to make a start with the computer she had already bought at her own expense.

We needed funds. OR couldn't ask the treasurer general, Thomas Nkobi, for money because he might raise awkward questions and suspect something was afoot, so on one of my trips to Britain, with OR's agreement, I raised a hundred thousand dollars—Joel Joffe was the donor—and that's how Vula was started.

Who Goes In?

By early 1987, OR and JS had selected me to go back into the country.* Chris Hani had been selected too. In my discussions with OR and JS, they hinted that they were contemplating selecting a third NEC member as well, perhaps JZ (Jacob Zuma).† This operation was never formally named Vula. I selected the name for the region I was going into. I originally chose *vulindlela,* Zulu for "open the road," which was shortened to *vula,* "open." I was working on the basis that the commanders for other regions would select their own names to distinguish one region from another and not let the enemy tumble onto a planned countrywide thrust. But today anyone who was in any region of the country at the time—like Charles Nqakula and Little John (Christopher Manye), who were preparing the way for Hani—regards himself as having been part of Operation Vula.

OR and JS intended to apply the strategy and planning for Vula to other regions, but it does not seem that they got far in preparing and sending in other members of the PMC and NEC.

Gebuza (Siphiwe Nyanda), the MK commander of the Transvaal urban military machinery, was chosen to be my deputy. Gebuza had a track record as a daring fighter. He was resourceful and innovative. The Transvaal machinery operated from Swaziland and Maputo. Some of his unit's actions became part of struggle's folklore. Gebuza seemed to have a charmed life, and his exploits in evading the South African security forces bore the touch of a Houdini. I couldn't have asked for a better deputy.

Preparations

I now began to phase myself out of other work, pretending that I was too ill to continue as secretary of the political underground. Two years—1986

---

*One of the fads in South Africa during the forties and fifties was addressing people by the first two initials of their names. Thus Oliver Reginald Tambo came to be known as OR and Joe Slovo as JS.

†Zuma says he was asked by Tambo to return to South Africa and that he agreed to provided he could handle all his own arrangements. However, before he could complete his arrangements, he was made chief of intelligence.[]maharaj/interviewees/[] Jacob Zuma (2005) embargoed until 2030.

to 1988—were spent in preparation, solving the communications problem, strategizing, creating a cover story, establishing the infrastructure for
survival, completely separate from anything else on the ground. This work
fell almost entirely on my shoulders. Rumor proved useful. It would be
said that I was in Canada for four days addressing a conference, say, or that
I was in a hospital; then I would be seen in Lusaka for a week; then it
would be said that I'd disappeared again. A rumor was put out that I was
in a hospital, that I was suffering from an increasingly debilitating illness
and that the doctors were having some difficulty finding out exactly what
was wrong with me. I had to prepare a cover that was so convincing that
even comrades in the NEC believed it. If they believed it, then perhaps the
regime would buy it too. In late 1987, Vladimir Shubin,[28] our key link on
the Soviet side, was brought into the loop by Tambo and JS. In Lusaka, Ivan
Pillay was appointed to take charge of the logistics, personnel, and other
services we would need. He had lived for years in Swaziland in the underground and since the late 1970s was also a member of the IPRD committee.

For military personnel, we could draw on either the pool of cadres in
the camps, who were already trained, or from those already deployed in
the forward areas or elsewhere. Once I was in the country, we could draw
on cadres in the MDM who knew the politics of the country and the areas
in which we would set up camp.

Refresher Courses

I took refresher courses in the GDR, Moscow, and Cuba. In the GDR, I
took a course on urban warfare because I felt that my limited training in
1962 was inadequate for our purposes and conditions. I also took one on
intelligence work, about developing an intelligence infrastructure and
penetrating the enemy.

In Moscow, I took a military course. My focus was going to be the urban areas because our strategic concept was to move toward a people's
war. We needed to create a relationship with the forces on the ground that
would bring what we had called the four pillars into a convergence.

I also went to Cuba. In Cuba's case, there were two organizations: the
July 26 Movement, led by Fidel Castro, and the Communist Party, led by
Blas Roca. Come the revolution, the real force was the July 26 Movement,
but later the two organizations came together and formed the United Socialist Party of Cuba. Even though they were separate—and Roca had earlier called the July 26 Movement "adventurists"—they came to respect
each other and eventually joined forces.

I wanted to learn from the Cuban experience. It had a bearing on both the way COSATU and the UDF worked together and how we worked with them. By studying the Cuban experience firsthand, I felt I would be better placed to handle such things.

Negotiations

The ANC always left the door open for negotiations. We had turned to the armed struggle only when the regime left us with no alternative. But that did not diminish our willingness to negotiate, as long as we believed the government was acting in good faith.

At Kabwe, OR briefed the conference about a bunch of businessmen who wanted to come and meet us. He said, "I cannot assure you that some people in this delegation will not go back and inform the government of what we talked about. Can we go ahead; can we engage?" And he got the conference's permission.

As early as 1986, feelers from Pretoria began to drift our way. Even I received a cryptic message on one occasion. I was in New York in June 1986 on my way to a conference on Long Island, New York, sponsored by the Ford Foundation, where the head of the Broederbond, Pieter de Lange, was due to make a presentation.[29] A high-level ANC delegation, including Thabo Mbeki, was attending. This in itself was a historic first, a sign of changing times—a face-to-face encounter between the movement and the voice of the Afrikaner establishment. At my hotel there was a message for me, "Ashley Wills, Washington, called. Please call him back at this number." So I called him back. He said, "I want to come and see you." He said that they (Washington) had reason to believe that Pretoria would start making overtures to the ANC, so he had come to appeal to me: should we receive such overtures, we should think carefully and respond positively.*[30]

---

*Ashley Wills attributes a lot more importance to the meeting than Mac does. In 1986, Wills, a career diplomat, was head of the Africa Desk in the State Department. His immediate superior was Chester Crocker, under secretary of state for Africa. Wills recalls: "I was officer in charge of the South Africa Desk in the State Department, and my boss, assistant secretary Chet Crocker, was musing one day about how it would be useful for us to establish contact with the ANC. I piped up and said, 'Well, I happen to know a senior person in the ANC.' There was astonishment all around. I sent word to our intelligence agencies that someone should let me know if Mac Maharaj was coming to the United States, and not long thereafter I got word that he was coming to New York. I arranged to go up there and marched into his hotel and rang him on the hotel phone. He was very surprised. We had a lovely reunion downstairs in the lobby and spent two or three hours chatting about what he had been doing in the intervening years and what the ANC's

He didn't appear to know that Mandela was already meeting with the South African government, but he certainly indicated that there were talks going on, with pressure from the Western powers, particularly the United States. I passed the message on to Thabo, and to OR when I got back to Lusaka, and that was the end of my involvement in the matter. But I assume that other overtures were being made to Thabo, OR, and others.

In October 1987, I attended a meeting of the NEC at which overtures from the regime were discussed. The NEC passed a resolution: no to bogus negotiations, yes to genuine negotiations. Our intelligence section was wary of these overtures and maintained that the government's National Intelligence Service (NIS) under Niel Barnard was following a twin-track strategy: the possibility of negotiations as well as the idea of weakening the ANC and splitting it.* We shared the view that if and when real negotiations came about, the apartheid regime would pursue such a strategy. This, after all, was the way Britain had handled negotiations over Zimbabwe. South Africa had used the same tactics in Namibia. At the same time, both within the country and outside, the pressures on Pretoria to move toward negotiations were mounting. Pressure was also mounting on the ANC—one more reason why we needed to do everything to hasten the struggle at home.[31]

---

view was, and I communicated to him the Reagan administration's wish to establish an informal contact with the ANC. He was cautious. It was a great surprise to him that I was communicating quite a significant signal, and he, as a good ANC official, didn't quite know how to interpret this and wasn't sure how his colleagues in Lusaka or wherever would react. So he took a reserved position, said he understood what I was saying to him and that he would pass it on and we would hear back. We did hear back.

"One thing led to another, and contact was established. A few months after that we invited Oliver Tambo to Washington to meet with secretary of state George Shultz. One of the photographs I have on my so-called me wall is my introducing Oliver Tambo, president of the ANC, to secretary of state George Shultz. That contact led eventually to all kinds of positive developments both in our relations with the ANC and the ANC's relations with the South African government, and eventually to Mr. Mandela's release. It was all initiated by this conversation between Mac and me, and that was possible because of our relationship going back several years earlier."

*Barnard rejects out of hand this analysis of his actions. He insists that talks with Mandela were initiated by P. W. Botha after much prodding from the NIS, which had concluded as early as 1985 that only a negotiated settlement would stave off the economic collapse of South Africa. [] o'malley interviews/1996/[] Niel Barnard, 17 September. Maritz Spaarwater, director of operations in the NIS, who, among other things, oversaw the analysis of economic data, recalls the morning when Botha himself visited his office, peered intently at the data on the wall, and said, "Does this mean the country is bankrupt?" []o'malley/interviews/[] Spaarwater.

Communications

Before Vula, I was already acutely aware that our movement had to find new answers in the field of communications. In 1982, Zarina and I bought a computer in Mexico, which was shipped via Canada, Britain, and Tanzania to Lusaka. It was very big, made by Ohio Computers in the United States, and we didn't want anybody to know that we owned it. With OR's and Nkobi's permission, we built a special building to house it. Govind Chiba (Chips), Zarina's former husband, an aeronautical engineer who had been in computers at Rolls-Royce, practically lived there; he slept and ate and drank and worked on that computer. Very few people knew about it. We were experimenting with data storage and retrieval. In 1985, Ronnie Kasrils became head of Military Intelligence, and he recruited a unit from South African comrades in London and brought in computers. By then the computer from Mexico was obsolete.

Jackie Molefe was the head of communications in the Revolutionary Council (RC). She had installed and successfully linked Luanda and Lusaka by radio. When Kasrils became head of Military Intelligence, he and Jackie put their heads together. Kasrils was able to equip an MK unit, the Broederstroom group, led by Damian de Lange,[32] and they were able to infiltrate the country with a mobile radio transmitter beaming to Luanda.

Transmission by radio signals was the best we could do, but I foresaw problems because once a transmitter went on the air, the regime could pinpoint with great speed where it was. Kasrils assured me his unit would compress the signals into a short sharp burst. In debriefing him, I realized they were still relying on manual encryption. There had to be a different answer, but I did not raise this with him. My instincts told me that the socialist countries, on which we were dependent for our techniques and communications equipment, would not reveal their latest innovations.

My views were confirmed when a Soviet general stationed in Angola offered help. He suggested satellite communications. "Who will decrypt?" I asked. He said, "My people." But I didn't want my communications to be seen by people I didn't know, including people in the Soviet Union.

Tim Jenkin and Ronnie Press in London were also working on communications problems. I sounded out Jenkin during one of his visits to Lusaka. When I outlined the problems, I found Jenkin had an instant understanding. He was really the only comrade who thought through the problem from the standpoint of the underground in South Africa. I knew

I had found the right person for the task. He was full of ideas, but he was also frustrated when so many of his ideas were dismissed by his comrades.

Jenkin and Press were way ahead of their time in developing such communication techniques; less technically inclined comrades thought them far-fetched. But once I had met the two of them, I knew I had struck gold. They were on the ANC's Technical Committee in London, which came up with innovative ways of smuggling things into South Africa and the like. They had been working with computers and encryption systems for some time but without any takers—until I came along.

With Zarina and me, working outside the loops of the movement, within the space of a year the four of us had developed the basic equipment and techniques that resolved the difficulties of speedy coding and decoding, of computerized encryption, and rapid transmission using the public telephone system.

We used a laptop computer, a tape recorder, an acoustic coupler that fitted snugly over the mouthpiece or earpiece of a phone for transmitting or receiving, the program disks for operating the system and the coding/decoding disk. Messages were typed on the computer, encrypted by it, and then the signals were transferred to the tape recorder. We attached the tape recorder to the acoustic coupler and went to a public phone and dialed a number in London. As soon as we were connected to London, we fixed the coupler to the mouthpiece and switched the tape recorder to Play.

Within the space of a minute we were able to send a two-thousand-word message. London picked up the message on a tape recorder, fed it into their computer to decrypt it, recoded the message, and sent it on in the same way to Lusaka. In short, with prearrangement we could be in touch with Lusaka within fifteen minutes. To receive messages, the procedure was reversed.

Without Jenkin, Press, and Zarina, this breakthrough in communications could not have happened. But Jenkin was the central figure.[33] I was simply the cheerleader.

Sleepers

First I sent in the expatriates: Bob and Helen Douglas, Canadians; Anita Kreuss, a German; and Susan Grabeck, another Canadian. They were unknown to one another. They had only one purpose: to set up safe accommodation without being told for what or for whom. We started working on building the rest of the forces, calling for others from outside, and creating the correct conditions for their arrival.

These trusted foreigners could come into South Africa, get jobs, find accommodation, live the lives of ordinary people, and never make contact with the movement. They would know nothing about us or about Operation Vula. I did rigorous screening. Just being active in the anti-apartheid movement didn't mean they were okay. I checked their political backgrounds.

Kreuss was a member of the German Communist Party and had served as a courier to South America. The Douglas couple were longstanding members of the Canadian Communist Party. Grabeck was a teacher with a record of progressive involvement. Our sleepers were not in any way to get involved in politics, or even to express political views in their social interactions.

Schiphol

We tasked Jenkin to scout international airports in Europe and check out their security systems. He traveled through various European airports and reported on the setup at each one. We found that Schiphol Airport in Amsterdam was the easiest place to arrive on a flight with one passport under one name, avoid immigration, change disguises in the transit lounge—it was a very busy airport—then buy a ticket with another passport for the next leg.

It wasn't easy because you couldn't book an outgoing ticket through a travel agent, but if you dressed like a wealthy businessman and bought a first-class ticket, you could walk over to the internal passenger counter, and the attendant wouldn't ask on which flight you had arrived. You'd say, "I'm Andrew Johnson and my secretary has booked a ticket for me to collect here for Nairobi." "Yes sir, yes sir, I'll check on my computer. Can I see your passport?" They would look only at the photograph, then at you. Gebuza and I used Schiphol to move between Moscow to Swaziland.

Disguises

I had met Connie Braam on a number of occasions. Connie was the pivot of the anti-apartheid movement in Holland from the 1970s on. Besides doing anti-apartheid work, she also got involved in gathering resources in Holland for all sorts of clandestine purposes. She is the one who blew the whistle with OR on Berend Schuitema, who was involved with the Okhela operation.* This happened while I was still in prison. Schuitema was an apartheid agent.[34]

Connie also helped different people in the underground structures—Ronnie Kasrils and others—and found safe people as couriers from Holland to Mozambique and Swaziland. She also was involved in providing assistance to Ebrahim Ebrahim, who used to be an adviser to Jacob Zuma.

I knew Connie had all kinds of contacts in the theater world. She had access to cosmetic artists, dentists, wigmakers who used human hair, makeup artists who could change one's appearance. So I tapped her for Vula and then delegated dealing with her to Ivan Pillay. I got Connie to do this for me without explaining the mission. Then because of the competence of the wigmakers and the dentists, I got her involved in helping disguise Gebuza. After Gebuza and I had been disguised and had entered the country, Jenkin and Ivan continued to use Connie for many other cadres coming in.

The key to a successful disguise is to alter the voice and the outward appearance, but the changes have to be incremental and small. It's a fallacy to think that you need a dramatic change. In my case, the biggest hurdle is my voice. It's a dead giveaway. Mannerisms must also be dealt with. All of these things need infinitesimal adjustments.

With mannerisms I had to train myself. I sat in Lusaka week after week with Zarina, asking, "Now, am I talking to you the wrong way?" She would say, "Stop flapping that hand of yours; that's typically you. Learn to get rid of that." Then, near departure day, we noticed a small giveaway. I normally wore a wedding ring, but I'd taken it off, thinking I was very clever, but Zarina said, "Look at the lighter skin where the ring was—a different color from the rest of your hand. You'd better get suntan lotion and start working on it to darken that ring space."

---

*Okhela was a political resistance organization at first called Atlas and then Okhela ("Spark" in Zulu), made up of South African whites living in European exile and collaborating with the ANC. Its purpose was to provide a white left alternative to the SACP, with a perspective that supported African nationalism. Founded by Afrikaans poet Breyten Breytenbach, who wrote its political program, the movement was infiltrated by the regime. Breytenbach, who returned to South Africa in disguise to recruit members, was arrested and sentenced to nine years in prison. Okhela fell apart within two years. See Luli Callinicos, "Oliver Tambo and the Politics of Class, Race and Ethnicity in the African National Congress of South Africa," *African Sociological Review*, 3, 1, 1999.

Final Touches

In mid-1988, I held meetings in Mauritius for a week with Yusuf Vawda, a member of Pravin Gordhan's underground unit in South Africa. By profession, Pravin was a pharmacist and by instinct, a community organizer. After Soweto 1976, when the enemy was on the rampage, he and his group decided that the only way to survive the regime's attention was to disappear and then reemerge in areas that were not under the spotlight of the regime. So they began to work with communities to organize them around small issues, like the improvement of their local services. That's how they built their structures.

I did not divulge to Vawda that I was coming into the country, but I was able to gauge, after our talks, whether they were the right people to take me and possibly Gebuza across the border from Swaziland. Having sounded him out, I told him we were about to implement a highly secret security operation, and I wanted to assess his unit's capability for receiving a person who would cross the border from Swaziland on foot and for transporting that person safely within the country.

I also asked his unit to get a safe accommodation in Durban. I wanted a place that was untainted, that would not come under the attention of the Security Branch. It should be rented in a very secure way; whoever they were picking up would move into that accommodation for as long as was required. Then I set up the mechanics for the process.

I knew that if I could get to Durban with their help, on my own I would be able to reach some very staunch cadres, like Billy Nair. Through Billy I would get access to intelligence and get a clear reading of the security situation. Then we would settle in. I didn't want to tell Durban I was heading for Jo'burg. I would let the Durban comrades think I'd gone back to Swaziland. As it happened, things didn't go exactly according to plan.

A Breach of Confidence

About a month before I left Lusaka, Joe Slovo surprised me at a Politburo meeting of the party when he informed them that very soon I would be going into the country on an ANC mission and that he now wanted the party to give me a mandate to perform its work.

I challenged him outside the meeting: "Why did you do that? This sort of thing is not even discussed in the Working Committee of the ANC." I said, "Only you and OR knew, but now you've gone and told all the members of the Politburo." I thought divulging this was wrong.

JS said he'd done it because unless the Politburo gave me their mandate, it would be very difficult to get the party to process any political reports I sent. Also, he said, there would be huge problems about my disappearance,* and for that reason he thought it should be properly done. I objected on security grounds, but it was done. I didn't take up the matter with OR. And, of course, the party gave me their mandate to represent them and to work inside the country.

But this meant that John Nkadimeng, Jacob Zuma, Thabo Mbeki, Chris Hani, and Sizakele Sixashe all knew. I would make two sets of reports. Whatever I reported to the ANC was in relation to ANC and MK work. What I reported to the party was on party work. Separate code names, but the same channel of communication. Joe, of course, would share information with the Politburo and some of the operational details with the internal committee of the party—that is, the committee dealing with the building of the party inside the country.

It was disturbing. I don't know whether OR ever knew that JS had let certain party members know or whether Joe had ever raised the matter with him. But it left me with an uncomfortable feeling. Too many people were beginning to know I was going home—the very thing I had gone to such great lengths to conceal.[35]

---

*I asked Mac about this, given that his cover had been so effectively accepted, but he insisted that this is what Slovo had said. More curiously still, while he was in South Africa but believed to be in the Soviet Union in a hospital in the Crimea, the Lusaka region of the SACP expelled him for nonattendance! Its decision was overturned by the Central Committee (it also expelled Slovo for the same reason). See []maharaj /interviews/ 2003/[] September 23.

12. HOME AGAIN

Introduction

THE STORY OF VULA is complex. Its narratives overlap, intertwine, and run off in different directions. They are rich in tension, spiced with comrades' often not-too-kind comments about one another, and they ring with the voices of strong personalities. It is a human drama as much as a political drama. And all under the nose of the Security Branch (SB), which boasted that no ANC operation was beyond its reach, while blithely unaware that it had been penetrated at the highest level. Information from its security files was going directly to ANC intelligence in South Africa, which fed it to Vula before dispatch to Lusaka.

In December 1988, four months after Mac Maharaj and Siphiwe Nyanda had crossed the Swazi border into South Africa, Tambo wrote to Mac:

> We need a sustained, ever growing and expanding military offensive. But we are unable to take off in any significant manner. We hit one disaster after another, continuously, year in and year out precisely because we sought to run before we could walk, and kept on walking.
>
> Vula must not follow the beaten path—it's a minefield. Vula must strike out on a new road—to lay the indispensable foundations for a viable armed struggle by first creating, building and consolidating a strong, resilient, extensive political network that is self-protective, absorbs shocks. This is precisely the task Vula has started tackling with startling vigour and effectiveness. In the result much has been achieved but much, much more has yet to be done, especially in consolidating the ground already covered. . . . You will note that we use the acronym APC and not RPC or RMPC. This is to emphasize the point that we are set-

ting up political leadership structures under which all functions (including military) fall.[1]

Yet more than a year beforehand, Tambo had instructed Thabo Mbeki to meet with a group of Afrikaner "intellectuals" led by Willie Esterhuyse, a Stellenbosch University professor who had contact with P. W. Botha and other senior South African government officials. The first meeting took place in October 1987. Over the following eighteen months, the Afrikaners and ANC officials—the groups varying in size and composition—met on a dozen occasions at Mells House Park, outside Bath in the United Kingdom. On the ANC side, Mbeki and Jacob Zuma were the key players.[2] The Afrikaners would become proxies for the NIS in exploring opportunities for a negotiated settlement.[3] The NWC (National Working Committee) received briefings on the substance of these meetings[4] although it did not become privy to the NIS connection until October 1989.[5]

Giving his benediction to both Thabo Mbeki and Mac Maharaj in their endeavors reflected Tambo's holistic approach to the struggle. Like any good CEO, he understood that in a volatile political marketplace you diversified your political holdings. Prudence required him to plan for different outcomes.

Thus he had to plan for a seizure of power as well as for a protracted armed struggle, ways of balancing the four pillars of struggle, strangling the regime through economic isolation, and a negotiated settlement. Each course of action had to be pursued. The various pursuits were interrelated: Mac's Vula and Mbeki's Mells House Park talks complemented each other. Tambo orchestrated the efforts of both, and he knew too, as a result of the visits of Ismail Ayob and George Bizos to Lusaka, that Mandela was in contact with the South Africa government.[6]

It is sometimes asserted that Mbeki opposed the armed struggle as early as the onset of the 1980s.[7] If so, whatever misgivings he may have expressed about it in private were not consonant with his behavior within party and ANC structures. As one of the six members of the SACP politburo, the party's highest organ, he had a role in formulating and approving "Path to Power," the party's blueprint for destroying the apartheid regime. "Path to Power" was presented to the party at its conference in Havana in April 1989. Mbeki chaired discussion of the document and did so brilliantly, according to Joe Slovo.[8] "Path to Power" forcefully advocated seizure of power as a way forward, even as Soviet communism was visibly crumbling.[9] It was adopted as the party's manifesto to great acclaim, much

of it for the intellectual impresario who had conducted the proceedings
with such panache. At a pivotal meeting of the NEC in February 1990,
within a week of Mandela's being released, when there was a wide-ranging
discussion of how the ANC should proceed in the new circumstances,
Mbeki countenanced that "[we] need to correct position that creation [of
understanding]* will make armed struggle unnecessary."[10] Nor did Mbeki
at any time, either in the NEC or the politburo, or to Tambo or Slovo in
private, convey reservations about Vula. Moreover, after Mandela was released and had taken charge, he authorized that Vula continue its clandestine operations even though the ANC was then legal.

2

Between August 1988 and May 1990, Vula embedded itself in Natal and to a
lesser extent in the Witwatersrand. Huge quantities of arms were imported
and stored across South Africa, ready for the day of national insurrection.

Vula was probably the ANC's most successful operation, a compensation for a long and distinguished history of failure. At one point, in response to a report from Mac on Vula's activities, Tambo enthused, "The
report is remarkable for its scope and its detail. It gives a clear vision of the
immense potential of the Vula concept but also its tremendous yield in
terms of what has been achieved within a short period of time. To Adam
[Mac] and Sylvester [Nyanda] Bravo!"[11]

Vula established a direct line of communication between Mandela and
Oliver Tambo at a delicate moment in the ANC's engagement with the
white regime. Within the MDM a core committee was established, including Cyril Ramaphosa, Sydney Mufamadi, Rev. Frank Chikane, and Father
Smangaliso Mkhatshwa which "set" the political agenda for COSATU and
the UDF in consultation with Lusaka via Mac. Mac smuggled a draft of the
Harare Declaration to Mandela and whisked his comments and those of
nine other internal leaders back to Lusaka within ten days. Nyanda trained
MK cadres for a people's army—not for immediate deployment on the
ground—and gave them a familiarity with the geopolitical landscape. Vula
provided logistical and manpower support for the war in KwaZulu-Natal,
and conveyed to Lusaka a copy of Mandela's memorandum to P. W. Botha
before Mandela's meeting with him in July 1989.

In April 1989, Mac contained the frenzy that erupted when Mandela
was perceived by some senior members of the MDM to be "selling out."

*See Appendix, section F, pp. 521–26.

He also provided feedback and analysis on the crisis around Winnie Mandela's involvement in the death of a child activist, a situation that would have caused immense trouble for Mandela on his release, pulling him between his wife and the MDM that had condemned her.

The accomplishments directly attributable to Vula were real, and they affected the course of the struggle. After Mac informed Tambo that he could open a line of direct communication between Tambo and Mandela, Tambo withheld approval until Mac could satisfactorily assure him on two counts. ("Firstly, exactly how would you ensure and be certain that the enemy was not picking up on the disclosure of your response to M [Mandela]. Secondly, how would you demonstrate to M the operation of the secret line and ensure that in the process the enemy is kept permanently unaware.") Within weeks Mac, who had first proposed opening a line of communication five months earlier, in November 1988, was able to convince the ever cautious Tambo to give him the nod.[12]

Vula also compelled Lusaka to face harsh realities that challenged cherished shibboleths, but at the same time it reinforced the need for operations like Vula itself. Vula had to try to disabuse Lusaka of some of its misconceptions about how spontaneous but chaotic youth uprisings could be used. The youth imposed their ideas of revolution, and infighting muddied the waters. In the absence of a real MK presence, self-armed youths took it upon themselves to impose their rule in townships that by now really were ungovernable, with or without the declaration of a people's war.

The leaders of the MDM were weaned in the post-Soweto years, and the group was composed of disparate structures. The UDF itself was loosely structured, comprising six hundred or so organizations that spanned the political-ideological spectrum, united only in their determination to bring down apartheid. Within the UDF there were groupings that were either affiliated with the ANC or SACP or were material for conversion. But others were not.

The MDM included COSATU, which had its own political orientation and constituency. Within COSATU was the independent power of NUM (National Union of Mineworkers), the largest single union in the country already baptized in combat and increasingly aware of the power it could yield.

The MDM was at the coal face. It got there not by following some battle plan handed down by the ANC in Lusaka, but by using the people—the grass roots and the instruments the masses used to organize themselves to disrupt, disorient, and engage the regime at the street level and on the economic front. But it was vital that such efforts be coordinated with those of the ANC, and Vula played a significant role in that process.

The quality of the leadership in the mass organizations was always bothersome, and in one frank exchange, two pivotal UDF leaders bluntly told Tambo and Slovo that a broad-based leadership simply didn't exist.[13]

Both Harry Gwala, former Robben Island prisoner and veteran Stalinist leader of the SACP and the ANC in the Natal Midlands, and Govan Mbeki, who was released from Robben Island in November 1987, presented problems of a different kind. Gwala, once back in Natal after his release in November 1988 and disgusted with the derelict state of the political organizations, decided to remedy matters on his own terms.[14] The Natal heartland was the scene of some of the fiercest fighting between the UDF/ANC and Inkatha, and Gwala declared a scorched-earth policy on Inkatha. Among all ANC leaders, Gwala came closest to being a warlord in his own right. He was not inclined to take orders from anyone.[15] He ranted about a so-called Indian cabal, and ranted when he learned that Mac, an Indian, had been charged with setting up the ANC's underground.[16] Yet Gwala had to be brought into line. A working accommodation was reached between him and Mac, his "loose talk" halted. But when he finally agreed to meet Mac, he did so in circumstances that maximized Mac's public exposure.

Govan Mbeki was the first of the Rivonia Trialists to be released. He saw himself as head of the ANC in the country. He immediately became involved with the UDF, both its tactics and strategies. Lusaka gave him permission to set up structures in the Port Elizabeth (PE) region, but Mbeki, too, was his own man and began to extend his mandate to the whole country, without proper authorization from Lusaka. He established a national collective and recruited national figures in the MDM.* This presented Lusaka with problems. Mbeki was an icon of the struggle, especially in the PE region, to which he was now restricted. He was not someone who could easily be told what to do or not do. Members of the MDM, unaware of the constraints on his theater of operation that Lusaka was attempting to impose, would follow Mbeki's directions, believing them to have the imprimatur of Lusaka. Since the SB had Mbeki under surveillance at all times, his more militant actions endangered not only himself but the leadership of the MDM. He, too, had to be brought into line, but with great subtlety and sufficient deference.

Thus, discussions about the demarcation of function and territory and the allocation of responsibilities for covert organization required high-

---

*Among those Govan Mbeki sought to recruit were Kgalema Motlanthe, Dullah Omar, Harry Gwala, and Cyril Ramaphosa.

wire balancing acts. Personalities had to be assuaged, egos stroked, and due respect accorded prickly and determined battle-hardened veterans. But the objective was always the same: to ensure that Vula emerged unscathed, able to shake free of the turf battles among different fledgling ANC underground structures in a country still under the heel of the apartheid government.[17]

3

The narrative of Vula and the role it played in the struggle against apartheid is chronicled in the communications (comms) transmitted, via London or Amsterdam, between Vula operatives and Lusaka. To read them is to see them as part spy novel, part cartoon. There are mix-ups and foul-ups; there are ANC spies spying on ANC spies. Vula was a sophisticated, secret arms-importation business as well as a propaganda and crisis-management operation in dealings with the MDM. The comms reveal the bureaucratic nightmare of ANC inefficiency in Lusaka, but they provide riveting details of the setting up of a direct and secure line between Oliver Tambo in Lusaka and Nelson Mandela in Victor Verster Prison. To succeed, Vula had to become an underground within the ANC itself.

But also running through the Vula comms is a tangible sense of excitement: of being behind enemy lines and relaying its movements to the outside. The comms between Tambo, Slovo, and Mac are exercises in exquisite minimalism. The voices become interchangeable, harmony of language achieved, the ANC in exile speaking as if it were on the ground in South Africa, the MDM relaying the same messages to the masses.

4

As the regime groped its way toward negotiations, the ANC played catch-up. The Vula comms catch the flavor of their dilemmas, the ruminations that preceded decisions. In the end, external pressures drove events. Was the regime serious about discussions, or was this one more ruse to buy time, divide the opposition? Were they duping Mandela, another attempt to divide? Yet, according to Mandela, there were some in the regime who regarded the ANC as "a worthy opponent."[18] Was the praise, feigned or not, a ruse?

Thus the Harare Declaration (the ANC's preconditions for negotiations with the regime and framework for a constitutional settlement) came as a response to "increasing internal and external pressure from friends and enemies" for recognition that the time to negotiate had come.[19] But the ANC had to leapfrog international efforts to get involved, especially Margaret Thatcher's ("that most terrible bitch," Joe Slovo's less-than-tempered assessment).[20] The ANC had to evade the proposals the South African government was bandying about on the diplomatic circuit and grab the higher ground. When Tambo began to "assemble" the document that would become the Harare Declaration, he had a road map to guide him: Mandela's document to P. W. Botha articulates a set of arguments and positions that would stand the test of the negotiating process in the 1990s.

The ANC's belief in the widest possible range of consultations on every matter of importance, and from the MDM in particular, comes across very clearly in the comms, but no one was quite sure exactly what the "negotiating concept" meant.[21] And, of course, one could not negotiate from a position of perceived weakness.[22] Negotiate, yes, but step up the struggle too. Perhaps Joe Slovo's final comment on the draft Harare Declaration to Mac reveals a muted ambivalence: "Will have to do, until the real thing."[23]

Having struggled for so long, the ANC now found itself hard put to deal with the prospects of a negotiated settlement. It never doubted that it would win, but when it faced negotiations, it hesitated—a psychological reaction, perhaps, to its justified suspicion of an unscrupulous regime.

The ANC did not want to appear to be suing for peace.[24] The masses had to be eased into supporting the new direction. Likewise, many in the ANC itself, some incorrigible militants and some timeworn skeptics, had to be prepared and a consensus broad enough to accommodate quite disparate points of view thrashed out.[25]

Govan Mbeki questioned not only the worth of Mandela's initiative from within prison but also accused Mandela of being in violation of the ANC's cardinal principle of collectivity. He wanted Mandela to desist from such talks. Yet it was precisely Mandela's lack of a doctrinaire standpoint that made negotiations possible and allowed him, on his release, to grab the ANC by the scruff of its aging neck and haul it along with him to the negotiating table.

Harry Gwala also opposed Mandela's prison talks with the government team. Both were committed to the overthrow of the regime by force of arms. But unlike Gwala, Govan's hard edge had a pragmatic bent.[26] Exchanges between Mac and Gebuza and Mac and Ronnie Kasrils, after Kasrils entered the country in early 1990, reflect the intensity of Mac's involvement. He was a hard taskmaster and made no bones about it.

5

Access to good intelligence was one reason, perhaps the primary one, why Vula remained one step ahead of the security forces and why it was safe, unlike most ANC structures, from infiltration. Vula had access to some of the information compiled by Operation Bible, which had a mandate to identify apartheid agents within the upper echelons of the movement.[27]

The origins of Operation Bible lay in the regime's penchant for brutality and torture. Watching the extreme torture of Yunus Shaik, head of the ANC's MJK unit of MK,* by the SB in Durban in 1985, a senior SB official "turned."[28] Out of disgust, shame, and remorse, he became a mole for the ANC. Moe Shaik, Yunus's younger brother, who had been detained and tortured by the SB at the same time, became his sole handler. When Tambo authorized Operation Bible, he placed it under the jurisdiction of the MJK unit. Bible reported to Jacob Zuma, both before and after he became head of intelligence.

MJK thus had extensive access to the SB files. "The reports [we received]," says Yunus Shaik, "indicated that the ANC was riddled with infiltration and so was the entire democratic movement."[29] The informant was code-named the Nightingale—not the same person as the air hostess who was given that name by Mac. He was a mother lode of information. He took records from the files, delivering them to Moe Shaik. Shaik immediately had them photocopied. Nightingale then returned the files to SB keeping.[30] To advance his career, MJK provided help. It recruited informants on his behalf to facilitate his promotion within the SB ranks.

Yunus Shaik says: "We came to learn of the SB's techniques, its tactics and strategy, competition for title and promotion, the tension between SB and other organs of state, but most importantly, we were able to scope its deployment knowledge of our activities and deployment. Armed with this information, we could then act with impunity."[31]

Nevertheless, a recurring preoccupation of the Vula comms is security. Tambo and Slovo obsessed about it. The ANC in general was obsessed with it. Conversations between comrades were reported to Lusaka and compared with information from other sources; comrades were "tested";

---

*Yunus Shaik formed the Mandla Judson Kuzwayo (MJK), since the unit fell under MK machinery headed by Kuzwayo, hence the name. Originally, it had three members: Yunis Shaik (code-named Mandla), Moe Shaik (code-named Judson), and Jayendra Naidoo (code-named Kuzwayo). The unit was placed under the command of Ivan Pillay, later a key Vula operative. MJK fell under the control of Jacob Zuma when he was in charge of ANC structures in Mozambique, before he was appointed head of ANC Intelligence.

Lusaka was inundated with messages from structures in the forward areas, one colleague telling tales on another. Rumor, gossip, and insinuation seeped into the inner machinery of the movement, stopping initiatives in their tracks, always raising questions. This was the inevitable result of the movement's having been infiltrated by South African agents, at all levels, and its own awareness of its limited capacity to keep them out.

No one was beyond suspicion: Francis Meli, member of the NEC; Cyril Ramaphosa, leader of NUM; Peter Mokoba, leader of SANYCO (South African National Youth Congress); Maxwell Zulu, executive member of NUMSA (National Union of Metalworkers of South Africa); Bulelani Ngcuka, leader of the National Association of Democratic Lawyers (NADEL). Even Zarina, Mac's wife, was viewed with suspicion because of her work with the British High Commission and the United Nations. The Central Committee of the SACP conducted a formal investigation into charges by one of its senior members that she worked for MI5, the British intelligence agency. Senior members of the SACP believed that Cyril Ramaphosa was working for the CIA, a matter Jacob Zuma was supposed to look into, but never reported back on.[32]

So deeply had the enemy penetrated the ANC that when the ANC, with the assistance of its own moles in the SB, turned on itself to weed out "suspects," it did so with a ruthlessness the SB admired.[33] In the process, errors were made, individuals and families ruined, careers brought to abrupt halts.

The ANC fought a just war, but it was aghast when, many years after it had ended, the TRC found that it had, on occasion, used unjust means. Yet the cadres who worked at the coal face of the struggle were not fazed. In a dirty war everyone plays dirty; you do not pause to consider the moral niceties when your survival is at stake.

At one point, Mandela was also in the shadow of this endemic distrust. To the post-Soweto generation of activists in South Africa, Mandela was the personification of the struggle, the symbol used to give the masses a human face with which they could identify. But although the ANC used him for this purpose while he was still in jail, it did so grudgingly and with whispers of concern. When he began to explore talks with the regime, initiative was mistaken for deviation and lack of discipline.

6

A symbiotic relationship evolved between Operation Vula and Operation Bible. Sharing of operational intelligence facilitated penetration of state agencies such as Home Affairs. People in the underground were able to obtain South African passports and birth certificates, allowing them to travel in and out of South Africa through the Jo'burg airport.

They also had mutual support systems in place with regard to money laundering related to bringing money into the country from abroad for the underground and in certain cases for the overt mass organizations. Foreign currency was smuggled in. This would then have to be exchanged on the black market. The underground also made contact through a separate network with individuals who wanted to take their money out of South Africa. Businessmen and professional people handed over hundreds of thousands of rand to the underground's middlemen. At the same time, instructions were conveyed to Lusaka or London to have equivalent sums in the designated foreign currency deposited in the relevant bank accounts abroad or to have accounts opened. The advantage of this arrangement was that it concealed the link between the payment abroad and the payment within South Africa. The Vula comms read like a banker's guide to double-entry accounting. Another variant involved setting up overt businesses abroad for the purpose of conducting business with a South African-based company. There were bank accounts in London, Geneva, Toronto, New York. Businesses were set up in South Africa that were the franchise outlets of U.S. or UK companies. The transfer of funds could then be concealed under the guise of legitimate business activities. Sometimes big risks were taken and big losses incurred. While the political sense may have been astute, business acumen was often lacking.*

The treasurer general's office in Lusaka and the PMC structures in the frontline states and their substructures, MK Command and Central Operations, were constantly trying to invent mechanisms that would facilitate a continual laundering of foreign currency into rands and a parallel market for exchanging rand for foreign currency to maintain their respective operations. Vula was a special case, since funding of its activities from the treasurer general's accounts had to be concealed in order to preserve its covert character. Thus Vula became heavily reliant on the mechanism whereby it received tens of thousands of rand collected within South Africa while the equivalence in foreign currency from front companies in

*One venture involved a company in the United States, Orangematic, which franchised machines for making fresh juices. An investment was made in this company for the purpose of establishing a company in South Africa, Orange-O, which had exclusive rights to make and sell Orangematic products in the local market. In the United States the company got into financial difficulties. Attempts to recoup the initial investment failed, and Orange-O never got off the ground. Large sums of money were lost, despite attempts to recoup.

Lusaka or London was deposited into accounts abroad. Its network of "currency traders" was paid on a commission basis. Exchange rates were bargained. Sometimes ANC members going from Lusaka to conferences in Europe or the United States or Canada were couriers for currency in nylon bags.

One of the structures assigned this task was the MJK unit. The actual task was entrusted to Schabir Shaik, an older brother of Yunus's and Moe's, who specialized in arranging for foreign currency to come into South Africa and trading on the black market for rands, which were then disbursed to underground activities, including Vula, although of course he had no idea what actually became of this money once he had completed his side of the task.[34] The older Shaik, among others, was also involved in trying to purchase companies in the United States and the United Kingdom and opening franchising outlets in South Africa as a way of laundering money. Some got off the ground; some didn't.

The cooperation on the ground between Vula and Bible grew so close that sometimes Jacob Zuma took exception because he found that highly confidential intelligence information was reaching OR via Vula even before it had reached him via Bible.[35] Despite this closeness, the two operations were kept separate at all times.

7

The South Africa to which Mac returned to implant Operation Vula was not the country he had left in 1977. Indeed, since 1964 Mac had spent less than six months on the soil of South Africa. He had to acclimate himself to a country now increasingly urbanized, one in which many of the pillars of apartheid had collapsed not because of protest or amended legislation or a change of heart on the part of the regime but for economic reasons.

He soon discovered that MK command structures in the forward areas were working with outmoded geographies; that makeshift political undergrounds, with a few exceptions, could not integrate themselves with the occasional MK units they managed to make contact with; that incoming MK units frequently had little knowledge of the terrain they were traversing. Often, military targets that were theirs for the taking were left untouched. Communication with the outside was difficult, and information often became distorted as it was passed on.

Yet back in South Africa, Mac thrived. Vula drew on all his strengths: the penchant for the clandestine, his indefatigable energy, his willingness to take enormous personal risks, his personal charisma and capacity for innovation. He was a leader on the ground who would never ask a subordinate to perform a task he himself would not do. Vula engaged his ability to think strategically and switch direction at the hint of a threat, never losing sight of the larger picture and adjusting operations to ensure that the focus of the mission stayed on course.

Nor did he ever lose sight of his parallel mission: establishing and strengthening SACP underground structures and maintaining a flow of correspondence with Slovo on party matters. Thus at Slovo's request he made several inputs into the party's new policy document, "Path to Power," which was presented to the ~~party congress in Havana in April 1989~~. Reviewing the final draft, he took issue with the emphasis on military action as having been at the core of party strategy and observed that "if anyone had a strategy, it was confined to the top," adding "theory and practice were wide apart."[36] In a message to congress, supposedly from someplace in the Crimea, he complained of the "dictatorship of the doctors" that precluded him from being present but reported, nevertheless, that within South Africa there was "a crisis of leadership at all levels,"[37] no doubt leaving his bemused colleagues to wonder how Mac, dying from all accounts and bedridden seven thousand miles from South Africa, could arrive at such definitive conclusions. The Politburo, however, in the wise, reelected him to the top leadership.*[38]

And, of course, Vula thrived on his arrogance. He loved his multiple disguises, assuming different personalities, the theater of role-playing; he enjoyed appearing out of nowhere, to the bewilderment of others. He took chances, often unnecessary ones, and laughed them off, intoxicated with the sheer exhilaration of the freedom he felt from being able to plot the overthrow of the regime from within the belly of the regime itself. He was also meticulous, although thoughtlessly careless on occasion,[39] a leader who always asked more of himself than of others.

From Moscow, before leaving on the last leg of his journey back to South Africa, he wrote Zarina: "The pain of missing you through physical separation always lives with me. But at this moment the intensity of the pain sears my heart and mind. It is a pain born out of the joy of living because you give me strength. Our beliefs, our commitment to doing whatever the struggle demands of us, becomes personal—intensely—because in concrete terms we seek to build a livable life for the Joeys and the Milous. I begin to feel deep down we will conquer, we will accomplish

---

*The Politburo members were Joe Slovo, Chris Hani, Thabo Mbeki, John Nkadimeng, Mac Maharaj, and one new member, Jacob Zuma.

things which will give pride to our family and particularly to the future of our lovely children."[40]

Once in South Africa, his ideas, commentary, and analyses flowed. Already he was thinking ahead to Mandela's release, of how to put the regime under more pressure to release him, as well as what facilities would be available to Mandela upon his release. His text books were General Vo Nguyen Giap's *People's War, People's Army* and General Nguyen Thong's *The Great Spring Offensive*; yet at the same time, his efforts made the ANC's negotiating position in talks with the NP stronger.

The constant interchange of views, feedback, questioning, and probing provided Tambo and Slovo with an analysis of the state of the struggle on the ground. Thus they were able to move the NEC in new directions, to integrate external and internal developments. Says Pillay: "We were getting a picture that the regime, particularly after 1986–87, couldn't rule in the old way, that things were changing within, that the NP itself was changing. But having said that, and I know different people would read it differently, I was very skeptical about a negotiated settlement, that it was a long way off. I still thought that it would not come soon."[41]

But in that regard he was not alone. Tambo was of a similar view.[42]

Mac

I HEADED FOR MOSCOW on 4 July 1988. Our disguises—the wigs, dentures, clothing with padding, hair dye—were ready for us. Moscow prepared some of the travel documents. Before I left, I bought about twenty-four postcards and dated each one with a particular month, for two years ahead. I addressed each one to Zarina, care of the ANC head office in Lusaka. I wrote a message on each, sometimes saying things were getting worse, sometimes better, or that I was fed up, missing the family, deeply loving them, and so on. Every month, Vladimir Shubin, who handled the ANC on the Soviet side, would send a card to Lusaka as if it were coming from me in a hospital in Moscow. It would go to the ANC office first, and thus reinforce the belief that I was hospitalized in the Soviet Union. Of course, people in the ANC office would tell other people, so the whole thing became self-perpetuating.

Gebuza and I arrived in Amsterdam, traveling separately and on different routes. We got London to arrange, under separate names, tickets reading London–Amsterdam–Nairobi–Mbabane, on different airlines wherever possible. When we got off at Schiphol Airport in Amsterdam, separately, we dumped the passports we had used to enter, collected tickets at the passenger counter without exiting, and then used different passports to travel by separate flights to Nairobi.

From Nairobi, we took a Royal Swazi flight via Dar es Salaam to Mbabane. We disembarked as passengers who didn't know each other. Ivan Pillay had arranged where we should go from the airport. He had prepared a safe house in Mbabane where we hid out while finalizing preparations for crossing.

The arrangements for crossing the Swazi border were in Ivan's hands. He had an infrastructure not only of ANC comrades but of Swazi citizens and expatriates to help him. He isolated the possible crossing point. I had linked Ivan to Pravin's unit, saying Ivan would make the arrangements for crossing—the day, hour, number of people, where to collect them, and so on—on the South African side of the border.

The Best Laid Plans . . .

About three days before crossing the border, my blazer was stolen from the bedroom of our hideout. In the blazer, which was part of my disguise, was three thousand dollars. The blazer had my pocket diary, in the inside cover of which I had written key contact numbers. We had to make ad hoc arrangements: buy another blazer, find money, find other contact numbers. To complicate matters further, there was a misunderstanding and the comrades who were supposed to pick us up headed off for the Zimbabwe border instead. Our meticulously planned operation was beginning to look like the Keystone Kops before we had even set foot in South Africa!

We drove to the border. Totsie Memela, a female member of the underground in Swaziland, served as our guide and escort. Totsie had been recruited for the specific job of ensuring that Vula comrades either entering South Africa or leaving Swaziland were able to cross the border undetected. She took Ivan and me to a Swazi family living in a village on the border with South Africa.

We discovered that the SADF had a lookout post on a hillock across from the village, each team serving a stint of a month before being relieved. At the end of each month, during the changeover, there was a gap of about six hours when the post was unmanned. The next changeover was due in two days, so we decided to make our crossing at midday on Sunday, 31 July 1988, at the foot of the hillock, right under nose of the lookout post. The crossing went like clockwork.

Since Pravin's people had gone missing, Ivan found an expatriate, a

Dutchman living in Swaziland, introduced to me only as André, to drive through the Swazi border post at Pongola, then drive to where we had crossed and pick us up. The idea was that he would drop us a hundred kilometers deep into South Africa, and from there we would find our own way. Since we could not rule out the possibility that the group that was supposed to pick us up had been captured, tortured, and talked, we decided to change our plans and head for Jo'burg. André drove us there. There were no hitches. I told him to drop us at the Carlton Hotel. As soon as he left, we took a taxi to the Kairos Hotel in Hillbrow, to break the link between him and us in case he was picked up by the security police.

I fully expected the receptionist to ask for and record the details of my ID book. I had already whipped it out. But as I was filling in the details from the ID book in the reception form, the receptionist told me not to bother—the first surprise. At great expense, with much effort and secrecy, the movement had got the Soviet Union and the GDR to produce forged ID books for us, and now they weren't necessary! I kicked myself for not having debriefed a cadre we had sent into the country, and who had returned safely, so that I could properly understand conditions at home. At no time during our stay in the country was I asked to produce an ID book.

I decided I would first make contact with Ismail Ayob. Ismail was Mandela's family lawyer and visited Madiba frequently. After spending the next day carefully reconnoitering his movements, I contacted him. Through him we made contact with Ismail Momoniat (Momo). Momo was in the Johannesburg District Committee of the SACP and was on the run because of the crackdown during the state of emergency.

Momo became indispensable to Vula. He was based in Johannesburg, and he was one of my key contacts there. I've seldom come across a more resourceful person. I could say to Momo, "Where do I find so and so?" and Momo would find him. He was unassuming and quiet, but what was remarkable about him was that even though the police were after him, he always managed to stay in touch with people, even if they were also on the run.

Momo was never late, never missed an appointment. It didn't matter what time I called him. I would send him pager messages telling him to meet me at certain times. We had arranged that whatever time we put on the pager was not the real time. If I said seven, he was to subtract one—so it meant six. My reasoning was that if ever the police detected a message and took the time as genuine, we would be gone by the time the police got there; but if we added an hour, they might still be hanging around.

Momo moved us to accommodations in Hyde Park. Within a week we'd received a report from Durban and from Ivan about what had happened to the comrades sent by Pravin to collect us at the Swazi border. There was no security problem. Momo found someone to drive me to Durban and made arrangements for me to meet Billy Nair.

I knew Billy well from our days on Robben Island, where he had served a twenty-year term. Billy is a slightly built fellow, but his looks are deceiving. On Robben Island he was in trouble with the warders every day, and when the High Organ passed messages from one block to the other to tell Billy to cool it, Billy would send a message back to say they were a lot of cowards! Once, in an argument with Madiba, Billy yelled out, "Madiba, you are nothing but a bloody feudal aristocrat masquerading as a socialist! I'm going to expose you!" We laughed. And, for once, Madiba had no comeback.

Intelligence

I knew that even though he was living under the scrutiny of the Security Branch, Billy would find a way to connect me with Moe Shaik's unit, the MJK unit, and its intelligence reports. Moe was a gold mine of operational information, so I switched tactics. Instead of making Jo'burg my primary area, where we were supposed to start, we decided to start in Durban because of the advantage Moe's intelligence gave us. So we found accommodations there.

Through its analysis of SB security files being slipped to it by Nightingale for photocopying and microfilming, and from other reports, Moe's unit was able to identify possible enemy agents planted in MDM or COSATU structures. My relationship with Moe's unit became very close. But their lines of command and communication were separate—they ran through London to intelligence headquarters in Zambia. Joe Nhlanhla was the head, and Zuma was the counterintelligence chief. He was in direct command of the MJK unit.

I first met Jacob Zuma (JZ) in 1978, when he was stationed in Maputo and in charge of smuggling weapons and explosives into South Africa. He had evaded arrest in 1975, when Harry Gwala and others were caught. JZ's success in counterintelligence was in part due to Moe's work. After Vula made contact with Operation Bible, for the first time we were able to establish a viable mechanism for operational intelligence to be made available to the underground—both political and military—which in turn provided the infrastructure for intelligence and counterintelligence activities to expand significantly.

OR knew of the developing relationship between Vula and Bible. But when JZ found out that OR was sometimes in possession of intelligence before he was, he began to suspect that I might be in the country. His inquiries could have inadvertently jeopardized Vula, so OR took him into the loop.[43]

Intelligence gathering from sources within the security forces was fraught with danger. We had to secure copies of SB documents, assess their reliability, and piece together various items to establish the thrust of the information. If we got information that suggested a comrade might be an apartheid agent, we always erred on the side of caution. We forwarded all such information, and our evaluation of it, to Lusaka. It was never a question of saying, "We are sure so-and-so works for the regime" or "There is a fifty-fifty chance that so-and-so works for the regime." The least suspicion that someone might be an enemy agent was sufficient to have him or her classified as a probable spy, reported to Lusaka, watched, and never, as far as could be ensured, allowed access to information that might imperil others. For Vula, the stakes were especially high. Any mistake would be fatal.

We were working underground in South Africa during one of the most violent periods of the struggle. The regime's death squads had been set loose. We would have been fools, most certainly dead fools, if we had ever let considerations such as "reasonable doubt" cloud our judgment. We were in a very dirty war. We didn't allow the possibility of being unfair to someone or mislabeling them as enemy agents to endanger our survival. We didn't have the luxury of checking and double-checking information that we plucked from the state's security files. We took what we got and did our best with it.

We made mistakes. Lots of them. In dirty wars, many people, including your own comrades, become casualties of unintended consequences. Whether the future may exonerate them has nothing to do with historical facts. We did what was required of us—above all, we had to keep the underground safe, create the political and military infrastructure to bring the leadership into the country, build the underground as the vanguard for a people's war.

In Jo'burg, I collected intelligence in more crude ways. Yusuf and Maud Mohammed ran a twenty-four-hour pharmacy in Hillbrow. I was introduced to them by Moe, and they became indispensable for many areas of our work. Hillbrow was the heart of Jo'burg's underworld and clubland. Maud and Yusuf lived in a flat in the Highpoint Building that was a stone's throw away from the pharmacy. Because of the round-the-clock hustle and bustle of Hillbrow, I could move into and out of the pharmacy and the flat with little danger of detection. They were always there, and I could reach them at any time of the day or night. Sometimes I would disguise myself and go behind the counter to help out. The pharmacy was a useful point for gathering information from a whole range of people, many of them from the army and police, who would come by late at night looking for drugs. We were able to tag potential sources of information.

The Structures

Back in Durban we set up three committees to supervise the structures we were creating in each of the townships and suburbs: the military, the political, and the overall politico-military. Gebuza headed the military committee. We did not include Moe's intelligence unit in these structures, much to Moe's chagrin.

The committee on the military side was a small one made up of Gebuza, Charles Ndaba, Mbuso Tshabalala, and Dipak Patel. Kevin, real name Teeruth Mistry, was kept separate because his primary responsibility was to develop ignition and timing devices from local sources—a specialized task. Mbuso Tshabalala was a teacher and a legend in the area for his work in the UDF. On the political committee were Jabu Sithole, Pravin Gordhan, Mpho Scott, and Vusi Tshabalala.

Dipak was working at that time for South African Breweries. Once he became a member of MK, he put me under intense pressure to guide him and advise him. It was clear what he wanted: to leave his job and be in the underground full time. He kept pestering me until I said OK.

The joint secretaries of the political committee were Pravin Gordhan and Mpho Scott. The chairman was Jabu Sithole, a mathematics lecturer at the University of Zululand. Jabu was a colorful character. I used to call him Chairman Mao. He wanted rigor in your reasoning, as well as terseness. Things were black or white—there was no in-between for Jabu. He was disabled and moved around on crutches with great difficulty, but he was amazingly active at the community level.

The structures in the forward areas* could send people into the country to establish political underground networks, so it was possible to have people accidentally bumping into one another. Sometimes they'd be working at cross-purposes. Our job was to be sensitive to all these people and craft how we integrated them into our structures.

---

*The forward areas were the countries contiguous to South Africa that were the accesible points of entry—Botswana, Lesotho, Swaziland, Mozambique, and Zimbabwe, after it became independent, although it was never used to the same degree as the others.

We didn't bring in a very large number of people—fifteen to twenty. The illegals were Gebuza, Dipou (Catherine) Mvelase, Susan Tshabalala, and I. Then there was Janet Love; Raymond Lala, who had only been in the country for a few days before Vula unraveled; Little John; and Kevin. Ronnie Kasrils came in later, after Mandela was released. There was also the Western Cape Operation, which included Charles Nqakula, Max Ozinsky, and others.

Catherine Mvelase was a comrade of the post-1976 generation who had been involved in the grassroots struggle in Alexandra, got out, did her military training, then came back. She had a very strong commitment.

Janet Love was my chief communications officer. She had been infiltrated into South Africa by the SACP in 1987 and instructed to lie low. We worked closely together. All messages to and from Lusaka went through Janet; she encrypted and encoded. Without Janet, I would have been lost. She became my eyes and ears. In a crisis she was cool headed and able to respond immediately to any threat. Janet was extraordinarily resilient.

Our fundamental task was to create units in the Durban region. Some of them were devoted to helping with military work: recruiting people, training them, finding places to cache arms, tailoring vehicles for smuggling in weapons, creating facilities for people to come in and settle or to go out and train. Other units were devoted to propaganda work. There was a systematic program of political education in all these units. At the same time, some individuals had to maintain contact with people in the MDM structures.

Another Nightingale

One of our safest couriers was a stewardess, Antoinette Voegelsang, who had risen to the rank of purser with KLM. She had been introduced to me by Connie Braam. We code-named her Nightingale because of her surname (Birdsong), though this might've been a bit of a giveaway. She was in charge of the stewardesses on each flight, and she put herself on the route from Amsterdam to Nairobi to South Africa. At Schiphol in those years, KLM crew were not screened before or after flights, either at departure or when they landed in Jo'burg, nor would they have to go through the normal passport control. They passed through rapidly. The plane would be in South Africa for three to four hours and would then go back to Nairobi, where it made its overnight stay. Nightingale originally brought in money for us, which would be in cash; later she managed to bring in some weapons in small quantities. Tim Jenkin would fly to Amsterdam and give her the parcel; she would then fly to Nairobi and on to Jo'burg, where the cabin crew rested in rooms at the Holiday Inn adjacent to the airport before they flew back to Nairobi. I would arrive in Jo'burg and book myself into the Holiday Inn. Antionette would come to my room, give me my parcels or whatever she had, and I would give her whatever we wanted her to take back. I would sometimes give her disks that I didn't want to run through the normal transmission system.

Communications with Lusaka

When I arrived in the country, the communications system was not yet perfect. My first communication was over an ordinary telephone line, unencrypted. We had sent couriers in to test the method—was it detectable? How fast could they detect it? How quickly were they able to intercept a message? Could they monitor it with mobile vehicles and pinpoint the transmission point? We got a London person to buy a portable telephone through an account that could not be traced. We sent our KLM Nightingale to collect it and deliver it to me. We used the acoustic coupler method developed by Tim Jenkin, and within months we had a system that was marginally short of putting Vula in touch with Lusaka on a real-time basis. From wherever I was in the country, I could send a message either to London or Amsterdam. Whoever picked it up would send the encrypted message to Tim, who would decipher it, reencrypt it with a separate code, and send it to Lusaka. It didn't take long by using computers.

In the beginning, Zarina ran the receiving and sending station in Lusaka. She did this after hours because she was working full time for the UN. The UN job came with a big house in the plush Chudleigh area of Lusaka, and we used several rooms for Vula work. Ivan had recruited Lucia Raadschelders,* a veteran of the Dutch Anti-Apartheid Movement, who had previously worked for the ANC in Swaziland, and when Zarina had her accident, Lucia took over the work. The computers were moved to a house in Kabwata, a township on the outskirts of Lusaka, out of which Lucia worked.

Ivan Pillay attended to many of our questions and communications himself, for example, messages about when, where, and how the next shipment of arms would be sent. We asked for propaganda material—at the beginning in hard copy, later electronically—and we began to ask for it to be formatted and laid out because we had developed printing capacities.

*Interview with Lucia Raadschelders at [] maharaj/interviewees/[] Lucia Raadschelders.

And Ivan, with his team of people, would take care of matters. He would report to Slovo and Tambo on progress.

In mid-1989, Saponet* was set up in South Africa. It was like an Internet service provider, but it used telephone lines through the post office. You could rent a telephone mailbox from Saponet and place messages, either in signal form or voice, in the mailbox for the cost of a local call. It was the electronic version of having a locker at a railway station. Once you had the key or the lock combination, you could use it to dump whatever you liked into it and then give others access to it, and you would never have to see one another. Jenkin knew the mailbox number and could access it from London. Janet Love sent the signals from Ismail Ayob's offices, for which we had spare keys. At night we went in to use his telephone, dumping messages on Saponet. Then we'd alert Jenkin by pager.

I was in almost daily communication with OR or JS or both. They were kept fully informed of everything we were doing and what was happening in the mass organizations.

Zarina's Accident

Zarina was in a serious car accident on 7 October 1988. At first, Lusaka didn't tell me. Then a message came—nothing to worry about; it's only a broken arm, and she'll be out of the hospital in a couple of days.[44] The next thing I heard, from Momo, was that she had nineteen fractures. Momo went with a delegation of Indians to Lusaka, and he visited her at the hospital. A week later, on his way home, he found Zarina on a stretcher being taken to the plane to Harare.

When he saw me in South Africa, he said, "Your wife's paralyzed." "What!" "Yes, she had an accident a week ago. She's been flown to Harare." "What about my kids?" He said, "I don't know." I sent a message to JS and Ivan: "Chaps, what's happened to my wife?" They wrote back, "Don't worry, everything is OK; the children are being looked after." "Tell me what's happened to her!" In the end, I sent a message saying, "You bastards, I want a medical certificate. I don't trust you. I want a full medical report." They said they were sending it to me, but they never did.

She was taken from Lusaka to Harare, where she was for a few months, then back to Lusaka, then to Moscow for four months, then back to

---

*Saponet: the South African Post Office NET; an electronic postbox into which someone with your electronic post office address could send electronic messages and which the addressee could use to send messages.

Lusaka and finally to London, at her own insistence. I kept asking myself, What would I have done if I'd known? I would have found a way, by hook or by crook, to go to see her, see the children—even though I would also have tried to get back as soon as possible.

That's a wound we never talk about. But with the churning in my mind, and trying to concentrate on the work at hand, it was hard. It gnawed at me.

The Mass Democratic Movement

Only Gebuza and Billy Nair, and later Janet Love, knew I was in contact with leaders in the MDM, in particular Jay Naidoo, Cyril Ramaphosa, Sydney Mufamadi, Chris Dlamini, the Reverend Frank Chikane, the Reverend Smangaliso Mkhatshwa, Ismail Momoniat, Diliza Mji, Mike Roussos, Kgalema Motlanthe, Murphy Morobe, and Valli Moosa. I maintained regular contact with this group and others to ensure that we shared a common outlook so that what they did in their mass organizations and in training was complementary and not contradictory to the overall thrust of the liberation struggle. We were all too familiar with the consequences of our failure to do so in the past. These comrades were told not to divulge that they were interacting with me and or that they were members of the ANC. We never told the mass organizations what to do. Together we explored ideas; then it was left to them to pursue what they considered best within the dynamics of the organizations in which they were serving.

We interacted with the political underground structures. Where structures did not exist, we created them. We discussed what the military should be doing and began to create a viable structure for propaganda work with the underground political units. We had operational units in fourteen out of the twenty-six districts in the Durban area doing clandestine work and being seasoned in the style of underground operations.

We steadily increased our capacity to produce and distribute leaflets. In the case of *Umsebenzi*, we were distributing at least five thousand copies per issue in the Durban region alone. We had begun writing, producing, and distributing ad hoc ANC leaflets tuned to the issues of the area. And we were doing so without suffering any major casualties. This was in addition to smuggling in and distributing copies of *Sechaba* and *Mayibuye*, which were written and produced abroad.

All these activities had to be fully alert to the rapidly changing situation in the country. Mass marches and rallies were becoming the order of the day. The mass organizations were forcing the pace and opening up spaces for the ANC to become more visibly active. The pressures on the leadership of the mass democratic organizations were enormous. Early in 1989, with the concurrence of OR and JS, I took steps to get Ramaphosa, Chikane, Mkhatshwa, and Mufamadi, who were part of the Committee of Nine, a reception committee established in late 1988 when there were rumors surfacing that Madiba might be released, to expand and diversify the committee with them as the key part of the secretariat that would ensure that Madiba would have direct access to Lusaka when he was released.[45] I was constantly on the move. I hardly spent more than two weeks at a stretch in Durban. But Gebuza and I were always in touch.

Slowly and patiently we had begun to establish contacts in the Jo'burg region. I traveled by car. Both for security and as a cover, I was more often than not accompanied by a female comrade who also doubled as a driver. Two comrades, Claudia Manning and Selina Pillay, were drawn from Moe's unit and the third, Sabera Bobak, came from structures created by Pravin Gordhan. Although at times I traveled alone, traveling as a couple drew less attention, especially going through roadblocks and speed traps. I felt my forged documents were my best protection, and I resisted the temptation to travel armed.

Getting Ready

Overall, there were now at least seventy people in our operations in the Durban region. With the support people who provided safe places for meetings or work, or hired cars, there were more than a hundred. But most did not know they were part of something called Vula. Other than knowing they belonged to an underground unit of the ANC or MK or the SACP, they had no contact with one another. I was comfortable. I could now begin to look at what tactics and strategy we could develop in the Jo'burg region.

Our primary mission was to build the long-term capability of MK to fight a protracted people's war. We came across potential targets, and I have to admit that my heartbeat quickened. I spent hours reconnoitering targets, checking their security and vulnerable points. Sometimes we were sorely tempted to engage in short-term actions, like other MK units, but there was always the steady hand of OR to keep us on track.

Our job was to build up stockpiles, select an officer corps, train people on the ground, and select candidates for outside training. We had to keep our military machinery in shape; acts of sabotage were kept to a minimum unless they were for training purposes.

Gebuza's recruits were being trained to join MK. They were told they were eventually to become armed combatants to engage in guerrilla warfare. If they raised the question of negotiations, once they had become a possibility, I would say, "Chaps, concentrate on your job here. Let Lusaka attend to the negotiations. The regime will only talk about negotiations when they see that the mass struggle and the underground struggle are heating up."

The Import Business: Matériel

Weapons were brought in and stored in different parts of the country, in readiness for the future. Lusaka could simply contact us, and we would release the weapons. We found that a particular make of car, the Toyota Cressida, had a fuel tank that could be detached from the body of the car very quickly. We bought secondhand Toyota Cressida tanks and created false compartments in them in which to store weapons. We went to a rental-car company, hired a Cressida, removed the tank, and inserted one with a false compartment.

We would find a legitimate reason for aboveground people to drive these cars to Botswana, where they would be parked at a certain place, the keys left under the mat. Someone else would arrive to take the car away. Within an hour, the car would be returned with a tank loaded with weapons, but as the tank's capacity was now less than normal, you had to keep it topped up.

Each person did a once-off mission. Each time, we used a different rental-car company and a different number plate. Once the driver returned to South Africa, the car was left in a specified garage, the tanks were swapped, and the following morning the driver would return it to the rental company. Although drivers knew they were collecting weapons, they didn't know where these were hidden, nor would they have been able to give names or descriptions of anyone else involved either in South Africa or Botswana. We moved out computer disks with detailed analyses of the situation on the ground and other messages that were too much for our communications system to handle in the same way, and we received responses on the return trips.

The matériel included AK-47s; dynamite; plastic explosives; detonators; RPG rocket launchers; land mines, both antipersonnel and antitank. We also began to collect arms within the country through the external ordnance department. Certain people had access to caches in Natal and Jo'burg, but only one person knew where every cache was.[46]

We also started making arrangements to purchase arms inside South Africa, but Lusaka said, "Hold it." They were concerned that buying stolen weapons from the SADF and the police would increase the danger of getting

caught; we were not there to start engaging in military action, only to prepare for it.

Tensions with Lusaka

As Vula rooted itself in the country, our demands on Lusaka multiplied
tenfold. Tim Jenkin in London was under pressure. The frequency and
length of our reports, our requirements for arms, matériel, and guidance
kept him hopping. Ivan, in Lusaka, was in charge of administrating Vula
and similar projects. It was his job to find OR or JS and prod them to respond to our requests. Whenever things did not work, I bared my fangs at
Lusaka. I know we were putting them under severe pressure, but my attitude was that if Vula was as important as they were saying in their messages, and if their congratulations on progress were sincere, then it was
their responsibility to keep up their side of the bargain. If Jenkin was over-
worked, they should allocate comrades to assist him. If Ivan was over-
stretched, they should provide him with help. In Vula we were working
twenty hours a day, seven days a week. My only relaxation was a tot of
brandy before I hit the sack at some early hour of the morning. On our
side, if Lusaka asked us to jump, we jumped.

I have a tendency to speak my mind, to shoot straight. It has gotten me
into trouble many times. I was harsh with OR and JS, even though I was
fully aware of the enormous burden they were under and the multiple duties they had to juggle. But we were all juggling, and if I dropped something, I didn't waste time bending down to pick it up. I just kept right
on juggling. At times I could detect frustration in Joe's responses. But
my communications with him reflected the complicated relationship we
had. With OR it was different. He avoided my barbs; he was, at heart, a
kind man.

There were instances where they criticized me and I them. Every time
it appeared that word of my presence in the country might leak out, they
would want me out, but I stayed put. They thought I was spreading myself
too thin, but I only saw more work to do.[47]

We made mistakes in Vula, but the mistakes were always noted quickly.
The fact that we operated for two years in such an intensive way shows we
were successfully avoiding the attentions of the security forces. Of course,
one of the things that gave us an enormous advantage was the intelligence
information we were receiving from Moe.

Loose Cannons

One of the many ironies of Vula is that sometimes our own comrades were a greater danger to us than the security forces. They almost succeeded in exposing us where the security forces had failed. Keeping Vula a secret from comrades consumed a lot of time and energy. I had to make myself known to them without letting on what I was up to. Moe's intelligence always allowed us to keep a few steps ahead of the SB. But our own comrades, stalwarts in the struggle, heroes to the masses, were a different matter.

Two in particular had convinced themselves that unless the struggle was conducted the way they thought it should be done, the struggle would not prevail. Perhaps they thought they had good reason for thinking that way. Both had spent many years on Robben Island—in Govan Mbeki's case, twenty-four years, and in Harry Gwala's, two stints of eight and eleven years. Both were deeply committed to the armed struggle.

Harry joined the Communist Party in 1942 and the ANC in 1944; Govan became active in the ANC in 1955 and then the underground SACP. What made it difficult for Lusaka to deal with them was the fact that in the late 1980s they were the two highest-profile African movement leaders in the country and could, in fact, mobilize people. Both were looked up to by leaders in the MDM. They were the visible presence of an ANC leadership in the country, and because they were in the country, both believed they had the right to a certain autonomy from Lusaka.

Harry Gwala

He became a major figure in the Inkatha/UDF conflict. His stance and ideology were uncompromising. He was blunt, single-minded in purpose, and obsessively territorial. When rumors reached him that I was in the country organizing structures in his domain, he saw this as a threat to his hegemony. He fueled the rumors. It was clear Harry would have been pleased if Vula was discovered. OR's advice: "Run, get out." Gebuza's advice was "Don't go." I saw Harry as a political problem: we had to find a way of dealing with him without making matters between us worse.

By April 1989, things were getting out of hand. Gwala's actions were endangering Vula.[48] I made overtures through intermediaries, but they were brushed aside. Eventually I told OR that Gwala simply rebuffed all attempts to get a dialogue going. OR said, "Listen, I've wanted to send a message to him, but I can't get a safe courier, but since you say the situation is becoming critical, I am preparing a lengthy report discussing these issues with him. I want you to deliver it. I want you to go and meet him."[49]

OR regarded Gwala as a loose cannon.[50] Gwala was paranoid that the ANC's structures in Natal were being corrupted by an "Indian cabal" and apoplectic when he learned that the ANC had chosen an Indian to organize its underground structures inside the country. Gwala, whom the comrades held in high esteem for the tenacity of his war against Mangosuthu Buthelezi, was in reality a high-risk threat to the struggle he thought he embodied.

I made numerous attempts to arrange a meeting with him through intermediaries. He ignored everyone, but we eventually met. He set a meeting for 11:00 A.M. in the consulting rooms of a medical doctor well known for his anti-apartheid activities. The consulting rooms were in Lancet House in Durban, a building known to house a nest of anti-apartheid activists and NGOs, and under constant surveillance by the SB.

My discussions with Gwala were mostly concerned with the violence between our supporters and Buthelezi's. My greatest concern was that when some of his own comrades disagreed with his hard-line position on violence, he encouraged other comrades to silence them. It's one thing to say he was mobilizing and acting against the enemy in warfare, but when he turned against our own people, he set out on a path that would have untold harmful consequences for the struggle and the future.

I gave him OR's communication, which urged on him the absolute necessity of keeping my presence in the country secret. For my part, I was conciliatory and cooperative. But Gwala kept none of the agreements we made. We had to make direct contact with activists in the Pietermaritzburg area to slowly build up a capacity to distribute printed propaganda in the area, without help from Gwala. But once he became aware of what we were doing, he began to see that many of his own people in the region were also involved with Vula and me. He became more amenable to cooperating with us.[51]

As I recall this incident so many years later, I can laugh it off. But there was nothing funny about it at the time. Here was a comrade who was endangering the entire Vula operation. He was telling comrades of my presence in the country. And he was trying to lobby support against me by alleging I was part of an Indian cabal. He thought that Natal was his territory and that he could do as he liked there as long as he engaged the enemy. He didn't want interference from "outsiders" in his area. There was a calculated hardheadedness, lack of scruple, and opportunism about his actions. It put a distance between us. I didn't trust him. He could have handed the apartheid security forces a coup.

Govan Mbeki

Madiba negotiated Govan's release with the regime. One of the conditions of his release, which Madiba relayed to Govan, was that he should keep a low profile. Madiba's analysis was that if Govan didn't go out of his way to bring himself to the attention of the regime, which would be watching him in any event, it would open the way for the release of Walter and company.[52]

But once free, Govan immersed himself in action. He had his own theories on how to organize the masses, and these did not always mesh with how the MDM wanted to move forward or with the ANC's long-term designs. The way he intended going about this would have opened the way for the regime to crush key elements of the MDM and arrest its leadership. He was failing to build firewalls between structures, and he was centralizing activity around himself, despite being so vulnerable. Besides, the SB was keeping him under constant surveillance, and everyone who visited him came under scrutiny. Govan by nature was tough to deal with. He emerged from prison with his reputation as a tough hard-liner intact. We had to get Lusaka, OR in particular, to brief him to ensure that the role he played was consistent with the strategy, tactics, and organization of the underground that had been developed over the decades he had been in prison.

He set up his own line of communication with Lusaka via a courier, the Reverend M. Xundu, someone I didn't have a high regard for. I once sent a message to OR: "I'm in Jo'burg at the moment, and yesterday I believe I saw Zizi's [Govan's] courier, the Reverend Xundu, at a hotel, and he was on his way to Lusaka. Xundu's reputation is controversial. If he's bringing you a verbal report, you have to assess it with a particular filter."

Xundu was controversial because he was often divisive. The UDF strategy was to broaden the reach of the struggle, and it didn't matter whether you agreed fully with the ANC strategy and tactics. Its purpose was to let the mass movement flower and encourage people to act. That's the first step in the politicization of the masses. You do not use the underground to tell them what to do, which is the approach Xundu used. There was an authoritarian streak, coming from Govan, which was divisive: we must all operate on instructions and under orders. In my opinion, authoritarian styles divide rather than encourage. You have to tap into what communities are thinking, what their local issues are, and from there develop their awareness of national issues.

I sent Dr. Diliza Mji, a confidant of Govan's from the Durban region, to meet OR. I had high regard for Mji; I'd seen the caliber of his work. But when I discussed matters with him, I could sense he was quietly reporting to Govan. Because Mji was of a younger generation, I didn't want to place him in the difficult position of having to choose between the differing approaches of two senior comrades, one of whom was regarded as a father of the struggle. So I felt it was important for Mji to have a face-to-face meeting with OR, who was very much impressed with him, and who agreed that Mji should not be caught in a push-pull situation between Govan and me.

Mji's meeting with OR went on for several days. When Mji wanted to take notes, OR said, "Don't make notes. When you get back to Durban, the person who arranged your coming here will have a full record of my discussions with you in writing, so you don't have to bother to smuggle it in." After Mji returned to Durban, he came to see me, and of course OR had sent me a comm enclosing the letter Mji was to deliver to Govan. I said, "Here's a lengthy report; read it." He did so. I said, "Is that an accurate record of your meeting with OR?" He said, "Absolutely accurate." I knew the warning bells were buzzing in his head. I said, "Now deliver it to Govan because that's what OR has told me you must do. I presume he has told you?" He said, "Yes, yes."

OR had gently advised Govan to confine his activities to Port Elizabeth (PE) and the border areas, that he, OR, was personally overseeing an Area Political Committee (APC) in the Durban region and was planning to do the same in Jo'burg. Above all, he wanted to dissuade Govan from pursuing his ideas for a national collective because the way Govan was going about it put the top leadership of the MDM in danger. But Govan continued to hold meetings with Kgalema Motlanthe, Cyril Ramaphosa, Dullah Omar, and others. None of them had any idea what instructions Govan had received from OR. As far as they were concerned, he was the voice of the ANC—whatever Govan said was the movement speaking. He continued to believe he could organize a national underground operation. He seemed not to understand what being under constant surveillance meant. Or maybe he was daring the regime to send him back to prison. Mji told me it would be difficult for him not to tell Govan that he was serving in our structures if Govan asked him about the situation in Natal.

The rumors about my presence intensified. From other sources it emerged that Jacob Zuma was conducting his own inquiries. So there were three sources of rumor and inquiry reinforcing each other. Again OR wanted me to pull out of the country for a while, to reappear in Lusaka—as if back from medical treatment—so that my physical presence there would squelch the rumors that I was at home. But I wasn't ready to leave yet. Again, I told OR I could handle the situation. I would go to see Govan. "He's had your briefing in writing," I said. "He's had time to study it. It's time for me to meet him." OR wasn't very keen. He thought the surveillance around Govan would make it impossible. Slovo wanted 95 percent security. I said I'd take care of things. They finally agreed, but very reluctantly.[53]

I sent Maud Leo and her partner, the pharmacist Yusuf Mohammed, and Soraya Shaik, Moe's wife, to do a reconnaissance of Port Elizabeth. We worked out an elaborate plan to shake off any SB surveillance so that we could pick up Govan and then take him to a room in the Elizabeth Hotel.

The plan worked like a charm. Govan and I met for five hours. We hugged each other—we had last seen each other thirteen years previously on Robben Island, and even though we'd had sharp differences in the past, there we sat and talked warmly. He was delighted but not surprised to see me in the country. I said that OR had sent me. I said, "We would like to see PE well organized. What help can we give you; what are your needs?"

Of course I told him nothing about Vula. Our discussions focused on the practical side of work, the support that PE comrades needed. I said, "You've got to separate the military and the political on the ground. You've got to avoid bringing the mass organizations' leadership into these underground structures, or there's a danger they could all be wiped out at one shot. What do you need?"

He said, "We've got MK units." I said, "How many units have you got? Who is the head? Can you put me in touch with him?" "No, I'll contact him." I said, "No, I don't want you back in jail; you're an inspiration out of jail. Tell me who the commander is, and I'll find who relates to him. I'll attend to his needs of training and equipment, etcetera. Tell me about your propaganda units; I'll arrange for propaganda to get to them and train them in the production of underground propaganda. But you, Zizi, you need to ensure that you stand above all this. So don't start mixing yourself with all those little details. Live so that if your commander gets caught, you're not linked to him. If it leads to me, they still have to catch me, but you—you're a sitting duck."

I didn't tell him that I was staying in the country indefinitely. I just said, "I'm here, any time you need me, send a message. I will find my way here."

So what could I tell OR? That despite OR's instructions, Govan was continuing to involve himself in military work. That I would have to monitor his activities, which meant using our resources to keep an eye on our own rather than getting on with the job we were there to do. That Govan had to be kept on a tight rein—if that was possible. But that was up to Lusaka. I could not be the movement's babysitter. On the other hand, Govan could not say he was unaware of my presence. He knew I spoke with the authority of Lusaka, that I had a fast and reliable line to Lusaka, that I was aware of what he was up to and would be reporting to Lusaka. Perhaps that would make him a little more circumspect, but as it turned out, not circumspect enough. After OR had his stroke and Walter Sisulu and the rest of the Rivonia Trialists were released, and the ANC was unbanned, Govan tried to put his own stamp on the composition of the leadership at home. He tried blindsiding both OR and Walter, but he failed and Mandela rapidly took command of developments at home.*

Dirty Tricks: Our Turn

Shortly after Madiba was released in February 1990, during the period when ANC emissaries were traveling from abroad to meet with South African government officials to arrange issues such as amnesty, commencement of bilateral talks, and so on, the ANC's head of counterintelligence, JZ, told me that a member of South Africa's military intelligence had contacted him about plans to eliminate Madiba. When asked to substantiate this, the MI man said he was part of the group assigned to carry out the task and that they had already been assigned the weapon, one with an optical sight. Because he did not intend to carry out this order, he was prepared to entrust the weapon to the ANC. JZ asked whether I could store the weapon safely inside South Africa. I said yes, and also suggested it could be of use to us.[54]

I was aware, from reports by Moe's Nightingale that Moe had shared with me, of tensions within the SB, specifically between two very senior Durban-based officers, Major von Sittert and Major Hentjie Botha, who were constantly undermining each other. Their rivalry showed how corrupt the system was. Informers were paid, but many were simply opportunists trying to get a slice of the pie. One of these officers kept putting in reports from an informant he called a gold mine, but the other chap felt overshadowed and tried to poach him. So they were at each other's throats. Courtesy of Moe, I had seen the actual reports, and I knew this in-

*See pages 337–39.

former wasn't connected to the movement but just cooking up his own stories.

I asked, "Which one is the bright one? Could we eliminate that one and make it look as though the other did it? That would distract them from the real security issues, make them point fingers at one another, force internal investigations because the weapon will be one of their own." Gebuza said, "Hey, we've discussed using this tactic for some time: how to force the enemy security forces to turn inward and self-destruct, provided we could do it the right way." But, unfortunately, the ripe opportunity never surfaced.

Western Cape

After Chris Hani became MK chief of staff in 1987, the question of his leading a Vula-type operation in the Western Cape was moot. However, an advance team of cadres had already been sent in to prepare the way for Chris. Lusaka felt that progress there was slow relative to what we had achieved. The comrades were not really integrated with the people's forces on the ground, so the question arose of how to bring them into a more dynamic command structure. In April/May 1989, Lusaka instructed me to expand Operation Vula to the Western Cape.[55] After discussions with Charles Nqakula and Little John, I found they hadn't done much more than stockpile weapons.[56] There were many organizational and communications problems to be addressed in the Western Cape.

13. VULA: CONFLICT IN KWAZULU-NATAL (KZN)

Introduction

SOME CALLED IT a civil war among Zulus. On the one side: Chief Mangosuthu Buthelezi, chief minister to the Zulu king, Goodwill Zwelithini, leader of the KwaZulu enclave and head of Inkatha. On the other: the UDF (United Democratic Front) with its ANC affiliations. It was a bitter conflict for political control of KwaZulu, then only part of the larger province of Natal, though scheduled for sectioning off as a homeland.

Many believed the conflict was orchestrated by the apartheid regime, which covertly supplied Inkatha with arms and training, but others called it an ethnic war when it spread into the Transvaal after 1990. Here the conflict was between migrant hostel dwellers, mostly Zulu and Inkatha supporting, and the people living in the townships adjacent to the hostels, invariably referred to by the Zulu migrants as Xhosa-speaking ANC. It was also seen as a clash between modernity and tradition: the democracy of the ANC versus the autocracy of Inkatha. And there was also the view that some of the violence was the unfinished business of other Zulu wars, clan wars, internecine rivalries, and a vendetta culture that honored retributive vengeance.

It was all of these things. There is no accurate count of the number of victims—perhaps between ten thousand and fifteen thousand. In this war between Africans, more African lives were lost than in the war waged by the apartheid state against the liberation movements between 1960 and 1993. As in many conflicts of oppression, the indigenous populations turned on one another with a ferocity that matched that of their colonial masters. The broader context is the pervasive devaluation of black life by the apartheid state.[1]

The ANC strenuously objected to having this conflict referred to as "black on black," on the grounds that to do so fed into the regime's attempts to fuel white fears that blacks were a bloodthirsty lot, incapable of settling disputes among themselves other than with violence. The ANC also objected on the grounds that the Inkatha warlords were acting with the support of the apartheid security forces, that they were in fact surrogates of apartheid. The regime argued that the conflict was a foretaste of what life in South Africa would be like under black rule, that the country would "go the way of the rest of Africa."

And the government did help to fund Inkatha: it trained some of its operatives and provided much indirect and sometimes direct assistance.[2] But when these factors are discounted, the conflict in KwaZulu remains one between two predominant black political alignments competing for power. And as in all conflicts, the blame for the carnage rests with all sides. The conflict was fought mostly in the rural areas, in the heart of the Natal Midlands and the townships abutting Pietermaritzburg and Durban. Territory changed hands and so did allegiances, since the cost of being accused of being on "the other side" could be fatal. No-go areas were established on both sides. To this day, memories are sharp, grievances stored, and beneath the surface of calm and normality of what is now the province of KwaZulu-Natal, there remain many scores to be settled. The peace achieved through much effort still needs assiduous nurturing.[3]

2

Ostensibly, the quarrel between the two movements revolved around the question of what strategy to use against the regime. The ANC might have tolerated Buthelezi's disagreement with its strategies on armed struggle and economic sanctions. It understood that the IFP had to exist in the legal space available within the country, and to ask the IFP to "endorse" the ANC's policies would defeat the purpose of establishing it as a quasi surrogate or at least ally.* But when Buthelezi's disagreements turned into public denunciations of the armed struggle and sanctions, it was seen as an act of apostasy by the ANC.

In the 1980s, his anti-ANC stance became increasingly belligerent.

_____

*Even the UDF was dissuaded from "endorsing" the armed struggle. (The ANC advised the UDF not to adopt the Freedom Charter so that it might attract as broad based a constituency as possible, but the UDF endorsed it anyway.)

He maintained that the regime could be more effectively attacked by mobilizing blacks politically to extract incremental concessions from the South African government. The ANC regarded Buthelezi's attitude toward violence as hypocritical and his stance on sanctions as collaborationist. Accusations flew. Tambo accused Buthelezi of dressing Inkatha in ANC colors—black, green, and gold—for his own political purposes. Buthelezi charged the ANC with wanting to hijack Inkatha and when that failed, of trying to destroy it.

Inkatha gained control of local-authority structures in townships within the borders of KwaZulu, preeminently Umlazi and KwaMashu, and of townships earmarked for incorporation into KwaZulu. It successfully applied its strategy by securing control of the KwaZulu legislative assembly. Yet Buthelezi's refusal to make KwaZulu an "independent" state along the lines of Transkei, Bophuthatswana, and Venda, all of which had opted for putative independence, threw the government's plans for Grand Apartheid into disarray, for unlike the other "independent" states, the KwaZulu Bantustan had the economic resources and infrastructure, if you included Natal, which Botha, in desperation, was prepared to do in order to give real clout to that "independence."

After the formation of the UDF in 1983, Inkatha found itself under fire from young comrades who opposed all apartheid-created institutions and responded to the ANC's call to make South Africa ungovernable. The ANC propaganda machine swung into action, describing Buthelezi as a puppet and a collaborator—labels which all too often carried a death sentence. John Nkadimeng, a member of the NEC, said in a Radio Freedom broadcast in late 1986: "It is clear that the puppet Gatsha* is being groomed by the West and the racist regime to become a Savimbi in a future free South Africa. The onus is on the people of South Africa to neutralize the Gatsha snake, which is poisoning the people of South Africa. It needs to be hit over the head."[4] Such talk was an incitement to kill. The TRC interpreted the State Security Council's call to "neutralize" someone as sanction for his murder; by the same yardstick, the ANC engaged in similar actions with regard to Buthelezi. Not that Buthelezi was any less culpable, despite protestations of adherence to nonviolence. Addressing the KwaZulu Assembly in the early 1980s, he exhorted his supporters in words they readily understood: "If someone hits you with a bare fist, must

*According to Ben Temkin, Buthelezi's biographer, "Gatsha is a familiar form of address and came to be used patronizingly and abusively in some of the media. Courtesy demands that his proper first name Mangosutho be used. . . ." Ben Temkin, *Buthelezi: A Biography* (London: Frank Cass, 2003), p. xviii.

you not take off the boxing gloves and hit back at him? Is it the right thing to run away and be branded a coward? If need be we will call for an eye for an eye and a tooth for a tooth."[5]

3

The conflict in KZN does not feature significantly in the Vula communications because the conflict was not part of Vula's mandate. Not to get involved required an exercise of discipline that was being instilled into the cadres in the underground. Although they strained to go to the help of the UDF, to do so would have endangered the mission. Vula's MK cadres were being trained as an army with a future mandate: when all elements of the preparations for a people's war were in place, and political leadership had matured, then it would engage. Nevertheless, Vula's MK structures did provide training to township comrades without exposing themselves or their mission,[6] and on one occasion Mac was willing to undertake the covert killing of warlords identified by Natal activists to preempt attacks on communities sympathetic to the ANC.[7]

The fact that underground political and military structures were being established within the conflict area unavoidably impinged on Vula. Vula recruits required special management to ensure they did not become part of either MK or UDF structures that were taking the fight to Inkatha. The threat of members recruited to the underground being detained by the SB increased commensurately with their involvement in activities outside their own unit.

But the comms reflect the ANC strategy for dealing with Buthelezi and the IFP during the last years of the 1980s.[8] They suggest there was so much distrust that no peace between the two sides was possible. The ANC's line was clear: nothing would be done in terms of peace initiatives that might legitimate Buthelezi's claim as being *pari passu* with the ANC. (Indeed, there was no basis for the IFP, with a Zulu constituency largely within one province, to claim the same footing as the ANC, a national movement spread across all African ethnic communities and over the whole of South Africa.) Inkatha was willingly taking assistance from the government. Buthelezi should be marginalized. The ANC failed to understand that support for Buthelezi, especially in rural areas, was real and not driven by a false consciousness somehow instilled by the regime.

Buthelezi attempted to meet with the MDM, at least partly to escape marginalization and establish parity of importance with the ANC. But COSATU and the UDF concluded that Buthelezi was "posturing and is not serious about the peace process." Thus the context for decisions: "GB [Gatsha Buthelezi] has always tried to portray MDM as proxies of ANC. The insistence on the quadripartite meeting on his part is an attempt to promote this stance, as well as to claim that the movement has finally acknowledged him as a power." And its final decision: "We cannot approve of a 'blackmail summit.' "[9]

When Buthelezi got Margaret Thatcher to signal to the ANC that he wanted to use her as an intermediary to "normalize" relations between Inkatha and the ANC,[10] her attempts were rebuffed on the grounds that "GB's attempts to break out of isolation are part of a bigger package involving the British government and other imperialist forces."[11]

Having successfully portrayed Buthelezi as a stooge of the regime in the latter part of the 1980s, the ANC found that attempts to defuse the climate of retaliatory violence were met by resistance from their own supporters in the most affected areas. Buthelezi, deeply hurt by the ANC's accusations, turned increasingly to the regime for assistance in resisting the ANC, and in the process he became what he was accused of being.

But Buthelezi, for all his faults—egomania and personal eccentricities—insistently called for the release of all political prisoners, and despite the blandishments of the regime, he refused to negotiate with it until Mandela was released. And, interestingly, he and Mandela maintained a warm correspondence.[12]

Mac

IN AUGUST 1988, the conflict between the UDF and Inkatha was at its height, and we trained people to defend themselves against Inkatha. The warfare on the ground was vicious. The Inkatha forces, assisted by the state, were on the rampage, and there were no-go areas. Here we had a situation that was a real dilemma: Gebuza was training an MK army for a people's war, and there was a war going on right beside him in which our guys were being killed. We had weapons; we had trained men; but we couldn't "Go and fight." That was the real problem for the movement. We were in an ongoing war, but if we immediately threw all our forces into the fight, we would never have been able to build a capacity and would have been out of weaponry in half an hour.

But we could assist: we gave them as much training as we could without endangering ourselves, making available some weaponry if we found they were really short but encouraging them to get it from the other side—there's never been a guerrilla situation where all the arms were imported.

I am sure that some comrades acted outside our mandate because the people on the ground would think with their blood. It's very difficult to resist the temptation when your own people are being mowed down. Jabu Sithole was living in Lamontville, one of the most fiercely contested areas. He was not just an ordinary citizen; he had a history of activism. We had Mpho Scott; he was from another hot spot. He was an activist, giving leadership on the ground—he would be involved, but we didn't prescribe and say you mustn't get involved in the violence. Because it wouldn't work.

We tried to assess the situation area by area, situation by situation. We knew where we were heading. We were planning on a long-term war. My first night back in Durban, I met with Billy Nair, and we drove around the C. R. Swart Building, HQ of the SB; he wanted us to prepare an attack on the building. I refused. He said, "That's the headquarters of the SB. There, the window there, that light on the eleventh floor shows where somebody is being interrogated and tortured. We can't stand for that. It's easy to blow up this building and attack it." I said, "That's not what I'm here for." Big quarrel between Billy and me. But I could afford to have that type of quarrel with Billy. He would understand.

When I arrived in the country, I knew I would have to make judgment calls on things like this. I couldn't have the same kind of debate with the rest of the structures as I could have with Billy. They'd tell me to fuck off, so I'd have to use a different argument: "Now, chaps, if we take this path, where you say it will be a stand-up fight, you can see that their forces are overwhelming; we'll be defeated, and what will be left?" So we gave assistance to the UDF without drawing them into our structure. We gave them equipment and guidance on how to train themselves to be better prepared. We also gave strategic advice: how effective were the tactics the comrades were using? We would engage in debate, analyze potential conflict situations, and assess the best alternatives to deal with the different kinds of attack used by Inkatha.

I remember an occasion in 1990 after Ronnie Kasrils had joined us. Gebuza and I were in Jo'burg, and a request came for us to release AK47s from the arsenal.[13] Gebuza and I independently said no and that we were coming down to Durban. I sent a message asking the structure to arrange for an all-night meeting with the military and political committee to debate this matter.

It was a long debate, and I was being pushed into a corner to articulate solutions I was not prepared to put before such a large meeting. I asked for the intelligence information and the identities of the warlords who had met and planned this Inkatha march. Outside the meeting during a break, one comrade cornered me and wanted to know whether all my position amounted to was pouring cold water on their proposal and having nothing to offer in return. I said to him, "Give us the names, identities, and addresses of those warlords, and we'll find ways to deal with them without fanfare." That way the march would not take place, a massacre would be avoided, and future marches would not happen. But I said that this was not a matter for a meeting such as the one we were holding.

It was not an easy debate, for it was charged with much emotion. But it was a necessary debate. It revolved around the strategy behind Vula. Gebuza and I hoped that by opening up the debate even at such an emotional time, we could use the occasion as a "seminar" on leadership and the role and strategy behind Vula.

Standing Not So Idly By

This was a dirty war between two groups of people who fought for the control of towns and villages right across KZN. One day the area would be in the hands of Inkatha, the next day it would be UDF territory, a week later it would be Inkatha again. People took sides depending on who was in control, and on who got killed. You killed my sister, so I will kill yours. And if I can't kill your sister, I'll kill your cousin. Time and again, Gebuza and I had discussions with comrades to get them to understand where retaliatory violence would lead. Mostly they were receptive, but not without a lot of give and take. And sometimes they went their own way with all the predictable consequences. The fact is that if you sent in an MK unit to operate in Pietermaritzburg, for survival's sake alone it had to relate to the mass of the people, and in that environment it would be impossible for it to avoid becoming involved in tit-for-tat violence

As senior figures, our job was not to go and say don't do this, don't do that. Our job was to interact with the leading figures both in the underground and the MDM—like the Billy Nairs, Pravin Gordhans, Jabu Sitholes, and Mpho Scotts—to debate tactics to be used so that they would come to an understanding that we were being driven into a no-win situation. Even with everything that was going on, it didn't mean that we should not try to open lines of communication with Buthelezi and those around him.

It was not part of my mandate to make an intervention in KZN. Lusaka had already reached a deadlock with Buthelezi. Since the collapse of the London meeting in 1979, Buthelezi had come out openly against us, and he'd come out against sanctions. How could you intervene except to say "keep the lines open"? If possible, you could use the influence of the South African Council of Churches or a foreign connection to talk to Buthelezi—anything to keep something open.

We had people: Siegfried Bengu and Joshua Zulu, chaps who had served in prison as ANC cadres. Siegfried Bengu had trained abroad and come into the country in 1964, before my first arrest. He was arrested, landed in Robben Island, was released after ten years, and joined Inkatha. I met Joshua Zulu when I came out of prison in 1977. He was in the single cells but released before I was. He was an ANC cadre; after he came out, he joined Inkatha and was their representative in Durban when I met him in 1977.

One of my tactics had always been to look inside the apartheid government structures to find people who sympathized with us, either to spy for us or act as political allies, so I did the same with Inkatha. When I came home, I tried to cultivate these contacts through others. I was able to confirm to Lusaka that the weaponry the IFP was getting came from the SADF's armory, as did their officer training, and that Inkatha and the state were cooperating. But I also raised concerns that a never-ending war against Inkatha was now taking our attention away from fighting apartheid.

14. MANDELA

Introduction

IN SOUTH AFRICA TODAY it is not possible to find former struggle activists who are prepared to admit that at one time they believed Nelson Mandela was selling out. By "selling out," they did not mean they thought Mandela was willing to barter his freedom (and that of other political prisoners) for the titular position of a Bantustan leader or that he would kowtow to Pretoria or betray the movement by cozying up to the government. Selling out conjured up scenarios of Mandela's having talks with the government and being willing to give his imprimatur to an agreement for less than the full exercise of the franchise by blacks, or one embracing "group rights" (code words to activists for maintaining white power), or perhaps power sharing of a kind that would ultimately give whites vetoes in key areas of the polity. In short, selling out meant that Mandela might convey the impression to the government that he would settle, and hence so would the black masses, for something less than majority rule.

The fears that Mandela might go it alone in talking with the government without consulting the ANC in exile grew out of the general paranoia that enveloped the ANC in Lusaka. The ANC in exile believed that a key element in the strategy of the government was to isolate Mandela, first in Pollsmoor Prison and then in Victor Verster Prison, in order to soften him up, and make him more amenable to their suggestions. The aim: split the ANC.

Niel Barnard, head of the NIS, pooh-poohs insinuations that the talks he and his colleagues held with Mandela in 1988–89 were intended to achieve this aim, but others, of course, would pooh-pooh whatever Barnard might say. Mandela asked the government to talk with him; P. W. Botha made the decision to respond positively. However, after the talks were well under way, Mandela became upset when he was informed by Barnard that the NIS was going to initiate secret talks with the ANC. Mandela, perhaps, suspected that this might be part of a strategy on the part of the government to try to exploit perceived differences between his exchanges with the team and NIS exchanges with the ANC in exile. Whatever the cause of his discomfort he nevertheless pressed ahead with his talks once a secure line of communication between him and Tambo was established.[1]

2

The facts are straightforward enough. When he was moved to Pollsmoor Prison in 1985, Mandela wrote to Kobie Coetsee, minister of justice, asking for a meeting to discuss talks between the ANC and the government. He had concluded that "the struggle could best be pushed forward through negotiations. . . . It was clear to me that a military victory was a distant if not impossible dream. It was time to talk."*[2]

In 1987, Mandela had several meetings with Coetsee at his residence. Coetsee told him that the government would appoint a team of senior officials to talk with him in private.[3] The State Security Council (SSC) had authorized the meetings.[4] The team comprised Niel Barnard, head of NIS; Fanie van der Merwe, director general of the Prisons Department; General W. H. Willemse; and Coetsee himself. It reported directly to Botha. In Mandela's count, there were forty-seven such meetings before he was released; in Barnard's, forty-eight.

A smuggled letter from Tambo expressed concerns over reports that Mandela was talking to the government. Mandela, using George Bizos as the conduit, tersely replied that he was talking to the government about the government talking to the NEC of the ANC.[5]

The regime didn't view the talks in quite the same light. As far as it was concerned, it was engaged in secret negotiations. The objective was to

*Between 1985 and 1987 the Commonwealth's Eminent Persons Group (EPG) embarked on an initiative to break the political impasse. (Its narrow frame of reference, agreed at the meeting of the British Commonwealth in Nassau in October 1985, was to determine whether international sanctions against South Africa were an appropriate tool to help end apartheid.) Subsequently, during its fact-finding trip to South Africa, the EPG met with Mandela at Pollsmoor and with P. W. Botha. In April 1986, months before the EPG was scheduled to release its reports and recommendations, Thabo Mbeki provided the NWC with the assessments of the EPG, as conveyed to him in London by the EPG. It had found Botha "unyielding. He offered nothing and was completely negative." For a summary of Mbeki's conversations with the EPG and of Johny Makathini's (NEC member) interactions with Frank Casey, the chairman of IBM and a member of the Schultz Advisory Commission on South Africa, go to []maharaj/documents and reports/ANC NWC/1986/[] Minutes of NWC Special Meeting 26 April; see also the Commonwealth Group of Eminent Persons, *Mission to South Africa.*

agree on the broad parameters of a settlement. According to members of the team, they and Mandela found common understanding on the most crucial issues. In the four years of formal negotiations between 1990 through 1994, the detailed settlement was hammered out within the framework they had established.[6]

In December 1988, Mandela was moved to a one-story cottage at Victor Verster Prison. Coetsee arrived with "a case of Cape wine as a house-warming gift." Coetsee told him "Victor Verster would be my last home before becoming a free man." The authorities "began to permit some of my ANC comrades and members of the United Democratic Front (UDF) and the Mass Democratic Movement (MDM) to visit."[7]

In April 1989, Mandela sent a memorandum to Botha in anticipation of a meeting with him, which he had been told had been scheduled. "I now consider it necessary in the national interest for the African National Congress and the government," he wrote, "to meet urgently to negotiate an effective political settlement."[8] He gave Ismail Ayob a copy of the document for delivery to Tambo. But Ayob, mistaking the import of its contents, gave a copy to Jay Naidoo, secretary-general of COSATU, who, in turn, disseminated copies to other MDM leaders. All interpreted the document to imply that Mandela was selling out. There was consternation. Mac moved with speed to assess the damage and then, in a series of decisive moves, quashed the rumors, brought the straying UDM leaders into line, and had them quickly reach out to their own structures to spread the word: Mandela was not selling out.[9]

3

When I interviewed the MDM leaders who were involved in the episode— Jay Naidoo, Valli Moosa, and Momoniat—to corroborate Mac's version of how events unfolded, all suffered from bouts of amnesia. So did Ismail Ayob, the man who triggered the outbreak of consternation among MDM leaders in April and May 1989. None has even a faint recollection of the events leading up to the call on MDM figures not to respond to Mandela's invitations to see him at Victor Verster; there are no recollections of ever having seen the document, no recall of hectic meetings called—all is a blank. At the same time, none was prepared to state categorically that Mac's account of the events was inaccurate.

Had I not gained access to a copy of the Vula communications, Mac's recollections of the events of that time would have remained uncorroborated except for one other—Billy Nair gave full confirmation of what Mac had told

me. But the comms allow us to give substance to the story. If Mac had not intervened, first through Valli Moosa in Jo'burg and then Billy Nair in Durban,
the results could have been disastrous. Mac dispatched Nair to straighten out
Govan Mbeki and Harry Gwala, who had added fuel to the fire by claiming
Mandela had jumped ship. Mbeki's standing as the most senior ANC leader in
the country, as a Rivonia Trialist and a legend to a younger generation of struggle leaders, gave his position the gravitas of the authentic voice of the ANC.

　　Without Mac's decisive action, the connections between Mandela and
the MDM, and the MDM and Lusaka, could have been severely disrupted.
At the least, misunderstanding, confusion, and distrust would have developed. When the matter had been resolved, Tambo wrote Mac: "IA [Ismail
Ayob] made a dangerous mistake. Imagine the massive damage had you
not intervened. You saved the movement from being plunged into a stun-
ning crisis. Thanks. Well done!"[10]

4

Not knowing it would go through Mac, Govan Mbeki sent a message to
Tambo accusing Mandela of violating the principle of collectivity and saying that Mandela had not been authorized to speak on behalf of the ANC.
On his own initiative, Mbeki instructed "lawyers" to visit Mandela "to
convey our disquiet about [his] initiative and to tell him to stop and suspend his initiative."[11]

　　In his response, Tambo emphatically rejected the assertion that Mandela had violated the principle of collectivity or that he was engaged in
negotiations. Lusaka, he said, construed Mandela's talks with the government team as an effort "to bring the major political bodies to the table,"
and hence gave them Lusaka's blessing. What was of concern, though, was
the content of the talks. Mandela, he told Mbeki, had been informed that
"nondisclosure is unacceptable. We insisted that he must now inform us of
the content of the discussions he has been having with the 'team,' noting
that while he observes strict confidentiality, the other side does not and
the regime is kept constantly and thoroughly briefed."[12]

　　Referring to the rumpus that exploded following Ayob's leaking of the
Mandela letter, Tambo cautioned that "the ease and speed with which a
perceived failure to conform is equated with open treachery is worrying,
especially where those who pass this severe judgment on a top leader can
hardly be regarded as merely rank and file."[13]

　　One is left to wonder who really were the loyal and disciplined members of the ANC.

5

Finding a way to communicate with Mandela preoccupied Mac. Within months of arriving in South Africa, he was able to inform Tambo that he thought he could arrange a secure line between Lusaka and Victor Verster. Tambo gave the nod, but with provisos that Mac was able to satisfy.

In April 1989, Mac was ready for the first step: letting Mandela know he was in the country, that he could arrange a safe line between Mandela and Tambo, that the decision was in Mandela's hands. Mandela agreed and the arrangement was made, although both Ismail Ayob, the family lawyer who was allowed to visit Mandela and would now act as the middleman, and Mandela had initial difficulties—nervousness—about making simple exchanges between each other (the comms refer to Mandela's trouble trying to open and reseal the "container").

On his first "run," Ayob delivered the container with messages from Lusaka and left it with Mandela. At his leisure, Mandela opened it, retrieved the message, and in due course inserted his response. On his next visit, Ayob brought another similar container with a new message from Tambo and swapped it for the one Mandela had. On Ayob's following visits, the same procedure was followed, Ayob and Mandela all the while maintaining a normal flow of conversation.*

"Mac," Ayob says, "tried to make a spy out of me. Mac taught me how to hide notes in hardcover books, taught me how to write with invisible ink. I then practiced this and became quite an expert at it; then I tried to make Nelson Mandela a spy, but it didn't work. The first time he was quite polite; he looked at it, and I indicated to him how he could open up the hardcover book and read the note inside it, and how he could reply, and here were the glue and all sorts of wonderful things. He took me outside on the second or the third occasion. He said, 'You're doing all these things for what? What more can they do to me? I've got life. You think they're going to hang me if I give you a message?' That was the end of my spying career. We went back to the traditional route. I would put things into my head and then make furious notes on the plane back to Johannesburg in order not to forget anything. Certainly, in the last year I did not travel to Lusaka at all. Mac was the person to whom I handed over information and whom I received information from."[14]

This exchange of containers (books with compartments for concealing correspondence built into the covers) between Ayob and Mandela went on

*On how the system worked, see Appendix, page 501.

for about six weeks, until Mac left South Africa in early July 1990. But it served its purpose, allowing Tambo to address Mandela directly about his talks with the government and to underscore the need for Lusaka to know their content. The first message from Mandela sent through Vula channels enabled Mandela to reiterate to Tambo that in his talks with the government team, he was "on side." He agreed on the importance of his getting reports to Lusaka but warned that giving written reports to Sekwati (Ayob) was a problem. "Sophitshi [Mandela] warns that Sekwati is a hot potato. It is clear that the other side knows that Sekwati shuttles between Ndima [Tambo] and Sophitshi. The possibility of a surprise swoop on him one day must not be excluded."[15]

Mandela did, however, provide a set of answers to the most pressing issues Tambo wanted him to address,* thus assuring Tambo that his talks with the government team at Victor Verster and Thabo Mbeki's talks with the Afrikaner proxies for the NIS at Mells Park complemented each other. After the release of Walter Sisulu and the other Rivonia Trialists in October 1989, restrictions on Mandela's communications with the outside were all but lifted; nevertheless, using the Vula transmission was the most secure route to his being in touch with Lusaka and Lusaka with him. Subsequent messages flowed to Joe Slovo and Alfred Nzo, especially after F. W. de Klerk assumed the presidency, including Mandela's correspondence with De Klerk and their meeting to try to reach agreement on the obstacles that stood in the way of the ANC's negotiating with the government.

Thus, as the countdown to his release began to accelerate, Mandela was fully informed of ANC thinking as it moved toward developing a negotiations manifesto, enabling him to shape his conversations with the team and ensuring congruence between what he was saying to the team and what the team was saying to Thabo Mbeki and Jacob Zuma at Mells Park.

Niel Barnard was central to both. If he was hoping to find differences between what Mandela was telling him and his team in Victor Verster, and what Mbeki and Zuma were saying to the "Afrikaner intellectuals" and later directly to his subordinates in Geneva, he would have come up empty-handed. But there are few reasons to believe that he was looking for such differences to exploit, although you would never find anyone in the ANC to agree. Barnard, after all, knew that when he dealt with Mandela he was dealing with the future president of South Africa,[16] something that had perhaps not yet crossed the minds of many in the ANC.

---

*See Appendix sections A and B, pages 501–8.

Mac

ON THE WAY BACK to Durban from seeing Govan in Port Elizabeth, I stopped over in Jo'burg on 20 April 1989 and saw Ismail Ayob, Mandela's family lawyer, who told me he had seen Madiba the day before.* He gave me a copy of the documents the following evening. These were transcripts of the meeting and a copy of the memorandum Mandela had sent to P. W. Botha in anticipation of meeting with him.

On the evening of the twenty-third, I got a shock when I learned from Sydney Mufamadi that Ayob had given a photocopy of his transcript of Mandela's memorandum to Jay Naidoo, and Jay had said that they had to call a meeting of COSATU/UDF right away to prevent Mandela from selling out. I got hold of Momo. Momo was full of the story. "Have you heard the rumor that Mandela is selling out?" he said. I said, "There's no sellout here. I want you to immediately go and find Valli or Sydney or Jay Naidoo. Find one of them, whoever you can find now, and bring them to a meeting with me this evening."

I sent him to Ayob with a message: "How come you did not tell me that you gave Jay Naidoo a copy of the documents? The documents were confidential, intended for OR's eyes only." I told him to withdraw the document immediately and freeze discussion.

Momo managed to contact Valli and brought him to the Constantia Center, where the old Thrupps used to be. There used to be a cinema complex and an outdoor restaurant on the first floor in a sort of open area, a vantage point from which I could see anybody.

Valli greeted me and said, "Have you heard Madiba is selling out?" I said, "Where did you get that from?" He said, "We have proof. We have a letter he's written to P. W. Botha." So I said, "Sit down, Valli." I think Momo went away at this point. I took out the letter and said, "Is this the letter?" He said, "Yes. Oh, you've got it too, I see." So I said, "Let's go through this letter," and I took him through it paragraph by paragraph. I said, "Is this a sellout? There's no sellout here. He is urging PW to have talks with the ANC in order to resolve the conflict in South Africa. He is not negotiating for himself. He explains the historical circumstances under which we turned to violence and says that by opening negotiations, the violence can end. Botha has an objection to talking to the ANC because it has an al-

---

*Ayob sent a report to Tambo in Lusaka via Beyers Naudé. See Mac to Tambo at [] maharaj/vula comms/1989/[] April 26.

liance with the Communist Party. Mandela goes on to justify and defend the alliance historically. In the letter he says that for negotiations to succeed, the negotiations between the government and the ANC will have to address the following issues."*

Then I systematically took him through the issues and said, "Where's the sellout? Have you chaps read this letter carefully?" Valli said, "Shit. I didn't understand this thing. I just thought this was proof that he's negotiating." I said, "It was not supposed to be for your hands. What have you all done?" He said, "We've met, and we are meeting again tomorrow morning." I said, "Who else is going to be at the meeting?" He said, "Kgalema Motlanthe. The four of us are meeting to discuss this."

I said, "Now are you satisfied there is no sellout?" He said, "Yes." I said, "Now that meeting tomorrow morning must happen, and it is your duty, Valli, to go to that meeting and take them through the letter word by word, as I have done with you, to show them there is no sellout." He said, "Sure, you can take it for granted it will be done."

I said, "What other damage is happening?" He said, "Mac, the word has also come from Port Elizabeth that he's selling out." I said, "From where?" He said, "From Govan. But it's the talk in the whole country." I said, "I'm heading for Durban." My line of communication with Govan was through Durban.

I left for Durban in the early hours of Monday morning. When I got there, I saw Billy Nair and went through the letter with him. Billy had heard the rumors too. But before I left for Durban, I had transmitted the text to OR with an explanation about what was happening and what steps I was taking to defuse the problem.

In Durban, I realized that the rumors were spreading like wildfire. Harry Gwala said an invitation to go and visit Madiba had been delivered to his home in Pietermaritzburg by a prison warder. So he had thought, "This is very suspicious; I don't trust it. What are the prison authorities doing? It means Madiba is selling out." He decided not to respond to the

---

*"The key to the whole situation is a negotiated settlement, and a meeting between the government and the ANC will be the first major step towards lasting peace in the country.... Two political issues will have to be addressed at such a meeting; firstly, the demand for majority rule in a unitary state, secondly, the concern of white South Africa over this demand, as well as the insistence of whites on structural guarantees that majority rule will not mean domination of the white minority by blacks. The most crucial task which will face the government and the ANC will be to reconcile these two positions. Such reconciliation will be achieved only if both parties are willing to compromise. The organisation will determine precisely how negotiations should be conducted." Extract from Mandela memorandum. Full memorandum at [] pre-transition/documents and reports/1989/[].

invitation, and he told others, if they received such invitations, they should do the same.

I sent Billy to see Gwala in Pietermaritzburg to correct the wrong impressions. I got a report from Valli that he and the others had met that morning—Sydney, Jay Naidoo, and himself. Kgalema had arrived late. Why? Kgalema had been to Port Elizabeth to see Govan. Govan had summoned him, so he had flown down on the Sunday and flown back early on Monday.

When Kgalema walked into the meeting, he said, "I've had word confirmed. Madiba is selling out." They said to him, "Where did you get this from?" He said, "From the ANC head office." They said, "What head office?" He said, "I've just seen Govan. I've just come from Port Elizabeth. Madiba is drinking wine, dressing up, asking people to come and visit him. No one must go." He had been sent to give them "instructions from above," which were not subject to any discussion. No one felt they could cross instructions coming from Govan.

Then they said, "Here's the letter." So Valli took them through the letter and showed them there was no sellout. But Motlanthe was insistent: "Govan is the boss until there is word from OR."

What was not clear to me was how the message had gotten to Govan. When I saw Ayob, I told him he had caused a major problem by acting incorrectly, that the letter had been for OR's eyes only and that he had made a mistake by showing it to comrades in the UDF. That was not his function. He took it well. He told me that Dullah Omar was present when Madiba briefed him. Dullah had flown to Port Elizabeth and given his verbal report to Govan; both had interpreted it as Mandela selling out.

The image of Mandela that Dullah conveyed was that Madiba was living in the lap of luxury. He was dressed in a suit, he offered Ayob wine in this house at Victor Verster, he was consorting with the enemy—and this was all proof that he was selling out. This idea fell on fertile ground because Govan had always harbored this suspicion. This, along with his strong differences with Mandela and Sisulu, caused havoc.

Govan gave Chris Dlamini a message for OR, but Chris gave it to me and I immediately transmitted it to OR. The message was strong:

1. No meaningful consultations are possible at Victor Verster.
2. The principle at stake, that any negotiations can only be by NEC, should under no circumstances be sidelined.
3. Nondisclosure of the government names is unacceptable.
4. It is incorrect for the comrade to give names of persons to be seen by him.

5. Lawyers have been instructed to convey our disquiet about the comrade's initiative and to tell him to stop and suspend his initiative.
6. We are taking immediate steps to consult MDM.
7. Harry Gwala was visited by a warder at his home and handed an invitation/permission to see Mandela.
8. Pending directions from you, we are directing that no one goes to Victor Verster.[17]

OR now sent me messages for Valli and company and for Govan and Gwala: he had seen the document and knew Madiba was not selling out—they were to put an immediate stop to such foolish rumors. Mandela had not violated any ANC principle of disciplined conduct. He had instructed Madiba to proceed with the talks but to keep him informed about their content.[18]

In the meantime, Valli and others started correcting the situation. Had we not been present, had we not acted as fast as we did—tracked it down and reported to Lusaka accurately—and taken steps to control the damage, the incident had the potential to split the movement, or at the very least cause major confusion among the leadership and the people.

For me, it was déjà vu. But the episode had disturbing implications. It was clear that when Madiba was released, he would have to watch himself; there would be some among his own comrades whose support he could not take for granted.

Communicating with Mandela

Within months of being in the country, an idea came to me: could we establish a truly secure line of communication between OR and Madiba? We knew talks were going on between Mandela and the government. It was crucial to set up a link between Mandela and OR so they could brief each other confidentially.

I raised the issue with OR and JS in November 1988.[19] It was not part of my mandate, but it was feasible. I had ideas about how it could be done. I contacted Jenkin and company: Could they make a pen with a concealed compartment? False book covers? Book spines? They came up with many ideas, not knowing, of course, the purpose for which these were intended.

OR had concerns. Contact with Madiba must not compromise Vula, and Madiba must not be caught trying to smuggle messages out of prison. I reassured OR: "It can be done." I got the mandate: "Yes, incorporate this function into your mission."[20]

After he was moved to Victor Verster Prison, Madiba's restrictions on visitors eased, and the environment was more relaxed. I was concerned about hidden cameras or listening devices, so I worked around that assumption. But what was the staffing situation? Ismail Ayob said the warder in charge was James Gregory, and Jack Swart was a warder who served as the cook. Neither monitored Madiba's visits. Madiba was free to move around; he had a sitting room where he could receive visitors. Usually he would sit on one side of the table and visitors would sit across from him. The table was stomach high. Listening devices and cameras were probably everywhere, but the outlets would be visible. Where was the strategic point for passing something to Madiba? Where couldn't the cameras see? Under his table!

I had to make assumptions about how the prison authorities were treating Madiba. I had to put myself in their shoes. We believed the regime wanted to use Madiba's release to try to split the ANC between the external and the internal mission. So they would treat him as though they trusted him; they would not treat him with overt suspicion. Since they were having talks with him, they were obviously, if subtly, trying to persuade him to agree to their mode of thinking. To do this, they would behave in a very relaxed way around him, despite all the hidden devices for keeping tabs on him. They would be satisfied to eavesdrop discreetly, to intercept messages. But they also knew that Madiba might suspect that they were up to something. So where might he go if he wanted to have a private conversation with someone? To the tree in his garden. Under the tree. And that's exactly where they put a bug, as we later found out from Kathy.*

I had to guess what Madiba's environment was like when he met Ayob, and work out how the first note could be slipped under the table. Of course, I couldn't guarantee there'd be no video camera under the table. That was a chance I had to take.

---

*According to Kathy, Mandela always assumed that Victor Verster was wired for conversation. Whenever he wanted to have a private conversation he would take his visitor into the garden. Sometime post-1990, Kathy took Sharon Gelman, who heads Artists for a New South Africa, on a visit to Victor Verster. The prison official then residing at the house pointed out to them a tree in the garden which, he said, had had a bug concealed among the branches when Mandela had been in residence. (Confirmed with Kathy on 6 September 2006.)

"Zwangendaba"

We went to work. First I had to let Madiba know I was in the country. Sometimes when I was in Jo'burg I'd go to Ayob's home in Fordsburg in the evenings, late at night. His wife, Zamilla, was always worried about my welfare: "Where are you living? You show up here at one in the morning!" And she would always say—typical Indian woman—"Food!" Straight into the kitchen to rustle up a meal!

One evening we were sitting and chatting. Ayob said, "I think I can take Zamilla along next time I visit Madiba." Zamilla was always nagging him, "You keep going to meet Mandela but you don't take me." And he would tell her, "But he always asks about you." I said, "Hey, this is fantastic! Do you meet him in his lounge?" He said they sat at the dining table.

Madiba had given me a code name when I left prison in 1976. It was the name of an African chief who had led wars against colonialism, a chief called Zwangendaba.* He said, "If I get a message, whether in a letter, or from any visitor who in the course of ordinary conversation drops the name Zwangendaba, then I will know that person is in touch with you, and I'll treat the conversation in a different way while talking about family problems." But that had been twelve long years ago; would he remember?

I said to Ayob, "OK, I'm going to write a note and roll it up very, very small so it can be hidden in the lining of your clothes. I want you to take Zamilla. I want her to distract the warder who is taking care of Madiba— that's Gregory. I want her to be the decoy to draw the attention of the cameras and listening devices. Describe where you normally sit and where Madiba sits at this table." He showed me. I said, "Keep this note, which is hardly wider than the length of a match stick, in a way that it cannot be seen by a camera, and while you are having your normal conversation with Madiba, I want you casually to introduce the name Zwangendaba. Then I want you to pass this note under the table into his hand. But," I said, "the key to his receiving it and knowing how to conduct himself is that you should use the name Zwangendaba. You should say, for example, if he raises a legal matter or a problem about Winnie and the children, 'Yes I'm handling it,' and in the course of telling him what you're doing, you should tell him you've also seen Zwangendaba to discuss the matter and after that touch his knee. Then if Zwangendaba's name clicks with him,

*Zwangendaba was a general under Zwide, who refused to be assimilated by Shaka. He and his followers fled north and settled in present-day Zimbabwe, Malawi, and Tanzania. Literally translated the name means "he who is heard of through the news."

he will realize, hey, there's a hand trying to give me something under this table."

That was how Madiba found out I was in the country. To read the note, he pretended to have a tummy upset and went to the toilet. In the meantime, Zamilla kept up a flow of conversation with the warder. The note said: "I'm in the country. I can offer you techniques for communicating with OR. You choose. You know your circumstances best. I can give you a special pen or a book with a secret compartment. I am told that you're allowed to watch videos: I can put a concealed space in a video cover."

I wanted Madiba to have confidence in my methods, to know it wouldn't be an amateurish job. In the end, I decided that a concealed compartment built into a book cover would be easiest for Madiba to use, since he would only have to insert his messages within the concealed space.[21]

Madiba Agrees

Madiba sent a note out with Ayob. He was a bit nervous. But his response was, "Yes, I will communicate, but, please, not an elaborate thing."

After the meetings, Ismail would return immediately to Jo'burg, where his offices were. I would head for Jo'burg and send a courier to Ayob's office—usually Momo—to pick up Madiba's responses. I would decrypt, encode, and send them. And presto, everything would be in Lusaka! When one of OR's responses came through, I reduced it and enclosed it in a compartment that Tim Jenkin had built into a book cover for Momo to deliver to Ismail along with other books so that Ismail never knew which book, if any, contained a message for Madiba.[22]

This system worked well for the month or so before I left the country, but it was a crucial month. Madiba was a bit shaky at the beginning and so was Ismail, but they had to get over it. The brief exchanges reassured OR that Mandela and the ANC were working in sync.

One of the items OR raised was that we would come under intense pressure from abroad around the question of negotiations: pressure to abandon sanctions, the armed struggle, and so on. OR said we had to be careful because while we wanted to push negotiations, we couldn't prematurely give up our weapons of struggle. If we were forced to give up anything, the one thing we couldn't abandon was international sanctions—they would take another twenty years to rebuild. Madiba had no problem with this perspective. In fact, he was grateful. There were no differences of opinion; he was only saying to the regime: talk to the ANC, not to me. We smuggled in a draft of the Harare Declaration and retrieved it with his comments.

Without going into great detail, Madiba briefed OR on what was happening in the talks on his side; he summarized the issues raised in the PW memorandum, which I had previously sent to OR. He dealt with the exact arguments he was using, and he said he'd been bolstered by the statement in the Harare draft declaration that cessation of hostilities was an item to be discussed, although Madiba never said we would "renounce violence," as the regime had demanded for years. The positions Madiba took fitted into the perspective outlined in the Harare Declaration. Madiba was comfortable with these developments and happy that the ANC was taking the initiative and becoming proactive about negotiations.

15. OUT OF SOUTH AFRICA

Introduction

IN HIS COMMUNICATION to Govan Mbeki following the Mandela-is-selling-out brouhaha, Tambo summarized the contents of the message he had sent to Mandela after receiving a copy of Mandela's memorandum to P. W. Botha. At this point, he had not tabled the memorandum with the NEC. His message reflected the state of thinking in Lusaka in late April 1989.

The issue he addressed was that of negotiations with the apartheid regime. He agreed with Mandela that negotiations with Botha's government should be approached "very seriously," but "also very cautiously, given the unreliable character of the regime." Despite the ongoing talks at Mells Park in Britain (by this stage, the NIS was indirectly involved), Tambo opined that "as far as we could observe [there was] no evidence whatever that the regime was serious about negotiations." Thus the ANC's "primary preoccupation is to wage struggle and take negotiation in our stride as we pursue our objective, instead of going out of our way to sue for it."[1]

Yet within weeks Tambo was focusing on the necessity for the ANC to grab the moral high ground on the issue of negotiations in the light of changes in the "external" situation. Gorbachev's opening up of the Soviet Union was pushing global relations in new directions. In April 1989, the UN Transition Assistance Group (UNTAG) embarked on the implementation of UN Resolution 435,* the first step toward the full independence of Namibia. The multilateral negotiations involving South Africa, the United States, the United Nations, the Soviet Union, Cuba, and Angola that preceded the implementation required the ANC to close its camps in Angola.[2] Cadres in the Angola camps were relocated to camps elsewhere, mostly in

---

*In 1978, the United Nations passed Resolution 435. The resolution accepted the de facto presence of South Africa in Namibia and assigned to it certain responsibilities to

Uganda and Tanzania. Overcrowded camps, taxed to limits beyond their resources, became more like holding centers than military commands. Rather than advancing the case for more MK incursions into South Africa, the influx of relocated cadres created huge logistical and administrative problems, buttressing the case for putting more resources into creating the infrastructure within South Africa for a self-sufficient people's war. The political landscape in southern Africa was also rapidly changing, and the ANC had to adjust. In Namibia, SWAPO had been left out of the negotiations that had agreed to the protocols leading to Namibia's independence. The ANC was intent on taking steps to ensure that it would not be similarly sidelined in South Africa.

On 17 May 1989, Tambo wrote Mac: "We're under intense pressure from friends & allies, & also because of MT [Margaret Thatcher]-led drive by the west to evolve a strategy that belongs to period following independence of Namibia. The race for who'll control developments in our country has started in earnest, & we should be in the lead. Our friends, no less than we, don't leave the running to MT & other allies of regime. The question being pressed on us from every corner is 'what is to be done? What is the new strategy, or new approach?' We need to evolve a kind of '435' for South Africa, formulated by us (ANC & MDM), sold to the FLS [frontline states] & used to control & channel pressures, including MT & co, that we take charge of what needs to be done in our country. Can you make input?"[3]

Another communication followed, referring to the "enormous pressures bearing down on the movement from everywhere calling for negotiations." The document being worked on at HQ would be designed "to guide world discussion on SA presented as an African position, & designed

---

carry out until a constituent assembly was elected to draw up a constitution and establish a government for a new, independent state. Under 435, a United Nations Transition Assistance Group for Namibia (UNTAG) was to be established by the UN secretary-general with a budget for a one-year operation. UNTAG was to be comprised of a military and civilian component, both headed by the special representative of the secretary-general, Mr. Martti Ahtisarri of Finland. UNTAG operations would be carried out in stages: cessation of all hostile acts by all parties and the withdrawal or demobilization of various armed forces; the conducting of free and fair elections to a constituent assembly. Preconditions included the repeal of all restrictive and discriminatory laws, the release of all political prisoners, the free and voluntary return of Namibians in exile, the establishment of effective monitoring of the transition process by the UN, and an adequate period for electoral campaigning; the third stage provided for the election of a constituent assembly to draw up a constitution and consequent independence. Almost eleven years passed before implementation of 435 got under way on 13 April 1989.

to pre-empt pressure groups, big & small, who desire to impose their own approach to the SA problem."[4]

Tambo had also been given to understand that "the US admin had up-graded the status of the ANC" and that President George Bush intended to meet him.[5] Also "there are signals from the regime that they've already firmly decided to release Cde Madiba after the September elections."[6]

The need for swift and decisive action was imperative. "The imperial-ists are moving carefully towards mediation at the present time," Tambo warned. "That is why we need the commitment of the FLS & OAU (Organization of African Unity).* The entire world is concerned about apartheid & no particular country or group can arrogate themselves the role of mediator."[7]

Mac brought Mandela into the loop so that he could bear these issues in mind as he continued his talks with the regime's team. Mac also urged Tambo to bring the mass movements into line with the ANC's efforts to develop a negotiations document, to make them understand clearly that the MDM was the key to bringing the masses on board. "Any negotiations scenario would likely send very mixed signals to the grass roots." But, he cautioned, the need for a strong negotiating position did not preclude pressing the regime on every front, and the masses could be used to ensure that a coherent strategy of resistance dovetailed with other efforts:

> The basic premise to any negotiating positions must be escalating the struggle & esp in this context the mass struggles. The push from our u/g structures in this regard has to be reinforced at your meetings with [MDM]. . . . We have to recognize great need to find the way (a) to force the Sep elections† [the September 89 "whites only" elections that saw the NP returned to power with a reduced majority and F. W. de Klerk elected president in his own right] off the headlines (b) give FW no breathing space, rather baptize him in fire (c) keep the DP under constant tension so that there is room to keep it shifting left (d) find the balance to re-structure IN ACTION [sic] and (e) give masses & activists a sense that there is a direction in wh we are moving & in this regard we must ensure

---

*The Organization of African States (OAU) was formed in Addis Ababa by thirty-two independent African states in 1963 to promote unity and solidarity and to eradicate all traces of colonialism from the continent. It adopted a principle of nonintervention in member state affairs. The fifty-three members of OAU replaced the OAU with the African Union (AU) in 2000, a body with a wider mandate to create an African eco-nomic community and to eventually bring about African political unity.
†South Africa's last "whites only" general election was held on September 6, 1989.

that the Constitutional Guidelines gives an added sense of whereto but not in an academic but rather mass action sense. The reality is that there is not even a debate within this sort of framework & what we shld be doing is not to prescribe the actual decisions etc, rather to generate this perspective for debate within the MDM . . . [which] will develop the campaign issues, the nature of the mass actions & sense of urgency & power the masses command.

What is crucial is that we shld mobilize for action around elections but select issues (not a whole shopping list) which focus masses on key issues, treat the elections with disdain yet subsume rejection of elections within the other issues, & thereby dominate election period.[8]

On 31 May, Mac received the first draft of the document that would ultimately become the Harare Declaration. He arranged, on the instructions of Lusaka, to get copies to Govan Mbeki and Harry Gwala. The document, Tambo said, represented "new thinking." "We ourselves feel that the time has come for us & the MDM to move & to take up a position which enables us to control & direct these pressures in the interests of our struggle & to keep the initiatives in our hands."[9]

Once again, Mac was able to get the message to Mandela for his comments and analysis.

Tambo accepted Mac's recommendation for how the ANC should handle the mass movements: "We will indicate to Cosatu/UDF that we are in the process of working out our positions & ask for an input from the visitors [a delegation was then visiting Lusaka]."[10] A committee would work out a redraft, based on these discussions, and the product would be presented to the NEC on 8 June for further input. Mac would receive an amended draft for circulation to a small group of MDM leaders—and, of course, the redoubtable Govan and Harry.

The MDM delegation, Tambo reported, "told [us] that there was general nervousness and suspicions among militants (e.g., Numsa* Conference). The need for maximum consultation and explanation was stressed. There was all round emphasis from both sides on the fact that negotiations must not be presented as a substitute for struggle and that the basic need was for an intensification of the struggle."[11]

Tambo continued, "The NEC met for 4 days thereafter. It covered similar

---

*The National Union of Metalworkers of South Africa (NUMSA) was the second largest union after the National Union of Mineworkers (NUM). It was also among the most militant.

ground on the internal situation, the campaigns and, more especially, the need for intensified activity in the pre-election period in order to sideline them. The general view squared with Tony's [Mac's] input which was read to the meeting as emanating from an internal collective. . . . From ANC side all political and military structures were instructed to engage in a most intense offensive leading up to the elections. The idea of 'a spring offensive' [September is spring on South African side of the equator] was emphasized.[12]

A new draft, with some considerable modifications, followed. Tambo: "Although the draft reflects the NEC consensus it was decided to leave the way open for amendments after we've canvassed the views of a selected list of individuals both within our ranks and trusted external friends, including selected FLS-leaders. Depending upon responses from all the latter, we may have to look at the document again."[13]

Mac was asked to get the draft for comment to Govan Mbeki, Dullah Omar, Valli Moosa, Murphy Morobe, Cyril Ramaphosa, Sydney Mufamadi, and Frank Chikane. And also to Madiba "if it can be done safely, to comment himself, collect all comments & return to Lusaka within two weeks."[14] For a second time, Mac managed to get a copy to Madiba.

The SACP, of course, also had its say. On 17 June, Slovo advised Mac that

> The negotiation document will be discussed by the PB in a few days time. But J [Slovo)] feels that already some of the dangers of the negotiation scenario are lurking. Part of the reason why our input at the MDM meeting on the WAY FORWARD was so scrappy is because the working cttee devoted all its days leading up to the MDM meeting to the discussion of the negotiation concept. We came to the MDM meeting without having discussed the WAY FORWARD in the coming period and we were left with a rather unsatisfactory PMC input on the latter. Of course we cannot avoid paying attention to the pressures on negotiation. But we must in practice (not only in theory) not do so at the expense of the real thing.[15]

Slovo's comments reflected his ambivalence. He wasn't quite ready to throw his hat into the negotiations ring. The "real thing" in Slovo's mind remained a people's war.

By 23 June, Mac had assembled the responses and comments from all and relayed them to Lusaka. The consensus: an elected Constituent Assembly was the key to making the package acceptable to the MDM. Meanwhile, Mac had sent the draft to "all units of the party," on Slovo's instructions, and their comments were also assembled and forwarded to Slovo.

Of all respondents in the MDM, ANC, and SACP, MDM leader Sydney Mufamadi was the most cautious:

> Just as we are agreed that the regime has given us nothing to negotiate about, the masses on the ground—at least the membership of the MDM in its various formations—will conceivably look at this unfolding situation with suspicion. It is our task to explain why as a movement we have to take advantage of the fact that, unable to break out of the crisis, the enemy finds himself with having to look for a political (negotiated) settlement, and to further amplify the positive aspects (we pushed the enemy into a corner and we therefore have to consolidate this gain).
>
> We are on record as saying that we should not allow the prospect of a negotiated settlement to demobilize us on crucial fronts—pressure must be intensified. The challenge is to get the membership to appreciate that in the light of both the pressure on ourselves & the regime as well as in the light of what is happening in the region, this is the route we have to take.[16]

Thus nine months before Mandela's release and the unbanning of the ANC, Lusaka was juggling with two sets of opposing circumstances that needed to be brought into balance. On the one hand, it believed there was little prospect of "real" negotiations. On the other, necessity demanded that it preempt the mounting pressures to negotiate coming from Western governments and the Soviet Union before they decided to cut some kind of deal that would also cut the negotiating ground from under the ANC.

Indeed, the comms reveal that the document the ANC was drawing up at the time, which became the Harare Declaration when it was adopted by the OAU on 21 August 1989, was not a proactive initiative on the part of the ANC. The ANC was pushed to formulate a position in response to Pretoria's making its interest in a negotiated settlement known in the West.[17] Perhaps, given the ANC's enormous distrust of Pretoria, it was wary of any signals from the regime. But despite "these reservations" Tambo gave Mandela Lusaka's approval to continue his talks with "the team." At the same time, however, Lusaka insisted on knowing to whom he was talking and what he was saying. "The other side would certainly have been receiving regular debriefings from their people." Meanwhile, Mac briefed Mandela via "the container."[18]

2

Of course, the event that triggered the rapid change of position in the National Party had taken place months earlier. After a stroke, P. W. Botha stepped down as leader of the National Party on 2 February 1989, although he retained his position as state president. His replacement as party head, F. W. de Klerk, had a reputation as a hard-liner and was the preferred choice of a small majority of the NP caucus over the perceived liberal and reformist finance minister Barend du Plessis. For the ANC, the appointment was no cause for celebration. Thus the imperative "to wage struggle."

By midyear, Botha appeared to be going out of his way to sabotage De Klerk. A bitter power struggle was under way, one that Botha lost when his own cabinet confronted him.[19]

Tambo had other problems. The rumors that Mandela was selling out had now mutated into a new form: Mandela, according to the new whispers, was negotiating with the government. This time the rumors reached Mandela, who raised the matter with Tambo. To forestall further "mischief," Mandela asked that his memorandum be read to a select number of MDM leaders, whom he himself specified.*

Mandela was, of course, unaware of the furor that had enveloped the MDM leadership after Ayob's indiscretion. As far as he was concerned, only Tambo had a copy. No one told him differently. Ironically, while a widening circle of MDM leaders knew of or had actually read Mandela's memorandum to P. W. Botha, no ANC leaders in Lusaka, other than Tambo and Slovo, were in the know. Tambo had not informed the NEC that Mandela had sent a discussion document to PW in anticipation of meeting with him. Tambo, it was clear, would have to address the issue.

As Mac's presence seemed to be becoming more difficult to conceal, Tambo called on Mac to consider taking a break. He was spreading himself too thin, working too hard, and rumors of his being home were becoming increasingly difficult to cover up—better that he come out, show he was not at home but still recuperating, and then return. And, of course, there was the question of Zarina, itself sufficiently compelling to warrant his exit.

*See Appendix, section B, pages 505–8.

3

Zarina's recollection of her automobile accident is vivid. She was working for the UN at the time, had just completed a project in the course of which she found that "certain officials in Geneva had been cutting huge corners . . ." in a UN project related to the Preferential Trade Area (PTA) of East, Central, and Southern Africa, had attended a reception for visiting PTA officials, and was returning home when she fell asleep at the wheel and crashed head-on into a tree.[20]

She was unconscious for forty-eight hours and awoke in a grimy hospital in Lusaka. The initial diagnosis was nineteen fractures, two in the spine. The hospital lacked rudimentary facilities, even painkillers. Joey and Milou were mistakenly brought to the hospital. "They crept under the bed and hid there the rest of the evening," she recalls. "I was covered in tubes and plasters and blood, and swollen. Joey thought her mummy was already gone, and Milou said, 'Don't worry, Joey, I'll look after you if she dies.' So that's what the kids remember."[21]

Joe Slovo came around. Getting her to a hospital in Harare, he told her, was the responsibility of the UN, her employer, not the ANC. But Tambo, who was abroad at the time of the accident, heard what had happened on his return, rushed to the hospital, and told her, "I'm going to send you out." She was flown to Harare and had multiple operations, but once back in Lusaka there were more problems, so Tambo again stepped in.

Back in Lusaka after two months in Moscow, "the two most depressing months of my life," her recovery kept being threatened by complications requiring more surgery. She was unable to cope with the children on her own and had now been apart from them for long periods. And even though she sometimes had the help of Mac's sister Shanthee and her own sister, Shirene, she was very distressed about the impact this was having on their well-being. And she needed more treatment. One option was to go back to Moscow, where she and the children would rendezvous with Mac, who was planning to go there to meet with Tambo and Slovo. After her surgery, they would enjoy a vacation together. Another option was London; the UN, anxious to get her back on the job, offered to send her there.

4

The comm correspondence between Mac and Zarina during this period reveals how they were prepared to put their personal needs aside in pursuit of the greater goal, but it also reveals how, when the welfare of their children, Joey and Milou, pushed itself to the foreground after Zarina's accident, their sense of priorities began to undergo a subtle transformation.* The accident, on 9 October, had repercussions neither could have envisaged. It changed everything. Slovo did try to get word to Mac right away, but Mac was not aware of this until I told him in August 2004, when I came across the comms.

Even as Mac prepared to leave South Africa, Zarina raised the issues her disablement posed for his continuing role in Vula. He would have to make choices. She wrote:

> I am somewhat confused. Janet [Slovo] told me in a recent discussion that you had indicated to her that you could be at Cathy's [London] on your way out. She also said that the decision for you to return where you are now after a month's break with us came entirely from your side & that not only did she & co not instruct you to be there, they do not feel they have any right to instruct you one way or another. Is this true? If so, I'm surprised I was not even consulted as to whether the kids & I are able to continue to cope in trying circumstances for another indefinite period of time. How do you envisage us in this scheme of things? No doubt you were planning to discuss this on holiday but it would be useful to me to have some idea of how the lands lie. . . .[22]

Mac's response was evasive: He was preoccupied with the problems of getting out: "exiting & re-entry make me even more nervous than being here in the midst of constant security scares. However, pls bear with me as I try to work out how, routes, legends."[23]

The future was problematic at best:

> At one point I received advice that I should come out for two months, both to see you & kids & to get out of the enemy way for security reasons (including the view that legend was fraying, & hence to reinforce the legend) & for discussions. This was from Janet [Slovo] & confirmed in subsequent msg from Alphons [Tambo]. At this end I have assumed that matters have been discussed from time to time with you. So for the moment I don't know how to respond to your question "how do you envisage us fitting into this scheme of things?"[24]

---

*For comm correspondence between Mac and Zarina go to []maharaj/family/correspondence[].

In his last months in South Africa, Mac juggled the vagaries of Harry Gwala; the brushfire of the Mandela "sellout"; a trip to Port Elizabeth to see Govan Mbeki; strategizing with Tambo and Slovo and the MDM; getting through to Mandela and securing his participation in the exchange of messages between him and Lusaka; setting up a two-way communication system between the two; getting the Harare Declaration to MDM leaders and to Mandela; collecting, summarizing, and returning their comments to Lusaka within ten days, finding a way to leave the country, arranging it, and making the physical adjustments to his appearance to fit with his passport photo. On top of this were his mounting anxieties over the extent of Zarina's injuries, where one operation simply led to another complication and another operation. The creeping realization that if his "disappearance" had not already left his children emotionally distraught, his wife's absences because of her need for medical treatment compounded their sense of abandonment would. Zarina's London treatment would leave her unable to cope.

On the eve of his departure to Moscow, the question "How do you envisage us in this scheme of things?" lingered, but Mac had no answer.*

5

Mac was in London with his family when Tambo had a stroke on 8 August 1989, causing a leadership vacuum in the ANC, exacerbated while they vacillated before deciding two months later that Tambo's condition was more serious than originally thought and the NEC named Secretary-General Alfred Nzo as acting president. Mac did what Tambo had asked him to do: he went to Lusaka and participated in the NEC meeting at which the Mandela memorandum was tabled.*

With a multitude of issues to deal with, including uncertainty about the ANC leadership and Mandela's release, Alfred Nzo was a "filler" leader. During his tenure, uncertainty prevailed at a time when decisive leadership was required. He may never have been fully apprised of Tambo's

*Apparently, the only point the NEC cautioned against was a meeting between the ANC and the government before the government took action to establish a climate for negotiation. See Mandela comm to Slovo and Nzo that advises "in future discussion with the Government emphasis will be put on the creation of a climate for negotiation before there is a meeting." Appendix, section D, p. 516.

grand design for Vula; if he was, he may not have understood the dynamics that drove it. But even if he had, a shift of seismic proportions was redrawing the global political terrain. Suddenly "people's war" seemed an archaic conception, a relic from the past that counted history in days, not decades.

In September 1989, the NEC approved setting up a core of national underground leaders. At this point, it was aware of something called Vula, but only as an umbrella for underground activities in South Africa. "The present Vula core,"* it decided, "should be expanded and reinforced to fulfil the mandate of building a national u/g organization."[25]

Also in September, De Klerk became president in his own right when the National Party was returned to power. But it lost seats to the Conservative Party on its right and the Democratic Party on its left. De Klerk interpreted the results, the combined vote for his party and the Democratic Party, as an acknowledgment by whites that the time had come to reach an accommodation with blacks, that the days of apartheid were over. The phrases he would use throughout the next four years, "group rights" and "protection of minorities," became part of the public discourse.[26] The ANC regarded them as code words for the protection of white privilege and a political veto over the will of the majority. The ANC waited for actions that would herald the beginning of rapprochement De Klerk hinted at.

But away from public clamor, the wheels of change were beginning to move, creakily at first but with an unmistakable momentum. At the direction of P. W. Botha, Niel Barnard, director of the National Intelligence Service, used the talks at Mells Park to signal a desire on the part of the NIS to meet with the ANC leadership. On the instructions of the ANC President's Committee, Thabo Mbeki and Jacob Zuma were authorized to do so. They met with Mike Louw, NIS deputy director, and Maritz Spaarwater, director of operations, in Lucerne, Switzerland, on 12 September 1989. According to the report on the meeting Jacob Zuma gave the NWC, the NIS was of the view that De Klerk (who was unaware at the time that the meeting had taken place) was "thinking of change" and "not playing political games" and that the main players were the National Party and the ANC. Whether the regime or the ANC liked it, pressure from outside for a settlement was going to grow. De Klerk "was compelled to be ambiguous be-

---

*The Vula core, which was unknown to the NEC, consisted of Mac and Nyanda at the national level; at the Durban level, Mac, Siphiwe Nyanda, Pravin Gordhan, Billy Nair, Mpho Scott, and Jabu Sithole. After he arrived in late March 1990, Ronnie Kasrils became a member of both.

cause of the impending elections, not because he was not committed to genuine change." De Klerk had to be given time; he was "serious and genuine" but had to overcome hurdles, like the police. They [NIS] were aware of the government's contacts with Mandela, did not want to undermine them, and believed that Mandela should have an opportunity to brief the ANC; the release of political prisoners "was no longer a question, only a formula for effecting this was desired." And they [NIS] "had taken the initiative" [to request the meeting] in the interests of coming to terms with reality.[27]

Meanwhile, at a meeting of an extended President's Committee,* Thabo Mbeki reported back on the meeting with the "Broeders" [the Afrikaner intellectuals] at which they said "the process of releasing the prisoners was about to start." They had also identified the obstacles to change: the NP did not want to lose control of the pace of change, fear of black domination, De Klerk's wanting to restructure the state security machinery, especially the State Security Council's distrust of the ANC, and being unconvinced that there was not some "secret agenda behind the Harare Declaration."[28]

When the media broke the story of the "Broederbond meeting," there was much grumbling in the National Working Committee about being left out of the loop. Chris Hani was angered at the absence of feedback, of collectivism.[29] Pallo Jordan was more incensed: the NEC had become "accustomed to a style of leadership counter to the principle of collective leadership, to irregularities, like the Broederbond." "We can't talk about collective leadership; it is something we defend with lies."[30]

On 19 October, days after the extended PC meeting, Sisulu and the last of the Rivonia Trialists were released, the outcome of Mandela's talks with the team. Their release was unconditional. The government feared that it would be used by the ANC to "worsen the current explosive situation in the country." Mandela tried to reassure. Before their release they met with Mandela, who conveyed the government's fears and what reassurances he had given.† He hoped the step would open the way for the release of other political prisoners and provide further leeway for the exploration of talks about talks.

But when Mandela counseled a "low key" role for the Rivonia prisoners after their release to an MDM visiting him, the delegation informed

*Thomas Nkobi, Dan Tloome, Thabo Mbeki, Jacob Zuma, Joe Modise, John Nkadimeng, and Steve Tshwete.
†Appendix, section D, pages 511–15.

Lusaka—and Lusaka concurred—that the "leaders should take their place at the head of the struggle."[31] Criticism of Mandela was quite sharp: "The struggle," Thabo Mbeki said, "is really not about Mandela; it is about other issues. . . . He will be released not because of 'low key' activity, but because of heightened activity." Chris Hani: "NM should consult to help us avoid public confrontation. He is in prison & does not understand. . . . It is difficult but he should canvas [sic] views."[32]

The NEC agreed. There was widespread expectation that the release of Mandela was imminent.

In Lusaka, the same month, the NEC addressed the question of leadership. Members were withering. Slovo: "The situation is unfolding inside in a unique way but we found ourselves at HQ where we couldn't say there was a leadership collective to do justice to that situation . . . the impression was created that events were beyond our control . . . it is a chaotic state we are in . . . there is a feeling abroad that we are not able or geared to respond adequately to the situation and yet the period ahead is bound to be even more hectic. . . . We have a gaping hole with the president not being with us. . . ."[33] Zuma called it "the problem of the ungovernability of the leadership.[34] The irony went unnoticed. John Nkadimeng referred to "weaknesses of implementation and accountability,"[35] and Jackie Selibi said that the word in Lusaka among the cadres was that the NEC was not a "leadership" but a "readership."[36]

A review of NEC and NWC minutes in October 1989 suggests that the ANC was unable to react timeously to developments.[37] They fretted about the intentions of the government, but without being able to formulate strategic responses to alternative scenarios. Assessments of the capabilities of MK were bleak, a regurgitation of old problems: ("we are baffled that some units are not active," "the big question is how to take fighters inside," "inside operatives don't strike when they are expected to," many people outside are no longer prepared to fight: "We still have to continue to hit the enemy and this has been our dilemma for years").[38] There was a sense of alarm that a grand moment of history had arrived but that they could not rise to the occasion. So they reverted to the thinking they were familiar with: the regime was trying to divide the exiles and the MDM.

In November, the "President's Projects' collective" (Slovo and Nzo) decided that the Vula "core" and the released prisoners constituted the internal national leadership.[39] Sisulu would be the overall head of the interim leadership collective while Mac would continue to head Vula.[40]

Also in November, the Berlin Wall came tumbling down, the cold war was over, and the ideology which had fueled the Total Onslaught crumbled. In December, Mandela met with De Klerk and raised the question of the conditions for a meeting between the ANC and the government and conveyed a summary of their conversation to Lusaka.* Operation Vula continued; the comms between Gebuza and Lusaka were now mostly concerned with logistics and operational details.[41] The focus of the action had shifted.

6

Mac was furious with Slovo for concealing the extent of Zarina's injuries from him. In Brighton his personal turmoil grew. He made his choice: he would not abandon the ANC, so he had to abandon his family. He was suffused with guilt, an emotion his life experiences had not equipped him to deal with. His personal turmoil was compounded by turmoil in the movement. Events were moving with a speed that left the ANC floundering. Without the guiding hand of Tambo, the leadership was unsure of itself. He had no contact other than a turnaround visit to Lusaka to resolve a technical problem. With the release of Sisulu, preoccupations were elsewhere. Mac was increasingly isolated without anyone with whom to share his political and personal anxieties, anxieties that now manifested themselves in contexts he was unfamiliar with.

In the last six months of 1989, the momentum toward a negotiated settlement gathered speed.[42] Mac was neither in South Africa nor Lusaka; he was in Brighton, looking after his wife and children. For the first time since his release from Robben Island, he was on the sidelines. He did not report to Slovo and Nzo on P. W. Botha's decline and fall, nor on the September 1989 elections in which De Klerk cemented his position as state president in his own right, nor on the state of the right wing, nor on the release of Walter Sisulu and others, nor on the increasing tempo of the mass movements, nor on the impending visit of the Rivonia prisoners to Lusaka. Nor were his views solicited. Of course, in Tambo's absence, Slovo's room to maneuver was cramped. His relationship with Tambo was special; with Nzo a relationship was lacking, so as the South Africa question began to climb the international community's ladder of attention, Nzo turned to others, among them Thabo Mbeki. Slovo did not instruct Mac to return to South Africa until late November.[43]

Mac felt let down, ignored, and very pissed off.

---

*Appendix, section E, pages 516–21.

Mac

WITH ALL THE LOOSE TALK going on, OR and JS became very concerned that too many people might get to know that I was in the country—the rumors were creating security problems. Better, they thought, that I come out for a while to strengthen my cover and then go back.[44]

In May 1989, I received a message from Tambo asking me to meet him in Moscow for a face-to-face debriefing, and he gave a date, 12 July, when I should be there. I had entered South Africa on foot, so I did not have any means, nor had the organization provided me with any, to travel in and out of the country. But OR's pressing request meant I had to find a way out and make my way to Moscow. He had also made it clear that I should exit in such a way that I would be able to return.

My travel arrangements needed some thought. I found a way to get a false passport, under the name Ibrahim Sheik, from Pretoria through our contacts in Home Affairs. I sent a message to London that I would travel under that name to Bombay. I also got London to collect the passport issued to me by the government of India under the name Robin Das, which I had left behind in Moscow, and send it to the Soviet mission in Delhi, and to book a flight under that name from Delhi to Moscow. So the person who left Jo'burg for Bombay had no connection to the one who traveled from Delhi to Moscow.

I met with OR, JS, and Ivan for intensive debriefing. OR had one more thing he wanted me to do. In Lusaka, he said, there were still rumors about Madiba's talks with the regime and that he was selling out.[45] My efforts to quash the rumors months earlier had not been entirely successful. Like most rumors, they had developed a life of their own.*

OR wanted a structured discussion in the NEC on signals from the regime about negotiations.[46] This was becoming increasingly difficult; some comrades continued to allude to these rumors. He wanted the NEC to understand that Madiba's talks with the regime were strictly in accord with ANC policy, that Madiba had told the regime it had to talk with the

---

*In *Long Walk to Freedom*, Mandela describes some of the emotions that swept through him when he met the ANC leadership in Lusaka on 27 Feb 1990: "I knew that over the previous few years some of the men who had been released had gone to Lusaka and whispered, 'Madiba has become soft. He has been bought off by the authorities. He is wearing three-piece-suits, drinking wine and eating fine food.' I knew of these whispers, and I intended to refute them," p. 498.

ANC and that he could not negotiate on its behalf. This is precisely what the Mandela memorandum said.

OR said to me, "I need to put the memorandum Mandela sent to PW in March before the NEC. You've read that memorandum carefully, and you've analyzed it. I want you to be present when we discuss it. I want you to find a way in the course of that discussion to stand up and analyze the memorandum so that people understand it properly." So I said, "But how do I get to Lusaka? What excuse do I make?" He said—and Slovo was there—that my story should be that I had taken such a battering from my treatment that the specialists had suggested I needed a break from the drug therapy. So I would be in Lusaka for a rest, and because I'd be there at the time of the NEC meeting, I would attend the meeting.

London

My next scheduled stop was London. I had a very good reason for going there. I should have left the country the moment I heard about Zarina's car accident in Zambia. I should have been with her and the children. I can make all sorts of excuses about why I didn't, but I don't know whether my decision not to leave at that stage was right. The collective will say—have no doubt about it—that it was the right decision; it was good for the struggle. But as an individual, the partner of my wife and the father of my two children, and for them as individuals, what was right or wrong?[47]

I was very anxious to see Zarina and the children. Her comms were worrying. With me away and with her absences for medical treatment, the children were beginning to feel the effects. They were frequently in the care of others, and neither of us was happy with that.

OR left Moscow while my disguise was being prepared. I needed a visa for London, and I left it to Shubin to organize. While I waited for my visa, I grew my beard and mustache. By arrangement with the British government, if the South Africa desk of the Foreign Office was told by the ANC office to grant somebody an entry visa to the UK, they just granted it. But for some reason, mine was held up. The ANC office in London was no help. I keep phoning, and finally one of the secretaries said, "Look, please understand that there are urgent visas we have to attend to. Yours is a run-of-the-mill one."

Maybe that was an indication of how effective my role had become or how quickly you become dispensable once you're no longer perceived to be a player of any significance. Eventually I just phoned the British embassy and said, "I'm flying tomorrow. With or without a visa I'm flying. I'm just informing you. You arrest me." The British in Moscow suddenly leaped into action, and by five o'clock in the afternoon they phoned, "Tell him to come here, we will give him his visa."

I arrived in London on 21 July. The UN had rented a flat for Zarina and the children in Mayfair, near Harley Street, where her doctors were. Zarina and I talked about my home mission. When I originally set out on Vula, she had asked me what I thought my chances were for coming back alive. She insisted I give her an estimate. I said, "About 5 percent." Now she told me how in the intervening period and particularly after her accident, with the children living in the care of strangers, she came to realize that although she supported my going home on rational grounds, it was difficult to accept at an emotional level. At the time, Milou was six and Joey was three. She knew the risks. She didn't flinch. She had said yes. But now she had to find a way to be in the UK near medical treatment and in better circumstances, and to be with the children. So she wouldn't be going back to Lusaka or her job with the UN. The family had to relocate to the UK.

She applied to Sussex University to do a master's degree in gender studies and was accepted. I fully agreed with her decision and made preparations to move her and the children to Brighton once she had completed her treatment. In Brighton, Zarina found a tiny one-room flat for her and the children.

Only in London did I learn of the full extent of what she had gone through. To begin with, JS had told me she had suffered "only minor injuries" and he had not wanted the party to pay for her to get treatment in Harare. He thought the UN should pay. All this while she lay in hospital in Lusaka in severe pain, not knowing the extent of her injuries. I was very angry about this. It was something I couldn't forget. Only after the matter was brought to OR's attention had there been any action.[48]

Lusaka Redux

In Lusaka, OR had a stroke on 8 August.[49] He was incapacitated, flown to London. What role, if any, OR had in mind for me at the upcoming meeting of the NEC in September was now moot. But I still intended to go to Lusaka as he had wanted me to do. Other than being there for the tabling of Madiba's memorandum, there was little to engage me. The Harare Declaration had been accepted by the OAU on 21 August; it clearly stated where the ANC stood in relation to negotiations, and the Mandela memorandum was fully in keeping with its provisions.

I went to Lusaka on 26 August. My return was hardly noticed. No "Mac is back" stuff. Some comrades dropped by the house to ask about my treatment and the likely prognosis, about which I was suitably vague; some avoided me completely. The NEC meeting was held on 21 September. At the meeting, Slovo and Alfred Nzo, now acting in place of Tambo, tabled the Madiba letter. A confidential copy of the memorandum had been circulated just prior to the meeting. Some comrades hadn't even had time to read it before our discussions started. Comrades got up, not arguing from what they had read but from their own perceptions of what was Mandela doing. Was he selling out?

After several comrades had spoken, I got up and said, "Can we go through this document?" And we did, and much as I had done with Valli, I made the same points. I said that I had seldom read such a brilliant defense of why we had resorted to armed struggle. I spoke as someone who had been in detention and prison. I also said I had seldom seen anyone defend the alliance with the Communist Party as Madiba had defended it from the perspective of the prisoner. I asked whether we defended the alliance with as much vigor as Mandela.*

My presence in Lusaka had been OR's decision. Clearly, he had an idea of how he was going to use me at the meeting. Whatever it was, Nzo didn't know. But the NEC did fully endorse the Madiba memorandum.[50]

I stayed in Lusaka until 17 October—two days after Walter and the remaining Rivonia Trialists were released.[51] I met with Ivan and JS and heard how they were evaluating developments at home and whether the impending release of Walter and others changed the perspectives and mandate of Vula, etcetera. It didn't. We also discussed Vula's progress and problems. I met with Ronnie Kasrils and Slovo about Ronnie's recruitment for Vula.

Ronnie's selection had been agreed to in Moscow with OR. Before OR had his stroke, he had had at least one discussion with Ronnie. JS would

---

*From Slovo to Nyanda on 22 September 1989, the following message was enclosed for Mandela: "Send ff to Sipho [Mandela]: from Shaun's father [Slovo], on behalf of Presidential Committee [Slovo and Nzo]: The National Executive Committee at yesterday's plenary session received a full report on Sipho's talks with the team. There was unanimous approval for the way he handled the whole situation. In particular, the meeting was overcome with his exposition of the movement's position on all the key issues in the document presented to the other side. The meeting felt very strongly that if the document could be published without jeopardizing the 'confidentiality' of the discussions, it would be a major mobiliser. The other side has spread a great deal of misinformation about his positions. Publication of the document could serve to correct wrong impressions." See Appendix, section C, pages 508–11.

also have had discussions with him, but now the actual preparation had to be arranged. The mechanics were left to Ronnie and me to work out. Slovo's job was to introduce us and say, "You have to work together. This is the nature of the project." So Ronnie and I met to decide on the mechanics of how to get home, but in the end, he didn't go back to South Africa until either the end of March or early April 1990, almost three months after the ANC had been unbanned and a year after OR first told him he was going home.[52]

I did not attend the October meetings of the NEC but stuck to my story: I was taking a breather. I still wasn't "well." Mostly I kept to myself.

Sabbatical

None of us knew how long I was going to be abroad. On my departure, we assumed I would be back in about a month's time. The plan at that point was for Zarina and the children to join me in Moscow, and then we'd have a month's holiday together. But OR's request for me to go to Lusaka threw all our plans out the window. Because of the extent of Zarina's injuries, she wasn't able to handle the move from Lusaka to London alone, never mind the kids. I had to be there.

Zarina gave up the flat on the Sussex campus when we found out that the older kids at Milou and Joey's school were bullying Milou unmercifully because of his color. We had to find a bigger place close to schools so that Zarina, given her state of health, could manage taking the children to school and going to the university. We had some money—while she worked for the University of Lusaka, she had been paid by the British Technical Service in sterling, paid into her British bank account, and she was also paid in dollars while she worked for the UN. We bought a house at 38 Gordon Road, Brighton, and settled in.

I lived quietly in Brighton, enjoyed my children, and watched Zarina get back on her feet. I took care of the kids and the household chores—a new experience.[53] I knew I couldn't just leave her and walk away.

My mind was in South Africa, but there was nobody to discuss it with. I received no messages from Ivan or JS; they were dealing directly with Gebuza. There was still some contact with South Africa. Occasionally I visited Tim Jenkin at his flat in London, or I'd contact Ivan or JS in Lusaka, or they'd call me using prearranged public phones. It wasn't entirely satisfactory, but at least kept me up to date. In a sense, I was on a sabbatical; there was no need for me to attend to the day-to-day problems of Vula. Things were up and running and going smoothly.

Gebuza was in sole charge during this period. I had no contact with him. He reported to Lusaka through Ivan and received responses and guidance from Lusaka. He had the assistance of Janet Love, Billy Nair, and the structures that had been established. Everything was being attended to by Ivan and JS.

When Walter, Kathy, Wilton, and the other Rivonia prisoners were released in October, I was not in the loop.[54] Following OR's stroke there was uncertainty and confusion.

Tambo and Nzo

OR had mastered the techniques of how to get people to address the same problem and how to bring the best out in them and get them to work together. He could preside over meetings of forty people, very strong-willed people, and steer them in such a way that by the time he summarized the meeting's consensus, he managed to include everyone.

For the ANC in exile, far from home, this ability to bring everyone together and hold them together with a common vision was vital. Every individual had to feel he or she was personally important to the struggle. OR kept them all in the fold and convinced them that we were moving forward. He never allowed the process to degenerate into recrimination or despair. OR had honed these skills to an extraordinary degree. There were times when we thought he should have been more decisive or taken a more radical position. But then you remembered how he was holding the movement together and taking it forward.

I saw OR in moments of firmness, in moments of anger, but I never saw him being unfair. In debates he was very sharp, but he never humiliated anyone. He was a man whose leadership you could not doubt because you could see that he gave everything of himself. I never questioned it when he told me, "I want you to go home." I never imagined, even for a moment, that if it had been his turn to go home and put his life on the line, as he expected me to do, he would hesitate. He didn't need to give me orders; all he had to do was ask and I would do it.

OR held the ANC together for twenty-five years, in part because the NEC would defer matters to him, and he would find a way to work through a problem. That was his uniqueness. Indeed, many members of the NEC were in the habit of relying on him to take care of things. His presence was taken for granted. In that sense, he was irreplaceable.

As acting president, Nzo simply didn't have OR's ability to make decisions. He didn't have OR's grasp of detail, his tactical sense, or his strategic vision. Nzo was unexpectedly put in an unenviable position, one he had neither aspired to nor was prepared for.[55]

I never met with Nzo regarding Vula, even though he passed through London a number of times. He never came to Brighton. Nzo gave me the impression that he took over the presidency in a laid-back way: whatever happens, happens.

We were in a totally new ball game, and it took time to get the players in place. The movement had to come to terms with the severity of OR's impairment, and that took some months. While OR was beginning to re-cover some of his speech, Sisulu and the rest were released. How did one steer a path in such a situation?

Getting Ready to Go Home

In early January 1990, Walter, Govan, and the rest of the Rivonia prisoners went to Lusaka. Great celebrations and joy—and more questions. What were the implications; what's coming? Walter et al. then went to Stockholm to meet with OR, where he was recuperating at a clinic. Nzo and Slovo also headed for Stockholm, and there they decided on the leadership that would reincarnate the ANC as a legal entity in South Africa. The core, as it was called, would be Walter (as the head) and Govan, Ray Mhlaba, Mandela (whose release was being anticipated), and me. But I wasn't aware of this decision because it was taken while I was on my way back home.[56]

My brief? The underground was to continue side by side with the overt ANC. I was to get in touch with Walter and draw up a list of names we would recommend to the NEC for inclusion in an expanded leadership. Walter was in overall charge, and I would be in charge of the underground. We would be in dynamic contact. The key focus was how to get the rest of the political prisoners out, because their release would continue to galvanize the country.

Before I left the UK on 24 January 1990, I went to visit OR, who was then in a London clinic. Adelaide, his wife, left me and OR alone. He was still weak but fully conscious and alert. He asked me what I was doing. I was about to say I was on my way home when he waved his hand and asked, "Are you going home?" I said, "Yes." He said, "Very good. Proceed."

I flew to Moscow and retraced my route—to New Delhi, Bombay, and on to Jo'burg. I was switching passports, so I needed about two weeks to get my appearance back to what it was for traveling into the country.

Moscow was like a magnet. Thabo Mbeki and Aziz Pahad were there in December and into January. JS and Alfred Nzo passed through on their way to see OR in Stockholm. And that's where we all were when the news came on 2 February 1990: F. W. de Klerk had unbanned the ANC and the SACP.

The inclusion of the MK and the SACP among the organizations unbanned came as a surprise. We'd expected the unbanning would come with a few hedges, especially around MK and/or the SACP. On 11 February, I think, I flew into Jo'burg from Delhi, and watched the release of Mandela on television in a hotel room in Jo'burg. Or I was still in New Delhi, in a hotel room watching CNN. It is odd that, as good as my memory is, for this momentous event it is blank.

Once again, we were in a state of play, for us a precarious one, fraught with damning consequences if we made the wrong decisions: were the regime's apparent overtures to be taken at face value or were they a play to lure us into a situation where our continued advocacy of armed struggle would lose us the moral high ground in the post–cold war political configuration, how to stop the momentum that had swung to De Klerk after his actions were widely applauded by apartheid's erstwhile enemies; whether to declare a moratorium on armed action; how to move forward in a progressive way yet prepare for worst case scenarios; how to persuade the international community, especially the United States, to keep pressure on the regime and not to relax sanctions; how to create unity within our own ranks and among all black liberation movements, and the question of how to deal with Gatsha. All daunting tasks requiring judicious assessments of the internal environment and a collaborative interaction among the exiled leadership, most of which had not set foot in South Africa for decades, the Robben Islanders, and the fragmented leadership of the MDM at home. My role now was to assess the new political environment as it unfolded and figure out what role the underground should play.

Zarina and My Family

In the weeks before I left, Zarina and I had talked about my going back. But the context of our conversation had changed. She poured out her feelings: how hard it had been on her emotionally and psychologically not knowing from one day to the next what might happen, that it was one thing to say yes when you had not experienced the insecurity and anxiety of the unknown but quite another to live with it every day. And then there was the turmoil that followed her accident. The children without a father and then without a mother. Their sense of abandonment. The dislocation of relocation to England.

My prolonged absence was affecting my family, causing grief for my children and pain between my wife and me. And now I was abandoning them again. When I was later arrested, in July 1990, my eight-year-old son actually said to his mother, "It's not about when we will see him, it's whether we will."

In January of that year, Zarina asked me: "Where are the others? Why is it always you who steps forward?" I didn't have an answer.

16. TRANSITIONS

Introduction

WITH THE UNBANNING of all political parties, especially the SACP, and Mandela's release, the ANC was thrown off balance.* It was taken by surprise by the sheer audacity of De Klerk's actions, despite signals since the late 1980s that Mandela's release was only a matter of time, and that by late 1988 a reception committee was already in place.[1]

Mostly, the ANC tacked its sails to the prevailing winds. Contradictions and rumors had a field day. The ANC wanted the government to respond to its overtures for talks but not too quickly; it couldn't be seen to be suing for peace. It also couldn't be seen as the party holding back. It had to prepare its constituency, which for years it had primed for armed insurgence.† Township youth and the comrades, led to believe that a seizure of power was imminent, had to be hauled into line.

In his discussions with De Klerk before he was released, the contents of which were relayed to Lusaka via the Vula communications system, Mandela, in concert with Lusaka, pushed De Klerk to agree to certain steps to create a climate conducive to negotiations before the ANC could agree to meet the government.[2] His release, ironically, would create a new set of dynamics that, paradoxically, made it more rather than less difficult to

---

*After meeting with the ANC in Lusaka in mid-January and being briefed by the leadership, the Rivonia Trialists traveled to Norway to meet with anti-apartheid stalwarts there before proceeding to Stockholm to meet with the ailing Oliver Tambo. In Oslo, Sisulu gave a press conference in which he expressed the hope that the ANC would be unbanned before the end of 1990. "ANC could be legal by end of year says Sisulu," *Citizen*, 30 January 1990.

†Nor were matters helped by Alfred Nzo's public remarks. In a briefing to the media, Nzo said: "Looking at the situation realistically, we must admit that we do not have the capacity within our country, in fact, to intensify the armed struggle in any meaningful

remove the obstacles to negotiations, which the ANC insisted on being addressed as a basic precondition for substantive talks.[3]

The ANC demanded immediate action from the government regarding the release of political prisoners and indemnity for exiles. The message from Pretoria via the Afrikaners at Mells House was reassuring: the government knew that the old order of apartheid South Africa was in its death throes and appeared anxious to get on with the burial arrangements.[4] At the same time, it was aware that De Klerk had not yet consolidated his own support base for his actions within the NP and could face being replaced or even a military coup.[5] Thus the strategic conundrum facing the ANC: it had to make demands on the government but not go beyond De Klerk's capacity, or it risked provoking a right-wing backlash that could threaten everything.* Neither could the ANC be seen as weak or soft, or it might lose its constituents.

In the early months of 1990, the government moved with confidence. De Klerk's popularity soared, especially among Africans, and the government was clearly determined to entrench itself as convenor of the peace process, the one who would draw up the rules of the negotiating process.

Two weeks after his release, Mandela went to Natal to try to mend the rift between Inkatha and the ANC. He told his supporters to throw their "pangas into the sea." The "young lions" howled their disapproval. The violence escalated. Perhaps ten thousand were killed between 1990 and 1994, mostly in KZN; Africans were killed by Africans, albeit in many cases the killings were abetted by the regime's security forces.[6] Inkatha accused the ANC of trying to wipe it out. The ANC accused the security forces of working with Inkatha and again denounced Buthelezi as a puppet of the regime.

Trying to ameliorate the war in KZN absorbed enormous amounts of time and energy.[7] On the national stage, the ANC accused the government of trying to be both player and referee, while in KZN it tried to act as peacemaker rather than see itself as a party to the conflict. It excoriated the

---

way." *Star*, 24 January 1990. Many political commentators (and probably more than a few in the ANC leadership) thought the remark extremely ill advised, a revelation you do not make with the possibility of real negotiations a distinct prospect. Shubin says: "According to specialist assessment in Moscow, Umkhonto already possessed arms and ammunition sufficient to sustain training and armed actions for at least a year." This assessment was made no later than May 1989, *A View from Moscow*, p. 350.

*On 25 January 1990, Mandela's memorandum to P. W. Botha found its way into the public domain, to the consternation of Mandela, who did not understand where the leak could have come from. Suddenly, Mandela's memorandum appeared to be setting the parameters of negotiations even before he was released or the ANC unbanned.

security forces' "third force,"[8] while the government obsessed about Communists trying to destabilize the state. Inkatha felt by turns either sidelined or wooed by the NP, and Buthelezi pouted.

The government repealed the acts that were the foundation of apartheid: the Group Areas Act, the Reservation of Separate Amenities Act, and the Population Registration Act.[9] De Klerk snatched his moment in the international political limelight. In March he attended the Namibian independence ceremonies and met with nine African heads of states in Windhoek, a first for a South African president. In May he visited nine European countries, which provided him with a false sense of legitimacy. He began to believe he could hold the moral high ground, build a coalition of parties opposed to the ANC, or fragment the ANC itself and win an election with a voters' roll open to all races. For a while he sought to promote himself as the country's father figure, above the dirty business of politics, magnificently oblivious to his own party's history of repression and wrongdoing.[10] "Group rights" and "the protection of minorities" became staples of the government's political discourse; to the ANC these were code words for the maintenance of white privilege and a political veto over the will of the majority.[11]

In September he visited the United States to meet with President George Bush, an auspicious occasion for De Klerk, the first South African head of government to visit the United States since Jan Smuts forty-five years earlier. He was received with full military honors, South African flags flying outside the White House, a cordial and receptive George Bush. He savored the moment. He had brought South Africa in from the cold. "As 1990 drew to a close," he wrote in his autobiography, *The Last Trek*, "there was much for which I could be thankful."[12]

2

The ANC's core of five* established at Stockholm was supposed to meet and submit its recommendations to the NEC prior to their meeting on 14–16 February. Before that meeting, Nzo received a call from Govan Mbeki, who said the core's recommendations were on their way to Lusaka

---

*The core: Walter Sisulu (chair), Govan Mbeki, Raymond Mhlaba, Mac, and a place reserved for Mandela. It was replaced in March with a new core that added Slovo and Nzo. There was also an Interim Leadership Committee (ILC). This was a national committee including both the core and the regional leadership cores tasked with establishing ANC structures across the country. The smaller body only met on occasion and then rarely with all members present.

with Reverend Xundu. Subsequently, the names of Cyril Ramaphosa, Kgalema Motlanthe, Harry Gwala, and Andrew Mlangeni were put before the NEC and ratified for inclusion in the core of internal leadership.[13] At a press conference after the NEC meeting, Nzo told a reporter from the *Sowetan* that a committee, under Sisulu's leadership, comprising Govan Mbeki, Mhlaba, Mlangeni, Ramaphosa, and Gwala, would be responsible for reestablishing the ANC in South Africa.

When Mac read about these appointments in the *Sowetan* on 19 February, he immediately sent Slovo a terse one-line resignation from both the ANC and SACP.[14] He said he would hand over to Nyanda (Gebuza), staying on for a month to ensure a smooth transition, before leaving for the UK. His decisions, he said, were "neither discussable nor revocable." His letter to Slovo has a tone of cold irritability and a formal correctness that convey a depth of real anger.

The NEC had failed to include members of the underground in the core, despite Mac's insistence that their participation in the internal leadership was crucial to establish a proper symmetry between overt and covert structures. Gwala's apparent inclusion was the last straw. Mac regarded Gwala as being entirely unsuited, by both temperament and rigid ideological disposition, for a leadership role.[15]

But things were not quite as they seemed. On 27 February, the NEC learned that Govan Mbeki's recommendations to Lusaka were "unmandated"—that is, they had not been approved by Walter Sisulu or any member of the core group. Indeed, Sisulu was completely in the dark about Mbeki's actions. In an attempt to redress the situation, but without inquiring into how it had arisen, the NEC decided that the expanded core should consist of the original five plus one person from each region, as well as some HQ departmental heads and all members of the NEC who could be deployed to South Africa.[16] The names Govan Mbeki had recommended were dropped. Gwala qualified for inclusion as ANC chief in the Natal Midlands.

We can only speculate about why Mbeki behaved as he did. Three of his recommendations (Ramaphosa, Motlanthe, and Gwala) belonged to his "national collective," which he had continued to run despite Tambo's instructions to confine his activities to Port Elizabeth and the border area. Perhaps he thought that by having members of his collective on the committee, he would have a louder voice in the selection of additional members. It suggests that in Govan's eyes, at least, the ideological scores of Robben Island were not yet settled. One can either interpret his actions as a power play, an audacious move to seize organizational control of the

ANC in South Africa, or as a not-too-subtle play for his preferred nominees. Either way, his move certainly lacked adherence to the principle of "collectivity," the same misdeed for which he had faulted Mandela. Nor should it be forgotten that there were some in Lusaka, recipients of a steady stream of messages from Govan from the time of his release in 1987, who still harbored doubts about Mandela.

But Mac was not appeased, even when Slovo gave him a detailed account of how matters had transpired.[17] Although Slovo acknowledged that Govan Mbeki's actions were unmandated, Mac was adamant: nothing was being done either to chastise Govan or haul him into line, or to prevent Nzo from putting his foot in his mouth again. Mac played the hard man. His resignation stood; he would retire from the field of action.

Mandela heard of Mac's "retirement" during his visit to Lusaka after his release, days after Mac had tendered it. Mandela sent Kathrada to speak to Mac, and when Kathrada failed, Sisulu tried to persuade him to withdraw his resignation. When Sisulu failed, Mandela himself intervened and "twisted" Mac's arm, prevailing upon on him to return. So once again Mac threw himself into the fray with his relentless vigor.

Yet a scant three months later, on 23 June 1990, the occasion of the first legal meeting of the NEC inside South Africa in thirty years, Mac announced once more that he intended to retire from politics in December of that year. His reason: Mandela had not had a promised discussion with him on the issues that had precipitated his resignation in the first place. The NEC noted Mac's statement with concern, and it was agreed that "the matter will be taken up in private if members want to."[18] But members didn't want to. More important, Mandela was not present at the meeting.

3

When Mac and I talked about this meeting, he told me Mandela had been present. Announcing his forthcoming resignation, Mac said, was sending "a shot across Mandela's bow." A year or so later, when I obtained a copy of the minutes of the NEC meeting and ascertained that Mandela did not attend the meeting, which was chaired by Walter Sisulu, Mac was unfazed. Sisulu, he said, would have informed Mandela. This was a leadership matter. Perhaps, but still an assumption on Mac's part, an assumption that goes begging.

Sisulu did not pursue the matter with him, nor did the NEC, perhaps because this was only the second appearance Mac had made at an ANC meeting in nearly two years. To the NEC, Mac was no longer a matter of interest. The world had changed since he had slowly faded into apparent ill health some years before. Now he appeared again, only to say what many had already concluded: that he was calling it a day. In late April, Mandela met with Mac, still an illegal in South Africa, for a couple of hours. Mandela instructed Slovo to give Mac unfettered access to him. Whenever Mac wanted to see him, Slovo was to make room on the schedule.[19]

But Mac never asked to see Mandela, other than the one occasion when it became clear to him to him that Vula was going to be exposed. When Mac was granted indemnity on 20 May, and met with Mandela shortly afterward to discuss his leaving the country and coming back legally, he said nothing about his intention to call it quits in December. In October, when Mandela visited him at St. Aidan's Hospital, where he was held by the government pending charges to do with Vula, again he didn't raise the matter.

The move, he implied in our conversations,[20] was up to Mandela. Mandela, who had traveled the world twice over since emerging from twenty-seven years of imprisonment; who was trying to establish some semblance of a personal life; who was adhering "in a loyal and disciplined way" to the punishing schedule his new staff had prepared for him; who was dealing with Buthelezi and Natal and De Klerk and negotiations, and with competing factions within the ANC, was being held to account by Mac for failing to remember that he, Mac, had made his return to "active" service conditional on his having a one-on-one discussion with Mandela on his "issues."

It seems incongruous. After Mandela's release, Mac's mind raced ahead to the challenges Mandela would face in dealing with the regime and negotiations as well as in his private life. Mac had talked of Mandela's burden, with only Walter to lean on, yet he, someone else Mandela could rely on, was putting his own needs first.

One can only take Mac at his word: for him, his family's needs were now paramount. Yet Mac had visited Zarina and the children in Brighton only two weeks earlier and hadn't raised with her his intention to resign. Nor was she pressing him on that point. Later, when I raised the matter with people Mac had worked with, I was given a rationale that would crop up again and again when other of Mac's behaviors needed explication: Mac was being Mac.

4

In late April, the first group of ANC leaders returned from exile, and in early May the first meeting between the ANC and the government took place. The Groote Schuur Minute[21] committed both to "a resolution of the existing climate of violence" and to a process of negotiations. The NP would start granting temporary immunity to members of the NEC, review security legislation, and lift the state of emergency. In late May the first indemnifications were granted (Mac was among the indemnified). In June the government lifted the state of emergency, except in KZN.

A review of the NEC minutes in the latter part of 1989,[22] the first part of 1990,[23] the SACP's analysis of where the ANC stood prior to its own launch,[24] the briefing paper for the joint NEC/ILC meeting,[25] the minutes of the first NEC meeting held in South Africa since the ANC's banning in 1960,[26] and the minutes of the ANC/ILC meeting that followed[27] captures the contradictions, confusions, and suspicions of the early days of negotiations as the alliance grappled with multitudinous demands. A common refrain runs through the proceedings of these meetings: The ANC cannot translate its decisions into action. Implementation simply doesn't happen.[28] ("We write beautiful documents but implementation seriously lacking. There is great confusion on the ground and little or no guidance from the top.")[29]

The ANC lacked leadership. Organizationally, it was bogged down in factional disputes,[30] personal incompatibilities,[31] inadequate personnel, poor communication lines, and mixed messages.[32] Most of the leadership had not been briefed on the Groote Schuur Minute; most did not know where negotiations stood.[33] The external wing and the newly established internal wing were frequently at odds, and both were often at odds with the MDM, which had its own fault lines and lack of leadership. No one was in charge. Too much was asked of the Rivonia Trialists. The ANC's slavish adherence to the tradition of seniority pushed some of the released prisoners to assume tasks and discharge responsibilities they were patently unsuited for.

There was one meeting at Mandela's home in Soweto in October 1990 that captures the surreal incongruities that permeated the ANC as it struggled to get a grip on the organizational and financial anarchy running riot in the movement. Attending the meeting were Treasurer General Thomas Nkobi, Thabo Mbeki, and a few others. Mandela opened the meeting in blunt, businesslike terms. "I've been reading the Statement of Expenditure up to July," he tells the group, "and was frightened. The statement does not appear to be related to our resources and I thought we would reach a tragedy soon if we don't control the situation." And then he conducted a small seminar in cost savings he had identified. Less than nine months out of prison after twenty-seven years of being incarcerated, Mandela tried to lay out the new financial guidelines: No more business class flying. Night flights save money. Rent: "we pay a lot of money. If the Americans appreciate our efforts they ought to feel an obligation." He had spoken to Bush but Bush had made no promises. Coca-Cola was a better bet. Accommodation: "We can arrange for people to stay in the townships." Equipment: "We could get it at half price or even without having to pay." And thus it went.[34]

In 1990, this absence of leadership almost overwhelmed the ANC as it struggled to establish itself inside South Africa, to set up national and regional offices and structures, deal with the return of exiles, the dismantling of camps in Tanzania, the future of MK, negotiations, the war in KZN, build a parallel underground, and introduce Mandela to the international community. The common complaint: the masses weren't the only people in the dark; the leadership was also for the most part in the dark. Chaos ruled at ANC headquarters on Sauer Street in Johannesburg.

Within the ANC, the leadership was confused about its own position, which was yes to negotiations if they were authentic, but at the same time a continuation of smuggling arms into the country and the recruitment and military training of cadres—not for a seizure of power or even as an insurance policy should negotiations fail, but as an ambivalent position somewhere in between. In a sense, this was as much a political statement as a strategic necessity to placate powerful elements of its constituency. The two were interrelated. The leadership reasoned that only if the regime believed that the ANC could in fact seize power would it negotiate in good faith—or at least sufficient faith.

5

The first six months of 1990 were months of political and personal upheavals for Mac. He retired from the ANC and then unretired. He had little time for Ronnie Kasrils, who had entered the country illegally in March to join Vula after Mandela's release but before indemnities were granted. Kasrils, he believed, was careless, had an adventurist streak, and had trouble adapting to being illegal in an environment where indemnity for ANC cadres was already being arranged.

In April, he had a run-in with "Terror" Lekota, the UDF leader who was appointed to take charge of the ANC's overt structures in the southern Natal region. Lekota refused to consult with the covert structures, which suddenly found themselves in a political wilderness. Mac attributed Lekota's high-handedness and impudence to immaturity and general unsuitability for the position. To resolve the impasse, he turned to Walter Sisulu.[35]

In May, Mac left South Africa after he was granted indemnity so that he could reenter the country legally, supposedly returning from exile where the South African government had assumed him to have been all along. Before returning, he stopped over in Brighton to see Zarina and the children, to tell them he had "recovered" and that the family would be relocating to South Africa.

Also in May, he had a bitter falling out with Joe Slovo over details of the Groote Schuur Minute, an argument with harsh words exchanged, mostly on Mac's part, and although they continued to work together, at a personal level their relationship never recovered.[36] His anger with Slovo had a personal dimension. He could not forgive him for the way he had treated Zarina after her accident, although he never raised this with him. Somewhere along the line he lost his respect for Slovo as a person, although he would never belittle Slovo's enormous contribution to the struggle.

His relationship with Slovo reflected the tension inherent in all Mac's working relationships, but with Slovo it was exacerbated. Mac once described their relationship as one of love/hate.[37] It was his most important working relationship; the two stimulated each other intellectually. Both were powerhouses in the SACP. Mac had a keen appreciation of Slovo's strategic sense, but he believed Slovo's actions frequently gave a hollow ring to his words. He complained that, to Slovo, whatever was the current focus of his attention was where the revolution was.[38] Ironically, it was a complaint that many directed at Mac himself.

In June, back in South Africa, Mac took Gebuza to task for having agreed to share Vula's communication with the ANC underground in the Western Cape.[39] He immediately revoked Nyanda's decision and chastized him for what he perceived as creeping slackness in Vula's activities. And then he announced his retirement from the ANC again, effective at year's end.

Meanwhile, while attending to Vula and the larger matter of the structures of an ANC underground that would continue to function even while the negotiations process was being finely calibrated, he spearheaded the organization of a clandestine conference at Tongaat, about seventy kilometers outside Durban, for a group of twenty of the party's leading members, most of whom had not received amnesty and were therefore subject to arrest and prosecution. The conference met between 16–20 May to discuss the role of the party in the negotiations process, the relaunch of the party as a legal entity in South Africa, and the thrust of its policy positions.[40] The Tongaat conference endorsed the document, which was sent to the Central Committee for ratification.

But within a month Mac had quit the party. Without a hint of apparent regret, and notwithstanding the enormous effort he had put into preparing the way for the party's resurfacing in South Africa, he walked out of the party to which he had given unswerving allegiance for forty-five years. Nevertheless, he agreed to introduce the new leadership, including Gwala, at the party's relaunch because he had committed himself to doing so. Thereafter he was in permanent retirement.

As both the government and the ANC circled each other like wary adversaries in the first half of 1990, probing each other's vulnerabilities, Mac was busy deconstructing the worlds he had inhabited since his days as a student in Durban. With the endgame of the struggle to which he had devoted forty years of his life in sight, he walked away. Henceforth, he averred, he would play a new role: family man, a role that once again would be short-lived.

Mac

WHEN I RETURNED to South Africa in February 1990, I knew that enormous opportunities had opened up.* I was also very conscious of the fact that the burden was going to rest primarily on Madiba's and Sisulu's shoulders. I was very aware that Tambo was incapacitated, but I knew that even in his absence Madiba had the capacity to lead and move things forward.

---

*Mac had a problem recollecting exactly when he arrived back in South Africa and had no recall of having either watched Mandela's release on television or listened to it on radio. At least two years after we had stopped trying to figure out where he was and why he might not have been among the global audience that watched Mandela's release, I came upon a comm that shed some light on the matter. Mac arrived in Johannesburg from New Delhi on Saturday evening, 10 February. He spent the night in a hotel. His modus operandi was never to go directly to where he was supposed to go or to meet anyone during his first day back in the country in case he was under surveillance. Then on

In the course of my involvement in the struggle, Madiba, Walter, and Tambo were the people I had direct experience with, and they stood head and shoulders above the rest of us. As a team, they were outstanding. OR had performed with consummate skill through the exile years, but his stroke had sidelined him. I wondered who Walter and Madiba could share the burden with.

Govan? I didn't think so. I remembered the friction between him and Madiba in prison.[41] The negotiations process had to be driven and had to be sold to the people. We had to project unity, that we shared a common agenda. We had to ensure that the Rivonia Trialists were at one, that the ANC in exile was at one with COSATU and the MDM. So we needed people of stature who could command broad support, who would be given the benefit of the doubt, especially when they made unpopular decisions. That is why Mandela, right up to OR's death, no matter how ill OR was, had OR by his side in public, or Walter or Slovo or Jay Naidoo, or even Govan and Harry Gwala, although he knew where both stood. The message to the constituency was always the same and had to be hammered home: we are as one. Neither the ANC constituency nor the broad black public could afford to be internally divided.

Mandela's first statement was hard-line, pronationalization. We knew that some of these things were inserted by the MDM, people he had consulted from Victor Verster. They said, "You must say it." He said it because he wasn't going to argue, the issue being that he had to pull everybody together.[42]

At the time of Mandela's release, there was the potential for negotiations, but the process had to be driven. How did you bring that about with balance, without halting the progress of mass politicization? Negotiations had to be promoted. How did you set about maneuvering in the international terrain, where you now had a unipolar world? How did you maneuver inside the country to sustain the tripartite alliance? How did you ensure, in the face of the enormous pain and anger that apartheid had generated among the people, that the constituency of the liberation struggle supported the switch to negotiations? How did you attend to

---

Sunday, after 2:00 P.M., he made his way to the garage at the home of Bob and Helen Douglas, the two Canadian sleepers who lived in Parkhurst, an upscale suburb of Jo'burg. The garage was one of the safe houses he used when he was in Jo'burg. He would not have made any contact with the Douglases. The garage was without a TV or radio, which would explain why he has no recollections of either watching or listening to Mandela's release. See Carl (Nyanda) from John (Tim Jerkin) at [] maharaj/vula comms/ 1990[]/ Jan. 21.

organizing the ANC in the space that had opened up, and at the same time find enough resources to get ready for an election that could happen at any time, without weakening your forces engaged in negotiations? And under no circumstance could you allow yourself to be maneuvered into a situation where De Klerk would say, "Agreed, let's have elections in six months," or even in 1992.

If De Klerk had said, after releasing Madiba, "I'm inviting Mandela and six people selected by him to come into my cabinet for the purposes of holding elections in twelve months," or if he had said, "While I continue to rule the country, I'm setting up an interim body made up of six from each side who will supervise elections," where would we have been? It would have been nearly impossible for us to refuse. Then De Klerk would have been seen as the driver of the process.

Concerns

In the underground, one of our key preoccupations was how, in this changed environment, we could ensure Madiba's safety. I had no concerns about what he would say politically. Even when he said on his release that De Klerk was a "man of integrity," which caused ripples in the democratic movement, it didn't worry me.[43] Nor did his call, during a visit to West Africa, to African countries to support the National Party and De Klerk. I saw that as an indication that he was driving the process to the point where a win-win formula for negotiations could emerge.

Something else preoccupied me at that stage: the tactics De Klerk's government would use. I felt it was outside their power to control the emotions and support that would well up with Madiba's release, but I expected they would yet play some dirty tricks to try to manipulate the release to serve their own ends. I was concerned that although the regime could not diminish the stature of Madiba, it would systematically try to undermine him by other means: not by attacking him but by attacking his immediate family. With everything that was going on, his wife, Winnie, was a target inviting attack.[44]

I outlined that scenario to Lusaka before I left South Africa in May 1989, and again with OR and Slovo in Moscow. I felt it was our duty, not Madiba's, to guard against this. I thought it would put an unfair responsibility on him, and I believed that on a personal level, his relationship with Winnie was going to be very, very difficult, so I wanted to protect him from the most devastating impact. But I also understood that he was an intensely private person who would not allow people like us to get involved. It saddened me, now that this moment in history had arrived—and he was the pivot of that moment—that he was going to have to fight so many battles on his own. It would be hard.

Mandela's Tasks

Mandela had to drive the negotiation process and give it a formal character, and he had to drive it to a speedy conclusion. I think history will show that if we had been able to shorten the period of time from Mandela's release to the 1994 elections, some of the scars we're still living with would have been minimized. In the post-1990 period, the social fabric of South Africa began to unravel. We got caught in a downward spiral. The more time elapsed, the further down the spiral we were spun.

We had characterized apartheid itself as an illegitimate, immoral, and discredited system. By implication, all apartheid's laws should be rejected. We had mobilized the public to the point where no law made by apartheid deserved any respect. They had license to do what they wanted to do.

And the apartheid powers were themselves hypocritical—prepared to break their own laws—so the idea that law is governed by a sense of fairness and morality had been eroded. The understanding that the law prevents anarchy was absent; the basic principles governing social relationships were rejected.

As areas in the country became ungovernable, the restrictions of an unfair state were being removed, but nothing replaced them. The situation was ready-made for nihilism. The need to reassert law and the morality underlying law, and to instill respect for the law, was urgent.

The liberation movement had to come into formal existence in a legal environment and to organize itself as such. That was a formidable problem. Thirty years of being illegal meant developing afresh methods of organization and work suited to aboveground, legal existence. And this had to take place in the context of international support for the anti-apartheid movement, which had to remain unfragmented to gain greater momentum.

Then there was the need to prepare for elections. Mandela knew that the playing fields would have to be leveled if we were to win an election against an entrenched state.

These were some of the tasks facing Mandela. If Tambo had been around, some of them would have been attended to more speedily and not fallen solely on Madiba's shoulders. One of the greatest weaknesses of that period was insufficient organization of the ANC and its allies.[45] In the negotiations phase, much of our activity was still conditioned by our history, by oppositional protest politics, yet we had to prepare the ANC membership and political machinery to go beyond protest, to start thinking in terms of governing.

The mass democratic movement was truly a popular movement, so when it was called upon, it came out en masse. We'd never had individual branches for organizing ordinary people at community level, so now little attention was being given to creating branch structures.[46]

Madiba was very aware that he not only had to position the ANC to fight the election politically, he also had to restructure its organization. And he knew we would need enormous resources if we were to succeed.

Subsequent events showed that Mandela was able to keep a clear focus on all these challenges. Despite all the uncertainties and the violence ravaging the country, he was able to steer a path to democracy.

Resigning

Yet back in South Africa, I often thought of retiring. It was churning in my mind, no longer a question of should I? but when? I had left Brighton unsettled; my conversations with Zarina lingered in my mind. The actual incident that triggered my decision was the launch of the ANC internal leadership.

On 16 February 1990, Alfred Nzo announced in Lusaka the appointments to the leadership group that would take charge of establishing the internal ANC. I learned of these appointments from the newspapers. It was very clear they had ignored my many messages that the unbannings were coming, that we needed to surface in a proper way to establish the ANC inside the country.

I had a growing sense of being told, "Keep it up. You are doing great work," but then being left to steer a ship without a rudder. Of course it was frustrating, and these frustrations were aggravated by my anger at Slovo over the way he had treated Zarina after her accident. That had been unforgivable, a fundamental breach of friendship and comradeship.

Once back, however, I soon realized that the movement was no more prepared for the events unfolding than it had been when I left. Then came the Lusaka announcement, which reached us through the South African newspapers. It was too much. I felt I had outlived my usefulness, that it was time to bow out. At the time, I was unaware that OR and the others had agreed on the core leadership in Stockholm and that I was to be in the group of five.

When I read the names of the new interim leadership, I was angry, and frustrated that they hadn't even bothered to inform me. Yes, I felt insulted. But more than that, it was the incompetence of the thing that irked me the most. They had taken no account of the leaders in the UDF or the unions who were also disciplined members of the ANC. They'd entrusted the task of building the internal ANC to certain people without considering who already had a structured relationship with the underground. My view was not that the underground people should be the leaders, but that at least a few of them should be a part of our leadership, with an explicit mandate to link them into the legal ANC.

I said, "Guys, you've put me in an untenable position—I retire." On 24 February, I sent a message to JS, informing him of my immediate retirement from both the ANC and SACP, and asking for Lusaka's assistance in getting to London after I had facilitated a smooth transfer of command to Gebuza, which I told them would take about a month.

JS and Ivan tried to soothe me. Nzo, they said, was not supposed to have made the announcement publicly, but had done so inadvertently while facing media questions. I didn't buy it. Would I have thought differently if they had first briefed me about the need to maintain both covert and overt structures? If they had shown there was still space to address the relationship between these two levels of organization and activity? Perhaps, but I can't say categorically that it would have helped. Clearly, they had been taken in by Govan's message purporting to come from the core group established at Stockholm. I am not sure they realized how unilaterally Govan had acted, and if they did, I don't think they had any idea how to confront it. Fortunately, the release of Madiba cut the ground from under Govan's feet.

I resigned because I knew that otherwise the underground would be in an impossible situation. We would have two authorities: the newly appointed, overt, interim leadership and the covert political underground. Who should listen to which authority? "You've put us into a rival situation," I warned. And, indeed, that is what happened.

Things were moving at such a speed that tensions began to surface. In the absence of a linkage between the interim leadership and the underground, people became insecure. What did it mean for Vula? What should we be doing? Had we become irrelevant? Did Lusaka think we were not significant enough to be included in the overt structures that were being created?

I left things to Gebuza. I went to Durban and I said, "I'm handing over command to you." Gebuza didn't know what to say. I gave him a copy of my letter to Lusaka. I also informed Billy Nair and Janet Love. But because I was back within a week, my "retirement" went unnoticed. I was available to Gebuza to assist him in what I thought would be a transitional phase.

Mandela Intervenes

Madiba went to Lusaka on 27 February. Slovo told him they had a problem on their hands if I retired. After a few days Mandela returned to South Africa. First he sent Kathy to see me, but Kathy couldn't move me; then he sent Walter, but Walter had no luck either. Then he sent me a message: "Can we meet?" We met in Ismail Ayob's office at about ten at night and we talked until two or three in the morning. After we'd greeted and hugged each other, and I'd inquired about his health and he'd done the same, he said to me, "You know, I'm an old man, I'm tired, I got up at five this morning and been on the go all day. Since I've come out of prison, I've received hundreds of presents and gifts. But there's one gift I needed, and no one has given it to me." I'm thinking, is he stuck for money? I said to myself, "I've got access to the underground; I can provide what he needs." I said, "Well, what's it you need? I'll get it for you." He said, "I know you can get it for me." I said, "Well, what is it you want?" He said, "Withdraw your retirement." I said, "No, wait. Let's discuss the issues." He said, "No, if you've retired, you're not an ANC member.* I can't discuss ANC matters with you. You first withdraw your retirement; then we will discuss issues." So we went around this mulberry bush until two or three in the morning. Madiba pleaded with me, twisted my arm: "But, Mac, I need you." I was in a corner. He said, "I need you to fight this war." Yet my family needed me too, but I couldn't say this to Madiba because he himself was sacrificing everything.

In the end, I said, "For your sake, for OR's sake and for Walter's sake, I withdraw my resignation, but temporarily—till we discuss the issues." Mandela said, "Yes! Thanks, Neef. Now I've got to go and sleep; I've got to be up at five." I said, "Let's discuss the issues." He said, "Later, later, not

*When I told Mac that retiring from the ANC does not mean that you lose your membership, he insisted on leaving the sentence as is; that, he says, is what Mandela said.

now." I said to him: "Madiba, I will stay on for six months and then I will retire. I will help you to bridge this period." So I never got to Brighton. It didn't come to pass.

Come early March, I was back. Everything was back to normal. We continued the work.

The Issues

The first issue was structural. We were organizing the ANC overtly yet maintaining a clandestine presence. I knew we could not maintain a clandestine organization without engaging it in some defined activity. We were moving toward negotiations, and any excuse could be used by either side to jettison things, but at the same time, we needed the underground, so we had to have our stratagems carefully thought out. We needed to be able to provide Madiba with plausible deniability at all times.

The second issue was associated with the first. We had to have clear lines of command. No confusion.[47]

The third issue was how the underground could participate, like any other ANC structure, in decision-making processes. After Vula was busted, the feedback I got about reactions within the movement was that although there was enormous sympathy and pride among ordinary ANC members, trade unions, and ordinary people, within the leadership there was confusion about it. This left the people on the ground in an insecure position because what they heard from the leadership about Vula depended on who the leader was. One might be explicitly dismissive of Vula, another would say we deserved what we got, and yet another would give an ambivalent answer. This caused confusion among the very people we were trying to organize in the underground.

These were the types of problems to be addressed. They wouldn't be solved overnight, but we needed to start discussing strategy. Had that been done, I think I would not have resigned. I would have soldiered on, but Madiba never came back to me to discuss the issues.

Whither the Underground?

A committee headed by Madiba was established in March. The members were Walter, Madiba, Nzo, Raymond Mhlaba, Govan, Joe Slovo, and me.*

---

*This replaced the committee established at Stockholm. It was the new Internal Leadership Committee.

The expanded core decided who would do what. We had to deal with the underground and the military in a way that took into account what was happening aboveground, in the negotiations. Because of Vula, I was accountable to the top leadership for covert operations.

I was told to prepare a proposal to present at our next meeting about what should become of the underground and the military within the new situation. To do so meant consulting underground units around the country; we needed their input as well, since I felt the relationship between the two levels, overt and covert, required more than my opinion alone. And many people didn't even know I was involved with the underground. In the end, the issue was never fully resolved.

Meanwhile, the Internal Political Committee (IPC)* in Lusaka, which may have been unaware that the core committee of seven existed, had prepared a document for the NEC in which it made recommendations regarding the future role of the underground.[48] Slovo, without the knowledge of the NEC, passed the document on to me, and I solicited the views of the Durban underground. "Chaps, this committee is going to discuss the role of the underground. Can I have your views?"[49] Ronnie believed we should maintain the underground as an insurance policy.[50] In my communication to Durban, however, I disagreed because such a strategy, if found out, could embarrass Madiba and the negotiators.

I also said we could no longer maintain the underground in the old way, as if we were totally illegal. We had to reform in a more overt way, but without alerting the enemy that we were the underground. We could, for instance, provide security for the forthcoming Madiba rally at King's Park. We took the system of marshals that had emerged in the MDM and put some of our trained military cadres into it. They would drill the marshals, who were already well known in the media. I argued that the marshals should become a paramilitary structure, and embedded within it would be our MK people, as trainers, part of the officer corps.

That plan would keep our machinery oiled, no longer engaged in sabotage but still very active and maintaining communications, with proper lines of command and control. If we were found out, I argued, our negotiators would have a legitimate excuse to say to the regime, "You are unable to secure our rallies, and we wouldn't accept it even if you did, so we have created our own paramilitary security structures." I put this option to the committee; they agreed.

*The Internal Political Committee (IPC) was the successor to the IPRD. Before he got "sick," Mac had been secretary of the IPC and, of course, its predecessor, the IPRD.

It has become common currency that Vula was conceived as an insurance policy, something we could fall back on if negotiations failed. But Vula had been conceived in 1986. The idea of it being an insurance policy only emerged in the 1990s. In fact, the interim leadership core had rejected this idea.[51]

We decided to continue training underground units, to bring MK units into South Africa, to go on smuggling in arms relative to what was happening at the overt level. Mass mobilization, openly organizing the legal ANC, and negotiations were now the primary focus. The money for our operations no longer came through Lusaka; it was delivered to me at home. On Mandela's instructions, it was given to me in hard cash, not through bank accounts, because I couldn't pay the underground in checks. Usually I'd get it in ten- and twenty-rand notes; we had learned that you don't flash big notes around.

From the time of his release onward, Madiba put his full support behind organizing the underground along the lines we suggested. On one occasion he told us that he had just come from a visit to the Free State, where there was great potential for putting underground structures in place, and that he could even give Vula local contacts.*

Madiba had to play many roles after he was released. Transforming the underground swiftly and efficiently was among his priorities, but it was one he could not discuss outside the core group, of course. When I let him know I was in the country, he knew what I was up to. He also knew that you never negotiated by putting all your cards on the table. We should not forget that he was the founding commander of MK.

The core (the March 1990 committee) that would straddle the overt and underground levels of the organization never did function on a regular basis. The work pressure and demands on everybody, particularly on Madiba, were just too great. The period was so hectic that you hardly ever found time to discuss anything with anybody, let alone Madiba. This was becoming increasingly difficult even with Slovo, because his mind was elsewhere.

It did decide, however, that the new Organizing Committee would

---

*Mandela maintained a "plausible denial" relationship with the underground. While he did not want sensitive documents to be sent to him, he wanted to receive periodic briefings. Mac was to be able to see him whenever he wanted to. He even had a suggestion or two. "Sipho [Mandela] did feel that there was great potential in the OFS and indicated that he could ensure that Vula could get in touch with reliable [sic] [contacts] in the OFS with potential for being drawn into the u-g." Theo (Mac) to Norman (Alfred Nzo) and Kay (Joe Slovo) at []maharaj/vula comms/1990[]/April 20.

provide the best cover for building the underground. It was agreed that Ronnie and I would become members of that committee, which was set up by the NEC for the purpose of establishing ANC structures at the regional and local levels. The committee was chaired by Steve Tshwete.* We were able to juggle things so that it had a significant representation of key Vula personnel on board.† Traveling around the country on legal ANC business allowed us to canvass the underground.

Breaking with Joe

In May, I had a bitter discussion in Jo'burg with Joe Slovo over the Groote Schuur Minute. The evening the minute was signed I met with him. It was only then that I saw the text of the minute. I said, "Slovo, what did you do?" He said, "What do you mean?" I said, "There is not one word in this statement about the safety and security of your illegal cadres living in the country, the MK units that are here, the Vula people, or the other comrades from abroad who are here illegally. You should have inserted a clause committing the government not to arrest or prosecute those who are illegally within the country. You should have told De Klerk, without disclosing anything, 'You know we are committing ourselves to negotiations, and you know that the movement has people that it has infiltrated over the years living here illegally. I won't disclose how many or who they are, but I do want you to give an undertaking that their safety will be assured.' "

Slovo said to me, "I assumed that it was there." I said, "No, let's read it." So we read. He said it was implied. I said, "Bullshit. Show me where the implication is. De Klerk is not going to protect us by implication. Show me where you've put it."

The debate became personal and heated because I said to him, "Joe, you were in that delegation as the man who knows the army, MK, and the political underground. You know about this mission. You are in charge of this mission. You are its commander in chief. It was your job to advise our delegation and Madiba that we needed this phrase inserted, and you didn't do it. You forgot the comrades you were charged with protecting." We had a very, very bitter discussion.‡

---

*Tshwete was appointed to chair the Organizing Committee by the NEC. Tshwete was not in the know about Vula. Mac had concerns and would have preferred to see him replaced. But Sisulu vetoed the idea. He would not overrule the NEC. Theo (Mac) to Carl (Nyanda) 26 June 1990 []maharaj/vula comms/1990/[]June 26.

†Ismail Momoniat (Momo), Ronnie Kasrils, Ivan Pillay, and Siphiwe Nyanda (Gebuza).

‡Momo attests to a very bitter discussion having taken place between the two.

I said, "Did you raise the matter?" And he became very embarrassed, and I accused him. I said, "Things went to your head. All the caution you were warning against you forgot in practice. How do I then say that I can put the life of the underground cadres in your hands?"

With Groote Schuur, I lost confidence in Joe.[52] The way I saw it was that Vula was under the command of OR and Slovo, and with OR incapacitated and JS heading the SACP, I believed he was the proper person for me to raise my concerns with. After all, he knew all about Vula—about everything. I still believe I was right to raise it with him. Regrettably, it was acrimonious.

Operation Eagle: Tongaat

A month or two after the ANC had launched itself, appointing an interim internal leadership group to take charge of the ANC in the country, the Communist Party came to me and asked, "Will you set up an interim leadership corps of the legal Communist Party to operate openly?" And they sent a list of proposed names of people in the country.

I said, "Wrong way. The ANC had to do it in a hurry. Now learn from their mistakes. To select the people who should go into the leadership, let's have a conference in the underground and discuss this with twenty key Communists in the country. Let's discuss the strategy of how to legalize the party."

We called it Operation Eagle.[53] The meeting was at Tongaat, scheduled for 19 and 20 May 1990. I offered to smuggle Joe Slovo in to open the conference, but the Central Committee people in Lusaka told JS he couldn't go. Then I said, "Well, can we have a statement from him to read out to the meeting?" And I mentioned some of the points that should be in his opening statement.

A message came back; they were trying to get Jeremy Cronin (who was then on the CC in Lusaka) to go to South Africa. It was uncertain how they would organize his indemnity. He would deliver the statement. I said, "What happens if he doesn't come through? Where are we? Can you not transmit the text of the message? Because I haven't received a message from you to say when Jeremy will be arriving, or how he expects to make his way to a venue the whereabouts of which is unknown to him. How is he supposed to find where we are meeting? It's a clandestine meeting. So please, guys, in the meantime, send me the text so that when we open this conference, one of us can read out the statement from the secretary-general." "No, don't worry; Jeremy is coming." The night before the meeting was due to start, there was still no text and no Jeremy. We either had to proceed with the meeting or cancel it.

I was very pissed off with the party and with Joe. We had gone to extraordinary lengths to organize a clandestine conference within a whisker of the enemy's reach, and Lusaka had failed to send even a simple message from the secretary-general. In fairness to Joe, I should add that I later found out he had indeed drafted a message and left it to Jeremy to transmit, but there were some slipups, so Jeremy never got around to it.

So what was going through my head was: Are the chaps taking seriously the reemergence of the party? Because to me it was nothing for Lusaka to sit down and type the message into a computer and shoot it off to London, from where it would have been with us in an hour. But they were totally ignoring our problem. I wondered what they were worrying about. Oh, perhaps Jeremy has the text in his pocket and he's still busy trying to see if he can get a flight.

I went to Tongaat and checked the logistics, the venue and the security arrangements, the recording equipment we had brought. I went to Janet and asked: "Still no message from Lusaka, from the party?" I asked Janet to send an urgent message. No reply. This is the night before the conference, about ten or eleven o'clock. "Send a message. We have no word when Jeremy is arriving; we are opening tomorrow morning, and we've got to be over by Sunday." This was Friday night. "Can you send us the text of the message? Urgent." Silence. Twelve o'clock at night. We've reviewed everything; it's all in place except for the missing opening statement. After midnight, I said, "OK, Janet, sit down. Come on, chaps, let's draft the opening statement."

I wrote the opening remarks in the early hours of the morning. The central theme was "Please let's not clothe ourselves with a sense of infallibility." Even at the level of ideology, I said that the different religions, which Marx said were the opium of the people, had made enormous contributions to humankind's progress and were playing an important role in our own country. I said that we, as a party, must reflect and remember that there are good people committed to the ideals of socialism who are not in the party, who come from their own ideological and religious perceptions but believe in the equality of man. So that was my theme; it was tuned to the space I saw beginning to open, a space to reexamine socialism by a broad spectrum of forces and viewpoints not confined simply to those traditionally regarded as "the left."[54]

I had devised an agenda, together with the comrades in the country, saying, "Let's discuss where the country is sitting now; and let's discuss negotiations and cover all the possibilities of where they might go." And in that context I asked Gebuza to present a discussion paper expressing his view that a people's war could triumph, which he did using the nom de guerre Joe.[55]

I presented a paper that set out my vision for a new party. It called for the SACP to acknowledge that some party members and structures still carried some baggage from the past; and that the new SACP would have to eradicate all remaining vestiges of Stalinism and make a clean break with those limitations on inner democracy and accountability that underground life and the drawbacks of exile had imposed.[56]

In the end, the meeting gave full support to negotiations; it endorsed my vision for the party, decided that the party should legalize itself, and that in the process of legalizing, it should set up an interim leadership corps, which would be made up of people from outside and inside South Africa. It also decided that the party would be legally launched on the anniversary of its formation on 29 July 1990.

The full report of the conference ran to about three hundred pages. It was the first meeting in South Africa that was recorded and typed as people were speaking and transmitted to Lusaka. The whole of the verbatim report was in Lusaka's hands by that Sunday evening.

Breaking with the SACP

On Sunday, 20 May, Ronnie's and my names appeared in the *Sunday Times*. We had received indemnity. I was in Durban at the Tongaat meeting. We discussed the matter and decided that I needed to get to Jo'burg to get guidance from Madiba.

I rushed to Jo'burg, met Madiba, and he said Ronnie and I should leave the country, illegally, and then return legally before 16 June. There was going to be a special National Executive meeting. But Gebuza was not to leave the country, and the other Vula people would stay here. This certainly was not Madiba who was saying, "What are you doing? We're in negotiations and your operation is a danger to these negotiations."

Ronnie and I returned to South Africa on 15 June. Now we were legal. We began to plan for the launch of the party. Some comrades wondered if we'd fill the stadium—Jabulani Stadium accommodates about thirty thousand people. We said we'd fill it—not a problem. We would do the organizing work, but we had to have time—June and July would be enough. We'd liaise with the unions and everything. In the meantime, Joe Slovo and I attended a press conference called by the SACP on 20 June to announce that the party launch would be at a mass rally on 29 July.[57]

We had a clandestine meeting of the extended Politburo in Troyeville, Johannesburg, some days later. We were not sure whether a number of comrades who were in the Central Committee and/or the Politburo would come. Some of them had raised the issue with Joe: Was it wise that they be identified with the party? JS and Chris Hani had said, "What crap. What disadvantage is it to you? Just go to the townships and see how popular the party is." I said, "Well, we must think strategically. You can't say that comrades must be there if they're doing it reluctantly." So that was the atmosphere—a noise in the system.

But both Chris and JS were in town and, of course, I was, so that was a quorum for a Politburo meeting. But the feeling was that we should augment the meeting by inviting everyone who was in the Central Committee who was also in town, so that our decision would be as broadly based as possible. The only other person I can remember who was invited, though, was Ronnie.*

We ran through a list of names for the leadership. At Tongaat we had canvassed the delegates for names for the internal leadership, and Harry Gwala's name featured. I didn't object at the meeting because I was not going to raise my criticisms of him at such a broad gathering. The Politburo was well aware of my criticisms of Harry; both Chris and Joe already knew where I stood on this particular issue.†

So I said to them: "Chaps, we're discussing this matter in a disjointed way. We need to be clear what type of space the Communist Party intends to occupy in the public mind. We are into negotiations. Negotiations are going to be a murky business. In my view, there is a danger that we will be perceived by our support base as compromising our principles. For that reason, it is important that the Communist Party, which is very popular on the ground, should occupy a space asserting the morality of our struggle and projecting the need for principle. The ANC would welcome the party occupying that space because whenever the government tries to smear us and confuse things, we will be there as one of the custodians of the struggle, to remind the mass movements that ours is not just a political struggle but a moral one. We assert that morality as a part of the alliance."

I continued, "In the course of the conduct of the struggle from the un-

*Kasrils was not a member of the Politburo.
†See note 15.

derground, I have reported to you aspects of our struggle that are dangerous." I don't remember the exact words that I used. "One example of that danger is that a number of our people have slipped into practices where they cannot distinguish between what is a legitimate instrument and what is an unacceptable instrument in dealing with our own colleagues.

"The biggest worry, which I have reported to Lusaka repeatedly, is that one of our leaders, Harry Gwala, whom you want to be part of the new leadership, sanctioned behavior in Natal that is contrary to everything we profess to stand for. In one instance, I supplied you all with the name of a youth leader who disagreed with Harry, and Harry encouraged another youth faction to kill him. They killed a very good comrade in the pursuit of their internal squabbles.

"You know the record of the man; he is a stalwart Communist, but he has never in his life had that moral fiber that would enable him to distinguish between how you fight the enemy and how you fight your own colleagues. A failure to make this distinction is unacceptable when it leads to the killing of a good comrade. We have to stamp that out because otherwise we will be riding a tiger that is going to bite us. This is the space that the party needs to occupy."

Everybody said, "Yes, you're right," but I could see they were impatient with the argument. They didn't want to grapple with the issue. I said, "Now if that's the framework, then Gwala cannot be put in the interim leadership." Hani responded to me. He said, "Look, you're right, there are these problems, but Comrade Gwala is an influential person. We need to put him in the leadership, and we will have a commission of inquiry on his conduct."* I said, "I don't buy that. I've seen commissions of inquiry before. Under the pressure of events, we will be forced to fudge it. This is what the ANC will have to do, but the party does not have to do it. The ANC has to make sure that everybody is behind it in its negotiations, but we, as the Communist Party, need to assert a voice as part of the alliance that is a countervailing force to the carpetbaggers, like the Bantustans and their apartheid puppets, who will probably be part of the negotiations." Now don't misunderstand me: we wanted it that way, but we were under no illusions that they were not bloody crooks and had no real commitment to democracy.

---

*In March 1990, Gwala was hauled over the coals by both Nzo and Slovo in the presence of Sisulu, apparently for his continuing to operate in a way that threatened to expose Vula and Mac's presence. K to Theo (Slovo to Mac) [] majaraj/vula comms/1990/[] March 16, 1A.

I said, "We've got to get rid of all traces of sectarianism and Stalinism and become a party that does not claim infallibility." My ideas were evolving, and they were directed particularly at the negotiation framework. Within this framework, what image could the party put forward to create a countervailing tendency to what could be a perception that the struggle was now about horse-trading?

Ronnie Kasrils then said, "What are you saying? Are you saying that unless we do what you want, you are not prepared to serve in the Communist Party?" I said, "Why do you ask that question?" He said, "Because the position you are taking, Mac, is the position of a traitor. You are betraying the Communist Party." He used those actual words. I said, "Stop there. To call me a traitor for what I'm saying is such a serious thing that it cannot be left at that. You have now personalized the issue. I will not tolerate that from you." I wanted to fight it out with him—I was ready to kill him for what he had just said.[58]

The meeting tried to pacify me. I said Ronnie had questioned my integrity and called me a betrayer. He had not listened to what I had to say. I said, "It's not acceptable to me." JS and Chris tried to pacify me. They said, "Ronnie didn't mean it that way." And Ronnie said, "I didn't mean it that way."[59] I said, "The harm is done. But, OK, let's put it aside. You appoint Gwala to the interim leadership group, and that's the last you see of me in the Communist Party." Slovo said, "Mac, what does this mean? Does it mean that you will not help to organize the rally?" I said, "No, I will organize the rally. It has been announced that I'm organizing the rally, and I will do it with passion, but when you announce the interim leadership that includes Gwala, please exclude my name because that's it. It's good-bye after the rally."

JS then said, "Will you introduce the people to the crowd, the members of the interim leadership?" I said, "Why?" He said, "Most activists in the country know of you." I said, "OK, I will introduce them, including Gwala, but please understand that my name must be excluded, and that will be my last act for the Communist Party." He said, "Will you think it over?" I said, "There's no need to think it over, Joe. After the rally I will have gone into retirement."

In retrospect, I have no doubt that my anger with Joe, or in a sense with the SACP as personified by Joe, had been growing for some time: first it was Joe and the party's casual attitude toward Zarina's accident, then it was the Groote Schuur Minute, and now this. I was lancing a boil.

As it happened, the party never explained why I had left. On one occasion, after more media reports and another letter from me, Joe came to see me and said it was a very difficult situation for him to handle. I said, "Fine, we'll part."

I had no sense of loss, because I had lived through the period. I've read about what has happened in so many countries where revolutions have gone haywire. In my view, the socialist countries ended the way they did because the experiment became badly flawed very early into the revolution.

The SACP was not an anomaly in the sense that parties from the British colonies grew up with their contact in London, and parties in the French colonies grew up with their contact in Paris. The SACP, however, was driven into clandestine existence at a time when all over the colonies Communist parties were coming into existence legally. The SACP came from legality and was driven into illegality. It had to go through a change of mind-set.

In our case, comrades were going for training in the socialist countries and were coming back well disposed toward communism. So most trained members of MK were Communists.

I had been taught to believe that a revolutionary had to die with his or her boots on, that the revolution took precedence over everything. But I came to believe otherwise. How could I struggle for human rights for all our people and yet deny my own children the right to have their father present when they were growing up? Was I never to see them? Was I to be a stranger to them and they to me? Was I to have no part in helping to form the value systems they would live by as adults?

Of course I am unhappy that relations between JS and me ended the way they did. It is not made easier now that he is no more. We shared a lifetime together in the trenches. It shouldn't have ended that way. It leaves a taste in my mouth that I don't like.

History: First Meeting of NEC in South Africa Since 1963

The first meeting of the NEC in South Africa took place on 16 June 1990, a day after I had returned to South Africa as a legal person. That is when the proposal was made to establish an organizing committee. Steve Tshwete headed it, but the committee included Ronnie Kasrils and me so we had the space in which to continue our underground work while we also did legal work aboveground.

But when they elected me to the Organizing Committee, I said, "Chaps, I'll do this work for six months only because I intend retiring. I will help you out for six months; then I'm out." Madiba was there; I was signaling to him that he hadn't yet had that discussion with me about the issues I wanted to have addressed.

17. VULA UNRAVELS

Introduction

AFTER NYANDA WAS ARRESTED on 13 July 1990 and it became clear that other arrests would follow, Mac and Janet Love cleaned out the safe houses in Johannesburg and got their sleepers out of the country. When the SB swooped, they found only empty nests. Mac raced to Durban with Ronnie Kasrils and there, with the help of Claudia Manning, cleaned out the safe house in which Vula had stored arms, and again, when the SB swooped, it came up empty handed.

On 22 July, three days before his own arrest, he attended a meeting of the NEC at which Slovo proposed (with the approval of Mandela, who would not have been in a position to make the proposal himself because it would give grist to the still-smoldering suspicions that he might have cut some deal with the regime to secure his release) that the ANC call a unilateral, albeit temporary, cessation of the armed struggle. Thabo Mbeki, Slovo, Kasrils, and Mac drafted the resolution, which was adopted by the NEC. The ANC intended to spring its surprise move on the government at the meeting between the two sides scheduled for 6 August in Pretoria and thereby once more seize the moral high ground.

With his arrest on 25 July, Vula was over, although the underground continued to function under Ronnie Kasrils, who managed to escape arrest but taunted the authorities with appearances in public places and cheeky letters to the media, earning him the sobriquets Red Ronnie and the Red Pimpernel.[1]

In its haste to achieve a propaganda coup and reinforce its own belief that the government was being seduced into believing that the ANC was genuine about negotiations while the SACP was hell-bent on a power grab, the Security Branch (SB) used some of the unencrypted comms on the computer disks it had seized to conclude that Vula was a red plot involving a plan masterminded by Mac and Jacob Zuma to assassinate Mandela—the single spark that would ignite the forest fire[2]—then accuse the regime and mobilize the fury of the masses to overthrow the government and seize power.[3] The SB also found a copy of a paper presented at Tongaat, written by someone called Joe, which outlined a scenario for the overthrow of the government by force.[4] Senior SB officials met with the NIS and briefed De Klerk. The sensational revelations reinforced every suspicion whites harbored: the ANC was a front for the SACP, whose real agenda was the imposition of a revolutionary Communist state on South Africa. Negotiations were pretense.[5]

The media had a field day—revolution, assassination, cunning Communists who were about to hijack the peace process and wreak mayhem. De Klerk demanded that Mandela drop Slovo from the ANC's negotiating team that was preparing for a meeting with the government on 6 August in Pretoria. But the SB had in its haste to publicly expose the conspiracy threatening the state incorrectly identified "Joe" as Joe Slovo. Slovo easily rubbished the charge that he had written the paper advocating seizure of power by proving he had not been in the country at the time of the Tongaat conference (the paper was commissioned by Mac and Gebuza wrote it—it was for discussion purposes only and not policy).[6] The Tongaat conference passed no resolution calling for armed struggle.[7] De Klerk backed down. He and Mandela met and the difficulties were smoothed over. They had dealt with this first crisis with their commitment to a negotiated settlement reaffirmed.

On 6 August, the ANC and the government met again in Pretoria.[8] In the Pretoria Minute, the ANC agreed to a unilateral suspension of the armed struggle, "in the interests of moving as speedily as possible towards a negotiated political settlement." The government agreed to start releasing political prisoners on 1 September.[9] Both sides agreed that "the way is open to proceed towards negotiations on a new constitution." But relations between the two rapidly deteriorated. The government refused to renew indemnity for Mac, Kasrils, and Chris Hani,[10] halted the release of political prisoners,[11] the ANC accused De Klerk of acting in bad faith,[12] and the ANC hinted that it might have to resume the armed struggle.[13]

Inkatha, fearful that the government and the ANC might become bedfellows and sideline it, signaled to the government that it, too, was ready to enter into talks. Parties began to line up to claim their seats at the negotiating table.

But within weeks of the Pretoria Minute, deep distrust between the government and the ANC added further poison to the political well. With the explosion of so-called black-on-black violence in the Vaal Triangle in September, South Africa began to lose its political balance.[14] The ANC blamed the regime;[15] Inkatha, the PAC, and AZAPO blamed the ANC.[16] The ANC, they said, had a history of political intolerance.[17]

SADF troops were deployed on the Reef to curb intensified violence in the townships.[18] Self-defense units (SDUs) were formed by ANC supporters.[19] The ANC was immovably convinced that these outbreaks of violence were being orchestrated by the government as a calculated dual strategy: negotiate with the ANC on the one hand; undermine it with violence on the other;[20] use Inkatha as a surrogate, and sanction violence between Inkatha-supporting hostel dwellers, aided by the security forces and ANC-supporting township residents.[21] Unsure of how to respond and without a strategy to deal with the violence, the ANC leadership weighed options as disparate as having De Klerk visit the conflict areas and suspending talks until the government could demonstrate its commitment to ending the violence.[22] For its part, the government, especially after the exposure of Vula, believed the ANC was pursuing its own dual strategy: organizing a legal political party while maintaining an underground for a mass insurrection.[23]

The death toll for the year reached 3,500,[24] at least half in KZN. There were rumors of police giving weapons to vigilante groups.[25] The fighting between the ANC and Inkatha was ferocious. Fears of an outright civil war in the province increased.

The goodwill of the early months following Mandela's release was replaced by fear and finger pointing.[26] De Klerk accused the ANC of reneging on the Pretoria Minute and continuing to use violence to eliminate other political parties. But there was also a not-so-subtle underlying message to blacks and whites alike:[27] what they were witnessing was a harbinger of what might happen under black majority rule, an outcome that at the end of 1990 was absolutely unacceptable to the National Party government.

Once again, Mac, languishing in St. Aidan's hospital in Durban, was out of the loop.

Mac

THE UNRAVELING OF VULA began with the arrests of Mbuso Tshabalala and Charles Ndaba. The first inkling we had was when they were due the weekend of Saturday 8 July in Inanda township (outside Durban) but did not turn up. On Monday, Catherine Mvelase raised her concerns. On Monday evening I got a message in Jo'burg to say that Charles and Mbuso had not returned.[28] It seems they were arrested on 8 July 1990; both were killed. An *askari** traveling in a police vehicle had spotted Ndaba in a public place in Durban. He recognized him as a cadre he knew from MK camps outside the country, and he immediately arrested him. The story then becomes unclear.[29]

Now they had two of our chaps, and it would appear that through torture the SB acquired information about a particular safe house in Durban. They monitored the house and arrested a few more people on Monday, Tuesday, and Wednesday. At the time, Gebuza was traveling to one of the hideouts only known to him, Pravin Gordhan, Mpho Scott, and me. It was a flat that belonged to Schabir Shaik. Gebuza and I used to work from the flat. On his way there, the police arrested him. That meant they knew which car to watch for.

They took him to the C. R. Swart building, HQ of the Security Branch. He later told me he had been put into a straitjacket and tortured.[30] How they got information about the third house where Gebuza was storing the disks, I don't know. They certainly found some keys in Gebuza's possession, and one of those keys was for that house. They hit the house a few days later.

Anyway, on 13 July, I got a message saying Gebuza had been picked up; it was a Thursday. I went to Walter Sisulu and said, "Some members of the structures I am working with have been arrested. There is danger coming. Our intelligence tells us that this danger is real." Walter said, "Madiba is arriving on the eighteenth, the day of his birthday, from India and Malaysia. You had better be at the airport, and we will find an opportunity to pull him aside so that you brief him." At the airport there was a rush of people. Walter managed to tell Madiba that he must see me. Madiba told me to come home with him to Soweto, where his birthday party was just starting. Madiba saw me in the kitchen and said, "We will find a chance to talk. Just stick around."

At half past ten, his bodyguards came and told me the old man was exhausted. Could I be there at seven o'clock in the morning? So the next day I briefed him. He immediately picked up the phone and contacted Jacob Zuma. He told Zuma to arrange an urgent meeting between himself and

---

*Askari, Arabic for soldier, first entered English from Swahili in East Africa during the British colonial era, but in South Africa it was used for MK soldiers who changed loyalties and joined the South African security forces.

De Klerk. He would raise the matter with De Klerk without divulging identities.*

On 20 July, the NEC met to discuss the upcoming meeting with the government on 6 August. Slovo proposed that we should go there with a mandate from the NEC for the unilateral suspension of the armed struggle, which would give us the moral high ground in negotiations. We drafted the resolution and the NEC approved.

By 22 July, I had realized I was under twenty-four-hour surveillance. I gave the surveillance team the slip and went to Madiba again. I told him three members of the NEC were going to be detained, and I was one of them. I thought the other two could be Slovo and Kasrils—if the SB had information on us, they'd know Joe and Ronnie were involved.[31]

After the arrests started, I began to take measures to break our links so that the arrests didn't go beyond a certain point, and also so that the SB didn't find the arms we had hidden, but I was also aware that the SB was following me. I told Madiba it was going to be very difficult to give them the slip. What should we do? Should I get out of the country? I said there was a danger I'd get caught trying to escape. We decided it would be best if I stayed at my overt legal post, which was working at the ANC office on Sauer Street as part of the Organizing Committee.

Simultaneously I would do all I could to prevent further arrests, taking whatever precautions I could. Janet Love displayed sterling leadership and helped others clean out their places. Ronnie Kasrils and I drove down to Durban to clean out a hidden cache, and then I drove back to Jo'burg. I sent messages to Moe to tell others to disperse.

I said to Madiba, "I must make sure that if they come to arrest me, they do it in broad daylight, where there are witnesses, so that the news gets published. Once it gets published, the structures in Cape Town, Durban, and Jo'burg, which I can't reach, will realize that they must take cover." Madiba agreed.

That is, in fact, what happened. Nobody other than me got arrested. The Cape Town comrades immediately fled to the Transkei. Bantu Holomisa† was in power there, so they were safe.

---

*There is no record that Mandela had this meeting with De Klerk. See Mandela, p. 510, and De Klerk, pp. 200–201. De Klerk says he met with Mandela on 26 July 1990 to discuss the issue, the first reference he makes to a meeting between the two on this matter.
†General Bantu Holomisa was head of government in Transkei and was openly supportive of the ANC and an ally of Chris Hani's. Interviews at [] o'malley/interviewees/[].

Arrest

I was arrested on 25 July, five days after the NEC meeting. They had arrested me as I drove up to Valli Moosa's home, where I was staying. I had my briefcase with me, and in it was the Pretoria Minute—not the typed version, but the original, in my handwriting! So the surprise element the Minute should have had was now gone.[32]

I was interrogated at the Sandton Police Station, near Jo'burg, from 25 July to 6 August. I tried to smuggle messages out to say that the resolution was caught with me. The messages never reached anyone. When Elsabe Wessels, Valli's wife, forced her way into Sandton Police Station to deliver me a tracksuit, I thought, "Hmm, opportunity!" and I hid a note in my old clothes. But they didn't allow her to see me.

With me in custody, the SB thought they'd hit the jackpot. They said to me, "Now tell us about Vula." I said, "Look, it's straightforward. I am the commander. What do you want to know?" "Who's who? What have you all been doing?" I said, "That I'm not prepared to discuss." They said, "We're going to beat the hell out of you."

There were between twenty to thirty officers coming in and out of the interrogation room at Sandton. It was a fairly big room, with chairs all round three walls; I was seated on one of them. I observed the security men's conduct to see who was giving deference to whom. I isolated a chap wearing a gray suit who kept coming into the room, threatening me verbally and marching out. "I'm coming back later. If you haven't talked by then, you're going to deal with me." He would leave and the others would come to cajole and threaten.

When he walked in again later that night, I was ready. He started to threaten me, and I said, "Excuse me, can I see you alone?" He thought I was going to talk. He took me into a private office down the corridor, sat behind the desk, and said to me, "Sit down. Right, start talking." I said, "I take it you're a colonel." He said, "Yes." Now he's thinking I'm only prepared to talk to a senior officer, that this is going to be a coup for him.

I said, "I asked to see you because your conduct is an incitement to your juniors to assault and torture me. My arrest comes at a very sensitive time. Your political bosses may well have to sacrifice you in favor of the talks. You know my rank; you know I am the commander of Operation Vula; you know I'm a member of the National Executive of the ANC. I think you ought to be very careful because if your junior officers mistreat me and this becomes a hot potato for your government, they will repudiate you and the buck will stop with you. They will put the blame on you.

I've asked to see you alone so that I can raise this with you away from the rest of your men."

He didn't know how to respond. He just shut up and escorted me back to the interrogation room. All the officers in the room who had seen us go out watched us with expectation. They were trying to work out what had transpired between us. I sat down, and the colonel left and never came back.

That night I kept demanding to see General Basie Smit, head of the security police. He arrived about seven the following morning. I'd been up all night under interrogation, and when Smit met me, I said, "You found that resolution. You'd better be careful how you handle this problem." Smit protested, "No, no, I'm police; I'm investigating a crime." I pretended to believe him. In fact, we both knew the real score.

I was interrogated that whole night, the whole of the following day and night, until finally I was taken to John Vorster Square, where I got my first sleep in three days. We now followed a routine. I was held in John Vorster but taken to Sandton every day for interrogation.

My first sense that something was brewing on the outside was when I saw the headline DE KLERK DEMANDS SLOVO BE DROPPED[33] on news posters as I was driven in the police van from Sandton to John Vorster. What had happened was that among the disks found by the SB were some left unencrypted, and one of them related to the meeting at Tongaat to discuss the relaunching of the SACP in South Africa.

When the SB read the minutes of that meeting, they zeroed in on Gebuza's paper evaluating the prospects of an armed uprising succeeding in South Africa, which he had written and presented under the pseudonym Joe. The regime thought this meant Slovo. It claimed this was the authoritative position of the meeting, that Joe Slovo was still advocating the overthrow of the government by force. De Klerk demanded that Madiba drop Slovo from the delegation to the Pretoria meeting scheduled for 6 August.

Mandela called Slovo and told him what they were saying. Joe said, "I wasn't even in the country." He showed Mandela his passport, which confirmed his statement. Mandela took this evidence to De Klerk and told him, "I will not drop Joe Slovo from my delegation. Here is the proof that you were wrong to say he was at Tongaat, and besides, you're not going to dictate who is going to be in my delegation."[34]

Madiba and his delegation were getting ready for Pretoria. They had a mandate for the suspension of the armed struggle. They were not aware that the mandate was known to the other side. De Klerk tried to sidetrack

them with the demand that they remove the Communists from the delegation, the Vula people because they were subverting negotiations.

Subsequently that became the prevailing myth: that Vula was nothing
more than a disgruntled group of hard-line militants plotting to sabotage
negotiations and overthrow the government. The fact that the NEC failed
to act decisively in acknowledging what Vula was can be forgiven; it was
not in the know, and events were moving rapidly. But Slovo was our commander in chief, and it was his duty to clarify the picture both in the NEC
of the ANC and the Central Committee of the SACP.

At John Vorster, they took me to the office of the commanding officer.
And who was it? The colonel from Sandton. I said, "Good afternoon,
Colonel." He just didn't know how to handle it! I never could remember
his name.

In the meantime, Madiba was demanding to see me, but they held him
off until after the Pretoria meeting ended in the early hours of 7 August.
Madiba came directly from Pretoria to the Sandton Police Station. I was
under interrogation when he arrived. Suddenly they called me from that
room and took me to another. Madiba and General Basie Smit were there,
and one or two other SB officers.

Madiba and I embraced and when we sat down, General Smit got up to
leave the room. He said, "I'll leave you two together." Madiba said, "No, no,
no, I want you to sit here." Smit sat and Madiba expressed his concerns
with the way I was being treated. I was preoccupied with what I wanted to
tell him about the resolution, and there was Basie Smit sitting next to us! I
simply said, "Madiba, they found that NEC resolution on me."

To him that was in the past because the Pretoria meeting had already
taken place. His mind was trained on safeguarding me and my comrades
who were in detention.

I told him, "The first night was rough; they attempted to assault me.
They have continued to threaten to assault me. They haven't yet, but they
are threatening me." Sleep, blankets, food—I went through the lot. Madiba
turned to Smit: "General, these conditions are not acceptable. You'd better
treat him properly. Decent food and no torture, no assaults." Smit said,
"Yes, yes, yes." Madiba said, "For the rest, Neef, we're handling the problems, don't worry."

When Madiba left, I was taken back to the interrogation room; the interrogators were still there. After Basie Smit saw Madiba off, he came into
the interrogation room and said, "Forget about any idea that you are here
on holiday or living in a hotel. It is clear to us that you have agents in my

security forces." I immediately knew they had somehow been able to access our comms. But how?

Smit said, "Whatever happens, there is no way I am going to stop this interrogation or modify it until you give us the names of our agents who are working for you. That you must tell me." I said, "There is no way you're getting anything from me." He said, 'I will give you the name of a member of your National Executive who is working for a foreign intelligence service, and you will give me the names of the agents in my ranks who are working for you." I said, "Don't come with that foreign agent story to me. Whoever it is, it's a nonissue; there's no trade-off. You release me and then we can talk. As a detainee, no trade." He said, "I'm not releasing you. I want that information, and we won't stop interrogating you until we get it." He walked out.

But just before he left, he turned to me and said out of the blue, "You're going to see violence hit this country that will make all previous violence look like a picnic." It worried the hell out of me. What were they up to? I couldn't work out what he was getting at. It was only when I was brought to trial that I put two and two together. When the train and hostel violence flared up to unprecedented heights in late August, and the regime described it as black-on-black violence, I understood that Basie Smit's statement meant that the security forces were involved.

I didn't know anything had been decrypted at this point. During their interrogations they kept feeding me with information to suggest that they knew everything. I thought perhaps they'd found the minutes of the Tongaat meeting because certainly I had left an unencrypted version with Jeremy Cronin. I didn't know who else they had picked up, but I knew that Gebuza had been. I didn't know who was talking, but I knew from the questions they were putting to me that they were really saying, "The game's up; we know everything you've been doing." They knew we had moles in the police. It was no longer important how they got it; the most important thing was what did they know?[35]

Assault

The first time they actually assaulted me was later on the morning of the seventh, after Madiba had visited me. The officer was Gideon Nieuwoudt,*

---

*Nieuwoudt was denied amnesty in connection with the Motherwell killings, called a congenital liar by the TRC, reapplied for amnesty, and was denied. He died from cancer in 2005 before prosecution.

a warrant officer. He slammed me against the wall, and I said to him, "Be careful what you are doing." In walked in a colonel who had been supervising the whole thing, one Frik Venter. He was wearing a camouflage jacket, and he was a huge guy. He stuck his face into my face, slammed me against the wall, and clouted me. I immediately said, "Colonel, I promise you, hit me once more, and I will kick you in the balls." This is in the presence of two of his juniors! He backed off. My reading was that they had been told to be careful.

I didn't know at that point that FW had backtracked on his demand that Madiba drop JS from the ANC delegation for the August 6 meeting, but the SB knew that. So there was an edginess now in how they handled me.

After they assaulted me, I raised the matter with senior officers and with the magistrate who visited me at John Vorster Square. I said, "Please go and check with General Erasmus." Erasmus was then commissioner of police in the Witwatersrand. "Check whether torture broke me in 1964. Go and ask the general whether this little bit of slapping and punching me around and threatening me will work. He and his whole team, with their license to torture, did not get me to talk. Do you think you are going to succeed?"

A few days later, when they threatened to assault me again, I said, "Have you been to the general? Have you asked him?" Of course I didn't know whether they had, but they said, "Yes, we have contacted him." I said, "Well, didn't he tell you that these threats are not going to work?" No answer.

But they made sure I understood that they had a lot of information. "You rented fourteen houses and flats," they said. "We know that nine are in Durban, and five are in Johannesburg. You brought weapons into the country, some as late as June." They took me to Berea and pointed out a flat, saying, "We know this is a place you used for certain meetings." I kept quiet. They took me to the Parkhurst house and said, "This is a house where you built a basement hiding place to cache arms." Now these two places were known to a very limited number of people: Gebuza, Janet, Momo, and me. But I knew Janet had escaped, and Momo had gone underground.

In a Blink: Yusuf Mohammed

During my stay at John Vorster, a black policeman I'd chatted up told me there was an Indian detainee there who was "in a bad way." I asked his name: it was Yusuf Mohammed. The policeman said he was "going off his head." I prevailed upon the policeman to let me see him, and one day he opened my cell and said, "He's in the bathroom. Go quickly and see him and then get out. I'll cover for you." I went to this huge bathroom. Yusuf was alone there. We had a quick chat; I tried to calm him. I said I'd take the rap and cover for him. He was shaking, but he was in control.

I bolstered his morale, and then I said, knowing he was a pharmacist, "Listen, how can I simulate a medical condition?" He said I could fake madness. "All you have to do is keep blinking your eyes rapidly for a long enough period. It will disorientate you, and you will not be able to walk steadily. You will even collapse." I said, "Fantastic!" The policeman was calling me, and I raced back to my cell. I thought this idea of blinking was an interesting gimmick. I'd keep it in reserve.

I was taken to Durban. When we set out, I had no idea where we were going. They had removed the number plates of the Kombi in my presence and put on false ones. I joked, "So, you're putting on false number plates." They said, "Well, we do what you do." I said, "But you don't need to do that; you control the state." They said, "We know you guys; we're not taking chances. You have been collecting information about our cars."

I wondered if they were doing this to scare me. We were on the road going past Witbank and Frik Venter asked me, "Do you know where you're going?" "No, I don't." "Do you know Piet Retief?" "I've heard of it." He said, "Well, I am sure you know that people who go to Piet Retief never come back alive." I asked myself if they were trying to build fear in me to make me crack up.

Piet Retief is a town near the Swaziland border. The security forces there made forays into Swaziland and intercepted people crossing in and out. Many of our cadres were taken to Piet Retief and brutally tortured there. At least one was killed. The SB in Piet Retief was known to act in a completely lawless way.

I thought, "Shit! They're taking me to Piet Retief, out of the way, to torture the hell out of me. Mac, it's time to start the blinking." So I started to blink. I blinked and blinked, but nothing happened.

We got to Piet Retief. Although nothing had happened, all that blinking had kept me from thinking, from being afraid. When they locked me up in Piet Retief, I sat there saying to myself, "Yusuf gave me a stupid, useless trick." Then I realized that the trick could only work for binocular vision because it creates a dysfunction in the images, and I've only got one fucking eye! I still joke when I meet Yusuf; I say, "Yusuf, you knew I only had one eye! Why did you give me this trick?"

The next day we drove on to Durban. On the way they stopped at the point at which Gebuza and I crossed into South Africa in 1988. They knew the exact spot. Only one person could have told them that: Gebuza.

Durban

I was put into Bellair Police Station in Durban and taken to C. R. Swart for interrogation. I now realized, from the questions they were throwing at me, that the SB had found unencrypted disks at our workplace. They quoted from our reports. When we came up for trial and I looked at the state evidence, it was clear they had found reams of material.

In Durban I was in full control. Within a week, I was in the hospital. I focused on two things: How do I avoid interrogation, and what do I do about the possibilities of escape? The first thing was to get to a doctor. I kept telling the SB I needed to see a doctor. I told them, "My neck is killing me. You know, Frik Venter assaulted me in Sandton, and my neck is in a terrible state. It was injured in 1964."

The office of the district surgeon was downstairs, in the Bellair building, and they made the mistake of taking me there. They sent two very young policemen to accompany me, and that was it. By five o'clock that afternoon I was in hospital. The district surgeon turned out to be an Indian chap called Vawda. When I walked into his room, one of the police officers walked in with me and the other stayed in the waiting room. I said to Vawda, "Doctor, I don't think it's acceptable that a police officer should be standing here while you examine me." He took that in his stride: "Yes. Officer, would you mind waiting in the waiting room?"

When I told the doctor the history of my neck injuries, he said, "I need to get a top orthopedic surgeon to examine you." He phoned a Dr. Naidoo and made an appointment. Immediately it was the talk of the entire building that Mac Maharaj was coming to see the doctor. As luck would have it, Pravin's wife, Vanitha, was working in the X-ray Department, and she immediately rushed up when I arrived. Pravin was in detention; he was a pharmacist and known in the medical fraternity.

Dr. Naidoo came to examine me. I said, "Should you examine me in the presence of a guard?" He did an unusual thing. Instead of telling the guard to leave, he said, "No, I don't mind his being present because you're a detainee, and I want to deal with you in a very open way." Pravin's wife had already sneaked in and told the doctor, "Whatever happens, you must put him in the hospital." So when he said he preferred the security policeman to be there, I knew that he understood and I was going to the hospital.

The doctor told the guard he thought I should be in a private ward. "You'll be able to guard him better." The policeman could only mumble yes.

I was taken back to C. R. Swart, and Venter was furious. He said, "I'm taking you to Pretoria and hospitalizing you in the prison hospital." I said, "Right. You take responsibility. The specialist says I must be put in the hospital immediately. If anything happens while you are transporting me, you'll take personal responsibility. I'll sue the pants off you."

Venter realized he'd lost control. He couldn't drive me the eight hours back to Pretoria. Times had changed.

Hospital: Sitting It Out

I arrived at St. Aidan's Hospital at about five o'clock. All the staff knew as soon as I got there. I was put in my room with two officers guarding me. At about eight o'clock that night, the nurses came and whispered to me that Billy Nair, who had had a heart attack and had surgery, was in intensive care. A little later, at about ten o'clock, another nurse came and said she'd take me to visit Billy. They said, "Just ask for a bit of exercise. As a patient, we believe you need exercise for your treatment." I said, "Sure." The officer said to the nurse that I couldn't walk outside. She said, "No, no, we'll walk in the corridors and through the wards." The poor guy didn't know what to do.

Next thing, I was in intensive care. The nurse said, "By the way, that's Billy Nair." I walked over and hugged him. The guard said, "You're not supposed to talk to him." I said, "Piss off, man, he's had a heart attack." The nurse said to him, "This man has had a heart attack, and they know each other. Let him help to boost Mr. Nair's morale." So I sat talking to Billy, just chatting.

Madiba Visits

Madiba visited me for the second time, on 14 October, at St. Aidan's Hospital. It created quite a stir. He told me he was fed up with the way the government was handling my detention. When he had gone abroad, he had left Walter to deal with the minister of police and law and order, Adriaan Vlok. Vlok had indicated that by 17 September they would either release me or charge me, but Madiba returned to find they had done nothing.

He said to me in the hospital ward that he thought the time had arrived to mount a campaign for my release. But he cautioned me that there were members of the leadership who were divided on this matter. Some felt he was giving my detention too much attention and that he should concentrate on the talks. But he felt he should pursue both.

My answer to him was "You have to assess what's the best thing to do politically. I'm sitting here in hospital having a right royal time. I'm under no pressure. I can sit it out for as long as you want. Do what you need to do to push negotiations."

In detention, and particularly in the hospital, I was getting information through doctors, my physiotherapist, and the nurses, and I was allowed visits. I could even phone my wife in Brighton from public call boxes in the hospital precinct, with the collaboration of the nursing staff. I knew there was divided opinion inside the ANC about my detention. I could have escaped, but I felt that this would jeopardize the chances of other detainees who might need hospitalization. I sent messages to Slovo but received no reply.

At St. Aidan's I had relative freedom, and I felt I was performing a useful role in the hospital because Billy was there, and Anesh Sankar, who had also been detained, was in another ward, also receiving medical attention. I was able to see both of these guys. I was able to strengthen their resolve not to talk under any further interrogation. The nurses kept me supplied with newspapers, so I was able to keep abreast of what was going on. I was comfortable.

Gebuza

The first time I had an opportunity to talk with Gebuza after our arrest came later, when we shared a cell as awaiting-trial prisoners. He acknowledged that he had left the disks at one of his safe houses, with Susan Tshabalala, who was working as his secretary. The disks, unencrypted, were in her possession when she was arrested. I asked why the disks had been left unencrypted. He had no explanation.

It seems that after I left, Gebuza thought it necessary to read the reports I had sent to Lusaka to bring himself up to speed. He didn't bother to reencrypt them—carelessness, laziness, or sheer overconfidence. It was a severe breach of discipline. But this was not an issue for us to discuss or for me to reprimand him for while we were standing trial.

Did Gebuza cooperate with the SB? It's a tough question. Our own experience of torture had taught us not to be judgmental of comrades who talked under torture. I did not raise the matter then, but I had come to certain conclusions. I believe it was a shock to his system when he was arrested.

His mind-set was that Mac and Ronnie had gotten indemnity, so with all these documents in the possession of the police, what could be the harm in mentioning that Mac and Ronnie were in the country? He thought he would get indemnity too. I don't know when he was interrogated. They might have told him they had arrested me long before they actually did because that's a technique of interrogation. They knew I was in the country, so they said, "Well, we've arrested him." So Gebuza believed they'd arrested me. He may have thought that protected him because they could not deal with him differently from the way they had dealt with me, and to deal with me they had to confront the issue of my indemnity. As it happened, they paid no regard to the indemnity. They made an assessment and decided to arrest me. And during my interrogation they told me that Gebuza was "like a sieve"—again an interrogation technique, but the SB did know about things, such as that in the Parkhurst house there was a basement under the bed. Only Gebuza, Janet, and I knew that, and Janet was never arrested.

They probably extracted Gebuza's cooperation in dribs and drabs as they confronted him with more and more information they already had. He therefore chose a particular way of responding. It's not unknown in a detention situation that when you cooperate on one thing that looks very innocent, it lays the basis in your mind for cooperation on another thing that also looks innocent, until at the end you are beginning to talk and talk and talk and cannot stop yourself, because you have so compromised yourself by talking that it's too late to draw the line. I wouldn't be surprised if that happened. I'll leave it an open question.

I readily acknowledged that I was the overall commander of Operation Vula, but beyond that admission I would not divulge anything of a secret nature. I claimed for myself the status of an officer who is a prisoner of war. So when they threw all sorts of information at me, including claims that Gebuza was talking, I remained unfazed: I was neither going to confirm nor deny anything. As a prisoner of war, they had no right to any information from me. For the rest, I kept looking for ways to evade interrogation either by escaping or, as happened, getting into the hospital.

By the time of the Vula trial, it was irrelevant whether Gebuza had talked. But later on when Madiba placed Gebuza in charge of the self-defense units (SDUs), I went to Madiba and said, "Haven't you made a mistake in whom you've appointed to take charge of the SDUs?" But he turned the tables on me. He said, "I know what you're going to say. You're going to say I have appointed some people who are weak. Don't raise that question, Mac, because you've already retired. I would have put you in charge but you were not there, so don't you come and question me about whether I've made the wrong choice." By the time I came out of jail, the six months I had given myself till retirement had passed.

Gebuza and I lived close together: three years in the underground, two of them in the country. Now I hardly even meet him socially. I don't go to his home; he doesn't come to my home. Now and again, at official functions, we meet, shake hands, laugh. I will give him support in the work he's doing if he asks me for help, but you can't say it is a friendship. Since his retirement we have begun to meet socially and there is always a warmth between us.

18. VULA ON TRIAL

Introduction

ANXIOUS TO KEEP the fledgling peace process on course, both the ANC and the South African government sought to downplay Vula after De Klerk had to back down on the question of Joe Slovo's inclusion in the ANC delegation that negotiated the Pretoria Minute. De Klerk and Mandela met, and Mandela obviously believed that the matter would soon be resolved expeditiously and the prisoners released. After reluctantly acknowledging that Vula was an ANC operation, the ANC virtually distanced itself from the arrestees.* The State Security Council (SSC), with De Klerk in attendance, met and decided that Michael Imber, the Natal attorney general, should charge Gebuza only with possession of firearms,† much to the chagrin of the SB, which believed that they had an ironclad case for charging him with treason based on the reams of Vula comms they had printed and

---

*Although the ANC decried the government's allegations that Vula was a Communist plot to overthrow the government, and there were scattered references in the media in which some ANC leaders alluded to Vula's having been authorized by Oliver Tambo sometime in the latter part of the 1980s, the ANC did not explicitly acknowledge Vula and take full responsibility for its actions or explain the circumstances in which it had been conceived and the internal chain of command until the Vula trials were about to start. Then Alfred Nzo issued a special circular to all "regions, branches, and other fraternal organizations" which provided the rank-and-file membership with a full briefing on the background to Vula. ("ANC Brief on Operation Vula," *Natal Witness,* 8 November 1990.) At this point the ANC was arguing that the prosecution was in contravention of an agreement reached between the ANC and De Klerk that political members implicated in acts committed before 8 October 1990 would be indemnified from prosecution. The only statement on the ANC's Web site concerning Vula during this period is the text of Mandela's statement on 22 June 1991. (See [] maharaj/vula other/Mandela statement on 22 June 1991 on Vula.)

†Interview with Peter Blomkamp, the state prosecutor assigned the case by Imber. Blomkamp accompanied Imber and Kobie Coetsee to the Union Buildings where the

deciphered and the materials they had uncovered. In the car that Nyanda (Gebuza) was driving when he was arrested they found a hidden compartment with the 45 Thompson submachine gun, N3A1 45 caliber, with one optical night sight and one silencer for the weapon and rifle ammunition, leading the SB to the conclusion, when they read the comms, that Mac was planning the assassination of Mandela.[*1] There is little doubt that Nyanda made the SB's case easier to construct and that he helped his interrogator, Christo Davidson, to decipher the comms and make sense of many.[†2] When he was informed that he would be charged only with possession of firearms, he was, says Davidson, disappointed, somehow diminished that given the range of his activities, the state should choose to charge him with such a lowly felony.[3]

When he was brought to court on 22 August 1990 to be charged, he sought bail, which opened him to wide-ranging questioning once he opted to enter the witness box on his own behalf. Peter Blomkamp, the state prosecutor, used the occasion to pepper Gebuza with questions drawn directly from the contents of the comms he had helped Davidson decipher.

SSC meeting took place. Blomkamp recalls being introduced to De Klerk before De Klerk went into the meeting. De Klerk was out of cigarettes and asked Blomkamp whether he had any. For reasons unstated, Blomkamp knew that De Klerk smoked John Rolfe. He smoked Paul Revere, which De Klerk accepted thankfully. Go to[] maharaj/interviewees/[] Blomkamp. Blomkamp's account of the SSC meeting was confirmed by General Johan van der Merwe, then commissioner of police.

*De Klerk met with Mandela on 26 July and "confronted him with some of the evidence that the security forces had acquired. . . . He seemed to be genuinely surprised by these revelations." De Klerk, 200–201. But certainly he was being a little disingenuous when he says in his autobiography that when "de Klerk . . . read me from documents he claimed to have been confiscated in the raid [,] I was taken aback because I knew nothing about it." And certainly when Slovo told him that "Vula was a moribund operation," Slovo, too, was being egregiously disingenuous. Mandela, *Long Walk to Freedom,* 510. Left out of both autobiographies are the machinations, especially on the government side, to rid itself of Vula, but a determined bureaucracy had other agendas.

†Janet Love, who frequently chastised Nyanda for his carelessness in not reencrypting, provides a sympathetic insight into the considerations a prisoner tries to balance when he gives information to the enemy, knowing that the enemy already possesses it or can have it confirmed by others. Decisions on what to respond to an interrogation should be governed by one criterion: Does the information you provide endanger a colleague or compromise the operation? []maharaj/interviewees/2005/[]Janet Love. Using this criterion, Nyanda walked a thin line. [] See also interview with Ivan Pillay/[]maharaj/interviewees/ 2002/December 11; Janet Love [] maharaj/interviewees/2002[] February 28b & March 15;/ 2004/May 15 maharaj/interviewees, and interviews with Mac on 9 October 2000, 10 September 2001, 12 March 2002, 26 September 2003, 28 May 2004, and 17 and 18 June 2004.

Gebuza admitted to everything: multiple disguises, trafficking in arms, providing military training, and planning to overthrow the government.[4] The media had the proverbial field day.[5] Reports of the scale of operations Vula had encompassed raised a ruckus among whites and mobilized the right wing, so the government changed course, now instructing prosecutors to throw the book at the lot of them.[6]

2

Eight Vula detainees appeared on 29 October 1990 in the Durban Regional Court to attend their bail hearing. They were charged with terrorism in terms of Section 54 of the Internal Security Act. On 8 November, the state offered no opposition to bail, and suggested the trial be postponed until January 1991 in order to give the accused the opportunity to apply for indemnity. For Mac, bail was set at eighty thousand rand; for Gebuza, sixty thousand; Pravin Gordhan, forty thousand; Raymond Lala, Catherine Mvelase, and Susan Tshabalala, thirty thousand; for Dipak Patel, twenty thousand; and for Anesh Sankar, five thousand. No one from the ANC was there to pay the bails. The movement had disassociated itself from those now tarred as deviants caught trying to orchestrate a "red" revolution aimed at seizing power and scuppering negotiations.

They were taken back to Westville to wait. The days wore on. Humiliation grew. Their friends frantically ran around Durban, calling on people they knew in an effort to cobble together the needed R295,000. They made it with ten minutes to spare before the court office closed. The Vula Eight were free after almost five months of incarceration, during which they had access to no one, some were subjected to sustained brutality, and all of them assaulted in some way. They went their separate ways. Vula might well have been something they had imagined. Except for a lingering doubt: Had one of their leaders broken down, made the state's case for the state, acted in a way that in another time would have been construed as turning state witness? But if any harbored doubt, each decided for his own personal reasons to keep it to himself. The ANC itself had all but turned its back on them: while not disowning them outright, the movement's silence conveyed its own message. But they kept their counsel. They all were, after all, loyal and disciplined members of the ANC.

3

Vula had no paper trail in the ANC files; although a vague authority had been given to Tambo to undertake an operation somewhat similar in nature to Vula, there was no subsequent feedback to suggest that any action had followed. Perhaps the leadership's collective memory had forgotten that the NEC had given Tambo a blank check in matters pertaining to the return of senior ANC members, including some of their own, to South Africa.

The ANC's hesitancy in being more forthright about Vula helped to form the impression that it was divided between negotiators and an SACP faction plotting to overthrow the government.[7]

Mac is a realist. He accepted that whatever public comments the ANC made in the matter were the result of due consideration and in the best interests of the movement. But when he learned that many of the same comrades decried Vula in private conversations with the media and in meetings of the NEC, he considered it tantamount to betrayal. Comrades don't disown other comrades in a time of war. In time, he let the NEC know precisely what he thought of some members.[8]

Ironically, Mac's creation of a "legend" that, he believed, would deceive the enemy only if it deceived the NEC as well succeeded far too brilliantly. The NEC was in the dark about the scope and range of Vula operations. There was no Tambo to explain. Nevertheless, Slovo was fully in the know, and Nzo had a lesser grasp but, unlike Tambo, had no investment in Vula's success. Mandela knew, and other members of the SACP Politburo—Chris Hani and Thabo Mbeki—were at least aware of Vula and Jacob Zuma was privy to some details.

Some members of the NEC with no connection to, association with, or understanding of Vula saw it as an obstacle to negotiations. Some were also furious that it should come to light less than two weeks before the Pretoria meeting. They acted, collectively, in a way that sought to rationalize their ignorance of what had been going on in the top echelons of the ANC. Hence the leaks about maverick operations.

4

The ANC's dual strategy at the time was known only to a few, and in the early months of 1990 the ANC was caught off guard. Without Tambo, upon whose presence the ANC in exile had become dependent to resolve its inner tensions, a lame-duck ANC leadership faltered. The underground was unprepared for unbanning, and for Vula operatives in particular what they assumed would be a blanket indemnity altered the psychological terrain of struggle. What only days before was a matter of life and death suddenly appeared to be only a matter of life.

When Vula was uncovered, the core committee members (Mandela, Mbeki, Nzo, Slovo, Sisulu, and Mac) were in the process of defining their new mandate. Vula was exposed at precisely the wrong moment: just before the crucial Pretoria meeting. The media jumped on the first reports of the Tongaat meeting with insinuations of a "red plot" to seize power, and that designation of Vula stuck. When the Vula trial got under way almost six months later, the government still stuck to the original script: Vula was a red plot aimed at the seizure of power through revolutionary means.[9] For the government, the discovery of Vula was a propaganda coup, which it used to put the ANC on the defensive; for the ANC, it could have been a disaster. Had De Klerk not thrown it a life jacket when he aggressively demanded that Mandela remove Slovo from the ANC delegation that was scheduled to meet the government in Pretoria, only to have to back down, appearing to have been foolishly informed and thus allowing the ANC to go back on the offensive, the ANC would have found itself in uncharted waters.

In part, the blame for this rests with the ANC itself. It did not robustly acknowledge Vula as an ANC operation. There was no emergency meeting of the NEC at which all members could be apprised of its origins.[10] Piecemeal accounts contributed to rumor and misinformation. The ANC's chief representative in the UK, Mendi Msimang, went on British television to state that Vula was not an ANC operation.[11] Slovo, publicly implicated in Vula, was silent. Priorities had shifted.

Mac

WE WERE BROUGHT to court on 29 October 1990. There were eight of us:* Catherine Mvelase, Susan Tshabalala, Pravin Gordhan, Dipak Patel, Gebuza, Anesh Sankar, Raymond Lala, and myself. The charge was terrorism, contravention of Section 54 of the Internal Security Act.

Various things were occupying my mind. How would we collectively defend ourselves and handle the defense, and how would we get bail? Who were our lawyers going to be? But there was great relief: we were out of

---

*Billy Nair, still recuperating from his heart attack, was at St. Aidan's.

detention, and we were going to deal with the matter politically. We were not going to say we were sorry for what we had done, nor were we going to expose the treatment we had been subjected to (once we had been brought together, we could hear how others had been tortured).

When we got to the courtroom, there was not one single member of the National Executive or the Central Committee there, not one. We'd been in detention for six months. This was the first day the eight of us were appearing in court. In spite of their many activities, the secretary-general of the party, the secretary-general of the ANC, and the general secretary of COSATU could have been mobilized to be at the courtroom so that when these comrades came out of the basement and walked to the dock, there were key people sitting in that audience. But there was nobody there. We were remanded until 8 November.

Zak Yacoob was our advocate. In a surprise move, the state withdrew its opposition to bail, and we were released. The total bail for the eight of us came to almost three hundred thousand rand. The court granted the bail before lunch. Yunus Mohammed and Zak Yacoob came and told us, "Chaps, we are pleading with the police to keep you here in the court cells because we've got to go and raise the money. Jo'burg promised us, but it's not here, so we've got to find the money, and you cannot be released until we find it. We are pleading with the court officials, and we are now going to go to individuals to chip in money."

We were taken back to Westville Prison and had to wait. Finally, at about five o'clock that afternoon, Yunus and Zak reappeared. They had raised the bail from different people in Durban, ten thousand rand here, twenty thousand there, and so on.

We appeared the following week, and the case was remanded again. We appeared again. Now some comrades began to ask, "Where's the leadership? Why don't they attend?" It was an event that should have galvanized people. I heard that the Working Committee had instructed at least some members of the National Executive to find time to be at the trial. At a later court appearance, I saw John Nkadimeng and one or two others. But no Slovo, no Nzo, no Jay Naidoo from COSATU. I thought, "Oh, they're having a problem explaining Vula." But it preyed on my mind.

The case was remanded several times. The trial proper started in January 1991, was adjourned until March, and then suddenly, on 25 March, Blomkamp, the prosecutor, got up and announced that President F. W. de Klerk had indemnified the entire group, and that was the end of the case.

Pointing Fingers

I had heard who in the ANC leadership was saying Vula was not an ANC operation, that it was a maverick operation. They were saying, "Don't bother about Mac; let him face the music." They said this to journalists and others. What annoyed me was that some of those who were in the know about Vula, including Politburo members such as Thabo Mbeki, Jacob Zuma, and Joe Slovo, were not doing anything to refute this talk.* Yes, I was angry. I understood why the ANC would want to play down Vula in the run-up to negotiations, but I could also see how Vula could be used to our advantage. Disowning us, when we had acted on the direct order of OR as mandated by the NEC, was something else altogether. That would have appalled OR. That should have appalled Slovo. Only Chris Hani publicly defended us.

I had lived through the sixties; I had seen how people stood by their own. You dealt with uncomfortable developments by explaining them to the masses and standing your ground. Madiba was standing his ground in defense of me, and so was Walter Sisulu. To be fair to JS, I did believe he was at least vocal in his support within the ANC.

Pointing Back

While awaiting trial and on bail, I attended an NEC meeting. It was a regular meeting to discuss all sorts of things, the first I had attended since being detained. I asked the chairman for permission to speak. I said I had a major criticism to make. I said, "Here we are entering the negotiations phase, which needs us to be united as never before. It's a difficult task to negotiate with the enemy. But individuals in the NEC are maligning their own colleagues, colleagues who are sitting in the enemy's den." I named

---

*On 15 August 2004, Mac and Zarina attended a function in honor of Solly Shoke, the new chief of the army. Minister of arts and culture Pallo Jordan was also present. He and Mac got talking about Vula. According to Mac's account of the conversation, Jordan said a number of NEC members in 1990 were saying: "What business does this chap have to go and hide arms? We are in negotiations now, what's he up to?" Jordan said he asked them: "But what should he be doing? Should he now stop everything?" Most agreed. But Jordan confirmed that the prevailing view of a number was "Let Mac and them stew, disown them." Even Zuma, it appears, questioned the operation. One wonders why since he was fully attuned to its operations. People like Slovo were lost, didn't know how to fight back. Thabo Mbeki's attitude, it appears, was more sophisticated, usually put as a question: "Shouldn't we leave that? We'll attend to it later. We'll attend to their release and things like that. Let's get on with the business of the moment."

some NEC members. I said, "You, Aziz [Pahad], this is what you have been saying to journalists. I do not understand this behavior." My attack was brutal, and I still make no apologies for it. Even Jacob Zuma, I learned, said things that surprised me. Thabo hadn't raised a voice to refute all the wild talk. I was making the point that unless we stopped such uncomradely conduct, we would make things even more difficult for ourselves in negotiations. I am sure those individuals have never forgiven me for it.

Out in the Cold

By the time of the December 1990 national consultative conference of the ANC, my six months were up. I had retired.[12] Zarina had gone back to Brighton to pack up our things. My children were now in school at Sacred Heart College in Observatory. I was living at Yeoville and driving the Toyota Conquest that belonged to Maud, Yusuf Mohammed's wife.

On a Saturday in February 1991, my kids had a swimming gala at Sacred Heart. It was their first school activity, and I was sitting there as a parent when I heard a car alarm go off in the car park. It didn't strike me that it might be my car. When the gala was over, the kids and I were having a jolly time when we jumped in the car. It was less than a kilometer to my house. But within two hundred meters, I saw the heat gauge go from zero to boiling, and I realized the alarm in the car park must have been from my car.

My kids were eight and six years old. I tried to pretend everything was OK, although I was thinking about an explosive. I stopped the car and told the kids to get out and stand a distance away on the pavement. I opened the trunk and found that the pipe to the radiator had been cut. I examined the engine and found a plastic bag stuck to the side of it. I calmly closed the car and said to the kids, "Why don't we walk home? The car seems to have some mechanical problem." I made it into a joke, and we walked home.

I phoned Yusuf Mohammed for help. He sent someone to look at the car. A few hours later he phoned me back. He said, "There appears to have been a bomb attached to your car, but the mechanic panicked and threw it down the drain."*

Madiba was out of the country. I phoned Walter and said I was going to phone General Basie Smit, head of the Security Branch, to tell him he'd

---

*Mac subsequently reported this to the Goldstone Commission in March 1993. See the footnote on page 402 for details regarding the genesis of the commission.

better stop or else. Walter didn't know what to do. I knew there wasn't much Walter could do, but I wanted to ensure that he was aware of what had happened and what I was doing.

I got hold of Basie Smit, and I told him what had happened. I said, "My children were in the car. If your rules have changed, and you don't care whether you kill my children, who are six and eight, you should remember that from my period in Vula I have access to explosives and arms, and I have the home addresses of many of your top people and the locations of the vehicles they drive. I am telling you that when you find them dying one by one, being blown up one after the other, don't come and complain." There were no further attempts or threats.

That was an extremely stressful period. I was in retirement, so I had to fight this battle myself. Maybe I was wrong; if I had turned to the movement for help, perhaps they would have come forward. I also had the strain of not having an income. Only Vella Pillay's brother Krishna helped—he offered me the job of managing a petrol station.

Mind-set Redux

Madiba never repudiated Vula, and he continued to defend the people involved. At all times, however, we had to dress him in the clothing of plausible deniability.

Immediately after the unbanning of the organizations and the first tentative steps toward negotiations, comrades got carried away. The gleam of light at the end of the long struggle distorted perspectives. The underground—comrades in South Africa, Vula, and those who had come into the country clandestinely for operations other than Vula—were forgotten. The political steamroller had left them behind.

Lusaka was far removed from the real conditions in South Africa. After the NEC returned to South Africa, they failed to see the use of Vula. In Lusaka they had been unaware of it; back in South Africa they couldn't believe that an active underground was in place, that provisions for a people's war were under way—arms stockpiled, personnel trained—and that the regime was unaware of it. Perhaps these NEC people felt resentful because they hadn't been trusted enough to be told about Vula. Or perhaps the momentum of events concentrated people's minds in new directions. Who wanted to start examining the present utility of a plan to overthrow the apartheid government, created in different circumstances under different assumptions, when time had made both the circumstances and assumptions redundant?

19. INTO THE NEW SOUTH AFRICA

Introduction

WHILE MAC WAS ON THE SIDELINES between December 1990 and July 1991, the negotiating process began to take shape. In February 1991, a further agreement—the D. F. Malan Accord[1]—tightened the Pretoria Minute.* The ANC would discontinue the infiltration of arms and personnel and cease to either create new underground structures or recruit cadres for training inside South Africa. But the ANC still refused to agree to surrender its arms caches or stop establishing self-defense units (SDUs).[2] The accord also removed obstacles relating to indemnities and the release of political prisoners, and set the stage for multiparty talks. By the end of March, three hundred political prisoners had been released. Outdoor political rallies were legalized for the first time in fifteen years.[3]

In May, the ANC announced it would not attend a proposed peace conference called by the government to address the question of violence because "implicit in it is the inference that the state is an impartial body standing above the violence. . . . We dismiss the implication."[4] For the ANC, the government wanted to be both the convenor of the peace negotiations and a participant—both referee and player.

Moreover, the ANC had become increasingly convinced that the government strategy was to outflank it among African voters by forging an electoral pact with Buthelezi's Inkatha Freedom Party (IFP).[5] At the time, the notion was by no means far-fetched. The NP had opened membership to nonwhites, and even though there were no recruitment drives in the townships, De Klerk's popularity among the African masses was high. They

*Despite the D. F. Malan Accord, MK and the underground continued to import and stockpile arms until the 1994 elections. See [] maharaj/interviewees/[] Aboobaker Ismail (Rashid); Ronnie Kasrils.

were still prepared to thank him for freeing Mandela, unbanning the liberation movements, and repealing the most repressive pieces of apartheid legislation. To many Africans, he was Comrade de Klerk. Indeed, some opinion polls indicated that he might carry as much as 30 percent of the African vote. Thus De Klerk,[6] the ANC believed, was not predisposed to ending the violence, because the violence strengthened the government's hand and weakened the ANC's.[7]

At the beginning of July the ANC held its first national conference in South Africa since 1959. It elected a new leadership and provided it with a mandate to pursue a negotiated settlement. Mandela was elected president; Walter Sisulu, deputy president;[8] and Cyril Ramaphosa, secretary-general.*[9] Mac, prevailed upon by senior ANC figures, came out of retirement and was elected to the NEC.[†]

2

Serious negotiations started on 20 December 1991 when nineteen parties, including ones from all the apartheid homelands and the four independent states, gathered at the Holiday Inn in Kempton Park, near Johannesburg. At this meeting the Declaration of Intent was adopted[10] and the appellation the Convention for a Democratic South Africa (CODESA) agreed on as the formal name of the negotiating process. Thereafter, CODESA met at the World Trade Center, also in Kempton Park, over a three-year period from 1991 to 1994.[11] Throughout, Mac and his government counterpart, Fanie van der Merwe, a senior civil servant who had been part of the team that visited Mandela at Victor Verster, played pivotal roles as the secretariat for CODESA, charged with overseeing the fluid operation of the negotiations process. And Mac, because of his long

---

*Walter Sisulu, a reluctant deputy president, was prevailed upon to stand for the position, unopposed, when a looming fight between Thabo Mbeki and Chris Hani for the position might have resulted in unseemly campaigning by both and opened divisions between the left-leaning wing of the party, supporting Hani, and the more centrist leaning, supporting Mbeki. The ANC was still only finding its feet; any hint of division would only have benefited the NP government in the run-up to negotiations. Mbeki was under the illusion that Ramaphosa would not stand against Nzo, that as part of an agreement, no member of the old order would be challenged. He regarded Ramaphosa's candidacy, which saw Nzo defeated, as a betrayal of an understanding he thought they had come to.

†For complete coverage of the Durban conference go to www.anc.org.za. According to Kasrils, Mac approached him at Durban and sought his assistance in making his "come back"[]maharaj/interviewees/[] Kasrils. Mac rejects the assertion with contempt.

association with Mandela and Mandela's absolute trust in him, worked behind the scenes as one of Mandela's troubleshooters. Mac and Van der Merwe quickly became close friends; their chemistry ensured that no operational problem ever became a stumbling block. In the negotiating forum, Mac was a key adviser to Cyril Ramaphosa, the ANC's chief negotiator, and part of the "channel," the small team of negotiators from the ANC and the NP that negotiated the Record of Understanding in September 1992.[12] That agreement got negotiations back on track when they stalled.

From the start, the process of negotiations was a stop-start business, moving through the phases of mutual mistrust and shifting allegiances. And they took place against a backdrop of unrest and conflict across the country, including concerted attacks by Inkatha supporters on other township dwellers, counterattacks by the ANC's SDUs, which often assumed an offensive character, and the ongoing Inkatha/ANC conflict in KZN.

On the night of 16 June 1992, forty-three residents of Boipatong, a township about fifty kilometers south of Johannesburg, were hacked to death by marauding residents of the nearby IFP hostel at KwaMadela. Immediate reports were that the police were involved in orchestrating and assisting the massacre.[13] In the face of black outrage, Mandela had no option—the ANC broke off negotiations with the government.* The ANC used Boipatong to demonize De Klerk in the townships,[14] to the point of practically accusing him of personally ordering the massacre. Whatever support he had in the townships was emasculated. Never again would he be referred to as Comrade De Klerk. Mandela and De Klerk exchanged long memoranda.[15] Each exchange between the two seemed to make things worse.

With the permission of their principals, Cyril Ramaphosa and Roelf Meyer,[16] the head of the government's negotiating team, established contact and put together small teams to work on a series of steps that would enable both sides to resume formal talks. Between June and September, Meyer and Ramaphosa, the "channel," met on forty-three occasions.

---

*When Mandela addressed a rally in Evaton, a township adjacent to Boipatong, he visited Boipatong, a few days after the massacre. He was greeted with chants of "You are lambs and the government is leading us to slaughter." Sparks, p. 146.

CODESA was not a failure. In four of the five working groups, consensus was reached and reports produced. Working Group 5, which had the task of deciding on the percentages that would be required for the adoption of the Bill of Rights and the adoption of the final constitution, failed to reach consensus on these issues. On 24 May 1992, CODESA adjourned to allow for further negotiation among the parties on these matters. The ANC broke off negotiations after Boipatong indefinitely.

The urgency of an expeditious resolution of their differences became overwhelming after a second massacre: twenty-nine people were killed when Ciskei Defense Force troops opened fire on ANC marchers gathered near Bisho Stadium on 7 September 1992.[17]

The Record of Understanding, signed by Mandela and De Klerk on 26 September 1992, opened the way for a resumption of negotiations. The ANC and the government committed themselves to an elected constitutional assembly to draw up the country's constitution, a schedule for the release of political prisoners, and the fencing of hostels to forestall attacks by hostel dwellers on adjacent communities. On the hostels, De Klerk balked, but Mandela stood firm. The Record of Understanding was a turning point in the process. It drove a wedge between the NP and the IFP. The government implicitly acknowledged that the ANC was its partner in a joint process. It left Buthelezi twisting in the wind.[18] The ANC had gained the psychological upper hand. Henceforth, it drove the process.

3

In April 1993, formal negotiations again got under way, this time under the rubric of the Multiparty Negotiating Process (MPNP).[19] Once again Van der Merwe and Mac were the secretariat. The outcome was agreement on an interim constitution, a bill of rights, and a five-year government of national unity (GNU). The two houses of parliament—the National Assembly and the Senate—sitting in joint session would constitute the Constitutional Assembly, the body charged with drawing up the country's final constitution.[20]

Before the government and the ANC could sign off on the agreement, two matters were outstanding: how decisions would be made in the cabinet and amnesty. On 17 November, Mac and Van der Merwe were assigned to draft a text that would resolve the issues. Their text, accepted by both parties, became the preamble to the Interim Constitution[21] and the constitutional mandate for the Truth and Reconciliation Commission.[22]

In the newly established Transitional Executive Council (TEC),[23] a body with members drawn from all parties to oversee the functioning of government until elections in April 1994, Van der Merwe and Mac were again chosen to direct the secretariat. The TEC had a specific mandate to ensure a level political playing field.* An Independent Electoral Commission (IEC) was established to conduct impartial elections, and the

---

*In some areas of governance the TEC enjoyed a virtual veto. The days of the NP's claiming sole authority as the governing party were over.

Independent Broadcasting Commission (IBC) and the Independent Media Commission (IMC) would ensure that the state did not abuse the state-controlled media, particularly radio and TV.

4

Mac's capacity for seeing the big picture, for taking the particulars of a situation and putting them in the context of a larger vision, helped to shape critical outcomes. On two pivotal occasions he, along with Van der Merwe, preempted what might have resulted in the right wing's either rising in revolt or seriously disrupting elections. The first involved Bophuthatswana (Bop), one of the "independent" states, where the president, Lucas Mangope,[24] was toying with secession, perhaps as a negotiating ploy.[25] Had it been followed through, in all likelihood, it would have caused Mangosuthu Buthelezi to do likewise in KZN, thus leaving the new South African government to deal with two secession battles. The second had to do directly with the IFP.

In the early months of 1994, unrest in Bop had grown, fueled in part by Mangope's vacillation over whether to participate in national elections, which would have meant its dissolution into the larger South Africa. By March, the unrest had boiled over into a popular, ANC-driven uprising that threatened to drive Mangope from power. Mangope called on General Constand Viljoen,[26] leader of the right-wing Afrikaner Volksfront (AVF) and Mangope's ally in COSAG,* an alliance opposed to majority rule in a unitary SA, to reestablish his authority.

Viljoen, a former SADF chief of staff and a legend among SADF rank and file, had only recently entered the political fray. A farmer since his retirement, he was called back into service by his people to help secure Afrikaner self-determination in the new dispensation. Viljoen maintained that he could muster the support of thirty thousand Afrikaner comman-

---

*On 6 October 1992, Buthelezi, Ciskei military ruler Oupa Gqozo, Bophuthatswana's Lucas Mangope, the Conservative Party (CP), its breakaway faction Afrikaner Volksunie (AVU), and the Afrikaner Freedom Foundation formed the Concerned South Africans Group (COSAG). COSAG was an alliance between black and white right-wing parties that united in their rejection of the Record of Understanding, which they believed would lead to ANC majoritarian rule. A year later, COSAG fragmented. Inkatha, Bophuthatswana, Ciskei, the CP, and the Afrikaner Volksfront (AVF) formed the Freedom Alliance. The AVF was formed by a group of former military leaders, including General Constand Viljoen, to support Afrikaner demands for self-determination.

dos, farmers, and former members of the military who composed the civilian arm of the defense force. True or not, the implied threat of rebellion with unforeseeable consequences, perhaps even racial war in the run-up to the elections, posed imminent danger. Moreover, because of his reputation, there was a fear that if Viljoen called on the members of the SADF to join him, many soldiers would rally to his cause, fragmenting the SADF and opening the way to anarchy.

Mangope asked only that Viljoen not use members of the Afrikaner Resistance Movement, the AWB, the paramilitary force led by the charismatic but often buffoonish (to his opponents) demagogue Eugène Terre'Blanche,[27] a white supremacist who had vowed to resist black rule. But the reckless Terre'Blanche refused to cooperate, seeing an opportunity to assert the AWB's military prowess. On Saturday, 14 March, *bakkie*-loads (*Afrikaans* shorthand for light delivery vehicles), of AWB "soldiers," many of them drunk, crossed into Bop and drove through the streets of the capital, Mmabatho, shooting at will. The results were a fiasco. The Bop army was outraged and struck back, repulsing the AWB in quick order. Televised images of a Bop soldier executing two AWB members as they lay wounded beside their car riveted South Africans. Never had the AWB, and the white right in general, seemed so incompetent, their myth of white supremacy so preposterous.

At this point, Mac secured the permission of the TEC for himself and Van der Merwe to fly to Mmabatho to assess the situation. They found Viljoen in the compound of the South African embassy in Mmabatho, conferring with General George Meiring,[28] head of the SADF. Fearing that a move was afoot to reinstate Mangope, who had retreated to the safety of his palace at Motswedi, Mac swiftly orchestrated a series of maneuvers whereby Mandela and De Klerk jointly ordered foreign minister Pik Botha to fly to Motswedi along with General Meiring, Van der Merwe, and himself, to inform Mangope that he was relieved of his office and under house arrest. With Bop now back under the control of the South African government, whatever disruptive plans Mangope might have harbored were aborted and the realistic Viljoen was convinced that Afrikaner self-determination could be better pursued by participating in the democratic process.*

The second intervention occurred in KZN weeks before the 1994 elec-

*He broke away from the AVU and founded a new political party, the Freedom Front, which participated in the April 1994 elections.

tion. Through intelligence contacts established during Vula, Mac got word that elements in the SADF were giving military training to some five thousand Inkatha operatives, under the direction of Philip Powell, a former SB officer who had joined the IFP, at a secluded camp at Mlaba in northern Natal.[29] Such an SADF-trained group could disrupt the elections in that area. Mac received the go-ahead from De Klerk and Mandela to organize a clandestine raid on the camp. Mac, Van der Merwe, a police general, and a member of the Goldstone Commission moved in on the camp, only to find that it was empty except for large amounts of weapons, almost assuredly because of tip-offs from within the SADF. But this swift, uncompromising action derailed such moves to disrupt the ballot in KZN.

On both occasions, Mac's experience in Vula, the extensive network of intelligence built during that period, and the continued presence of Nightingale in the Security Branch were essential in averting disaster. While others dithered, Mac acted. Van der Merwe says, "Mac is one of the most moral people I have ever met. If he ordered me killed, I'd know it would be for a good cause."[30] A jest? Hardly. It resonates with authenticity, encapsulating in the fewest words what Van der Merwe perceives as the essence of Mac.

Ramaphosa's assessment of the man he worked closely with when he was leader of NUM and Mac underground in Vula and who worked closely with him during negotiations strikes a different tone: "Mac," he says, "was one of the leading strategic thinkers in the ANC, part of a brains trust triumvirate made up of Thabo Mbeki, Joe Slovo, and himself. During negotiations, Mac's strategic mind and incisive intellect were invaluable. He always had a solution to many of the intractable problems we had to resolve. Mac was a joy to work with."[31]

Life in the New South Africa

Mac served a distinguished four years in Mandela's cabinet as minister of transport. "Mac," says Ketso Gordhan, who served as his general director for much of his tenure in transport, "was not just an able strategist, but a keen manager who was able to extract the best from the people he worked with, endeared a great loyalty, and led by example. His focus on getting to an outcome while being pragmatic about how he got there was his greatest strength." He was later lauded as one of the world's best ministers dealing with infrastructure development by the influential journal *Infrastructure Finance*. In 1999, to accolades for his initiatives in that sector, especially the construction of the Maputo corridor,* Mac retired from government.[32] He joined First Rand, one of South Africa's premier banking groups, as a nonexecutive director, and settled into a "normal" life. He served on the ANC's NEC until 2000, and then he bowed out.

In retirement he devoted himself to the welfare of comrades he had served with—especially his old comrade and friend Walter Sisulu. He edited and oversaw publication of *Reflections in Prison*, essays written by eight senior struggle leaders, including Mandela, Sisulu, and Govan Mbeki, written while all were in jail.[33] His friendship with Mandela grew and he was among that group of old and trusted comrades Madiba looked to for advice—and to share memories. Zarina began to write a fortnightly column for *Business Report*, a highly regarded daily newspaper, set up a consultancy business, and ventured into a few business enterprises. The children were growing up. He quit smoking. The old revolutionary, it seemed, would get his wish: to die in his rocking chair, boots off.

But in the years after Thabo Mbeki succeeded Mandela as president, there were oddities, a slowly growing sense of being marginalized. When the new wing to the Johannesburg International Airport, a project Mac had spearheaded as transport minister, had directed, and brought to realization, was opened by President Mbeki, he was not among the dignitaries invited. He was not invited to any state function by Mbeki. While other veterans of the struggle, including Little Rivonia Trialists Wilton Mkwayi and Laloo Chiba, received the highest honor the state can confer in recognition of their contribution to the struggle, Mac received nothing.

There would be no settled ending to his tale.

Mac

ON THE FRIDAY EVENING before the meeting on the Record of Understanding was due to begin on 25 September 1992, we reported to Madiba

---

*The Maputo development corridor (MDC) toll road, a joint project of South Africa and Mozambique, was one of Africa's most ambitious regional development projects. The 1.5 billion rand (1998 rand value), 525-kilometer toll road ran between Witbank in South Africa and Maputo in Mozambique. The corridor opened a trade route between South Africa and Mozambique because Maputo is the logical port for South Africa's Mpumalanga province and much of Gauteng. The MDC was a prototype for BEE in the roads sector as it empowered communities along the route through the targeted transfer of skills training and procurement.

on what the working group and the channel had worked out for the meeting the next day on the release of comrades who had been sentenced to death and were serving their sentences on death row. They included Robert McBride.* Mandela was unhappy that we had not secured the release of McBride and company before the summit was to take place.[34] He then personally took the matter up by phone with De Klerk and insisted that unless McBride and the others were released before the start of the meeting, the meeting was off. I must confess we thought he was pushing things a bit far. Was it worth jeopardizing the meetings for releases that were going to take place anyway? But Madiba was adamant. After much toing and froing over the phone, De Klerk eventually acceded and the releases were effected. De Klerk had yielded on a matter of considerable emotion in his own constituency, which would accuse him of releasing murderers.[35]

During the negotiations leading up to the meeting, we had insisted that the hostels be secured and that people shouldn't be allowed to move out. De Klerk had resisted. On the question of carrying arms in public, at demonstrations, De Klerk said, "I can't do anything," although he had revoked the law that prohibited the carrying of weapons early in 1992. This made it possible for the IFP to allow its supporters to go rampaging. We said, "Ban the carrying of weapons. Fence the hostels. Upgrade them, yes, but fence them so that there is control. De Klerk kept saying that it was legal, but we would have to examine the law, and the law advisers would have to sit over it before he could do anything.[36] We knew that the principle of fencing the hostels was going to drive a wedge between the National Party and the IFP, but we weren't going to broadcast that to the public.†

Madiba had, in my view, reached a point where he felt that FW was being dishonest with him over the violence, and he now wanted to assert a relationship that would make De Klerk act.[37] Our respective teams had agreed on a series of actions for the government to take to secure the hostels. We reached the point where this agreement only required the signatures of Mandela and De Klerk.

---

*Robert McBride, Mzondeleli Nondula, and Mthetheleli Mncube had been convicted of murder, sentenced to death, and granted a reprieve. McBride was convicted in a bombing at a Magoos Bar in which nine people died. In white South Africa he was synonomous with the ANC campaign of violence and its targeting of civilians. For the constitutional issues McBride's release posed, see Hassen Ebrahim, Soul of a Nation, pp. 139, 291, at www.omalley.co.za, and "The Mind of a Bomber," International Herald Tribune, 19 October 1992.
†On his release Mandela wanted to meet with Buthelezi, but because of the vociferous objections of the ANC in Natal, he delayed doing so until January 1991, when the spiraling violence made the meeting imperative.

When they met to discuss the issue, FW said, "I do not sign documents without knowing the contents. I have not seen the report, the detailed report on the hostels question. In general, I am sympathetic to what you are raising. Can we leave it out of the Record of Understanding and attend to it later?" But we had information that the cabinet had discussed it the previous night, so De Klerk was fully acquainted with the detailed report. So we slipped a note to Madiba to let him know this and told him that FW was going to try to wriggle out of it: "Don't let him. We have information that they have discussed it and that they are divided on the issue."

So after FW made this speech, Madiba, calmly and simply, said, "Well, Mr. President, we can go on the way you are suggesting, but when we leave this room and meet the media, I will have to pronounce this meeting a failure. Whatever else we have agreed; I will pronounce it a failure." FW then said, "Let's discuss this matter a little later in the agenda." Madiba said, "Fine, we'll discuss it later."

When the tea break came, I was watching to see whom FW would talk to. Among others, he talked to Hernus Kriel, the minister of law and order and a real hard-liner.[38] We came back into the meeting and proceeded with the rest of the agenda, but FW didn't mention the hostels.

Lunchtime was approaching. There was nothing left on the agenda other than the hostel question. There was a pregnant silence; we didn't want to remind De Klerk. We wanted to see what he was going to do. He said, "May I suggest that while we are having a lunch break, a working group be put together to look at that agreement?" And Madiba said, "Fine, you name your side and we'll name our side." Now during the tea break earlier, we had already planted this idea with Roelf Meyer and Leon Wessels.[39]

When the lunch break came, I said, either to Roelf or to Leon, "If Hernus Kriel is on your team, the whole thing will collapse." And they said, "Don't worry, it's on track; we'll be there." The working group met and cleared everything, with hardly any alteration to the content.

FW now had to sign the agreement for the hostels to be fenced and upgraded. The prohibition on carrying arms was also agreed on, but it was never implemented.

The Record of Understanding brought the negotiations back on track.[40] But the real advance was the recognition on the part of the NP that its real allies in this process were the ANC and not Inkatha or the cluster of Bantustan parties they had cobbled together. This was a multiparty process; we had agreed that every party, legitimate or illegitimate, apartheid creation or not, should come to the table. The NP thought that

most of them would be on their side because they were apartheid crea-
tions. They thought that together they would be able to overwhelm
the ANC.

All along, we had said that whatever interim arrangements were made,
the end point had to be a final constitution written by the people of South
Africa through an elected structure. The Record of Understanding committed the NP to that. But the real paradigm shift was their recognition
that without the ANC there would be no negotiated solution. They had to
accept that we were partners in a process. The Record of Understanding
fractured the alliance between the NP and the IFP.[41] There is distrust
among any band of crooks, even highway robbers. They unite over the
robbery, but each is looking at what happens to the spoils.

At the meeting, the shift in relationship between Mandela and De Klerk
was dramatically visible. On the release of McBride, FW was going against
his constituency. By agreeing to fencing hostels and the carrying of weapons at public gatherings, he was abandoning his strategy of an alliance between his party and the IFP against the ANC. On both scores, he was
driven into retreat, and at the risk of much schism and unhappiness inside
his own cabinet.[42]

Looking back now over this period, it is clear to me that it also marks
the point at which De Klerk actually acknowledged that his term of rule
had reached the point where he alone could not rule South Africa anymore. He may have had hopes, ambitions that he could survive into the
future, but it was now clear he could only move into the future South
Africa through some understanding and relationship with the ANC.

The Final Resolution

When the negotiations resumed after the Record of Understanding, there
was a lot of very difficult discussion to get through. We kept asking what
the government's bottom line was. It was a shock, as we negotiated details
on the resumption of talks, to realize gradually that the bottom line was
one of very narrow self-interest. The civil service, pensions—everything
had to do with their pensions. They could not say, crudely, "Guarantee us,
the politicians, our pensions," but once we understood that that was what
they wanted, we realized that their bottom line was so base that we could
drive them on substantive issues. Joe Slovo (JS) set out our thinking in a
paper on sunset clauses.[43] These assured the civil service of their pensions
and of job security for a period of five years, at which point the guarantee
would fall away.

One of the last issues to be resolved was the cabinet and its functions. In an interim government based on power sharing, not only the overall winning party would have cabinet posts. But how this would work, exactly, was the last stumbling block.

A meeting took place at the NP's offices at the World Trade Centre on 16 November 1993. Roelf Meyer, Leon Wessels, Fanie van der Merwe, and Niel Barnard were there from their side; on our side were Cyril Ramaphosa, Joe Slovo, and I. We argued about how cabinet posts would be distributed after the election in a way that would be equitable in terms of the percentage of votes gained by each party, but would also satisfy the need to share power. Was this going to be a democratic cabinet, or would it have minority veto powers? We said our commitment to a government of national unity was a real one, which meant no one could have a veto power. Mandela had been explicit in his guidance to us: a cabinet that functions by simple majority rule.

Fanie and I were told to draft an appropriate clause and also one for the amnesty question, which had gotten bogged down because Kobie Coetsee, the minister of justice, had played his cards too close to his chest. Early in the process, back in 1990, we had offered an unconditional amnesty for everyone.[44] The NP team had agreed until Kobie got wind of it and kiboshed the whole thing. Kobie thought he could use the issue as a bargaining chip with us, but as we got to the endgame, power had shifted. Clearly, we were going to be in charge, and the security forces and the NP were out on a limb, not knowing what would happen. The trade-off for me was: How does cabinet function versus this last item they are concerned with—amnesty? But they couldn't say it outright. I said to Fanie, "When we finalize this, the two of us, is there a deal?" He said, "I think so." So Fanie and I disposed of the amnesty question by inserting "shall" not "there may be amnesty."[45]

We went back to the working group with the draft. Cyril then said, "Now before we finalize this thing and say we're done, let's get back to the cabinet question. Do you still have a problem because I want to tell you that we will not agree to any form of veto and troika control?" They looked at what Fanie and I had drafted, namely, the section that said the cabinet would function in the spirit of seeking consensus, and when all else failed, take decisions in the normal way, that is, by majority decision.[46] And they said, "We're satisfied." In the end, we did not spend even five minutes on settling the issue of cabinet decision making at the follow-up meeting.

Everyone was relieved. The next day we went into the negotiating

chamber and put forward this last resolution, which became the postam-
ble to the interim constitution. All the parties signed. We had an impromptu celebration at the WTC on 17 November, which coincided with
Cyril's fortieth birthday.

Roelf Meyer was happy because he could tell De Klerk and Kobie Coetsee that he had extracted an agreement that "there shall be amnesty" from
us. Now they were able to get the security forces to buy into the deal.

Slovo, on the other hand, was surprised. He never thought they would
agree to majority cabinet decision making, and he had been preparing a
formula to try to deal with it. But the NP was more concerned about
amnesty than the details of cabinet decision making.

The NP, and De Klerk in particular, I believe, failed in the long term
because they started off with a dual strategy: negotiate, but use state power
to try to weaken the ANC. On the other hand, Mandela's position from
day one was to negotiate in the belief that those who negotiate are all going to come out better and stronger. He kept saying, "Mr. De Klerk, if we
do this together, I want you to be stronger, to grow stronger." He actually
said so. "The stronger each of us grows as parties by working together, the
better for the country." What he meant was: the better each would be able
to deliver on the agreements reached.

And More Dirty Tricks

Still, even though things were going well at the official level, there were
strange things going on elsewhere. At about midnight one night in October 1992, while we were living at 27 Muller Street in Yeoville, the bell at my
gate rang. I got up and spoke over the intercom: "Who's there?" A white
woman's voice, frantic: "Help me, help me, I'm in trouble. I'm in danger."
"Who are you?" "I'm Pearlie Joubert of the *Vrye Weekblad*."*

I opened the gate to let her in, and there was this young Afrikaner
woman in her early twenties—first time I'd ever seen her. She said, "I'm
sorry to have given you the impression that I was being attacked. I wanted
you to let me in because I have to speak to you." I said, "OK, what's the
problem? What's happening?" She said, "Mac, at the Goldstone Commis-
sion† it is going to be alleged that you are behind a Mozambican by the

---

Vrye Weekblad (Free Weekly Journal) was a left-of-center Afrikaans-language publication that was highly critical of the NP government.
†The Commission of Inquiry for the Prevention of Public Violence and Intimidation, under the chairmanship of Judge Richard Goldstone, was established in 1991. Between 1991

name of Cunas.* He has confessed to certain sabotage activities, and he is giving evidence at the commission that he was involved with Military Intelligence. He says the planning of all that was done in your house, in your presence, and you are the head of it all."[47]

I asked who this Cunas was. She said he was an MI operative whom the military had decided to sacrifice when he was accidentally arrested. Then they visited him in detention and suddenly his story changed—now he was fingering me. He claimed I was planning "third force" activity, the state-sponsored death squads that had recently been revealed.

I contacted the Goldstone Commission to ask what was going on. The Goldstone investigators came to see me. They indicated that they didn't believe Cunas's story but were obliged to question me. He had described a room in my house where these meetings had allegedly taken place. We agreed that certain questions should be put to this man in my presence.

Then they pulled a trick on me. I went to Pretoria to meet the Goldstone Commission people in their offices. Unbeknownst to me, they had put this Cunas in the foyer of their building so I would see him as I arrived. They wanted to see if I would recognize him. As I walked in, they were watching me. But I'd never seen the man before; I didn't even look at him. They could see from my lack of reaction that I did not recognize Cunas. My evidence of denial was accepted by the commission and Cunas's allegations came to nothing.[48]

Then, in February 1994, another odd incident: I was out of the house—we were now living in Observatory—when my wife called me at about ten-thirty one night and asked me to come home. I raced home and found two ANC comrades, Moe Shaik and Yusuf Mohammed. Moe said, "The police are going to raid your house tonight." "Tonight? For what?" He said, "I don't know. I've got the information that they're raiding your house tonight, and it's going to be a high-profile raid." I said, "In connection with what?" He said, "Criminal activities, stolen cars—I don't know the details."

and 1994 the commission conducted a number of public inquiries into incidents of violence. The findings more often than not were highly critical of the actions of the security forces, sometimes of Inkatha, and on occasion of the ANC, especially with regard to investigations of violence on the Rand. He was as evenhanded as was possible in circumstances where all parties had vested interests in withholding information or scoring political points. Interviews with Richard Goldstone at []o'malley interviews/[] Richard Goldstone.
*Joao Cunas was a Mozambican army deserter who approached *Vrye Weekblad* claiming that he had visited Mac at his home, where Mac had instructed him to fabricate accounts of SAP hit squad activities.

I was amazed. Yes, I had weapons there, for my protection—illegal weapons, but Fanie van der Merwe and Niel Barnard knew about them. I had been refused a license. It was a joke at the World Trade Centre.

Later, Moe came back with more information. He said there was going to be a police press conference in Pretoria that night.

Apparently, a group called the Boeremafia (an Afrikaner crime syndicate) had been arrested. Among them were right-wingers engaged in criminal activities. But the police also paraded an Indian person called Maharaj. They claimed at the media conference that he was my nephew. They said there was a huge stolen-car racket.[49]

I said to Moe, "This is a set-up." We got out some weapons and got ready. I said, "Chaps, whoever comes to the gate, even if they are wearing police uniforms, we're not letting them in. I'll decide whether we fire on them."

I phoned General van der Merwe,[50] head of the South African Police. It was now about 11 P.M. I said to him, "General, I have a report that your police want to raid my place tonight." He said, "I know nothing about it." I said, "Well, I don't know who's going to be coming. Are they right-wingers? Is it the police? I'm sitting here armed, and no matter who comes to my gate tonight, I'm not letting them in; I'm opening fire. I'm defending myself."

He said, "Now hold on, Mac; don't do that. Phone the head of Witwatersrand Police, General Calitz." I phoned Calitz, and I told him the same thing. He also said he knew nothing of it. I said, "The fact that you, the general in charge of Witwatersrand Police, are telling me that you know nothing means that if anybody appears at my gate tonight, I'm opening fire." He said, "I'll call you back."

I went back to Moe. He had confirmed that there had been a press conference. One hour later, Calitz got back to me. He said, "Mac, there'll be no raid on your place." I said, "General, was there going to be a raid?" He didn't answer the question.

The night passed. The next day, in the *Citizen* newspaper there was a story linking me, the Boeremafia, and stolen cars.[51] Two months before the election! I phoned General van der Merwe. I said, "General, it's very clear from today's newspaper reports that the raid was on. By my phoning you and General Calitz, I preempted the raid; otherwise the headlines were going to be 'Mac Maharaj's home raided for stolen cars.' "

He denied it. I asked if the police had verified whether this man claiming to be my nephew was in fact my nephew. I called the *Citizen:* "Did you phone me to check?" They said, "No, it was sufficient for us that the police said he was your nephew."

I called my lawyers at Cheadle, Thompson and Haysom and sent the police a letter demanding a retraction. In March they retracted their statements.[52] I believe they were trying to destroy me and, in the process, trying to damage the ANC's election chances.[53]

In Government

I was made minister of transport in Mandela's cabinet. We had to enter government and start changing a civil service that hadn't even seen our program. Until then, we'd had no contact with the civil service.

And what the hell did I know about Transport? But it was not as if the NEC had left me unarmed; our appointments to the cabinet were preceded by policy-making conferences and were encapsulated in a comprehensive RDP* document. We went in equipped with that. I wasn't part of the process of developing it in any detailed way because I was busy with negotiations. But as soon as I knew I was going to be a minister, I thought, "Let me read this document carefully. What sort of road map does it provide for me? What are the implications for Transport?"

The day we were sworn in, I asked where the offices of the ministry of transport were. No one knew. I sat in the president's office in the Union Building in Pretoria with his staff and asked: "Hey, who has got the ministry's address?" Somebody said, "Oh, here's a book. It's the Forum Building, Struben Street." I drove over there.

They were not expecting me. They thought I would be coming in the next day. They were in a flurry. The previous minister of transport was not there. I never saw him. There was no handover. That seems to have been

---

*The Reconstruction and Development Program was the ANC's blueprint for the Mandela presidency. Implementation was given to Jay Naidoo, former head of COSATU and new minister without portfolio in the Mandela government. The program was idealistic, labor friendly, and set unrealistic goals for redressing the lack of basic services in black communities. Implementation was hampered by several constraints: a civil service in transition; the need to immediately address the mess in the treasury; budgetary limitations; the need to get South Africa's economic house in order; a huge escalation in crime; a culture of entitlement in townships used to paying no rates, no rents, and no service fees (during the "make the country ungovernable" phase of the struggle in the eighties, not paying was your patriotic duty) being told that these services had to be paid for; lack of coordination and weak lines of authority: every minister was left to implement his/her version of the RDP.

the experience of our other new ministers as well. The previous incumbents disappeared. They weren't even at the door to welcome us.

The director general (DG), Dr. C. F. Scheepers, eventually turned up to see me. He was in a flurry and said welcome, and so on. I asked him, "What happens here?" He said, "Minister, we've prepared a briefing document. Here's your copy."

I said to myself, "Hey, who is this guy?" I'd never heard of him. He'd arrived. He'd told me he was the DG, and he introduced me to a few people. And he'd told me his own tenure would expire in six months, but he was prepared to serve me if I wanted to extend his contract, and if I didn't, he was prepared to leave.

Those of us who came into the cabinet from the ANC had a huge sense of wariness about the existing civil service. At the same time, the civil servants had a huge sense of unease about us. They just didn't know how to relate to us. Some of our people's wariness was so strong that it literally translated to "I won't show it, but I'm going to get rid of this bastard as quickly as possible. Not because the man is bad, but because I proceed from the assumption that he comes from the old guard. I want somebody else I have confidence in from my ranks. So until then, I'll just interact civilly."

But I said to myself, "Wait a minute. I don't even know who I'm going to appoint; I don't even know the job. Wait. I'll give myself a month. I must understand the job. I must understand how it is structured. I must understand who the key management people are, and I must question them and relate to them. I must put them at ease, question them about how things stand, develop an understanding, and question them about what they have done in preparation." But I told myself that before I began even contemplating how I would rock the boat, I must first understand who was on this boat and put them at ease.

When a deputy DG came to my office, and I said, "Will you now brief me on passenger transport?" he typically (because they also had no experience of this change) did the "Yes, Minister" act; that is, he just flooded me with documents. But in the discussion I was evaluating him: was he summarizing effectively? Was he answering my question directly, or was he evading it and simply giving me a mass of documents?

I got to know Scheepers during several chats. He was a career civil servant with an academic record, a doctorate. He had worked in various departments as DG. He used to play golf with former president F. W. de Klerk. He was fine. I never had an unpleasant moment with him. I knew he had walked into it because he had offered to leave when I became minister. To facilitate the transition, I hired Ketso Gordhan, who was about to become my new DG, as a special adviser for the last three months of Dr. Scheepers's contract and then Dr. Scheepers as my special adviser for the first three months of Ketso's so that Ketso would be thoroughly familiar with all facets of the department. Our parting was amicable. He found a job in academia.

But the race gulf between Dr. Scheepers and me had been huge. I could sense, at times, that he didn't know how to read my body language. He came from a different cultural background, and he had never interacted with us. He would become insecure because he had grown up in a culture and a bureaucracy that told him: "Watch the minister's body language; say the right things to him." Now he no longer knew what the right thing to say was, so he was no longer at ease. I was comfortable now because he was uncomfortable. "He's unsure now what the right thing to say to me is. Leave it like that."

For example, after I studied the RDP, I decided that before I embarked on new initiatives we should conduct a comprehensive review of existing policies sector by sector with all the relevant role players participating. I told Scheepers we needed to make sure that everybody was on board. "Oh, Minister, yes, you're right. There is the Transport and General Workers Union.[54] Would you want them there?" Obviously, they had to be there. But was that the only union, I asked him? "Oh, I think there is another one." I said, "Don't the white workers have a union?" "Yes, Minister, they have." I said, "Well, invite them." He said, "Are you sure?" I said, "Yes, I'm very sure." Then it turns out, as I'm questioning him, that he knows by name all the white workers' union leadership and has met them. But he doesn't know the Transport and General, which is the black union. He didn't suggest the white workers because he assumed that I might say we shouldn't have them. He was a bit surprised when I say they must be present.

I didn't feel the old guard were putting obstacles in my way, although other ministers had different experiences. It remained an assumption that the civil service would be an obstacle, either because it works slowly or because it adheres to the principle that ministers come and go, and anyway, policy making was their field.

I did not want to approach the matter as if there were a conspiracy in the civil service. There was a mind-set. There was a fear of the new government, and there was a fear about losing their positions. Under the Interim Constitution they were guaranteed their jobs for five years, not their positions. I could redeploy a deputy DG as a door janitor if I wished, but I would have to continue to pay him at the level and with the perks of a deputy DG. They themselves had made certain assumptions. Similarly on our side, there were certain assumptions, and those assumptions involved suspicion. But the question was whether that suspicion had moved to a point of distrust.

Was I distrustful of Scheepers? No. I got rid of him because he was not suitable for managing the consultative process that I wanted to inculcate as the key instrument in policy making—one that would ensure that the concerns of all stakeholders were taken into consideration. The DG had to be someone who would come in with confidence and would have the personality to win the confidence of all the role players. I needed a person who would relate to all the players without transmitting his suspicion and who would respect facts. Dr. Scheepers was not suitable for that role. But I did not interfere with other senior staff. I said, "Ketso, that's your baby. You are going to be the DG. You have time to assess people, but I don't want the boat to be rocked to the point where it stops moving. That's the guideline."

Plant?

Also in my office was my secretary. I found this chap to be extraordinarily efficient. He knew how to get me my airline tickets. He knew where to get this or that, and he knew whom to go to in the department to answer my questions. I found myself helplessly dependent on him. So one day I called him into my office, ordered a cup of coffee, and sat down with him. I praised him and he preened himself. He turned out to be a personality who liked to praise himself. He told me how great he was and that he could solve any problem for me. He knew who was who, not only in our department, but across the departments. Then I happened to ask him what his previous posting had been before he had come into my office, and it turned out he had been made secretary in my office one week before my appointment. So I said, "What were you doing before that?" He said, "I left Minister Magnus Malan, and I was put into the Department of Transport as Communications head, and then a week before your appointment the DG approached me about becoming your secretary."

I said to myself, "Mm, that's interesting. There's something problematic here. Why did he leave Magnus Malan, the forestry minister,* go into

*Magnus Malan was minister of defense until the ANC forced his redeployment after Inkathagate, the revelations that the South African government had been funding activi-

Communications at Transport, and was then posted to me? He's been earmarked to be my secretary, but he had to go into Communications to get some working knowledge of the Department of Transport. Fine, this guy I'm getting rid of. This is a man who, in his helpfulness, will block me from understanding how government is functioning. Because I can't say boo without turning to him, and everything I ask him he tells me." I began to find that he had even done things before I could raise them. This was superefficiency. But I said to myself: "He's been put here. This is one person I don't want."

After Ketso had settled down in the adviser's role prior to becoming DG, I said to him, "I'm getting rid of this guy." Ketso said, "But you're getting rid of a very good guy." I said, "I don't have facts. All I have is someone who's going to be a gatekeeper around my responses, but who is superefficient. I don't want him. I suspect him." Ketso said, "You are wrong." I said, "Well, if I'm wrong, you can take him into your department because he officially came from Communications, so he can go back to Communications." Ketso said, "Indeed I will take him because I think you're wrong, Mac." When Ketso became DG, he took him. Two months later Ketso was at my door. "What's the problem?" He said, "Mac, I want to get rid of that bastard." So I said, "Oh, you're joining the club?" He said, "If there's one man I'm getting rid of it's that man." "That's your baby, Ketso. You took him on; you find a legal way to get rid of him. I'm thankful that you took him off my hands."

In the civil service top management, there was a fear, a need for security. Therefore, when individuals were amenable, you didn't know whether they were being amenable just to secure their jobs. But it was a futile exercise to analyze the problem because there you were, new, with your mind overwhelmed with how to get on top of your job. And you knew that getting on top of your job meant that there was going to be a radical transformation of policy. There was going to be a policy shift, but from where was the policy shifting, and to where? You didn't know. All you knew, as an individual minister, was that you had to engage and begin to understand where your department was and where you wanted to lead it. But having decided on an approximate course, you also knew there was a general perception that the civil service was not seen as a servant of the people. So you said, "I want policies to serve the people, policies that begin to deliver to the people."

ties of the IFP, which emerged in a series of exposés in the *Weekly Mail* (now the *Mail & Guardian*) in January 1992. De Klerk appointed him minister of forestry. For interview go to []o'malley interviews/ []Magnus Malan.

The Transport Portfolio

The significance of Transport in the macro pigeonhole was minimal. The departure from or the further development of policy for Transport would be reported to the NEC, but I do not recall an instance where it became the centerpiece of debate, where the National Executive members said they were unhappy. But it was not efficient.

Yes, all those policies touching on the economy and the economic transformation were put together in a single report. And when it was tabled at the NEC, the debate would take place around GEAR,* around labor. There was hardly any debate on Transport. Yet in the cabinet, as far back as December 1995, there was a special cabinet meeting that had recognized Transport as one of the five critical areas that needed to be addressed in terms of our total restructuring of the economy.[55]

What do I mean by total restructuring? I mean we were taking a closed economy and integrating it into a world economy, and saying that the basis of that was that the South African economy had to become more of a manufacturing export economy and competitive on the world market. The transportation costs were a vital element of that. Whatever understanding people have of globalization, this modern phase of globalization has been driven by two issues: increased speed of movement and reduction of the costs of transportation of goods and telecommunications.

---

*In 1996, the RDP was replaced with the Growth, Employment and Redistribution (GEAR) program, which placed the premium on South Africa getting its "economic fundamentals" in order and attracting FDI to generate economic growth and create jobs. GEAR was market friendly; privatization entered the political lexicon much to the horror of the SACP and COSATU. The RDP, GEAR, and commentary on the early years of economic transformation are available at []transition/documents and reports/1994/ []post-transition/documents and reports/ 1996/[] and []transformation/documents and reports/2005/[] respectively. See also interviews with Jay Naidoo, former minister without portfolio; Tito Mboweni, former minister of labor, current governor of the Reserve Bank; Derek Keyes, former minister of finance; Chris Lansberg, former minister of finance; Sam Shilowa, former general secretary (GS) of COSATU, current premier of Gauteng; Mahlmola Skhosana, then deputy SG, now SG of NACTU (National Council of Trade Unions); Jeremy Cronin, deputy GS of SACP; Charles Nqakula, former GS of the SACP, current chairperson and minister for safety and security; Blade Nzimande, GS of the SACP; Popo Molefe, former premier of the North West province; and Pravin Gordhan, former ANC MP, current head of SARS (South African Revenue Service), on the government's economic policies and their efficacy. See also Alan Hirsch, *Season of Hope: Economic Reform Under Mandela and Mbeki* (Scottsville: University of Natal Press, 2005); Raymond Parsons, ed., *Manuel, Markets and Money: Essays in Appraisal* (Cape Town: Double Storey, 2004).

Those are the two things that have driven the increase of trade between states around the world.

So it was pivotal. But the understanding of dealing with that in detail, the role it played and how to reduce transportation costs, was at this stage overwhelmed by an assumption among most people that the 60 percent ownership of the transport industry by the state should be maintained. And yet what we had inherited from the parastatals was total inefficiency. So the debates about that inefficiency and how to deal with it—bringing about efficiency and reducing costs—was really taking place inside the cabinet. And although it may have been referred to in the debate in the NEC and the Policy Unit, it was never pursued in any significant way.

In the case of my department I found that 60 percent of the transport industry was controlled by parastatals, which were accountable to the minister of public enterprises. When I went to Stella Sigcau, the new ANC minister, and said, "This is what the RDP says," the minister said, "Hmm," and ignored the RDP. She wouldn't cooperate. But she never said she wouldn't cooperate. She had inherited an empire, and she was not going to dismantle it or diminish her power. So the parastatals stayed where they were—in the wrong place—and the problems with trying to integrate them into a strategic transport strategy became virtually impossible.

One year after I retired, I visited one of the ministers, Geraldine Fraser-Moleketi, quite a dynamic minister in charge of the public service, and she said to me, "You know, Mac, many of us distrusted what you were doing in Transport in terms of the agencies that you set up, the autonomous agencies. I now realize that what you did in creating those agencies was very significant and that we should be looking at the model and trying to emulate it in other government departments." I said to her, "What do you mean, you distrusted? You were sitting in the cabinet and approving my memoranda." She said, "Yes, we approved, but we didn't really trust. We thought you were dealing with it in a liberal way, that you were a neoliberal." So I said, "That's a great and sad comment." She asked why. "Because it means that you did not put your reservations on the table so that what I was doing could be informed by debate. You were saying that I can't be bothered to investigate this thing and examine it. Let's just pass it. But you were saying you didn't believe in it, and, therefore, you were transmitting a message to the membership that you didn't believe in it. Now should we be surprised if our delivery is not as effective as it should be?"

Race

When I decided to appoint Ketso as DG, I went to Madiba before I took the matter to the cabinet. I was conscious that I'm of Indian origin and I was appointing a person of Indian origin, although one with an impeccable record in the ANC. I had tried to find other people, but I couldn't persuade the people I approached. Either they didn't want the job, or they wanted too high a salary, or they were not available.

This was before I had decided on Ketso. So I went to Mandela and said, "Madiba, here is my problem, and this is the person I want to appoint. What do you think?" And he said, "Very good choice. I support you." Months later I got wind of murmurings among some of the ANC comrades. I think it was in a publication called *Tribune*, a black magazine (although I'm not sure) that was run by Jon Quelane at the time. They ran a general article commenting that ministers were appointing people from similar race groups, and in particular they made that remark about me. So there was this murmuring going on and then—surprise, surprise—I learned from Madiba one day during a casual chat that one of the veterans of the ANC who was in parliament and on the Transport Committee had gone to Madiba to complain about the appointment of Ketso.

So the matter stayed on the public agenda. When *The Star* reported one day on some matter to do with transport, in 1997 or 1998, Kaiser Nyatsumba attacked me in a column and said that I was employing only Indians. I didn't bother responding. But when Nyatsumba became the executive editor of *The Star*, he invited me to a lunch. We had a very nice lunch with key people in *The Star*, most of them white. Kaiser was the host. We had a good discussion on transport questions. They asked me about wider issues in a very nice way over lunch and then, just as the lunch was finishing and Kaiser was thanking me for coming, he raised the question, criticizing me for appointing Indians. This was done at the conclusion of the lunch.

So I said, "No, we don't do this. You have raised matters which you should have raised in the question time, and I now insist that we carry on." I was due to fly to Cape Town that day at about three o'clock. I called my personal assistant to cancel my flight because, I said, "I won't leave this matter like this." So I insisted that they all sit down and we tackle the question. I set about explaining and Kaiser went on to the defensive. I said, "No, here is a report that you wrote some weeks ago on this same matter. Now what I'm offering you here, in front of your whole management, is a visit to my department, no restrictions. You walk through the whole department. You meet anybody you want to. You talk to anybody you like from the DG down. And you question them about the figures: How many appointments were there? What did we inherit? What was the racial composition? What are the changes? Who's been appointed? Who's at middle management? Who's at top management? Ask everything." I said, "I want you to come and see everybody, and when you have seen the department, I want you to have the guts to publish a correction. That's the condition. You will report on what you see, and you will publicly acknowledge that you were wrong if the facts show you that. But if the facts show you anything else, don't apologize. Hammer me."

It was a very rough discussion. I was really angry with him, and I went for him. He came to the ministry. He didn't even bother to meet Ketso. He didn't bother to walk through. He came and sat in my office, and I put the overall picture to him. He published a stingy correction.

20. BACK IN THE COLD

Introduction

ON 16 FEBRUARY 2003, the *Sunday Times* ran a front-page story suggesting that Mac, while minister of transport, had received a kickback from Schabir Shaik, brother of Yunus and Moe. This alleged kickback related to a R265 million contract awarded in February 1997 to the consortium Probida, which included Nkobi Holdings (a Shaik company), to produce the new credit-card driver's license. It also related to a R2.6 billion contract to upgrade the toll road between Johannesburg and Durban, awarded to the N3 Toll Road Consortium, of which Nkobi Investments (another Shaik company) was a member.

The kickback of R535,000 to Mac, the *Sunday Times* alleged, was paid into Zarina and Mac's bank accounts over five years. In media accounts of the payments, it was never reported that the driver's license contract had been awarded by the State Tender Board and the toll road contract by the National Roads Agency, or that neither Mac nor the Ministry of Transport had any say in the awarding of either contract.

Whether the Scorpions, the elite crime unit of the National Prosecuting Authority (NPA), began to investigate Schabir Shaik or Jacob Zuma[1] first in connection with the South African arms deal[*2] of 1998 is moot.[3] In June 2001, they conducted a search-and-seize operation on the offices and home of Schabir Shaik. Among the materials seized were documents that suggested that the then deputy president Jacob Zuma had been promised

*South Africa announced a massive arms deal in 1998 to reequip the South African military forces. The first phase of the deal involved the purchase of patrol corvettes, light helicopters, submarines, Hawk jet trainers, and light fighter aircraft from manufacturers in France, Britain, Italy, Germany, and Sweden. Within one year, the cost of the deal had skyrocketed from R29.9 billion to R43 billion (US $5 billion)—an increase of more than 42 percent.

annual payments of R500,000 in exchange for protecting a consortium headed by Thomson-CSF from being investigated in connection with the arms deal. Nkobi Holdings had a 5 percent stake in Thomson's successful R6.6 billion bid. Schabir Shaik controlled Nkobi Holdings, and he was also Zuma's financial adviser, in control of his personal affairs. Among the alleged crimes the Scorpions were investigating was whether Shaik had solicited the bribe on Zuma's behalf. Schabir Shaik was arrested in November 2001 and charged on a number of counts, including corruption.

2

In the wake of the *Sunday Times* story, Mac stepped down from his position at First Rand to allow it to investigate the allegations. Bulelani Ngcuka,[4] director of the NPA, confirmed that Mac and Zarina Maharaj would be questioned in connection with the matter, although he denied that either was the target of an investigation. The Scorpions subpoenaed thirty to forty officials from the Department of Transport, the state Tender Board, and the National Roads Agency. The Maharajes were asked to answer a series of questions under Section 28 of the National Prosecutorial Act, which requires individuals to respond to questions put to them by the NPA, whether or not they are targets of an investigation and whether or not the responses are self-incriminatory. Refusal to respond is a criminal offense.[5]

In a seemingly unrelated matter, the Scorpions sent Zuma thirty-five questions relating to their probe into the arms deal. Zuma refused to answer them on the grounds that the government had already investigated the arms deal and had found no evidence of wrongdoing.[6] The cases of the deputy president and Mac became intertwined when Ngcuka made Mac's exoneration conditional on his securing Zuma's cooperation in addressing the questions.

After the *Sunday Times* published its allegations of corruption on the part of Mac, several attempts, all initiated by Ngcuka or on behalf of Ngcuka, were made to convey the message to Mac that the Scorpions had nothing to charge him with. Ngcuka said so to Ismail Ayob, Mac's attorney.[7] But, Ayob was told, no statement to that effect from the NPA would be forthcoming unless Mac secured the cooperation of Schabir Shaik in relation to a plea bargain as well as Zuma's responses to the questions the Scorpions had sent him. It is unclear why the Scorpions felt Mac had influence in this matter, unless they believed that people who had worked in the underground inside South Africa in the 1980s had special bonds of loyalty and commitment to each other that would supersede the legal strictures of the state they helped create. For his part, Zuma rejected offers of mediation out of hand. Cyril Ramaphosa was drawn into the matter and had made arrangements to meet with Ngcuka, once canceled, and due to be rescheduled[8] when the *Sunday Times* ran a story with the caption that he had been approached to play the role of interlocutor between Ngcuka and Mac.[9] Ramaphosa bowed out.

First Rand issued its report on 14 August, clearing Mac. Yet in the absence of any statement from the NPA to indicate that Mac was no longer under investigation, First Rand and Mac agreed that he should resign his position. Which he did, with a settlement of one million rand.

He lost his reputation. His forty years of being at the cutting edge of the struggle counted for naught. He was smeared with the brush of corruption. He fought back, accusing Ngcuka of abusing his office, daring Ngcuka to charge him. He became obsessed with the abuse of power in the office of the Directorate of Public Prosecutions. He read every book he could find on J. Edgar Hoover, the first director of the FBI, who maintained his position of power by having something on every president of the United States. Nothing could convince Mac that Ngcuka was not out to maintain secret files on the country's leadership and presidential aspirants. Now, with me, he could talk of nothing else.

3

Since Vula, Moe Shaik's career and Mac's had moved in different directions. In the government of national unity, Moe served as deputy cocoordinator of intelligence in the Ministry of Intelligence, where he worked under Joe Nhlanhla. Nhlanhla instructed Moe to continue to update Operation Bible, which he did.[10] In 1997, Moe moved to the Department of Foreign Affairs, and in 1999, he became South Africa's ambassador to Algeria and subsequently special assistant to Dr. Nkosazana Dlamini-Zuma, the minister of foreign affairs. He became a close friend and confidant of his former Intelligence boss Jacob Zuma. Moe and Mac maintained a casual friendship. The *Sunday Times* story on Mac brought them together and linked their fates in ways neither could have imagined.

In 2002, press reports began to circulate, which were confirmed by Ngcuka, that the Scorpions were investigating alleged criminal activities involving Moe's brother Schabir and Zuma. Moe issued a public statement that he had no objection to his brother's being investigated but that the Scorpions should "lay off" the deputy president.

Zuma's career had taken unexpected turns. He had been secretly brought in to South Africa by the National Intelligence Service (NIS) in early 1990 to coordinate arrangements for the Groote Schuur meeting between the government and the ANC. In July 1991, he was elected to the position of deputy secretary general of the ANC. During the negotiations, he was primarily deployed to KZN, where he and the IFP's general secretary Frank Mdlalose tried to put a brake on the spiraling violence. It was a difficult and hazardous task, and Zuma deserves much of the credit for brokering the uneasy truce that eventually emerged between the two movements.* He was elected national chairperson of the ANC in 1994, chairperson of the ANC in KZN, and nominated the ANC's candidate for premier. When the IFP won the province, Zuma became minister of economic affairs and tourism in the power-sharing government in KZN. In 1997, he was elected deputy president of the ANC, and when Mbeki became president, he appointed Zuma deputy president. When Mbeki was reelected in 2004, Zuma was also reappointed.

Moe Shaik was convinced that the NPA's attempts to link Zuma to wrongdoing because he had been the recipient of large sums of money from Moe's brother Schabir were intended to derail Zuma's chances of succeeding Mbeki as president.† He resurrected a file Operation Bible had opened on Ngcuka in 1988 and brought it to Mac's attention. In 1989, Operation Bible had found that there were sufficient grounds to conclude that Bulelani Ngcuka was "probably a spy"—and that he could be identified as the spy code-named Agent RS 452. On 23 August, Mac brought the matter to the attention of President Thabo Mbeki, who looked over the reconstructed Intelligence file on Ngcuka, but gave no hint as to what, if anything, he might do. Later the same day, Ngcuka and Penuell Maduna,[11] the minister of justice, held a press conference at which they announced that although they had a prima facie case of corruption against Zuma, they would not prosecute him because they did not believe they had a winnable case.

4

Bulelani Ngcuka had risen fast in the ANC hierarchy. After graduating from the University of Fort Hare, he went to Durban in 1978 and served

---

*For his efforts and his participation in the peace process in Burundi, he was honored in October 1998, in Washington, D.C., with the Nelson Mandela Award for Outstanding Leadership.
†Under the constitution a president can only serve two terms.

his articles of clerkship in the law office of Griffith Mxenge, a well-known anti-apartheid activist who was later assassinated by the SB in 1985. Ngcuka was admitted as an attorney in 1980 and opened a law practice in 1981. Throughout this period he was active in the ANC underground in the Durban area. In November 1981, shortly after the arrest of Patrick Maqubela, he was detained. At the subsequent trial of Maqubela on a charge of high treason, Ngcuka refused to testify for the state. As a result, he was sentenced to three years' imprisonment, during which he completed his studies for an LLB degree by correspondence. After release in 1985, he left the country for Switzerland, traveling on a South African passport that had been issued to him in 1981. He worked for the International Labor Organization, lived in Geneva, and traveled extensively in Europe on behalf of the ANC. He returned to South Africa in 1987, became active in the UDF and, in time, UDF chairperson in the Western Cape. He was detained twice. After the ANC was unbanned, he became a member of the ANC's constitutional committee and later a member of the ANC delegation to CODESA and the multiparty negotiations in Kempton Park. In the new constitutional legislative structures, he became deputy chair of the National Council of Provinces, the second chamber of parliament, and in August 1998 he was appointed national director of the National Prosecuting Authority (NPA). In that capacity, he had overall control of the institution and conduct of criminal proceedings on behalf of the state and of the Directorate of Special Operations (DSO)—the Scorpions—a body with considerable investigative and prosecutorial powers designed to halt corruption in all spheres. It was lodged in the Ministry of Justice as opposed to the police. When Mbeki became president, he appointed Ngcuka's wife, Phumzile Mlambo-Ngcuka, to the position of minister of minerals and energy, replacing Penuell Maduna, who became minister of justice.

5

Mac had begun to question whether there was a connection between the Operation Bible finding and what he perceived as Ngcuka's abuse of power, not just in relation to his case but in other cases it had investigated.* Mac had irrefutable evidence that the Scorpions had deliberately

*I asked Mac on several occasions to specify which cases he was alluding to. The cases he mentioned were ones that he said were leaked to the media: the case of Dr. Zweli Mkhize of the ANC from KwaZulu-Natal, who, the media reported, was about to be arrested for gun running and murder. It was reported, Mac said, that he would be arrested together with Philip Powell of the IFP. Powell himself was the center of the second case. Powell

leaked aspects of the investigation of himself and Zarina to the press in violation of its statutory obligations—that the NPA itself had committed a crime. (He tape-recorded a conversation with Jovial Rantao, a political correspondent for Independent Newspapers, during which Jovial told him that he had received information regarding his case from sources within the Scorpions.) The documents published in the *Sunday Times* included check stubs and could only have been leaked by the Scorpions. Mac wanted the matter brought into the open.

On 7 September 2003, *City Press*, a widely read Sunday newspaper, led with the story that Ngcuka had been investigated by ANC Intelligence, which had concluded that he probably was a spy. On 8 September, Mac confirmed the *City Press* story. But the media failed to make a clear distinction between his confirming that Bible's findings had been conveyed to him by Moe Shaik in 1989 and his having some independent corroboration of the finding itself. Thus the distinction between a confirmation of the findings of 1989 and an accusation that Ngcuka had been a spy was blurred. Nevertheless, Mac had absolute confidence in Moe's findings. During Vula, Moe's intelligence unit had saved his life on numerous occasions and now, in the absence of any information that had come Moe's way to suggest otherwise, he believed Moe's findings were correct: Bulelani Ngcuka had probably been an apartheid spy.

It would be naive to believe that Mac's motives were entirely altruistic. He was deeply angry at Ngcuka for his refusal to clear him, which cost him his job and encouraged the media to imply wrongdoing on his part because

---

had run the camp Mac had arranged to have raided prior to the elections in 1994. When the Scorpions discovered large arms caches in KZN, rather than Powell being arrested he was allowed to go to the UK under an arrangement never made public. Zweli's name, Mac maintains, has never been cleared. Accusations were also made in respect to Popo Molefe, premier of North West, who was alleged to have molested a young girl; leaks were already circulating at the time about Jacob Zuma; Kgalema had already made a statement condemning the "Hollywood-style" operations of the Scorpions.

The most important case in which the NPA appears to have abused its power had not yet come to the fore. The Ngoako Ramathlodi case had not hit the media by that time. When Ramathlodi was premier of Limpopo two of his associates, Solomon Mohale and Gideon Serote, were alleged to have won tenders to distribute old-age pensions in exchange for financial favors to Ramathlodi at the time. The Scorpions raided their businesses and seized documents. Mohale and Gideon took the Scorpions to court and in February 2006 Justice N. M. Mavundla ruled in the Pretoria High Court that the documents should be returned. He found that they had been illegally seized by the Scorpions on the basis of warrants obtained under false pretense. The investigation was believed to have scuppered Ramathlodi's chances of succeeding Ngcuka as head of the NPA or of becoming a member of Mbeki's cabinet in 2005. Ramathlodi is still under investigation (2007).

he would not play along with Ngcuka's mediation overtures. Moreover, he had been informed that at an off-the-record briefing Ngcuka had held with seven black newspaper editors on 24 July,[12] Ngcuka had allegedly called him a liar, said that the way to get at Mac was through his wife, and that he was going to charge Zarina Maharaj with tax evasion.[13]

Mac, says Janet Love, his Vula colleague and as loyal a friend as anyone could have, should have added a caveat to his confirmation of the spy allegations: he should have noted that such investigations during the struggle years were conducted under difficult and dangerous circumstances, and that conclusions reached then with regard to specific individuals should be revisited before being aired in public as if they were facts. Mistakes were often made. By not acknowledging these, she says, Mac lost the moral high ground.

Mac is never one to admit to anger or, indeed, to ever having made a mistake. That is who he is. He had not exhausted all alternative means for pursuing the matter, but he has never found it necessary to acknowledge that he might have handled matters differently, with perhaps less disastrous consequences for himself and his family. He behaved as he always had, serving notice that he would not be intimidated by the Scorpions or be more circumspect about drawing attention to what he perceived as their high-handed behavior. It was inevitable, perhaps, that the Scorpions, given their wide powers (including the sole mandate to investigate wrongdoing within its own ranks), would sometimes act in an arbitrary, persecuting manner. But Mac, like the agency, also acted arrogantly, believing he was acting to preserve constitutional checks on the abuse of power.

Moe Shaik's motives were more clear-cut. Either independently or with Zuma's blessing, he sought to out Ngcuka and protect Zuma. When Mac confirmed that in 1988–89, Operation Bible, under the direction of Moe, had conducted an investigation into Ngcuka, this was widely interpreted as support for Zuma's perceived attempts to discredit Ngcuka. Impugning Mac was a form of counterattack. The more Mac protested that his actions were triggered solely by what he considered an egregious breach of power by the NPA—an attempt to convict him in the media for a matter on which it could not charge him—the more he was seen to be in the Zuma camp.

On 16 September, Moe Shaik and Sipho Ngwema, the spokesperson for Ngcuka, appeared on a prerecorded eTV news program in the course of which Moe said that his post-1994 investigations had enabled him to establish that Ngcuka was not RS 452.[14] "RS 452," he said, "was a false flag or strat-com operation." (A "false flag" is a procedure whereby intelligence from one informant is hidden under the code number of another in order to protect the former's identity.) Ngwena indicated that the NPA had established the identity of RS 452—"a white person from the Eastern Cape."[15]

6

On 19 September, Thabo Mbeki appointed retired judge Joos Hefer as the chairperson and sole member of a commission of inquiry to determine whether Ngcuka was either RS 452 or an agent of the apartheid state, under any code name, at any stage prior to 1994. On 7 October, the commission's terms of reference were extended to determine whether Ngcuka, "due to past obligations to the apartheid regime," had abused the powers of his office. But on 11 November, Mbeki once again redefined the terms of reference. Now the commission would report on the "allegations by Messrs. Maharaj and Shaik" that Ngcuka was RS 452. Thus if Hefer found him not to have been a spy, specifically RS 452, the need to address the second question (abuse of office) was obviated. Why the president would reformulate the commission in this way and for what purpose is a question that only he can answer since no one was accusing Ngcuka at this point of being RS 452.

The reformulated terms of reference shifted the goalposts. Now Mac and Shaik were being asked to prove not that Ngcuka had been a spy, or even that Ngcuka had been investigated and found probably to have been a spy, but that Ngcuka was RS 452, something neither Shaik nor Mac had accused him of being. State intelligence and security agencies refused to cooperate with the commission on the grounds that all intelligence files were classified, and no information would be disclosed that might reveal the identity of RS 452. Similarly, security personnel were prohibited from testifying. The ANC adopted a similar stance: Jacob Zuma, the former head of Intelligence, informed the commission that he "was not at liberty to disclose information, without the express mandate and direction of my organization," which was not forthcoming. The situation, Hefer reported, had become "insufferable."

Nevertheless, beyond this one small outburst of exacerbation, he uncomplainingly accepted the constraints imposed on him by the shrinking frame of reference and pressed ahead. But relief was at hand.

Also on 11 November, the Reverend Frank Chikane, the president's chief of staff, wrote Hefer that the president had "unfettered access to all information in possession of the state intelligence and security structures that bear on the matters being considered by the commission," that "these structures have made no allegations that bear on the matters being considered by the Commission," and that the basis for appointing the commission related "to information held by persons outside state structures." Thus there was no need for anyone from the state security services to give testimony before the commission.

But the president chose not to inform either Hefer or the public that he had already seen the contents of the file containing the basis for the allegations made by Shaik and Mac and could have determined their veracity in the weeks following 23 August with a few inquiries to his own intelligence services, or by asking Messrs. Maharaj and Shaik to share their information with the security services. There was, in fact, no need for the commission.

No members of Moe Shaik's former unit or any member of ANC Intelligence in Lusaka came forward to support his claims (nor did he ask them to). Hefer refused to subpoena them on the not unreasonable grounds that they had only to step forward.

The assertion that Ngcuka was agent RS 452 was disproved when Vanessa Brereton, now living in London, owned up to having spied for the government under that code name. Information available in 2003 but unavailable to an ANC unit operating underground in 1988–89 exposed the flaws and mistaken assumptions in Moe Shaik's analysis.

Three attorneys, Jabuta Moerane for Ngcuka, Norman Arendse for Penuell Maduna, and Kessie Naidu for the commission, took turns cross-examining Mac and Shaik. Mac confirmed that the investigation had been carried out by Shaik's unit and that he had been "persuaded" by its findings. But, finally, Mac had to say, in the light of information now available, he "did not know" whether Ngcuka had been a spy. Moerane, seizing the perfect sound bite before the television cameras (the hearings were televised and broadcast live—a first in the country), proclaimed with a magnificent flourish: "Now all of South Africa knows that Mac Maharaj does not know whether Bulelani Ngcuka was a spy!" Grand theater. Great headlines. Mac and Moe as bumbling begrudgers stripped of honor.

The media portrayed Mac as someone prepared to help defend Zuma, by foul means, against corruption charges that Zuma had not even bothered to rebut. Zuma kept complaining he was being given a trial by media, but refused to speak to the media about the issue and was prepared to use his old intelligence connections to smear Ngcuka. Mac was seen as an instrument of the smear. The issue at this point was not that Mac was corrupt, but that he was prepared to help derail an investigation that might show that Zuma was. It looked like he was doing Zuma's dirty work. The influential *Mail & Guardian* weekly ran an editorial on Mac with the headline THE TRAGIC FALL OF AN ICON.[16]

7

The Hefer Commission of Inquiry found that Ngcuka "probably never at any time before 1994 acted as an agent for a state security service" and that "the suspicion of a small number of distrustful individuals harbored against him fourteen years ago was the result of ill-founded inferences and groundless assumptions." Hefer insinuated that Shaik's finding, even in a "war situation which demanded a low level of suspicion [for reporting individuals to Lusaka as probable spies]," was unwarranted when he made it in the light of information then available, which probably would, had it been pursued, have led him to a different conclusion.[17]

It is ironic that Hefer should trash the way Shaik had weighed probabilities, using impossible-to-weigh probabilities to do so. Hefer's first assertion is itself a probable, and it is interdependent with the second assertion. This latter is hypothetical, a purely subjective judgment on the part of a member of the Afrikaner establishment, whose processes of analysis were irreversibly rooted in a culture of thinking germane to apartheid's perceptions of its enemies and their modus operandi. He assumed he could make a determination of what information ANC operatives, working in clandestine and highly dangerous conditions, *should* have been capable of gathering, of how they *should* have analyzed information at hand—and this during a dirty war in which there were no rules of engagement. Moreover, he was similarly incapable of divining what might constitute "a low threshold of suspicion."*

*I talked with Judge Hefer on 24 March 2006. He was quite forthcoming. In response to my questions, he said that Moe Shaik had conducted a sloppy investigation, and with the information then available to him, he *should* have been able to deduce that Vanessa Brereton was RS 452. He also said that he had made a "judgment" on the quality of Shaik's Bible report rather than saying Shaik had just gotten it wrong "because the idea was to say that it wasn't worth much because of the *bad work* that they had done." What struck me was the judge's assuming to have some special facility that allowed him to divine what constituted "good" and "bad" work performed by individuals who, if they did not remain underground in every sense of the term, were, if caught, subject to summary termination or abduction and torture and execution like their colleagues Vusi Tshabalala and Charles Ndaba. Or ordeals like Catherine Mvelase's. The experience of the ANC—that the regime was exceptionally successful in turning trusted comrades—had made it paranoid about everyone. The Vula comms are littered with references to inquiries, suspicions, follow-ups, insinuations, and so on.

Not a single voice emerged from the ranks of the ANC elite to question the basis of Hefer's extraordinary deductive powers. For the sake of political expediency, the ANC elite was willing to have its own history trashed.

8

Subsequent to the Hefer Commission, I talked with key people from ANC Intelligence and people from all branches of the former security forces, including officials who liaised with apartheid-era employees of the Department of Home Affairs, none of whom appeared before the Hefer Commission. The interviews are embargoed until 2030.

Was Bulelani Ngcuka investigated by Moe Shaik's Bible unit and found probably to have been a spy? Yes. Was that report forwarded to Lusaka? Yes. Did ANC Intelligence in Lusaka accept that finding? Yes.* Was Moe Shaik instructed to continue with his investigation? Yes. In the light of information available in 2003, was the ANC's finding—not Moe Shaik's—regarding Ngcuka incorrect? Yes. Indeed, one can go a step further and say with as close to certitude as one can get in the labyrinthine world of intelligence and counterintelligence that Bulelani Ngcuka never worked for the South African Police.

Mac and Shaik erred in trying to prove that a 1998–89 finding could have been correctly arrived at with information available in 2003. Hefer erred in trying to show that Shaik (ANC Intelligence) should not have made the finding he did in 1988–89 because he either overlooked or did not studiously pursue information then available that would have led him to a different conclusion. Determining whether the 1988–89 finding was *justified* was not part of Hefer's authority. Beyond that, he was imminently unqualified to make any determination in the matter.

Operation Bible's conclusions were not based on "the suspicion of a small number of distrustful individuals" or on "ill-founded inferences and groundless assumptions." Leaving aside the issue of how he received a passport, one of the questions the commission had to address was how Ngcuka had his passport renewed in Geneva. In Geneva, he adopted a high-profile anti-apartheid, pro-ANC posture and traveled across Europe castigating the apartheid regime. The ILO, the organization for which he

*In response to my question: if you had been able to verify that Moe Shaik's report had been forwarded to Lusaka and its finding that Ngcuka was "probably a spy" accepted by Lusaka, would the allegation that Ngcuka was found to have "probably been a spy" stand as valid, despite the *fact* of his not having been one in the light of your investigation, Judge Hefer answered yes.

worked, was monitored by the security services.* Wanting to return to
South Africa in 1987 and finding that his passport had expired, he went to
the South African consulate in Geneva and had his request for renewal approved as a matter of routine. The resident NIS agent never flagged the application, it seems.† Hefer concluded primarily on the basis of the
testimony of an official from the former Department of Home Affairs that
there was nothing out of the ordinary in this. But my conversations with
former SB members, former NIS agents, and former employees of Home
Affairs regarding the ways in which passports were issued and renewed
during the 1980s make it clear that the granting of this passport, and especially the manner of its renewal, was something out of the ordinary.‡ Sufficient grounds, at the very least, to warrant suspicion. The new orthodoxy
promulgated at the Hefer Commission that there was not extensive collusion between the security forces and the Department of Home Affairs resulting in blacklisting individuals who were not to receive passports is
simply a rewriting of the past.

*The SB file number for ILO was S.32/1/18.
†In South African embassies, which did not count among their staff officials of the Department of Home Affairs, passport applications and applications for renewal were handled by the NIS contingent in the embassy. Known agitators, i.e., people on whom the
NIS kept a file or known activists, especially ones who had been convicted on struggle-
related charges, would usually have their applications summarily dismissed. There
would, if thought necessary, be consultation with the SAP, but decisions where consideration was deferred for security reasons usually took time. Conversation with senior NIS
officials on 31 July 2006; source embargoed until 2030.
‡Depending on who I talked with, I got a different account of how passports were issued,
how and whether blacklists were maintained, where they were maintained, and how they
worked. But no one denied that they did exist. In the case of Bulelani Ngcuka I was told
that when he applied for renewal his application would have been passed to the NIS official in the embassy. Given Ngcuka's status and the fact that the SB and NIS kept security
tabs on the ILO, and that the NIS would have opened a file on him, the NIS agent would
have forwarded the application to HQ, which would write an "opinion" in the matter
that would be sent to SB HQ. The SB would take the final decision. Sometimes it would
override the opinion of the NIS. Or in the case of high-profile cases it would refer the
decision to the political authorities—Ngcuka, the source said, would hardly qualify for
that categorization. All this would take time. If a passport was granted, it would be
tagged to monitor its future use. One case I came across where a passport was denied to
a South African applying for a passport renewal involved Dr. G. V. (Freddy) Reddy, who
moved to London in the late 1950s (he knew Mac there) and then to Norway, where he
became a psychiatrist and founded the Norwegian Anti-Apartheid Movement. Between
1979 and 1989, Reddy spent part of each year working in ANC camps. On his first application for a renewal of his passport it was renewed but was refused on an application
when he sought to have it renewed again. On this occasion the Department of Home Affairs would grant him only a docucment that would allow him to travel in South Africa.
He refused the document and remained in exile up until post-1990. (See interview with

Hefer's implicit conclusion that Moe Shaik alone conducted the Ngcuka investigation is incorrect. Others worked with Shaik on the Ngcuka file. Zuma knew that Ngcuka was under investigation. Zuma concurred with Bible's findings. Suspicions about Ngcuka were brought to Tambo's attention in November 1988 by Mac,[18] and were referred to again in a comm to Tambo and Slovo from Mac regarding confidentiality of information passing through London in February 1989;[19] Tambo and Zuma discussed the matter of an investigation relating to Ngcuka and "a certain number" (RS 452) in May 1989.[20] Mac himself discussed Ngcuka with Mandela in late April 1990 in the presence of Alfred Nzo.[21] I have talked with one of the few persons who had access to the Vula comms and Tambo, and he unhesitatingly corroborated the statement that it was his understanding that Tambo concurred with the Intelligence finding that Bulelani probably was RS 452.*

Hefer's report is without context. Unwilling to test the commission's powers of subpoena and the extent of its authority, he had virtually no input from officials from the apartheid government's many intelligence agencies to ascertain how they gathered and evaluated intelligence on the ANC, how they uncovered ANC intelligence moles, or the role of probability in intelligence decisions. He received no information from officials in ANC intelligence to explain how the Department of Intelligence and

---

Dr. Reddy at []maharaj/interviewees/[] Reddy.) No doubt having an influence on Shaik's analysis was the fact that while he was a student at the University of Durban at Westville he was denied a passport on several occasions. At the time he was a student activist but not aligned overtly with any organization. And of course, he, like just about every black activist, knew numerous people who had been denied passports, some with only tenuous ties to the anti-apartheid movements. Among the recommendations in a report prepared by Karl Edwards (handler of Vanessa Brereton) for the NIS in 1980 on the NIC were a number relating to travel restrictions. Because of the contacts a number of Indians had with the ANC/CP, he said that "for this reason travel documents must be withdrawn from those Indians who are abusing them, and not issued to those who (upon reasonable suspicion) intend to abuse them. . . . In order to clarify this issue of travel documents it is suggested that Mrs. Labuschagne of Section B screen passport applicants in the light of this report. With this in mind, two procedures can then be followed: a list of individuals must be made whose passports must definitely be removed on the ground of their present ANC/CP involvement; [and] a list of additional suspects, friends, and relations must be prepared for the purposes of search at border points." Go to [] maharaj/documents and reports/security files/[]NIS: In-depth Analysis of NIC with emphasis on ANC/CP links; for duplicates of passport applications and assorted SAP comments about whether applicants should receive one, go to [] maharaj/documents and reports/security files/[]passports.

*Interview embargoed until 2030.

Security (NAT) worked,* and the special place of Operation Bible in the larger intelligence picture. He had no understanding of the level of paranoia within the ANC, why important strategic and operational decisions were not disclosed to members of the NEC, and no idea of the scope of the apartheid state's intelligence infiltration of the ANC leadership.

Because, in the absence of anyone's stepping forward to testify, Hefer could not confirm that Operation Bible reports were routed through Shaheen Bawa, an ANC intelligence operative in London who had received specialized training in the GDR in ways to courier information to avoid detection or that Bawa delivered these reports personally to Zuma when the latter visited London or otherwise had them conveyed to him in Lusaka.[22] For the same reason, Hefer could not establish that Pingla Udit worked with Moe Shaik at the NIA, post-1994, upgrading Operation Bible files.[23] In the world of intelligence, where information and disinformation have equal currency, the books are rarely closed, much like the way in which the NPA itself sometimes appears to operate.†

In *Move Your Shadow*, Pulitzer Prize–winning author Joseph Lelyveld recounts Oliver Tambo's response when he told him that a certain Colonel Coetsee, an SB official in Pretoria, had boasted that government intelligence could infiltrate the ANC at will. Rather than offering some rejoinder, Lelyveld says Tambo exclaimed: "He was right! He was right!" Some of the ANC's members, who were "highly respected, who had behaved very well, were disciplined, sounded very committed and certainly performed all their tasks very satisfactorily," turned out to be apartheid agents.[24] SB official Hentie Botha, who had recruited Charles Ndaba before he came

---

*During our conversation, Judge Hefer expressed some puzzlement as to why the ANC would not have taken some action against Ngcuka if it, in fact, had concluded that he was probably a spy: "You know what to expect if they discover a spy in their midst, but nothing like that happened. It just occurs to me now it is strange that nothing was done about it." But, of course, part of the failure of the commission was its inability to establish exactly how the ANC dealt with spies in its midst. On many occasions, especially at the level of a Ngcuka and higher echelons, NAT did nothing overtly. I raised a similar question with Jacob Zuma with regard to an individual uncovered as probably a spy who was a member of the NEC, and I subsequently came upon documents showing that this individual, despite this finding, was still sitting in on meetings of the NEC. Zuma smiled and said, "That's not the way we operated." But the fact that the Hefer Commission could entertain a null hypothesis, that is, that all things being equal, the ANC was likely to take action against someone if it found that he or she was a spy and that the absence of any action predisposes one to accept the hypothesis that the individual is not a spy is flawed and indicates his unfamiliarity with the way in which NAT worked.
†See []maharaj/footnotes [] 427.

into South Africa and then, when Vula was being uncovered, shot him dead because his utility had expired,[25] could have recounted how the SB fed the ANC misinformation about Thami Zulu, the MK chief in Swaziland, in the knowledge that Zulu would be recalled to Lusaka and arrested by NAT.[26] When Maxwell Zulu was exposed, Mac told Tambo he would have him assassinated,[27] but Tambo forbade it.[28]

Had Mac not been so protective, he might have informed the commission that many others had been investigated too—Siphiwe Nyanda and Susan Tshabalala, the Vula operative infiltrated into South Africa in late 1989—or that one of the SACP's highest ranking officials accused his wife, Zarina, of working for MI5, a charge investigated by the SACP's Central Committee,[29] or that some of Cyril Ramaphosa's colleagues in the MDM believed that he worked for the CIA.[30]

Absent from Hefer's report is any sense that there had been a mortal battle between an apartheid government obsessed with crushing the ANC using whatever means and without regard for the life of *anyone* who stood in its way and a dysfunctional liberation movement often gripped by paranoia induced by the knowledge that the comrade who appeared to be the most motivated and driven might be working for the enemy. ("It seems to me," Hefer said, "that the whole organisation wasn't as good as it seemed on the face of it, well not as effective.")

In 2006, three years after his report was released, Hefer looked back and summed up: "There are questions which remain unanswered," he said, "and it's a pity that one couldn't see what's in the records because there is something there; they wouldn't have hedged like that if there wasn't something. There are still questions that I would like to see answers to."[31]

9

Even though it did not fall within Hefer's purview to address abuse of power by the NPA unless he found that Ngcuka had been a spy, Hefer was sufficiently perturbed by Mac's evidence, in his opening statement, that he did address the question in a limited way, reaching perhaps his most unequivocal conclusions:

> I find Mr Maharaj's evidence most disturbing . . . it is beyond doubt that leaks occurred . . . and highly likely that the guilty party was within Mr Ngcuka's party. Months have elapsed since Mr Maharaj was questioned by members of the Investigating Directorate and although Mr

Ngcuka has assured me that the investigation has not been completed, no charges have yet been preferred against Mr Maharaj or against his wife. In the meanwhile press reports about the allegations against them kept appearing. In a country such as ours where human dignity is a basic constitutional value and every person is presumed to be innocent until he or she has been found guilty, this is wholly unacceptable.

For the sake of completeness I must also mention that Mr Maharaj avers that Mr Ngcuka at one stage attempted to persuade him to become a party to a mediation process in order to bring the investigation against him, his wife, Mr Zuma and Mr Schabir Shaik to a satisfactory conclusion. Mr Ngcuka has denied the allegation and I am unable to make a finding.

Ngcuka was either not being truthful or availed himself of some legalistic interpretations of the questions put to him. (Mac and Shaik's lawyer's performance wavered between the anemic and the inept.)

While Mac maintains that Hefer's finding regarding possible abuse of power was a vindication of his decision to give evidence, the finding went entirely ignored and Mbeki never acted to address it.*

Of more import but as ignored was a matter relating to Ngcuka's testimony. Under cross-examination by Stephen Joseph, advocate for Mac and Shaik, regarding the alleged remarks he made at his meeting with the black editors, Ngcuka refused to answer questions on the grounds that because the meeting was off the record and the editors bound to confidentiality, he, too, was bound by the same constraints of disclosure. When asked by Judge Hefer whether he was aware of the consequences of refusing

---

*Following Nguka's press statement by Nguka that the NPA had a prima facie case of corruption against him, but would not prosecute because it had not a winnable case, Zuma lodged a complaint with the public protector that his human rights had been violated. Lawrence Mushwana, the public prosecutor, reported his findings on 24 May 2004 that Ncguka had "unjustifiably infringed on Zuma's constitutional right to human dignity and caused him to be improperly prejudiced." In the ugly public spat among Ngcuka, Maduna, and Mushwana that followed, Maduna abruptly resigned as minister of justice. It also emerged in Mushwana's report that the president had conducted an internal investigation into the actions of the NPA in compliance with Hefer's recommendations. That investigation exonerated Ngcuka from being party to the leaking of information but arrived at the somewhat unstartling conclusion that "strong circumstantial evidence that privileged material in the possession of the NPA found its way to unauthorized persons outside its structures." See [] maharaj/documents and reports/Jacob Zuma/[] report of the public prosecutor May 2004. The president's inquiry did not address the issue of Ngcuka's refusal to answer questions put to him at the commission presumably because the powers to investigate this matter were vested in the NPA.

to answer questions put to him while he was under oath before a presidential commission of inquiry, Ngcuka answered that he was.

The consequences?* Not to answer these questions was prima facie evidence of a criminal offense. The NPA should have investigated the matter, acting in compliance with an order from its director, and a court of law had determined whether there was "just reason," i.e., whether it could be shown that the legal responsibility not to respond had outweighed the legal obligation to do so. In the circumstances of 2003, this was tantamount to asking Ngcuka to investigate himself or, at the very least, to recuse himself while authorizing a deputy to do so. The fact that the NPA never carried out such an investigation went to the heart of the question of abuse of power: Who investigates possible wrongdoing on the part of the prosecuting authority when investigations of the kind called for are vested in the prosecuting authority itself? No doubt unwittingly, Ngcuka, cognizant that he could with impunity, given the powers of his office, afford to be in contempt of the commission underscored the inherent potential for abuse of power that resided in the office of the national prosecutor. Ironically, on this issue Ngcuka was Mac's best witness.[†] The man who had publicly proclaimed that he had a prima facie case of corruption against the deputy president himself committed a prima facie offense before the commission.

To support today what Mac said he accepted in 1989 is not an accusation that Ngcuka was a spy; it is to acknowledge that Mac confirmed in 2003 that an investigation had been carried out in 1988–89 and that he was made aware of its findings. The mistake Mac and Moe Shaik made was to attempt to find information in 2003 that would validate a conclusion reached in 1989.

Months after Hefer released his report, Yunus Shaik met with Ngcuka, apologized to him for the pain the revelations of the spy allegations had caused him, and made a pilgrimage to Mecca on his behalf. Ngcuka, he avers, is a good man. Moe Shaik is satisfied with the Hefer report. Hefer, he believes, had met his allegations halfway: Hefer was unable to say that Ngcuka was not a spy. And Mac, of course, has his own sense of vindication, one that would grow as further events unfolded.

---

*The consequences were laid out for me by Judge Hefer in a conversation we had in mid-July 2006 when we discussed the exchange between him, Ngcuka, and Stephen on the matter. The excerpt in question is available at [] maharaj/documents and reports/ Hefer Commission/ [] extract from cross-examination of Bulelani Ngcuka.

†I read this paragraph to Judge Hefer on 29 July 2006 to ensure that I had not misconstrued anything he had said in our earlier conversation. He said the paragraph was "100 percent" correct.

I met with Bulelani Ngcuka, whom I have known since 1992 and interviewed on several occasions, with a view to getting his reflections on the spy allegations and the Hefer Commission in the hope of clarifying the apparent discrepancies between what he told Hefer regarding mediation and the statements of others that there were efforts made in that regard. But before I could raise any issue, Ngcuka made his position on the spy allegations and the Hefer Commission definitively clear: He had no comment whatsoever to make. All those who had made allegations against him had had their chance to have their say. The matter was behind him. He had moved on. Nothing further in the matter was of interest to him.

10

Mac had pleaded with Ngcuka to charge him so he could clear his name. This did not happen. The "investigation" lingered. Mac's reputation took a battering. He was subjected to innuendos of sleaziness and corruption; he was ostracized by the ANC and politically sidelined.

Mac never told me that Ngcuka had been investigated as a spy. I first read of it in *City Press*. But once the story broke and the Hefer Commission had been established, Mac leaped into action, embarking on the search to prove that the 1989 conclusion had stood the test of time. Everyone who knew him tried to dissuade him, in the full certainty that he wouldn't pay the slightest attention. He had made his decision. To him, once again, it was all about a fundamental question of principle. When Mbeki narrowed the frame of reference to the impossible, he could have bowed out. He had never said he had proof that Ngcuka was a spy. But no—Mac plowed ahead regardless. He confused obstinacy with integrity, assumptions with facts, and the pursuit of justice for himself with the pursuit of justice for all.

Former comrades who could have validated parts of his evidence preferred to remain silent, either because they thought he should not have become embroiled in the Ngcuka spy scandal or because they did not want to "expose" themselves, especially when the findings of the Hefer Commission were regarded as a foregone conclusion. Mac and Moe were the butt of jokes, ridiculed, the bumbling stars of "The Moe and Mac Show." Many in the ANC leadership who had winced when they were targets of his cutting tongue were now smugly delighted. The great Mac had received a long overdue comeuppance.

The media failed to critique Hefer's report and has subsequently distorted its conclusions. It has insinuated repeatedly that Mac harbored sinister motivations.[32] The media has never examined itself and its failure to disentangle the issues.

11

When Hefer released his report in January 2004, Mbeki informed the country in his weekly online *Letter from the President* that "the ANC knew of the allegations against Bulelani Ngcuka even before we returned from exile. We never took any action to isolate him or otherwise break his links with the movement. . . . The fact, however, is that this leadership was certain that it had never been presented with such convincing evidence as would have required it to act against the person accused, in defence of the revolution."[33]

The president's statement is at odds with the concerns of the likes of Oliver Tambo and what was brought to the attention of the likes of Nelson Mandela and Alfred Nzo and Joe Slovo[34] and what can be attested to by at least one individual with access to ANC cross-border communications traffic. Mbeki's online admonishments beg the obvious: Why did he not share this information with Mac on 23 August? Or with Hefer? Why not ask Lindiwe Sisulu, then minister of intelligence, to check security files on Ngcuka's status? Why restrict Hefer to investigating abuse of power by the NPA only if he found that Ngcuka had been a spy, rather than allowing him to address the larger issue in its own right? Why his disinterest in issues of abuse of power by state investigative organs? Why not tell the cabinet that Mac had come to him with Ngcuka's reconstructed file before asking for its imprimatur to establish a commission?

Could Maduna and Ngcuka have made their statement that the NPA had a prima facie case of corruption against Zuma, but wouldn't prosecute because it probably wasn't winnable, without the foreknowledge and approval of the president? It seems unlikely. Maduna insisted that the president was not forewarned and only learned of his decision when he, Maduna, announced it publicly.[35] But it boggles the mind to think that a minister would not have informed his president of an impending decision of such potentially far-reaching consequence.

The purpose of the exercise, for the pedagogical president, was, as he wrote in his online letter, that "the Ngcuka affair must teach us all the important lesson that all of us must stop speculating about non-existent lists of apartheid spies. None of us should ever again seek to win whatever battles we are waging by labeling others as having been apartheid spies."[36]

He wanted a public humiliation of Mac and Moe—the better to teach the lesson.

In *Thabo Mbeki and the Battle for the Soul of the ANC*, an influential book published in 2005,[37] William Gumede writes that the Hefer Commission "could turn out to be one of Mbeki's shrewdest political maneuvers." Beyond saying that it gave Mbeki "an opportunity to pull the plug on two people he perceived as political opponents: Mac Maharaj, whose alleged private criticism of his leadership had long irked Mbeki, and Jacob Zuma, whom he suspected of becoming a rival within the ANC," he offers no analysis of how and why he arrived at this rather extraordinary conclusion. And no one has questioned it: rather, such is the level of critical analysis in South Africa, that his conclusion has been accepted by most political commentators.

Rather than Mbeki's shrewdest move, his support of the Hefer Commission might better be characterized as his most venal move. Whether for reasons great or petty, he gave the thumbs-up for the revolution, like most revolutionary movements in history, to start eating its own—a time to settle old scores, personal and ideological, a time to get down to what postrevolutionary movements do best: marginalize old comrades and trample on others in the stampede for power. Some did it with the guillotine, some with civil wars, some with show trials, and some with show commissions.*

Gumede's Mbeki is not someone who allows perceived slights to go unaddressed. Most insiders I have spoken to swear there is bad blood between Mbeki and Mac, but when pressed, no one could point to a specific incident or series of events. At most, some mentioned that Mac supported Cyril Ramaphosa over Thabo Mbeki as head of the ANC's negotiations team in 1991, when Mbeki saw the position as being rightfully his. But Mac did not; he was "in retirement" when that decision was made. Some say Mbeki never forgave Mac for supporting Ramaphosa over him to

---

*At the ANC National Conference in Mafeking in 2001 at which former president Mandela formally handed over the presidency of the ANC to South African President Thabo Mbeki, who had been elected unopposed to the office, Mandela made some off-the-cuff remarks at a farewell function in his honor. "There is a heavy responsibility for a leader elected unopposed." He said, "He may use that powerful position to settle scores with his detractors, to marginalize . . . to get rid of them and surround themselves with yes-men and women. His first duty is to allay the concerns of his colleagues to enable them to discuss freely without fear within internal structures." "Chronology of ANC Power Play," *Sunday Independent (SA)*, 29 April 2001.

succeed Mandela as president. Mac says he had no say in the matter, that the issue was decided by the ANC's NWC, of which he was not then a member. Certainly there is no love lost between Mandela and Mbeki, and Mandela's support of Ramaphosa for president riled Mbeki. Whatever the truth, what is abundantly clear is that Thabo Mbeki never forgets. Perhaps he was simply paying Mac back for a slight of fifteen years ago, when Mac reminded him before the RC that the file he inherited on the IPRD for Swaziland, previously Mbeki's territory, in which his career nearly became derailed, was empty.

Despite my pressing Mac on numerous occasions about his relationship with Mbeki, he remained adamant that their paths had infrequently crossed; his "harshest" criticism of Mbeki was that he was nonconfrontational; his most insightful observation was that Mbeki was prone, at meetings that he participated in, to say little but to volunteer to write the minutes or draft the necessary resolutions, thus effectively controlling the statement of the outcome. Mac's working relationship with Thabo was mostly confined to drafting assignments—he and Thabo were often given the task by various working committees on which they sat of drafting statements and the like; they seemed, Mac said, to think along the same lines.[38] Not a word of criticism.

12

In July 2004, Ngcuka resigned as director of the NPA. His company, Amabubesi Investments, secured a major stake in a lucrative golf and luxury residential estate near George, in the Western Cape, in a development headed by Colonel Jan Breytenbach, a renowned former Special Forces operative. Some time in 2006 he sold his interest in Amabubesi and moved into different ventures. He also has a share in insurance giant Sanlam's black economic empowerment (BEE) roll-out. Also in 2004, Penuell Maduna quit as justice minister, and joined Sasol. He is also involved in a number of BEE deals. And the NPA hosts an annual Penuell Maduna classic golf tournament.

In June 2005, in the Durban High Court, Judge Hillary Squires found Schabir Shaik guilty on two counts of corruption and one count of fraud after a marathon trial, during which the state presented some 140 volumes of documentation. Most seriously, Squires found that the payments Shaik admitted to having made to Zuma—and Zuma admitted to having recieved—were made "corruptly," that his intention was to influence Zuma to "use the weight of his political offices to protect or further Shaik's business interests."[39] Squires's 162-page judgment pulled no punches; he sentenced Schabir Shaik to fifteen years' imprisonment on the two corruption charges and five years on the fraud conviction, sentences to run concurrently and with leave to appeal. (Between October 1995 and September 2002, Zuma was the recipient of R1.27 million from Shaik or one of his companies. Neither Shaik nor Zuma denied that the payments had been made. However, although both insist that the transactions were loans, the NPA investigated them as payments to Zuma for either favors received or a down payment for favors to come.)

The Shaik brothers are unrepentant. "After the verdict," says Yunus, "Moe and I discussed among ourselves whether Schabir could have done things differently. And we agreed there was a lot he could have done differently but that he should have done what he did. He honored the bonds of friendship. We are proud of our brother. We are there for people. The Shaiks do not take life lightly. If that leads you to prison, so be it. We would do it again. Life is insufferably lonely if you don't look out for your friends." Indeed, the old bonds of struggle loyalty are deep and fiercely held; friendship overcomes any sense of what is a proper financial relationship with an elected official.

In the media, Squires's judgment was widely reported as his having determined that there was "a generally corrupt relationship" between Zuma and Shaik, and this formulation of the verdict quickly became a staple of political discourse and public commentary. Weeks after Squires's judgment, Mbeki addressed a joint session of parliament and dismissed Zuma as deputy president after Zuma had refused to step down. Mbeki appointed Phumzile Mlambo-Ngcuka, then minister of minerals and energy, and wife of Bulelani Ngcuka, as deputy president. Almost immediately, Zuma was charged with two counts of corruption. The trial date was set for July 2006.

With Zuma's firing and subsequent indictment, revolt among the grassroots erupted. Divided loyalties within the ANC NEC became clear, and Mbeki for a period lost control of the ANC.[40] Important factions within COSATU, the SACP, and the ANC Youth League threw their support behind Zuma, claiming he was the victim of a political conspiracy to prevent him from succeeding to the presidency, a claim rejected by the NEC after its own investigation.[41] COSATU demanded that the charges against Zuma be dropped and that he be restored to the position of deputy president. The hairline fractures in the alliance became open fissures.[42] The ANC, riven by divisions, hunkered down to weather the biggest political crisis it has faced since the Group of Eight was expelled in the 1970s.

Soon after, Billy Masetlha, director of the NIA, and two other senior intelligence officials were suspended for allegedly approving NIA surveillance of Saki Macozoma, a prominent businessman, member of the NEC, and ally of Mbeki.[43] Adding to the stew of intrigue and political malevolence, the ANC came into possession of seventy-three pages of e-mails purportedly between Frank Chikane and Bulelani Ngcuka, among others, with details of a scheme on the part of Mbeki (read anti-Zuma) insiders to discredit Zuma and ANC secretary-general (SG) Kgalema Motlanthe.[44] And then when matters seemed to be heading to a climactic head, Zuma was charged on 6 December 2005 with raping a thirty-one-year-old HIV-positive AIDS activist, the daughter of an old friend and struggle hero, who had died in Swaziland. He stepped down from his position as deputy president of the ANC and from all other positions.

A report by Zolile Ngcakani, the inspector general of intelligence, uncovered Project Avani—an intelligence probe into potential threats posed by the presidential succession race, poor service delivery, and Zuma's legal troubles undertaken by Masetlha without executive sanction. Masetlha used Avani, the report concluded, to create and disseminate hoax e-mails, to fabricate a case for there being a conspiracy among the highest echelons in the ANC to prevent Zuma from becoming president, which he later presented to Mbeki.[45]

The telephones of prominent individuals, it emerged, including such ANC heavyweights as Cyril Ramaphosa, had been tapped, or rather attempts to tap them were unsuccessfully made.[46] The fabricated e-mails were so amateurish and replete with elementary mistakes that one could not help but wonder whether they were, in fact, intended to be uncovered. Whatever the eventual outcome of legal and political wrangling, the damage was done. State institutions were enmeshed in the succession race and manipulated by supporters of either Mbeki or, with the political demise of Zuma, anti-Mbekites.

In March 2006, local elections were held across South Africa. The ANC closed ranks, alliance partners got behind the party, and it recorded unprecedented success. Once the elections were over, it returned to its internal warring ways. The manner in which different factions were using state institutions to fight turf wars and gain the upper hand in the succession stakes received scant attention. No thunder clouds of apprehension that the institution charged with overseeing the security of the people—for which the government is responsible, that is, with assuring that the state was adhering to its responsibilities to the people in terms of its constitutional obligations—were desecrating the constitution to advance the positions of some in the politicking for power within the ANC. The president saw no need for a commission of inquiry (no rush to a Hefer here). Rather, he announced that all was well in the country that prides itself on having the world's most progressive constitution.

Zuma was acquitted on the rape charge in May 2006. What happened on the streets outside the courthouse during the six-week trial was as telling a political statement as the proceedings of the legal process within were a test of judicial integrity. On one side, Zuma supporters, many bused in from KwaZulu-Natal, maintained a daily vigil, denigrating Zuma's accuser, chanting Zuma's praises, convinced, like Zuma himself, that the rape charge had been contrived, the woman part of the political conspiracy Mbeki acolytes had contrived to destroy him. Their behavior was a national disgrace, ugly, abusive, violence always imminent, the touch of menace a reminder that the boundaries of the permissible were slowly disappearing. Zuma did nothing to assuage the situation. After his acquittal he addressed them, joining in the singing of his signature tune, *Umshin Wami*, "Bring Me My Machine Gun," the words loaded with sexual innuendo and a subliminal incitement to his supporters. Never once did he admonish them or tell them to behave themselves.

On the other side, women's groups protested the woman's treatment, sexual violence, abuse in general, and the fact that in South Africa rape had become so pervasive that even the ugliest and most obscene sexual assault elicits little more than a shrug of disgusted indifference. Outcry had become so commonplace it had lost its voice.

In court, Zuma spoke only Zulu, was cross-examined in Zulu, provided graphic details of his sexual encounter, testifying that it had been consensual, citing the woman's short dress as a sexual come-on, telling the court that in Zulu culture to leave unfulfilled a woman you have sexually aroused was tantamount to rape in the woman's eyes, thus his obligation to consummate the sexual act despite the woman's HIV status, and that while he did not use a condom he took a shower immediately afterward to lessen his chances of becoming infected with the HIV virus.

The media excoriated him as unfit to hold any office of state or party. Here was the person who was the head of the National AIDS Council, in charge of the Moral Regeneration Program, admitting he had not followed one of the cardinal rules of sexual behavior that he was charged with drumming into the people's minds—to use a condom—cavalierly dispensing with the rule himself and implicitly suggesting that taking a shower after having sex with an HIV-infected partner made you less liable to contract HIV was met with howls of disbelief and anger by HIV/AIDS activists and the medical community. Even the *New York Times* got into the act, giving Zuma the distinction, dubious given the content, of an editorial which concluded scathingly that "[t]hose who are now welcoming him back to political life—including the secretary general of the African National Congress—are doing the country a disservice. He has been acquitted of rape but is still unfit for office."[47] But the *Times* is hardly a must-read in South Africa.

13

Mac has been unemployed since stepping down from First Rand. With the issues surrounding the Scorpions investigation still unresolved, he is unemployable. He was not invited to a single official event celebrating the tenth anniversary of the new South Africa. In official ANC circles, he is a pariah. On one occasion, he says, the ANC secretary general Kgalema Motlanthe told him he might be asked to appear before an ANC disciplinary hearing for behavior that "had brought the ANC into disrepute" but that he would only receive a slap on the wrist. Presumed guilty before being heard, Mac told Motlanthe to have the ANC expel him.[48]

On the day after the NPA announced that it was going to charge Zuma with two counts of fraud, the conservative *Citizen* daily newspaper ran a half-page headline on its front page: MAHARAJ NEXT?[49]

On 16 July 2005, nearly two years after last contacting him, the Scorpions came knocking on Mac's door again. More questions for him to answer. But this time, Mac was not prepared to give the Scorpions the willing cooperation he had extended in June 2003. He had not forgotten that Hefer had categorically concluded that the leaks to the *Sunday Times* regarding the Scorpions' inquiries into allegations of corruption on his part had come from the Scorpions themselves. Or that Hefer had concluded that an abuse of power on the part of the Scorpions occurred in relation to their handling of his case. Or that two years had elapsed since Hefer submitted his report to the president calling attention to abuse of power, and yet no steps had been taken or procedures put in place to ensure that such abuse would not happen again. In short, nothing had changed.

A response to some questions the Scorpions posed would require great confidentiality, given their sensitivity in relation to aspects of the struggle against the apartheid government. The Scorpions seemed unwilling to say that they would provide assurances of absolute confidentiality; that is, they would not guarantee that strict measures could be put in place to ensure that neither some of their questions nor Mac's responses would find their way into the public domain without any accompanying context, thus further destroying his name and humiliating his family. In the absence of assurances he could trust, Mac decided he would only answer their questions in a court of law, but that if they charged him, he would contest the constitutionality of Section 28 (6), (8), and (10) of the NPA Act.

Other questions related to his associations with people back in the mid-1980s, people who had played roles, although they were not aware of it, in relation to Vula activities. He was outraged. The NPA had no jurisdictional authority with regard to the actions of people that were designed to bring about the destruction of a state the liberation movement regarded as illegitimate. The questions made it appear to him that the Scorpions were acting on behalf of a state that no longer existed.

He took the questions and his responses to them together with the requisite documentation to a committee of "ANC stalwarts" appointed by Kgalema Motlanthe. The stalwarts accepted that his actions, which led to the Scorpions' questions almost twenty years later, were performed on behalf of the struggle.

Mac's mind is at rest. Ready to do battle again—against the "good boys" this time—but sometimes the good guys, he believes, can get carried away with their own sense of self-righteousness—an observation he is well equipped to make.

Mac

BEFORE THE *Sunday Times* ran its story alleging corruption on my part in relation to payments made to Zarina and me by Schabir Shaik and the awarding of contracts to his company, Nkobi Holdings, during my tenure as minister of transport, I called Bulelani Ngcuka. It was one of several calls between us. He said I was clean, but he could not issue a report until he could do so in the context of the entire arms deal. (I gave the Hefer Commission a list of the dates of some of the calls listed on my mobile phone, and their duration, to indicate that the discussions were not just idle.)

My contact with Schabir while I was minister of transport came when the consortium, of which Nkobi and Investec Bank were a part, lost a tender for the Maputo Corridor. This was in 1997. There was a protest from the consortium. I called a meeting with my counterpart Paulo Mushanga, the Mozambican minister of transport. On a Saturday morning in Johannesburg, with the entire consortium present, we heard the complaints from Schabir and others. Ketso Gordhan, my DG, and I then had a meeting with Mushanga and his DG to ask them to give us explanations of all the criticisms raised in the meeting, which they did. Then we asked the two DGs to leave the room, and the minister and I discussed the matter. We agreed that the criticisms of the tender process did not stand the test, and that the explanations offered by our officials satisfied us. We told Schabir and the others this, and we said we would meet them later for a fuller explanation if need be.

After the *Sunday Times* story, I told First Rand, where I was working, that I would take a six-month leave of absence while they conducted their investigation, which I requested them to do because I was a member of First Rand's board of directors. Two audits were completed. The first, by Hofmeyr, Herbstein, & Gihwala, was seen by First Rand as clearing me of any wrongdoing, but they felt it was not sufficiently robust. They then called in Deloitte & Touche, who did a further investigation. This report also cleared me of all wrongdoing, although there were two items, to the tune of R19,000, that the reports could not satisfactorily account for. One concerned a trip to Disney World that Zarina and the children and I made as guests of South African Airlines at the Olympic Games in Atlanta in 1996.* The second one concerned the amount of R100,000 ($16,000) deposited into my account, for which the bank was unable to provide a copy of the deposit slip, the check, or any information as to who had made that deposit.

Interrogation

Zarina and I went to the Scorpions, each for a day, in June 2003. In my direct telephone discussions with Ngcuka, he had said the newspaper revelations had caused a problem, but that he had found nothing to suggest corruption on my part. I believed him because he'd been a member of the ANC, and he was now occupying a high position. He also told me that the reason why he could not issue a statement to clear me was that he had promised parliament to investigate the arms deal further. He said he first had to make that report, and it was only in that context that he could clear me—that if he did so for me individually, then everybody would start

---

*Mac told the auditors, and subsequently the Scorpions, that he had paid in travelers' checks, as was his wont when he traveled abroad—a matter that could be confirmed by his personal assistant (PA) in the Department of Transport; the auditors found that they were paid with an American Express card but could not determine whose card it was and, on investigation, they found that the card had never been validated.

pressuring him to clear him or her. Again, I found this plausible, so I was willing to answer questions in a trusting frame of mind.

I accepted Ngcuka's word. He said, "Come and answer these questions," and when I answered them, he said, "Also, please persuade Schabir to come and answer questions so that I can close this aspect of the investigation." That is what he had said to me on the phone. I was relaxed, I was comfortable, I was not fearful. I was open. I expected the matter to be over by the time Schabir had given his evidence to the Scorpions, but it didn't happen.

Mediation

In early August, there was talk of mediation involving Cyril Ramaphosa, but it broke down. The idea was put to Yunus Shaik by members of the Scorpions and directly to me through Dipak Patel, who had been DG of transport when I retired in 1999. There was telephonic contact between Cyril and Ngcuka, and they had agreed to meet when the media got wind of it and Cyril bowed out. At Ngcuka's instigation, my attorney, Ismail Ayob, met with Ngcuka, who outlined the basis of a deal involving a plea bargain on Schabir's part—he would plead guilty to unspecified charges—and Jacob Zuma would answer thirty-five questions about the allegation of a bribe solicited from Thomson-CSF. Ngcuka told Ayob the Scorpions had nothing against me, but that Zarina had to plead guilty to contraventions of the Company Act for failing to declare her earnings and pay her tax and that there could be a resolution by plea bargain.[50]

I did ask Schabir to cooperate in answering questions about his dealings with my department, which he did. At that point, Ngcuka had intimated through others and to me that he would call First Rand before it issued its report to say that the Scorpions had found nothing to charge me with. Had he done so, I would not have had to resign my job. But on his other demands—that I persuade Schabir to plead guilty to some unspecified charges, persuade Zuma to answer the questions the Scorpions had put to him—I asked, "Why, when you've got nothing to charge me with?" I felt it was blackmail. I said to Ayob, "Tell him I have no response. I have noted his message."

I was of the view that it was Ngcuka's machinery that had leaked the information to the *Sunday Times*, and now we were all tarred with the same brush. I was saying, "If you're investigating me and you have undiluted power to prosecute, why the leak? Just get on with it. It's clear to me now that you have nothing on which to prosecute me, but you throw it into the public arena so that I am tainted and my reputation is destroyed.

Now if nothing further happens, what renews my reputation? Nothing. What help is it that there's a statement made in public that the Scorpions and I have resolved the matter and that there are no charges? The damage is done."

Once Bulelani proposed mediation because he thought I could influence Zuma and Schabir, I began to feel that there was a far larger game at play, one involving not just me but also Zuma. I began to ask myself what his motivation was. I was reminded by Moe of the 1988 security reports that Ngcuka may have been an apartheid spy. I also had information about some of the people from the old order who now held important positions in the Scorpions, and I began to feel there was another agenda at work. I went back to those 1988 reports to try to understand why Ngcuka was abusing his power in such an unscrupulous way. What was his agenda? I can't say.

I believe it was about who would succeed Thabo Mbeki; it was about the direction this country takes; it was about whether it will be undiluted GEAR (the government's economic policy)[51] or a regulated market; and about who can make the most from black economic empowerment.[52] It seemed to be about who becomes the kingmakers in South Africa. If Ngcuka had been able to reach a deal with Zuma, a relationship would have been established of some level of indebtedness and some level of fear. There is a great deal of fear of the Scorpions. Whenever people stand up to them, their investigations are leaked to the media. The Scorpions don't even have to charge anyone for the damage to be done.* That's the peculiarity of this form of intimidation.

---

*On 18 August 2005, the Scorpions carried out early-morning raids on Zuma's townhouse in Johannesburg; his traditional home in Nkandla, KwaZulu-Natal; his former home at the Union Building; the offices of his attorneys, Michael Hulley and Julekha Mohammed; and the home of Pierre Moynot, managing director of Thint Holdings, the South African Thomson-CSF offshoot; and more than a dozen other people all publicly named. Both Mohammed and Hulley went to court demanding the return of documents seized on grounds of breach of client/lawyer privilege. Moynot filed a complaint against the Scorpions for searching through her underwear. Mohammed won her case but the NPA has appealed. Hulley's case is still before the courts. At Zuma's Johannesburg home there was a tense standoff between his bodyguards and machine-gun-toting Scorpions.

Informing President Thabo Mbeki

I made an appointment to meet with the president; I said I had something to discuss with him. He didn't ask what it was about, but he did agree to see me at 2:00 P.M. on Saturday, 23 August, at his home in Pretoria. We met for just under an hour.

I told Mbeki, "I have not come here about my personal problem; let that unfold in the proper way. I have come here because I don't understand the conduct of the Scorpions, the abuse of power that is going on." Earlier, I had done the same with Kgalema Motlanthe, the secretary-general of the ANC, with whom I had already met at least twice. He had gone on record, saying the Scorpions used "cowboy tactics."[53] I was searching for an explanation of Ngcuka's conduct: if it was true he had been investigated as an apartheid spy, this would explain why he was acting like this.* I gave the president the reports that had so far been unearthed—Moe's analysis of whether Ngcuka had been a spy. I handed him the reports.[†] He looked at them. He then asked me, "What should we do?" I was not suggesting he should accept what was in those reports or that he should act on my word. Instead, I suggested to him that as the president of the country, he could quietly appoint a group of top analysts to look into all the information available, what I could give him as well as whatever was in the state's files. This panel could examine everything, evaluate it, and give him a considered report. On the basis of such a report, he would be able to come to a more considered view of the matter.

Mbeki asked me to suggest who these analysts might be. I said to him, "I don't know. You must have people in the NIA, in the various intelligence services. You could even quietly call in some experts from outside the state. You have Moe Shaik around too, and you should make them all part of the team because you want a well-evaluated report." He said,

---

*Mac and I argued over this. I was of the opinion that if Ngcuka had been investigated and found to have been a spy, the last thing in the world he would do is to start investigating those who had investigated him in case they went public with their own investigation. He argued that the more Bulelani gathered incriminating information on people who might have some inkling as to his past activities, the more he insured himself against exposure.

†Mac says that after his meeting with Mbeki, he and Moe Shaik discussed whether they should have the report dusted for the president's fingerprints. They decided that it would be dishonorable to do so, that they would never put themselves in a position that would open them to accusations of incriminating the president of South Africa in a way that might be perceived as blackmail.

"Good, I'll think about it."* I also told him I had heard there would be a press conference, that very day, called by Bulelani and the minister of justice, Penuell Maduna, in which they would take a Pontius Pilate approach on Jacob Zuma—they would say there is a prima facie case against him, but not a winnable one.

The Scorpions were giving one-to-one briefings to the media, preparatory to the press conference, and one of my contacts passed the information on to me. I told the president that the rumors were that the conference would take place that very day. He said, "Is that so?" I said, "Yes, that's my information."

We parted on the basis that if there was anything new, I would tell him, and that we should keep an open mind. When I got into my car and drove away from the residence down Church Street, I switched on the radio, and the three o'clock news on Radio 702 was all about that very press conference. I immediately phoned the president's home. The switchboard said he was not available, so I left a message for him to call me at his convenience. He called me back at 4:00 P.M. I told him that the press conference had taken place, and again he said, "Oh, is that so? Thanks for telling me, I'm going to make sure that I immediately get a transcript." And we left it at that.

Of course, I was sure he must have been briefed before the press conference was held, and that he was aware it was taking place. Yet he did not say to me, "I know about that." He did not use the opportunity to say to me, as he did afterward on the ANC Web site, that he was aware of the spy claims against Bulelani, that the matter had been looked into by the ANC, or that Bulelani had been cleared. He had the chance to tell me, and he had no reason to believe I would not have respected his views. But he did not, and that left me with a funny feeling.

---

*I first e-mailed Murphy Morobe, then the president's spokesperson, on 6 October 2005, to renew our acquaintance and bring his attention to my prior interviews with him going back to 1985. I then forwarded him questions for the president, e-mailed on 24 November 2005. His office acknowledged receipt and that Morobe had seen the questions. Some e-mails later, his spokesperson took my cell number and said he would call me. Thereafter, little response came of my efforts to follow up other than a stream of electronic acknowledgments of my e-mails in this regard. When I asked in my last e-mail whether I should take his electronic acknowledgments of my previous e-mail as his final response in the matter I received an electronic acknowledgment. Interviews with Morobe at [] o'malley interviews/[]Murphy Morobe. For questions to President Mbeki, go to []maharaj/documents and reports/Hefer Commission/[] Questions for President Mbeki.

The Scorpions Leak Again . . .

I received a phone call from Jovial Rantao, editor of the *Star*, who told me he had learned from the highest authorities in the NPA that the Scorpions were going to charge Zarina with a violation of income tax, a conversation I taped and presented to Hefer. I was outraged. This was a complete breach of faith by Ngcuka. It changed my attitude. Previously I might have been persuaded to believe that the leak to the *Sunday Times* was accidental, but now we had the head of the NPA himself abusing the information he had. That changed my mind-set. It made me singularly concerned about the abuse of authority that was taking place. Whatever the gains of our democracy—and they are many—I felt that the seeds of its destruction could be sown with this type of abuse of power, this co-opting of the media to print privileged information, with the sole purpose of having people convicted in the press. I saw this as a real threat to freedom.

Then we learned of the briefing of newspaper editors on 23 July and what Ngcuka had said. He said I was a liar, and he demeaned my wife. He said he understood my vulnerability, that he would get at me through my wife.[54] With that the gloves came off. As far as I was concerned, Ngcuka was engaging in an egregious abuse of his office. I felt free to confirm in the public arena that I was aware that an ANC intelligence report in 1988–89 had concluded that Ngcuka probably was a spy.

Soon after that, on 7 September, *City Press* published the spy allegations against Ngcuka, which I confirmed, and eTV followed with a documentary in which I said that I believed the intelligence report prepared by Moe, because during Vula, Moe's intelligence had saved Vula—and my life—on a number of occasions. I had absolute trust in him. And still have.

Hefer

When Mbeki narrowed the Hefer Commission's terms of reference, I could have said, just like every other person who could have thrown light on the matter, that I was no longer going to cooperate. But I didn't. I could have pulled out when the state refused to pick up our legal costs or even pay for our stopovers in Bloemfontein. I could have pulled out, but I didn't. I said I would assist Hefer to the best of my abilities, and I did. For me it was vindication enough that Hefer had been sufficiently perturbed by what appeared to be abuse of power within the NPA that he made a point of expressing his concerns in his report addressed to the president, even though he was not supposed to make comments on the issue after concluding that Ngcuka was probably not a spy.

The Return of the Scorpions

Almost two years went by before I heard from the Scorpions again. At the end of July 2005, Piet Pieterse arrived at my house one morning with two sets of questions in writing—one for me, one for my wife—in sealed envelopes. He opened the envelopes in our presence, said we must read the contents and sign an acknowledgment of receipt. Then he placed this in an envelope and said, "Look, I'm sealing the envelope. I haven't read the document."

I looked at this charade, and I said, "Why are you?" Why was he performing this elaborate charade? He said he wanted to be sure it was all being done properly. But I was already suspicious. I thought they were doing it this way so that when it was leaked to the media, they would be able to blame me.

I felt the way I had toward the apartheid police—but with the difference that with the apartheid police I had been aggressive, whereas with the Scorpions I was measured in my response. The public still has faith in them, and the media has refused to address the threat caused by the Scorpions' abuse of power. The reaction to my views has been "Oh, he's being investigated; that's why he's saying it." This question was put to me at a press conference, and I said, "Society has never corrected itself until people whose shoe is pinching stand up."

Some questions wanted me to address aspects of my activities in the 1980s. They wanted me to give them permission to access my income tax returns, and if I refused, to state my reasons for refusing. Only SARS (South African Revenue Service) has the authority to examine tax returns and to investigate cases where there are suspicions that a person is failing to disclose income or is otherwise acting fraudulently. If the Scorpions have reasons to believe that a suspect is concealing income, they have to turn the matter over to SARS for investigation, and SARS gets back to them with its findings. If they thought I'd been squirreling away income somewhere, they should have gone to SARS to request an investigation and got on with it. But no, instead they played the game in which I am supposed to provide them with reasons why I don't want them to review my tax returns, something they are not legally authorized to do!

Thirteen Years On: Whither South Africa?

To talk about the state of South Africa's democracy is difficult just thirteen years after the advent of its democracy. Our democracy is still so young, so vulnerable, so much desired that any criticisms are perceived as letting the side down. Yet it is important to take stock to assess how far we have traveled, what obstacles we are encountering, and what we should be doing to overcome them.

What has happened to me should not color the prism through which I look at events. I must put a distance between my own situation and the overall picture. In thirteen years, we have registered enormous gains under an ANC-led government. That cannot be gainsaid. These years have been marked by a measure of stability that has been unprecedented in more than five decades of previous rule in South Africa.

We have managed to bring about fiscal prudence in the economy to reduce the deficit, creating stability at the economic level. After a slow start, the rate of growth has picked up. The hope that in 2006 we will register 6 percent is no longer unrealistic. We inherited a closed economy. We had to open it, often at a painful cost to ourselves, and integrate it into a global economy. Much has been done in that regard, often at a pace faster than world organizations expected us to achieve.

The sources of instability in our society are not all uniquely South African. Some are imposed on us by external factors over which we have very little or no control.

The biggest threat to South Africa's stability and democracy is in the high unemployment rate.* The second is the extremely sharp disparities of income that have emerged. Third, the educational system is unable to produce the skilled workers we need to achieve sustainable levels of high growth. And fourth, it is a matter of common knowledge that the HIV/AIDS pandemic is wreaking havoc on our economy and has already substantially lowered the life expectancy of South Africans.

---

*In January 2006, South Africa's official unemployment rate was the highest among the sixty-one countries tracked by Bloomberg. The unemployment rate has increased every year since 1994, and in 2006, it was either 4.6 million or 8.4, depending on whether one uses official or expanded unemployment figures, either 28 percent or 41 percent. The official definition of unemployment requires that a person must have looked for a job in the four weeks prior to the survey interview. Given the nature of the labor market, it is accepted by most commentators other than the government that the rate is closer to 40 percent than to the official figure. For expanded footnote go to [] maharaj/footnotes/[] 447.

Jobless growth is, of course, not unique to South Africa. It is a problem of the world economy, and there is no doubt in my mind that part of the reason behind jobless growth is the way in which the world economic order is structured. The global economy is biased in favor of the rich and against the poor. South Africa is largely an insignificant player, and many of the factors that contribute to high growth are simply beyond our control, especially because we are reliant on foreign investment and export-driven growth; hence, access to the markets of rich countries is crucial. Nevertheless, there is still an extraordinary buoyancy of optimism among our people that they will have a better future. If optimism alone was the barometer of success, South Africa would certainly rank among the most successful countries in the world.

Much has been written about the achievements of our first thirteen years; they are many and we can be justly proud, but that should not blind us to low-key warning signals, perhaps false warnings, but they are there and it is our task to look beneath the surface for the signs that point to dangers ahead.

Dangers That Lurk

Ironically, the first of these dangers arises from one of the strengths of the South African struggle pre-1994. Then there was a high level of mass politicization among our people and a plethora of NGOs, ratepayers, and civic community-based organizations. It was the proliferation of these organizations drawn together under the umbrella of the UDF and supported by COSATU that gave our struggle one of its special strengths. In our constitution there is even special mention for the place of civic organizations in our society.

But since 1994, the record is very different. There are three hundred to four hundred NGOs in South Africa, but they do not register anywhere on the political Richter scale.* Government and civil society have not found

*After the ANC was unbanned in 1990, the UDF disbanded and folded itself into the ANC. The UDF was the umbrella under which large segments of civil society had gathered. Many believed that with the return of the ANC, there was no further need for their existence. Many civic organizations, encouraged by the ANC, followed a similar course, thus weakening civil society with the object of strengthening the ANC prior to the 1994 elections. Mbeki's plans for the transformation of South African society are sweeping. Unfortunately, criticism of transformation as articulated by the ANC was equated with opposition to change, that is, wanting to maintain the status quo. Harsh condemnation from the ANC of such postures and the insinuation that any opposition to change was indicative of wanting to maintain apartheid's remnants silenced many

ways of working together without undermining each other's independence. Their relationship still simmers with latent tension, and this has taken an unhealthy form. At best, government tends to smother civil society; at worst, it is downright antagonistic toward it. For example, the relationship between the Treatment Action Campaign (TAC) on HIV/AIDS and the government and the Department of Health is seriously skewed.* There is no doubt that the TAC has done an enormous amount of good work in making people conscious of the threats and dangers of HIV/AIDS and on challenging the big pharmaceutical companies about their pricing structures. What should have been a relationship of independent allies working together toward a common goal is perceived as a relationship of antagonists. And the fault lies primarily on the side of government.†

Moreover, there have been statements by government, including some by President Mbeki, that have questioned the bona fides of some NGOs on the basis of their funding.[55] This is a dangerous development with its implicit suggestion that these NGOs, most of which have worked here since apartheid days and at the forefront of the struggle against apartheid, have agendas that are not in the best interests of our country.

We should be doing a lot more to encourage civic and community-based organizations to come into existence and to get into relationships where they, with government, could be cobuilders of our new South

---

NGOs. And many who held their ground were perceived as being anti-ANC and, eventually, as being racist.

*The Treatment Action Campaign was launched on 10 December 1998, International Human Rights Day. Its main objective is to campaign for greater access to HIV treatment for all South Africans by raising public awareness and understanding about issues surrounding the availability, affordability, and use of HIV treatments. In the ensuing years it has engaged the government, especially the minister of health, Dr. Manto Tshabalala-Msimang, in a running battle over the provision of antiretroviral (ARV) treatment for people infected with HIV/AIDS. In August 2001 it took its case against the government to the Constitutional Court, which found in its favor in July 2002. The government, however, has proceeded very slowly to implement the court's decision. At the beginning of 2006, three and a half years after the court's ruling, only 122,000 people were receiving free ARVs in contrast to the 1 million estimated by the ASSA model project. See endnote 59, Chapter 22.

†Challenged by TAC at every point for the inadequacy of its HIV/AIDS programs and the absence of political leadership at the national level, the counterproductive behavior of Dr. Manto Tshabalala-Msimang, which has confused the public and often sent life-threatening signals to people, the government retaliated in 2006 when it banned TAC and the AIDS Law Project from attending the UN General Assembly on HIV/AIDS on the grounds that they would attack the government and had nothing otherwise to contribute. The government's actions caused uproar among other NGOs and the minister backpedaled.

Africa. Even with the African Peer Review Mechanism (APRM)* well under way, the government is leading the process and civil society is playing catch-up. The situation should be the other way around. Government should not be the key actor in deciding the extent to which it is advancing democracy. Given the serious shortcomings of the political opposition and the fact that the government dismisses out of hand most of the criticism, civil society has a greater role to play.

The second issue that concerns me is abuse of power by organs of the state. I have consistently said I have no problem with any proper investigation being done into my affairs, but I do have a problem with the way in which those powers are exercised. I believe state power is sometimes used in a way that constitutes abuse in terms of the statutory obligations of the state organs in question, and here I unhesitatingly point my finger at the Directorate of Special Operations (DSO)—the Scorpions—and the NPA. Unfortunately, the issue of abuse of power is ignored whenever I raise it because I am perceived as wanting to deflect attention from some wrong-doing of mine.†

*The APRM is a process agreed among countries in the African Union whereby each submits itself to a review by a team from participating countries to assess the progress each is making toward the adoption of policies and practices contained in the Declaration on Democracy, Political, Economic, and Corporate Governance. The goal is to promote political stability, high economic growth, and sustainable development. Through the sharing of experience, the implementation of successful and best practice is reinforced, deficiencies identified, and the capacity-building needs assessed. In July 2006, South Africa submitted its self-assessment, which was prepared by the National Governing Council under the direction of Geraldine Frazier Moleketi, to Professor Adebayo Adedeji of Nigeria, a former UN under-secretary-general, who is responsible for leading the review process on behalf of the AU APRM panel. The final report will include both South Africa's self-assessment and what his team observes during their stays in South Africa. Go to www.aprm.org.za. See Paddy Harper, "South Africa Criticizes Itself. Sort of," *Sunday Times,* 16 July 2006; "Women are not safe in SA, says Peer Review Report," *City Press,* 23 July 2006; Geraldine Frazier Moleketi, "Report to peer review is 'quite frank,' " *Sunday Independent (SA),* 23 July 2006; Brendan Boyle, "SA's peer report masks some scars," *Sunday Times,* 30 July 2006.
†The question of whether the Scorpions should continue to exist as a separate law enforcement entity reporting directly to the minister of justice or be folded into one of the existing agencies, such as the SAPS, was first mooted in 2003. Mbeki established a one-person commission under Judge Sisi Khampepe in March 2005 to determine their future. Other than the media, it appeared the Scorpions had few friends. Minister for Justice Brigitte Mabandla, under whose jurisdiction the Scorpions fell, Minister for Safety and Security Charles Nqakula, the Police and Prisons Civil Rights Union (POPCRU), the National Intelligence Agency, and SAPS all called for relocation within the SAPS. Only Ronnie Kasrils, minister for intelligence services, argued that the status quo should be maintained. Khampepe's recommendation, accepted by the president, was Solomon-like: The NPA remains under the jurisdiction of the minister for justice, but while the

The degree to which abuse of authority occurs is a measure of whether a democracy is moving in the right direction. Here in South Africa this situation is far from healthy. For several years, prominent people—in business, government, and senior cadres in the ANC—have been wary about talking on phones for fear their phones are tapped. This wariness, I believe, arises from the perceived abuse of power, and this threatens our constitutional freedom. There is a growing undercurrent of fear: fear of getting on the wrong side of investigating authorities and ending up being investigated. People have apologized to me for not being able to give me work. They simply fear the potential repercussions. Not that they can point to anything specific—they just believe they will be in for the kind of attention from state authorities they would rather do without. They fear the rumor mill that would start rolling if the Scorpions started to look into their affairs or that their contracts for state business would dry up.

It is the same with offers of helping me with money: it has to be cash. Nobody wants to write a check to me with his or her name on it. In my case, Judge Hefer found that the information the Scorpions leaked to the *Sunday Times* in 2003 was in violation of the law. You cannot understand the fear factor this kind of leakage induces unless you understand what harm it does. It destroys your life, it destroys your opportunity to earn a livelihood, it constantly makes you look over your shoulder—are they coming tomorrow to detain me? And certainly in the case of my family it breeds disillusionment, confusion, and cynicism. A week after Jacob Zuma was charged, one newspaper ran the headline MAC NEXT? Another periodical stated as a fact that I was going to be charged. What does that do your ability to live a normal life, your ability to generate an income? Your life enters a state of limbo.

Everybody is now afraid to blow a warning whistle because they don't want to draw attention to themselves in case they are made the subject of a similar enquiry. The point is not whether the allegations are true or not, it is that abuse of power breeds fear and with fear comes self-censorship—you become a party to the diminution of your own freedom. And that is a dangerous syndrome.

The touchstone seems to be pure politicking. Hefer referred to the abuse, and he regarded it as unacceptable and intolerable. That was in January 2004. This is now 2006. Even though the judge said, "I see abuse here and it is not acceptable," nothing has been done about it—nothing.

Scorpions will continue to remain part of the NPA, they will fall under the jurisdiction of the minister of safety and security,

The fact of the matter is that the president has not seriously looked at the problem. I raised the question of who prosecutes the national prosecutor in terms of the constitution. Is there a gap in the law? Again, silence.[56]

Our public intellectuals rarely raise their voices where issues of possible abuse are concerned. They are trapped in a space that keeps telling them that these are institutions created by our democracy, that they are good institutions and that criticism undermines them. That goes for the media itself. The only time the media stands up and howls is when it perceives itself as coming under threat.

At the moment, the issue is framed in terms of only one issue: corruption. I agree corruption is a critical issue in any society. But in South Africa abuse of power has been pushed off the public agenda, and there is a singular preoccupation with corruption. When you look at allegations of corruption, you find investigations are extremely selective. All things being equal, if you are perceived to be a friend of the president's or within his political circle, the less likelihood there is of being investigated by the Scorpions. In a certain sense, corruption and abuse of power are two sides of the same coin. In the case of corruption, people in positions of power use their positions in a manner contrary to the statutory obligations prescribing the way in which that power is to be used, or in a way that is just plain unlawful. In my book, that is a form of abuse of power. I'm not making a judgment call on the matter, but if a preoccupation with the issue of corruption is stopping commentators and public discourse from addressing the instances of abuse of power, beware that we do not find our freedoms eroded by stealth. The fault will be all ours.

The third issue on my list of dangers we have to be on the look out for is how the tasks of defining and managing transformation are conducted. These are enormously complex tasks, and from time to time we need to look back and do some rethinking. Take the question of the transformation of the judiciary. It was clear that the law that we had inherited, both statutory and common, from the apartheid system had to be reinterpreted and brought into sync with the spirit and content of the constitution, including the Bill of Rights and the reality of a constitutional state. It also meant that the composition of the judiciary and the entire justice system had to rapidly reflect the mix of the South African population and its control taken out of the hands of previously privileged white minority.

One of the reasons why we created the Constitutional Court over and above the existing courts, including the Supreme Court of Appeal, as the final arbiter on matters relating to the interpretation of constitutional disputes was that the existing courts were in the control of the white minority who had grown up in a system governed by the interests of that community and in which the law recognized and implemented racial discrimination.

But transformation cannot be conceived and managed as a simple top-down affair. Looking back, we erred when we allowed the judiciary (both judges and magistrates) to avoid attending and accounting for its role in the perpetration of gross violations of human rights before the TRC. It is understandable that some in the judiciary were concerned about the insta-bility and jitters public hearings would create for the judiciary as an insti-tution and for its individual officers. But the decision also sent a signal to the ordinary people that they had no role to play in the transformation of the judiciary. Thirteen years into our democracy there is concern among people about the pace and depth of the transformation of the judiciary.

Of greater concern is the tendency to lock civil society out of the processes of evaluating the changes going on and the further development of transformation. Recent changes to the constitution proposed by the government would have undermined the independence of the judiciary.*
In the end the president reined in his ministers but not before people like George Bizos and Arthur Chaskalson, the former chief justice of the con-stitutional court, jurists in the international community, and others had voiced their concerns in public. But the fact is the executive side was will-ing to test the limits to which it might encroach on the domain of another branch of governemnt before it drew back. It was a close call. The govern-ment's Films and Publication Amendment Bill contained provisions that could be used to curtail freedom of expression and curtail the media's ability to report the news. Again, at the last moment, just before the bill was to be tabled in parliament, the government exempted the media from the provisions of the bill after vociferous objections from the Media Insti-tute of Southern Africa, the Freedom of Expression Institute, and the South Africa National Editors Forum. (See "Editors spell out fears over censor bill," Cape Argus, 11 October 2006.)

---

*The government gazetted the changes in December/January 2005. During the summer vacation period (mid-December through the end of January) South Africa closes down for summer holidays. The proposed thirteenth and fourteenth amendments to the con-stitution would have provided for far-reaching changes in the structure of the judiciary, given the executive a role in the administration of justice, curtailed some judicial powers in relation to ordering the suspension of the implementation of legislation pending a test of its constitutionality, and given the president more power in relation to the ap-

We have to be very careful. There is a danger that the need for ongoing transformation of the judiciary may be used to erode the independence of the judiciary. But there is also a danger that the transformation of the judiciary will continue to remain in the hands of the judiciary. The former is immediate and arises from the proposed changes to the constitution under consideration by parliament; the latter has its roots in the late 1990s, when we allowed the judiciary to avoid appearing before the TRC, where the role and nature of the judiciary under apartheid would have received proper exposure to the public. This was a mistake for which the government, the leaders of the judiciary, and the TRC must share blame.

This is an ANC government. We should encourage constant debate and the interchange of ideas, and we should invite public criticism, taking it as being honestly offered and meriting honest response. We should engage more with the opposition parties, and foster a parliamentary climate that gives better expression to the spirit of a multiparty democracy. Nobody, no matter how good his or her performance in the past, has a guarantee of perpetual excellence. The health of a society is in its body politic; therefore, the question should constantly be arising, "But do these absolute powers open the road to abuse? And when abuse occurs, what happens? Who suffers?"*

---

pointment of judges. Had the *Sunday Times* not learned that the government had gazetted the bills without the knowledge of the judiciary, the new bills might have become law in their original form. Following an outcry, much of it from leading jurists across the racial divide, the government provided more time for a more judicious consideration of the bills. Ultimately, the bills were referred to President Mbeki. On 30 July 2006 he announced that the judicial reform bills were to be taken off parliament's agenda until a white paper on judicial transformation was completed (perhaps by December 2006) and widely debated in the profession and among the public. The president indicated that there would be more consultation with the judiciary on the parts of the two bills that were controversial and on aspects they were concerned with. See Anthony Holiday, "Threat to an Independent Judiciary," *Cape Times*, 23 January 2006; Fikile-Ntsikelelo Moya, "Judges to Talk Tough at Key Meeting," *Mail & Guardian*, 27 January–2 February 2006; Angela Quintal, "Top Legal Minds Hint at Battle Between Judiciary, Legislature," *Star*, 22 February 2006; Jan Steyn, "Violations of a Sacred Agreement," *Business Day*, 16 March 2006; Nigel Wills, "Guard the Future of our Freedoms," *Business Day*, 15 March 2006; Angela Quintal, "Judges to Be Given Chance to Discuss Judicial Reforms," *Cape Times*, 31 July 2006.

*Certainly, the most infamous example of how power is employed to curb, not by threat, but by fear of offending or incurring the displeasure of South Africa's ruling elite was President Mbeki's frontal verbal assault on Archbishop Tutu after Tutu in the course of a speech to the Nelson Mandela Foundation lamented the lack of debate in the political arena. Tutu had called for "a vigorous debate that is characteristic of a 'vibrant community' where 'people play the ball and not the person and not think that those who disagree, who express dissent, are ipso facto disloyal or unpatriotic.' " And he went on: "An unthinking, uncritical, kowtowing party-line toeing is fatal to a vibrant democracy. I am

The check on the ANC is a healthy civil society. The check is a society that is debating. The check is a society that does not look only at corruption but also at the abuse of power, one that recognizes that the abuse of state power is a threat to freedom, one that debates the danger. The check is a society that does not say, "Because you, the government say so, therefore it's right." It says, "I believe you, but I would like to be convinced." The vibrancy of civil society that was present at the height of the anti-apartheid struggle has significantly diminished. Yet the challenge for South Africa is whether we will succeed in deepening and realizing a participatory democracy, or whether we will allow our democracy to become frozen in formal trappings and structures. Participatory democracy requires that we encourage and stimulate the development of civil society. Instead, we see signs that those in power tend to see citizen debate as an annoyance, something they have to tolerate.

Transparency is difficult, all the more so perhaps for the ANC because we come from a culture of nontransparency, where information and the dissemination of information had to be closely guarded. We knew not who within us was working for the enemy, and even the most trustworthy of comrades, either out of carelessness or lack of discipline, was not above sharing information with others that could endanger the lives of others. On our part, therefore, there has to be a constant striving toward openness. It is a dynamic process.

I'm not sure whether this question of concentration of power under the presidency of Thabo Mbeki has been correctly formulated. The push toward centralization arose from very real problems, temporary or longer term, but the solutions we devised are delivering consequences that were not foreseen. To call the proliferation of institutions under Mbeki's presidency centralization is fine provided you do not then conclude it has happened simply because Thabo likes to wield power.

Everybody wants service delivery. When you interviewed me on the eve of the end of the first ANC government, I expressed the hope that we would relook at the provincial powers because I believed the delivery

concerned to see how many have so easily been seemingly cowed and apparently intimidated to apply." Proportional representation fostered subservience to party leaders; those not foolhardy "opted for silence to become voting cattle for the party." Nelson Mandela Lecture, Wits University, 23 November 2004. Mbeki responded in his On Line Letter. Among others whose verbal or written statements merited robust rebuttal by the president using his On Line Letter (which became the headlines in the Sunday newspapers) were indirectly Charlene Smith, a rape survivor, and Anthony Trahar, then CEO of Anglo-American corporation. For expanded endnote, go to [] maharaj/footnotes/455.

point should be local government structures and that we needed to strengthen those structures.[57] But I also expressed the fear that if we didn't address it soon, we would let the opportunity slide. What I see now is that government has developed a habit of addressing every problem by creating a new institution. Even if the problem is temporary, the result is an institution that will live on long after it has outlived its purpose. Vested interests are created that have nothing to do with doing things for the people, but which continue to exist for reasons beyond the rationale for which they were brought into existence.

By comparing dictatorship and democracy, one can put the trade-offs that are necessary for efficient service delivery into context. In a new democracy, service delivery is invariably slow until the democracy and its institutions find their feet. In a benign dictatorship, service delivery may be far better. But because we value our democracy so much, we accept that trade-off. We accept the inefficiencies as part of the price of our freedom. Democracy gives you the space to relook at a decision, to revisit a problem, to backtrack and retrace your steps. Democracy allows you to find new paths and to do so in a way that is empowering. Dictatorship does not backtrack or even allow the space to do so.

In these past thirteen years there have been signs of backtracking but never openly. Let me give you an example. Government has changed its position on privatization, but it has not said that it changed its position, because the results were A, B, and C, and it will now backtrack because what it wanted to achieve were D, E, and F. The reason this is important to me is because this is the way you educate the public to become an active participant in democracy. You have to explain things publicly: why you took those previous steps, what you had intended would happen, why the outcomes have been different to what you had intended, and therefore why you are now retracing your steps and what you hope to achieve by doing so.

So that is what you've got to be looking at, the strategy that has got to be present, but my final word on this matter is that everybody justifies what they did by explaining their intentions. I think that's the worst crime. Intentions have little to do with it; it's the outcome that should be the issue. Politicians, like businesspeople, keep talking about intentions, intentions, intentions, and yet in reality there is nowhere in the world, in any form of activity, where intentions always lead to the desired outcomes. The real issue we should be looking at is outcomes. Are we empowering our people? Is hope growing or is it diminishing? Is unity broadening or is it narrowing?

But we also need to look beyond the pluses and minuses of achievements and failures. The advent of democracy in 1994 opened South Africa to an era of profound social and economic change that will encompass future generations. The ANC and its alliance partners, COSATU and the SACP, remain the organized forces leading that change. But change is characterized by challenges and obstacles. It breeds insecurities, both among the people and the elites competing for power, that have to be managed. No matter how desperately people want change, they fear the uncertainty that change brings. We can manage this change with the people when they are participants in the process, or for the people when they are bystanders. If we take the latter course, we are in for trouble.

Even with the people on board, mistakes are inevitable. Above all, we have to be on guard that the mistakes in the way we manage the insecurities I have mentioned do not reach a point where we lose the trust of the people. That will take us into a zone where calamity would be unavoidable.

21. FAMILY: STRUGGLE AND DAMAGE

Introduction

MAC'S DAYS in the underground inside South Africa were purchased at a terrible price. The toll on his family was extraordinary. That the children would feel abandoned was inevitable; inevitable too was that such embedded feelings would later affect their relationships with their father. In their early years, the family had lived a lie.

When the truth later emerged, the children could only feel manipulated by their own parents. They had gone through deep feelings of mourning for a lost parent, fear that he was dead and that Mum was about to die. There was no one around them to confide in, to trust, to feel safe with.

When Mac went about making his meticulous preparations for Vula, he knew he had to create a cover story that would withstand every effort to unravel it, every doubt about its authenticity. It had to be sustainable over time. What he didn't realize was that his children would unwittingly become part of the Vula web of deceit.

Mac lived a lie from 1987 on: his bad health, his having to go abroad for treatment, missing NEC meetings; he was less ebullient, hunched, walked with a stick, produced endless complaints, meanwhile carefully preparing the way for what everyone would regard as the natural outcome of such protracted deterioration in his physical condition. Everyone in Lusaka had to be deceived so that the informants among them could pass the word on to the regime: Mac is fading, is no longer the threat he once was—physically debilitated, mentally spent, and starting to act like a hypochondriac. Five minutes of conversation and he's back to talking about how awful he feels.

Zarina, of course, had to sustain the lie. "Mac's not feeling good; complains all the time." And then, after a visit to Moscow, the diagnosis: kidney disease with lung complications. He'll need extended treatment. What a great loss to the struggle. And the children had to be "recruited," told that Daddy had to go away to hospital. But one lie led to the next: "Look, another card from Daddy. He's getting better. The treatment is working."

The story took root, became a staple of Lusaka life. The lie became real. Zarina lied to the Lusaka community, to her children. The NEC was lied to (by omission) by Slovo and Tambo. For the Party Congress in Havana, Cuba, in April 1989, Slovo suggested "a letter to Congress from Tony [Mac] purporting to come from Fatman's area [Moscow] ... making some point about his illness and dictatorship of doctors which does not enable him to attend."[1] Slovo, in turn, reported back with obvious satisfaction that Mac's message was well received and he had been reelected to the PB.[2] Zarina also reports, "I spent ten days in the Crimea strengthening your legend."[3] In a comm forwarded to Vladimir Shubin thanking him for looking after Zarina when she was in Moscow receiving care and for embellishing the seriousness of his own "illness to all inquiries from ANC and SACP comrades passing through Moscow," he advises, "Keep telling effective lies about me," adding the self-derisory comment, "Oh, how one lie will lead to a lifetime of lives!"[4]

For Mac, of course, the construction of a cover story, the credibility of which depended on the web of lies that underpinned it, did not begin with Vula. It went back to the sixties underground. He became comfortable with disguises, enjoying his ability to evade detection. But for every lie there is a day of reckoning. For Mac it came from a direction he had never factored into his equations of risk: his children. Milou knew the truth, but said nothing:

> My mom told us for years that he was having a kidney transplant in Russia, [he says] and we honestly believed that, but when we moved to England, my dad came for a few weeks to settle us down and then he left again. But I could see that he was perfectly healthy. I was eight. With the background in Lusaka, and all the things my mother had told us, I figured out that he must be working in South Africa. I was very happy to see him. I idolized him. And I loved him very much, and I was very happy to spend some time with him. And so I knew then, and even though my mom continued to say that he was having an operation and that he was in Russia in a hospital, I knew he wasn't. And I was actually quite disturbed by it.[5]

When Mac arrived in London in July 1989, Zarina almost immediately raised the question of his future plans. Almost eleven years earlier Tim had asked him the same question when he came to London, after a far lengthier absence. In both cases, Mac's answer was the same: I'm going back to South Africa. Zarina was upset. She had lost the use of her left arm and shoulder and the sight in her right eye. There was no way she could handle Lusaka, with its food shortages and queuing for hours to buy food. "I just couldn't face that again on my own." She had her limits.

In Brighton, Milou drifted into his own fantasy world, but even that was not a safe place. A strange country. Isolation. Loneliness. Recurring anxiety about his father. Unable to communicate his fears to his mother. And anger that he was being lied to.

> My mom was working at the university, and we had moved house so that my sister and I could go to the same school. But they only accepted my sister. So my mom started a huge legal battle with the council to get me put into the school. That lasted six months and during that time I was alone at home. She would be there but she would be working. I remember she told me that her computer was her AK47, and her words her bullets. . . . She became the first person to single-handedly defeat the council, and they took me into that school. But during the six months before that, I was at home living in my imagination and fantasy, TV a bit. But mostly in fantasy. I would go backwards thinking of how my Dad was being tortured.
>
> It was terrible. I didn't know anybody. I was very isolated, did not see anybody, and just lived in my own fantasy [world]. I seemed all right at the time, but I was very disturbed. . . . I lived in a bunk bed, and my sister often slept with my mother. I never demanded attention, so I didn't get much attention. One of the things I used to do, I recall, was urinate on the wall from the top of the bunk bed.[6]

A cry for help.

Joey's reactions to her father's absence were similar, but not as severe because she, at least, did not know the truth:

> He [her father] came to Brighton to take my brother and me to school. He woke us up and it was so dark outside. I didn't like him. I thought, "Oh, God, what is this asshole doing here?" I couldn't stand my dad for a very long time because I didn't understand where he had gone and why he had gone. I just felt pretty abandoned by him. . . . I didn't speak to him at all. I was really horrible to him.[7]

And then within weeks he was gone again, and again there were repercussions. Zarina:

> As soon as he left, they went into a depression, especially Milou, who had always felt, it turned out later, totally abandoned by Mac. When Mac left, he felt that Mac didn't really care for him . . . he never actually articulated it, but he subsequently told us that that was the biggest blow in his life . . . he was very, very attached to Mac . . . and when Mac left again it was such a blow. Then on top of it all, Milou isn't accepted into the school, and, like a fool, . . . I decide to take on the Sussex County Council. . . . So I keep Milou out of school for six months. . . . Milou is at home all this time, going totally berserk. I was going to classes. Milou was on his own. He was about six. . . . Yes, I would go and come, but he still felt very, very isolated because Joey was at school all day, and even when I was at home, I was so preoccupied with the court case against Sussex County Council that actually I forgot he was in the house.[8]

But within six months Dad was back. This time the news was different. He was better, on his way back to South Africa to prepare for the family to come home. Once again, everyone would be uprooted, but this time for a joyous homecoming. But, once again, things were not what they seemed. Zarina:

> He sent for us at the end of July [1990], and we were about to board a flight when a telephone call came through saying Mac's been arrested. Steve and Beverley Naidoo came to fetch us from Brighton when they heard the news; they didn't even consult us—they just came in their car, packed us into the car, and took us away, which was very nice, and looked after the kids. . . . I was incapable of looking after my kids at that point; I was shocked, devastated. They filled in, but Joey and Milou were devastated. . . . They kept saying, "When are we going home, when are we going home?"
>
> With Vella and Patsy Pillay and the AAM [Anti-Apartheid Movement], we went on a campaign for his release. I went to speak at the UN Committee on Human Rights. Quite a lot was published about Mac's case based on what I had told them. The UN intervened with the SA government to release Mac. Then the AAM asked me if I would be prepared to go on a European tour to Holland, Belgium, and Germany to speak to the politicians and public and media there and tell them the

story and try and persuade them to intervene, which was very successful. I went on that tour. I left the children with my friends in Sussex. I went on this tour of Europe, a very successful tour. I was on television, radio, in newspapers nonstop.[9]

The campaign to release Mac, with demonstrations outside South Africa House in Trafalgar Square, was not an ANC campaign and did not receive its endorsement. Rather, the ANC frowned on a campaign not approved by movement structures. Mendi Msimang, then the ANC's representative in the UK, appeared on television to say that Vula was not an ANC operation, but Zarina also went on television, contradicting him.

The children were bewildered. Zarina:

> I think that really was the beginning of Milou's breakdown. It had started long before that, but it was just too much for a boy of six [or] seven. . . . When you promise to take a child to a circus or a movie and they get so excited, and then for some reason you can't go, they are so devastated. Well, multiply that by a million times. They had been trying to work out what their Dad looked like; they were arguing with each other; they couldn't remember his face; they hadn't seen him for so long, and they were like, "Oh, I'd love to know what he looks like" and "We'll be home by the weekend." It was devastating stuff, completely devastating. We had sold up the house . . . all the furniture, sold the car, everything, and there we were sitting in an empty house ready to leave for the airport next evening. It was an absolute shock.[10]

Joey:

> We were let down again. That was like the last letdown because we had nothing; we had sold the car, everything. My brother and I lay awake drawing pictures of how he looked because I couldn't really remember. We heard he smoked cigarettes and he had a beard . . . the time was flying because no matter how angry I was with my dad, I was so excited to see him. That's something you can't get rid of . . . I was so excited but . . . before I knew it the phone was ringing; it was about four o'clock in the morning, and I just heard my mother swear and my brother and I both knew . . . well, I didn't know that my father had been arrested . . . but just by the tone in my mother's voice I knew that we weren't going to SA. . . . How do you tell kids we're not going home anymore? My brother was staring at her; I didn't understand why he was looking at her like that.

Now, when I look back, the reason that he was looking at her like that, he was just in so much shock because he knew that my dad had been arrested and she wasn't telling us. . . . The only time he ever forgave my dad for that was when they were having a chat, and he said, "How could you not tell me?" He said to my mom the one night, "Mommy, you treat me like the enemy.". . . And I think she realized he knew everything, and he was very hurt . . . one day my dad and him were chatting . . . and my brother said, "I had a right to know . . . do you know how betrayed I felt for years?"[11]

Back in South Africa and a pupil at Sacred Heart College (Primary School) in Johannesburg, Joey bubbled over with anger at her father:

He'd tell me to brush my teeth, and I'd say, "You're not my father; don't tell me what to do." Or when we first went to school, we used to have injections at school for measles and stuff, and I used to write with an art liner "I hate my Dad; I wish he would die," on my arm so that when they rolled up my school shirt, people would see. I just wanted everyone to know that biologically he's my father, but otherwise he's not.[12]

Feeling abandoned by both parents, moving around, lacking explanations, Joey and Milou came perilously close to psychological collapse.

2

In 1990, as a nine-year-old student at Crawford College, Johannesburg, Milou wrote his Grade 6 English essay "The Satisfaction of Achieving":

When we moved to England after seven years of my growth in Zambia, a deep, aching, emotional wound was opened. The culture shock that my sister and me experienced was like no other. The discomfort was eased during a period of four days when my father came to help us settle into a new country. There was sheer joy about seeing his face, an image I had lost completely by this point. As soon as he had come, he was gone and I was left to deal not only with a new culture but a new education system.

When finally my mother won the case [against the council] and I was admitted to the school that lay across the road for the past few months, I had completely lost all the knowledge that I had learned before. Catching up was made more difficult considering that I had just learnt my father had now been arrested back in SA. I would go to class and strain to remember systems and processes I knew I had known before. In Math I could remember that I had been good at multiplication, but I could not remember what the process was. The teacher attempted to reteach it to me, telling me that two times two is four. He tried several times, refusing to believe that I had known the process before. After periods of intense concentration I finally crashed the code to multiplication. I remember the feeling of sheer elation knowing that with all the pressures around me I had been able to understand and solve this foreign problem completely on my own. Airs of confidence and self-understanding flowed through me. These were short-lived, but I know that when I solved that problem, I had learned an important lesson about myself. I believe that multiplication was the greatest single achievement of mine.

Soon after that I was moved to my unseen home, South Africa, new cultures, new education systems, more challenges.[13]

And more problems. Since the mid-1990s, Milou has had periodic nervous breakdowns induced by the trauma of his past. The proceedings of the Hefer Commission broke him, destroyed the small trust he had painstakingly built in the world around him, left him withdrawn, safer in the solitude he seeks than in a world that always managed to break his heart. His life in limbo, the rich rewards of the new South Africa are yet his to find.

3

The allegations of corruption in the *Sunday Times*, Mac losing his job at First Rand, the Bulelani Ngcuka saga, the Hefer Commission and its fallout—all exacted a toll on Zarina and their children that was incalculable, perhaps far greater than the toll of believing that their father might be dying in some hospital thousands of miles away. Joey and Milou had tentatively begun to reassemble their lives after the trauma of the years of charade, but now they had to face the public humiliation of their father. They found themselves the target of derisory taunts that their father was nothing but a crook who struck back by smearing his accusers with the most damning of allegations—that the state's most senior investigative officer was nothing but a two-bit former apartheid spy posturing as the fisher of corrupt men.

Zarina:

The very sad part about it is that the children, in all those years in exile, felt that one day when they came home and they get their dad back, for them it was enough reward that their father was regarded as a hero of the struggle . . . [but] then what happens is that Bulelani Ngcuka stuff and the fuss and the children are told their father is the most corrupt man in SA. And having lived through the nightmare of not having him around when they were kids but feeling, well, at least he's a father of the nation in a way; we may have lost him to the nation, but at least he is somebody. To be told your father is the most corrupt man in SA at school and things—it's made them both so ill. . . .

In a way I'm biding my time because I know deep down that this is just a phase and the truth will prevail, and Mac will come out of it . . . and will reclaim a place in the struggle and in the movement. Yes. But it has been extremely painful, extremely tragic, for me anyway.

I paid a very heavy price for being Mac's wife. It's not enough that they were persecuting Mac, they had to get at me too. But they haven't been able to crush us.

Mac is very hurt. . . . It's very sad that it should have gone this way. The worst is that he felt Milou paid the ultimate price for the struggle. You know children of the struggle have been very neglected by definition. . . . I was so distracted myself that the children actually felt very unloved. . . . You don't regard it as a sacrifice; you chose that you wanted to do it. That's what you believe in, that's what your ideals were. But when it turns out that your own comrades turn against you afterwards, I think that's a particularly bitter pill to swallow. . . .

Mac doesn't really even talk to me that much about it because he's always looking for the positive. You know Mac's whole thing, "Focus on the future; focus on what we can do to make it better." . . . He doesn't allow himself to feel the grief, to immerse himself in the grief. . . . The reason I feel I'm healing is that I've allowed myself to grieve. . . . I don't think I'm bitter, but I am grief stricken. . . .

Joey is amazing. Very sad though. Very sad about what's happened to her family. She's going to be the politician in this family, you mark my words. She's going to change things. She's going to pick up the baton from Mac. Just give her time. She's a powerful little lady.

I think what broke Mac was Milou's illness more than anything. It was the last straw. . . . All the other stuff was horrendous, but this was devastating. But the fact that he's getting better, we can't count our blessings enough, and we are coming through this whole thing. You know they say—if it doesn't break you, it builds you. Well, it hasn't broken us, so it must be building us.[14]

Joey:

It [the Hefer Commission] just about killed my mother. She's strong and she's come through it, but after everything, my mom felt that enough is enough. "When are our comrades going to be our comrades?" My mother didn't even talk about Vula; people never knew she was involved. She couldn't even speak about things to our own comrades then, and now this thing happened. I think it really killed her. For me, it was just horrible. Milou was ill then, and I felt I was losing too much of what meant everything to me too quickly. The way I view my brother and my father are very important to me. To have that taken away isn't nice, and I remember standing in Woolworths with my dad at the checkout; all the attendants in the shop recognized him. . . . I was standing next to the newspaper rack, and it had his face all over it, and it was the first time in my life I ever felt embarrassed to stand next to him. . . .

It had a shocking effect on my father too. Most men have some sort of self-worth issue as they age, but to be told you weren't a good enough father because look what's happened to your son, and your daughter's embarrassed to be seen with you, you've lost your job, you're of no financial value to your family . . . he won't speak about it, but I think it was devastating for him, and his sense of worth was really crushed. Luckily enough, even though he couldn't recognize that, my mother and I can. . . . I told him every single day that I support his decision a hundred percent.

With the Hefer Commission and with the thing with my brother . . . when I was being bullied at school, whenever I had a problem, I used to think, I lived through that year when my mother was in hospital and I didn't know where my dad was—[I told myself] I survived that, I can survive anything, and that's how I spur myself on.[15]

4

And Joey spurred herself, graduating from the University of Witwatersrand in 2005 with a double major in law and economics, readying herself for graduate study either in South Africa or the United States.

That the family has survived, strengthened, and drawn closer is a tribute to their love for one another. That Mac has damaged all who love him is something he has to live with. They have forgiven him. The toll on him has also been enormous. But Mac finds it difficult to talk about this. The family voices, he seems to feel, speak for themselves, obviating the need for his. Of course they don't. But that he will have to discover for himself or within the fold of his family, and perhaps he has.

Mac

ONE IS NOT BORN A LEADER; one does not rise to leading positions by birth. It happens in the course of time, and through work. *Shades of Difference* is about a person who has been prepared to conduct himself with all the risks and responsibilities that go with being a foot soldier, and at different times, a person who has held important positions. I would like my epitaph to be that I conducted myself with the same sense of responsibility that one looks for in a leader as well as with the sense of duty that one demands of a foot soldier.

Mandela knew I had the qualities and the commitment to stay the course and shoulder those responsibilities. Of course, he can say that I have been extremely troublesome to him, that he had to learn how to interact with me, but he knew that the stuff of all revolutions is made up of different personalities.

More important is that my own life, I would like to think, illustrates that I never succumbed to a sense of victimhood. Yes, I was born into oppression in an oppressive system and was at the receiving end of that system, but I made choices that led to a life of dignity and fulfillment. Whether it brought happiness is an open question.

Kathy tells a story of when we were in jail. One morning I said to him, "I was having a hell of an argument last night." He says I gave him a blow-by-blow account of the argument. When I finished, he said to me, "But Mac, we're locked up in individual cells; who were you arguing with?" I said, "I was arguing with myself." I still do, but I'm now more uncertain about who is winning.

In my youth, one of the Marxist classics I was brought up on was Liu Shao-Chi's *How to Be a Good Communist*. During the Cultural Revolution, Mao Tse-tung (Zedong) had it burned. But Liu Shao-Chi said a good Communist puts the interests of the party first, and all his or her other interests are subsumed. There is no such thing as allowing a contradiction to arise between your personal interests and the party's interests. You see that in my political activities. It's all or nothing.

Which is why Vula left deep scars on Zarina and me. Which is why my children's freedom has come at a very high price to them.

Mine has been a great life, with many painful moments, many bitter moments, but you cannot live life if you allow the painful, bitter moments to overwhelm your consciousness. You will never be engaged to your own limits if you cannot generate passion. And in that I've been very fortunate.

I feel extraordinarily privileged to have had a great life. From time to time, when I hit a bad patch in my own mind, I remind myself: What an extraordinary gift that I'm still alive. I'm still alive! When I have a headache with my son or my daughter or my wife, or I get fed up, I say to myself, "What's your problem? Aren't they wonderful? Yes, they are, so what's your problem? You're still alive and relish it."

22. HUSH! APARTHEID THOUGHTS
OF A DIFFERENT KIND

1

ONCE ACQUITTED of the charge of rape, Zuma was reappointed to his posts in the ANC. Rather than fade into the political wilderness, with some aplomb he apologized to his accuser and the country, and with that behind him he embarked on a high-profile string of appearances at events across the country. He was sufficiently embraced by the SACP and COSATU to reinvigorate his ambition to become president of the ANC in 2007 and thereafter president of South Africa. Elements of the media and big business were added to the conspiracy mix.

Within weeks of the trial's end, both COSATU and the SACP made scathing attacks on what they increasingly dubbed Mbeki's ANC. The SACP condemned his style of governing the party and country, the centralization of all power in the presidency (what it called the presidentializing of the executive), the emasculation of state institutions, misuse of the same for political purposes, usurpation of the functions of the ANC's SG, and initiated a debate on whether it should perhaps contest elections in its own right. COSATU went further, accusing the president of taking the country down the road to dictatorship, of going the Mugabe route.[2] Both intimated that they had begun to seriously consider leaving the alliance,[3] but if this happens it will almost certainly be after the ANC's National Conference in December 2007, at which the new president, officers, and NEC will be elected.[4] According to all accounts, except the ANC's, the

FN.s: p. 602 →

ANC is rent by divisions a decade in the making, more bitter because they are now more personal.

That Mbeki was, pre-1990, a member of the SACP's highest organ, the politburo, itself a clandestine organ within a clandestine party that adhered with the fervor of the true believer to Stalinist centralism until communism as we know it imploded, is never mentioned. That he might have had a predilection to organize his presidency along the Communist lines in which he was schooled is not unreasonable to postulate. That Jacob Zuma was elevated to the same politiburo in 1989 is also never mentioned.[5] And just what Zuma is schooled in remains opaque.

Before the alliance partners embark on their future courses, they will pause. If the SACP, with the backing of COSATU, was to contest elections in 2009 in its own right after a divisive 2007 ANC conference that split the movement along lines of ethnicity, class, and personality, all differences will be ineluctably compressed into two factions: one pro-Mbeki and one pro-Zuma. One has only to recall the scenes of Mbeki's photo image on banners and posters being burned outside the Durban courthouse in 2005 when Zuma was arraigned on corruption charges, the vituperation the crowd directed at the president, and the scenes again outside the courthouse in Johannesburg in 2006 during Zuma's rape trial to ask whether this democracy, at this point in its young life, could withstand electioneering in a highly polarized situation without widespread localized violence. Certainly KwaZulu-Natal, the scene not so long ago of South Africa's forgotten African war, would be highly combustible.[6]

Zuma's immersion in his Zulu heritage, his assiduous attention *to be seen* as being Zulu, is not happenstance but the cold calculation of a political poker player who, whatever the denouement of his corruption trial, has played his hand with a deftness and steeliness of will that has left his political enemies flat-footed. And certainly, too, the hostels that still stretch across the Vaal Triangle, where Zulu migrants celebrated Zuma's rape acquittal with raucous jubilation, the ties that link them to their adjacent townships are fragile and the memories of the ferocious war they waged with ANC-aligned township residents are still fresh. They still vote for the IFP, still harbor feelings of marginalization, and are among the most likely to believe that Zuma's troubles arise from the connivance of his enemies.

South Africa is a constitutional democracy and seems to work as one. People of all races, creeds, and color are equal under the law. People can work and live where they like, are free to think what they like and express themselves however they want. Political activity is open to all; elections are free and fair and conducted according to electoral cycles. But the ANC's hegemony is close to absolute, and with that come the usual perils of absolute power. The question that South Africa must address is how the ANC is using the hegemony, for what purpose and whose benefit.

Since coming to power in 1994, the ANC has engaged in a number of practices that narrow rather than expand the political space for democratic participation. With more than a two-thirds representation in parliament, it has amended the constitution, hammered out first in interim form in CODESA over a two-year period and finalized in the people's Constitutional Assembly over a further eighteen months twelve times, with the thirteenth and fourteenth amendments in parliamentary bill form before being shelved by Mbeki for the time being in July 2006. More disturbing, a precedent has been set; as amendment becomes routine, the practice is internalized in the emerging political culture.

The ANC's Deployment Committee "redeploys" party members—from parliament to business, from prominence to obscurity, from anonymity to importance, from well-paying jobs to wealth through BEE initiatives that are government sanctioned. Party members who engage in actions deemed to bring the party into disrepute may be hauled before a disciplinary committee, and if found "guilty," severely reprimanded or redeployed.[7] The electoral system of proportional representation means that members of parliament are drawn from their place on their party's list, because voters only select parties, not individuals. Thus one's loyalty is to the party, not the public, and although "constituencies" are allotted to members of parliament, few people know who their local member of parliament (MP) is. Government rejected with little fanfare and less public debate a review of the electoral system, mandated by the constitution after five years, that proposed an electoral system based on half of parliament's seats being filled by members elected from delimited constituencies and half by the current part-proportional system.[8] Parliament cannot amend the national budget, exercises little oversight, and performs more as a rubber stamp for the executive than as an independent branch of government.[9]

A practice known as cross-stitution, permitted by a loophole in the constitution—which the ANC could fix but hasn't because it works to its advantage—allows MPs elected on one party's slate to cross the floor and join another during a stipulated period after an election.* Most floor

---

*Under the constitution there is a window period after parliamentary/provincial and local elections during which national/provincial MPs or local councilors belonging to a particular party may join another party and take their seats with them or form a new party. This period is open for fifteen days in the second year following the date of the election. Since the legislation stipulates that 10 percent of a party's caucus must defect

crossing is from minority parties to the ANC, since the ANC can offer inducements and the patronage power brings that other parties can't, thus artificially increasing the already huge number of seats it wins at the ballot box.[10]

Power is inordinately concentrated in the presidency. Under Mbeki, the president appoints the premiers in ANC-controlled provinces (now all nine), as well as the directors general of the national government departments and provincial government. The propensity for the institutions of governance to supersede the structures of the party, except at the highest levels, has disempowered the constituency-based structures of the ANC, especially in the regions, depriving them of patronage and leverage, asphyxiating the voices of the grassroots, and generating resentment at these levels.

A further twist emerged in 2005 after candidates selected by local ANC branches for the local government elections were unceremoniously dumped by the party's national lists committee because they were deemed to be inappropriate choices for office on the basis of their past records of nonperformance, "populism," skullduggery, or other nonredeemable attributes.[11] ANC candidates for mayor, normally the individual who heads the ticket, were not announced prior to the March 2006 municipal elections, but appointed by President Mbeki after the election. Some mayors were not even on the party list for which people voted. And to ensure efficiency, the ANC national leadership also assumed the prerogative to choose a mayor's executive staff. By every yardstick, it was democratic centralism gone berserk, fashioned by the man who was once one of the most senior African members of the SACP's politburo.

So voracious is the ANC's appetite for power that in the case of the only metropolitan city (Cape Town) out of the country's nine, where the ANC failed in 2006 to be returned to government (gained by cross-stitution in 2002, not by the ballot box), it engaged in extreme efforts following the municipal elections to bring down the Democratic Alliance coalition before wiser heads prevailed.[12]

These practices create a democratic deficit,[13] centralize excessive power in the presidency, discourage criticism that calls the party to account, and instill insecurity among party apparatchiks who serve in any capacity at the party's pleasure. Despite "their" party commanding unparalleled political power, the African masses are still politically powerless in many re-

---

before one member can, the big winner to date has been the ANC and the smaller parties the biggest losers. See []majarah/documents and reports/other[] IDASA floor cross briefing.

spects. At national and provincial levels there are no elected individuals who are accountable; the centers of power are remote and inaccessible. They have the right to vote, the right to a nonracial franchise for which the struggle was fought, but, paradoxically, little room to choose.

But to call attention in a public way to any implications ANC practices may have for entrenching democratic practice in what is still a fledgling democracy is to be targeted as being a member of "those" people who are intent on savaging South Africa's nascent democracy. The country's main opposition party, the Democratic Alliance (DA), should know. The ANC dismisses it as a racist irrelevance bent on bringing the country down.[14] For a party that preaches tolerance, the ANC is intolerant of those who disagree with it. You either agree with its policies for transformation, or you are labeled (especially if white) as wanting to preserve the privileges of the apartheid past.[15] The National Democratic Revolution must show no letup. There is an enemy. There is always an enemy.[16] All values are collapsed into one: loyalty to the ANC.*

2

Race, not surprisingly, continues to predominate matters of public discourse. Among sections of the black elite there is a preoccupation with it, and with President Thabo Mbeki, a virtual obsession. Which is unfortunate because rather than opening up the domain of debate, his frequent forays into the question of race relations have discouraged serious-minded people from becoming engaged in an open-minded exchange of views without being disparaged as racist. If whites criticize how South Africa has performed since the advent of democracy, they are dismissed as racist, unless they wrap their criticism in expansive tributes to how well the government has done.[17] There is still a simmering low-intensity resentment of liberal whites, including those who opposed apartheid,[18] who claim the right to assume the role of critic, since they, too, were, by virtue of the color of their skins, beneficiaries of apartheid. Moreover, the ANC believes that implicit in this criticism is the message that Africans can't govern. Hypersensitivity to less than flattering reviews is part of the

*In the course of an interview with R. W. Johnson following the charges of corruption against him being dropped, at least temporarily, Zuma said: "The ANC is a collective. Policy is decided together. I don't want to say anything which might seem critical of government policy. That would be seen as disloyal and in the ANC you have no future if you are disloyal." R. W. Johnhon, "Zuma Phenomenon: All eyes on the man from Inkandla," *Business Day*, 10 October 2006.

process of maturation. The healing of the human psyche is a delicate process.

Among ordinary people, however, there is a remarkable degree of reconciliation, given where whites were and what blacks had to endure. There is no perceptible overt bitterness among blacks toward whites, and many whites seem resigned, albeit not happily, to the reality of the way things are.[19] But most whites in South Africa cannot remember the past because they can't find a past to remember that includes blacks other than as objects, housemaids, garden boys, gas station attendants, and the like. The physical distance created by apartheid also created a psychological distance, giving their memories little to recall. While the TRC was cathartic for some blacks, especially those involved in the process—victims who came face to face with perpetrators—most whites saw it as just that, an opportunity for blacks to express grievance and loss, a vehicle for them to vent outrage and get on with life. Now the country was theirs. Winners had little reason to whine.

Among whites there is little sense that collectively they were part of a criminal injustice carried out with brutal indifference to the welfare of blacks. And there is no sense of the need for apology for wrong done.[20] Rather, they reserve the right to whine, despite retaining comfortable control of the wealth of the country—their 10 percent of the population controls 69 percent of the companies listed on the Johannesburg Stock Exchange either directly or through equity, compared with 4 percent controlled by blacks (27 percent is in foreign control); more than a hundred thousand whites earn more than sixty thousand dollars annually compared to five thousand blacks who earn that much.[21] Among whites, still privileged, petulant complaints of being deprived of opportunity are merely a reminder of how really privileged they were—in 2006, their level of unemployment (5 percent) was lower than unemployment rates in most first-world predominantly white countries.[22]

Yet an ANC enveloped in the abundance of almost total power may yet become as ideologically doctrinaire in imposing a system of racial representativity to redress the injustices of apartheid as the National Party was in imposing nonrepresentativity. The NP defined national identity in terms of exclusivity; the ANC likes to think it does so in terms of inclusivity, but in practice it implements a policy of racial representativity in all spheres of economic and social activity as a way of reversing the legacy of apartheid; the two, it maintains, are different, since the ends for which they are employed are different. True, perhaps, but it is a rationale that leaves others who see themselves as minorities in an overwhelmingly

African country—whites, Coloureds, and Indians—feeling marginalized and alienated. For Coloureds there are few benefits in BEE leftovers, and the bitter competition for resources between Coloureds and Africans, who in ever increasing numbers pour into the Western Cape province, home to most Coloureds, from the poverty-ridden rural areas of the Eastern Cape, belies the usual shibboleths about racism. Indians, their numbers minuscule, stick to themselves.

For reasons not difficult to fathom, elections are still racial head counts. Other than the ANC, Africans in particular have no credible alternative party to which they might turn, and none with legitimate struggle credentials other than the hapless PAC. Moreover, their bond with the ANC is derived from a sense of ingrained identification with something bigger than themselves that transcends quarrels and infighting, a sense of the ANC as family with all the small tyrannies that family members subject each other to. The ANC embodies them in the narrative of their own struggle, personifies and encapsulates the sacrifice of Robben Island, the hardship of exile, the oppression of apartheid, the communion of opposition to racism.

3

Mac, as with much else in his life, took the struggle at its word. He never entertained the thought that the ANC opened membership to non-Africans because it needed to, not necessarily because it wanted to, or that there was an unspoken understanding that membership was conditional on their being of assistance to Africans in their struggle and not wanting to supplant them in its leadership.[23] And if positions in the leadership were to emerge, the understanding was that they would be auxiliaries.

After becoming secretary of the IPRD, the first non-African to hold the post, Mac became the fourth non-African member of the Revolutionary Council (RC), one of only three non-Africans on the Political Military Council (PMC), and one of four non-Africans elected to the now nonracial NEC in 1985.*

As one of the few non-Africans on every structure he was either appointed or elected to, Mac should perhaps have kept his mouth shut more often. But given his talents and commitment, he rose up the ANC ladder. He took nonracialism at face value, believing that leadership is color blind. He believed that he had as much right to chew out an African comrade as an Indian one.

*Under apartheid, Africans, Coloureds, and Indians were collectively categorized as black.

Mac made this African struggle his own. Who else could claim to have the complete confidence of Mandela, Sisulu, and Tambo? He connected the ANC in exile with the ANC in the single cells on Robben Island, the people's war with the birth of negotiations through Mandela.

Few could match his range of activities. He interacted with the three different but complementary struggle cultures: the Robben Island strand, with Nelson Mandela at its head; the exile strand headquartered in Lusaka, with Oliver Tambo at its head; and the internal strand that evolved out of the UDF and the MDM. He bridged the often uncomfortable gulf among the three.

He roamed free, wherever the struggle was and in whatever form one could find his fingerprints: London and the AAM; South Africa and the underground in the early 1960s; Robben Island and the single cells; Mandela's autobiography; the IPRD and building an underground political network in South Africa; moving the emphasis from the military to the political; hammering the point that waging a revolutionary war against the apartheid regime could only be accomplished by building the army within South Africa itself and heading willingly back to South Africa to do just that; linking Tambo and Mandela, the MDM, and Lusaka; putting out internal fires; shuffling drafts of the Harare Declaration among key internals and getting their comments back to Lusaka; connecting Mandela with the underground; relaunching the ANC in South Africa and preparing the way for the SACP to redefine its role in the alliance, part of Ramaphosa's back channel; opportunistically stepping into the political vacuum in Bophuthatswana; codrafting the final clause that made possible the constitutional settlement and opened the way for the TRC.

A man shaped by revolution, loyal to a trinity—Mandela, Sisulu, and Tambo—and then to the ANC; a man who did not take negligence, inefficiency, nondelivery, laziness, or a lack of anything less than absolute commitment lightly. No one who worked with him found him anything other than a hard taskmaster: arrogant and dismissive of the opinions of others, but a leader.

"We love him and we loathe him," says Ronnie Kasrils. "He's done great things in the struggle, but he's really hurt countless comrades to the marrow."[24] He made enemies. His statement to the RC that he had inherited an empty folder when he became secretary of the IPRD was a rebuke to the Africans who had been charged with this task, among them Thabo Mbeki. (When Mac first recounted to me the state of affairs he found in the IPRD after he took over, he was blunt and very undiplomatic. With time and as his own troubles mounted, he wanted to tone down his language, make the situation more amorphous, absolve everybody, especially Mbeki, of any insinuation of being ineffectual. He did not want to appear divisive.)[25]

"Mac," says Ramaphosa, "has a beautiful mind that is full of wonderful ideas. He was an utter joy to work with, even though at times he is too complex and comes across in a complicated way—a way that many people struggle to grasp. But he is clever." Jay Naidoo, the first secretary general of COSATU, a key MDM leader, and a minister in Mandela's government, echoes Ramaphosa's sentiments. "Mac," he says, "is a superbly intelligent person. He was a bloody clever operator and he's made a fantastic contribution to the liberation of this country. He's an operator and that's how he survived and that's the role he's played."

Being seen as "clever," an "operator," is a millstone around Mac's neck. During the struggle, many of the negative connotations associated with either word—devious, scheming, cunning, sly, evasive, contrivance, guile, up to no good, all attributes that Mac exercised in abundance to survive, outwit the apartheid regime, and advance the struggle—were seen as positive attributes. In the new dispensation, however, they conjure up negative connotations. They convey intimations of shadiness, of Machiavellian intent, of trying to put something across or get away with something. Thus the wariness with which he is treated in public circles.

Our collective subconscious errs on the side of believing that clever people deserve what they get, that they are invariably too clever for their own good, their misfortunes the product of their own machinations and hence not deserving of empathy. Hence, too, our predisposition for wanting to see the clever among us put in their proper places.

In Mac's case, the juxtaposition of his being seen as clever, a public perception, and his own sense of integrity, a private recess, leaves little room for him to assert a moral presence that withstands public scrutiny, and so he is deprived of a public forum from which to articulate the things he cares about the most. Public perceptions of his cleverness emasculate public perceptions of his integrity. When he said that what concerned him most, after he confirmed that Bulelani Ngcuka had been investigated by the ANC and found probably to have been a spy, was not his personal situation with the Scorpions but the larger issue of abuse of power, no one believed him. Even when Hefer did draw attention to abuse of power with regard to his treatment by the Scorpions, no one thought much of it because he did not fit the profile of someone who had been wronged. When Hefer exonerated Ngcuka, Mac became the sinner rather than the sinned against.

Prior to his release, Mac was interviewed by the prison administration. The report cautioned:

This man will give the authorities no end of trouble wherever possible to the best of his capabilities. He will have to be kept under strict supervision upon his release. He is potentially a great risk/danger/threat to safety and security in the country after release.

The prisoner won't suddenly release or forgo his current beliefs and principles. . . . [26]

After meeting Mac in London in 1979, when he was still in the employ of the South African government, apartheid superspy Craig Williamson* wrote to his superiors: "Maharaj is the most dedicated, intelligent and well-trained leftist that I have ever met. He is totally dangerous and if his organization of internal networks is accomplished, there is going to be really big trouble inside South Africa. I feel that for the first time an accomplished and well-trained person is pulling together the strings of an ANC network inside South Africa."[27]

Among the apartheid state's records was a psychological profile prepared in 1980 by Karl Edwards, an SB agent, for Williamson, his superior. Edwards, who in subsequent years was Agent Vanessa Brereton's handler (RS 452), wrote:

Maharaj is the single most important person in the IPRD and possibly in the entire ANC/CP network. From old photographs of Maharaj it is evident he has changed his appearance entirely. His hair style is short and pushed arrogantly to the side, and he wears a "pirate's eye patch" over his blind eye. His dress is casual and his whole appearance is designed to give the impression of a dashing revolutionary. This appearance, linked with an arrogant and egotistical personality completes the picture. There is no doubt that his look is effective. He is a tireless worker and obviously has a large following that idolize[s] him wherever he puts in an appearance. His conjures up among his following the true image of the indestruc-

---

*Craig Williamson secured a job as deputy director of the International University Exchange Fund (IUEF) in Geneva to facilitate the awarding of IUEF scholarships to African students. He was in a position to direct scholarships to South Africans, which enabled him to infiltrate the ANC at the highest levels. Eventually he was exposed as a spy for the South African Police (he first held the rank of captain, then major) in 1980. He received amnesty for the letter bomb murders of Ruth First, assassinated in 1982, and Jeanette Schoon and her daughter Kathryn, assassinated in 1984. The Schoons and First were close friends of Mac's. For Mac's interactions with Williamson go to []maharaj/interviews/[]. For accounts of Mac's interactions with Williamson, go to Mac interviews on 8 January 2002, 15 January 2003, 5 November 2001, 16 October 2002, 25 October 2002, and 25 September 2003.

tible and all-powerful revolutionary. Should the ANC ever lose Maharaj, it would be an extremely harsh practical and psychological blow to them.[28]

Often his enemies thought more of him than his colleagues.

4

Cassius Make, a member of the NEC, remarked to Phyllis Naidoo that in NEC meetings Mac should watch his tongue, that not all members had the privilege of a university education.[29] Mac was aggressive in a culture where aggressiveness was a negative attribute. There is a huge cultural divide between the way the Indian community in South Africa engages in the process of decision making and the African mode.[30] Mac was resented and disliked; he had colleagues but few friends.[31] Mac, says Jacob Zuma, pissed off a lot of people. And Zuma laughed.[32]

In the paradoxical and contradictory ways apartheid worked, whites like Joe Slovo occupied a more privileged place in the struggle than Indians. "Struggle whites" put their careers and positions in society on the line. Such whites were special. They brought special skills, world-ranging experiences, special insights into the ways in which the regime thought. They were to be listened to. "Struggle Indians" were not seen in a similar light.[33] When Mac was invited by the RC to attend meetings in order to brief it on the activities of the IPRD, he was not asked to sit beside IPRD chairman John Motsabi but behind him. One can hardly imagine Joe Slovo being treated in a similar way.

Zarina Maharaj, who had her own difficulties with the ANC in exile and harbors, unsurprisingly, her own prejudices in the matter, attributes his lack of popularity among his colleagues to his utter obliviousness to the role of *place* in the ANC:

> I've got pictures of Mac and Thabo as young men [she says], just shortly after Mac's release from prison. I think by then already Thabo was beginning to sense a threat from Mac. Mac upstaged him in all these meetings, I am sure. He was just a bit too brilliant and a bit too unapologetic as an Indian, because it was already floating around that the trouble with Mac is that he talks as if he's an African; he has no sense of apology about him. There was this element in Lusaka, if you were nonwhite, if you were classified as Indian or Coloured, because you had had some privileges relative to the African majority, you had to feel a bit guilty somehow and you had to pander a bit and you had to know your

place in the hierarchy and Mac didn't know his place. That was his biggest crime. He is not apologetic enough. He didn't know his place. He didn't know how to take a backseat.

Mac has such confidence in who he is, in his place in the struggle, that he has no sense that he must play second fiddle to anybody just because he is Indian rather than African. I've always felt that if Mac had been a bit more submissive, a bit more apologetic, a bit less brilliant and less clear about the way he was heading and what he wanted, and if he were less committed even, it would have been to his advantage.

Had Thabo reached out to Mac, he probably would have stayed on [in government]. When he decided that he had to leave, he asked to see Thabo. Thabo gave him five minutes and didn't even try to persuade him not to leave. He just said, "OK, fine." He didn't even sit Mac down for a chat, not even "Maybe we should go out next week, let's have a drink together, let's talk."[34]

And that was it. A lifetime in struggle netted him, it seems, one brief visit to the office of the president-in-waiting.

5

Breaking the physical chains of oppression, repealing the legislation of oppression, celebrating the symbols of newfound freedoms, creating the political space for freedom of speech are the easy parts of establishing a new national identity. Breaking the mental chains takes a generation or two. In most deeply divided societies where one group has oppressed the other for centuries, the systemic domination embeds a sense of inferiority in the psyche of the oppressed that continues to inhabit the mind even when they are freed and assume the political power previously the exclusive preserve of their oppressors.

This sense of inferiority in South Africa expresses itself in innumerable ways: an inverted sense of superiority leads to claims of being the regional, perhaps even the continent's superpower; exaggerated statements of achievement since the advent of democracy; of having one of the world's best constitutional democracies with a deeper commitment to human rights than others; of being more deserving than others because of its apartheid past; an obsession with being first or best in every endeavor in which South Africa competes; of disproportionate response to perceived slight.

At the root of national identity is a myth that underpins a country's relationship to its sense of self. In the new South Africa, it is the myth of nonracialism. The ANC wraps itself in the fiction of being a nonracial movement. The promulgation of historical conceit is not just the province of South Africa, but a universal one; each nation state nurtures its own comforting accounts from whence it has emerged.

For the new South Africa to overcome the formidable array of challenges on every economic, social, and political front it faces, a long slog of decades of work will be required. There are no shortcuts.

Among the challenges are the dual needs to foster national unity and to create a sustainable national identity. The two are not necessarily mutually inclusive. Fundamental to the new identity is the need to instill among the African masses a sense of pride in being African, a sense of connection with their own past that engenders self-worth and increases self-esteem, all the more important given the level of unemployment (a range of 26 to 40 percent). In the short term, not much can be done to eliminate the appalling disparities of income and wealth that are the hallmark of apartheid's legacy.[35] Hence the great need to provide a psychological upliftment that will compensate for the absence of material improvements in socioeconomic conditions.

Germane to this endeavor is the inculcation of the belief among Africans that anything whites can do, Africans can do as good or even better. It goes to the core of erasing the inferiority complex that centuries of slavery, colonization, exploitation, and dehumanization have implanted.

The intellectual core of the African renaissance is the deracialization of thought.* An African renaissance, according to the script, will impart to Africans, continentwide, a sense of the history of their own glorious past, of African civilizations that predate the ancient civilizations of the Greeks and Romans; resurrect breakthroughs in math and science that were in

---

*It is a "sad fact that the racialised notion of Africa is pervasive throughout this continent. It is an indicator of how colonised we have become mentally. This is, of course, why an intellectual rebirth, a reawakening of the mind, is an urgent need. It is this new sense of self, born of a different sense of history and one's place in it, that we call African renaissance. Let us recall that every major development of historical significance must rethink and rewrite history, and thereby redefine its place in history so as to give itself a sense of self-worth and a renewed sense of agency. Only those who have little to hope for from historical change can refer to great movements for changes in consciousness as a 'brain-washing' exercise." Mahmood Mamdani, "There can be no African Renaissance without an Africa focused Intelligentsia" in Maleqapuru William Makgoba, ed., *African Renaissance* (Cape Town: Tafelberg; Sandton: Mafube, 1999). The cause of deracialization of thought was not furthered by the revelation in May 2006 that a group of African intellectuals had formed a racially exclusive forum called the Natives Club to nurture/foster African intellectual life. In the wake of the adverse publicity and comparisons with the NP's Broederbond, the Native Club opened its doors to all.

time co-opted by Europeans and claimed as being their own; of art and architecture as great as anything the Renaissance in Europe produced.*

Coming of age when national identities are undergoing repostulation as counterpoints to encroaching globalization, South Africa under Mbeki has to assert itself with more aggressiveness to authenticate its claim to speak on behalf of Africa at global forums. However, in South Africa, "Africanization" and Africans have become virtually interchangeable.[36] It has acquired an exclusivity. Aggressive affirmative action and BEE policies, unfortunately, have aggravated perceptions. As should be the case, Africans, the most disadvantaged under apartheid, have benefited the most in the postapartheid era. But "disadvantaged" is a relative concept, and many Indians and Coloureds are reluctant to give ground to Africans on the issue.[37]

National identity is not created within a decade or even a generation. It evolves as a country immerses itself in shared experiences, struggles to reconcile its differences, acquires the psychological glue for social cohesion, accommodates the "other," and melds the commonalities that begin to slowly emerge in a transformative process out of which it creates a shared sense of national selfhood. In South Africa, hosting the World Soccer Cup in 2010 may perhaps provide the psychological glue that will act as a therapeutic catalyst drawing all peoples together in a common endeavor, instilling a unity of purpose from which all can take pride, and incubate the seeds of self-esteem germane to national reconstruction, as important as more obvious material yardsticks. In rising to the occasion, all South Africans will rise together. I say "perhaps" because in South Africa the sense of relative deprivation among the poor is high, the potential for social upheaval probably more likely than in other countries at the same stage of development. "Perhaps," too, because already one can sense an emerging expectation that the World Cup will be a panacea for all that ails the country, that another "miracle" is around the corner. A backlash, if the expected benefits do not trickle down to the poor, may as easily eviscerate whatever social cohesion the great occasion will generate.

In the meantime, the constancy of such emphasis on Africanness, a secondary identity at best but easy for the majority to readily identify with,

---

*"After sheltering the first forms of life on earth up to *Homo sapiens* and then peopling the planet through the Isthmus of Suez and the Strait of Gibraltar, Africa was the initiator of a brilliant civilization, the light of which has illuminated and educated the ancient world for millennia along the Valley of the Nile, from its Ugandan source to its Mediterranean delta. This was unanimously attested by ancient Greek authors, and cannot be rebutted today by any *bona fide* scholar." Dialo Diop, "Africa: Mankind's Past and Future" in *The African Renaissance*.

is that it requires history to rewrite itself to comply with the new definition of things.[38] In the new mythology, there is little room for an Indian dimension, little room for the likes of Mac Maharaj. He is an anachronism, an artifact of the struggle. To which he would say, "That's life."

Mac told of a question he put to Tambo in 1988:

> Before I left and OR had given me my orders, I said to him, "Are you finished?" He said, "Yes." I said, "OR, I have a question to ask you; I don't want you to answer, but you think about it. I'm going to do what you're asking me to do, but why is it that you are sending me among others to the province of Natal, where there are very, very serious racial tensions and you're not sending an African member of the NEC?" Now it wasn't my choice. People may think what they want to, but the record is there: OR asked me to go. I was mindful that it would have been better if an African went, but I wasn't going to sit back and say, "No, I'm not going to go until you've sent an African."[39]

Tambo did not say a word in reply.

Among Indians who played important roles in Mac's story, grievances linger. Paul and Dasu Joseph feel that their participation in the struggle in the early dangerous days after the ANC took to the armed struggle has been rejected because the government will not provide official recognition that they were members of MK. They look for the recognition not for themselves but for their grandchildren. Vella Pillay and Ameen Cajee (Doha) died unsung and unrecognized. Hassim Seedat, Mac's flatmate in London in the late 1950s, feels the Indian community has marginalized itself. Tim Naidoo, Mac's first wife, is bitter. Zarina, his current wife, rails at his enemies.[40] A shared oppression does not make for a shared identity.

At Mac's surprise seventieth birthday party, struggle Indians paid simple but eloquent tribute to his courage and leadership; only a handful of struggle Africans was present.

"The Asian knows only too well what is required of him in order to qualify in the mind of the African as a true citizen," Shiva Naipaul wrote. "He must disappear into the land. He must cease to exist."[41]

Not a sentiment Mac would agree with.[42]

6

Going into its second decade of democracy, South Africa faces the realities of chronic unemployment, poverty, the AIDS epidemic, and the mounting disparities between the haves and the ubiquitous have-nots. The haves are increasingly members of the burgeoning new black bourgeoisie,[43] and the have-nots are the bulk of the impoverished African masses whose lives are not much better, in material terms, than they were under apartheid.[44] Much has been done in the way of basic services such as housing,[45] electricity, sanitation, water, and education, but by no means nearly enough.[46] The majority of Africans are condemned by the circumstances of their birth to lives that are harsh and hard, and often brutally short.[47]

The proportion of the population living in poverty and the degree of income inequality between the new elite and the poor have increased.[48] More people than ever live in squatter camps, euphemistically referred to as informal housing;[49] education, supposedly free for all, is not free for some.[50] BEE has become a synonym for avarice and crony capitalism.* The avarice feeds the party's coffers.† Ostentatious consumption among the newly empowered elite, some of whom were once leading lights in the SACP, laughs in the face of the Freedom Charter.[51] Corruption, especially at provincial and local levels of government, seems to be winning the battle despite intensified prosecutorial efforts to weed it out.‡ Violent

---

*Among the NEC members in empowerment deals: Kgalema Motlanthe, Manne Dipico, Saki Macozoma, Penuell Maduna, Popo Molefe, Mohammed Valli Moosa, Smuts Ngonyama, Matthews Phosa, Cyril Ramaphosa, and Max Sisulu. Of these nine, seven are either former government ministers, premiers, or senior parliamentarians. NEC members whose spouses are in empowerment deals: Collins Chabane, Enoch Godongwana, Phumzile Mlambo-Ngcuka, Naledi Pandor, Jeff Radebe, Ngoako Ramatlhodi, Zola Skweyiya, Sam Shilowa, and Makhenkesi Stofile. See "ANC Incorporated Takes Over," *City Press,* 27 November 2005. Among senior government officials are Murphy Morobe, head of communications in the presidency; foreign affairs spokesperson Ronnie Mamoepa; presidential adviser Titus Mafolo; South African ambassador to the Netherlands Hlengiwe Mkhize; former ambassador to Britain Cheryl Carolus. See Kevin Davie, "Rich Pickings of the WaBEEnzi," *Mail & Guardian Online,* 11 to 22 November 2005. The ANC's five wealthiest NEC members are Saki Macozoma (thirty-fifth richest in the country), Cyril Ramaphosa (thirty-seventh), Popo Molefe (sixty-fourth), Valli Moosa (sixty-fifth), and Smuts Ngonyama. The five have a combined wealth of R1.5 billion ($220 million). See "ANC Turns on Fat Cat Comrades," *Sunday Times,* 6 August 2006.

†There is no legislation limiting the amounts political parties in South Africa may accept from individuals, corporations, or in donations by foreign individual or governments. There are no disclosure laws, hence no transparency in the financing of political parties and the individual or corporate entities they may be beholden to.

‡Among the many outcomes Mbeki wanted to use his presidency to achieve, the alleviation of poverty among the poorest of the poor, job creation, and bridging the gap between the "two nations" that live within the physical boundaries of South Africa were certainly among the most important. But midway through his second term, it was apparent that his efforts would fall short, not because of a lack of will on his part but simply because the rate at which backlogs accumulated outpaced the ability to address

crime, especially crime against women, appears to be getting the better of law enforcement. It is random, so gratuitous that even the most heinous act fails to evoke more than mechanical outrage, so pervasive that it has become "acceptable," nothing out of the ordinary, something you expect to read about in the morning newspapers or hear on the radio.[52]

Delivery of basic services at the local level is stymied by incompetence and corruption.[53] As the poor watch the new African elite preen themselves amid the trappings of conspicuous wealth, they are beginning to suspect that the benefits of liberation have accrued to the politically connected, that there is a convenient convergence of enrichment, opportunism, and cronyism.[54] "Minirevolts" in desperate townships in 2004–5 were suppressed on occasion in a manner reminiscent of apartheid.[55]

In a scathing assessment of where South Africa stood in 2004–5, the Institute for Justice and Reconciliation, one of the country's most respected think tanks, wrote:

> Most dramatically in the course of 2004–2005, countrywide conflict and widespread citizen protests at non delivery by local governments—often led by activists from the 1980s and 1990s—has precipitated our most visible crisis of governance since 1994. That social conflict is not worse is attributable to the fact that the number of people on grants now nears 10 million. To the prescient remark that unemployment near 50 percent would see people rioting in the streets, one can only note that this is indeed the case.
>
> While we acknowledge our achievements, we must also candidly admit that it is an increasing part of popular public perception that policy is made and implementation managed from behind closed doors, often on the basis of internal party politics, involving political connections, favoritism, and power trade-offs. In the short run, the character of economic transformation would seem to be held hostage to political transformation.[56]

---

them, to say little of cutting deeply into past backlogs, massive skills shortage, lack of investment in infrastructure, and maintenance of existing facilities put limits to growth, failure to deliver was systemic and direct foreign investment (DFI) shied away. With Zuma's indictment on corruption charges, Mbeki nailed his future to the mast of anti-corruption. The more the Zuma camp denounced the charges against Zuma as an effort to preclude his ascendancy to the presidency of South Africa, the more Mbeki castigated the purveyors of corruption as a corrosive threat to democracy. For further details go to [] maharaj/footnotes/[]485.

But transitions to democracy never quite turn out the way they are supposed to; new dispensations can rarely match the promise of their constitutions. The disparities and inequities, corruption and incompetence, violence and crime that typify South Africa can be found in other midlevel countries emerging from poverty and conflict. The study of such phenomena has created an industry of economists, sociologists, and political scientists. Nothing startlingly out of the ordinary in South Africa, their research tells us. But that is where similarity stops.

What made South Africa special was that the destruction of apartheid was for a generation of people across the world the embodiment of a great moral crusade. With freedom came ordinariness. But what is out of the ordinary is the new South Africa's slide into a moral oblivion that belittles the values freedom supposedly brought. "Ours is a moral struggle," the ANC preached from a corner in Hyde Park in London to the chambers of the United Nations in New York to the cavernous halls of the Kremlin. Yet with freedom has come silence. Not a silenced press or of any form of expression, but a silenced public life that conflates loyalty to the ANC with loyalty to South Africa, the self-silence that comes when there are fears of a new kind of marginalization.[57]

The struggle to have blacks recognized as human beings, to have the value of their humanity put on an equal footing with the humanity of whites, to erase centuries of stigmatization of inferiority and state-sanctioned racism has metastasized into something hollow and cynical that gives the lie to official proclamations that the pursuit of equality and empowerment of the poor are still the guiding principles of a continuing "national democratic revolution." While such ringing declarations of intent urge organs of state to rise to every revolutionary occasion, not a single member of the ANC's leadership—national, provincial, or local—has spoken out since 1999 against President Mbeki's misguided ideas on HIV/AIDS. His denialism—a whim of his convoluted understanding of science—has contributed to the deaths of hundreds of thousands *every* year because it infects the actions or lack thereof of his government as truly and deadly as the virus infects human beings.[58] The government's willfully passive and neglectful policies have condemned millions to death.[59] In his annual addresses to parliament on the state of the nation, the pandemic merits passing reference, the flip of a half sentence between a deep breath and a semicolon.[60]

No cabinet minister takes issue with the minister of health, Dr. Manto Tshabalala-Msiamang, who is perceived to advocate a traditional African diet of potatoes and garlic as an alternative to the use of antiretrovirals for

HIV-positive people.[61] In the end her own defiance of science was her undoing. At the 16th International HIV/AIDS conference in Toronto in August 2006, the South African government's information stand promoting the importance of beetroot, African potatoes, and lemons for HIV-positive persons with almost no presentation on the necessity of taking ARVs created an uproar. Stephen Lewis, the UN special envoy on AIDS, lambasted the South African government's policies at the conference's final plenary session, a group of eighty-one of the world's leading scientists, including codiscoverer of HIV Robert Gallo and Nobel laureate David Baltimore petitioned Mbeki to fire Tshabalala-Msiamang, and Mbeki, always sensitive to South Africa's international image, bowed a little. In September 2006 sole responsibility for implementing government policies relating to HIV/AIDS was delegated to a cabinet committee headed by Deputy President Mlambo-Ngcuka.*

Within the next ten years, an estimated 4.4 million people will die of HIV/AIDS—more than 10 percent of the current population. One in four people is HIV positive. Life expectancy, sixty-three years in 1991, is now fifty-one and will drop to below forty, perhaps as low as thirty-six years, by 2010.[†62] The United Nations Human Development Index for South Africa worsened from 0.73 in 1994 to 0.67 in 2002 to in 0.653 in 2004,[63] one place above Tajikistan, one behind Equatorial Guinea, ranking 121st out of the 177 countries surveyed.[‡]

Had an apartheid government ever dared to pursue the HIV/AIDS policies of the ANC, we would have seen UN resolutions, worldwide condemnation, cries of genocide, thousands demonstrating outside South African embassies across the world, calls for sanctions, for the intervention of the international community, and for a redefinition of what constitutes a crime against humanity.[§]

---

*See endnote 59, p. 609.

†In 2005, with more than six million infections, South Africa had more people living with HIV than any other country, only recently having been overtaken by India. See endnote 62, pp. 609–10.

‡The human development index (HDI) is a composite indicator. It covers three dimensions of human welfare: income, education, and health. The HDI is a barometer for changes in human well-being and for comparing progress in different regions. Between 1990 and 2003, in sub-Saharan Africa the interaction of economic stagnation, slow progress in education, and the spread of HIV/AIDS produced a free fall in HDI rankings. Southern Africa accounted for some of the steepest declines—a fall of thirty-five places for South Africa, twenty-three places for Zimbabwe, and twenty-one places for Botswana.

§After South Africa was humiliated at the XXVI International AIDS conference in Toronto in August 2006 by the actions of Tshabalala Msimang (see endnote 59), Mbeki was compelled to take action. He established a new interministerial committee under the

No one speaks out against the egregious abuse of human rights being perpetrated by the regime of Zimbabwe's Robert Mugabe against his own people. Indeed, to raise the matter in South Africa may earn you the ruling party's label as a white neoliberal, your professed concern merely a smoke-screen for your real concern: the interests of white farmers whose lands you believe were forcibly seized from their rightful owners rather than being returned to them.[64] As it does about much else, the ANC believes it has a monopoly on what human rights are.

Something has gone terribly wrong.[65]

7

When Jacob Zuma's corruption case came before the Pietermaritzburg High Court on 31 July 2006, the state requested a postponement until February 2007 because it was not yet ready to present its case. Already the proceedings had been recast into political theater by Zuma's lawyers and supporters, the indictment lambasted as a contrivance by pro-Mbeki elements within the ruling elite who did not want Zuma to become president. Zuma's lawyers argued that the court should order the NPA to proceed with the case forthwith or, in the event of its being unable to do so, should either strike the case from the rolls or dismiss the charges permanently.

In a further hearing on 6 September 2006, Judge Herbert Msimang, to whom the case had been assigned, became visibly incredulous when the NPA informed him that it was using documents seized during the dawn raid on 25 August 2005 from the premises of Zuma's lawyers, Julia Mahoomed and Michael Hulley, and on all of Zuma's homes and offices, including the office at Union Buildings from which he worked when he was deputy president,* to prepare the final indictment, despite the fact that judges in Johannesburg and Durban had instructed the NPA to return all documents seized and copies made pending the outcome of appeals. The NPA, Msimang chastised, was in "double contempt of court."[66]

---

direction of Deputy President Phumzile Mlambo-Ngcuka to monitor and strengthen the implementation of the state's HIV/AIDS program. Mlambo-Ngcuka moved quickly to beef up the National Aids Council (SANAC), which she chairs, and mend relations with NGOs, including the Treatment Action Campaign (TAC). Mbeki's action effectively moved HIV/AIDS from the Tshabalala Msimang's health portfolio.

*Judge Msimang found, inter alia, that the NPA had falsely claimed under oath that the state had given KPMG (a company that conducts forensic audits) contested documents after reaching "agreement in principle" with Zuma and his advisers about the seized documents. Text of the SCA's judgment is at []maharaj/documents and reports/Jacob Zuma/[]. (See endnote 59, p. 609.)

On 20 September he struck the charges against Zuma from the rolls. The NPA's case, he wrote in his judgment, "had limped from one disaster to another";[67] the NPA had "jettisoned" standard legal practice "in favour of some non procedural policy" and "ill-advised decision making." It had "ignored judicial guidelines on the use of disputed evidence," made claims "under oath that were false," gave unlawfully seized documents to auditors to prepare a report into Zuma's financial affairs. The "social prejudice" to which Zuma had ben subjected, he declared, "closely resemble[d] the kind of punishment that [can] only be imposed on convicted persons and is therefore inimical to the right to be presumed innocent enshrined in the constitution."[68] In essence Judge Msimang found that the NPA's actions, after it had charged Zuma, were characterized by an abuse of its powers and possible criminal offenses.

For Zuma and his supporters the reprieve was tantamount to total victory.* The consipiracy, they claimed, had been exposed for what it was: a mendacious attempt hatched in the upper echelons of the ANC and business to deny Zuma the ANC presidency in 2007,[69] the NPA as party to a surreptitious undertaking to derail Zuma's political aspirations and prepared to go to any lengths to pursue him even to the point of operating in contravention of its own prosecutorial mandate. But the sense of absolute vindication was short-lived. Within a month the Supreme Court of Appeals upheld Schabir Shaik's corruption and fraud convictions on all counts,† opening the way for the NPA to reindict Zuma sometime in 2007 when it has its act properly together.

However, the SCA's findings contained an error of indeterminate consequences. In one section of the judgment Judge President Craig Howie wrote that "between 1996 and 2002, Shaik and Mr. Jacob Zuma engaged in what the trial court (Squires) appropriately called 'a generally corrupt relationship' . . ." Squires had made no such finding and ventured a public statement that he could not have made such a judgment because he could not speak for Zuma's frame of mind when he received the payments from Shaik. Thus the SCA had inadvertently attributed to Squires a legal finding

---

*Within hours of Msimang's verdict, the Scorpions raided an accountant's firm linked to Schabir Shaik. See "Scorpions Mount Fresh Zuma Raid," *Sunday Independent*, 24 September 2006.
†"In our view," wrote Appeals Court Judge Craig Howe, "the sustained corrupt relationship over the years between Zuma and Shaik had the effect that Shaik could use one of the most powerful politicians in the country when it suited him. In our view this was an aggravating factor." "New Zuma Trial Is on the Cards," *Cape Argus*, 7 November 2006. Text of the SCA's judgment is at []maharaj/documents and reports/Jacob Zuma/[].

he had never made. And although the SCA immediately issued a clarification upholding a finding of there being a "generally corrupt relationship" between Zuma and Shaik irrespective of whatever words Squires had used, the political damage was done. For Zuma's supporters this was manna from heaven. The public, they argued, had internalized, as it appeared the SCA had, the language widely promulgated by the media, which was a willing shill for the conspiracy against Zuma, of what was presumed to be a verbatim account of Squires's finding. They claimed that this account, now exposed as a canard, had, by virtue of the media's unrelenting repetitive use of the phrase, shaped the public perceptions of Zuma and his fitness for high office; for Zuma's lawyers more grounds to argue, should Zuma be reindicted, that the former deputy president cannot get a fair trial. The country waits.

That different factions within the alliance should trade allegations of conspiracy in pursuit of their respective agendas as they try to stage-manage their ascension to power is not surprising. Apartheid was replete with narratives of conspiracy and secrecy where the inventions of the whites to buttress a sense of siege and justify apartheid and the inventions of blacks as they weaved and bobbed around apartheid laws, found livelihoods within the system, made their own petty bargains with repression to eke out the meager coexisted, accusations of conspiracy found willing ears, more willing ones perhaps among Zulus susceptible to the suggestion that the Xhosa elite would not give up their hold on the presidency to a Zulu.

Indeed, Mbeki himself gave the people their first taste of conspiracy cocktails. In October 2000, eighteen months into his presidency he told parliamentarians that criticism of his HIV/AIDS policies* was a plot on the part of the CIA working in cahoots with the drug companies.[70] The following year, the EU was supposedly out to discredit him;[71] and then in April 2001, Steve Tshwete, his minister of safety and security, publicly fingered Tokyo Sexwale, Matthews Phosa, Cyril Ramaphosa, who had been Mandela's personal choice to succeed him, as being joined in a conspiracy to overthrow Mbeki.[72] Of course it was all preposterous nonsense,[73] but the three, all powerful members of the NEC and presidential material by any yardstick, found themselves in the invidious position of having to appear to publicly disavow having presidential aspirations, thus removing themselves in 2001 as possible rivals to Mbeki's reelection to the presidency of the ANC in 2002 and hence to his reelection as president of South Africa in 2005. And Jacob Zuma, too, fell under the scrutiny of the

---

*"Does a virus cause a syndrome? It can't. A virus causes a disease."

loyalty radar. Weeks before Tshwete's accusations of a plot to unseat Mbeki, Zuma, for reasons never revealed, felt compelled to publicly avow his loyalty to Mbeki and reiterate that he harbored no presidential ambitions.[74] At the time the statement seemed bizarre, given the absence of any context and the fact that an election was four years away, until subsequent events unfolded.

"It's a conspiratorial thing," Mbeki said during a TV interview. "The best way of dealing with the matter is to have open debate about everything, including the presidency. Because once you start a conspiratorial thing, you are implanting a destructive process."[75] The fallout of Tshwete's allegations cemented Mbeki's hold on power at an early stage in his presidency.

8

My journey through the decades of the struggle against apartheid as seen through the prism of Mac's life and the trajectory of the forces that are shaping the new South Africa have led to me to conclusions I would rather not have reached.

The ANC in exile developed a self-perpetuating inability to deliver on *any* aspect of its internal struggle against the apartheid government; the ANC in government continues to use the paradigm of exile to govern and transform South Africa, thus reinventing the exigencies of exile in a post-liberation South Africa and similar incapacities to deliver on the pledges it makes to the people.

The ANC never had to face the consequences of its own failures as a liberation movement. Whenever it engaged in a reexamination of the way it conducted the struggle, it failed to implement corrective policies and regressed to old, entrenched habits. Its leadership, immune to external criticism and responsive only to itself, sanctioned the recruitment and training of thousands of young men and women for an armed struggle and continued to bind itself more assiduously to this course even as the cumulative evidence became unmistakable: the armed struggle was not succeeding and could not succeed. In government, the ANC is still immune to external criticism and is responsive only to itself—on only one occasion in fourteen years has a cabinet reshuffle resulted in a minister's being relieved of his portfolio, and the minister in question was back in the cabinet within two years—and it binds itself ever more assiduously to policies on Zimbabwe and HIV/AIDS: the policies have been disastrous, a blot on all the ANC supposedly stands for.

The ANC is crippled by a chronic inability to implement well-thought-out public sector programs, a mirror image of the ANC's chronic inability in exile to implement its struggle strategies, many extremely sophisticated, but lost in the patchwork of small tasks gone undone, unattended to.

The ANC claims ownership of the revolution, only begrudgingly giving others who could make an equal claim to having been integral to the demise of apartheid a passing acknowledgment. Perhaps this might be attributed to a postapartheid schizophrenia: On the one hand, the ANC claims to have been a revolutionary movement in the image of other great revolutionary traditions, but it wasn't. On the other, it asserts that it overthrew the illegitimate apartheid regime, but it didn't. Trying to find congruency between these sets of contradictions has created an identity crisis. In exile, it could comfortably afford to clothe itself in the tradition of African liberation; in government, the fabric quickly wore thin; but where to find new clothing? Unable to, it continues to dress itself in the old ways, clinging to rhetoric that has become jargon, beating the last drop of usage out of old bogeys. When in doubt, resort to the legacy of apartheid.

In exile, the ANC leadership was secretive, conspiratorial, and paranoid, decidedly nondemocratic—and with good reason. The SACP was convulsed at times with bouts of distrust, paranoia, and a penchant for the clandestine and nondemocratic command systems. Good learned behavior for revolutionary movements infected with state security agents at every level of leadership. Deviousness was a necessary antidote, though rarely a sufficient one. In government the ANC has yet to unlearn these behaviors.[76] Mbeki's leadership of the country and command of the ANC have been matters of intense scrutiny since he assumed the helm in 1999, ranging from the harebrained to the keenly perceptive. But there is a common theme: whether he is in control of the ANC and how he is exercising his power to ensure that he is.[77]

Some characterize the succession war that Jacob Zuma had come to personify as a war about ideas, that Zuma served as a lightning rod for factions of the ANC disgruntled and marginalized (pro-poor and pro-redistribution) and factions entrenched (pro-business and pro-growth) in the structures of the state under Mbeki, and not particularly disposed to seeing someone other than a loyal Mbeki acolyte succeed him. But it looks less grand. There is a new terrain of struggle. The struggle for power, and in this struggle what the pundits call a battle for the soul of the ANC is increasingly becoming the battle for a large empty space.

POSTSCRIPT

IN EARLY 2006, Zarina Maharaj published her memoir, *Dancing to a Different Rhythm*. In October, *Mandela: The Authorized Portrait* was published in twenty-two countries simultaneously. Mac and Ahmed Kathrada (Kathy) were the editorial consultants for the book, a labor of love for both.

And Mac found an intellectual home. Bennington College is a small liberal arts college in Vermont. In 2005, it established a Democracy Project and chose Mac as part of a select team to conduct classes and seminars and develop the program. He teaches and writes for some part of both semesters in the prestigious school, nestled into the landscape of the beautiful New England countryside. He has found in the United States a place from which his voice can speak to young people about Africa and South Africa's struggle and any matter his eclectic mind might turn to, a place no institution of learning in South Africa thought of offering him.

Thus the final irony: able to share with eager young minds nine thousand miles from South Africa, but no forum in his own country to share with its young people.

ACKNOWLEDGMENTS

IN THE WRITING OF *Shades of Difference* there are numerous people to thank for assistance and encouragement. There is, of course, Mac himself, who always made himself available, although he did not always answer the questions, which kept me on my toes—Mac at his elusive best! Even in the dark days—the events that led to his resignation from First Rand Bank, the Hefer Commission, and the darker days that followed the publication of the commission's report—he continued to converse with me for hours at a time on matters that had nothing to do with these events, testimony to his remarkable ability to compartmentalize and focus, attributes essential to being a successful revolutionary, but even more essential to surviving underground in a South Africa where the regime made one final push in the late 1980s to crush resistance.

My deepest thanks, too, to his wife, Zarina, and two children, Joey and Milou, who spoke openly and with a breathtaking honesty about events that were painful and left lasting scars. Ironic that the course of life he chose to free them and all the children of South Africa should list them too among the casualties.

And to Madiba, my gratitude for taking time to write such a forceful and reflective foreword; his empathy with the suffering that the struggle brought to the Maharaj family is striking, a manifestation of his having to bear witness to the suffering that his twenty-seven years of imprisonment brought to his own family, something that has weighed heavily with him over the years.

Among those I interviewed in connection with Mac's life I recall with fond memories the late Vella Pillay and his wife, Patsy; the late Wilton Mkwayi and his wife, Patty; the Josephs, Paul in London and Dasu on his visits here; Nandha Naidoo, who wept openly at what he perceived as the attempts of the new South Africa to destroy his friend; Michael Dingake, only met over the phone in long conversations but the ring of laughter lingering long afterward; Ahmed Kathrada (Kathy), for his insights into life on Robben Island, our many years of friendship, his example of tolerance and forgiveness that is a beacon of hope in a South Africa often short on tolerance, and still, unsurprising, unforgiving in the many ways that escape easy notice; Indres Naidoo and the entire Naidoo family also exude the hope and optimism that years of struggle have not dimmed; Shanthee Maharaj, Mac's sister, for sharing her memories of Mac and childhood and for going out of her way to be accommodating, full of magical energy and even more magical thoughts; Tim Naidoo, Mac's first wife, for giving me the opportunity to visit with her, her lively conversation and tart wit, willingness to revisit times that brought up painful memories and face them with me when the "safe" thing to do would have been to show me the door; Ivan Pillay, ever helpful, guiding me, providing documents, taking time; Dipak Patel, who shared memories of Vula and met the test of loyalty with trust, the only test that counts; Janet Love, another who shared memories of Vula and insights into life underground in South Africa in the brutal years that preceded the demise of apartheid; Ismail Ayob, who taught me much about the Indian experience in South Africa and gave, unstintingly, too, of time; Totsie Memela, her courage emblematic of the courage of thousands of young people who lived through the last years of apartheid and today form the nucleus of the best in the new South Africa; Dipuo (Catherine) Mvelase, for sharing memories of a young man she loved very much who was killed by the security forces in a shootout in Alex, but whose courage raged in her heart when the Security Branch tried to break her; Phyllis Naidoo, for digging through overflowing boxes to find the one specific document so that she could damn you with faint praise; the late Walter Sisulu, who loved Mac like a son and loved the Irish playwright Sean O'Casey with an equal passion.

There are others, all deserving of thanks not just for assisting me but for the courage they drew on to break the apartheid state and give life to the new South Africa, which, for all its warts, is still a mere youngster and prone to the vanities of the young.

For almost eleven years Judy Drew scheduled interviews and transcribed hundreds of hours of the taped interviews, many conducted under near inaudible conditions. And having transcribed the tapes, she then, years later, waded through them again to edit and make sense of what you have read. Judy's diligence is exceeded only by her dedication.

To my editor in South Africa, Shaun de Waal, I will always be indebted for his incisiveness, skill in being able to separate the essence from excess verbiage, his willingness to question what I wrote, and his familiarity with the politics of South Africa. My thanks, too, to Maureen Brady, for additional editorial input that tightened up the manuscript and for her extensive knowledge of South African history that allowed me to complete numerous incomplete endnotes and footnotes. Also, my thanks to Bridget Theron, who fact-checked the manuscript, prepared the glossary, and assisted in the preparation of endnotes and footnotes.

Leanne Smith was researcher par excellence. She would follow every lead, disappear for days into the basements of libraries, come up with documents from the most unlikely sources. Leanne worked with me for three years before moving to a more rewarding position. Susan de Villiers had the hapless task of trying to decipher the transcripts of the early years before she, too, also moved on. Andrea Crowell was like the substitute brought on in injury time, and then with the clock ticking hits the back of the net twice in the dying seconds of the game. Together we clawed our way through the copyedited hard-copy manuscript, marked repeatedly on every page with one kind of inquiry or another. Denise Ackermann undertook the painstaking task of transcribing the Vula communications, often difficult to decipher, with diligence and good humor, and brought an equal diligence to proofreading.

To my editors at Viking, Kathryn Court, who stayed the course when less believing editors might have thrown in the towel, and Ali Bothwell Mancini, who labored through innumerable drafts until the word "cut" became the single-word mantra I repeated as I stretched myself to reduce an enormous bulk of a manuscript to manageable proportions.

From 1989 to 2006, many individuals energetically contributed their skill, time, and intellect. They were motivated by their personal enthusiasm for the importance of this information to future generations who could draw lessons from the South African experience in the transition from apartheid to democracy. The following is a short list of those who participated. The recognition of these people represents many others who performed like tasks: Andre Titus, Faisal Sultan, Henry Tshabalala, Kate Doerr, Mandla Khanyile, Matt Vasconcellos, Nomsa Ngakane, Vusi Buthelezi, Roger Berry, and Zweli Tshabalala.

To my colleagues at the University of the Western Cape and the Mayibuye Center I am indebted for technical support and unearthing documents and reports hidden in dusty places.

Special thanks go to Tim Jenkin, for reconstructing part of the Vula communications, and to an individual who wishes to remain anonymous for providing me with a set. These comms are the stuff of history and it is my intention to donate them to an institute/library/university in South Africa that will treat them with the attention they deserve. Jan Wagener opened the way for me to talk with former members of the security forces who provided insights into how the apartheid security apparatus worked.

Jill Kneerim acted generously and magnanimously on my behalf and John Taylor "Ike" Williams has had a direct or indirect influence on much of my life, always with my best interests in mind. My brother Peter facilitated an introduction to the late Robie Macauley that was to change the course of my life. Had he not done so it is doubtful whether I would ever have put a pen to page. That he had faith in me where my own was so lacking I remain profoundly grateful. The McCormack Graduate School of Studies at the University of Massachusetts Boston has been my home. Ed Beard, during his tenure as dean, had abiding faith in me. The measure of a good scholar, he says, lies in his being able to take the measure of his own abilities. Pat Peterson, my colleague on the *New England Journal of Public Policy*, provided editorial assistance when I was in dire need of some; Margery O'Donnell brought a love of Africa that inspired me to do better—and do more; Sandy Blanchette, Candyce Garragher, Jamie Ennis, and Mike McPhee always had the little word of encouragement that opened blue skies. To other stalwarts of the McCormack's tenth floor, my thanks for providing support willingly whenever I asked for it. Two others, Joe Corcoran and Fred Clark, stood steadfast in making other dreams possible.

My work in South Africa has benefited from the assistance of several foundations and individuals: the Open Society Institute—George Soros and Frederik van Zyl Slabbert, who brought me to the attention of OSI; the Charles Stewart Mott Foundation—William White, Christa Kuljian, and Russell Ally; and Atlantic Philanthropies—Gerald Kraak. And to Dr. Marcy Murninghan, a special recognition for bringing me to the attention of the Mott Foundation, an introduction that provided financial support for this undertaking.

Learning 24 designed and maintains The "Heart of Hope" Web site at www.omalley.co.za that contains the transcripts of some 1,500 interviews I conducted in South Africa between 1990 and 2000. The site is also the repository of the transcripts of my interviews with Mac Maharaj between 1993 and 2006 and with the individuals I interviewed in connection with *Shades of Difference*, transcripts of the Vula comms, and most of the research I conducted to document the events in Mac's life, which encompasses the history of South Africa throughout the apartheid era, documentation of negotiations and transition to a democratic South Africa, and the transformation of South Africa under the presidencies of Nelson Mandela and Thabo Mbeki. For the work in this regard I am indebted to the vision of Anton van Dorsten and the professionalism of Annemie Stoman, Tahnya Schutte, and the Learning 24 team.

To the many who spoke to me under conditions of anonymity, I can only say that your willingness to help shed light on some events in South Africa's turbulent past adds a little to historical accuracy and helps to demolish the foundations of historical absolutism and debunk myth, of which there is already an unhealthy abundance in circulation.

I would have liked to conclude by thanking the African National Congress for enabling me to access some documents that would have confirmed certain proceedings at different points in time, especially after 1985, but refused to do so on the most spurious grounds. In itself that is not important. What is important is that the ANC has provided similar documentation to other writers and scholars, sometimes attaching conditions to access, thus creating the impression that it is trying to shape the writing of history. Again, perhaps understandable in a country still in its infancy, still learning and growing, and still overly sensitive to criticism and unduly reactive to perceived slight. However, for every document there is a copy somewhere.

And finally there is Pat Keefer, who deserves much more than a book dedication, and Gladwin, the joy of my life, who is the future of South Africa, proud of her country, full of hope for the future, of ambitions declared and undeclared, free of hate, for whom apartheid is something "old" people talk about, open to opportunities previous generations of children thought unimaginable, for whom race is a thing you do on a track.

—Padraig O'Malley

APPENDIX

Correspondence between Nelson Mandela and Lusaka smuggled out of Victor Verster Prison concealed in a book cover (the container) and forwarded via the Vula communication system. Responses were sent in the reverse order.

So far the container we are using is getting through. Only Sophitshi [Mandela] has not mastered how to open & re-seal it. The idea is that Sekwati [Ayob] will take in the container and leave it with Sophitshi, so that by next time Sophitshi will have time to retrieve material, prepare his reply etc, insert it & have it ready for handling over the next time. Each time Sekwati will have another container with in going material, so that all that will happen is that containers are swopped. However, even in this case it will be important that the conversation at the visits does not abruptly and drastically change in content. Apparently this last time both Sop & Sek were nervous but they'll get over it.

Tony (Mac) to Alphons (Oliver Tambo) and Janet (Joe Slovo)
[]maharaj/Vula comms/1989/May 29, part 6

SECTION A

24 May 1989

Alphons (Oliver Tambo) and Janet (Joe Slovo) to Tony (Mac)
For Rachel (Govan Mbeki) and, of course, for you.

Please ensure that R gets it soonest.

Report: on 7th April Alphons raised the following matters with NM [Nelson Mandela], through IA [Ismail Ayob]. We have just received the answers. Further questions were raised with NM in middle of May. We're waiting for these answers and we shall be reporting further to GM [Govan Mbeki].

1. What is the subject matter of these talks?
There is one, and only one, subject matter of the talks, namely a

meeting between ANC and the government. Right from the start of the talks M [Mandela] attempted to define this position as clearly as he could. He emphasized that he was not a negotiator, and that his only concern was to bring the organisation and the government to the negotiating table. As would be expected, a host of matters have been raised in the process. Although he attempted to outline the policy of the organisation on each point, his basic attitude has throughout been that all these issues be put directly to the organisation itself when the meeting is held.

2. It is our idea that we should not negotiate in fragmented formation as this will promote fragmented approaches when the government comes with a coherent plan.

M agrees that fragmented negotiations would be dangerous, and that this should be avoided at all costs. He is, however, not aware that the government is talking with some of our members other than himself. He makes it quite clear that if that is what the government is in fact doing he will immediately back off his own discussions. His intention in urging the government to talk with the organisation is precisely to forestall such a fragmented approach on our part.

3. If negotiation is not handled we will discourage such pressures as sanctions.

M can think of no better method of conducting negotiations than to bring the government and the organisation together to work out a solution acceptable to all parties. He has, however, insisted that there can be no change in the position of the organisation, as well as its operations, until a proper settlement is reached. Naturally, the international community will continue to pressure us to negotiate as they are already doing right now. But we have fairly powerful machinery and very able and dedicated leaders inside and outside the country, who ought to experience no real difficulties in convincing the world that there should be no easing of pressure until an effective settlement is reached.

4. The organisation insists that all leaders, inside and outside prison, should be there when negotiations take place:

This is an objective worth striving for and its immense advantages are too obvious to require further emphasis. But we must accept that it may not be so easy for the organisation to secure the release from prison of all leaders required at such negotiations, and the leadership outside prison may be compelled to enter talks without those inside.

5. What M is discussing with the government is not known to the organisation:

It is perfectly natural for the organisation to be worried when a member engages in serious discussions with the government without a mandate from his organisation. It is worse when that member is a long term prisoner separated from his own fellow prisoners. However, from the very start of the talks M expressed the hope that the government would, in due course, allow him to report to his colleagues inside and outside the country, a point which he is presently hammering in these discussions. One may add that M has kept his colleagues at Pollsmoor Prison informed on the discussions, even though for reasons which he explained to them, he was unable to be as detailed in his report as he would have liked. He also reported to Bribri Wilton Mleway: when the latter was transferred from Robben Island on 17 March 1989.

6. Request to see GM and to get his views on internal leaders to be consulted:

Despite the fact that the government has repeatedly turned down M's request to see GM, he continues to urge the government to allow this visit. He had discussions with GM on three different occasions before the latter was released from prison, and he stressed the importance of regular contact between them so that he (M) could keep abreast of the thinking of the NE on the political situation in the country generally and on the talks in particular. As pointed out in (7) below, M is no longer pressing to report first to the internal leadership before he meets the NE [National Executive].

7. Report to the NE on the talks:

As pointed out under (5) above, M is urging the government to allow him to report to the NEC on the talks, and to get its views on the whole matter. He was of the opinion that the NEC would probably want to know the views of the internal leadership on these issues before it makes a firm decision. He would have preferred to consult with representations elected by the internal leaders themselves. But the team with whom he is discussing insisted on getting the names of the proposed representatives for the purpose of considering the request. It was under these circumstances that he suggested certain names on a regional basis. M stressed to the team that if the consultation was to have any significance, top leaders from each region would have to be included. Some of these leaders, he pointed out, were serving prison sentences, others were in detention while still others were restricted. All of them would have to be free to attend. M has, however, noted your deep concern on this particular point. It is clear that he did not examine very carefully some of the ticklish problems to which the organisation has drawn attention. He is consequently no longer pressing for such consultations, and would now prefer to report first to the NEC. The next step would be taken after full consultation with the NE.

8. Release of political prisoners serving life imprisonment:

M is definitely negotiating with the government on this issue, and the release of GM is the result of such negotiations. This particular development must, however, be seen against the background of the massive campaign for the release of political prisoners by the democratic movement and by our friends throughout the world during the last 25 years. No single individual can, therefore, claim credit for the release of any of our political prisoners. But M has been discussing the matter with the government since July 1986. The expectation was that GM and WS [Walter Sisulu] would be released at the same time. But this was not to be. Nevertheless, it was a happy moment indeed when M informed GM that he was being released at last, and without conditions. GM's release was significant in several respects:

(a) The government has insisted throughout the years that a person serving life imprisonment could never be released from prison, life imprisonment meant just that. GM's release put an end to that approach.

(b) The government released him without conditions, which meant that the movement would now have an experienced man who would be free to move around the country helping in settling problems.

(c) GM's release was also a test, and the release of the remaining lifers would be influenced mainly by what he did outside prison. For these reasons M advised that, subject to what the organization outside prison might decide, GM should avoid addressing public meetings. M is still of the opinion that lifers, and only lifers, who are released because of old age, health grounds or whatever, should be used very cautiously by the mass democratic movement in order to facilitate the release of those still in prison.

Conclusion:

As pointed out above, a host of issues were raised in the course of the discussions with the government. The attitude of the organisation on questions such as violence, the SACP, majority rule, sanctions and other forms of external pressure is fairly clear and one can state it accurately.

But there were other matters on which the views of the organisation were not so clear to M. An issue of this nature, which repeatedly came up, was the fact that the government had repeatedly announced that they would never talk with the organisation. How would they retain credibility to their supporters, they asked, if they now changed their stand and sat down to talk with the same organisation.

M's own assessment of the line-up within the establishment, especially during the last three years, is that whatever the hawks may say in public, there is a strong government lobby that regards the organisation and its leaders as worthy opponents, with whom negotiations could be fruitfully considered. This is but natural, because what dominates the political scene in SA today is the fact that the organisation has far outclassed the government both in its ability to mount effective operations inside the country in the face of the most massive machinery of repression this country has ever seen. Equally important has been the success of the organisation in the diplomatic field. In any negotiation situation we would not enter the talks from a position of weakness. Obviously the wheels of government grind very slowly, and almost three years of discussion is by any standard a long time. Moreover M's illness and that of others from the other side were regrettable setbacks which seriously disrupted the tempo of the talks. Now the forthcoming general election and changes in the top echelons of the NP and government mean that no significant advance should be expected until about the end of the year. M feels that there has been fairly good progress. At the same time he has made it abundantly clear that if the NEC is, for any reason, of the opinion that he should pull out of the talks, he will do so immediately.

SECTION B

29 May 1989

To Alphons (Oliver Tambo) and Janet (Joe Slovo)

Sophitshi [Mandela]: (a) Reply to Ndima [Oliver Tambo]: Sophitshi is happy to know that you support the initiative he has taken to talk to the team, and your acceptance that he sees himself as merely facilitating talks between us and the other side. He accepts your observation that both you and him are at a total disadvantage in regards to this initiative, since on our side he is the only one who knows the contents of his talks. He will accordingly give you a full report of his discussions at the earliest possible convenience.

But you must advise him without delay just how the report should be made available to you. There are three options. The first, which Sophitshi prefers, is to continue pressing the other side, as he has been doing, to allow him to come over to report to you. The team [Niel Barnard et al] agrees with this point of view, but the final decision does not rest on them. It is doubtful whether this is likely to happen before the forthcoming general election. The second option is to brief Xhamela [Walter Sisulu] as you suggested. This will be extremely difficult to do. Altho Sophitshi's discussions with visitors are never visibly monitored by an official, it must be assumed that in actual fact we are never alone. We cannot give him a written report as he might be searched on release. The 3rd option is to continue using Sekwati [Ismail Ayob] to whom we can give a written report for your attention. But Sophitshi warns that Sekwati is a hot potato. It is clear that the other side knows that Sekwati shuttles between Ndima [Oliver Tambo] and Sophitshi. The possibility of a surprise swoop on him one day must not be excluded. Sophitshi will consider carefully your guidance on this aspect. You state that Sophitshi seems to be concentrating on the internal clash between black & whites & not on our set objectives & external pressure. This impression is not correct & is based solely on the part of his comments in which he defines his exact role in the discussions. The forthcoming report will probably clear the issue. However, in the actual discussions Sophitshi has deliberately underplayed the importance of external pressure.

Sophitshi has already informed you that he has abandoned his plan of consulting the regions. But he intends seeing Archie [Gumede]. Sophitshi has already seen Dullah from WP and Harry, separately of course. He hopes to see Dlamini [Govan Mbeki] & Ntsiki [Albertina Sisulu] soon. It may not be wise to appear as treating Archie differently. Sophitshi will indicate to each what his original plan was but that he has dropped it on your advice.

A resolution adopted by the recent NUMSA conference suggests that somebody is going around saying one of us is negotiating with the govt. Sophitshi proposes that the mischief should be countered without delay by reading to the under-mentioned individuals the statement in which Sophitshi has defined his role in the ongoing discussions.* This must be strictly confidential: Elijah Barayi & Jay Naidoo, Cyril & Mahlatsi, Cassim Saloojee, Essop Jassat & Firoz Cachalia, . . . Archie & George Sewpersadh. I will acquaint Albertina & Murphy personally.

The concluding two paras which I did not read out to you are as [follows]: "I must add that the purpose of this discussion are not only to urge the urge to talk to the ANC, but it is also to acquaint you with views current among blacks, especially those in the liberation movement. If I am unable

---

*This is a reference to the memorandum Mandela had prepared for his meeting with P. W. Botha, which took place on 9 July 1989. Mandela was not aware of the brouhaha that had erupted after Ayob mistakenly distributed copies of the document to certain MDM leaders. For the text of the memorandum go to [] pretransition/documents and reports/1989/[].

to express these views frankly & freely, you will never know how the majority of South Africans think on the policy & reactions of the govt: you will never know how to deal with their grievances & demands.

It is perhaps to remind you that the media here & abroad has given certain public figures in this country, but also in respect of their prescriptive stance when dealing with black leaders generally. This impression is shared not only by the vast majority of blacks, but also by a substantial section of the whites. If I had allowed myself to be influenced by this impression I would not have even thought of making this move. Nevertheless, I come here with an open mind, & the impression I will carry away from this meeting will be determined almost exclusively by the manner in which you respond to my proposal. It is in this spirit that I have undertaken this mission, & I sincerely hope that nothing will be done or said here which will force me to revise my views on this aspect."

This introduction is followed by 10 pages in which I state our policy on violence, alliance with SACP, majority rule and sanctions. ends msg to Ndima [Oliver Tambo]. (b) Here follows response to Tony's [Mac's] note: Sophitshi was pleasantly surprised by your message & it revived warm recollections of the comradeship to which you refer.

You have, however, been in our thoughts all these years. It was quite proper for you to concentrate on the technical aspects (ie of communications) and Sophitshi has noted all your suggestions. Keep[ing] in touch will be of crucial importance to us all & Sekwati will be the best channel of communication (i.e. carrying the camouflaged goods). He is, however, very hot as the establishment is by now probably aware of his shuttling between Ndima & Sophitshi. We must seriously reckon with the danger of a surprise swoop on him. As you know, Sophitshi is no longer in regular contact with Ntakobusi & they are not likely to meet soon. Sophitshi will accordingly not be in a position to convey the information to him, which is probably good. Sophitshi is in full agreement with everything you have said & expects a further communication from you. Meantime fondest regards. Ends. According to Sekwati the only point that arose in the verbal part related to Fatima and the books question. Sophitshi mentioned that there is some major hitch regard to Xhamela's release. Plus he asked Sekwati to go to Durban personally to tell Archie and George Sewpersadh that Sophitshi saw HG [Harry Gwala] only to discuss his personal matters as Sop [Sophitshi]. Feared that HG would be restricted. There was also the question of his passport. Whilst HG was with him he discussed other matters. Sop wants them to know that the impression created by HG that Sop holds his views higher than theirs is not correct & he would also like to meet them. Ends (Tony's note: it seems that Fatima conveyed this re what HG is saying, though I have not heard that HG has said this to anyone! Seems there is no shortage of mischiefmakers!)

SECTION C

22 September 1989

Shaun (Joe Slovo) to Carl (Siphiwe Nyanda): Send ff to Sipho (Nelson Mandela) from Shaun's father (Joe Slovo) on behalf of Presidential Committee:

The National Executive Committee at yesterday's plenary session received a full report on Sipho's talks with the team. There was unanimous approval for the way he handled the whole situation. In particular, the meeting was overcome with his exposition of the movement's position on all the key issues in the document presented to the other side. The meeting felt very strongly that if the document could be published without jeopardizing the "confidentiality" of the discussions, it would be a major mobilizer. The other side has spread a great deal of misinformation about his positions. Publication of the document could serve to correct wrong impressions. If, however, he feels that such action is premature, the following alternate proposals are suggested:

Here's 2/2

(i) the document be circulated to the leadership, taking into account the necessary security precautions.

(ii) the document be shown to selected leaders of the Frontline States & the Socialist World. We want to stress that we will be bound by his assessment as to whether we should risk circulating the document in one of the above ways or not at all. Two points made by Sipho in the last few paragraphs: (i) on allaying white fears; & (ii) that negotiations be preceded by meetings to work out the pre-conditions for a proper climate for negotiations, are to be further discussed. Our thinking will be forwarded to you.

24 September 1989

Kay (Joe Slovo) to Carl (Siphiwe Nyanda) [to forward]: from Shaun (Joe Slovo) to Sipho (Nelson Mandela)

\1\ A plenary session of the NEC [21 September] has once again discussed the exchanges between you and the "team" in the light of the additional information contained in their reply. We are launching a full investigation as to the source of the leak. The document came to us in two stages. (a) A report from the lawyer on the first portion (of about 5 pages) which was read but not circulated to a small NEC group selected by the president. Unknown to us, the lawyer subsequently circulated these pages to a number of individuals in the MDM. (b) The first time that the document, or any part of it, was known to the NEC as a whole was at last week's meeting. At all stages the absolute confidentiality of the document was insisted upon and at the Lusaka end none other than the president and Shaun's father have ever had possession of the actual document. We do not rule out the possibility of a deliberate leak by the team.

\2\ The NEC is of the view that a meeting between the two sides to work out pre-conditions for the creation of a proper climate for negotiations is premature and, especially in the light of recent developments, could have negative consequences. The points we have in mind are the following.

\2.2\ The initiative launched by the NEC to gain acceptance of our negotiating concept has received overwhelming international endorsement. It was accepted virtually without amendment by all the Frontline States and subsequently unanimously by the OAU which publicly identified the document as having been prepared by the ANC. Since then a similar endorsement was made at the Belgrade meeting of the Non-Aligned Movement. At the OAU meeting the lone dissenting voice came from the head of PAC whose demagogical stand against any prospect of negotiation was rejected even by Mugabe. Moves are now being considered to get the UN itself to accept the positions in the document.

\2.3\ A key element of the document (going to its very roots) is on insistence that the regime is obliged to take steps to carry out the pre-conditions upon which the document insists in order to create the atmosphere for the beginning of negotiations. It is of the utmost importance to note that virtually all the leaders of the western world (U.S., U.K., France, West Germany, etc) have, without referring to the actual document, accepted in their public pronouncements that the onus is on the regime to implement some or all of the conditions to open the way for meaningful negotiations. Indeed Bush has threatened that unless this happens further sanction measures may be implemented. Even the hardline Thatcher has been compelled by the force of international popular opinion to assert that she will find it difficult to maintain her stubborn opposition to sanctions if the regime does not fulfil some, at least, of the pre-conditions. In her tour of Southern Africa she refused to include SA on her itinerary insisting that before she could go the pre-conditions such as the release of political prisoners would have to be met. All this is of great significance for the forthcoming October Commonwealth Conference.

\2.4\ In the light of the above, a move by the ANC at this stage to engage in talks about pre-conditions would take the steam out of the unprecedented momentum which we have built up internationally on this question. It would also provide an excuse to our reluctant "friends" (Bush, Thatcher, etc) to opt out of their more recent positions into which they have been pushed by popular pressure. Many of our people may conceive it as a retreat, and it is likely to trigger off divisions within the MDM and between the MDM and those on its periphery. We have to take into account that it has not been straight sailing to gain broad acceptance for the very concept of negotiations among our supporters in the MDM. We have, in general, succeeded in allaying understandable suspicions and reservations. If we are seen to move away from an insistence on the pre-condition measures (so universally accepted) we can expect a most unfortunate reaction.

\3\ Our insistence that the regime creates conditions to make the idea of "talks" meaningful is clearly not a tactical maneouvre, it goes to the very root of the problem. As things stand at the moment only the regime has the freedom to consult. We are all cut off from legality and deprived of any real possibility of meeting collectively with those of our leaders in the prisons and, on the ground, in the mass movement.

\4\ So far it is extremely uncertain whether De Klerk will move in any substantial way from the policies of his predecessors on the really fundamental issues. What he has said before and after the election suggests a stubborn adherence to the concept that there will "never be majority rule" and a commitment to a constitutional mechanism which is not much of a departure from the old "Great Indaba". We felt that the responses of the team to the 1st part of your document is not only insolent but confirms their "old thinking". We believe that their implied readiness to contemplate talks with the ANC about pre-conditions is designed to depose escalating international pressure.

\5\ The NEC stresses that it has no reservations whatsoever about your initiatives to engage the enemy in the exchanges which have taken place. We believe generally that the question of negotiations is a terrain of struggle in which we must also take the high ground. We therefore believe that you should persist in your contact initiatives. But for the reasons outlined we do not believe that, especially at this moment, it would be appropriate for us to agree to skip the stage of insisting that the regime takes measures not only to demonstrate its bona fides but also to create at least some of the key conditions in which we have the freedom to exist and consult without let or hindrance in preparation for possible negotiations.

\6\ Your get well message to Timo [Oliver Tambo] will be delivered. Your suggestions about Adi and reducing his work burden are well-taken. Shaun's father will be in Cleo [London] next week and will update you on his condition. Please also accept my personal affection, comradeship and brotherliness. It's been too long but it does really look like we can get there.

SECTION D

13 October 1989

From Carl (Siphiwe Nyanda) for Norman (Alfred Nzo) and Kay (Joe Slovo): Report dictated to Sekwati (Ismail Ayob)

1. Makgoto [Mandela's son by his first marriage] came at 7 a.m. and stayed until 8 a.m.

2. At 7.45 p.m. on Monday evening the 9 October 1989 whilst he was watching TV they came and told him that Kobie Coetsee with another Cabinet Minister would come to see him at 9 a.m. on Tuesday. They also told him that the Pollsmoor colleagues with Oscar Mpetha would arrive at 1 p.m.

They said that at 5 p.m. the other five would arrive. They had earlier asked him who should come with Albertina Sisulu. They had then asked what should happen if one or more of them should not be available; the answer was that they should decide.

3. Makgoto arrived at 7 a.m. and stayed until 8 a.m. He was supposed to have stayed for the whole day. They telephoned Farida Omar and said to her that he could only stay for one hour. Yesterday (Thursday 12 October 1989) Professors De Kock and Strauss from Tygerberg came. They said

that the operation had gone very well. He has to see him again on the 11 December 1989 and you have to make the arrangements. He will visit NM on 10 December 1989.

4. A little after 9 a.m. Kobie Coetsee and Gerrit Viljoen arrived. They were there for a while and then were joined by General Willemse and Fanie van der Merwe, advisor to the Minister of Constitutional Affairs. He used to be Director General of Justice and started as Public Prosecutor at the Johannesburg Magistrates Court.

I have been discussing with the government the release of my colleagues. On 18 September 1989 I met with Kobie Coetsee at my request and I reminded him of the release of my colleagues and was no longer concentrating on the release of Walter but on all the colleagues and Mpetha and Masemola and two others from the time of Robben Island, that is Mathew Meyewe and Zakhele Mdlalose. I said that all must be handled as one package. I said that I would expect the new State President in his first major policy statement to highlight the release of the political prisoners. I included Mathew and Zakhele because in the later 1960s and early 70s they had done 8 years for terrorism. Then in 1978 they came back, doing life with Gwala and now had already done 11 years of their life sentences. I pointed out to Kobie Coetsee that if you add 8 years to the eleven they had already served 19 years and theirs must be treated as a special case. I had also, after discussing the matter with Kobie, discussed the matter with General Willemse. He then made the statement that they had no difficulty at all with the releases except these two. This raised my hopes. He gave us their reasons for not releasing Mathew and Zakhele that they had done 11 years of their life sentences only and it was not enough in terms of the rules for people doing life. I still pressed him and said these were not normal rules for prisoners doing life but required as a special case. He said that he would go into the matter.

5. On Tuesday morning the two Ministers said that our approach is identical with yours. The Government has decided to release these eight and they repeated what the General had said about the other two. I urged them to take the matter up with the State President and to indicate to him that I would be a lot happier if the request was to be granted in respect of these two prisoners as well and I went to great lengths to support my case. They said that they would go into it but then, later, during the day, the General and Van Der Merwe came back to me and showed me a statement that they were going to make that night and wanted me to approve it. This is what normally happened in the past. I approved the statement. This was already when Albertina and the others were here. I altered some of it. I

thought that it would not be tactful for me to make a statement without my having consulted. I was not arguing about the correctness of the statement but I wanted to consult first. Yesterday I signed the corrected statement after it had been typed.

6. One thing I was expected to raise and that is the impression the government is giving that there is a difference between the Organisation and myself on the question of working for peace in the country. I pointed out to them that this is very dangerous and in conflict with the spirit which characterizes the discussions which we have had, but I was very warm in thanking them for the decision to release the colleagues and the two ministers who must have been very strong in deciding that this release must be accepted.

7. As far as Mr. Coetsee is concerned, I have given you my assessment of him. He has, throughout, projected himself as a man of integrity. He is a member of the National Party and is bound to carry out its policy, but subject to that, he is a man with whom you would like to discuss problems. He makes it easy to discuss sensitive problems without tension. He pointed out that he had brought along Dr Viljoen so that I could make his acquaintance, as the man who would handle negotiations. My first impression of Viljoen was also a positive one. He appeared confident and relaxed. And apart from the fact that he is handling a difficult department he is the best qualified person.

8. They are having difficulties amongst themselves. Like Walter. When they came in March to tell me that he was being released, I asked when— weeks, months. No, they said, within days. Months passed and nothing happened. I raised it with them and they said that the government had decided not to release him. I was shocked, I raised it with the State President when we met. He said, as soon as we have the green light we will release him. That did not help.

9. At 1 p.m. I saw Walter and the others.

10. On the next day, Wednesday, I went past all the journalists who were gathered outside Pollsmoor. They looked and did not recognize me. The General said to me after my meeting with PW that the journalists had made life very difficult for him after Winnie said that I would be making my own statement.

11. I explained to the colleagues my whole position. They were very constructive. To be released without conditions is very important. They must be aware that if they are not careful the government will simply clamp down on them and we will not gain anything.

12. I don't think they should be involved. There are another five chaps

to be released before Christmas from Natal. If our own chaps are not involved in whipping up the level of agitation. I know that we are involved in a campaign for the release of all political prisoners. We on the inside are doing our best to get all long-term colleagues out. With regard to these two, Gwala said that please include them. I hope leadership will cooperate. They must make it easy for the released colleagues. We discussed it in full. They were very constructive.

13. Then they left at about 5 p.m.

14. At about 6 p.m. Albertina Sisulu, Cyril Ramaphosa [CR], Murphy Morobe and Cas Saloojee came and stayed until 11 p.m.

15. He looked at IA's notes on the Ramaphosa discussion and confirmed that this was correct.

NB from Carl. What follows is a copy of what appears to be the CR notes referred to. Sekwati says he gave CR a copy of the above report.

1. Sisulu must be seen with the others was his insistence.

2. Mbeki and Gwala conduct after release.

3. De Klerk speech 18/9. He made reps for 10. Mdlalose and Mayewa but forgot 5 others. They agreed.

4. The 8 said they were resp leaders they would have to re to ANC. He was happy.

5. Then asked each of group. They said some restraint but could not hold back masses spontaneous meetings not a problem. Govt [sic] not worried about mass meetings of 100's of thousands. Said marches and demos diff to hold back. Will rep to org.

6. He would like org to discuss the matter and fears and concerns of govt.

7. He called General then came back said Stm [statement] would be made. They wanted him to say that he thought FW was on way to reform. He refused, but agreed his own release not issue.

8. He has prepared document which has not been shown to anyone. 14 pages long.

9. 2 phases—pre conditions then negotiating process.

10. ANC against proposal of pre cond.

11. Defiance campaign, peoples assembly.

12. Look at creating ideas.

13. Graduation ceremony at request of UNISA.

14. House in Umtata for children and grandchildren.

15. Holomisa [General Bantu Holomisa, military dictator in Transkei at the time] S/M is correct he cannot move to Transkei.

16. CR will go to Lusaka on 13/14—10. Need to receive the leaders. Will

have to hold meetings and rallies. We need to raise the centrality of the ANC and it is the pressure that has led to release.

I had app. with CR to, among other things, clarify some aspects of this report. He failed to show up. But I still hope to see him before I leave this area.

1 November 1989

Carl (Siphiwe Nyanda) to Norman (Alfred Nzo), Kay (Joe Slovo)

Here follows Sipho's (Mandela's) verbatim report:

On 18 September Sipho stressed to the Minister K. C. that the release of p[olitical] prisoners should be highlighted in F. W.'s first major policy statement. Ten names were given to him, including that of Mpama's Jeff Masemola.

Early on 10 October S discussed the matter at length with ministers KI.C. [Kobie Coetsee] and G. V. [Gerrit Viljoen]. They indicated that the government had agreed to release 8 prisoners without conditions, and that an announcement to the effect would be made the same day. As expected, they were much concerned about the possibility of their release worsening the current explosive situation in the country. It was pointed out to the ministers that, apart from Jeff, the p. prisoners involved were loyal ANC members and they would accordingly report to the organisation and carry out whatever directives might be given. It was stressed that these were re-sponsible and experienced men, and that all S. would do would be to con-vey to them the Government's concern.

At 1 o'clock the same day S. discussed the matter with the Pollsmoor Comrades and OM and later with Albertina, Murphy, Cyril and Cassim. Unfortunately Elijah did not come as expected. They will give you the re-port in due course. S. recommends that, apart from purely spontaneous welcome rallies on release, these comrades should not be involved in the ongoing demonstrations and other gatherings except on very special and carefully selected occasions.

S. also used the opportunity to warn the Government against any at-tempts to drive a wedge between the organisation and himself. Such an at-tempt, it was pointed out, was contrary to the whole spirit that up to now has characterized the discussions. S. has since received your comment on the document, reconsidered the question of its "leaking". It may well be that he himself was responsible for the "leak" as it was read to his Pollsmoor

Comrades on 2 August. However, he would advise against publication at this stage, but fully agrees with its circulation to the membership and to selected leaders of the Front Line States and the Socialist World. Circulation to some Western governments, organisations and key figures could be considered. Your comment on the document was read out to the Pollsmoor Comrades and OM on 10 October, and although there was no time to discuss the matter S. has noted the observation that a meeting between the ANC and the Government would be premature at this stage. In future discussion with the Government emphasis will be put on the creation of the climate for negotiation before there is a meeting.

The release of the Comrades has induced S. to request Murphy and others to set communication-consultation machinery through whom reports can swiftly be made. Communications with Lusaka entails long delays, which are inconvenient in emergency situations.

Lastly, OM informs S. that a certain Mandela from the W. Cape was sent on a mission to Lusaka, but he now refuses to report on the trip. He will appreciate any assistance you can give on the matter.

You are all in our thoughts. Best Wishes.

P.S.: It is assumed that these communications will be made available to Shaun [Oliver Tambo] without any specific request from S.

SECTION E

2 January 1990

From Timo (Oliver Tambo) and Kay (Joe Slovo) to Xhamela (Walter Sisulu)

Carl (Siphiwe Nyanda)—pls pass the 2 attached documents to Xhamela. The NEC requests him to show it to the other ANC leaders internally. We would like a feedback on these documents at the earliest but not later than Jan 12th.

Report of Cde [Comrade] Sipho (Nelson Mandela) to the NEC of the ANC, dated 19 December 1989

My meeting with State President De Klerk, which I requested on 5 December 1989, is now a matter of public knowledge. The views I expressed to him are set out in the attached document, the original of which reached him on the day before the meeting. Mr De Klerk regarded the document as disconcerting but noted the fact that it was intended to create a climate of understanding. He then suggested that it should not be used as a basis for discussion, and invited me to state my case. The status given to these documents never worries me, as long as they clearly set out our views on all the key issues under discussion.

In my remarks I made the simple point that a meeting between the ANC and the Government had become urgent, but that such a meeting could only take place after the Government had created a proper climate for negotiations. I concentrated on this issue and criticized the concept of group rights. I pointed out that these two issues were matters of concern, not only to the ANC and the mass democratic movement, but to the people right across the board, as well as to important sections of the Afrikaans press including the *Burger*, mouthpiece of the Cape National Party. You are probably aware that its columnist, Dawie, has of late been unusually frank in his criticism of aspects of Government policy. Recently he warned the Government that, by committing itself to the concept of group rights, they had created a minefield for themselves. It was his opinion that the Government would find it almost impossible to answer the accusation that this concept is a disguised form of apartheid. I closed my brief remarks by stressing that the creation by the Govt of a proper climate for discussion between the two parties, and a drastic review of the concept would be a positive contribution to the spirit of reconciliation which he so eloquently highlighted in his inaugural address.

In his response, Mr De Klerk pointed out that our discussion should focus on the process of negotiation itself. In this regard, two issues would have to be addressed, namely: (1) the legalisation of banned organizations, and (2) the establishment of a vehicle to act as an intermediate stage; it would consist of a small, compact and highly powered body of leading figures.

The legalisation of banned organizations.
In dealing with this aspect, he referred to the steps the Govt has already taken to normalize the political situation: the relaxation on protest marches, release of political prisoners and the Soweto Welcome Rally. He argued that these were important signals to which he had expected constructive response from the ANC and its allies. Instead the ANC continued to shift its goalposts, an attitude he described as one of our biggest problems in the negotiation of a settlement. The ANC, he maintained, considered these Govt initiatives as a sign of weakness on its part, and as victory for the movement, and that calls were being made for the intensification of all kinds of pressure against the Govt. He added that at the CDF, he was denigrated and his integrity questioned.

This, in turn, was causing widespread consternation among his closest supporters everywhere, making it impossible to normalize. This state of affairs was giving lethal ammunition to the right-wing to mount a formidable onslaught on the Govt. If events continued on this course, we would soon be knocking at Tuynhuys to see Dr Treurnicht [leader of the Conservative Party], except that he would not speak to us. The Govt would not allow these developments to persist, and he may reach a stage when he would be compelled to abandon all efforts to normalize.

His people were already asking the question: how had his initiatives helped to normalize the country's situation? The ANC must not expect him to put a knife in the hearts of his people. He said the biggest mistake we had made was to think that the Government was acting from a position of weakness. He was careful to explain that he was not making this statement in a spirit of confrontation or threat, but in order to reach understanding with us.

He pointed out that in his inaugural address on 20 September, he committed his Government to an active effort on its part to remove the actual or imagined obstacles on the road to peace and understanding. Where necessary a completely new approach to remove obstacles would be used.

He went on to explain that this commitment meant, in effect, that the Government would lift the state of emergency, unban the ANC, allow exiles to return, and release political prisoners. But the claims and activities of the ANC were making it difficult for the Government to normalize without losing credibility to its supporters.

He went further and said that the Government wanted to talk to the ANC, and that our meeting at that moment, and that of his predecessor and myself last July, were evidence of that fact. He denied the allegation that the Government was not prepared to see the ANC alone. There were indeed issues which would require a meeting between these two parties. But what they had said was that these meetings would not be confined to the ANC only. Other organizations would also be met.

He said that it was a misconception to say that the Government did not want to speak to the UDF. He had publicly stated that he was prepared to see all political leaders. It was in pursuance of this declaration that he had seen Archbishop Desmond Tutu and Co when they asked for an interview. He was also willing to see Murphy Morobe if he asked.

He referred to the statement on page 1 of the attached document, to the effect that no serious political organization would ever talk peace when an aggressive war was being waged against it. He argued that this position also applied to them. No Government could normalize while war was being waged against it.

He also explained the stand of the Government on group rights. The notion "group" was not in itself a dirty word. It also figured in the Freedom Charter and in the constitutions of several democratic countries. In the NP five-year plan, it was used in the sense that we should address the fear of the whites of domination by the blacks. To him this was essentially a question of formulation which the Government was prepared to look into.

He stressed the importance of readiness to compromise from all sides. None could succeed if we had hidden agendas.

The concern of Afrikaners related not only to political issues, but to economic questions as well. One of the challenging problems of our society had to be addressed & corrected. He concluded by pointing out that it was important that in search for permanent peace, South Africans should reach this goal without victors or losers.

I should add that on 4 December, I was visited by General van der Merwe, the new Commissioner of Police & General Smit, Head of Security Police. They made points similar to those raised by Mr De Klerk: the movement (ANC & MDM) regarded the concessions made by the Government as a sign of weakness etc. In the course of the discussion, they referred to a document allegedly seized from HG on his return from London. It dealt with the four pillars of the policy and strategy of the ANC and called for the intensification of mass action, especially from the beginning of December. They stressed the duty of the police to maintain law & order, & to protect all South Africans irrespective of their colour, a step which would adversely affect the peaceful atmosphere the Government was striving to create in the country.

On December 5 I was visited by members of the team & this was again the main subject of discussion. I informed both delegations, as well as Mr De Klerk, that they had raised matters beyond my power & that there was nothing whatsoever I could do about them. They were problems that should be taken up directly with the NEC in Lusaka.

I pointed out to all of them that during the last three years I had urged the Government to meet the ANC, & that if they had heeded my request these problems would probably long have been settled. Nevertheless, I considered it necessary to discuss this situation with Mr De Klerk, & that was why I asked to see him.

After Mr De Klerk had responded, I made a suggestion, subject to what the NEC might decide, which the other side seemed to welcome. I suggested a public declaration by the ANC committing itself to a peaceful settlement, & the simultaneous issue of a statement by the Government lifting the state of emergency, unbanning the ANC, allowing exiles to return and releasing political prisoners: Mr De Klerk insisting on a narrower definition, covering only those political prisoners convicted of promoting the activities of banned organizations and similar offences, but excluding persons sentenced for offences like murder and necklacing.

I argued for a wider definition, which would include all prisoners convicted for offences committed in the course of their anti-apartheid activities. I referred to their own struggle against British imperialism, when murders and assaults were wantonly committed by Afrikaners against other Afrikaners whom they regarded as sell-outs. I stressed that it would now be very difficult for the same community to favour a definition they emphatically rejected during their own struggle. But we ultimately decided to leave this aspect for discussion with Lusaka.

In this connection, an interesting point was made by Minister Kobie Coetsee when he said that the simultaneous declarations by the ANC and the Government did not rule out the possibility of unilateral action by the Government in this area.

The establishment of a vehicle to act as an intermediate stage.
As pointed out above, this vehicle would be made up of a small, compact and highly powered body of leading figures. I, however, refused to be drawn into this aspect of the discussion, and pointed out that this was one of those issues which would better be . . .

Assessment of Mr De Klerk
My assessment of Mr De Klerk is that of a strong, cautious but flexible man who is prepared to adapt to new ideas and to meet new challenges. He seems to be conscious of what it means for a public figure not to honour his undertaking. In this regard, he is complemented by Ministers like Mr Kobie Coetsee and Dr Gerrit Viljoen, who are clearly among the more enlightened in the NP.

However, these are but personal impressions. As an organization we should be guided not by personal impressions, but by harsh reality.

And the reality is that the actual policy of the ruling party has brought untold suffering to our people, and dragged the country to the brink of disaster. There is a wide gap between rhetoric and deeds, and one of the crucial questions to be answered is whether Mr De Klerk will be able to carry his people along on the basic issues. This is a question I cannot answer at this stage.

On the question of the release of Comrade Meyiwa and three others,

IA was informed that Mr Kobie Coetsee would look into the matter after the New Year.

SECTION F

Document Forwarded by Cde Sipho [Mandela] to F. W. de Klerk on 12 December, 1989, entitled: A Document to Create a Climate of Understanding

Mr President

I hope that Ministers Kobie Coetsee and Gerrit Viljoen have informed you that I deeply appreciate your decision in terms of which eight fellow-prisoners were freed on 15 October 1989, and for advising me of the fact in advance. The release was clearly a major development which rightly brooked praise here and abroad.

In my view it has now become urgent to take other measures to end the present deadlock, and this will certainly be achieved if the Government first creates a proper climate for negotiation, followed by a meeting with the ANC. The conflict which is presently draining South Africa's lifeblood, either in the form of peaceful demonstrations, acts of violence or external pressure, will never be settled until there is an agreement with the ANC. To this end I have spent more than three years urging the Government to negotiate with the ANC. I hope I will not leave this place with empty hands.

The Government insists on the ANC making an honest commitment to peace before it will talk to the organization. This is the pre-condition we are required to meet before the Government will negotiate with us. It must be made clear at the outset that the ANC will never make such commitment at the insistence of the Government, or any other source for that matter. We would have thought that the history of this country's liberation movement, especially during the last 41 years, would have made that point perfectly clear.

The whole approach of the Government to the question of negotiation with the ANC is totally unacceptable, and requires to be drastically changed. No serious political organization will ever talk peace when an aggressive war is being waged against it. No proud people will ever obey orders from those who . . . .

Besides the pre-condition that we should commit ourselves to peace

is inconsistent with the statement you made in Nigel shortly before the last general election, in which you appealed to black leaders to come forward to negotiate with the Government, and to refrain from setting preconditions for such negotiations.

It was generally assumed that the appeal was addressed to blacks as a whole and not, as now appears, only to those who work in apartheid structures.

In the light of subsequent Government policy statements, the perception has deepened that the Nigel statement was no more than mere rhetoric. Although the Government called on blacks to set no pre-conditions it considers itself free to do exactly that. That is the reason why it prescribes to us to make a commitment to peace before we can talk.

The Government ought to be aware that readiness to negotiate is in itself an honest commitment to peace. In this regard, the ANC is far ahead of the Government. It has repeatedly declared its willingness to negotiate, provided a proper climate for such negotiations exists. The organization has recently published a clear and detailed plan to this effect, which has already been approved by the Frontline States, the OAU, the Non-Aligned Movement and by almost all the members of the Commonwealth of Nations.

Equally relevant is the fact that on many occasions in the past, the ANC has explicitly acknowledged its commitment to peaceful solutions, if channels for doing so are available. As recently as 24 October 1989, *The Star* reported as follows: "The ANC says it is committed to a peaceful solution in South Africa but accuses the Government of rhetoric. . . . At present there is really no serious indication from the Government itself about a peaceful solution to the political crisis. . . . Five years ago, President P.W. Botha spoke virtually the same words but nothing happened. It is history now that the ANC has made impassioned overtures to every single Government of South Africa in vain. Every manoeuvre was met with a negative response, & at times violence."

This & similar other previous statements clearly show that the ANC has an established record of commitment to peace, & that its armed struggle is a purely defensive measure against the violence of the Government. This point was stressed by Mr Oliver Tambo, President of the ANC, during an interview with *Cape Times* editor, Anthony Heard, on 4 November 1985, when he said: "The unfortunate thing is that people tend to be worried about the violence that comes from the oppressed. . . . Really, there would be no violence at all if we did not have the violence of the apartheid system."

There is neither logic nor common sense in asking the ANC to do now what it has consistently done on countless occasions before. It is the Government, not the ANC, that started civil war in this country, and that does not want reconciliation and peace. How does one work for reconciliation and peace under a state of emergency, with black areas under military occupation, when people's organizations are banned, leaders are either in exile, prison or restricted, when the policy of apartheid with its violence is still being enforced, and when no conditions for free political expression exist?

Serious doubts have also been expressed as to whether the Government would be prepared to meet the ANC even when it fully complied with your .... discussions you and other Government members held recently with the "homeland" leaders and their urban counterparts, you avoided meeting the very organizations which, together with the ANC, hold the key to peace in the country. The UDF and its main affiliates, COSATU, NIC and TIC, are all non-violent and peaceful organizations. Why did the Government ignore them if commitment to peace is the only qualification for participation in negotiations?

In your inaugural address on 20 September 1989 you made an important statement which must have had a formidable impact inside and outside the country. You said: "There is but one way to peace, to justice for all: that is the way of reconciliation, of together seeking mutually acceptable solutions, of together discussing what the new South Africa should look like, of constitutional negotiation with a view to a permanent understanding."

The cornerstone of that address was the idea of reconciliation, in which you pleaded for a new spirit and approach. By reconciliation, in this context, was understood the situation where opponents, and even enemies for that matter, would sink their differences and lay down their arms for the purpose of working out a peaceful solution, where the injustices and grievances of the past would be buried and forgotten, and a fresh start made. That is the spirit in which the people of South Africa would like to work together for peace; those are the principles which should guide those who love their country and its people; who want to turn South Africa into a land of hope. In highlighting this theme in your address, you sparked a groundswell of expectations from far and wide. Many people felt that, at last, the South Africa of their dreams was about to be born.

We also understood your appeal for reconciliation and justice for all, not to be directed to [the]se blacks who operate apartheid structures. Apart from a few notable exceptions, the blacks are the creation of the National

Party and, throughout the years, they have served as its loyal agents in its various strategies to cling to minority rule. Their principal role has been, and still is, to make the struggle for majority rule in a unitary state far more difficult to achieve. For the last three decades, they have been used to defend the NP's policy of group domination—now referred to as group rights—and they have no tradition of militant resistance against racial discrimination. There is thus no conflict to be reconciled between the NP and these people.

The appeal could not have been directed to any of the opposition parties in Parliament either.

Although the NP has made positive initiatives here and there, its public image is still tarnished by a cloud of distrust and suspicion, and by an inherent vagueness and indecision as far as the really basic issues are concerned. Many people see no fundamental difference between its policies and those of the Conservative Party. Both are regarded as apartheid parties, the only difference being that one is more blunt than the other in its defence of white privilege.

Although the Democratic Party is the most progressive parliamentary party, and despite the existence of important policy differences between that party and the NP, the relations between the two parties are not so bitter as to justify a call for reconciliation and peace by a head of state. The fairly even relations between the two parties is clearly illustrated by the fact that the DP is not banned, none of its leaders are restricted, imprisoned, driven into exile or executed for purely political . . . .

The conflict which we believed you wanted to settle was that between the Government, on the one hand, and the ANC and other extra-parliamentary organizations, on the other. It is the activities of these organizations which have turned South Africa into a land of acute tensions and fear. It is on this level that the country desperately yearns for reconciliation and justice for all. As pointed out on another occasion, dialogue with the ANC and the mass democratic movement is the only way of stopping violence and bringing peace to the country. It is, therefore, ironical that it is precisely these organizations with whom the Government is not at all prepared to talk.

It is common knowledge that the Government has been sharply criticized, and even condemned, in the past, for squandering precious resources, and for wasting much energy and time discussing with people who can play no significant role in the resolution of the current conflict in the country. Past experience shows that the Government would prefer to make peace with those who accept its policies, rather than those who reject them, with its friends rather than its opponents. It is to be hoped that this time the Government will not repeat that costly mistake. To continue to ignore this criticism, and to confine consultations on the political crisis almost entirely to those individuals and organizations which help the Government to maintain the "status quo," will certainly deepen the distrust and suspicion which impede real progress on negotiations.

In my lengthy discussions with the team of Government officials, I repeatedly urged that negotiation between the ANC and the Government should preferably be in two stages: the first being where the Government and the ANC would together work out the pre-conditions for negotiations. The second stage would consist of the actual negotiations themselves when the climate for doing so was ripe. These were my personal views and not those of the ANC which sees the problem quite differently.

It seems to me that now I am aware of the attitude of the ANC on the matter, an attitude which is perfectly sound, we should work on the formula indicated by the organization for the resolution of the present obstacle to negotiation.

The principal source of almost all our problems in this country is undoubtedly the policy of apartheid, which the Government now admits is an unjust system, and from which it claims to be moving away. This means that organizations and people who were banned, restricted, driven into exile, imprisoned or executed for their anti-apartheid activities were unjustly condemned. The very first step on the way to reconciliation is obviously the dismantling of apartheid, and all measures used to enforce it. To talk of reconciliation before this major step is taken is totally unrealistic.

The five-year plan of the NP, with its outdated concept of group rights, has aggravated the position almost beyond repair. It is yet another example of the Government's attempt "to modernize apartheid without abandoning it." What the plan means, in effect, is that after resisting racial oppression for so many years, and after making such heavy sacrifices during which countless lives were lost, we should at the height of that heroic struggle, yield to a disguised form of minority rule. In a nutshell, the plan means that blacks will taste real freedom in the world to come. In this one, whites will go on preaching reconciliation and peace, but continue to hold firmly and defiantly to power, to enforce racial separation, the very . . . .

I would like to believe that my exploratory efforts during the last three years have not been in vain, that I have an important role still to play in helping to bring about a peaceful settlement, that the initiative you have already taken will soon be followed by other developments on the really fundamental issues that are agitating our people, and that in our life-time our country will rid itself of the pestilence of racialism in all its forms.

In conclusion, Mr President, I should add that, in helping to promote dialogue between the ANC and the Government, I hope to be able to avoid any act which may be interpreted as an attempt on my part to drive a wedge between you and the NP, or to portray in a manner not consistent with your public image. I trust that you and other members of the Government will fully reciprocate.*

SECTION G

11 January 1990

From X [Walter Sisulu] to Timo [Oliver Tambo] and Kay [Joe Slovo]

On behalf of my comrades, I would like to thank you for the comm. As requested, I managed to get those comrades who are based in this town to

---

*Some peculiar claims have been made regarding the steps that preceded the onset of the negotiating process "proper" in South Africa. Most notable are the assertions in the "Biographical Sketch of Thabo Mbeki," in Thabo Mbeki, *Africa: Define Yourself* (Cape Town: Tafelberg, 2002), pp. 295–316. It is stated that ". . . Mbeki was to lead the process of preparing the document which, after approval by the Organization of African Unity at a meeting in Harare, became known as the Harare Declaration.

"By September 1989, the discussions between the Mbeki delegation and the South African government delegation now led by Fanie van der Merwe, director general for constitutional affairs, had reached agreement on a number of important points.

"It was agreed that all political prisoners, including Nelson Mandela, should be released, political parties unbanned, exiles allowed to return, subsequent to which negotiations for a new South Africa would begin, as visualized in the Harare Declaration.

"There were many within the ANC and its supporters within South Africa . . . who thought it was impossible for the apartheid regime to agree to all these things. They were therefore convinced that Mbeki and his team had betrayed the struggle by holding out the illusion of a negotiated settlement, a sentiment which had to be dealt with at the time that the very concept of a Harare Declaration was under discussion.

"Later, at the ANC 1990 Consultative Conference of the ANC Mbeki had to present to the delegates another controversial position of the ANC leadership: the decision to suspend the armed struggle. He did so unflinchingly . . . by his impeccable logic and reasoning he convinced the delegates of the correctness of that decision."

Suffice to say that the most informed sources on the former South African government's side simply scoff at these claims, the processes that guided discussion of the statement that became the Harare Declaration are dealt with in this book, and the Mandela discussions as detailed in this Appendix put paid to other claims that the decision to suspend the armed struggle was taken five months before the consultative meeting referred to.

come together to consider the contents of cde Sipho's report to the NEC. GM also managed to come up and he also participated in the discussion.

The contents of the document, coupled with the fact that the other side seems to have known and accepted that cde S was going to contact the NEC, convinced us that these signals have to be taken seriously. It seemed to us that the main issues to be considered by the movement at this stage are the ff:

1. The creation of a climate of understanding;
2. The establishment of a vehicle to act as an intermediate stage; and
3. A simultaneous declaration by the other side and ourselves.

1. The creation of a Climate of Understanding.

As pointed out in the document, De Klerk is of the view that he has already taken some steps to normalize the political situation. He also feels that we have not reciprocated this. Indeed, the outlook of the movement is that De Klerk has been pushed to take the steps he has taken by the pressure of our all-round struggles. This is a correct statement, politically speaking. To the extent that some of our public pronouncements may be acting as a breaking mechanism as far as De Klerk's professed intentions are concerned, perhaps there may be a need for us to be cautious. However, we feel we have not been that reckless. In the light of these developments, it may indeed be incorrect to mount platforms with a view to scoring points against De Klerk. After all, it has never been the aim of our movement to do so.

2. The Establishment of a Vehicle . . . .

In a situation where something unequivocal and tangible has been put forward by the other side, the establishment of such a machinery is unavoidable and desirable. Is it not about time that if De Klerk means what he is saying, then he must raise this directly with the movement? Cde S's report seems to indicate that he (Sipho) did intimate this in his encounter with De Klerk. We accept this in principle. However, we leave it to the NEC to determine the form thereof.

3. Simultaneous Declaration . . . .

Commitment to peace and a peaceful resolution of the SA question has always been the movement's position. The Harare Declaration shows that this commitment is still basic to our position. The OAU declaration does point to the hurdles which successive NP governments have put on the path of a peaceful settlement. If De Klerk feels that this declaration will empower him to clear the environment of these hurdles, there can be nothing wrong with the parties making the declarations simultaneously. For our part, this will not in any way constitute a departure from our principled position. What we said on point 2 above is of relevance here. For if the declaration is to be made simultaneously, it has to be as a result of the two parties having synchronized their positions through direct contact.

In conclusion, we wish to point out that we had very little time within which to discuss these issues. However, our views are as outlined above.

THE WEB SITE

The official site name is "Heart of Hope" at www.omalley.co.za. Unless otherwise stated all Web references can be found at this site.

[]O'Malley Interviews 1989–2000
[]pre transition/
[]transition/
[]post transition/
[]transformation/post transition

[]general information/

[]maharaj/
    Glossary/[]
    Bios/[]
    Maps/[]

    Mac Interviews/year/[]
    Family/
        Interviews[]
        Correspondence[]
    Interviewees/[]

[]maharaj/vula comms/year/[]date
    vula other[]

[]maharaj/documents and reports/
    ANC/year/[]
    ANC NEC/year[]
    ANC NWC/year/[]
    SACP/year

/Tongaat/[]
Other/year

Alliance documents 2006/
    ANC/[]
    COSATU/[]
    SACP[]

Hefer Commission/[]
Little Rivonia/[]

Security files/[]

Jacob Zuma []

Other[]

[]maharaj/chapter no./[] page no.

[]maharaj/footnotes/
    Page/[]

ACRONYMS:
PARTIES AND ORGANIZATIONS

For short histories of parties and organizations, go to []maharaj/glossary/[]; [] general information/organizations/[].

AAM: Anti-Apartheid Movement
ALLIANCE: Tripartite Alliance
ANC: African National Congress
ANCYL: African National Congress Youth League
APLA: Azanian People's Liberation Army
AVF: Afrikaner Volksfront
AWB: Afrikaner Weerstandsbeweging (Afrikaner Resistance Movement)
AZAPO: Azanian People's Organization
BC: Black Consciousness
CA: Constitutional Assembly
CoD: Congress of Democrats
CODESA: Convention for a Democratic South Africa
Congress Alliance
COSATU: Congress of South African Trade Unions
CP: Conservative Party
CPC: Coloured People's Congress
CPSA: Communist Party of South Africa (see also SACP)
DA: Democratic Alliance
DP: Democratic Party
IFP: Inkatha Freedom Party
Inkatha
MDM: Mass Democratic Movement
MK: Umkhonto we Sizwe ("Spear of the Nation")
MPNF: Multi-Party Negotiating Forum
NEC: National Executive Committee (ANC)

NEUM: Non-European Unity Movement
NIC: Natal Indian Congress
NP: National Party
NUSAS: National Union of African Students
NWC: National Working Committee (ANC)
PAC: Pan-Africanist Congress of Azania
PFP: Progressive Federal Party
PMC: Politico-Military Council
RC: Revolutionary Council
SACP: South African Communist Party (see also CPSA)
SACTU: South African Councils of Trade Unions
SADF: South African Defense Force
SAIC: South African Indian Congress
SAP: South African Police
SASO: South African Students' Organisation
SB: Security Branch
SSC: State Security Council
TIC: Transvaal Indian Congress
TRC: Truth and Reconciliation Commission
UDF: United Democratic Front

A NOTE ON BIOGRAPHIES

For short biographies, go to [] maharaj/biographies/[] and [] general information/Biographies/[].

A NOTE ON INTERVIEWEES

Interviewees who spoke on or off the record; sources who wish to remain anonymous are conspicuous by their absence. Interviews are available at []/maharaj/interviewees/[].

Aboobaker, Ismail
Ahmed, Kathrada
Ayob, Ismail
Badsha, Omar
Barnard, Niel
Bernstein, Hilda
Bizos, George
Blomkamp, Peter
Botha, Hentie
Botha, Pik
Bunting, Brian
Cajee, Amien
Chaskalson, Arthur
Chiba, Laloo
Davidson, Christo
Dingake, Michael
Ebrahim, Hassen
Gordhan, Pravin
Hefer, Joos
Howard, Randall
Hutchings, Gillian
Jenkin, Tim
Joffe, Joel
Joseph, Daso
Joseph, Paul
Kasrils, Ronnie
Love, Janet

Maduna, Penuell
Maharaj, Joey
Maharaj, Milou
Maharaj, Shanthee
Maharaj, Zarina
Mahomed, Yusuf
Makgoale, Omry
Manning, Claudia
Masondo, Andrew
Meiring, Georg
Memela, Totsie
Mkhatshwa, Smalgaliso
Mkwayi, Wilton
Moleketi, Jabu
Momoniat, Ismail
Moosa, M. Valli
Mvelase, Dipuo (Catherine)
Naidoo, Indres
Naidoo, Jay
Naidoo, Murthi
Naidoo, Nandha (Steve)
Naidoo, Phyllis
Naidoo, Tim
Nair, Billy
Ngcuka, Bulelani
Nyanda, Siphiwe
Patel, Dipak

Pillay, Ivan
Pillay, Vella and Patsy
Raadschelders, Lucia
Ramaphosa, Cyril
Reddy, Fred
Scott, Mpho
Seedat, Hassim
Shaik, Moe (and the Nightingale)
Shaik, Yunus
Shubin, Vladimir
Sithole, Jabu
Taylor, Jimmy

Trewala, Paul
Tshabalala, Vuso
Van der Merwe, Fanie
Van der Merwe, Johan
Wagener, Jan
Weinberg, Sheila
Wills, Ashley
Viljoen, Constand
Vlok, Adriaan
Yacoob, Zac
Zuma, Jacob

A NOTE ON
MAC MAHARAJ INTERVIEWS

For interviewees with Mac, go to []maharaj/interviews/year/[].

Chapter 1: Childhood and Youth

9 October 2000
28 March 2002
9 May 2002
8 August 2002
12 August 2002
29 August 2002
1 November 2002

Chapter 2: Durban Days

9 October 2000
28 March 2002
29 August 2002
17 September 2002
13 October 2004

Chapter 3: London Days

9 October 2000
17 September 2002

Chapter 4: GDR Days

9 October 2000
18 September 2002
27 September 2002
1 November 2002
4 November 2002
7 November 2002

Chapter 5: Going Home

28 March 2002
29 August 2002
8 October 2002
9 October 2002
11 October 2002
12 December 2002
8 January 2003
9 January 2003

Chapter 6: Detention and Torture

9 October 2000
27 September 2001
23 August 2002
9 October 2002
11 October 2002
9 January 2003

Chapter 7: Little Rivonia

31 October 2001
2 April 2002
11 October 2002
8 January 2003
13 October 2004

Chapter 8: Robben Island

2 April 2002
8 April 2002

9 May 2002
23 August 2002
28 August 2002
8 October 2002
16 October 2002
8 January 2003

Chapter 9: Banned in Durban

17 October 2002
11 December 2002
9 January 2003

Chapter 10: Lusaka and London

9 October 2000
8 April 2002
29 April 2002
27 September 2002
9 October 2002
25 October 2002
1 November 2002
5 November 2002
7 November 2002
12 December 2002
31 December 2002
9 January 2003
30 October 2002
1 November 2002
8 January 2003
9 January 2003
10 January 2003
15 January 2003
16 September 2003

Chapter 11: Vula: Getting Started

24 August 1998
21 August 2000
10 September 2001
7 March 2002
28 March 2002
29 April 2002
13 March 2003

1 November 2002
4 November 2002
7 November 2002
12 December 2002
8 January 2003
10 January 2003
15 January 2003
16 September 2003
19 September 2003
2 April 2004
28 May 2004
29 May 2004
18/21 June 2004
6 September 2004
20/21/26 June 2005

Chapter 12: Home Again

21 August 2000
10 September 2001
15 October 2001
22 March 2002
28 March 2002
30 October 2002
5 November 2002
7 November 2002
11 December 2002
12 December 2002
31 December 2002
9 June 2003
16 September 2003
19 September 2003
23 September 2003
24 September 2003
26 September 2003
2 April 2004
28 May 2004
17 June 2004
17/18 June 2004
18/21 June 2004
21 June 2004
19 August 2004
20 August 2004

27 August 2004
6 September 2004
16 September 2004
20 September 2004
24 April 2005
6 June 2005
26 June 2005
17 October 2005

Chapter 13: Vula: Conflict in KwaZulu-Natal

7 November 2002
11 December 2002
23 September 2003
28 May 2004
17 June 2004
21 June 2004

Chapter 14: Mandela

24 August 1998
12 December 2002
23 September 2003

Chapter 15: Out of South Africa

21 August 2000
9 October 2000
15 October 2001
22 March 2002
9 September 2002
12 December 2002
23 September 2003
25 September 2005
28 May 2004
17 June 2004
16 September 2004

Chapter 16: Transitions

24 August 1998
29 November 1999
21 August 2000
18 September 2000

9 October 2000
10 September 2001
31 October 2001
13 December 2001
12/13 March 2002
22 March 2002
28 March 2002
23 August 2002
5 September 2002
17 September 2002
27 September 2002
30 October 2002
12 December 2002
31 December 2002
23 September 2003
24 September 2003
25 September 2003
26 September 2003
29 September 2003
10 January 2003
28 May 2004
17 June 2004
17/18 June 2004
18/21 June 2004
21 June 2004
19 August 2004
20 August 2004
5 September 2004
6 September 2004
20 September 2004
13 October 2004

Chapter 17: Vula Unravels

18 September 2000
9 October 2000
31 October 2001
12 March 2002
12/13 March 2002
22 March 2002
28 March 2002
30 October 2002
4 November 2002

24 September 2003
25 September 2003
26 September 2003
28 May 2004
17/18 June 2004
21 June 2004
22 June 2004
19 August 2004
5 September 2004

Chapter 18: Vula on Trial

13 March 1997
9 October 2000
12/13 March 2002
23 August 2002
30 October 2002
24 September 2003
26 September 2003
17/18 June 2004
24 April 2005

Chapter 19: Into the New South Africa

18 August 1993
27 February 1995
13 March 1997
16 October 1997
24 August 1998
29 November 1999
6 December 1999
21 August 2000
18 September 2000
5 October 2000
9 October 2000
27 September 2001
15 October 2001
31 October 2001
5 November 2001
13 December 2001
22 March 2002
8 April 2002
12 August 202
23 August 2002

5 September 2002
9 September 2002
18 September 2002
30 October 2002
31 October 2002
7 November 2002
15 November 2002
12 December 2002
30 December 2002
31 December 2002
6 January 2003
7 January 2003
25 September 2003
17/18 June 2004
19 August 2004
13 June 2005
17 October 2005

Chapter 20: Back in the Cold

23 August 2002
31 October 2002
30 December 2002
6 June 2005
10 June 2005
12 June 2005
13 June 2005
21 June 2005
11 October 2005
12 October 2005
17 October 2005
29 December 2005

Chapter 21: Family: Struggle and Damage

9 October 2000
23 August 2002
29 August 2002
9 September 2002
7 January 2003
24 September 2003
13 June 2005
29 December 2005

NOTES

Introduction

1. T.R.H. Davenport, *South Africa: A Modern History*, 4th ed. (London: Macmillan, 1991), pp. 22–23.

2. Quoted in Christopher Saunders and Nicholas Southey, *A Dictionary of South African History* (Cape Town: David Philip, 1998).

3. Hermann Giliomee, *The Afrikaners: Biography of a People* (Cape Town: Tafelberg, 2003).

4. "Old Wine in New Bottles: The Persistence of Narrative Structures in the Historiography of the Mfecane and the Great Trek" in C. Hamilton, ed., *The Mfecane Aftermath: Reconstructive Debates in Southern African History* (Johannesburg: Witwatersrand University Press, 1995), pp. 35–49.

5. L. Switzer, *Power and Resistance, in an African Society: The Ciskei Xhosa and the Making of South Africa* (Madison: University of Wisconsin, 1993).

6. Ibid.

7. Jeff Peires, *The Dead Will Arise: Nongqawuse and the Great Xhosa Cattle-Killing Movement of 1856–7* (Cape Town: Jonathan Ball, 2003). First published 1989 by Ravan Press.

8. Leonard Thompson, *The Political Mythology of Apartheid* (New Haven: Yale University Press, 1985).

9. See for example H.H.W. de Villiers, *Rivonia: Operation Mayibuye* (Johannesburg: Afrikaanse Pers-Boekhandel, 1964), pp. 61–63. De Villiers, former judge president of the Eastern Cape Division of the Supreme Court, came from a family line that included nine members who sat on the Supreme Court in South Africa, including two chief justices before the union (one colonial and one republican) and two after the union.

10. Thomas Pakenham, *The Boer War;* I. Smith, *The Origins of the South African War* (London: Long Maw, 1996).

11. For the text of this and other legislation referenced between 1911 and 1948, go to [] pre transition/documents and reports/[] racial legislation 1806–1947.

12. James Leatt and others, eds., *Contending Ideologies in South Africa* (Cape Town: David Philip, 1986).

13. J. Serfontein, *Brotherhood of Power: An Exposé of the Secret Afrikaner Broederbond* (London: Rex Collings Ltd., 1979).

14. For a history of Afrikaner nationalism, see H. Giliomee, *The Afrikaners*; G. le May, *The Afrikaners, a Historical Interpretation* (Oxford: Blackwell Publishers, 1995).

15. For the text of apartheid legislation from 1948–1990, go to [] pre transition/ the apartheid state/[] apartheid legislation 1948–1990.

16. See the National Party's first submission to the Truth and Reconciliation Commission (TRC) at [] post transition/ TRC/ submissions/ [].

17. See the ANC's first submission to the TRC at []post transition/ TRC/ submissions/[].

18. For the ANCYL founding policy document, go to [] general information/ organizations/ ANCYL/[] policy document 1948.

19. [] general information/organizations/ANCYL/[] programme of action.

20. Nelson Mandela, *Long Walk to Freedom* (New York: Little, Brown, 1994), p. 121. This figure is also used by Elinor Sisulu in *In Our Lifetime: Walter and Albertina Sisulu* (Cape Town: David Philip, 2002), p. 106; and by Luli Callinicos, *Oliver Tambo: Beyond the Engeli Mountains* (Cape Town: David Philip, 2004), p. 185.

21. Stanley Wolpert, *Gandhi's Passion: The Life and Legacy of Mahatma Gandhi* (New York: Oxford University Press, 2001), pp. 40–41.

22. On Indians, the ANCYL policy document had this to say: "Although, like the Africans, the Indians are oppressed as a group, yet they differ from the Africans in their historical and cultural background among other things. They have their mother-country, India, but thousands of them made South Africa and Africa their home. They, however, did not come as conquerors and exploiters, but as the exploited. As long as they do not undermine or impede our liberation struggle we should not regard them as intruders or enemies." See [] general information/ organizations/ ANCYL/[] policy document 1948.

23. Mandela, p. 107.

24. Ibid.

25. See minutes of ANC NEC in Lusaka from 27–31 August 1971 at [] maharaj/ documents and reports / ANC NEC/ 1971 [].

1. Childhood and Youth

1. *From Cane Fields to Freedom: A Chronicle of Indian South African Life*, Uma Dhupelia-Mesthrie, ed. (Cape Town: Kwela Books, 2000), pp. 9–31.

2. Wolpert, pp. 34–35.

3. "The Role of the Indian People in the South African Revolution." Interview with Dr. Yusuf Dadoo, 1 January 1968, in the Yusuf Dadoo Collection at www.liberation.org.za/collections/sacp/dadoo.

4. For an account of the riots and the subsequent inquiry into their causes go to [] general information/SAIRR/[] 1949/.

5. Ibid.

6. *Newcastle Advertiser*, 21 January 1949, text at []general information/SAIRR 1949-53/ [] extracts from *Newcastle Advertiser* 1949–53.

7. Ibid.

8. Maharaj/family/[] Shanthee Maharaj 25 October 2003; 17 December 2003.

9. Mandela, pp. 79, 80, 90, 238, 273.

2. Durban Days

1. Dale T. McKinley, *The ANC and the Liberation Struggle* (London: Pluto Press, 1997), pp. 6–8.

2. In 1919, the ANC dispatched a special delegation to London to plead its cause. In an open letter to Viscount Milner, it emphasized that "we have come not to ask for independence but for an admission into British citizenship as British subjects so that we may also enjoy the free institutions which are the foundation and pillars of this great Commonwealth." Quoted in Peter Walshe, *The Rise of African Nationalism in South Africa: The African National Congress 1912–1952* (Los Angeles: University of California Press, 1971), p. 64. See also Francis Meli, *A History of the ANC* (Harare: Zimbabwe Publishing House, 1988), p. 47.

3. Walshe, p. 65.

4. Ibid., p. 389.

5. The African Mine Workers Union (AMWU) was created in the early 1940s at the initiative of J. B. Marks and others. At the time of the strike, Marks, a long-time member of the ANC and the Communist Party, was president of the AMWU. There were perhaps four hundred thousand African miners working on the Reef. See McKinley, p. 12; and Mandela, pp. 89–90.

6. The founding of the ANCYL was met with resistance from the conservative ANC leadership, who had to be convinced that it was not a breakaway organization. One of the agreements that assuaged these fears was the stipulation that anyone over seventeen years of age joining the Youth League had to be a member of the ANC. See Sisulu, *In Our Lifetime*, pp. 66–69.

7. For the text of the ANCYL Manifesto, go to [] general information/ organizations/ ANCYL/[] Manifesto 1944. See also Nelson Mandela, *The Struggle Is My Life* (London: International Defence & Aid Fund for Southern Africa, 1978), pp. 11–20, 20–27.

8. For the text of the Basic Policy Document, go to [] general information/ organizations/ANCYL/[] policy document 1948. See also Mandela, *The Struggle Is My Life*, pp. 20–27.

9. For the text of the ANCYL program of action adopted at the ANC annual conference on 17 December 1949, go to [] general information/organizations/ ANCYL[] programme of action 1949. See also Mandela, *The Struggle Is My Life*, pp. 28–30.

10. Eddy Maloka, *The South African Communist Party in Exile, 1963–1990* (Pretoria: African Institute of Africa, 2002).

11. During his lifetime, Sisulu's involvement with the Communist Party (he was

a member of the Central Committee) was not in the public domain. According to Mac, when he was leaving Robben Island, Sisulu had one request: that when he died, it should be made public that he was a Communist.

12. See Sisulu, *In Our Lifetime*, pp. 97–106; Mandela, pp. 111–22. The Defiance Campaign was a joint undertaking of the ANC and the SAIC. It lasted six months, from 26 June to December 1952.

13. Mandela, p. 121; Sisulu, p. 106.

14. The idea for a Congress of the People came from Professor Z. K. Matthews, under whom both Mandela and Tambo had studied at Fort Hare. A National Action Council was created composed of eight members from the sponsoring organizations—the ANC, CoD, SAIC, and SACPO—under the chairmanship of chief Albert Luthuli, president of the ANC. The congress took place at Kliptown on 25/26 June 1955, and the Freedom Charter was endorsed. Within the ANC there was some friction between the strict "Africanists" and multiracial elements. See Mandela, *Long Walk to Freedom*, p. 153. He wrote an article for the June 1956 issue of *Liberation*, a monthly journal, disputing claims that the Freedom Charter favored a socialist order and was influenced by Communist ideology. For text of the Freedom Charter go to [] pre transition/documents and reports / 1956/ [] Freedom Charter. For the text of Mandela's article in Liberation go to [] pre transition/documents and reports/1956/[] Liberation.

15. The Africanists argued that the Freedom Charter was one more deviation by the ANC from the ANCYL Program of Action, that before Africans could develop an effective political organization they had to develop a national consciousness, and that a national consciousness could only be built by unifying Africans under the umbrella of African nationalism. See Benjamin Pogrund, *How Can Man Die Better: The Life of Robert Sobukwe* (Johannesburg: Jonathan Ball, 1997), pp. 60–88.

16. McKinley, p. 23.

17. [] maharaj/interviewees/ Nandha Naidoo, 28 November 2003.

18. Ismail Meer, *A Fortunate Man* (Johannesburg: Zebra Press, 2002), p. 67.

3. London Days

1. Giliomee, pp. 524–25.

2. Grand Apartheid embodied the concept of "separate freedoms." See Dan O'Meara, *Forty Years Lost: The Apartheid State and the Politics of the National Party, 1948–1994* (Johannesburg: Ravan Press, 1996), pp. 64–74.

3. Extracts from *Winds of Change* at [] maharaj/documents and reports/other/ 1960/ [] "winds of change."

4. See Giliomee, pp. 525–58. Following the referendum, it appears that Verwoerd was more concerned with containing Afrikaner dissent over what to do with Coloured people—between Afrikaners who wanted them included in the franchise as part of the "white" community and those who supported Verwoerd's unwavering position of exclusion, pp. 525–31; see also Tom Lodge, *Black Politics in*

South Africa Since 1945 (Johannesburg: Ravan Press, 1983; fourth impression, 1990), "The Sharpeville Crisis," pp. 201–30.

5. Go to [] post transition/TRC/ report of the truth and reconciliation commission/ Vol 3/Chapter 6/[] paras 1–4; pre- []general information/SAIRR/[] 1959/60, pp. 56–62.

6. For the text of Mandela's testimony to the court at the Treason Trial go to []pre transition/documents and reports/1960/[] Treason Trial: Mandela.

7. Muriel Horrell, *A Survey of Race Relations in South Africa* (Johannesburg: SAIRR, 1963), p. 109. Go to [] general information/SAIRR/[] 1963.

8. Thomas Karis and Gail Gerhart, "Challenge and Violence," p. 364, Vol. 3 of *From Protest to Challenge* (Bloomington and Indianapolis: Indiana University Press, 1977). For Mandela's statement on behalf of the National Action Council following the strike go to [] pre transition/the struggle/strikes and mass action/[] General Strike-statement by Nelson Mandela. During 1961, Mandela also wrote to Verwoerd on two occasions, first on 25 April 1961 calling on him on behalf of the National Action Council to summon a national convention and again on 26 June 1961 warning Verwoerd of the consequences of his failure to respond to the demand to summon a convention. "You may choose to persist with the present policies which are cruel and dishonest and which are opposed by millions of people here and abroad," he wrote. "For our own part, we wish to make it perfectly clear that we shall never cease to fight against repression and injustice, and we are resuming active opposition against your regime. In taking this decision we must again stress that we have no illusions of the serious implications of our decision." The text of both letters is available at [] pre transition/ documents and reports/1961[].

9. Roger Fieldhouse, *Anti-Apartheid: A History of the Movement in Britain* (London: The Merlin Press, 2005), pp. 8–10.

10. The South Africa Boycott Committee was formed in the fall of 1959 as a subcommittee of the Committee of African Organizations (CAO). SAFA accounted for the largest block of representatives on the committee. On 29 December, the committee reconvened as the Boycott Movement. Ibid., p. 14.

11. The Boycott Movement had its last meeting on 30 March 1960. It was renamed the Anti-Apartheid Movement. Ibid., pp. 21–22.

12. Ibid., pp. 27, 93.

13. [] maharaj/interviewees/[] Vella Pillay.

14. Fieldhouse, p. 8.

15. C. Gurney, "A Great Cause: The Origins of the Anti-Apartheid Movement, June 1959–March 1960." *Journal of Southern African Studies* 26 (1) (March 2000), pp. 123–44; see also [] maharaj/documents and reports/ other/[]reddy: the anti apartheid movement 1959–79.

4. GDR DAYS

1. The largest, the Free German Association of Trade Unions, had a membership of almost 90 percent of the total employee population. See Kurt Sontheimer

and William Bleek, *The Government and Politics of East Germany* (London: Hutchinson University Library, 1975), pp. 120–21.

2. Ibid., p. 103.

3. Charles S. Maier, *Dissolution: The Crisis of Communism and the End of East Germany* (Princeton: Princeton University Press, 1997), p. 20.

4. Timothy Garth Ash, *The File: A Personal History* (New York: Random House, 1997), p. 84. He calculated that one in every fifty adults had a direct connection with the Stasi.

5. Gareth M. Winrow, *The Foreign Policy of the GDR in Africa* (Cambridge: Cambridge University Press, 1990).

6. For a detailed discussion of some conflicting views on how the ANC turned to armed struggle see SADET, *The Road to Democracy. Vol. I, 1960–1970*, pp. 68–91. There is broad consensus that the SACP arrived at the decision and had operational units in the field before the ANC took the decision. However, the discussions in the SACP and the ANC as to which course each movement should take were virtually between the same people, as the senior leadership of the SACP and the ANC were for all intents and purposes the same people. As Walter Sisulu succinctly put it, "They were the same people who had been discussing it from a different way." (Quoted in *The Road to Democracy*, p. 83). For Mandela's account see *Long Walk to Freedom* (Boston: Little, Brown, 1994), pp. 325–27, 333–35, 336–39, 351, 429; Raymond Mlaba's recollections of the events leading to the formation of MK can be found in his memoir *Personal Memoirs: Reminiscing from Rwanda and Uganda*, narrated to Thembeka Mufamadi (Cape Town: HSRC, 2001); Joe Slovo, *Slovo: The Unfinished Autobiography* (Johannesburg: Ravan Press, 1995), pp. 145–58. Ronnie Kasrils describes being recruited by M. P. Naicker during a walk on the beachfront in Durban in July 1961 in *Armed and Dangerous*, p. 38.

7. In *Long Walk*, Mandela says that he, Sisulu, and Slovo formed the High Command (p. 239); SADET says Mandela, Sisulu, Slovo, and Mhlaba (p. 90), and then without explanation adds Govan Mbeki (p. 117); Mandela says that in October 1961, he moved, undercover, to Lilliesleaf Farm, where he was joined by Raymond Mhlaba for a few weeks. "He had been chosen by the ANC to be one of the first recruits for Umkhonto. He had come to prepare for his departure, with three others, for military training in the People's Republic of China. . . . I also enlisted his assistance in writing the MK constitution. We were joined by Joe Slovo and Rusty Bernstein, who both had hands in drafting it"(p. 244). In *Walter and Albertina Sisulu*, Elinor Sisulu lists Mandela as chairman and Walter Sisulu as political commissar; Govan Mbeki, Joe Slovo, Andrew Mlangeni, and Raymond Mhlaba, she writes, were "recruited to the original High Command" (p. 47). Slovo says that he and Mandela were the original High Command and that at different stages Govan Mbeki, Walter Sisulu, and Joe Modise were co-opted and that Mhlaba, Andrew Mlangeni, Wilton Mkwayi, Joe Gqabi, and Patrick Mtembu, who were sent to China for six months of training by the SACP in September 1961, became members on their return (p. 148). See extract from Mandela's 1964 ad-

dress to the court where he sets out why the ANC turned to armed struggle. [] pre transition/the struggle/MK/[].

8. Vincent Crapanzano, *Waiting: The Whites of South Africa* (New York: Random House, 1985), "[a book] about the discourse of a people who are privileged by [the] power [of domination] and, paradoxically, in their privilege victims of it" (p. xiii).

5. Going Home

1. See "The Homelands: from 1960 to 1990" [] post transition/ TRC/report of the truth and reconciliation commission/ Vol 2/[] Chapter 5; O'Meara, pp. 72–74; Giliomee, pp. 515–42.

2. See [] pre transition/racial legislation 1802–1947/[]Native Land Act No. 27 1923/ Native Trust and Land Act No. 18, 1936.

3. A group of researchers calling themselves the Surplus People Project published an unofficial five-volume report, *Forced Removals in South Africa*, in 1982, a summary of the five volumes, *The Surplus People: Forced Removals in South Africa*, Laurine Platzky and Cherryl Walker, eds. (Johannesburg: Ravan Press, 1985). See T.R.H. Davenport, *South Africa: A Modern History*, 4th ed. (London: Macmillan, 1991), pp. 403–4.

4. SADET, *The Road to Democracy in South Africa*, Vol. 1 *(1960–1970)* (Cape Town: Zebra Press, 2004), pp. 41–43.

5. Maloka, p. 5.

6. Ibid.

7. Quoted in editorial, "African Communist," *Quarterly Journal of the SACP* 10 (July/August 1962). http://www.sacp.org.za/ac/ac10.html.

8. For the text of Operation Mayibuye, go to [] general information/ organizations/MK/[] Operation Mayibuye.

9. Stephen Clingman, *Bram Fischer: Afrikaner Revolutionary* (Cape Town: David Philips, 2002), p. 313.

10. For the background to the Naidoo family, go to [] post transition/TRC/ witness hearings/special hearings (prisons)/[]; and O'Malley interview with Indres Naidoo at []maharaj/interviewees/[] Indres Naidoo.

11. [] maharaj/interviewees/[] Indres Naidoo (14 October).

12. [] general information/organizations/MK/[] Operation Mayibuye.

13. Ibid.

14. []maharaj/interviewees/[] Wilton Mkwayi.

15. [] maharaj/interviewees/[] Paul Joseph.

16. [] maharaj/interviewees/[] Laloo Chiba.

17. [] maharaj/interviewees/2003/[] Dasu Joseph.

18. Ibid.

19. For text of Mandela's statement to the court, go to [] pre transition/ documents and reports/[]/1962.

20. Mandela, pp. 210–11.

21. For her account in solitary confinement, see Ruth First, *117 Days* (New York: Monthly Review Press, 1989), first published in 1965 by Stein and Day.

22. For accounts of the Rivonia Trial see *Long Walk*, pp. 305–30; *Walter and Albertina*, pp. 159–77; *Memoirs*, pp. 165–94.

23. Tom Lodge, *Black Politics in South Africa Since 1945* (Johannesburg: Ravan Press, 1983; fourth impression, 1990), Chapter 10, "Guerillas and Insurrectionists," 1961–1965, pp. 231–60.

6. Detention and Torture

1. For a full overview of torture in custody in South Africa, including methods of torture, the use of torture in the arrest and interrogation of detainees, and the deaths of detainees held in custody, go to []post transition/TRC/report of the Truth and Reconciliation Commission/Vol 2/ Chapter 3/[] "Torture and Death in Custody," paras 91–166.

2. []pre transition/the apartheid state/apartheid legislation 1948–1990/[]1962 Sabotage Act, 1965 Criminal Amendment Act.

3. See [] post transition/TRC/ report of the Truth and Reconciliation Commission/ Vol 2/Chapter 3/[] para 91.

4. See Don Foster, with Dennis Davis and Diane Sandler, *Detention and Torture in South Africa* (Cape Town: David Philip, 1987), which provides the findings about the posttraumatic stress disorders associated with detainment in solitary confinement without trial in South Africa.

5. Ms. Zahrah Narkedien's testimony to the TRC about her experience of being held in isolation in a cell the size of a small bathroom for seven months. [] Vol 2/Chapter 3/[] par 119.

6. Kate Millet, *The Politics of Cruelty* (New York: Norton, 1994); Elaine Scarry, *The Body in Pain* (London: Oxford University Press, 1985); John Conroy, *Unspeakable Acts, Ordinary People: The Dynamics of Torture* (New York: Knopf, 2000).

7. Mandela, p. 313.

8. [] post transition/TRC/report of the truth and reconciliation commission/ Vol 2/ Chapter 3[] paras 122–25.

9. Ibid., Chapter 2, para 54.

10. Ibid., para 55.

11. Ibid., para 128.

12. Ibid., para 98.

13. First, p. 59.

14. Hilda Bernstein interviewing Zarina and Mac (undated), Mayibuye Archives, Mayibuye Centre, University of the Western Cape. Go to [] maharaj/jula/other[]Hilda Bernstein interviews Mac and Zarina Maharaj.

15. []maharaj/interviewees/[] Murthi Naidoo.

16. First, *117 Days*.

7. Little Rivonia

1. [] post transition/ TRC/ report of the truth and reconciliation commission/ Vol 2/[]. Chapter 4, but especially paragraphs 32–33. "Perhaps the most common form of subservience can be captured in the maxim *qui facet consentire* (silence gives consent)."

2. Heinrich H. W. de Villiers, "Rivonia, Operation Mayibuye: A review of the Rivonia Trial" (Afrikaanse Pers Boekhandel, Pretoria: 1964).

3. Ibid., pp. 63–64.

4. []post transition/TRC/ report of the truth and reconciliation commission/ Vol 2/Chapter 3/[] paras 21 to 37.

5. []maharaj/interviewees/[] Laloo Chiba.

6. []maharaj/interviewees/ [] Wilton Mkwayi.

7. [] maharaj/interviewees/ [] Joel Joffe.

8. Ibid.

9. For a transcript of Lionel Gay's evidence for the state, go to []maharaj/ documents and reports/1964[] Little Rivonia/[]Lionel Gay.

10. For text of Mac's remarks, go to [] maharaj/documents and reports/1964/ Little Rivonia Trial/[](accused no. 5 (Maharaj)), pp. 1–2.

11. For the text of Maharaj's statement to the court go to [] maharaj/ documents and reports/1964/[]Little Rivonia trial/[].

8. Robben Island

1. Moses Dlamini, *Hell-Hole, Robben Island, Prisoner No. 872/63: Reminiscences of a Political Prisoner* (Nottingham, UK: Spokesman, 1984).

2. Ibid.

3. Fran Lisa Buntman, *Robben Island and Prisoner Resistance to Apartheid* (Cambridge: Cambridge University Press, 2003), pp. 48–51. Her book is the best account of the prison lives, the resistance, and the complexities of prison life on Robben Island.

4. [] maharaj/TRC/witness hearings/special hearings (prisons)/[] Indres Naidoo; [] general information/miscellaneous documents/[] memoirs of the island; Nelson Mandela, *Long Walk to Freedom*; Indres Naidoo, *Island in Chains*; Michael Dingake, *My Fight Against Apartheid*; Ahmed Kathrada, *Letters from Robben Island* and *Memoirs*; Elinor Sisulu, *Walter and Albertina Sisulu*; Thembeka Mufamadi, *Raymond Mhlaba's Personal Memoirs*; Alexander Neville, *Robben Island Dossier 1964–1974*.

5. SAIRR Survey, 1970. [] general information/SAIRR/[] 1970.

6. Michael Dingake, *My Fight Against Apartheid* (London: Kliptown Books, 1987), pp. 140–41.

7. Buntman, p. 65.

8. []maharaj/ interviewees/[] Laloo Chiba.

9. [] maharaj/interviewees/[] Michael Dingake.

10. Thomas G. Karis and Gail M. Gerhart, "Robben Island: The Early Years," in *From Protest to Challenge: A Documentary History of African Politics in South Africa 1882–1990*, pp. 30–34; Vol. 5: *Nadir and Resurgence, 1964–1979*; Mandela, *Long Walk*, pp. 374–75.

11. [] maharaj/interviewees/[] Michael Dingake.

12. In his memoirs Kathrada refers to the quarreling over the leadership and to some prisoners, supportive of Mbeki's position, arguing that in a poll on the issue only Africans as bona fide members of the ANC should have the right to vote. Mac says that Mbeki himself supported this position. Michael Dingake, who now lives in Botswana, confirmed Mac's recollection of these events. See Kathrada, p. 292; conversation with Michael Dingake, 9 September 2006.

13. Kathrada, p. 293.

14. Buntman, p. 101; Michael Dingake interview.

15. Mandela, p. 385.

16. Kathrada, p. 292.

17. According to Dingake, M.D., Naidoo became a member of the High Organ when he arrived in 1967 (see also allusion to his appointment in *From Protest to Challenge*, note 37 to Chapter 2, "The Liberation Movements, 1964–1975," p. 61). Dingake also says that at one point, he, Billy Nair, Wilton Mkwayi, and Andrew Masondo constituted the High Organ. Kathrada does not address the issue, but Mandela (p. 386) says that he served as a fifth rotating member for five years and that Laloo Chiba also served for a period. [] maharaj/ interviewees/2003/ Michael Dingake.

18. See Karis and Gerhart, pp. 157–88.

19. Mandela, pp. 388–90.

20. See Mandela, pp. 413–14, and for Wilton Mkwayi's account, see [] maharaj/interviewees/[] Wilton Mkwayi.

21. Mandela, p. 414; Eddie Daniels served fifteen years in the single cells, the lone member of the African Resistance Movement (ARM). He came up with an ingenious scheme to snatch Mandela from the courtyard using a helicopter with a large basket and net in its underbelly. He had observed many such helicopters flying close to the island on the way to service oil tankers sailing around the Cape of Good Hope. The High Organ approved the plan on condition that the leadership in Lusaka approve. The time and date were set: 9:15 A.M., 1 January 1981. Even though he was banned after his release, he managed to get details of the plan to Lusaka, where it was destroyed before it could be considered because Lusaka was bracing itself for a raid from the SADF. See Eddie Daniels, "Escapes That Never Were," in *There & Back: Robben Island 1964–1979* (Cape Town: CTP Printers, third edition, 2002), pp. 211–18.

22. [] maharaj/ documents and reports/ security files[] Robben Island/ prerelease assessment.

23. Mac's account was verified by Vella Pillay before he died. See [] maharaj/ interviewees/[] Vella and Patsy Pillay.

24. These essays were deciphered by Mac in 1999/2000 and published in a book,

Reflections in Prison (Cape Town: Zebra Press, 2001), which Mac edited. Remarkably, all but one of the authors were alive at the time of publication.

25. Phyllis Naidoo told me that it was she who picked Mac up. [] maharaj/ interviewees/[] Phyllis Naidoo/. However, I talked with Kithar's widow, Mayna Maharaj, who verified that it was she and Kithar who picked Mac up. Both concur on Mac's wanting to get into the driver's seat and test his long dormant driving skills.

9. Banned in Durban

1. For a review of the South African economy during any period between 1943 and 1999, see the annual surveys of SAIRR at [] general information/ SAIRR[].

2. "The average rate of return on investment in apartheid South Africa after 1964 was among the highest if not the highest in the world. As late as 1994, the average American corporation received an 18 per cent return on its South African investment, as compared with only 8 per cent in Britain." Dan O'Meara, *Forty Lost Years: The Apartheid State and the Politics of the National Party, 1948–1994* (Athens, Ohio: Ohio University Press, 1996), p. 174. See also *The Road to Democracy*, pp. 41–47.

3. O'Meara, pp.176–78.

4. Leonard Thompson, *A History of South Africa* (New Haven: Yale University Press, 2001), pp. 221–25.

5. See Vladimir Shubin, *ANC: A View from Moscow* (Cape Town: Mayibuye Books, University of the Western Cape, 1999), pp. 84–93.

6. Ibid.

7. For the full text of "Strategy and Tactics," go to [] pre transition/documents and reports/1969/[] Strategy and Tactics/.

8. On Robben Island there was a great deal of discussion about Black Consciousness. See Nelson Mandela, "Whither the Black Consciousness Movement? An Assessment" in *Reflections in Prison*.

9. Nancy Clark and William Worger, *South Africa: The Rise and Fall of Apartheid* (Edinburgh: Pearson Education, 2004), p. 76.

10. Ibid.

11. Quoted in Frank Welsh, *A History of South Africa* (London: HarperCollins, 2000), quoted p. 475.

12. Thompson, *A History of South Africa*, p. 200.

13. Ibid.

14. Kenneth W. Grundy, *The Militarization of South African Politics* (London, Tauris, 1986), p. 21.

15. Thompson, pp. 200–201.

16. BOSS (Bureau of State Security) was established in 1968. It became the Department of National Security (DONS) in 1979 and in 1980 the National Intelligence Service (NIS). In the decade of its existence, BOSS's full-time employees increased from 500 to more than 1,000. Grundy, pp. 42–43.

17. Karis and Gerhart, *From Protest to Challenge*, Vol. 5, pp. 279–86; 300–305.

10. Lusaka and London

1. For an account of SADF activities in Mozambique, see Hilton Hamann, *Days of the Generals* (Cape Town: Zebra Press, 2001), pp. 103–22: [] post transition/ TRC/report of the truth and reconciliation commission/Vol 2/ Chapter 2/[] paras 189–99.

2. O'Meara, pp. 219–24; Peter Stiff, *The Silent War: South African Recce Operations, 1969–1994* (Johannesburg: Galago, 1999), pp. 96–141; Hamann, pp. 21–45, 63–101.

3. The TRC, Volume 2, Chapter 2, "The State Outside South Africa Between 1960 and 1990," provides an account of South Africa's wars in Angola between 1975 and 1988. This can be found at []post transition/ TRC/ report of the truth and reconciliation commission/ Vol 2/ Chapter 2/[] paras 10 to 72. The same chapter details accounts of the South African state in covert activities in Mozambique, Botswana, Zambia, Lesotho, and South West Africa (Namibia); see also Jannie Geldenhuys, *A General's Story: From an Era of War and Peace* (Johannesburg: Jonathan Ball, 1995); Colonel Jan Breytenbach, *The Buffalo Soldiers* (Johannesburg: Galago, 2002); and Stiff, pp. 182–215, 234–38, 351–68, 530–55.

4. Republic of South Africa, Department of Defence, White Paper on Defence and Armaments Supply, 1977 (p. 5); quoted in O'Meara, p. 225.

5. Dan O'Meara, "Neo Apartheid: The Botha Reforms" in *Forty Lost Years*, pp. 272–87; see also Dr. Frederik van Zyl Slabbert: "From Apartheid to Reform: Preparations for the Total Onslaught"; "The Dynamics of Reform: Co-Optive Domination—Power Sharing Without Losing Any"; "The Dynamics of Reform: Patterns of Resistance and Revolt" (Cape Town: Institute for a Democratic South Africa Occasional Papers, 1987).

6. "By 1988, a Joint National Management Centre (JNMC) presided over 12 Joint Management Systems (JMCs), 60 sub-JMCs, 448 mini-JMCs (covering local municipalities and an unknown number of Local Management Centres [LMCs] covering the area of jurisdiction of a local police station)," O'Meara, *Forty Lost Years*, p. 286. LMCs reported to mini-JMCs, which reported to sub-JMCs up the line to the NMJC and the SSC. "Every government institution had to participate in a committee of the National Management Security System (NMSS)." Ibid. For a graphic representation of the NMSS, go to [] pre transition/ the apartheid state/ state security apparatus/ [] organizational structure of the SA state. The TRC's review of the SSC and related structures appears at [] post transition/ TRC/ Vol 2/ chapter 3/[] Appendix paras 1 to 9; the TRC's overview of the evolution of the SA state security machinery between 1979 and 1984 at [] post transition/TRC/ report of the truth and reconciliation commission/ Vol 2 Chapter I[] paras 108–39.

7. Go to []maharaj/glossary/[]tricameral parliament. For further information on the tricameral parliament and enabling legislation, see [] pre transition/ apartheid state/[] tricameral parliament.

8. Go to []maharaj/glossary/[] Black Local Authorities (BLAs).

9. For an account of the policy differences that led Dr. Andries Treurnicht, the

powerful leader of the National Party in the Transvaal, to break with P. W. Botha, see "Split in the National Party," in F. W. de Klerk, *The Last Trek—A New Beginning* (London: Macmillan, 1998), pp. 79–89.

10. Go to []maharaj/glossary/[] United Democratic Front (UDF). See also Jeremy Seekings, *The UDF: A History of the Democratic Front* (Cape Town: David Philip, 2000); for an extended note on the UDF and related references go to [] general information/organizations/[]United Democratic Front/.

11. Tom Lodge, "The Vaal Uprising, 1984–1985," in *South Africa: Time Running Out*, eds. Tom Lodge et al (Cape Town: David Philip, 1991), pp. 65–77; [] post transition/ TRC/ report of the truth and reconciliation commission/Vol 3/ Chapter 6/ [] paras 260–313.

12. For a summary history of Inkatha, see [] post transition/TRC/report of the truth and reconciliation commission/ Vol 2/ Chapter 5/[] paras 195–206.

13. An account of the London meeting between Inkatha and the ANC in October 1979 at [] post transition/ TRC/ report of the truth and reconciliation commission/ Vol 2/ Chapter 5 / [] paras 207 to 210. For an account from the ANC perspective, see Luli Callinicos, *Oliver Tambo: Beyond the Engeli Mountains* (Claremont: David Philip, 2004), pp. 397–402. For an account from Buthelezi's perspective, see Ben Temkin, *Buthelezi: A Biography* (Balgowan, South Africa: JB Publishers, 2003), pp. 205–8. See also Anthea Jeffery, *The Natal Story: 16 Years of Conflict* (Johannesburg: SAIRR, 1997), pp. 32–37.

14. For an account of the violence in the early 1980s, go to [] post transition/ TRC/ report of the truth and reconciliation commission/ Vol 2/ Chapter 5 / [] the early 1980s: The beginning of institutional violence within Inkatha, paras 211 to 232. For the latter 1980s, go to paras 233 to 278, which include an account of Operation Marion, the first instance of covert military assistance between Inkatha and the South African government. Out of this emerged the clandestine training of some two hundred Inkatha supporters in offensive action by the Special Forces arm of the SADF in the Caprivi Strip in South West Africa/Namibia in 1986.

15. See Barrell, "Conscripts to Their Age." "The most compelling reason for the ANC's persistence with armed activity regardless of the cost was the prestige, influence, and popularity that armed struggle gave it among potential supporters both inside South Africa and abroad. Indeed, the heavier the ANC losses, the higher that return was: the more MK cadres being buried or marching off to jail, the greater the evidence that the ANC had *dared to struggle* against a brutal, powerful, and internationally infamous enemy. Therein lies the explanation for the paradox of the ANC's trajectory: how it found its success in failure." Go to [] general information/Howard Barrell: "Conscripts to Their Age"/[]Conclusion p. 468.

16. In its second submission to the TRC, the ANC submitted a list of MK activities in South Africa from the 1960s through 1990. The list was drawn from data first published by the SAIRR. See [] general information/ organizations/ MK/ [] List of MK operations.

17. Vincent Crapanzano, *Waiting: The Whites of South Africa* (New York: Random House, 1985).

18. Howard Barrell, *The ANC's Armed Struggle* (Johannesburg: Penguin, 1990), p. 32.

19. [] maharaj/interviews/2005/[]April 25/.

20. For the text of "Strategy and Tactics," go to [] maharaj/documents and reports/ANC/1969/[] "Strategy and Tactics," Morogoro.

21. [] general information/ organizations/MK/[] Manifesto of Umkhonto we Sizwe 16 Dec 1961.

22. Report of the Politico-Military Strategy Commission to the ANC National Executive Committee, August 1979 (The Green Book). For text, go to [] maharaj/documents and reports/1979/[] Green Book.

23. "The armed struggle must be based on, and grow out of, mass political support and it must eventually involve our whole people. All military activities must, at every stage, be guided and determined by the need to generate political mobilisation, organisation and resistance, with the aim of progressively weakening the enemy's grip on his reins of political, economic, social and military power, by a combination of political and military action." Ibid.

24. Barrell, "Conclusion" in *Conscripts to Their Age* at [] general information/ Howard Barrell: Conscripts to their Age/ [] Conclusion, pp. 449–69.

25. Green Book.

26. Ibid.

27. See 5.3, "Toward People's War and People's Power" in ANC: "Stages of Struggle and Policy Foundations 1960–1994" at []post transition/TRC/submissions/ANC/[] statement to TRC, August 1996.

28. Ibid.

29. Ibid.

30. For the ANC NEC January 8, 1985 statement, go to [] maharaj/documents and reports/ANC NEC/1985/[] January 8 statement.

31. *Sechaba*, August 1985.

32. See Nancy L. Clark and William H. Worger, *South Africa: The Rise and Fall of Apartheid* (Edinburgh: Pearson Education, 2004), p. 96.

33. Text at [] general information/organizations/MK/[] statement on 26th anniversary of Umkhonto.

34. General Giap, *People's War* Text at [] maharaj/ documents and reports / other/[] People's War, People's Army. For extended endnote go to []maharaj/endnotes/ chapter 10 [] endnote 34.

35. Joseph Lelyveld, *Move Your Shadow: South Africa, Black and White* (New York: Time Books, 1985), pp. 331–32.

36. In Walter Sisulu's essay "We Shall Overcome!" at [] pre transition/The struggle/Reflections in prison/[] Walter Sisulu.

37. Green Book.

38. On 28 November 1980, the ANC signed the Geneva Accords. Captured members of the South African Defense Force would be treated as prisoners of war. Go to [] general information/organizations/MK/[] Statement on Signing Declaration; statement issued by ANC.

39. See [] general information/organizations/[] End Conscription Campaign.

40. See text at [] maharaj/ documents and reports/ ANC 1985/ [] Commission on Strategy and Tactics, Kabwe.

41. See [] maharaj/ documents and reports/ ANC 1985/ [] Commission on Strategy and Tactics, Kabwe/ and Oliver Tambo's statement on "soft targets."

11. Vula: Getting Started

1. Address by state president P. W. Botha at the opening of the Natal National Party Congress, Durban, 15 August 1985. (The Rubicon Speech) [] pre transition/ documents and reports/ 1985/[] Rubicon Speech.

2. O'Meara, p. 330. In his testimony to the TRC, former foreign minister Pik Botha said that he included these lines in a draft of Botha's speech but that they were deleted by Botha. For a further account of the shenanigans surrounding the preparation of the Botha speech and Botha's reactions to what he perceived as an attempt by some of his ministers, especially foreign minister Pik Botha, to put words in his mouth, see Patti Waldmeir, *Anatomy of a Miracle: The End of Apartheid and the Birth of a New South Africa* (New York: Norton, 1997), pp. 53–57.

3. Author conversation with Pik Botha, a former minister for foreign affairs, in P. W. Botha's government on 31 March 2006.

4. Rubicon speech.

5. See De Klerk, *The Long Trek*, for what Botha in his address to the Cape Congress of the National Party had in mind when he used the phrase "but within structures of South Africa's own choosing," p. 106. His statement was an example of the terminological confusion that bedeviled government thinking on constitutional matters.

6. *The Citizen*, 1 February 1986.

7. O'Meara, p. 335.

8. Data published in the South African Reserve Bank *Quarterly Bulletin* for the period draw a bleak picture of the unraveling of the South African economy. To prop up an already faltering economy external borrowing soared: from $16.9 billion in 1980 to $24.4 billion at 1984. The ratio of external debt to GDP increased from 20.3 percent to 45.7 percent; the cost of debt servicing doubled. Short-term loans from external creditors rose from 19 percent of total foreign liabilities in 1980 to 42 percent in 1984. Following Botha's Rubicon speech, all foreign banks refused to renew some $10 million in short-term loans maturing at the end of the month. The rand depreciated by one third in a week. South Africa had to suspend debt repayments and institute exchange controls to stem the flow of outward disinvestments. In 1984 forty U.S. companies pulled out of South Africa; another fifty followed in 1985. See interview with Maritz Spaarwater, former director of operations of NIS, at []maharaj/interviewees/[]Maritz Spaarwater.

9. Clark and Worger, p. 96.

10. See Fink Haysom, "Mabangalala: The Rise of Right-Wing Vigilantes in

South Africa" (Center for Applied Legal Studies, University of Witwatersrand, Johannesburg, 1986).

11. See Annexure A, "Political Assassinations of Anti-Apartheid Activists," for a list of 225 assassinations carried out between February 1971 and February 1991 in Jacques Pauw, *In the Heart of the Whore: The Story of Apartheid's Hit Squads* (Johannesburg: Southern Book Publishers, 1991); John Kane-Berman, "Violence and the State," in *Political Violence in South Africa* available at [] general information/ violence/ countrywide/ Political Violence in South Africa/ [] violence and the state; post transition/TRC/ truth and reconciliation commisson/Vol 2/Chapter 1/paras 140–65 (1985–1989: the war comes home): "The need to eliminate the ANC as a threat led to the adoption of an internal strategy of counter revolutionary warfare (para 155). . . . The security forces themselves became covertly involved in extra judicial killings, acts of arson and sabotage and other reprisals" (para 159).

12. O'Meara, pp. 272–87.

13. Interview with Magnus Malan []o'malley interviews/ 2001/[] September 17; O'Meara, p. 346; Hilton Hamann, *The Day of the Generals* (Cape Town: Zebra Press, 2001), pp. 58–63.

14. O'Meara, p. 343.

15. Three times the number of work days were lost in 1984 compared to 1983; the number doubled again in 1985, doubled again in 1986, and multiplied sixfold between 1986 and 1987. Clark and Worger, pp. 91, 96.

16. Hilton Hamann, *Days of the Generals*, pp. 54–56. The SADF prescription for victory: "80 percent political and 20 percent military," O'Meara, p. 323.

17. F. W. de Klerk, p. 109.

18. Ibid. "[The new policy] sought to strike a balance between the ideal of having one nation on the one hand, and the reality of our cultural diversity on the other."

19. Archbishop Desmond Tutu was chairperson of the TRC. In *No Future Without Forgiveness* (London: Rider, 1999) he writes, "The minutes of the State Security Council from the 1980s bristle with quite extraordinary vocabulary— 'neutralizing' and 'eliminating' people, for instance, which leaders of the apartheid government disingenuously wanted us to believe was really quite innocuous language meaning nothing more sinister than to detain or to ban. Those who carried out these orders almost consistently understood them to kill, murder and assassinate" (p. 193). In testimony before the TRC, General Johan van der Merwe, police commissioner under P. W. Botha, said, "All the powers given to the security forces were to avoid the ANC/SACP achieving their revolutionary aims and often with the approval of the previous government we had to move outside the boundaries of the law. That inevitably led to the fact the capabilities of the SAP, especially the security forces, included illegal acts" (Van der Merwe quoted in Tutu, p. 194). See also [] post transition/ TRC/ report of the truth and reconciliation commission/ Vol 2/ Chapter 1/ paras 154–56.

20. Vlakplaas, "Farm on the Plains," was a 44-hectare farm, about 30 kilometers outside Pretoria, bought by the SAP in 1981 for the purpose of training *askaris*

(members of the ANC or other liberations who had "turned" and were now working for the state). Vlakplaas was HQ for the C1 Unit, the covert and operational section of the SAP's counterinsurgency unit, commanded at various times by Dirk Coetzee (who fled the country in November 1989, joined the ANC, later got amnesty for the killing of Griffith Mxenge, and told all about Vlakplaas's death squad) and then by Eugene de Kock ("Prime Evil") in 1985. In 1993, De Kock was arraigned on 129 counts of murder and fraud. In October 1996, he was sentenced to two life sentences plus 212 years. De Kock, of course, did not operate as some freelance killer. He was given orders to kill. Most of his superiors neither appeared before the TRC nor have been brought to account. For a very insightful account of De Kock and an understanding of what drove Vlakplaas operatives to "motiveless malignity" in the conduct of their small "industry" of murder, see Eugene de Kock as told to Jeremy Gordin in *A Long Night's Damage* (Johannesburg: Contra Press, 1998).

21. The source for this is a secret SSC document that came into the possession of the TRC. Go to[] post transition/TRC/ report of the truth and reconciliation commission/Vol 3/Chapter 3/[] par 177.

22. "Notes of PMC 'Working Committee' with M (Murphy Morobe) & V (Valli Moosa)" []maharaj/vula comms/1989/[] Feb 11.

23. The cabal referred to "certain Indians and Whites" in the MDM "regarded as leaders in the struggle," who were supposedly manipulating the MDM, causing disunity. See [] maharaj/ documents and reports/ other/[] report and recommendations of commission on the cabal.

24. Author interview with Ivan Pillay at [] maharaj/interviewees/[]Ivan Pillay/ December 11, 2002.

25. Ibid. There is a revealing exchange between Nyanda and Slovo in October 1989. On 16 October 1989, Nyanda expresses his extreme dissatisfaction with the way in which Lusaka is servicing Vula, especially with regard to its demands for more personnel and resources. See Carl (Nyanda) to Kay (Slovo) [] maharaj/vula comms/1989/[]October 16. In response Slovo takes him through the history of Vula and bluntly says it is very difficult to get cadres of the right caliber who are willing to go home and more or less tells Nyanda to stop the complaining and be thankful he has what he has. Kay (Slovo) to Carl (Nyanda) [] maharaj/vula comms/1989/ [] October 25.

26. Janet (Slovo) to Tony (Mac) (11 February 1989) [] maharaj/vula comms/ 1989[] Feb 11/ Notes of PMC 'Working Committee' with M (Murphy Morobe) and V (Valli Moosa).

27. In *Anatomy of a Miracle*, Patti Waldmeir asserts that "as he [Mac] tells it, ANC leader Oliver Tambo authorized his mission in 1986—as soon as it became clear that negotiations with Pretoria were on the horizon," p. 82. In our numerous conversations on Vula, Mac never said anything of the sort. Negotiations with Pretoria were not on the horizon (see "Report to GM" included in Tambo to Mac [] maharaj/vula comms/1989/ [] May 2, parts 2/4 and 3/4). There is an insinuation here of Tambo wanting to have what became known in the parlance as "an insurance policy" in the event of negotiations, whenever they occurred, failing. It

was nothing of the sort. Vula as conceptualized and carried out was to prepare for a people's war. To the end (his stroke in August 1988) Tambo was skeptical about "real" negotiations.

28. See Vladimir Shubin, *ANC: A View from Moscow*, pp. 332–39, for his understanding of the role of the USSR in Vula.

29. For an account of the meeting, and the near eruption when a very belligerent Seretse Choabe, a senior ANC official, threatened to kill De Lange and Mac's initiative in defusing the situation, see Patti Waldmeir, *Anatomy of a Miracle*, pp. 63–64. For Mac's account, go to [] maharaj/interviews/2002/[] October 9 (2). This interview also throws some light on Mac's perceptions of his relationship with Thabo Mbeki in that it was one of their being for the most part on complementary lines—allies, not adversaries.

30. For Ashley Wills's account of the circumstances of this meeting, go to [] maharaj/interviewees/[] Ashley Wills.

31. For a review of the debate going on within the ANC, see Tom Lodge, "People's War or Negotiation? African National Congress Strategies in the 1980's" in G. Moss and I. Obery, eds., *South African Review*, no. 5 (Johannesburg: Ravan Press, 1989), p. 42.

32. Damien de Lange was the commander of a guerrilla unit of four white males organized by Ronnie Kasrils, then head of military intelligence. With guidance from Kasrils, the group infiltrated South Africa, traveling from Malanje-Angola to Botswana, across the Kalahari Desert into the Northern Cape and from there to Johannesburg. In 1987, the unit, including De Lange and his girlfriend, Susan Westcott, who had been trained as the unit's radio operator, were arrested in Broederstroom, north of Johannesburg. One member of the group attempted to desert, a second surrendered himself to the police and led them to the others. In court he testified against them. De Lange was tried and sentenced to twenty-five years in prison, Westcott to eight. They later married. See Ronnie Kasrils, *Armed and Dangerous* (Cape Town: Mayibuye Books and Jonathan Ball, 1998), pp. 277–78, 280, 290–91, 317–19, 416.

33. For how the system worked, see interviews with Jenkin [] maharaj/interviewees/[] Tim Jenkin, March 22, 2002 and May 19, 2004; and Tim Jenkin at [] marahaj/vula/other/[] Talking with Vula. See []maharaj/interviews/2001/[] 10 September, /2002/December 12, /2003/ September 16 and /2004/June 24; and Janet Love, May 19, 2004. There was a two-stage process in writing messages: they were encrypted and then encoded. Both codes and encryption were changed on a regular basis.

34. Barend Schuitema was an Afrikaner engineer who fled to Amsterdam in 1969. In 1971 he founded the Dutch Anti-Apartheid Movement (AABN) and was co-founder of Okhela. The *Sunday Times* "outed" Schuitema as an apartheid spy, a view supported for years by many, including his ex-lover Conny Bram. It seems, however, that the *Sunday Times* story was planted by the apartheid regime to discredit Schuitema. See Bart Luirink, "The Rumour: Barend Schuitema—Anti-Apartheid

Fighter or a Double Spy?" *Haagse Post/ De Tijd*, November 11, 1993, pp. 1–3. Go to [] maharaj/ documents and reports / other/[] The Rumour.

35. When rumors about his presence in South Africa began to surface in the early part of 1989, frantic efforts were embarked on to ascertain where they might be coming from. Jacob Zuma was an obvious choice because Operation Bible, which was working with Mac, reported to him. In a message to Slovo, tagged "For Janet [Slovo] only," Mac speculates: "Not clear of all facts and do not want to cause problems. . . . But leaks *cld* be from PB [politburo] end too—Moshoshoe can't be at ease given how I keep picking his loose talk! Hope J has not spread it to Mamba, Sue etc. Once we know facts, have to find ways to contain info. Decide if you want this known to A [Tambo] at this stage—careful probs may have arisen from PB side!" Tony (Maharaj) to Janet (Slovo), []maharaj/vula comms/1989/[] March 4.

12. Home Again

1. Comm Tambo to Mac (11/Dec 1988) []maharaj/vula comms/1988/[] Dec 11. For the SACP assessment of where the struggle stood when Mac and Nyanda entered the country, go to []marahaj/documents and reports/SACP/1990[] other/ assessment 1985–1988.

2. Since 1994, much has been written about cliques of "insurrectionists" and "diplomats" in the ANC, the former supposedly led by Chris Hani, the latter by Thabo Mbeki. In reality, no such cliques existed in any organized form. Individuals may have had a proclivity for one or the other viewpoint, but the real battle was about how to implement the strategy for a "people's war." See Patti Waldmeir, *Anatomy of a Miracle*, pp. 49–51, 75–80; Allister Sparks, *Tomorrow Is Another Country* (Cape Town: Struik, 1996, sixth impression; first published in 1994), pp. 72–86. Waldmeir creates a false dichotomy in her analysis of the Mells House talks and Vula. Thabo Mbeki is portrayed as the lonely figure in the ANC advocating peace talks as the way forward as far back as 1985, only with the support of Tambo; others (and she refers to Maharaj specifically) "preferred to fight [their] way to the table." The Vula comms provide a more complicated reading of the situation. Pigeonholing ANC leaders into different camps only contributes to a misreading of their positions and rather than throwing light on their behavior adds confusion. The comms suggest that the ANC was prepared to fight its way to the table if the government continued to stall or block attempts at negotiations. To suggest that Thabo Mbeki, member of the SACP politburo, was somehow advancing a line to which none of his colleagues would listen is misleading. For an excellent discourse on "hardliners" and "soft liners" see []maharaj/interviews/[] Dipak Patel.

3. See ANC NWC meetings on 22 February 1988, at which the subject of the talks first emerges. Prior to this the NEC was unaware of the talks. Chris Hani was very upset, demanding to know "on whose authority Cde [Comrade] Thabo entered into discussions with these Afrikaner intellectuals? Does the NEC/NWC know anything of this?" Neither Tambo nor Mbeki was at the meeting. At the end

of the discussion, Hani said, "Let the minutes record that we register our extreme displeasure that Cde Thabo has unilaterally gone to London without any consultation and without a mandate from the NWC." Hani's resolution is supported by the NWC. See [] maharaj/ documents and reports/ ANC NEC/ 1988/[] Feb 22. Matters got more complicated. At the NWC meeting on 9 March 1988, when the minutes of the previous meeting were read, James Stuart, who had not attended the February meeting, said he recalled an NWC decision authorizing Mbeki to make the London connection. A long discussion followed with the resolution that "there can be no deviation from the principle of the NWC choosing delegations." Mac attended this meeting but not the February one. Reports of meetings with the Afrikaners were provided at subsequent meetings.

4. See NWC meetings of 22/23 June 1988 and 8 September 1988 at []/ ANC/NWC/1988/ [].

5. []maharaj/documents and reports/ANC NWC/1989/[] Special Meeting of the NWC on 15 October 1989.

6. Mandela, p. 466.

7. Waldmeir, pp. 62–83.

8. Comm Slovo to Mac, 23 April 1989, Janet (Slovo) to Tony (Mac) at []maharaj/ vula /comms/1989/[] April 23 (no. 1 of 5).

9. For text of "Path to Power" go to [] general information/organizations/ SACP [].

10. Go to []maharaj/documents and reports/ANC NEC/1990/[] Special []NEC Meeting, February 15/16.

11. Comm Alphons (Tambo) to Tony (Mac) at [] maharaj/vula comms/1988/[] Dec 11.

12. Comm Tambo to Mac 2 May 1989 [] maharaj/vula comms/1989/ [] May 2. When Mac raised the matter in November 1988, Tambo replied in December that "a secure line [Madiba-Reggie-Madiba] is welcome" & "maximum collective functioning of the Rivonia group is vital including special contact between Zizi [Govan Mbeki] and Madiba." Tambo to Mac at [] maharaj/vula comms/1988/[] December 11

13. See "Notes of Meeting of PNC 'Working Committee' " with M [Murphy Morobe] and V [Valli Moosa] in comm. Slovo to Mac []maharaj/vula comms/ 1989/[] Feb 10: "There is a serious crisis of leadership within the MDM as a whole; current leadership not capable of working out strategic direction; no forum for strategizing; lack of cohesiveness; only responding to crises; there is urgent need to find answers to the fundamental question of lifting MDM from state of unconscious existence. The UDF in particular is plagued by many weaknesses. . . ." (Murphy and Valli).

14. After Harry Gwala had returned to Natal on his release from Robben Island, he sent his assessment of the situation there to Tambo with a catalogue of the initiatives he intended taking to straighten matters out and resuscitate ANC underground structures. Tambo sent Gwala's report to Mac. "Here at home," he reported, "we are in a shabby state of organization. It would appear that the organization of

internal structures has either been neglected or people have shied away from it. . . ." For full text go to []maharaj/vula comms/1989/[] May 2, (para 5.3.7).

15. In his second incarceration on Robben Island, Gwala was openly opposed to the leadership of the single cells and to Mandela's nationalism; for Gwala, communism—a socialist state—was the end of the struggle. At one point he refused to meet with the "older" leaders in the single cells to resolve the "battle of ideas" that raged between Gwala and a post-Soweto generation of young prisoners in the communal cells and ANC leadership in the single cells, with the possible exception of Govan Mbeki. See Buntman, pp. 99–102.

16. Mac to Slovo (28 Apr 89), "Tony [Mac] was told by two independent cdes at Sello's that HG had told each that Tony was at Zola's; that he was with the cabal; the cabal had destroyed and was destroying all organisations in the area; that the org. outside did not understand the cabal problem; that the org should not have sent an Indian to build the ANC u/g; [the independent comrades were Kgalema Motlanthe & Sydney Mufamadi]." Go to [] maharaj/ vula comms/1989/[] Apr 28. Tambo to Mac (17 May 89): "He [Harry Gwala] does have problems about cabal. His correspondence about it is ferocious & furious—to a degree, which seems to allow no space in his mind for u/g org of Inqindi [the liberation movement] as fundamental to maintenance of structures & the guaranteeing of a sustained offensive at mass level." Full text at [] maharaj/vula comms/1989/ [] May 17.

17. Just months after Mac returned to South Africa, Tambo and Slovo concluded a comm to him with a plaintive: "What best way to putting end to some of unhappy infighting in our broad ranks." Comm, Slovo to Mac (23 October 88) [] maharaj/vula comms/1988/ [] Oct 23(3).

Govan Mbeki had established his own structures in the PE region once he was released. He also attempted to form a national structure. How to manage territory and jurisdictional overlaps, especially when Vula was clandestine became a problem. So too did Govan Mbeki's national unit, which had members who were part of Vula. They were exposed to the attention of the security forces active when they visited Govan Mbeki in PE. [] maharaj/vula comms/1988/ [] Dec 5, Dec 27, 28/29.

In one comm (28/29 Dec), Tambo refers to the first meeting of Mbeki's national collective: "The approach which characterized the first national get-together was clearly a recipe for another Rivonia disaster."

See also Slovo to Mac (10 Feb. 89): "The whole question of division of labour between the different structures engaged in the same area is beginning to loom. There are more than half dozen outfits theoretically involved in internal building (IPC, JO, SACTU, NAT, MK, President's Project, Rachel &, very theoretically, youth, women etc). How to prevent duplication, achieve co-ordination and, at the same time, maintain the absolutely necessary security wall around Vula?" [] maharaj/ vula comms/1989/[] Feb 10.

18. See Mandela's comment, Appendix, Section A, p. 499.

19. Tambo to Mac (17 May 89): "In the light of the enormous pressures bearing down on the movement from everywhere calling for negotiations, a document is

being worked out at HQ, to be discussed with the MDM & then with the FLS before presentation to the OAU for adoption as a kind of 435 for South Africa. It's
designed to guide world discussion on SA presented as an African position, &
designed to pre-empt pressure groups, big & small, who desire to impose their
own approach to the SA problem. A first draft will be sent to you, GM & HG
for your input." [] maharaj/vula comms/1989/ [] May 17. In a report to Mac on
16 June, covering their meeting with a delegation from MDM to discuss the issue
of negotiations, Tambo and Slovo say: "On our side we gave info about the mounting pressure for a political settlement from a variety of external forces (both
friends & enemies)." Tambo and Slovo to Mac [] maharaj/ vula comms/1989/
June 16.

20. Slovo to Mac (6 October 1988) [] maharaj/vula comms/1988/[] Oct. 6.

21. A (Tambo) and J (Slovo) to Tony (Mac) at/[] maharaj/vula comms/1989/[]
June 16 (3/7).

22. The TRC refers to a special meeting convened by the KIK (Coordinating Intelligence Committee) in October 1985 attended by top-level generals and intelligence personnel to discuss the possibility of a settlement with the ANC. While
clear differences of emphasis are evident the consensus was that "any negotiation
should take place from a position of strength, not weakness and a settlement
should be avoided until the balance of power could be shifted. In the words of
General Groenewald: 'This is a stage where one can negotiate from a position of
strength and can afford to accommodate the other party, given that it has largely
been eliminated as a threat.' " [] post-transition/TRC/ report of the truth and reconciliation commission/ Vol 2/Chapter 7/to/Chapter 1/[] para 154. Thus, it would
appear that while the generals saw an accommodation as inevitable, it wanted to
delay inevitability until it had sufficiently weakened the ANC.

23. "Of course we cannot avoid paying attention to the pressure on negotiation.
But we must in practice (not in theory) not do so at the expense of the real thing."
Slovo to Mac in comm, 16 June 89 at [] maharaj/ vula comms/1989/[] June 16 (3/7).

24. In a long comm, Tambo and Slovo to Mac, the former outline the diversity
of opinion within the MDM regarding negotiations and the need to assuage militants. At NEC discussions on these issues, Mac's input was "read to the meeting as
emanating from an internal collective." At this NEC meeting in early June the
ANC's position on negotiations [Draft Harare Declaration] "was discussed para
by para." [] maharaj/vula comms/1989/[] June 16 (1/7) through (7/7).

25. Ibid.

26. See comm. Mac to Tambo and Slovo forwarding the comments of Govan
Mbeki and Dullah Omar on the draft Harare Declaration. Govan was concerned
about the lack of preparation among the grass roots for what would appear to
them to be a major shift in strategy, as the issue of negotiations was rarely raised
at this level, the sole emphasis being on the armed struggle. See comm. Tony
(Mac) to A (Tambo) and J (Slovo) at []maraharj/vula comms/1989/[]22 June.
Gwala was not among the select number asked to provide comment.

27. Interview Moe Shaik; [] maharaj/interviewees/[] Moe Shaik/May 7, 2003.

28. Yunus Shaik []maharaj/interviewees/[]Yunus Shaik/ May 28, 2004.

29. Ibid.

30. Interviews Moe Shaik and Nightingale [] maharaj/ interviewees/[] Moe Shaik and Nightingale, 2004.

31. []maharaj/interviewees/[] Yunus Shaik/May 28, 2004.

32. Theo (Mac) to Jean (Ronnie Kasrils), Marsha (Billy Nair) and Carl (Siphiwe Nyanda) at [] maharaj/vula comms/1990/April 25.

33. []maharaj/interviewees/[] Hentie Botha, 2006.

34. On occasion, Mac expressed his displeasure at what he considered the excessive sums Schabir Shaik levied on transactions as his fee for facilitating transactions. On one occasion he wrote Slovo: "Although the sums we received were more than we had estimated while we were working on the budget, I still think Pits (Schabir Shaik) is making a killing from the deals. He is giving us 10 % and I doubt his claim of the rate having been 4.08 on the date the deposit was made. Anyway this is how he worked out the exchange: 36,470 @ 4.08 = R148, 797, + 10 % (R14, 879) = R163,677. I suggest that you also look for other sources at Jessy's (Jo'burg) with whom we will make business in the future." Lara [Mac] to Kay [Slovo] []maharaj/vula comms/1990/[] April 10 comm: Mac complaining about Schabir's take.

35. Slovo to Mac (2 Apr 89) [] maharaj/ vula comms/1989/[] Apr 2.

36. "Having decided on the armed struggle we conducted ourselves as if simply by that decision, that form of struggle was already the dominant form." He warned that "the enduring people's militancy cannot be equated with our having transformed the masses into political revolutionary bases." For full text, go to Mac to Slovo 28 March 89, []maharaj/vula comms/ 1989/[]March 28 parts 4 and 5.

37. Mac's letter of 8 March 1989 to the general secretary of the SACP at []maharaj/vula comms/1989/[]March 8 (received in Lusaka on 25 March 1989).

38. Comm Slovo to Mac 23 April 1989, Janet (Slovo) to Tony (Mac) at []maharaj/vula comms/1989/[] April 23 (no. 2 of 5).

39. On 9 July 1988, in a letter from Moscow to Zarina, Mac, on his way back to South Africa, described how he left critical disks with his hand luggage, which was put through an X-ray machine at Budapest airport; go to []maharaj/family/correspondence/[]. In Swaziland someone put his hand through an open window in the hotel he was staying at and stole his coat with all his contact numbers and money. When he was arrested in July 1990 in his briefcase he had a draft of an ANC NEC resolution suspending the armed struggle, which was going to be a surprise move on the part of the ANC at the Pretoria meeting with the government on August 7, when he *knew* he was going to be arrested.

40. []maharaj/family/correspondence/[].

41. Interview Ivan Pillay; [] maharaj/interviewees/[] Pillay/ October 11, 2002.

42. In his response to Govan Mbeki's intervention following disclosure of Mandela's memorandum, Tambo enclosed a summary of a message in the matter that he had sent Mandela, which included the observation that "there was as far as we could observe no evidence whatsoever that the regime was serious about negotiations." Tambo to Mac, 1 May 1989. Go to []maharaj/vula comms/ 1989/[] May 1.

43. In comm. to Tambo and Slovo 4 March 1989 [] maharaj/vula comms/1989/ [] March 4 Mac informs both that Jacob Zuma knows he is in South Africa; Slovo to Mac 2 Apr 89, confirms that he and Tambo have confirmed that Zuma knows. On 2 May 89, Tambo and Slovo write a "Reply to yours of 28/4/89," "Janet (Slovo) and Alphons (Tambo) were very angry with JZ. . . . Ultimately, Alphons decided he would have to confront him. . . . JZ hadn't been irresponsible" []maharaj/vula comms/1989/[] May 2 (2/4) and (3/4).

44. Because the sequence of events following Zarina's accident had a profound impact on the personal relationship between Mac and Joe Slovo, see the comms that passed among them at []maharaj/endnotes/Chapter 12/[] 44.

45. Adam [Mac] to Reggie [Tambo] and Robin [Slovo] (22 October 1988) []maharaj/vula comms/1988/[] October 22; Reggie [Tambo] and Robin [Slovo] to Adam [Mac] (27 October 1988), []maharaj/vula comms/1988/[] October 27; Mac to Tambo and Slovo 13 November, Tambo and Slovo to Mac /17& 21 November.

46. See Slovo to Mac (25 Feb 88), "Further to your report re storing equipment in Para 9.8 of the last report that came with John, Alphons [Tambo] is apprehensive about the impression that it is intended to have large storage places. He prefers greater decentralization." []maharaj/vula comms/1988/[] Feb 25.

47. Slovo to Mac (6 March 89): "Your reports and from others show that you're overworking. Shouldn't you slow down for a limited period? []maharaj/vula comms/1989/[] March 6; from Zarina [Elsa] on March 20 via Ivan: "Saw Janet [Slovo] yesterday who advised that you've been asked to consider a break with us." But Mac was not ready to come out. See Mac to Tambo and Slovo []maharaj/vula comms/[] March 21, 2 (c).

48. Mac to Tambo (28 April 89), "We cannot minimize the danger to Vula [he wrote OR]. Our sources are more or less disciplined cadres. (Who else he [Harry Gwala] has told and is telling is another question!) The fact that none, when told by HG [Harry Gwala] saw fit to draw attention to the danger he was exposing Vula [to] and the organization is really a question of inadequate development of the political culture that goes with the nature of our struggle and it is likely that these problems will give advance cadres a better understanding of what it means to protect the organization. At the same time we cannot help feeling that HG seems to be getting support for his positions from someone or other at HQ. We have begun changing our style of working, begun implementing security precautions to protect Vula from enemy and are closely monitoring the situation. In our courier report we shall give you more on our assessment etc but we think we can not only survive but play our part in solving the problems which are fundamentally political. But we would appreciate your ascertaining who at HQ has a line to HG and getting urgent word to him not to endanger our lives." Mac to Slovo and Tambo []maharaj/vula comms/1989/[] April 28 Part six.

49. Tambo message for Harry Gwala inc. in Tambo to Mac 17 May 89 []maharaj/ vula comms/1989/[] May17, part 4 of 9.

50. Gwala's high-handed antics in KwaZulu-Natal, refusal to meet with Mac, his lividness with the fact that an Indian had been sent in from exile to organize the

ANC underground in South Africa, his obsession with the "cabal" exasperated the ever patient Tambo. Outlining the scope of Gwala's grievances and activities, Tambo sums things up: "We're stuck—at least at the moment of writing. Do you have any brain waves? We're encouraging him to come out for treatment so that we can talk with him. In the meantime we are trying to get him to stop talking." Alphons [Tambo] to Tony [Mac] (2 May 1989) []maharaj/vula comms/1989/[] May 2.

51. In his first brief message to Tambo following meeting with Gwala, Mac sounds a little less sanguine: "Succeeded in meeting H for one and a half hours on 2 May. Went quite well if we go by his immediate responses, tone & attitude by end of meeting. . . . [But] he has a tendency of saying there are no probs. and then continuing with his own line." Mac to Slovo (9 May 89/May 3 resent).

52. See Appendix, section D., pp. 505–16. The problem also arose when Mandela and the "team" had agreed on the details of the releases of Walter Sisulu and the other Rivonia Trialists. See [] maharaj/ documents and reports/ANC NWC/1989/[] Minutes of Special Meeting of the NWC on 15 October 1989. These minutes include a summary by Joe Slovo of the report given to some NEC members in London (including Slovo) by Sydney Mufamadi after an MDM delegation met with Mandela prior to the release of Sisulu and others. ". . . they had suspected that he wanted to counsel a 'low key' reception. They (MDM) were opposed to this idea. NM had proceeded to give them a detailed picture of the negotiations that had been going on. He had dealt with the history of the releases, how he had negotiated release of HG and GM. He had been critical that they had not played a 'low key [role]' and HG's picture addressing meetings in an agitated mood had been shown to him. He had not raised his own position but had said undertaking with the regime was that they play a low key [role]. . . . He had said that he had seen all seven before their removal and they had agreed to play a low key [role]. Syd said the delegation came back surprised, but they did not hammer the need for the leaders to stand at the head of the mobilization campaign."

53. "Tony's (Mac's) visit to Rachel (Mbeki) requires a 95% security shield otherwise it should not be risked." Janet (Slovo) report to Tony (Mac) []maharaj/ vula comms/1989/[] February 10.

54. Comm Theo (Mac) to Carl (Nyanda) (24 June 1990) []maharaj/vula comms/1990/[] June 24, "In the meantime we have had word from Cleo [London] that Donald [code name for person known only to Tambo, Slovo, and Mac, never employed] will be coming into the country around the end of June. Besides the equipment you already have, it appears that Ntaba's [Zuma's] outfit is currently required to store two pieces which were in the hands of the enemy group planning Madiba's assassination. From the description that Ntaba gave me, one of the pieces seems to have an optical sight and given the internascent struggle within the enemy camp I am attracted to borrowing one of those pieces if it is suitable for use by us even if on a temporary basis. It would be good to know how you feel about that aspect of the project and whether our information is being updated re those potential targets."

55. See Theo (Mac) to Carl (Nyanda) (18 June 1990) []maharaj/vula comms/1990/[] June 18 (4).

56. After being granted indemnity on 20 May 1990, Mac, on Mandela's instructions, left South Africa so that he could return as a "legal" person. On his return on 15 June, he found that Nyanda had moved with some speed to establish more direct contacts with the Western Cape, including sharing the Vula communication system. Mac called an immediate halt to these efforts and took Nyanda to task in a stinging rebuke, spelling out the unreadiness of the Western Cape operation to be included in Vula—or Vula under another name. For text, go to Mac to Nyanda (18 June 90) []maharaj/vula comms/1990/[] June 18.

13. Vula: Conflict in KwaZulu-Natal (KZN)

1. For overviews of the conflict in the latter part of the 1980s: the human rights violations claimed by Inkatha see [] post transition/ TRC/ report of the truth and reconciliation commission/ Vol 2 Chapter 4/[] paras 71–78; Inkatha and collusion with the South African security forces, Vol 2, Chapter 5, paras 233–56; the KwaZulu police, Vol 2 Chapter 5, paras 258–78; 1990s: IFP–ANC war for hegemony on KwaZulu-Natal and the PWV, Vol 2 Chapter 5, paras 279–88; Regional Profile: Natal & KwaZulu, Vol 3, Chapter 3 paras 1–215; Anthea Jeffery, *The Natal Story*, pp. 61–126, 127–211, 213–313. See also [] general information/ violence /KwaZulu-Natal/Caprivi training camps [] and the Reports of the Commission of Inquiry Regarding Public Violence and Intimidation (The Goldstone Commission): "Second Interim Report," 29 April 1992 and "Interim Report on Criminal Violence by Elements within the South African Police, the KwaZulu Police and the Inkatha Freedom Party," 18 March 1994.

2. The TRC found that there was no difference of any significance between Inkatha and the government of KwaZulu. Thus government resources allocated to KwaZulu were also used to fund either directly or indirectly the activities of Inkatha. The SADF bore the cost of training and salaries of Inkatha members at Caprivi until they were incorporated into the KwaZulu police in 1989; the Inkatha-oriented United Workers' Union of South Africa (UWUSA) and various demonstrations (Inkathagate) Jeffery, pp. 218, 251, 299, 345–46, 583, 685, 691–92, 704, 742, 778; [] post-transition/ TRC (solidus) report of the truth and reconciliation commission/ Vol2/Chapter 5/ [] paras 197–206.

3. According to the TRC, "The IFP [was] the major perpetrator of killings on a national scale, being allegedly responsible for over 4,500 killings compared to 2,700 attributed to the SAP and 1,300 to the ANC." And "the IFP was responsible for approximately 3.5 killings for every one attributed to the ANC." Yet the TRC itself places a question mark over its findings, since it received many more accounts of the political violence from UDF/ANC supporters, "creating the impression that the violations suffered by the UDF/ANC outnumbered those suffered by Inkatha by five to one." [] post transition/ TRC/ report of the truth and reconciliation commission/ []. The TRC was also limited by the unwillingness of Inkatha to

cooperate and its instructions to victims of violence not to appear before the commission (until the last minute, when compensation was being mooted). Nor did the TRC have the cooperation of P. W. Botha, the SSC, or the major security and intelligence agencies. Thus the scale and scope of the TRC's investigation were compromised from the start and the resources at its disposal to unravel the conflict's multiple layers were simply insufficient for the task.

The report, however, does establish that for about a decade of its existence Inkatha functioned as an ally or auxiliary of the South African government: "Inkatha's initial opposition to the SA government's policies had changed to covert collaboration by the latter half of the 1980s and [that] the two had united against a common enemy 'the UDF and their affiliates.' "

The TRC also provides convincing evidence that Inkatha colluded with the security forces of the apartheid regime in actions aimed at crushing the ANC in the four years after the latter was unbanned in 1990 and that the 200-odd Inkatha members who were trained by the SADF during 1986 in Caprivi, Namibia, were not trained solely to fulfill a defensive role by protecting Inkatha leaders from ANC assassins. They were trained to undertake offensive actions against the enemies of the regime.

4. John Nkadimeng, in a Radio Freedom broadcast from Addis Ababa, Ethiopia, 21 November 1986. SACTU called him "a leader of a Bantustan Gestapo and a junior partner in oppression and murder." See Jeffery, p. 192. UDF activists used to call Buthelezi *"inja,"* which is Zulu for dog and rhymes with Gatsha.

5. For a fuller account of Buthelezi's remarks, go to [] post transition/ TRC/truth and reconciliation commission/ Vol 2/Chapter5/[] par 232.

6. Interview Dipuo (Catherine) Mvelase [] maharaj/interviewees/[].

7. There was great pressure on Vula to supply combat units to fight Inkatha. See comm from Carl (Nyanda) on 24 April 1990 for Cha Cha (Kasrils) and Suzanna (Janet Love) at [] maharaj/ vula comms/ 1990/ April 24; Dan (Kasrils) to Theo (Mac) 4 May. "The situation demands that we proceed with greater urgency in setting up combat & enemy forces structures. We have rated the combat structures as the top priority. Saturday: Met DPC today ... what the programme does not show is our decision to prioritize Umlazi following report we received that war lords are planning to attack the area on 13 July. We have decided: a) a crash course in use of firearms & tactics this week for Umlazi APC & combat unit. . . . Can Carl immediately inform us where and how we can obtain weapons to arm a minimum of six Umlazi trainees & a maximum of 12"; Theo (Mac) to Daniels (Kasrils) and Marsha (Billy Nair) on 6 May, (vi) ". . . Neither Joe (Nyanda) nor Theo have had a chance to look at your draft programme re MK work. But go ahead, we will just have to make modifications in our stride. The important thing is extreme secrecy and avoiding casualties at all costs. Any exposure could put our negotiating comrades under premature and unnecessary pressure. We are waiting to discuss with Joe your request re weapons for Umlazi but again we have to temper the real pressures on the ground with the need to ensure the fullest discipline and control over how the weaponry is used." See also interview

with Catherine Mvelase. In comm. Kasrils to Mac, Kasrils expresses his disappointment that the weaponry he requested is not forthcoming. []maharaj/vula comms/1990/[]May 6.

8. See Slovo to Mac (6 October 88) [] maharaj/vula comms/1988/[] Oct 6 (Thatcher as peacemaker and Slovo's response); Tambo to Mac and Nyanda (17 May 89) [] vula comms/1989/[] May 17 (2/9) (NEC statement on campaign for peace in Natal; the Archbishop Hurley initiative and Buthelezi's response, Buthelezi's insistence on a meeting of "presidents").

9. Tambo to Mac and Nyanda (17 May 89) []maharaj/vula comms/1989/[] May 17: 6/9, 7/9, 8/9, 9/9.

10. Slovo to Mac (5 October 88), quoting from a report prepared by Thabo Mbeki for the ANC NWC: "Thatcher had told us that Buthelezi wants to normalize relations with the ANC and that she is willing to assist in this process if she is so required." []maharaj/vula comms/1988/[] October 5.

11. In October 1988 Thabo Mbeki reported to the NWC that Buthelezi had met with British Prime Minister Margaret Thatcher and that Buthelezi told her that "the conflict between Inkatha and the ANC should stop and that he had said the same to Gen. Obsasanjo. In his view it required a prominent statesman to intervene. Thatcher had agreed with Gatsha that the conflict should end and had expressed a willingness to make peace." In the discussion that followed the NWC agreed that "time has not arrived to speak with Gatsha or even Thatcher." [] maharaj/ documents and reports/ ANC NWC/1988/[] Meeting of NWC on 4 October.

12. "On a personal level, my relationships with Chief Buthelezi were close and respectful. . . ." Mandela, pp. 501–2; see *A Prisoner in the Garden: Opening Nelson Mandela's Prison Archive* (Johannesburg: Penguin, 2005), pp. 179–80 for reproduction of a couple of Mandela's letters to Buthelezi.

13. Dan (Kasrils) to Theo (Mac) []maharaj/vula comms/1990/[] May 5 (4).

14. Mandela

1. Source embargoed until 2030.

2. Mandela, p. 457.

3. Ibid., pp. 464–65.

4. According to Barnard, despite the perception that P. W. Botha simply had his way in everything, he had to convince some members of the SSC who opposed opening talks with Mandela that this was the best political course the regime could pursue. Interview with Niel Barnard [] o'malley/interviews/1996/[] Barnard.

5. Mandela, p. 466.

6. Source sealed until 2030.

7. Mandela, p. 474.

8. For "Notes prepared by Nelson Mandela for his meeting with P. W. Botha on 5 July 1989," go to [] pre transition/documents and reports/1989/[].

9. For Mac's account of the sequence of events that he relayed to Lusaka immediately after setting in motion the actions that would douse the rumors of "Man-

dela is selling out," see comm, Mac to Ivan Pillay (for Tambo) (26 Apr 89) []maharaj/vula comms/1989/[] Apr 26 parts 1 to 3; Apr 27 parts 4 to 8. The account, interestingly, suggests that not many in the MDM leadership were willing to give Mandela the benefit of the doubt; on the contrary, they jumped to the conclusion that the document meant he was selling out. Convincing them that he had *not* sold out required a lot more effort. It also illustrates the hold Govan Mbeki had on the MDM. Instructions coming from Govan were seen as orders that had to be followed because Govan, to MDM leaders, was the head of the ANC in South Africa. With some frustration, Mac reports to Tambo (4.8.6.): "On reflection Diana [Valli Moosa] stated that she saw how the steps they had been instructed to take by Kqalema may cause serious problems but that, given that these instructions were coming from Rachel [Govan Mbeki], people like Diana could not intervene with Rachel." Mac to Slovo and Tambo []maharaj/vula comms/1989/[]April 27, part 8.

10. Tambo to Mac (2 May 89) []maharaj/vula comms/1989/[] May 2.

11. See Part six of Mac to Ivan Pillay (for Tambo) 27 April 89 []maharaj/vula comms/1989/[] April 27.

12. Tambo to Mac (2 May 89) []maharaj/vula comms/1989/[] May 2 "Report to GM."

13. Ibid.

14. []maharaj/interviewees/ [] Ismail Ayob/October 24, 2002.

15. Mandela, at this point, believed that Ismail Ayob was under surveillance by the authorities and that having him carry out messages, other than those that might be conveyed in the container, had become problematic. See Appendix, section B, p. 505.

16. Source embargoed until 2030.

17. The text of the message Govan Mbeki sent to Tambo representing "the collective views" of the circle that had seen the Mandela memorandum. Mac to Tambo (27 April 89) []maharaj/vula comms/1989/[] Part five.

18. Alphons (Tambo) to Tony (Mac) (2 May 89) []maharaj/vula comms/1989/[] May 2 (3 of 4).

19. Tambo's handwritten response to Mac written in November 1988 in the author's possession.

20. Tambo to Mac (12 Dec 88): "A secure line (Madiba-Reggie-Madiba) is welcome." []maharaj/vula comms/1988/[] Dec 12; Mac to Tambo 26 April 89, in which Mac discussed Mandela's mind-set, how conscious he was of being bugged, and how he was going about making him receptive to using a secure way to communicate with Tambo; Tambo to Mac on 2 May 89: "Re comms with Madiba: There are two central questions: firstly, exactly how you would ensure & be certain the enemy was not picking up the disclosure of your response to M. Secondly, how would you demonstrate to M the operation of the secret line & ensure that in the process the enemy is permanently kept unaware. In regard to the disclosure to P per se, we think this would be good news for him provided he's made aware of the deep secrecy of your presence." []maharaj/vula comms/1989/[] May 2, 2/4.

21. Mac to Ken [Jenkin] (9 May 89): "Like book containers, can you send with J some more plus variations? Want to use one to reach Madiba (so it better be good)!" []maharaj/vula communications/1989/[] May 3 (resend).

22. For Mac's account of Ayob communicating to Mandela that he [Mac] was in South Africa and wanted to communicate, see Mac to Tambo []maharaj/vula comms/1989/[] May 25; / Mac to Tambo and Slovo (29 May 89) includes Mandela's first message carried out in a book with a concealed compartment (container) by Ayob, picked up by Momo, received by Mac, and transmitted to Lusaka (Ndima).

15. Out of South Africa

1. "Report to GM" included in Tambo to Mac []maharaj/vula comms/1989/[] May 2, 2/4 and 3/4.

2. See New York Principles July 1988, http://www.c-r.org/accord/ang/accord15/c03.shtml. Upon acceptance of these principles by Angola, Cuba, and South Africa, a number of bilateral and tripartite agreements resulted, including one calling for the withdrawal of all South African forces from Angola by September 1988, the closing of ANC camps and withdrawal of MK cadres at the same time, and an agreement between Angola and Cuba calling for the phased withdrawal of Cuban troops.

3. Tony (Mac) and Isabel (Nyanda) from Alphons (Tambo) at []maharaj/vula comms/1989/[] May 17, 1 of 9.

4. Mac and Nyanda from Tambo, May 17, 5 of 9.

5. Ibid.

6. Ibid.

7. Ibid. In July 1987, an ANC memorandum prepared for the NEC outlined the steps being taken by the USA, the UK, and West Germany to facilitate a negotiated settlement. "We presume," the memorandum noted, "that these powers are preparing this initiative with the Pretoria regime." ("Pointers towards an Initiative Aimed at Imposing Negotiations on the ANC," 23 July 1987, document E22, Mayibuye Archives, University of the Western Cape. A year later the South African government, Cuba, the USSR, and Angola negotiated the future of Namibia without involving SWAPO. Tambo was determined that a similar situation would not arise with respect to the future of South Africa. See Luli Callinicos, *Oliver Tambo: Beyond the Engeli Mountains* (Cape Town: David Philip, 2004), pp. 604–6. Ironically, on the government side, Niel Barnard was as vehement at ensuring that negotiations would involve just South Africans with no role for outside mediators. []o'malley interviews/[] Niel Barnard, 17 September 1996, of 23rd November 1999/[]. In October 1988, after the New York Accords, which settled the future of Namibia, were signed, Joe Slovo raised similar concerns, endorsed by Thabo Mbeki, that a diplomatic offensive was afoot to pressure the ANC into a negotiated settlement. In Slovo's words, "The ANC was being surrounded in a diplomatic offensive . . ." See [] maharaj/documents and reports/ANC NWC/1988[] Meeting of

NWC on October 4. In June 1989, the ANC distributed a discussion paper on the issue of negotiations in which it asserts that "all manner of forces, both within our country and internationally, will be taking various initiatives on the issue of negotiations." The tone of the document resonates with paranoia: the apartheid regime, taking advantage of the changing international climate, is trying to grab the moral high ground, using Margaret Thatcher as its stalking horse. Outsiders will try to set the parameters of negotiations, pressure the ANC. Hence, "We must treat the issue of negotiations as . . . struggle by other means." Go to [] maharaj/documents and reports/ANC/1989/[] ANC Discussion Paper on the Issue of Negotiations June 16 1989.

8. Mac to Tambo and Slovo []maharaj/vula comms/1989/[]/May 31.

9. Tambo and Slovo to Mac for G Mbeki and Harry Gwala []maharaj/vula comms/1989/[] May 31.

10. Tambo and Slovo to Mac []maharaj/vula comms/1989/[] June 5, first of three messages.

11. Tambo and Slovo to Mac []maharaj/vula comms/1989/[] June 16, 1 of 7.

12. Ibid., 2 of 7.

13. See Appendix A, pp. 501–5.

14. See comm A & J (Tambo & Slovo) to Tony (Mac) on 16 June 1989: "Tony is asked to get the document to the following individuals: Govan and Omar, Valli and Murphy, Cyril and Sydney & FC [Frank Chikane]. Pls also get a copy to Madiba if it can be done safely. And of course Tony" at [] maharaj/ vula comms/1989/[] June 16 (2/7). See also Janet (Slovo) to Tony (Mac) 17 June 1989: "Alphons [Tambo] would like feedback on negotiation proposals if possible by not later than June 24. Slovo to Mac at [] maharaj /vula comms/1989/[] June 17.

15. Ibid., special note from Janet [Slovo] 3 of 7. See also endnotes 7 and 42.

16. Mac to Tambo and Slovo []maharaj/vula comms/1988/[] June 23/ comments by Syd.

17. Tambo to Mac and Nyanda []maharaj/vula comms/1988/[] May 17, 5/9; Callinicos, p. 602.

18. Tambo and Slovo to Mac []maharaj/vula comms/1988/[] May 24 part 1, which includes a comm from Sophitshi [Mandela]. See Appendix, Section A, pp. 501–5.

19. F. W. de Klerk, *The Last Trek*, pp. 136–48.

20. []maharaj/family/interviews/[] Zarina/ 15 and 22 August 2004; see also Zarina Maharaj, *Dancing to a Different Rhythm*, pp. 156–61.

21. Zarina interviews 15/22 August 2004.

22. From Elsa [Zarina], dictated, included in Tambo and Slovo to Mac [] maharaj/vula comms/1989/[] June 4.

23. [] maharaj/family/correspondence/ Mac to Elsa [Zarina] []maharaj/vula comms/1989/[] June 4.

24. Ibid.

25. Pete [Ivan] Pillay to Carl [Nyanda] (9 Dec 89): []maharaj/vula comms/1989/[] 9 Dec.

26. In June 1989 the NP published its five-year plan, its manifesto for the September elections. Black leaders rejected the plan but it signified important shifts in the NP's positions. It did envisage negotiations with black South Africans and did offer a one person one vote for everyone within five years. The NP was now thinking in terms of a federal dispensation that would ensure that there would be no domination of any one group by another. See "NP Announces Its Five Year Plan," *Citizen*, 29 June 1989; "Scrap Apartheid, Say Black Leaders," *Star*, 30 June 1989.

27. []maharaj/ documents and reports/ANC NWC/1989 /[] October: Special National Working Committee (NWC) meeting 13 October 1989.

28. []maharaj/ documents and reports /ANC/1989/[] Extended President's Committee meeting 9 October 1989.

29. NWC Meeting 13 October 1989.

30. See []maharaj/documents and reports/ 1989/ANC NEC/[] Resumed Meeting of NEC 27 October. Thabo Mbeki's meeting with "Afrikaner intellectuals" was first raised at the NWC meeting on 22 February 1988 with Chris Hani demanding to know on whose authority Mbeki had entered into discussions. ("It is very disturbing that a member of the NEC leaves to have discussion with Afrikaner intellectuals without prior consultation with NWC or at least PMC. I cannot understand why the NWC and PMC were not apprised. Anyone who goes to such a meeting should be delegated by the movement." The minutes note that there "was general acclamation of approval of these remarks.") At a meeting of NWC on 8 September 1988, Thabo Mbeki refers to the report he had already given on the October 1987 meeting with the Afrikaners and that reports of 1988 meetings were outstanding but were being consolidated into a single report for presentation to the NWC. Chris Hani attended this meeting. Given that the NWC was aware of at least some of the substance of the meetings, its sense of being left out of the loop, expressed in October 20, 1989, is a little difficult to fathom.

The minutes of the meeting of 22 February are revealing. Members do not recall either discussion documents/policy papers circulated at previous meetings, of decisions taken, of the cumbersome machinery of the decision-making process, of the propensity of some NEC members to go off on their own ways without "prior consultation" of the accuracy of the minutes of NEC/NWC meetings, etc. Tambo was not present at this meeting. Zuma was but said nothing. It is not clear whether nonattending NEC/NWC members read the minutes of meetings they did not attend, hence of decisions taken. See [] maharaj/documents and reports/ANC NWC/1988/[] February 22. See also [] maharaj/documents and reports/ANC NWC 1988/[] March 9; October 20.

31. []maharaj/ documents and reports/1989/ANC NWC/[] Special Meeting of the NWC on 15 October.

32. Ibid.

33. []maharaj/documents and reports/ANC NWC/1989[] Reconvened Meeting of the NEC 27 October 1989.

34. Ibid.

35. Ibid.

36. Ibid.

37. []maharaj/documents and reports/ANC NWC/ 1989 [] October.

38. []maharaj/ documents and reports/ ANC NEC/ 1989/[] Resumed meeting of the NEC 27 October 1989.

39. Pete [Ivan] to Carl [Nyanda] (9 Dec 89) []maharaj/vula comms/1989/[] Dec 9.

40. According to Elinor Sisulu, "Within days of [Walter Sisulu's] release the ANC set up an internal leadership core headed by Walter, Mandela (still in prison at the time), Govan Mbeki, Raymond Mhlaba and Mac Maharaj" (Sisulu, p. 402). The core she refers to was established in Stockholm in February 1990.

41. Carl [Nyanda] to Norman [Nzo] & Kay [Slovo] (October 2) []maharaj/vula comms/1989/[] Oct 2: "Since the departure of Comrade Theo there have been no significant developments infrastructurally." For Nyanda's Vula report, go to []maharaj/ vula comms/1989/[] October 16.

42. After the September elections, the pressure on De Klerk from all quarters to engage in negotiations increased—from the United States, the United Kingdom, big business in South Africa, the UN, and the EC. See "FW Told Business Can Help Create Negotiation Climate," Business Day, 13 November 1989; "SA Is Not Moving Fast Enough—EC," Star, 11 December 1989; "Group Areas Act Is Negotiable, Says Viljoen," Star, 8 December 1989; "Talks About Talks," Business Day, 14 December 1989.

43. Carl (Nyanda) from Pete (Ivan)[]maharaj/vula comms/1989/[]/Nov 29: "Hi, Theo—re-entry targeted for +- 23/1/90. Please prepare ff: #Rendezvous point.# Bleeper numbers #Codes to trigger meeting."

44. Slovo to Mac: [] maharaj/vula comms/1989/[] April 2; Tambo to Mac []maharaj/vula comms/1989/[]May 2, and 4/4.

45. See Anthony Sampson, Mandela: The Authorized Biography, pp. 377–78 for an overview of Tambo's apprehensions and the paranoia in Lusaka on the issue of whether Mandela was "selling out."

46. See, for example, the minutes of the NWC of the NEC on 2 May 1989. The report for the meeting was prepared by Chris Hani, then head of MK. He alludes to the pressure on the ANC coming from the West, to "academics and individuals [in the USSR] Foreign Affairs Ministry [declaring] in favour of a negotiated settlement in South Africa." They argued that "the regime had come out on top in South Africa and the MDM is exhausted and burnt out. These views have had an effect on the membership, some of whom believe we are preparing for negotiations." Shubin, The View From Moscow, p. 352. Shubin argued: "Hani's argument did not mean he was against negotiations, but he and apparently the majority of the ANC leaders thought that the time had not yet come. They argued that the ANC would need to be stronger before negotiations. The underground had to be strengthened, training inside SA had to be intensified, and the penetration of cadres from outside had to be increased. An overriding concern of the meeting was: 'We need to reassure people that we are not selling out.' " Op. cit., pp. 352–53.

47. On 22 March 89, Zarina sent a comm saying that she understood from Slovo that he been asked to consider taking a break. Mac [Tony] replies to Tambo and Slovo, "Appreciate your concern re Tony's safety but (and it's difficult when we have to also consider matters such as Elsa & co) the work is at such a formative stage, the complicated questions of logistics of getting out and coming back and the timing thereof lead the two of us to feel that Tony cannot leave at the moment. The solutions to so many issues are so much at a formative stage. Maybe you shld apply your minds to how we shld reinforce our legends." []maharaj/vula comms/1989/[] March 21 Part Two (c).

48. See []maharaj/family/interviews/[] Zarina 22 and 27 August 2004 for Zarina Maharaj's account of what she considered very inconsiderate treatment on the part of Joe Slovo. It is clear from my interviews with Zarina that she did not have a particularly high regard for Slovo.

49. Tambo attended a special meeting of the NEC on 8 August 1989 to discuss the Declaration of the OAU Ad Hoc Committee on Southern Africa. For his report to the NWC see [] maharaj/documents and reports/ANC NWC/1989/[] Special Meeting of the NWC on 8 August. Following the meeting Tambo suffered a debilitating stroke that essentially sidelined him from further participation in the forthcoming events that culminated in the settlement that brought democracy to South Africa.

50. While the NEC enthusiastically approved Mandela's memorandum to P. W. Botha and wanted to distribute it to a number of regional leaders (with Mandela's consent), it had two concerns: one regarding his proposition that negotiations be preceded by meetings between the ANC and the South African government to work out the preconditions for a proper climate for negotiations and the second about his concerns about white fears. See Appendix, Section C, pp. 508–11.

51. For details regarding Mandela's negotiations with the government over their release, see Appendix, Section D, pp. 511–15 and Section E, pp. 515–16.

52. Kasrils's name as a possible NEC member who would join Vula was first raised in November 1988. When Kasrils became chief of Military Intelligence, that seemed to be the end of the matter. However, when Mac met with Tambo and Slovo in June 1989, the latter agreed to have Kasrils join Mac, the intention being that Kasrils would take over the running of the Durban area while Mac would concentrate his activities in Jo'burg. It took another ten months before Kasrils set foot in South Africa, in which the political scene had been turned on its head. The ANC was unbanned, Mandela free, the first meeting between the South African government and the ANC about to take place.

53. []maharaj/family/interviews/[]Zarina Maharaj.

54. Walter and the other Rivonia Trialists were released on 15 October 1989. Sisulu was informed of there being "senior comrades" in the country and of the existence of the comm system, which he was urged to use to communicate with Lusaka. Slovo sent a message of congratulations on his release through the system to Sisulu. Slovo and Nzo to Carl (Nyanda) for forwarding to Sisulu (24 October 89) []maharaj/vula comms/1989/[] October 24.

55. Some South African newspapers referred to the ANC being run as a triumvirate: Alfred Nzo, Thabo Mbeki, and Thomas Nkobi (treasurer); and there was also some speculation about Thabo Mbeki succeeding Tambo. See *Business Day*, 8 January 1990.

56. For details of the leadership arrangements access Slovo to Mac (27 Feb 90) []maharaj/vula comms/1990/[] February 27 (3).

16. Transitions

1. Comm (20 Oct 88): Mac to Tambo and Slovo [] maharaj/vula comms/1988/ [] Oct 20; Comm (28 Oct 88) Tambo to Mac: [] maharaj/ vula comms/1988/[] Oct 28; Comm Mac to Slovo (1 Nov 88): [] maharaj/vula comms/1988/[] Nov 1.

2. At Mandela's request, De Klerk met with Mandela on 13 Dec 1989 to discuss the document "A Document to Create a Climate of Understanding," which had been forwarded to De Klerk on 12 December. See Appendix, Section F, pp. 521–26.

3. See []post transition/ TRC/report of the truth and reconciliation commission/ Vol 3/Chapter 6/ paras 530–34; for extended note, go to []maharaj/ endnotes/chapter 16/[]3.

4. See Special NEC meeting 14–16 February 1990 at [] maharaj/documents and reports/ANC NEC/1990/[] February 14–16. The minutes summarize Mbeki's report on his meeting in the UK with "a group of Afrikaners" led by Willie Esterhuyse the weekend of Mandela's release (10–11 February). According to Thabo Mbeki, the group conveyed to him that its canvassing of opinion in high places led it to believe that "the government finally recognized they had to deal with the ANC for a solution; that the Nats accept that in maximum 5 years they will not be the ruling party (possibly disappear). They consider this a decisive break, psychologically & very important." (Confirmed by Willie Estherhuyse in conversation with the author 21 June 2006.) See "ANC to Send Team for Talks with FW," *Star*, 17 February 1990.

5. These possibilities were discussed at the 15 February 1990 NEC meeting.

6. For a comprehensive overview of the violence in KZN between 1990 and elections in April 1994, go to []general information/violence/countrywide [] scroll to TRC extract "Political Violence in the 90s period of transition" (Truth and Reconciliation Commission Report Vol. 2 Chapter 7); for an overview of KZN, go to [] general information/violence/ kwazulu/natal [], which addresses the activities of IFP members given training by the SADF in Caprivi. And to Jeffery, pp. 691–92, 696–97.

7. Even as the violence worsened, the ANC, especially within South Africa, remained opposed to Mandela meeting with Buthelezi. It would not countenance action that would "elevate Gatsha," putting Inkatha on a par with the ANC. See [] maharaj/documents and reports /ANC NWC/1990/[] April 3. For the ANC's analysis of where things stood in mid-1990, go to [] maharaj/documents and reports/ANC/1990/[]Natal—Violence: Assessment of Forces. (Mandela's position regarding Buthelezi was opposite to the ANC's. When the issue of his possible

release first surfaced in November 1988, there were a number of exchanges between Mac and Tambo and Slovo as to how to proceed if he was released. On the question of meeting with Buthelezi, Tambo informed Mac that "having given him a thorough briefing, we should leave him to handle matter as he deems fit, for this is a matter on which he feels very strongly—he believes that it is wrong not to meet GB." See []maharaj/vula comms/1988/[]Nov 17 (4).

8. []General information/violence/countrywide [] scroll to "The Third Force."

9. [] pre-transition/ the apartheid state/[].

10. De Klerk, pp. 162–63.

11. See, for example, "Minority Rights or Majority Rule? The Choice for a New South Africa," *Sunday Tribune*, 13 May 1990; Ken Owen, "Cry Out Against the Tyranny of the Majority," *Business Day*, 21 May 1990.

12. A survey conducted in the latter part of 1990 found that "the overwhelming majority of blacks, Coloureds, Asians and whites felt that State President de Klerk was doing a good job." Paper delivered by Research Surveys at the 12th South African Marketing Research Association (SAMRA). See *Saturday Star*, 20 October 1990. Polling throughout 1991 continued to buttress this conclusion with some polls (June 1991) showing that in terms of political party preference 29 percent supported the NP, 4 percent the CP, and 29 percent the ANC. Among Africans support for the ANC hovered around 50 percent. Even among Africans, majorities believed that De Klerk was trustworthy and doing a good job, his leadership was admired. (*Information Update*, published by the Group for Information Dynamics of the Human Sciences Research Council [HSRC], Pretoria 1991.) See [] maharaj/documents and reports/ other/[] Information Update. De Klerk believed that he could cobble together a coalition of parties—Inkatha and other Homeland parties—and win a majority of seats in a parliamentary election. At the NP Congress held in Bloemfontein in September 1991 he told attendees that the NP had "drastically" increased its support base because the party had opened its membership to all races. "NP will be in majority," *Business Day*, 5 September 1991. In *Anatomy of a Miracle* (p. 203) Patti Waldmeir recounts a meeting De Klerk, she, and fellow journalists had following the stalemate at CODESA in May 1992 where he expressed confidence that he could get over 50 percent of the vote by leading an anti-ANC coalition.

13. Comm (27 Feb. 1990), Slovo to Mac at []maharaj/vula comms/1990/[] Feb 27.

14. Comm (24 Feb. 1990), Mac to Slovo at []maharaj/vula comms/1990/[] Feb 24.

15. Comm, 16 June 1989, Mac to Slovo at [] maharaj/vula comms/1989/[] June 16: "Confidentially HG who leaves this week has been playing a pretty destructive role in many parts of the country on a host of issues. I hope you folks bear this in mind in your discussions." Comm, Slovo to Mac (17 June), at []maharaj/vula comms/1989/[] June 17: "It would be useful if you provided details on HG's negative role. On which issues?" Comm Mac to Slovo (21 June) at []maharaj/vula comms/1989/[] June 21: "Am caught in a hectic cycle of attending to immediate work, trying to ensure that everything keeps on track while absent. HG etc will

have to wait until I get out." The TRC found that Gwala was party to gross violations of human rights. Go to []post transition/TRC/report of the truth and reconciliation commission/Vol 3/Chapter 3/[] paras 161–62.

16. Kay (Slovo) to Theo (Mac) (27 Feb 90) []maharaj/vula comms/1990/[] Feb 27.

17. Ibid. See also NEC minutes [] maharaj/documents and reports/ANC NEC/
90/[] February 15.

18. [] maharaj/ documents and reports/ANC NEC/1990/June 23.

19. Comm, Mac to Slovo (20 April 90), at [] maharaj/vula comms/1990/[]
Apr 20.

20. []maharaj/interviews/ September 5, 2002, December 11, 2002, September
23, 2003.

21. Text of Groote Schuur Minute available at []transition/ documents and
reports /1990/[] Groote Schuur Minute.

22. [] maharaj/documents and reports/ANC NEC/1989/[]; []maharaj/
documents and reports/ANC NWC/ 1989/[].

23. [] maharaj/documents and reports/ANC NEC/ 1990/[]; []maharaj/
documents and reports/ANC NWC/ 1990/[].

24. See []maharaj/documents and reports/SACP/1990/[] other/SACP analysis
of ANC, May 1990. (Go to 2.1 "ANC Regional Presence," forwarded by Mac to
Jean (Kasrils) and Marsha (Billy Nair) on 4 May 1990. The document also includes a sobering SACP self-analysis that draws attention to many of the structural and political factors that would contribute to the hemorrhaging of the
party's influence in the 1990s.

25. "Mass action has not been tied together into a combined thrust against
apartheid power because the activists are not fully grasping the character and demands of the present situation. . . . The masses have not been present in the
process leading to negotiations. . . . The leadership is often perceived by the people as always telling them what not to do. . . . The calls for discipline need to be
contextualized . . . the role of the activist layer is crucial." And "we need to take
immediate steps to reduce the bureaucratised, commandist way in which the organization has been set up. . . ." Go to [] maharaj/documents and reports/
ANC/1990/ [] Political Report for Presentation to Joint NEC/ILC meeting,
June 20. The report also outlines the ANC's understanding of De Klerk's strategic
situation, acknowledges that he could be sidelined—no reason for supporting
him. The report sounds a caution: "It is essential to have the masses with us." Two
years later when the massacre at Boipatong occurred, it took its cue from the
masses and broke off negotiations with the government.

26. [] maharaj/documents and reports/ ANC NEC/ 1990/[]June 23.

27. [] maharaj/ documents and reports/ANC/ 1990/[] ANC/ILC meeting June 20.

28. "The problem at HQ centres around our inability to implement the original
plan that was set out in the document 'Building the ANC Legally.' " [] maharaj/
documents and reports/ANC /1990/[]ANC-ILC Meeting, June 20 access "Building the ANC Legally" at Carl [Nyanda] & Theo [Mac] from Pete [Ivan Pillay] at
[]maharaj/vula comms/1990/[] 8 March.

29. See ANC-ILC meeting, June 20, point 14. "The ILC is charged with the task of setting up branches, recruitment, etc., but there is no programme of action. Therefore we are doing this in a vacuum. Every meeting we call for a new strategy, failing to look at the previous drawn up and adopted one."

30. See Carl (Nyanda) to Theo (Mac) two reports: from Jackie on establishment of ANC branch, Overport, Sydenham, Asherville, Clare Estate, Pantal Hills, Springfield; from Brenda on KwaMashu (included in file date 20 June 1990/ [] maharaj/ vula comms/ 1990/[] June 20).

31. See comm, Theo (Mac), Urgent message to HQ, 15 March 1990 at [] maharaj/vula comms/ANC/1990/[] March 15.

32. See [] maharaj [] ANC NEC/ 1990/NEC Meeting, February 15 see comm. Pete (Pillay) to Theo (Mac) at [] maharaj/vula comms/1990/[]June 1/. This comm. includes a report from "Sam" via Rory forwarded to Pillay for Mac. The report provides a vivid description of the travails besetting the coordinating committee and confronting the Communist Party or the movement in general in the opening months of 1990, after the unbanning. Things were done and decisions made on an ad hoc basis. Trevor Manuel, then a party member and minister of finance (1999–), was only told "at 11 am on the day of the meeting that he would be part of Mandela's delegation that would meet with De Klerk at 4.00 pm to discuss the shootings at Sebokeng, leaving no time to meet with the rest of the delegation to strategize for the meeting." Cheryl Carolus, another prominent UDF leader and party member, only learned through the media that "she had been included in the team to meet de Klerk's government on May 2 [sic]" [the Groote Schuur meeting on 4 May 1990]. She didn't know why she was included or what was expected of her.

See also Main Points of Discussion at the Extended NEC Meeting of 12 & 14 September 1990 at [] maharaj/documents and reports/ANC NEC/1990/ [] ". . . the point was made that we need to look at ourselves very frankly. The best evident characteristic of our work is that we drag our feet and do not implement decisions. This is unfortunately our style of work. We must pull ourselves together and act with speed. A loss of confidence in the ANC is taking place and must be stemmed."

33. "Despite participation in discussions of the last few days, lack of clarity of where we are in relation to the whole issue of negotiations"; "When one asks comrades at NEC how we judge and access the stage we are at, no one really seems to understand." [] maharaj/ documents and reports/ANC NEC/ 1990/ June 23.

34. See [] maharaj/documents and reports/ANC/1990/[] Consultative Office Meeting, October 11.

35. Mosiuoa (Patrick) "Terror" Lekota was appointed by the ILC to organize the ANC in the southern Natal region. Lekota refused to integrate members of the underground into the leadership on the grounds that it was not part of his mandate. This caused friction between Lekota, Mac, and Billy Nair and necessitated a meeting with Walter Sisulu to straighten things out. See comms: Theo (Mac) to Carl (Nyanda), Marsha (Billy Nair), and Daniels (Ronnie Kasrils) on 20 April

1990 at []maharaj/vula comms/1990/[] April 20; Jean (Kasrils) from Theo (Mac) on 21 April, Daniels (Kasrils) to Theo (Mac) 21 April and Daniels to Theo 4 May. See also "Establishment of ANC Branch in Overport etc." and enclosed "Meeting of the Task Force," included in Carl (Nyanda) to Suzy (Janet Love) 29 June 1990. Despite the problems he had with Lekota, minister of defense (2001–) and national chairperson of the ANC (2001–), Mac recommended him as someone who should be considered for the chair/convenor of the central organizational committee "despite substantial complaints about the position he is taking at the moment and the way in which he is going about establishing the Southern Natal ILC but in the belief that he is basically good and in the proper collective would develop his potential." See Theo (Mac) to Norman (Alfred) Nzo and Kay (Slovo) 20 April 1990 at []maharaj/vula comms/1990/[] April 20.

36. Interview Ismail Momoniat []maharaj/interviewees/ (embargoed until 2030).

37. Mac interview with Howard Barrell, 1990 [] maharaj/vula/ other/ [] Barrell interviews/. Mac: "I think there is a fundamental tension between JS and myself, a fundamental tension both at the personality level and at the approach level—and the fact that they had got somebody appointed to the IRD who would just be a . . . Barrell: Soft option? Mac: He's going to be a quiet [inaudible]—leave him there. Barrell: They misjudged you Mac! I think they had that problem very badly."

38. Ibid.

39. Comm, Mac to Nyanda (18 June 1990) at [] maharaj/vula comms/1990/[] June 18; see Nyanda's response to Mac at June 19 and Mac's rejoinder at June 20.

40. For some of the Tongaat papers, go to [] maharaj/ documents and reports/SACP/1990/Tongaat/papers/[].

41. Conversations with the author February 2006.

42. On 25 January 1990, weeks before the ANC and SACP were unbanned and his own imminent release announced, Mandela issued a statement from Victor Verster to rebut what UDF spokesperson Terror Lekota called "innuendo in the media that he [Mandela] had revised his position on a policy formulated in the Freedom Charter." Mandela's statement read: "The nationalization of the mines, banks, and monopoly industries is the policy of the ANC and a change or modification of our views in this regard is inconceivable. Black economic empowerment is a goal that we fully support and encourage, but in our situation state control of certain sectors of the economy is unavoidable." *Business Day*, 26 January 1990.

43. For text of Mandela remarks in Cape Town on 11 February 1990, go to []maharaj/documents and reports/other/[]; Mandela's remarks in Cape Town on 11 February 1990; in *Long Walk*, p. 494, Mandela ruefully observes, "And then in words that came back to haunt me, I called Mr. De Klerk 'a man of integrity.' These words were flung back at me many times when Mr. De Klerk seemed not to live up to them."

44. In 1989, the ANC found itself trying to manage the increasingly erratic and dangerous behavior of Winnie Mandela, who had become a law unto herself in certain areas of Soweto. Her "bodyguards," the Football Club, were little more than thugs and sowed mayhem and fear in the community. They certainly wouldn't

have been able to get away with their activities had it not been for the patronage and association with Winnie. But with the death of Stompie Seipei, and Winnie's apparent involvement, the community's patience gave out. The situation became, in Mac's word, "explosive." The Crisis Committee, which had been trying to get a grip on things, stepped out of the picture. Sydney Mufamadi and Frank Chikane stepped in. There were a series of communications between Mac and Tambo, with Mac feeding Tambo advice, and Tambo, in turn, feeding it back to Mufamadi and Chikane. Tambo tried repeatedly to get Winnie to disband the Football Club. When the MDM publicly disassociated itself from her and harshly condemned her activities, all the ingredients were there to provoke a split in the MDM and put Mandela in an extremely awkward position. In Mac's view, the ANC should seek to broaden the blame for the Football Club's activities, somehow find a peg to point the finger at the government. The ANC could not support the MDM's position. Otherwise, the situation would place Mandela in the untenable position of having to choose to defend his wife or side with the movement, a potential disconnection that the government would seek to use for its own purposes. No matter what action the ANC took, it had to ensure that it did not end up aligning itself with the SAP (South African Police) in the event of SAP investigation into Stompie's death and possible charges against Winnie. See comms, []maharaj/vula comms/1989/[] 13 Feb, 14 Feb, and 25 Feb. (2) Slovo to Mac: "Alphons [Tambo] is in constant contact with Winnie, emphasing the matters you [Mac] mention re statements, football club etc. We'll raise with Alphons the question of resuscitating the Crisis Ctee to speak on behalf of the family etc." See Fred Bridgland, *Katiza's Journey: Beneath the Surface of South Africa's Shame* (London: Sidgwick & Jackson, 1997); Anne Marie du Preez Bezdrob, *Winnie Mandela: A Life* (Cape Town, Zebra Press, 2004), pp. 222–29, 253–55, 256–61.

45. Extract from comm (19 May 90) from Mac to Billy Nair, Ronnie Kasrils, and Nyanda: "Kay [Joe Slovo] also stated that there was recognition at HQ that the work of organising the ANC was proceeding in an unsatisfactory way." [] maharaj/vula comms/1990/[] May 19, part 5.

46. See "Notes of Meeting 'PMC Working Committee' with M [Murphy Morobe] and V [Valli Moosa]" in comm, Slovo to Mac []maharaj/vula comms/1989/[] 11 Feb: "There is a serious crisis of leadership within the MDM as a whole; current leadership not capable of working out strategic direction; no forum for strategizing; lack of cohesiveness; only responding to crises; there is urgent need to find answers to the fundamental question of lifting MDM from state of unconscious existence. The UDF in particular is plagued by many weaknesses. . . ."

47. Throughout the struggle, cases of where the lack of clear lines of command or personality difference or lack of accountability plagued the ANC. One example, from the files of the ANC's National Intelligence and Security, "Security Reports on Individuals," is contained in the Report of Mathabatha Peter Sexwale on his resignation from ANC. The report is undated. Sexwale chronicles the animosity between Chris Hani and Lehlohonolo Moloi; the two were in charge of the ANC underground structures in Lesotho. Relations between the two men became

so bitter that cadres rallied to one or the other and those aligned to one would not take orders from the other. The result, says Sexwale, was that "conflicts in the region remained almost perpetual. . . . []maharaj/documents and reports/other/undated/[] Mathabatha Peter Sexwale.

48. The IPC submitted a document to the NEC in April 1990, "Building the ANC Underground." It called for "an underground which is continuously expanding and expanding all the time," "a massive recruitment drive for MK"; "[an] underground [that] must have the capacity to provide the organizational fallback in a situation where the legal activity of the ANC is threatened or even stopped." And "only one leadership body for the entire underground." For "a leadership that would fall under the leadership of the NEC and . . . the leader of the underground to be a member of the NEC." Among its tasks "the building of a strong and effective army, under an MK general staff." In conclusion it posed a question: "When we are legal, how are we going to justify the existence of an active underground?" Go to [] maharaj/documents and reports/ANC/1990/[] IPC u/g document.

49. Slovo, unbeknownst to the IPC, sent a copy of the IPC paper to Mac, and Mac in turn sent copies to Kasrils and Nair on 24 April 1990.

50. On 5 May [sic] 1990, Kasrils forwarded both Billy Nair's and his response to Mac. Nair stressed that "we must not make the mistake of leaving the building of our underground revolutionary forces in the hands of MK; that we must learn from the mistakes of the attacks on the Wimpy bar targets; that there must be firm political control which can only be exercised on the ground by the u/g." Kasrils argued for much more than an insurance policy. He regarded an insurance policy as a "passive" concept. In his view: "We must steadfastly avoid a situation where we feel everything and all things are dependent on negotiations. A strategy which encompasses the uprising perspective means that we must have a strong u/g machinery which has an active rather than a passive 'reserve' function." See Kasrils to Mac []maharaj/vula comms/1990/[] May 4 "Comments on Building the ANC u/g—IPC Document." What is clear is that in the first half of 1990, negotiations were clearly seen as one more front in the struggle, a fifth pillar that complemented the other four. The weight accorded to each would be determined by the "balance of forces" at a given time and strategic objectives. The memorandum dated 12 June 1990 addressed to "Chief" but unsigned provides a number of insights into the difficulties the underground had in finding its place in the new environment and the apparent lack of leadership coming from the top echelons of the ANC in the matter. This memorandum was written while Mac and Kasrils were both out of the counry so that they could resurface legally.

51. [] maharaj/ documents and reports/ ANC/1990/ ILC/ANC meeting June 20; Mac to Nyanda and Kasrils []maharaj/vula comms/1990/[] June 24 and 26.

52. For Mac's most open perspective on Slovo go to his interview with Howard Barrell in November 1990; it was a period when Mac was "out in the cold" and relatively uninhibited in what he said. Barrell's interviews with Mac can be found at [] maharaj/ vula/other/[] Barrell interviews.

53. Search "Operation Eagle." www.omalley.co.2a.

54. []maharaj/documents and reports/SACP/1990/[]Tongaat/papers/ Mac's opening remarks.

55. Ibid. / Joe's [Nyanda's] paper at []maharaj/documents and reports/SACP/ 1990/[] Tongaat/papers/ Joe's [Nyanda's] paper.

56. Mac's paper at [] maharaj/ documents and reports/SACP/1990/[] Tongaat/ papers/ Mac's paper.

57. For press statement at prelaunch press conference, go to []maharaj/ documents and reports/SACP/[] 1990/other/prerelease statement.

58. Mac interviews on December 12, 2002 (2), September 24, 2003, June 18/21, 2005 at maharaj/interviews/[].

59. For Kasrils's account of this meeting, go to []maharaj/interviewees/.

17. Vula Unravels

1. Ronnie Kasrils, *Armed and Dangerous*, pp. 324–34; "Red Pimpernel, I won't give up," *Sunday Star*, 9 December 1990.

2. Jimmy Taylor was a colonel in the SB whose specialty was intelligence analysis. Early in 1990 he had come across an article in the *African Communist* (first quarter 1990) written by Tebogo Kgope entitled "A Single Spark Can Start a Forest Fire." After Nyanda was arrested, Taylor was called in to assist in the investigation. In the course of their conversation on people's war, Nyanda, according to Taylor, uttered words to the effect that "a single spark can start a forest fire," immediately allowing Taylor to identify him as Kgope, much, he says, to Nyanda's surprise. The SB subsequently found a sniper weapon in a secret compartment of the car Nyanda was driving at the time of his arrest. After they decoded the comm of 24 June 1990 from Mac to Nyanda with its allusion to the rifle, which two members were supposed to use to assassinate Mandela, the SB jumped to the conclusion that Mac, Zuma, and Nyanda were involved in a plot to use the weapon to assassinate Mandela and blame the assassination on the government, thus providing the spark for mass insurrection and seizure of power. The SB duly told their superiors, who informed De Klerk. See [] maharaj/interviewees/[] Jimmy Taylor, 17 May 2005, Major General HD Stadler; *The Other Side of the Story*, pp. 90–98; Chapter 12, "Dirty Tricks: Our Turn."

3. See for example, "Mandela: Plot Claim an Insult," *Citizen*, 30 July 1990; "Maggie Dragged into 'Red Plot' Row," *Sunday Star*, 29 July 1990: "The discovery of the plot has placed a great strain on the peace process and could also cost the ANC-SACP alliance dearly. Observers say Mandela could suffer damage to his credibility unless he condemns it." "Police Analysing SACP Plot Info," *Sowetan*, 30 July 1990; "Reds in the Open," *Citizen*, 31 July 1990.

4. The paper presented at Tongaat by Nyanda was titled "Path to Power: Aspects from the Program in Relation to Our Strategies for Obtaining Power in the Current Situation." Discussion introduced by Comrade Joe. The paper, like all papers at the conference, was not a policy position. For text of the paper, go to [] maharaj/ documents and reports/SACP/Tongaat/papers[] Joe's [Nyanda's] paper.

5. "For a moment the whole negotiation process was in jeopardy." See De Klerk, pp. 200–202. The U.S. embassy sent the State Department a cable recounting a briefing to ambassadors on 24 July by Pik Botha on the secret SACP Tongaat conference and the contents of the documents downloaded from computer disks. Both Joe Slovo and Jacob Zuma, he said, were implicated. In 2005 Hentie Botha, the SAP officer who had arrested Nyanda and was then hot on the trail of others as the decoded computer documents revealed their names, told me that when the order came down to arrest them, the SAP was told not to arrest Jacob Zuma or Joe Slovo. The U.S. cable referred to in 5 also relayed the content of a conversation purportedly between a journalist and Mac on 25 July, the day of his arrest, in which Mac told him that "one of the contingency plans of Vula for triggering a 'national insurrection' called for the assassination of Mandela." The cable was unclassified in 1995. Who the journalist was who worked for the embassy and what his connection to South African intelligence remains a mystery. The U.S. State Department cable is available at []maharaj/documents and reports/other/1990/[] U.S. State Dept. cable on Vula unraveling.

6. On 25 May 1990, on his way out of South Africa, Mac advised Nyanda and Billy Nair on how to write aspects of the report on the Tongaat Conference, which they were preparing for forwarding to HQ in Lusaka. "Personally, I should not use formulations such as insurrection, insurrectionary overthrow. This entire item on the agenda [Nyanda's paper] could be a brief 2–3 paragraph report which should bring out the fact that there is no incompatibility between the pursuit of a negotiated resolution . . . and our pursuit of a strategy based on protracted all-round people's struggle for the transfer of power." Comm (25 May 90) Mac to Kasrils, Nair [Marsha] and Nyanda [Carl] [] maharaj/vula comms/1990/[]/May 25.

7. See recommendations forwarded by the Tongaat Conference to the SACP in Lusaka at []maharaj/ documents and reports/ SACP/1990/ Tongaat/ recommendation of Tongaat Conference.

8. Text of Pretoria minute at [] transition/documents and reports /1990[]. In a press conference after the signing of the minute Mandela said that the suspension of the armed struggle meant that there would be no infiltration of men or arms into South Africa, nor any activity related to military action. See Hassan Ebrahim, *The Soul of the Nation*, note 84, p. 281. Interpretation of the minute became contentious within weeks. See [] maharaj/documents and reports/ ANC NWC/ 1990/ [] ANC National Working Committee Meeting, August 30.

9. "Freedom for 3000 Prisoners by April," *Sunday Star*, 12 August 1990.

10. "Indemnity Under Fire," *Business Day*, 21 August 1990; "ANC Condemns Indemnity Decision" *Daily Mail*, 22 August 1990; "Indemnity Demand Made by ANC," *Business Day*, 22 August 1990; "Maharaj to Be Charged as Probe into Hani Goes On," *Daily Mail*, 23 August 1990. The focus of the indemnity dispute quickly became Hani. He argued that armed actions had been suspended, not armed struggle, and instructed MK cadres to "remain in their trenches." Hassan Ebrahim, *The Soul of a Nation*, note 106, p. 283. "Defiant Hani 'Won't Bow to Pik,' " *Business Day*, 22 August 1990. The minutes of the NWC meeting of 30 August

1990 suggest that Hani was correct. [] maharaj/documents and reports/ ANC NWC/1990/[] Working Committee Meeting August 30.

11. "Government halts release of prisoners," *Saturday Star*, 13 October 1990.

12. "ANC in surprise attack on FW's integrity," *Weekly Mail*, 12–18 October 1990.

13. "ANC may be forced to resume armed struggle," *Star*, 12 October 1990.

14. Within three days of the signing of the Pretoria minute violence had claimed at least twenty-three lives in township violence in Port Elizabeth. John Carlin, "Violence Follows ANC Pact," *Independent* (UK), 10 August 1990. Within a week the violence had spread from the Rand to Sebokeng, Thokoza, Katlehong, Vosloorus, townships about twenty miles south and southeast of Johannesburg where supporters of hostel workers, mostly migrants from KwaZulu who supported the IFP, and township residents, mostly supporters of the ANC, engaged in ferocious attacks on each other. By the end of August the violence had flared in all but three of the fifteen townships that made up the East and West Rand. There were fifty-six hostels in these townships, housing some two hundred thousand migrant workers. Some complexes could house twenty-nine thousand workers in eighty single-bed dormitories. Living conditions were primitive. See *Sowetan*, 24 August 1990. O'Malley interview with hostel dwellers at [] o'malley interviews/ search Thokoza residents; Thokoza hostel residents, Abraham Mzizi, Gertrude Mzizi. The media reported the violence as primarily ethnic—Zulu-speaking hostel workers supporting Buthelezi and the IFP pitted against Xhosa-speaking township residents supporting the ANC. See Alan Cowell, "140 Blacks Slain in South Africa as Factions Clash," *New York Times*, 16 August 1990; "Death Toll Is now 510," *Citizen*, 23 August 1990; Alan Cowell, "Thousands in South Africa Protest Ethnic Violence," *New York Times*, 18 August 1990; Allister Sparks, "Natal's Violence Spreads to Other Areas of South Africa," *Washington Post*, 19 August 1990; Roger Thurow, "South African Political Violence Assuming Look of Tribal Violence," *Washington Post*, 20 August 1990; John Carlin, "Pretoria Talks Under Threat After a Week of Ethnic Violence," *Independent*, 20 August 1990; "A Frightened Voice from the Centre of Violence," *Weekly Mail*, 24–26 August 1990; "Soweto's Killingfields," *Weekly Mail*, 24–26 August 1990; Hermann Giliomee, "Explaining the Slaughter," *The Star*, 24 August 1990; *Weekly Mail*, 7–13 December 1990, "3,400 die in SA Violence," *The Star*, December 14, 1990; "Roots of the Reef War," *New Nation*, 24–30 August 1990; "With Darkness Come the Zulus," *Weekly Mail*, 7–13 December 1990; Alan Cowell, "100 More Die as Rival South African Blacks Fight," *New York Times*, 23 August 1990; Alan Fine, "Thokoza Reveals the Chilling Depths of Hatred," *Business Day*, 4 December 1990; "What Really Happened at Phola Park," *Weekly Mail*, 7–13 December 1990.

15. See Main Points of Discussion at the Extended NEC Meeting of 12 and 14 September 1990 at [] maharaj/documents and reports/ ANC NEC/1990/[]. The ANC was rattled by the violence and how to respond. "There was a serious crisis of confidence developing and people were publicly tearing up their membership cards. The enemy was having some success in discrediting the ANC and the whole negotiating process." The ANC's committee on violence was not "functioning

properly," the violence was the cornerstone of the two-pronged policy (to negotiate with the ANC and simultaneously work to undermine it) Buthelezi was working for the government. "Extensive discussion was held on the recommendation
by the Deputy President (Mandela) that we suspend the talks."

Mandela was quoted in the *Citizen* on 12 September 1990 as saying that
"the government could not conduct negotiations and wage war against the people
at the same time," and on 18 September the *Citizen* reported, "ANC may quit
talks: Mandela." On 8 October Mandela handed affidavits to De Klerk supporting
his assertions that elements of the security forces were behind much of the violence. "Mandela Names the Third Force," *Sunday Star*, 7 October 1990.

16. Between 1990 and 1994, political violence claimed approximately 15,000
lives in contrast with 3,500 lives between 1984 and 1989. [] post transition/ TRC/
report of the truth and reconciliation commission/ Vol 3/chapter 6/ paras 526–76;
author interviews with Benny Alexander, Strini Moodley, Mangosuthu Buthelezi,
Barney Desai: go to []o'malley/interviews[].

17. The degree of animosity and suspicion some senior members of the ANC
harbored against the PAC is apparent from the minutes of an NWC in November
1986. See [] maharaj/ documents and reports/ ANC NWC/1986/[] November 17.

18. Alan Cowell, "Pretoria's Force Impose Tense Peace in Towns," *New York
Times*, 26 August 1990; "Police Cordon Off Kagiso Hostels to Separate Warring
Parties," *Business Day*, 24 August 1990.

19. The Human Rights Commission (HRC) estimated that between July 1990
and June 1993, there were a total of 3,653 deaths in KwaZulu-Natal. Between July
1993 and April 1994, conflict steadily intensified, so that by election month it was
two and a half times its previous levels. In the PWV (Pretoria-Witwatersrand-
Vereeniging) region in the Transvaal, the HRC estimated that between July 1990
and June 1993, 4,756 people were killed in politically related violence. In the period immediately following the announcement of an election date (May 1993),
the death toll in the PWV region rose to four times its previous levels. The TRC
report stated that "the escalation of violence coincided with the establishment of
Inkatha as a national political party, the Inkatha Freedom Party (IFP), in July
1990, and its attempts to develop a political base in the Transvaal. The development of self-defence units (SDUs) in largely ANC/UDF strongholds led to an escalation of violence in both provinces. Many came to believe that a 'hidden hand'
or 'third force' lay behind the random violence, which included military-style attacks on trains, drive-by shootings and a series of massacres and assassinations.
The train violence swept the Rand from 1990 onwards. By June 1993 it had caused
some 400 deaths and countless more injuries, and left thousands of commuters
consumed with fear on a daily basis. Such attacks frequently generated further
violence." Go to [] post transition/ TRC/ report of the truth and reconciliation
commission/ Vol 2/ Chapter 7/[] paras 7–11; [] general information/violence/
countrywide/ []. Of the 9,042 statements received by the TRC on killings, 5,695
occurred during the period 1990–1994.

20. NEC meeting 12 and 14 September 1990 at [] maharaj/ documents and

reports/ ANC NEC/ 1990/ [] Main Points of Discussion at Extended NEC meeting 12 and 14 September.

21. "Inquiry into Police Role," *New Nation*, 24–30 August 1990.

22. NEC meeting 12 and 14 September 1990 [] maharaj/documents and reports/ ANC NEC/1990 [].

23. De Klerk, pp. 187–88, 197–204; "Mandela . . . somewhat disingenuously [denied] that Operation Vula constituted a double agenda on the part of the ANC. On the contrary he said that it strengthened the negotiations rather than undermined them" (p. 201). "Alleged ANC/SACP Plot a Breach of Trust—Pik," *Citizen*, 16 August 1990.

24. "1990 most violent year in SA history, says Prof," *Citizen*, 26 October 1990; "Reef Death Toll Now Exceeds 1976 Unrest," *Star*, 24 August 1990; "3,460 die in SA violence," *Star*, 14 December 1990.

25. "Thokoza attacks: Were they policemen or not?" *Weekly Mail*, 7–13 December 1990.

26. "Mandela Now Doubts De Klerk," *New Nation*, 12–18 October 1990; "Talks in Danger, Says Slovo," *City Press*, 9 December 1990.

27. John Carlin, "Slaughter to Make Liberals Fear Botha Was Right," *Independent*, 21 August 1990.

28. We have a probable security problem at hand. Francis [Charles Ndaba] has been missing since the weekend. David [Vusi Tshabalala] also did not turn up for a meeting on Monday. He may have been with Francis on some task weekend. Nobody knows what their exact program was. Carl [Nyanda] to Lara [Mac] [] maharaj/vula comms/1990/[] July 11.

29. [] post transition/ TRC/amnesty hearings/assassinations/2002/[].

30. See author interview with Siphiwe Nyanda (Gebuza) on 27 October 2001 for his account of his arrest and torture. []maharaj/interviewees/[].

31. "ANC Secret Cell Shock," *Sunday Times*, 22 July 1990; "Red Plot Allegations Denied by SACP's Slovo," *Natal Witness*, 24 July 1990; "Communist Plot's Secret Plan Revealed," *Daily News*, 26 July 1990; "More Talks About Slovo," *Natal Witness*, 28 July 1990.

32. De Klerk and Mandela met on 26 July, the day after Mac's arrest, to discuss the report the SB had prepared alleging that there was a plot within the ANC's military wing, Umkhonto we Sizwe, to seize power. The report was based on what the police had uncovered in the unencrypted Vula communications. For varying interpretations of the meeting: "There Was No Plot," *Star*, 25 July 1990; "Gov't and the ANC Confident That Obstacles to Talks Will Be Swept Away," *Business Day*, 26 July 1990; David Ottaway, "De Klerk, Mandela Meet Over Allegations of ANC Uprising Plot," *Washington Post*, 27 July 1990, and "Opposition's Arms Buildup Hinders Search for Accord in South Africa," *Washington Post*, 1 August 1990.

33. "ANC Secret Cell Shock," *Sunday Times*, 22 July 1990; " 'Red Plot' Allegations Denied by SACP's Slovo," *Natal Witness*, 24 July 1990; "Communist Plot's Secret Plan Revealed," *Daily News*, 26 July 1990; "More Talks about Slovo," *Natal Witness*, 28 July 1990.

34. "ANC Stands by Red Joe," *Sunday Times*, 29 July 1990; "Mandela Will Insist on Slovo for Vital Talks," *Natal Mercury*, 1 August 1990; Mandela, at his own request, met with De Klerk again on 1 August and reported afterward that the meeting was very cordial: "I made an undertaking that I personally, together with the NEC, will do whatever we can do to ensure strict adherence to the Groote Schuur Minute." "Talks Will Go on and Joe Slovo Will Be There," *Business Day*, 2 August 1990; "Mandela and De Klerk Conciliatory after Talks," *Natal Witness*, 2 August 1990; "FW Did Not Demand Slovo Be Excluded, Says Mandela," *Sowetan*, 2 August 1990.

35. On 13 August, at an ANC meeting in Johannesburg attended by about four hundred members, Pallo Jordan, then head of information for the ANC, urged ANC supporters to be ready "to take to the streets" in support of the demand to free Mac and other Vula operatives held under the Internal Security Act, *Daily Mail*, 14 August 1990.

18. Vula on Trial

1. See pages 290–91. See also Maj.-Gen. H. D. Stadler, *The Other Side of the Story* (Pretoria: Sigma Press, 1997), pp. 90–98.

2. Interviews, all at [] maharaj/ interviewees/ 2000–2005: Christo Davidson (2000–1), Peter Blomkamp (2003), Yak Yacoob (2004), Catherine Mvelase (2003), Ivan Pillay (2002), Janet Love (2002–1), (February 2002–1, March 2002, 2004, 2005).

3. Interview Christo Davidson at []maharaj/interviewees/ 2002/2005.

4. Transcript of Siphiwe Nyanda's court hearing at [] maharaj/ vula other/[] Nyanda: court transcript, 1990.

5. "Dramatic Court Evidence on Vula Operation," *Natal Witness*, 23 August 1990; "Court Hears of Foreign Funds for Operation Vula," *Natal Mercury*, 23 August 1990; "Nyanda or Moosa or O'Reily or More," *Natal Witness*, 24 August 1990; "Nyanda: A Master of Disguise," *Daily News*, 25 August 1990; "Court Told of Cloak and Dagger Tactics," *Sunday Tribune*, 26 August 1990.

6. After it was announced that Mac and seven others would be charged, the ANC released a statement on 18 October 1990 saying that the government and the ANC had reached an agreement on 7 October in Cape Town that political offenders implicated in acts committed before 8 October would be granted immunity from prosecution. *Natal Witness*, 19 October 1990.

7. See, for example, Waldmeir, p. 81.

8. See Mac interviews, 25 September 2003, 19 August 2004, 24 April 2005, 12 June 2005.

9. "SACP 'Smeared,' Claims Joe Slovo," *Sunday Times*, 4 November 1990; "Court Told of Secret Operation Vula Plans," *Post*, 31 October–3 November 1990; "Hunt for 7 ANC Moles," *Sunday Times*, 4 November 1990; "The Vula Dossier," *Sunday Times*, Special Report, 4 November 1990; "Operation Vula: Eight Charged with Planning to Seize Power," *Daily Dispatch*, 30 October 1990; "Raised Fists Greet Vula Trialists," *Natal Mercury*, 30 October 1990.

10. Even when the NEC was a "little" informed about Vula—with no mention

of who was involved—it failed to elicit a groundswell of support. After Nyanda sent Slovo a Vula Report (16 October 1989) in which he complained about how the remit of Vula was being undercut by lack of resources, especially lack of personnel (see [] maharaj/vula /other [] October 16: Vula Report), Slovo responded in some detail, setting about the genesis of Vula and cataloguing the delays in getting things started—Mac was supposed to have been in South Africa six months after the operation was agreed; instead it took two years—and the difficulties in acquiring resources and personnel for a clandestine operation. The first report back the NEC received on Vula was in early October 1989. Slovo: "For security reasons, the President decided to make no reports to the NEC on the progress of the project. It was only six weeks ago [Slovo was writing on 25 November] that it was judged timeous to make such a report in general terms. This unavoidable delay infected the response of key individuals to our needs. At the NEC meeting, Kay (Slovo) made the point that the process of getting help was like drawing teeth. As you know narrow competitiveness in the politics of exile structures doesn't lose its tenacity overnight." Kay (Slovo) to Carl (Nyanda) 25 October 1989 at []maharaj/vula comms/1989/[] October 25, and Nyanda's response of October 26.

11. Zarina Maharaj, *Dancing to a Different Rhythm*, p. 22. Mac identified the official as Mendi Msimang, the ANC chief representative in London, ANC treasurer general (2001–). See [] maharaj/interviews/2003/[] September 15.

12. On 17 December 1990, Essop Pahad said: "In June this year, Comrade Mac informed both the ANC and the SACP that he intended to retire in the middle of December. He had indicated to us that his retirement was related to personal reasons. But everybody knows that Comrade Mac is not very well." *Natal Witness*, December 18, 1990. When I brought this statement to Mac's attention, he had one comment: "Essop was neither in the Politburo nor the NEC; where he got his 'facts' from one can only guess."

Alfred Nzo, ANC secretary-general, said that the ANC had previously been informed of Mac's decision to retire, but his resignation had not been confirmed. "We have heard of the news but we have not seen or spoken to Maharaj himself. Before the ANC can make any comment, it is crucial that we speak to Comrade Maharaj in person." Ibid.

Following his retirement, the ANC had to refute on a number of occasions that Mac had "retired" because "the organization had failed to secure his release when detained in connection with Operation Vula," as had been reported. The "who" in "as has been reported" was never identified in accounts. See *Business Day*, 18 December 1990. In its account of his retirement the *Star* put the word "retired" in quotation marks, again suggesting that he was doing it in a bout of pique and was not to be taken seriously. His subsequent "unretirement" gave credence to these interpretations of his actions and less credence to his denials. "Mac Maharaj Retires from the ANC," *Star*, 18 December 2003. During the events leading up to the Hefer Commission in 2003, the media also tended not to believe his accounts of events; there was always the niggling belief that he was hiding something, playing to a different agenda (see Chapter 20).

Mac's retirement was perceived as a setback to ANC militants by the newly emerged crop of "political analysts," still unconvinced by any explanation of Vula that did not support the "Red Plot" thesis. The ANC Consultative Conference the previous week was seen as a "resounding victory for hardliners at the expense of pragmatists within the organization." Following the conference, the ANC had suspended the joint working group between the ANC and the government and set 30 April as the deadline for the government to meet certain conditions. For a report of consultative conference go to []maharaj/documents and reports/ANC/1990/[].

19. Into the New South Africa

1. For full text, go to []transition/documents and reports/1991/[] D. F. Malan Accord.

2. For "Advance to National Democracy: Guidelines on Strategy and Tactics of the ANC," go to [] maharaj/documents and reports/ANC/1991/[].

3. For perspectives on the negotiations' process and the "miracle" of the new South Africa, see Allister Sparks, *Tomorrow Is Another Country*; Patti Waldmeir, *Anatomy of a Miracle*; Heribert Adam et al., *Comrades in Business*; Patrick Bond, *Elite Transition*; Hassen Ebrahim, *The Soul of the Nation*; Richard Spitz et al., *The Politics of Transition*. See also []transition/[] and o'malley interviews 1990–1996.

4. Joe Slovo quoted in *Sunday Times*, 19 May 1991.

5. Interviews at []o'malley interviews/ Mangosuthu Buthelezi.

6. Interviews at []o'malley/interviews/ F. W. de Klerk.

7. At a meeting in early April 1991, the NEC discussed what Joe Slovo, speaking on behalf of the President's Committee, called the ANC's "gravest crisis since February 1990." Mandela bluntly told members that the lack of response of the ANC to the violence was having devastating repercussions among its supporters. There was a perception, Joe Slovo said, that the ANC was "so hooked into negotiations that all we will do is issue condemnatory statements but we go on with the process." This had created a "gap between the leadership and the people." "To put it bluntly," said Mandela, "our problem is whether we should continue talking to the government in the light of the crisis facing us." See [] maharaj/documents and reports/ ANC NEC/1991[]April 4: National Executive Committee.

8. Interviews at []o'malley/interviews/Walter Sisulu.

9. Interviews at []o'malley/interviews/Cyril Ramaphosa.

10. The meeting on 20–21 December 1991 resulted in sixteen of the nineteen parties signing the Declaration of Intent, which committed them to the principles of a nonracial, multiparty democracy in which the constitution would be supreme and regular elections were guaranteed. The IFP and the governments of the "independent states" Ciskei and Bophuthatswana did not sign because the declaration's reference to the word *undivided* to describe South Africa seemed to rule out a federal option. See Declaration of Intent at []/transition/documents and reports/1991[].

11. To review documents and reports relating to the structure of CODESA, its objectives, decision-making mechanisms, participants, composition and terms of references, reports of its working groups, and an analysis of how and why it broke down, go to []transition/constitution making/CODESA/[]Reports and Agreements/.

12. For text of the Record of Understanding, go to [] transition/documents and reports/1992/[].

13. Although the TRC found that there was police collusion in the massacre at Boipatong, its conclusions are incorrect. There was no investigation by the TRC into the massacre. The TRC findings were an almost verbatim repetition of a pamphlet published within days of the massacre by an NGO considered highly biased in favor of the ANC. In their applications for amnesty the KwaMadala hostel dwellers arrested for the atrocity said there had been no police involvement, which jeopardized the granting of amnesty because had they been found not to have been telling the truth, they would not have received amnesty. The TRC findings were published while their applications were pending. Despite the TRC findings, the applicants stuck with their sworn statements, and after extensive hearings the Amnesty Committee found in their favor. My own research supports the position that there was no police involvement.

For a comprehensive review of all investigations and analyses relating to Boipatong, TRC findings, my interviews with both police investigators, TRC investigators, Boipatong residents, and others, go to []/transition/events during transition []. For the Boipatong amnesty applications and hearings, go to []post transition/TRC/amnesty hearings/[] Boipatong.

14. See Anthony Sampson, *Mandela: The Authorized Biography* (New York: Alfred Knopf, 1999), pp. 454–55.

15. For the memoranda: Mandela to De Klerk, 26 June 1992; De Klerk to Mandela, 2 July 1992, and Mandela to De Klerk, 9 July 1992, go to []transition/documents and reports/1992/[].

16. Interviews at [] o'malley/interviews/ Roelf Meyer.

17. The ANC's march to Bisho, capital of the Ciskei, took place on 7 September 1992. The ANC was demanding the resignation of Brigadier Oupa Gqozo (then military ruler of Ciskei), and free political activity in Ciskei was part of this campaign. Ciskei Defense Force (CDF) soldiers opened fire on the march, killing twenty-nine ANC supporters and one CDF soldier. At least two hundred CDF soldiers and seventy thousand to eighty thousand ANC supporters were involved. Prominent ANC leaders who were part of the march included Chris Hani, Ronnie Kasrils, and Cyril Ramaphosa. The TRC found that Brigadier Oupa Gqozo and three generals of the CDF committed gross violations of human rights. It also found that the actions of the Alliance contributed to the incident. Interviews with Gqozo at []o'malley/interviews/ Gqozo. See also []transition/ events during transition/[] Bisho.

18. Buthelezi was quoted in the *Financial Times* on 11 August 1990 as saying that bilateral relations between the ANC and the NP were "a threat to democracy." "Buthelezi out of Talks," *Citizen*, 28 September 1992; "Buthelezi Rejects Overtures," *Business Day*, 29 September 1992; Patrick Laurence, "IFP out to Match

Mandela," *Star*, 30 September 1992; "Fury of a Zulu Chief Scorned," *Sunday Times*, 4 October 1992; "South Africa: Gatsha's Last Stand," *Africa Confidential*, 23 October 1992; "Buthelezi Threatens to Form a New State," *Financial Times*, 2 December 1990. When I interviewed him in 1993, I asked him what was the one thing he would die for. His response was "a federal state." []o'malley/interviews/ Mangosuthu Buthelezi/1993.

19. As a starting point, the MPNP adopted the reports of the working groups that reached consensus in their deliberations in CODESA. Negotiations were intense. Between 1 April and 17 November 1993 the Negotiating Council met on seventy-four occasions. The structures of the MPNP are available at []/transition/ Constitution Making/ MPNP/ documents and reports.

20. See []/transition/constitution making/ MPNP/[].

21. For the text of the Interim Constitution, go to []/ transition/ constitution making/[].

22. The five volumes of the TRC Report, including the background to the enabling legislation setting up the commission (Volume 1, Chapter 1) are available at []/post transition/TRC/ report of the truth and reconciliation commission/. For commentary on the TRC and critiques of its methodologies and findings, go to []/ post transition/TRC/TRC reports/ commentary[]. The TRC also provides an excellent overview of the conflict. This is available at []/post transition/ TRC/ report of the truth and reconciliation commission/ Vol 2/[]Chapter 1.

23. For an overview of the Transitional Executive Council (TEC)—structure, composition, and functions—go to [] transition/Transitional Executive Council (TEC)/[].

24. Interviews at []o'malley/interviews/Lucas Mangope.

25. For an overview of the events that led to the overthrow of Lucas Mangope and interviews with the various role players, go to []transition/events during transition/ collapse of Bophuthatswana/[]. Fanie van der Merwe, who was in Mac's presence for virtually the entire period of the crisis, confirms the main facts of Mac's account of the fall. Ramaphosa also confirms Mac's accounts of the event. For Mac's account of the fall of Bop, go to []maharaj/interviews/[]2000; for Ramaphosa's go to []maharaj/interviewees/2000/[]; Fanie van der Merwe's account is embargoed until 2030. For other accounts that differ in some respects or take issue with aspects of Mac's account go to George Meiring (2000), General Constand Viljoen (2000), and Pik Botha (2000).

26. Interviews at []o'malley/interviews/[]Constand Viljoen.

27. Interviews at []o'malley/interviews/[]Eugène Terre'Blanche. See, too, "Police Report Says AWB Has 15,000 in Commandos," *Citizen*, 25 September 1992.

28. Interviews at [] o'malley/interviews/[]George Meiring.

29. For details regarding the supply of weapons to Camp Mlaba, go to [] post transition/TRC/report of the truth and reconciliation commission/ Vol. 2/Chapter 7[] paras 100–123.

30. Conversation with Fanie van der Merwe, 3 August 2006.

31. E-mail from Cyril Ramaphosa, 27 July, 2006.

32. When Mac announced that he would not stand for parliament again, he frequently found himself in the position of having to deny that he was doing so because he would not serve in a Mbeki government due to friction between himself and Mbeki. See Alan Fine, "Maharaj Decides to Put His Family First: Conflict with Mbeki Not the Reason," *Business Day*, 18 November 1998.

33. For *Reflections in Prison*, go to [] pre transition/ the struggle/ [].

34. "Deadlock at Talks," *Citizen*, 24 September 1992.

35. "The Government regards as 'atrocious and morally inexcusable' many of the crimes committed by the prisoners it is releasing . . ." in "Crimes Atrocious, But Slate Must Be Wiped Clean," *Star*, 28 September 1992; "Amnesty applies to all affiliations," *Star*, 28 September 1992; "Amnesty to Go Ahead, Says FW," *Star*, 28 September 1992.

36. The issues relating to phasing out the hostels, banning the use of cultural weapons, and the release of political prisoners bedeviled negotiations from the onset. For an excellent free-ranging discussion of how the ANC viewed the state of negotiations, especially in regard to these issues, its assessment of the sincerity of De Klerk and his commitment to negotiations and how the ANC should pursue its strategic objectives, go to [] maharaj/ documents and reports/ ANC NEC/1991[] Extended NEC Meeting, May 17.

Mandela's assessment: "Is De Klerk honest about negotiations? This is a relevant point, but we must not forget that firstly when we made the point that this is a man of integrity, we also added that what is important in formulating our strategy is not the honesty of the individual, but the policy of the party represented, and that there was no change in the policy of the NP, which should determine our strategy. If De Klerk is not committed to negotiations, we must make him committed. We are succeeding in this. We are forcing the government on all these issues." The Record of Understanding, agreed in September 1992, represented that point of commitment by De Klerk.

For the TRC's documentation of the violence emanating from the hostels, go to [] general information/organizations/Inkatha Freedom Party/ General/ KwaZulu [] scroll to paras 281–88. I was a frequent visitor to the hostels in Thokoza from 1990 through the elections in 1994. The hostel dwellers were all Zulu. They believed that the Xhosa-speaking ANC was determined to destroy the Zulu nation. That in any new dispensation they would be forced to submit to Xhosa hegemony. Repeated interviews with the hostel dwellers and IFP members Abraham and Gertrude Mzizi all reiterated the same points over and over. When fencing was placed around the hostels on Buthelezi Street, the hostel dwellers were outraged. This was a fundamental insult to their dignity. They were caged in like animals. They had as much regard for De Klerk and the NP as they had for the ANC. For interviews relating to perceptions of the roots of the violence from an IFP perspective, go to [] o'malley/interviews/[] Thokoza interview (1995), Thokoza hostels (1990), Gavin Woods (1991, 1992), Musa Zondi (1991), Harriet Ngubane (1992), Musa Myena (1992, 1994, 1995), Themba Khoza (1992, 1993, 1994), Abraham & Gertrude Mzizi (1992 [3]).

37. See Frederik van Zyl Slabbert, "Will Mandela's Writ Run?" *Star*, 24 September 1992, for an overview of the challenges from within his own ranks facing Mandela as he embarked on the summit with De Klerk. "Nelson Mandela," he writes, "finds himself in a lonely spot. Over the next few weeks history will begin to shape its judgment of him as a leader." Within two months of the signing of the Record of Understanding, the Goldstone Commission seized five files from an operations unit of military intelligence that elicited the first direct evidence of the existence of a Third Force orchestrating much of the violence. See "The Goldstone Raid: Violence—the Rot and the Cure," *Star*, 17 November 1992, for the text of the statement released by the Goldstone Commission. See also Ken Owen, "NP's Evil Past Stalks a Battered De Klerk," *Sunday Times*, 22 November 1992; "Ominous Signs," *Business Day*, 24 November 1992.

38. Interviews at []/o'malley/interviews/[]Hernus Kriel.

39. Interviews at []/o'malley interviews/[]Leon Wessels and author's profile of Wessels, "Leon Wessels: The Good Boer," at /[]padraig o'malley/o'malley writings on South Africa []. In "The Good Boer," Wessels comes across as a liberal NP leader, then deputy minister of foreign affairs, who was seduced by Mandela's graciousness to him at the Oslo conference on "The Anatomy of Hate: Resolving Conflict Through Dialogue and Democracy" convened by the Foundation and the Norwegian Nobel Committee in 1990. In his address Wessels spoke to an audience about desiring "real justice in our land," of wanting to "cast off the apartheid albatross." Mandela said in response, "We shall endlessly challenge the infamous seeds of hatred wherever these are found. This is the spirit in which we have come to Oslo. The spirit which has sustained us during the many lonely years of our imprisonment. The spirit which will form the basis of our new society." Indeed, looking at F. W. de Klerk's negotiating team, one is hard put not to conclude that he gave an enormous amount of rope to negotiators who were not too bothered by the prospect of the ANC becoming the country's majority political party and subsequent majority rule.

40. "ANC, Govt Remove Most CODESA Snags," *Citizen*, 28 September 1992.

41. Following the announcement of the agreement between the ANC and the government, Mangosuthu Buthelezi, the IFP leader, said, "The government and the ANC are making deals behind our backs. If this happens, Zulus will not listen. I see at the very least massive civil disobedience in Natal, and at the most civil war. I shudder when I say this, because it is something you do not say lightly. KwaZulu will not disappear. At least not without a bloody fight." Quoted in "These Are the Terms," *Sunday Tribune*, 4 October 1992; "Govt Laws Will Be Rejected," *Star*, 28 September 1992; "Homeland Leaders Reject Govt-ANC Pact," *Star*, 30 September 1992.

42. "Clinching a Tough Deal," *Sunday Star*, 27 September 1992; "De Klerk on a Tightrope," *Sunday Star*, 27 September 1992; Michael Hamlyn, "De Klerk Faces Challenge from Within," *Times*, 31 October 1992.

43. Joe Slovo, "Negotiations: What Room to Compromise," *African Communist*, no. 131, 1992; go to [] /transition/constitution making/CODESA/[]ANC debate/ African Communist/ No. 131. The debate his paper generated is available at the

same place. Interviews at [] o'malley/interviews/[]Joe Slovo. See also *New Nation*, 6–12 November 1992; "Drawn in the Slovo Sunset," *Weekly Mail*, 13–19 November 1992; Jeremy Cronin, "Nothing to Gain from All or Nothing Tactics," *Weekly Mail*, 13–19 November 1992; "ANC Opens Way for Amnesty Talks," *Weekly Mail*, 20–26 November 1992.

44. Kobie Coetsee on amnesty at []o'malley interviews/ 1998/[] Kobie Coetsee/ September 5 (1) & (2); /1999/Kobie Coetsee/ November 6.

45. For text of the last chapter of the Interim Constitution, "National Unity and Reconciliation" (Chapter 16), go to [] maharaj/ documents and reports/ other/ 1993/Interim Constitution: Chapter 16. The first sentence of the penultimate paragraph reads: "In order to advance such reconciliation and reconstruction, amnesty shall be granted in respect of acts, omissions and offenses associated with political objectives and committed in the course of the conflicts of the past." This paragraph was drafted by Mac and Fanie van der Merwe—Mac gives credit to Van der Merwe for doing most of the drafting and for insisting that they insert the word "shall."

46. The Mac and Van der Merwe draft read: "Cabinet shall function in a manner which gives consideration to the consensus seeking spirit underlying the concept of a government of national unity as well as the need for effective unity." It was incorporated into the Interim Constitution as sec 89 (2), Act 200, 1993.

47. Joao Cunas told the Goldstone Commission that an Indian man matching Mac's description and living in his house told him to fabricate a report about hit-squad activity after he denied a story in *Vrye Weekblad* in which he had claimed that he was paid by the police to kill ANC supporters in Natal. During his appearance before the commission, Cunas was evasive, and allegations could not be substantiated. Charlene Smith, "I Know of No Dirty Tricks, Says Mac," *Sunday Times*, 29 November 1992. Mac appeared before the commission on 12 January 1993 and refuted all allegations by Cunas. Goldstone's investigators could find no evidence to back Cunas's claims.

48. See Jacques Pauw, "Bomb Found in My Car, Says ANC Man," *Star*, 12 January 1993. At the commission, Mac revealed that a bomb had been placed in his car in the incident referred to in Chapter 18. "Maharaj Denies Meeting Deserter," *Citizen*, 13 January 1993. See also "AWB Planned to Kill Maharaj," *Star*, 30 January 1993. The ANC alleged that Mac was the target of two AWB members lying in tall grass, one of whom allegedly had a rifle with a telescopic sight, who were found when the AWB disrupted the opening of the ANC's Midrand branch in Noordwyk on 29 January 1993.

49. "Maharaj Denies Ties to 'Boeremafia' Man," *Weekly Mail*, 25 February 1994.

50. Interviews with Johan van der Merwe at []o'malley/interviews/[]; his interview in connection with Mac is embargoed until 2030.

51. Surren Maharaj was arrested on 20 February 1994 during a nationwide police swoop on organized crime. On 20 February, a police spokesman told a news conference that evidence in a bail application in 1993 was that Mac was Surren Maharaj's uncle. *Citizen*, 21 February 1994.

52. Surren Maharaj appeared in court on 7 March 1993 and was charged with

fraud involving R250 million, including trading in illegal weapons and hand grenades. Police Commissioner Johan van der Merwe issued a statement saying that the SAP regretted any embarrassment caused to Mac Maharaj by the SAP's incorrect statement that Surrei Maharaj was related to Mac Maharaj. "Crime Boss Loses Second Bid for Bail," *Business Day*, 8 March 1994.

53. For other incidents of strange goings-on around the Maharaj household during these early years, see Zarina Maharaj, *Dancing to a Different Rhythm*, pp. 171–80.

54. See interview with Randall Howard, secretary-general of the General Transport & Workers Union, on Mac's relationship with the union and on his performance as transport minister. []/maharaj/interviewees/[]Randall Howard.

55. The importance of transport as a key element for creating the infrastructure essential to promoting rapid economic growth was not recognized until the Accelerated and Shared Growth Initiative (ASGI) was launched in late 2005. ASGI replaced GEAR. ASGI was designed to accelerate growth to 6 percent per year. The government committed to spending R165 billion ($27.5 billion) on transport and electricity. In the transport sector, Transnet will drive the investment. For text of GEAR, go to []post transition/documents and reports/1996/[]. For text of ASGI, go to []transformation/ documents and reports/2005[].

20. Back in the Cold

1. Interviews at []o'malley/interviews/Jacob Zuma.

2. The government justified the huge expenditure on the arms deal on the grounds that it would generate 65,000 new jobs. It claimed that local companies, including the state arms manufacturer Denel, would benefit from billions of rand of investment in new technology. Chippie Shaik, the then chief director of procurement for the Department of Defense, is a brother of Shabir, a director of Thomson-CSF, the French arms manufacturer, which was awarded a contract to supply management technology for four corvette patrol vessels for the South African navy. Shabir was also the director of African Defense Systems (ADS), a Thomson-CSF subsidiary, which was involved in the same deal. ADS employed Chippie's wife, Zarina. Nkobi Holdings was a shareholder in ADS. Andrew Feinstein, the ANC cochairman of the parliamentary public accounts (SCOPA) watchdog committee, was fired from his position after he supported calls for an investigation into the arms deal amid allegations that senior ANC members had benefited from kickbacks. On 26 February 2001, three senior government ministers, Trevor Manuel (Finance), Alec Erwin (Trade and Industry), and Jeff Radebe (Public Enterprises), called a press conference to deny that there was any evidence of corruption. They castigated the public accounts committee (Scopa), which was chaired by Gavin Woods, an IFP MP, for being "incompetent and irresponsible and not knowing how the arms deal worked." "Arms Deals Squeaky Clean, Ministers Say," *Mail & Guardian* [online edition], 27 February 2001. The first casualty of the affair was Tony Yengeni, the ANC parliamentary whip with impeccable struggle credentials, who was charged by the Scorpions and subsequently found guilty of having accepted a big discount on a luxury 4×4 Mercedes

Benz. For a detailed narrative of the arms deal and the torturous course of attempts to investigate it, see www.sundaytimes.co.za/special reports/yengeni and www. sundaytimes.co.za/special reports/ zuma.

3. Questions about the arms deal began to surface in 2000. See "Improper Influence Behind Arms Deal Probed," *Mail & Guardian*, 31 October 2000; "Arms Deal: the Shaik Link Deepens," 12 January 2001; "Arms Deal Kingpin Helped Jacob Zuma out of a Money Crisis," 30 March 2001.

4. Interviews at []o'malley/interviews/[]Bulelani Ngcuka.

5. Section 28 of the National Prosecuting Act provides the NPA with extraordinary powers to combat organized criminal syndicates that were threatening to establish a stranglehold over South Africa in the years following the advent of democracy in 1994. Statements under section 28 could not be used as evidence in a court of law against individuals providing them, although they could be used to derive other evidence to substantiated charges being laid.

6. www.sundaytimes.co.za/special reports/zuma.

7. Interview with Ismail Ayob, 7 May 2004.

8. Confirmed by Cyril Ramaphosa, 20 September 2004.

9. "Ramaphosa Steps into Arms Row," *Sunday Times*, 18 July 2003.

10. Verified on 29 July 2006 by Pingla Udit, who worked with Moe Shaik in the NIA updating Operation Bible files.

11. Interviews at []o'malley/interviews/[]Penuell Maduna.

12. Mathatha Tsedu (*Sunday Times*); Jovial Rantao (*Star*); Vusi Mona (*City Press*); Phalane Motale (*Sunday Sun*); Jimmy Seepe (*City Press*); John Dludlu (*Sowetan*); Mondli Makhanya (*Mail & Guardian*).

13. Ayob, 7 May 2004.

14. Documents relating to the Bulelani Ngcuka spy allegations and Hefer Commission, including a copy of the reconstructed RS 452 intelligence file, Vusi Mona's affidavit regarding the editors' meeting, transcript of eTV News Special Report of 16 September 2003, Moe Shaik's and Mac's time line reconstructions of events that resulted in Moe Shaik's publicly "outing" that Ngcuka had been found to have probably been a government spy by his intelligence unit, an extract from Steven Joseph's cross-examination of Ngcuka and Maharaj's final summation before the commission at [] maharaj/ documents and reports/ Hefer Commission/[].

15. Ibid.

16. *Mail & Guardian*, 21 November 2003. For an examination of the media's performance during the Hefer Commission, see Guy Berger, "Media Ethics and the Hefer Commission," in *Balancing Secrecy and Transparency in a Democracy* (Pretoria: South African National Academy of Intelligence, 2004), pp. 103–41. Berger concludes that "South Africa's media overstepped its station during 2003, becoming deeply embroiled in fierce political battles. [It was] a case of questionable actions and various abuses of office by journalists. It was also a case where unethical conduct undercut the role that a free media ought to play in a democracy."

17. [] maharaj/ documents and reports/Hefer Commission/[]Report.

18. After Mac had asked Moe Shaik to "investigate" the leaders of the National Association of Democratic Lawyers (NADEL), with which he wished to make a secure contact, Shaik came back to him to say that Bible had suspicions regarding Bulelani Ngcuka. Mac passed this information to Tambo, and Tambo replied in the course of a communication on 11 December 1988, "All your security info is being passed onto the right quarters. Please give all information re basis of suspicion against Bulelani." Tambo to Mac (11 December 1988) at [] maharaj/vula comms/1988/[] December 11.

19. Mac to Tambo and Slovo (13 Feb 1989) []maharaj/vula comms/1989/ []February 13.

20. Extract of communication from Tambo to Mac on 2 May 1989: "Janet [Slovo] & Alphons [Tambo] were very angry with JZ [Zuma] but wanted to avoid confirming any suspicion he may have had. Ultimately Alphons decided he would confront him. Just then he came to see Alphons to lodge a bitter complaint (see below). He volunteered that he'd been told of Tony's [Mac's] presence by one of his men (see below). It was then put to him that in fact he'd asked his man to confirm such presence. He flatly denied this & wondered where that piece of information came from.

"He went on to say, however, that being aware of earlier plans to put leadership inside (remember he'd started making preparations himself before his name was dropped) he'd become suspicious over Tony's endless treatment. Tony was specifically mentioned in the course of explaining the fact that the Bible was perused by someone outside JZ's outfit & information extracted from it before the Bible reached JZ. There were other instances of the crossing of wires which pointed to the presence of a superior authority & led to Tony being mentioned.

"On the question whether JZ had gone sniffing around, Alphons having heard the above explanation felt relieved. JZ hadn't been irresponsible. He was however bitter when he met Alphons: This was over the FM affair. He'd received information about FM from Janet, & then later, exactly the same information gathered expressly on his instructions being impounded en route by Vula & passed on elsewhere. Unfortunately, earlier, Alphons [Tambo] had received a certain number relating to an agent believed to be Bulelani, &, unaware of the implications, had passed the number to JZ, warning him it might turn out in the Bible. It did but I didn't know this until the day of the complaint when he cited it as an example of interception." Tambo to Mac: [] maharaj/vula comms/1989/[] May 2. (Reply to yours of 28/4/89.)

21. On 20 April 1990, Mac met with Mandela and Alfred Nzo in Johannesburg. The meeting was broad ranging. At one point the issue of security arose. Extract from Vula communication from Mac to Joe Slovo and Alfred Nzo on 20 April 1990: "Several detailed aspects around security questions arose. We also exchanged some views around Bulelani, Peter Mokaba and Maxwell Xulu. . . ." []maharaj/ vula comms/1990/[] April 20(1).

22. Conversation with Shaheen Bawa, 27 July 2006.

23. Conversation with Pingla Udit, 29 July 2006.

24. Joseph Lelyveld, *Move Your Shadow: South Africa, Black and White* (New York: Times Books, 1985), pp. 331–32.

25. Interview with Hentie Botha at [] maharaj/interviewees/ 2005/[].

26. Ibid.

27. []maharaj/interviews/ 2005/[] 6 June.

28. "Re Xulu: Hold your horses!" Tambo to Mac, [] maharaj/vula comms/ 1988/[]Dec. 12, 9c.

29. See []maharaj/interviews/2003/[] January 10 (2) [name of accuser blocked].

30. The SACP wanted to recruit Cyril Ramaphosa and have him on the platform at the relaunch of the party. Cyril, as chief ANC negotiator at the time, would be a prized recruit. But there were rumors within the MDM that he worked for the CIA. Zuma undertook to look into it but there is no record of anything ever happening. Theo (Mac) to Jean (Kasrils), Marsha (Nair), and Carl (Nyanda) at [] maharaj/ vula comms/ 1990/[] April 25.

31. Notes of my conversation with Judge Hefer, 24 March 2006.

32. See *Business Day* editorial, "Mbeki Is Not Alone," 1 September 2005: "The Hefer commission into allegations that Bulelani Ngcuka was an apartheid era spy revealed for all the world to see the blatant lies of the intriguers who tried to frame him." And in the same issue: Xolela Mangcu, "When your world turns into a B-movie, roll with the punches. The people behind that rather pathetic attempt (to tag Ngcuka as an apartheid era spy) were exposed for being gossipmongers of the most dangerous order."

33. *ANC Today*, Letter from the President, 23 January 2004. Go to []maharaj/ documents and reports/Hefer Commission/[].

34. Mac's comms were invariably to both Tambo and Slovo. And, of course, it is clear from Mac's comm of 20 April 1990 to Slovo, after his meeting with Mandela and Nzo, that Slovo also knew. I have also separately verified that Nzo knew. (Source identity embargoed until 2030.)

35. Interview []maharaj/interviewees/[]Penuell Maduna.

36. *ANC Today*, 23 January 2004.

37. William Gumede, *Thabo Mbeki and the Battle for the Soul of the ANC* (Johannesburg: Struik, 2005).

38. Interview with Mac at []maharaj/interviews/[] October 9 (2).

39. For the full judgment, go to []maharaj/documents and reports/Jacob Zuma/ [] Judge Hillary Squires: Judgment in the case of Schabir Shaik.

40. After his dismissal as South Africa's deputy president, following his indictment on charges of corruption, the ANC's NEC accepted Zuma's offer to withdraw from party activities until his corruption trial was over. His offer, it was generally believed, was not made willingly. However, at the ANC's National General Council (NGC) meeting in Pretoria at the beginning of July 2005, delegates demanded that Zuma be reinstated to his positions, and in the face of what amounted to mass action inside the meeting hall, the leadership had to give way

and allow Zuma to reengage in his duties as deputy president of the ANC, member of the NEC, and the NWC. The outcome of the meeting was a humiliation for Mbeki. See S'Thembiso Msomi and Paddy Harper, "Zero to Hero in an Afternoon," *Sunday Times*, 3 July 2005; William Mervin Gumede, "Autocratic Leadership Style Has Returned to Haunt President," *Sunday Independent*, 3 July 2005; Wonder Hlongwa, "Zuma Rides Wave of Support," *City Press*, 3 July 2005.

41. See ANC NEC statement of 21 November 2005 at []maharaj/documents and reports/Jacob Zuma/[] ANC NEC: "There is no conspiracy."

42. The Zuma crisis aside, the state of the ANC, which SG Kgalema Motlanthe reported on, revealed a party at war with itself; at the grassroots with branches that were riven by greed, factionalism, and, in general, organizational chaos. For the full text go to [] www.anc.org.za and search "Motlanthe National General Council." [] See also Karima Brown and Vukani Mde, "Symptoms of a Deeper ANC Rot," *Business Day*, 25 November 2005.

43. Billy Masethla was suspended on 20 October 2005. SABC news later reported that he had been suspended in Mbeki's presence. SABCnews.com, November 15, 2005. He was dismissed by President Mbeki on 22 March 2006. "Mbeki Fired Suspended NIA Boss," SABCnews.com, 22 March 2006.

44. "A picture of a grand conspiracy," *Mail & Guardian*, 15–22 December 2005.

45. See report of inspector general at []maharaj/documents and reports/other/[]. But Kgalema Motlanthe, secretary-general of the ANC, rejected the report (the hoax e-mails also sought to discredit him as well as Zuma) and the ANC set up a task force under the direction of veteran James Stuart to conduct its own investigation. At the time of going to press this task force had not reported back to the NEC.

46. *Sunday Argus*, 26 March 2006. Others whose telephones were being monitored were Mbulelo Goniwe, then ANC chief whip; Smuts Ngonyama, ANC spokesperson; and the offices of the Democratic Alliance, the main opposition party. It is not clear to what degree any of the attempts to monitor conversations on phones was successful.

47. *New York Times*, 10 May 2006.

48. Mac's report to the author of the conversation he had with Motlanthe on 21 August 2004 on the occasion of the launch of Ahmed Kathrada's book, *Memoire*, in Lenasia, the previously apartheid-designated residential area for Indians, outside Johannesburg.

49. The banner legend on page 1 of the *Citizen* on 21 June 2005 read MAC NEXT? And the sub-legend "As Zuma Faces Charges, Shaik Taint also Reaches Out to Touch Maharaj." The July 2005 issue 69 of the investigative magazine *Noseweek* went further: In its "Dear Reader" column, with the legend "We Told You So," it said: (in *Noseweek* 47) " 'Watch this space,' we concluded. Now that it has been announced that charges are to be brought against Maharaj, to our dear friends at First Rand: you can't say we didn't warn you."

50. For Zarina Maharaj's account of the Maharajes' dealings with the NPA and the subsequent fallout, see *Dancing to a Different Rhythm*, pp. 186–91.

51. Relations among the alliance partners began to sour when the ANC, for all practical purposes, ditched the RDP in 1996 and replaced it with Growth Employment and Redistribution (GEAR). GEAR emphasized a free-market economy and fiscal and financial prudence as prerequisites for attracting direct foreign investment (DFI), which was seen as the engine that would drive economic growth. The DFI did not materialize. Relations between the partners worsened in 2002, when Mbeki launched bitter attacks on those within the "broad democratic movement" he characterized as "ultra leftists." By that he meant those who, broadly speaking, opposed GEAR. In 2006, GEAR was replaced with the ASGI (Accelerated and Shared Growth Initiative), which provides for the expenditure of some R400 billion over four years in targeted invested infrastructure, a more robust industrial policy, labor market and regulatory reform, and more emphasis on redistribution to bring the growth rate to six by 2010. For extended endnote, go to [] maharaj/ endnotes/Chapter 20/[]51.

52. Black Economic Empowerment (BEE) is a set of legislative measures to ensure that black South Africans can participate on an equitable basis in the economy in terms of ownership, income sharing, and decision making. Ownership of the economy in 1994 was almost entirely concentrated in the white minority. BEE seeks to rectify that. However, in the first "wave" of empowerment, a small group of former liberation activists with excellent political connections, some members of the ANC NEC, were increasingly perceived as the main beneficiaries, raising questions as to the "broadness" of empowerment. In her article "Black Corporate Ownership: Complex Codes Can Impede," in *Conflict and Governance*, Jenny Cargill writes, "A substantial proportion of labour, left wing and populist organizations see little distinction between corruption and the sometimes dazzling enrichment sponsored by BEE." She concludes that "while BEE ownership answers a strong political need right now, the numbers suggest that if commercial value cannot be injected into the process, the net results could be extremely negative for the economy in the medium to longer term—growth and poverty alleviation could be put at risk." See also Patrick Laurence, "Rising Black Elite Haunts Cosatu," *Star*, 7 Dec 2004. For expanded endnote, [] maharaj/ endnotes/Chapter 20/[]52.

53. Quoted in the *Sunday Times* on 3 August 2003 as referring to Scorpions on 31 July 2003 using "Hollywood theatrics" in some of their operations.

54. On 3 October 2003, Vusi Mona, editor of *City Press*, submitted an affidavit to the Public Protector, the Human Rights Commission, the Constitutional Court and Justice Minister Penuell Maduna setting out the contents of the Ngcuka briefing. His affidavit was supported by a sworn statement from Phalane Motale, editor of the *Sunday Sun*, who had also attended the briefing. (See pages 429–30.) Mona affidavit and certification of Mona's account of "what transpired" at the meeting of black editors on July 24, 2003, by Phalane Motale, then editor of the *Sunday Sun* at [] maharaj/documents and reports/Hefer commission/[] Vusi Mona: affidavit filed on 3 October 2003. At the Hefer Commission Mona was thoroughly discredited as a witness. Hefer dismissed his testimony on the grounds

that "his credibility had been reduced to nil." Yet Mona stuck to the substance of his October 3 statement. Motale was not called as a witness and Ngcuka refused to answer questions relating to the briefing. In his replying affidavit submitted to the Pietermaritzburg High Court on 23 August 2006, Zuma referred to the affidavit Mona had written as evidence that the Ngcuka editors' briefing was an egregious abuse of power. He also referred to Ngcuka's affidavit before the court in his own trial and drew attention to the fact that while Ngcuka flatly denied the allegations in Mona's affidavit he refused to reveal what had been said at the briefing (see pages 429–30). For Zuma's and Ngcuka's affidavits and other documents relating to the Zuma saga, go to []maharaj/ documents and reports/ Jacob Zuma[].

55. Thabo Mbeki, "Foreign Funding and Donor Agendas Tax NGOs as Much as the Government," *Cape Times*, 15 November 2005. His remarks on NGOs were made in the context of criticisms by a number of NGOs of the way in which South Africa was going to submit itself to review under the African Peer Review Mechanism (APRM), a key part of the New Partnership for Africa's Development (NEPAD) process being conducted throughout the continent by the African Union (AU). See also William MacLean, "Changing Africa's Face to Suit Western Ideals," *Southern Africa Report*, 20 September 2005, and Reuters, "Array of Global NGOs Serve Continent's Needs," *Business Day*, 19 October 2005. For extended endnote go to []maharaj/endnotes/chapter 20/[]56.

56. See Bob Amato, "Zuma's Day in Court Will Be the End of a Long, Sorry Saga," *Sunday Independent*, 11 December 2005. "The office of the chief prosecutor," he concludes, "is, seemingly, above any kind of oversight. Perhaps this is the case in other countries."

57. [] maharaj/interviews/2002/[]August 12; see Vicki Robinson, "ANC Move to Scrap Provinces," *Mail & Guardian*, 28 July to 3 August 2006.

21. Family: Struggle and Damage

1. Leo (Slovo) to Tony (Mac) on 14 March 1989 at [] maharaj/vula comms/1989/ [] March 14.

2. Leo (Slovo) to Tony (Mac) on 23 April 1989 at [] maharaj/vula comms/ 1989/[]April 23.

3. Gemma (Zarina) to Tony (Mac) on 4 March 1989 at []maharaj/vula comms/1989/[] March 4.

4. Mac to Ivan Pillay for forwarding to Vladimir Shubin via Oliver Tambo []maharaj/vula comms/ 1989/[] March 4.

5. []maharaj/ family/ [] interviews/Milou.

6. Ibid.

7. []maharaj/family/[]interviews/Joey.

8. []maharaj/family/[]interviews/Zarina, August 27, 2004.

9. Ibid.

10. Ibid.

11. []maharaj/family/[]interviews/Joey.

12. Ibid.

13. For an account of the impact on Joey and Milou of their parents' involvement in Vula, their mother's accident in Lusaka and its aftermath, and the subsequent impact of the allegations of bribery, the Hefer Commission, and the investigations of the Scorpions see Zarina Maharaj, *Dancing to a Different Rhythm* (Cape Town: Struik, 2006), pp. 3–17, 33–38, 160–63, 166–85, 194.

14. []maharaj/family/[]Zarina, August 27, 2004.

15. []maharaj/family[]interviews/Joey.

22. Hush! Apartheid Thoughts of a Different Kind

1. "SACP Blames 'Powerful Presidency' for ANC Ills," *Business Day*, 22 May 2000.

2. "COSATU Sees S. Africa Drift Toward 'Dictatorship,' " *Reuters*, 25 May 2006 at reuters_news@reuters.com.

3. "COSATU Flights Poll Pact with SACP," *Business Day*, 15 June 2006. All three members of the alliance issued discussion documents analyzing the options open to each and the probable consequences of the exercise of these options. For a summary of the respective papers, see *Sunday Times*, 18 June 2006. Documents available at discussion documents of the ANC, SACP, and COSATU at []maharaj/documents and reports/Alliance documents 2006/.

4. Most political commentators agree that whatever the divisions among the partners no imminent split is in the making. S'Thembiso Msomi, "Alliance Split Option Just Noise," *City Press*, 25 June 2006; Christelle Terreblanche, "There's a Bumpy Ride Ahead, but Alliance Will Stay," *Sunday Independent*, 25 June 2006. See also SACP Deputy Secretary-General Jeremy Cronin's remarks to the Cape Town press club in "Cronin: Alliance Split Will Damage SA," *Mail & Guardian Online*, 27 June 2006.

5. Zuma was elected to the Politburo at the party's seventh conference in Havana, Cuba, in April 1989. Mbeki also attended the conference. See Leo (Slovo) to Tony (Mac) at [] maharaj/ vula comms/1989/[] April 23 (A). Pedro is Zuma. Mbeki left the party in 1990. What Zuma did is not known. The meeting of the NEC on 23 June 1990 discussed the question of which members of the ANC leadership should "out" themselves as being members of the SACP when the SACP relaunched itself in South Africa on 29 July 1990. "If we go the full way it will be problematic, but if we do nothing it will also be problematic." []maharaj/ documents and reports/ ANC NEC/1990/[] NEC Meeting, June 23.

6. "Splits in the African National Congress during local elections continue to plague the Durban township of Umlazi, with violent infighting causing at least three deaths," Niren Tolsi in "Violence Plagues KZN Elections," *Mail & Guardian*, 26 May–2 June 2006.

7. For the case of Jeremy Cronin, deputy president of the SACP and a member of the NEC, in an interview with an Irish academic, warned against "Zanu-fication"

of the ANC. He was brought before the ANC's disciplinary committee and reprimanded. He apologized profusely. See []maharaj/endnotes/Chapter 22/[]7.

8. Electoral Reform Task Force (2003) headed by Frederik van Zyl Slabbert. See report at []maharaj/documents and reports/other/[].

9. Judith February, "More Than a Lawmaking Production Line: The Oversight Role of Parliament," in *South Africa 2005–2006: The State of the Nation* (Pretoria: HRSC, 2005). In mid-2006, with the succession "war" again in full swing, the SACP issued a scathing critique of the ANC, charging that Mbeki's presidential style and management were undermining parliament, had usurped the functions of the secretary-general of the ANC, alienated ordinary members from the ANC, and had made it more difficult to cut unemployment and eradicate poverty. The SACP discussion document was debated at the party's Central Committee meeting 24–26 June 1990. Discussion document at [] maharaj/documents and reports/ Alliance documents 2006/SACP/[]. " 'Mbeki Undermining Parliament'—SACP," *Cape Times*, 19 June 2006. See also Nic Dawes, "MPs Seek New Powers," *Mail & Guardian*, 28 July to 3 August 2006: "South Africa's weak and poorly resourced parliament can only find its voice if it is given new powers in the Budget process, and the resources to live up to them, a growing number of MPs and parliamentary officials believe." Of most concern to MPs is their ceremonial role in the budget process. The budget is subject to committee hearings and a final vote, but its components remain the same.

10. In 2005, during the "window of opportunity," fifty-one party members defected to other parties in the National Assembly and the provincial legislatures. In the National Assembly, the ANC gained fourteen members of parliament and in the provinces ten new members. Mpumelelo Mkhabela, "Politics of the Absurd in SA," *City Press*, 18 September 2005. See also Bob Amato, "Why Election Reform Stays Through the Grid," *Focus* 36 2004, Helen Suzman Foundation.

11. At a media briefing on 6 January 2006, ANC deputy secretary general Sankie Mthembi-Mahanyele announced that the ANC had ensured that candidates "with the skills necessary for running local authorities" had been included on its election lists. According to *Business Day*, election lists submitted by the Eastern Cape and KwaZulu-Natal had ignored the criteria set by the party. *Business Day*, 6 January 2006.

12. The Democratic Alliance (DA) won ninety seats, the ANC eighty-one seats, the Independent Democrats (ID) twenty-three seats. Among the smaller parties the African Christian Democratic Party (ACDP) won seven seats, the Muslim Party three seats, the UDM two seats, and the PAC, the United Independent Front (UIF), and the Universal Party (UP) one seat each. After much political maneuvering, the DA, led by Helen Zille, a white woman with impeccable anti-apartheid credentials, cobbled together a coalition made up of all parties other than the ANC and the ID with the PAC abstaining. On the vote for mayor, the PAC abstained, the Independent Democrats, which had campaigned not to form a coalition with any party, voted for the outgoing ANC major, Ms. Nomaindia Mfeketo, and the coalition and one member of the ID voted for Zille. In the opening

months of the new administration, the ANC went to great lengths to try to break the coalition. At one point ANC supporters, encouraged by the local ward councilor, chased Zille out of a ward in Crossroads, a township that is part of the Cape Town metropolitan area. In the by-election for the seat vacated by the renegade member of the ID, who stood as the DA candidate, the DA won the seat, giving the coalition a cushion of two seats. Matters only returned to some semblance of normalcy when the national leadership instructed the provincial structure to ease up. Within months Western Cape provincial Minister of Local Government and Housing Richard Dyanti announced that he intended to change the municipal structure of the city of Cape Town from an executive mayoral system to a collective executive system, which would strip Zille of her executive powers, making her little more than a figurehead. The ANC national leadership sanctioned the action. See "ANC Leaders Give Go-ahead to Council Bid," *Cape Argus*, 10 October 2006; "Defiant Dyanti presses on," *Cape Argus,* 17 October 2006. To forestall what might have become a constitutional issue, Zille and the provincial ANC reached a compromise. Zille's DA-led coalition remains intact while an additional two ANC-headed subcouncils were added to the twenty existing subcouncils, five of which are ANC controlled. "Calm Cape After the Cape Storm," *Mail & Guardian,* November 3–9, 2006. The ANC is confident that come the floor-crossing period in September 2007 it will induce sufficient numbers of coalition councilors to join the ANC and thus regain the city in time to host the World Cup in 2010. (The ANC didn't "win" the previous election in 2001. It became the governing party in Cape Town after the floor-crossing period in September 2002.) See "Cape Town Turmoil: Province Steps In," *Mail & Guardian*, 21–27 April 2006. See also Allister Sparks, "Is Political Power Addictive?" *Star*, 19 April 2006; Rhoda Kadalie, "Moves to Undermine Cape Coalition Bode Ill for SA," *Business Day*, 20 April 2006; Xolela Mangcu, "Absence of Political Competition a Primary Cause of SA's Malaise," *Business Day*, 20 April 2006.

13. The Harrismith disturbances in 2004 and the official response suggest an official leadership out of touch with a wide swath of its electorate. Go to []maharaj/endnotes/Chapter 22/[]13.

14. Interview with Kgalema Motlanthe at []o'malley/interviews/2004/[].

15. Ibid.

16. See [] maharaj/endnotes/Chapter 22/[]16: Mbeki speeches 2002.

17. See []maharaj/endnotes/chapter 20/[]17.

18. For an excellent analysis of the attitudes of whites post-apartheid, see Gerald L'Ange, "Freedom's Fruits," in *The White Africans: From Colonisation to Liberation* (Johannesburg: Jonathan Ball, 2006), Chapter 58.

19. James L. Gibson, *Overcoming Apartheid: Can Truth Reconcile a Divided Nation?* (Cape Town: HRSC Press, 2004).

20. At a conference commemorating the tenth anniversary of the establishment of the TRC, Archbishop Emeritus Desmond Tutu said, "My deepest sadness is that by and large, the South African white community has not acknowledged the incredible generosity of the black community. I would say the white political leaders

should tell their supporters you don't know how damned lucky you are." "Tutu Lashes Out at White South Africans in TRC Debate," *City Press*, 23 April 2006. Within days, Douglas Gibson, chief whip of the Democratic Alliance, responded, "It is quite clear," he said, "that the vast majority [of white South Africans] are good citizens who make a very significant contribution in terms of skills, investment, and hard work. It is no secret that the majority of our country's tax base is constituted around the contribution made by white South Africans. Almost all of the government's social development programs are reliant on tax contributions. If white South Africans did not believe in, or contribute to, South Africa's new democracy, it simply would not work." "Tutu Ignores Important Role of Whites—DA," *Cape Times*, 24 April 2006. Unwittingly, his response only reinforced the point Tutu had made.

21. "The Rand Barons," *Time*, 6 June 2005.

22. Unemployment among whites in South Africa hovers around 5 percent. Unemployment rates in the developed countries are invariably considerably higher: In France, Germany, and Spain rates are over 9 percent, in Italy approaching 8 percent, in Canada approaching 7 percent, in Australia and the United States just over 5 percent, and in the UK slowly approaching 5 percent. See Organization for Economic Cooperation and Development (OECD) at www.oecd.org.

23. NEC Minutes, Lusaka, 27th August 1971; go to []maharaj/documents and reports/ANC NEC/1971/[].

24. Interview Ronnie Kasrils at []maharaj/interviewees/[] Ronnie Kasrils.

25. See [] maharaj/interviews/[]2002/ October 25 and 2003(2) January 9.

26. []maharaj/documents and reports/security files/[]maharaj: Robben Island: prerelease assessment.

27. Craig Williamson quoted in NIS report at []maharaj/ documents and reports/security files/[]Karl Edwards: The Internal Reconstruction and Development Department [sic]. For accounts of Mac's interactions with Williams, go to Mac interviews on 8 January 2002, 15 January 2003, 5 November 2001, 16 October 2002, 25 October 2002, and 25 September 2003.

28. Go to [] maharaj/documents and reports/security files/[]Karl Edwards: "Personality, Appearances and Political Outlook."

29. Interview with Phyllis Naidoo at []maharaj/interviewees/2003/[] Phyllis Naidoo 26 October/.

30. With cultural comparisons in mind, Eskom commissioned the African Leadership Study, a two-year study to analyze the different leadership modes of Africans, Indians, Coloureds, English-speaking whites, Afrikaners, and Jews in South Africa. The purpose was to establish whether there were distinct leadership characteristics associated with leadership and the processes of decision making in each community. The research was carried out by Africa Now, a South African think tank headed by Eric Mafuna. The study's findings in 2003, admittedly stereotypical, became the basis of a series of leadership forums in subsequent years. (See Mathatha Tsedu, "Why Can't Africans Measure Up to the Job of Leadership?," *Sunday Times*, 13 July 2003.) Reuel J. Khoza, the CEO of Eskom, used the

study's findings as the basis for a book, *Let Africa Lead*, published by Eskom in 2004. The foundational study is available at []maharaj/documents and reports/ other/[]. (The full title of the report is "A Foundational Report of Findings and Observations from an Exploratory Assessment of the History and Evolution of the Concept of Leadership with Reference to the Development of an African Leadership Approach.") In July 2006, the African Leadership Foundation (ALF) and the African Leadership Development (ALD) company were launched in Johannesburg under the direction of Eric Mafuna, the African Leadership Group (ALG) chairperson, the umbrella group overseeing the ALD and the ALF. Both the foundation and the company will explore the dimensions of African leadership. In the past, Mafuna contends, Western concepts of leadership have been imposed on the continent. See Makhudu, "New Impetus for African Leadership," *City Press*, 9 July 2006; "African leadership starts from within, says Mbeki," an edited summary of his address at the launch of the initiative in *City Press*, 16 July 2006.

31. Interview with Jacob Zuma, 2005, embargoed until 2030.

32. Ibid.

33. The ANC set up a commission, "Commission on the Cabal," to look into "the problems of disunity within the ranks of the MDM due to the manipulating role of certain Indians and Whites regarded as leaders of the struggle." It prepared a report and made recommendations in March 1990. "We were unanimous in our belief that it [the Cabal] manipulates strategy, lacks democratic practices and stifles free and open debate." Among those the commission identified as members or supporters of the cabal in Natal were Pravin Gordan [sic], Zac Yacoob, Alf Carrim, Yunus Mohammed, Farouk Meer, Jerry Coovadia, Billy Nair—"all members of the NIC." Blacks in Natal under the influence of the NIC included Diliza Mjil [sic]. In the Transvaal the cabal's number included Eric Molobi and Amos Masondo. In the Western Cape, Dullah Omar was suspect. At the national level Valli Moosa and Murphy Morobe were singled out, although it noted that efforts were being made to reorient Morobe. It was hoped the impending release of Terror Lekota and Popo Molefe would stem the tide. For report of the commission, go to [] maharaj/ documents and reports/other/ The incomplete report of the commission on the Cabal.

34. Interview with Zarina Maharaj at [] maharaj/family/ interviews/[] Zarina, 27 August 2004.

35. On the intellectual legacy of apartheid, see Mahmood Mamdani, "There Can Be No African Renaissance Without an Africa-Focused Intelligentsia" in Malegapuru Makgoba, ed., *African Renaissance* (Johannesburg: Mafube, 1999).

36. In a perceptive essay, "Resolving the 'Native Question,'" *Business Day*, 25 May 2005, Professor Sipho Seepe, one of South Africa's leading intellectuals, addresses the question of African identity. "[For] many South African whites . . . blacks do not exist except to be at their beck and call." For the extended endnote, go to [] maharaj/endnotes/Chapter 22/[]36.

37. Ibid. See also Alan Boesak's address to the National Union of Metalworkers'

conference on nonracialism in Cape Town in July 2006. "Return to Racial Classification a Mistake, Says Boesak," *Sunday Independent (SA)*, 23 July 2006.

38. Steven Burgess, *SA Tribes* (Cape Town: David Philip, 2002), pp. 84–93.

39. Interview [] maharaj/interviews/2003/[] Jan 8, (3).

40. Zarina Maharaj, *Dancing to a Different Rhythm*.

41. Shiva Naipaul, *North of South: An African Journey* (London: Penguin Books, 1979), p. 121.

42. The African-Indian relationship in South Africa is one that is fraught with potential for misunderstanding. There is the historic mistrust, which Mandela himself admits to having harbored, Indian fears (riots in 1949, which fixed for decades Indian fears of Africans), and although the overwhelming number of Indians live in Natal, mostly in the Durban metro in KwaZulu-Natal, they were only a small proportion of the African population with the inevitable tensions of being overwhelmed that is a product of such disproportion. Throughout the comms there are not only numerous references to the "cabal," mostly of Indians trying to hijack the MDM, but of complaints that there were too many Indians in leadership positions to the exclusion of Africans. For an extended endnote, go to [] maharaj/ endnotes/ Chapter 22/[] 42.

43. A study conducted by the Unilever Institute at the University of Cape Town suggests that the African middle class now approximates two million, i.e., about one in ten of the adult African population of twenty-two million. The average monthly income of the new middle class is estimated to be R5,900 (about $900 to $1,000, depending on the rate of exchange). The research also suggests that only one hundred thousand Africans comprise the so-called buppies (black urban professionals). Research quoted in "New Black Middle Class Reaches 2m," *Cape Times*, 10 July 2006.

44. According to research carried out by Eighty20, a South African financial research group, in 2004, half of South Africa's households lived on less than R20 (about $3.50) a day. Overall only 328,000 households (3 percent of total households) lived on R280 ($35.00) or more per person per day. "Half of SA Survives on R20 a Day," *Business Report*, 13 July 2006. In their 2004 paper, "Measuring Recent Changes in South African Inequality and Poverty Using 1996 and 2001 Census Data," Murray Leibbrandt and others, using their own estimates and citing comparable calculations by Whiteford and Van Seventer (2000), show that the contribution of intragroup inequality to overall income inequality has increased from 38 percent in 1975 to 60 percent in 2001 and the contribution of inequality between racial groups to overall income distribution decreased from 62 percent in 1975 to 40 percent in 2001.

The authors show that the intragroup inequality is further highlighted by the steep increase in the income Gini (inequality) coefficients for each population grouping. The Gini coefficient for the black group has increased from 47 in 1975 to 66 (one of the most unequal in the world) in 2001, within the Coloured group it has increased from 51 to 60, for the Indian population it has increased from 45 to 56, and within the white population it has increased from 36 to 51. The national income Gini coefficient is shown to have increased from 68 points in 1975 to 73 in 2001. (The Leibbrandt Papers in Susan Brown and Alta Folscher, eds., *Taking Power in the Economy: Gains and Directions* [Cape Town: Institute for Justice and Reconciliation, 2004]). More details on living standards and poverty are available at [] maharaj endnotes/chapter 22/[] 44.

Further evidence is presented by Sampie Terreblanche in his book *A History of Inequality in South Africa, 1652–2002,* in which he shows that the top 17 percent of the population receive 72 percent of the income and the bottom 50 percent only about 3 percent. See Rejane Woodroffe, "Putting the Gini Back in the Bottle," *Mail & Guardian,* 2 December 2005. In 2005, South Africa had a 15.9 percent growth in the number of dollar millionaires compared with a global average of 6.5 percent. The number of new millionaires—5,880—brought the total number to 43,000, up from 25,000 in 2002. South Africa was ranked fourth among the countries with the fastest growing dollar millionaire populations, behind South Korea, India, and Russia. See statistics quoted from the World Wealth Report (2006) compiled by Merrill Lynch in *Sunday Times,* 9 July 2006. Ernst & Young's annual merger and acquisitions review of 2005 that 238 empowerment deals worth R56.2 billion (roughly $9.4 billion) were signed in 2005. Among the new millionaires: former communications director-general Andile Ncgaba, head of the ANC presidency Smuts Ngonyama, and SABC CEO Dali Mpofu. More than 50 percent of Africa's estimated 83,000 dollar millionaires come from South Africa.

45. For statistics, go to [] maharaj/endnotes/chapter 22/[]45.

46. For statistics, go to [] maharaj/endnotes/chapter 22/[]46.

47. Because of the impact of HIV/AIDS, average life expectancy has declined significantly. From 62 in 1994 (female 66, male 58) to 51 (female 53, male 49) in 2006. Actuarial Society of South Africa AIDS and Demographic Model 2003. The figures for 2006 reflect the latest data available from StatsSA. It estimated mid-2006 average life expectancy at birth for the overall population at 51 years (53 for women, 49 for men).

48. See endnote 44 and extended endnote at []maharaj/endnotes/chapter 22/[] 44.

49. See extended endnote at []maharaj/endnotes/ chapter 22/[] 49.

50. See extended endnote at []maharaj/endnotes/chapter 22/[] 50.

51. In "The Freedom Charter Scorecard," *City Press,* 26 June 2005, the late Jimmy Seepe examined how far the ANC in government had lived up to the ideals of the Freedom Charter. See extended endnote at []maharaj/endnotes/chapter 22/[]51.

52. Magabo Matlala, the four-year-old grandchild of Transvaal Judge-President Bernard Ngoepe, was strangled to death on 9 March 2006 in Lenasia. A fifty-seven-year-old woman caring for her was gang raped by three men in the course of a robbery. At first police thought the little girl had been abducted and more than one hundred policemen combed Lenasia looking for her. Two days later her body was found under the bed in her parents' bedroom. She was naked, her hands were tied with electric cord behind her back, and she had been "strangled with

such force with one of her father's pants that she bled from her nose." There was a national outcry, much spoken and written about how such a hideous crime could occur. Weeks later it was back to normal, the memory of the atrocity replaced by yet another. For a brief sampling of the rising concern about violence in 2006, see André Brink, "Our Model Democracy Is a Lost Dream," *Sunday Independent,* 9 July 2006; "Comparisons Show SA Has Problems," *Weekend Argus,* 29 July 2006; "Crime Spike Spooks State," *Mail & Guardian,* 14–20 July 2006; "Probe into Violent Crime," *Cape Times,* 2 August 2006; "South Africa Fear Factor," *Economist,* 5 August 2006; John Kane Berman, "Fight Against Crime: From the Heart or off the Cuff?" *Business Day,* 17 August 2006; "SAPS's New Crime Initiative to Fight Crime Kicks into Gear," *Star,* 27 September 2006; "SA Sitting on Inequality Time Bomb," *City Press,* 24 September 2006; "How Can We Win the War on Crime?" *City Press,* 1 October 2006; "Why Criminals Are Walking Free," *Sunday Times,* 1 October 2006; "This Is a Crisis, Not Just a Problem," front-page editorial in *Sunday Times,* 1 October 2006. For extended endnote, go to [] maharaj/endnotes/chapter 22/[]52.

53. For an overview of the extent of government corruption, parliamentary corruption, and issues that call into questions the dubious propriety of some of the ANC's financial transactions, go to []maharaj/endnotes/Chapter 22/[]53.

54. According to Bob Mattes of the Institute for Democracy in South Africa (IDASA), surveys conducted by Afrobarometer in January and February 2006 indicated that 45 percent of South Africans believe that all or most of their elected local councilors and officials are involved in some form of corruption. "Voters Losing Faith in Councils—Study," *Cape Times,* 16 June 2006.

55. For a small cross section of reports on the swelling waves of protest in 2005, see Jan Hofmeyr, "Municipalities Face Credibility Crisis," *Sunday Independent,* 18 December 2005; Teddy Nemeroff, "Services Crisis Needs New Dialogue," *Cape Times,* 28 November 2005; David Henson and Michael O'Donovan, "South Africa's Poor Demand a Better Deal," *Cape Argus,* 30 November 2005; Edwin Naidu, "Government Sits on Delivery Timebomb," *Sunday Independent,* 27 November 2005; Max du Preeez, "Desperate Plea from Dispossessed Falls on Deaf Elitist Ears," *Cape Argus,* 17 November 2005; Bryan Rostron, "High Water Rising in the Cape," *Business Day,* 23 December 2005; "Residents on the March Demand Houses Now," *Cape Times,* 17 November 2005; "A Lot of Toyi-Toying and Chaos Countrywide for a Living Wage," *City Press,* 31 July 2005; "Things Fall Apart," *Business Day,* 13 December 2005; "5000 Riot in Secunda Over Municipal Services Failure," *Southern Africa Report,* 18 March 2005. Other areas of protest, often dispersed by the police: Khayelitsha and Gugulethu in Cape Town, Kyalitshe, Free State, at the entry to Happy Valley near Blackheath Bay, Cape Town, black townships on the outskirts of Port Elizabeth. See Mpumelelo Mkhabela, "Something Is Very Rotten in Local Govt," *City Press,* 18 September 2005; Liepollo Lebohang Pheko, "As Long as State Ignores the Poor, There Will Be Riots," *Cape Times,* 1 December 2005; Yolandi Groenewald, "Why the Free State Burns," *Mail & Guardian,* 9–15 September, 2005; Rapule Tabane, "Residents Threaten Another Vaal Uprising,"

Mail & Guardian, 7–13 October, 2005. More comment at [] maharaj/endnotes/ chapter 22/[]55.

56. Susan Brown and Alta Folscher, "Growth Is Not Enough," in *Conflict and Governance*.

57. Nithaya Chetty, "Black Intellectuals Must Speak Up," *Cape Times*, 10 March 2006. In May 2006, the SABC canceled the showing of a documentary it had commissioned on President Mbeki and prohibited the producers from either discussing it in public or showing it to members of the media. "Academics Afraid to Criticize the Government," *Cape Times*, 4 December 2005.

58. For a brief overview of Mbeki's views on HIV/AIDS, go to []maharaj/ footnotes/chapter 22[]/58.

59. On the South African government's policies and attitude toward the pandemic, outspoken Stephen Lewis, Kofi Annan's special envoy to Africa on HIV/AIDS, in *Race Against Time,* writes that virtually every other nation in eastern and southern Africa "is working harder at treatment than is South Africa with relatively fewer resources, and in most cases nowhere near the infrastructure or human capacity of South Africa," and that "every senior U.N. official, engaged directly or indirectly in the struggle against AIDS, to whom I have spoken about South Africa, is completely bewildered by the policies of President Mbeki." His colleagues, he writes, are "incredulous" at how health minister Manto Tshabalala-Msimang has exaggerated the possible side effects of antiretroviral drugs and wrongly suggested that a diet of sweet potatoes and garlic can be as important as antiretrovirals in treating AIDS. See *Race Against Time* (Toronto: House of Anansi Press, 2005). See "UN Envoy Sharply Criticizes South Africa's AIDS Program," *New York Times*, 25 October 2005.

In Toronto, where the XVI International AIDS Conference was held in August 2006, Lewis, addressing the final plenary session, was unsparing: ". . . on the issue of treatment," he said, "I am bound to raise South Africa. South Africa is the unkindest cut of all. It is the only country in Africa, amongst all the countries I have traversed in the last five years, whose government is still obtuse, dilatory and negligent about rolling out treatment. It is the only country in Africa whose government continues to propound theories more worthy of a lunatic fringe than of a concerned and compassionate state. Between six and eight hundred people a day die of AIDS in South Africa. The government has a lot to atone for. I'm of the opinion that they can never achieve redemption. According to a 170-page mortality report prepared by Barbara Anderson and Heston Philips for Stats South Africa, the death rate for women aged 20 to 39 more than tripled between 1997 and 2004 while deaths among men aged 30 to 44 more than doubled." See "Death Rate of Women Has Tripled in Seven Years," *Cape Times*, 8 September 2006. For full text of Lewis's Toronto address and further details of HIV/AIDS and other health statistics in South Africa, go to []maharaj/endnotes/ chapter 22/[]59.

60. In surveys, HIV/AID rarely turns up as the issue most people are preoccupied with. This is not surprising. Across countries, surveys show that people's "main issues" are associated with their immediate concerns: economic security

(jobs and inflation), personal security (crime), and shelter (housing). HIV/AIDS is perceived as an issue other people should be concerned about as people who do not know their HIV status believe they are not at risk of getting the disease. HIV/AIDS is a disease that other people get.

61. For details of actions by Tshabalala Msimang that were harmful to HIV awareness or contributed to delays in effecting HIV/AIDS treatments or the dissemination of AIDS' prevention messages and encouraged HIV-positive persons to use alternatives, go to []maharaj/endnotes/chapter 22/[]61.

62. The Human Sciences Research Council (HSRC) study "The South African National HIV Prevalence, HIV Incidence, Behaviour and Communication Survey," released in November 2005. The survey concluded that 10.8 percent of all South Africans are living with HIV/AIDS. More details at[] maharaj/endnotes/chapter 22/[]62.

63. Human Development Report 2006 (Cape Town: United Nations Development Program, 2006). For the extended endnote, go to []maharaj/ endnotes Chapter 22[]63.

64. Allister Sparks (*The Mind of South Africa* and *Beyond the Miracle*) recalls a conversation with Thabo Mbeki in 2002 on the subject of Zimbabwe: "The conversation turned edgy when I asked about the gathering crisis in Zimbabwe. The fuss over what was happening there, he said, reflected a racist perspective on the part of white South Africans and the white developed world generally.

"The reason Zimbabwe is such a preoccupation here [he said] in the United Kingdom and the United States and Sweden and elsewhere is because a handful of white people died. And white people were deprived of their property. . . . All they want to talk about is Zimbabwe, Zimbabwe, Zimbabwe, he [Mbeki] declared in tones of rising agitation. Why? It's because 12 white people died! Zimbabwe is a big obsession here (among whites) but it isn't elsewhere on the African continent." Allister Sparks, "Now It's a Crime Against Humanity," *Cape Times*, 29 June 2005. For Mbeki and his "quiet diplomacy" in Zimbabwe go to []maharaj/ endnotes/ Chapter 22[]64.

The huge differences between whites and blacks on this issue are telling and juxtapose issues of identity. Go to []marahaj/endnotes/chapter 22/[]64.

65. Mondli Makhanya, "Getting Back Our Morality," *Sunday Times*, 9 July 2006.

66. Karen Maughan, "Zuma Judge Explodes," *Star*, 17 October 2006.

67. "State Limped from One Disaster to Another—Judge," *Star*, 21 September 2006.

68. "The Zuma Judgment," *Star*, 21 September 2006.

69. R. W. Johnson, "Zuma Phenomenon: All Eyes on the Man from Inkandla," *Business Day*, 10 October 2006.

70. Chris McGreal, "Thabo Mbeki's Catastrophe," *Prospect Magazine*, www.Prospect-magazine.co.uk/article_details.php?id= 4995; "Mbeki Says CIA Had Role in HIV/AIDS Conspiracy," *United Press International*, 6 October 2000 at http://www.aegis.com/news/upi/up0001001.html; Howard Barrell, "Mbeki Fingers CIA in AIDS Controversy," *Guardian*, 6 October 2000.

71. "Mbeki in Thrall to Fear and Suspicion," *Mail & Guardian*, 24 April 2001.

72. "Government Accuses Business Men of Plot to Oust Mbeki," www.archives.ie/breakingnews/2001/04/05 story 10857.asp. http://www.sabcnews.com/features/plot_mbeki/timeline.ftml.

73. "Theatre of the Bizarre," *Cape Times*, 26 April 2001; "Mandela: I Believe in Ramaphosa," *Cape Times*, 27 April 2001; "The alleged plot to overthrow President Thabo Mbeki is a smokescreen for the fact the ANC's top leadership wants to prevent deputy president Jacob Zuma from running for office again," "Mbeki's Turbulent Journey to Power," *Sunday Independent*, 29 April 2001; "Chronology of ANC Power Play," *Sunday Independent*, 29 April 2001.

74. "Plot Is a Smokescreen for Ousting Jacob Zuma, Says ANC MP," *Sunday Independent*, 29 April 2001.

75. "Gov. Accuses Business Leaders of Plot to Oust Mbeki," www.archives.tcm.ie/breakingnews/2001/25 / story 10857.asp. Mbeki was interviewed on eTV's program *3rd degree* by Debora Patta.

76. See Wally Mbhele and Moipone Malefane, "A House Divided Cripples ANC," *Sunday Times*, 9 July 2006; Karima Brown, "Descent into Politics of 'Total Garbage' and Smear," *Business Day*, 18 July 2006.

77. William Gumede, *Thabo Mbeki and the Battle for the Soul of the ANC* (Cape Town: Zebra Press, 2005); Shaun Johnson, "True Colours," *Leadership*, Vol. 18, No. 1, 1999; Sean Jacobs, "Time for Mbeki to Give South Africans Vision," *Cape Times*, 27 April 2001; James Myburgh, "Mbeki and the 'Total Formula,' " *Sunday Independent (SA)*, 1 April 2001; Dumisani Makhaye, "Democratic Centralism Is Not Totalitarianism," *Sunday Independent (SA)*, 22 April 20001; Drew Forrest, "Mbeki Reaps Ashes Sowed," *Mail & Guardian*, 28 October 2005.

BIBLIOGRAPHY

Adam, Heribert. *Modernizing Racial Domination: South Africa's Political Dynamics.* Berkeley: University of California Press, 1971.

———, and Kogila Moodley. *South Africa Without Apartheid: Dismantling Racial Domination.* Berkeley: University of California Press, 1986.

———. *The Negotiated Revolution: Society and Politics in Post-Apartheid South Africa.* Johannesburg: Jonathan Ball, 1993.

Adam, Heribert, Frederik van Zyl, Slabbert, and Kogila Moodley. *Comrades in Business.* Cape Town: Tafelberg, 1997.

Adebian, Iraj, Tania Ajam, and Laura Walker. *Promises, Plans and Priorities.* Cape Town: Idasa, 1997.

Adedeji, Adebayo. *Comprehending and Mastering African Conflicts.* London: Zed Books, 1999.

Akenson, Donald Harman. *God's People.* Ithaca: Cornell University Press, 1992.

Alexander, Neville, *Robben Island Dossier 1964–1974.* Cape Town: University of Cape Town Press, 1994.

———. *An Ordinary Country.* Pietermaritzburg: University of Natal Press, 2002.

Ali, Shanti Sadiq. *Gandhi and South Africa.* New Delhi: Hind Pocket Books, 1994.

Alperson, Myra. *Foundations for a New Democracy.* Johannesburg: Ravan Press, 1995.

Amnesty International. *South Africa: State of Fear, Security Force Complicity in Torture and Political Killings, 1990–1992.* New York: Amnesty International USA, 1992.

Andrews, Penelope and Stephen Ellmann, eds. *Post-Apartheid Constitutions: Perspectives on South Africa's Basic Law.* Johannesburg: Witwatersrand University Press, 2001.

Anyidoho, Kofi. *The Word Behind Bars and the Paradox of Exile.* Evanston, IL: Northwestern University Press, 1997.

Asmal, Kader, et al., eds., "Why South Africa Matters," *Daedalus,* Vol. 130, No. 1, Proceedings of the American Academy of Arts and Sciences, 2001.

Asmal, Kader, Louise Asmal, and Ronald Suresh Roberts. *Reconciliation Through Truth: A Reckoning of South Africa's Criminal Government.* Cape Town: David Philip, 1996.

Asmal, Kader, David Chidester, and Wilmot James, eds. *Nelson Mandela: From Freedom to the Future. Tributes and Speeches.* Johannesburg: Jonathan Ball, 2003.

Asmal, Kader, and Wilmot James, eds. *Spirit of the Nation: Reflections on South Africa's Educational Ethos.* Cape Town: New Africa Education and the Human Sciences Research Council in Association with the Department of Education, 2002.

Asmal, Kader with David Chidester and Cassius Lubisi, eds. *Legacy of Freedom: The ANC's Human Rights Tradition.* Johannesburg: Jonathan Ball, 2005.

Attridge, Derek, and Rosemary Jolly. *Writing South Africa.* Cambridge: Cambridge University Press, **?** 1998.

Basner, Mariam. *Am I an African? The Political Memoirs of H M Basner.* Johannesburg: Witwatersrand University Press, 1993.

Barber, James. *Mandela's World.* Oxford: James Currey, 2004.

———. *South Africa's Foreign Policy, 1945–1970.* London: Oxford University Press, 1973.

Barberton, Conrad, Michael Blake, and Hermien Kotzé. *Creating Action Space*. Cape Town: David Philip, 1998.

Barrell, Howard, "Conscripts to Their Age: African National Congress Operational Strategy 1976–1986," Ph.D. thesis. London: Oxford University, 1993.

———. *MK: The ANC's Armed Struggle*. London: Penguin, 1990.

———, "The Turn to the Masses: The African National Congress' Strategic Review of 1978–79," *Journal of Southern African Studies*, Vol.18, No.1, March 1991, pp. 64–92.

Baskin, Jeremy. *Striking Back: A History of COSATU*. Johannesburg: Ravan Press, 1991.

Basson, Dion. *South Africa's Interim Constitution*. Cape Town: Juta, 1994.

Beck, Don, and Graham Linscott. *The Crucible: Forging South Africa's Future*. JDenton, Texas: New Paradigm Press, 1991.

Beinart, William. *Twentieth-Century South Africa*. New York: Oxford University Press, 1994.

———, and Saul Dubow, eds. *Segregation and Apartheid*. London: Routledge, 1995.

Bell, Terry, in collaboration with Dumisa Ntsebeza. *Unfinished Business*. Cape Town: RedWorks, 2001.

Benjamin, Larry, and Christopher Gregory, eds. *Southern Africa at the Crossroads?* Johannesburg: Justified Press, 1992.

Benson, Mary. *A Far Cry*. London: Viking, 1989.

———. *Nelson Mandela*. New York: Norton, 1986.

Bernstein, Lionel "Rusty." *Memory Against Forgetting: Memoirs of a Life in South African Politics, 1938–1964*. London: Viking, 1999.

Bezdrob, Anné Mariè du Preez. *Winnie Mandela: A Life*. Cape Town: Zebra Press, 2003.

Biko, Steven. *I Write What I Like*. New York: Harper and Row, 1983.

Bizos, George. *No One to Blame*. Cape Town: David Philip, 1998.

Blumenfeld, Jesmond. *South Africa in Crisis*. London: Croom Helm for the Royal Institute of International Affairs, 1987.

Boesak, Allan. *Black and Reformed*. Johannesburg: Skotaville, 1984.

Bond, Patrick. *Against Global Apartheid*. Cape Town: University of Cape Town Press, 2001.

———. *Cities of Gold, Townships of Coal*. Trenton: Africa World Press, Inc., 2000.

———. *Elite Transition*. London: Pluto, 2000.

———. *Unsustainable South Africa*. Pietermaritzburg: University of Natal Press, 2002.

Bopela, Thula, and Daluxolo' Luthuli. *Umkhonto we Sizwe: Fighting for a Divided People*. Alberton: Galago, 2005.

Boraine, Alex. *A Country Unmasked*. London: Oxford University Press, 2000.

———, Janet Levy, and Ronel Scheffer, eds. *Dealing with the Past: Theological and Psychological Reflections on Truth and Reconciliation*. Cape Town: Idasa, 1997.

Botman, H. Russel, and Robin M. Petersen. *To Remember and to Heal*. Cape Town: Human and Rousseau, 1996.

Bozzoli, Belinda. *Theatres of Struggle and the End of Apartheid*. Johannesburg: University of Witwatersrand Press, 2004.

Braam, Conny. *Operation Vula*. Johannesburg: Jacana, 2004.

Brewer, John D. *After Soweto: An Unfinished Journey*. Oxford: Clarendon Press, 1986.

Breytenbach, Breyten. *The True Confessions of an Albino Terrorist*. New York: Farrar, Straus & Giroux, 1985.

Breytenbach, Cloete. *The New South Africa: The Zulu Factor*. Montagu, SA: Luga, 1991.

Breytenbach, Jan. *Eden's Exiles*. Cape Town: Queillerie, 1997.

———. *The Buffalo Soldiers: The Story of South Africa's 32 Battalion 1975–1993*. Alberton: Galago, 2002.

Bridgland, Fred. *Katiza's Journey*. London: Sidgwick & Jackson, 1997.

Brink, André. *Reinventing a Continent: Writing and Politics in South Africa 1982–1995*. London: Secker & Warburg, 1996.

Brink, Elsabé, et al. *Soweto 16 June 1976: It All Started with a Dog . . .* Cape Town: Kwela Books, 2001.

Brooks, Alan, and Jeremy Brickhill. *Whirlwind Before the Storm*. London: International Defence and Aid Fund for Southern Africa, 1980.

Brotz, Howard. *The Politics of South Africa: Democracy and Racial Diversity.* London: Oxford University Press, 1977.

Brown, Susan, ed. *Money and Morality.* Cape Town: Institute for Justice and Reconciliation, 2006.

———. *Conflict and Governance.* Cape Town: Institute for Justice and Reconciliation, 2005.

Buhlungu Sakhela, ed. *Trade Unions and Democracy.* Cape Town: HSRC Press, 2006.

———, et al., eds. *State of the Nation—South Africa 2005–2006.* Cape Town: Human Sciences Research Council, 2006.

Bundy, Colin. *The Rise and Fall of the South African Peasantry.* Berkeley: University of California Press, 1979.

Bunting, Brian. *Moses Kotane: South African Revolutionary.* London: Inkululeko Publications, 1975.

———. *The Rise of the South African Reich.* London: International Defence and Aid Fund for Southern Africa, 1986.

Buntman, Fran Lisa. *Robben Island and Prisoner Resistance to Apartheid.* Cambridge: Cambridge University Press, 2003.

Burgess, Steven. *SA Tribes.* Cape Town: David Philip, 2002.

Buthelezi, Mangosuthu G. *South Africa: My Vision of the Future.* London: George Weidenfeld & Nicolson, 1990.

Butler, Jeffrey, Richard Elphick, and David Welsh, eds. *Democratic Liberalism in South Africa.* Cape Town: David Philip, 1986.

Callinicos, Luli. *Gold and Workers 1886–1924.* Johannesburg: Ravan Press, 1985.

———. *Oliver Tambo: Beyond the Engeli Mountains.* Claremont: David Philips, 2004.

Camerer, Lala, and Suzette Kotze, eds. *Special Report on Victim Empowerment in South Africa—Victim Empowerment Report.* Johannesburg: Institute for Security Studies, 1998.

Cawthra, Gavin. *Brutal Force.* London: International Defence and Aid Fund for Southern Africa, 1986.

Cell, John Whitson. *The Highest State of White Supremacy: The Origins of Segregation in South Africa and the American South.* Cambridge: Cambridge University Press, 1982.

Centre for Policy Studies. *South Africa at the End of the Eighties: Policy Perspectives 1989.* Johannesburg: Centre for Policy Studies, University of the Witwatersrand, 1989.

Chidester, David. *Shots in the Streets: Violence and Religion in South Africa.* Cape Town: Oxford University Press, 1992.

———. Phillip Dexter, and Wilmot James, eds. *What Holds Us Together—Social Cohesion in South Africa.* Cape Town: HSRC Press, 2003.

Chimeloane, Rrekgetsi. *The Hostel Dwellers: A First-Hand Account.* Cape Town: Kwela Books, 1998.

Christopher, A.J. *The Atlas of Changing South Africa.* London: Routledge, 1994.

Chubb, Karin, and Lutz Van Dijk. *Between Anger and Hope: South Africa's Youth in the TRC.* Johannesburg: Witwatersrand University Press, 2001.

Clark, Nancy L, and William H. Worger. *South Africa—The Rise and Fall of Apartheid.* London: Pearson Longman, 2004.

Cling, Jean-Pierre. *From Isolation to Integration: The Post-Apartheid South African Economy.* Pretoria: Protea Book House & IFAS, 2001.

Clingman, Stephen. *Bram Fischer.* Cape Town: David Philip, 1998.

Cloete, Fanie, Lawrence Schlemmer, and Daan van Vuuren, eds. *Policy Options for a New South Africa.* Pretoria: HSRC, 1991.

Cochrane, James, John de Gruchy, and Stephen Martin, eds. *Facing the Truth.* Cape Town: David Philip, 1999.

Cohen, Robin. *Endgame in South Africa?* London: J Currey, 1986.

Cohen, Robin, Yvonne Muthien, and Abede Zegeye, eds. *Repression and Resistance: Insiders' Accounts of Apartheid.* London: Zell Centre for Modern African Studies, 1990.

Coker, Christopher. *South Africa's Security Dilemmas.* London: Praeger, 1987.

Cole, Josette. *Crossroads—The Politics of Reform and Repression 1976–1986.* Johannesburg: Ravan Press, 1987.

Coleman, Keith. *Nationalisation Beyond the Slogans.* Johannesburg: Ravan Press, 1991.

Coleman, Max, ed. *A Crime Against Humanity.* Cape Town: David Philip, 1998.

Commonwealth Eminent Persons Group on Southern Africa. *Mission to South Africa: The Commonwealth Report.* Harmondsworth: Penguin Books for the Commonwealth Secretariat, 1986.

Connor, Bernard F. *The Difficult Traverse: From Amnesty to Reconciliation.* Pietermaritzburg: Cluster, 1998.

Corrigan, Terence. *Mbeki: His Time Has Come.* Johannesburg: South African Institute of Race Relations, 1999.

Crapanzano, Vincent. *Waiting: The Whites of South Africa.* New York: Random House, 1985.

Cross, Michael. *Resistance and Transformation.* Johannesburg: Skotaville, 1992.

Crush, Jonathan, and Wilmot James, eds. *Crossing Boundaries: Mine Migrancy in Democratic South Africa.* Cape Town: Institute for Democracy in South Africa, 1995.

——, and Vincent Williams. *The New South Africans?* Cape Town: Southern African Migration Project, 1999.

Danaher, Kevin. *The Political Economy of US Policy Toward South Africa.* Boulder: Westview Press, 1985.

Daniel, John, Adam Habib, and Roger Southall, eds. *State of the Nation—South Africa 2003–2004.* Cape Town: Human Sciences Research Council Press, 2003.

——, Roger Southall, and Jessica Lutchman, eds. *State of the Nation—South Africa 2004–2005.* Cape Town: Human Sciences Research Council Press, 2005.

Daniels, Eddie. *There and Back: Robben Island 1964–1979.* Cape Town: Mayibuye Books 2002, third edition.

Davenport, T.R.H. *South Africa—A Modern History.* London: Macmillan, 1977.

——. *The Transfer of Power.* Cape Town: David Philip, 1998.

Davies, Robert H. *Capital, State, and White Labour in South Africa, 1900–1960.* Atlantic Highlands: Humanities Press, 1979.

——, Dan O'Meara, and Sipho Dlamini, eds. *The Struggle for South Africa: A Reference Guide.* London and New Jersey: Zed Books, 1984.

Davis, David. *African Workers and Apartheid.* London: International Defence & Aid Fund, 1976.

Davis, Stephen M. *Apartheid's Rebels: Inside South Africa's Hidden War.* New Haven: Yale University Press, 1987.

Deacon, Harriet. *The Island.* Cape Town: David Philip, 1996.

Debray, Regis. *Strategy for Revolution.* New York: Monthly Review Press, 1971.

De Grucht, John W. *The Church Struggle in South Africa.* Cape Town: David Philip, 1990.

——. *Reconciliation: Restoring Justice.* Cape Town: David Philip, 2002.

De Klerk, F.W. *The Last Trek—A New Beginning.* London: Macmillan, 1998.

De Klerk, W.A. *The Puritans in Africa: The Story of Afrikanerdom.* London: Rex Collings, 1975.

De Kock, Eugene. *A Long Night's Damage: Working for the Apartheid State.* Johannesburg: Contra Press, 1998.

Denis, Philippe, ed. *Orality, Memory & the Past.* Pietermaritzburg: Cluster, 2000.

Denoon, Donald. *Settler Capitalism.* Oxford: Clarendon Press, 1983.

Desmond, Cosmas. *The Discarded People: An Account of African Resettlement in South Africa.* Harmondsworth, Middlesex: Penguin, 1971.

De Villiers, H.H.W. *Rivonia—Operation Mayibuye.* Johannesburg: Afrikaanse Pers-Boekhandel, 1964.

De Villiers, B., D.J. Van Vuuren, and M. Wiechers. *Human Rights: Documents That Paved the Way.* Pretoria: HSRC, 1992.

De Villiers, Bertus. *Regional Government in the New South Africa.* Pretoria: HSRC, 1992.

——, ed. *State of the Nation 1997/8.* Pretoria: HSRC, 1998.

De Villiers, Riaan, and Doreen Atkinson, eds. *Developing Democracy.* Johannesburg: Centre for Policy Studies, 1993.

De Villiers, Riaan, ed. *Governability During the Transition.* Johannesburg: Centre for Policy Studies, 1993.

De Villiers, Simon. *Robben Island: Out of Reach. Out of Mind.* Cape Town: Struik, 1971.

Dialego. *Philosophy and Class Struggle: The Basic Principles of Marxism as Seen in the Context of the South African Liberation Struggle.* London: Inkululeko Publications, 1987.

Dingake, Michael. *My Fight Against Apartheid.* London: Kliptown Books, 1987.

Distiller, Natasha, and Melissa Steyn, eds. *Under Construction: "Race" and Identity in South Africa Today.* Johannesburg: Heinemann, 2004.

Dlamini, Moses. *Robben Island Hell-Hole: Reminiscences of a Political Prisoner in South Africa.* Trenton, NJ: Africa World Press, 1986.

Dorrian, Paul. *The Making of South Africa Inc.* Cape Town: Zebra Press, 2005.

Driver, C.J. *Patrick Duncan—South African and Pan-African.* Cape Town: David Philip, 1980.

Dubow, Saul. *The African National Congress.* Johannesburg: Jonathan Ball, 2000.

Dugard, John, ed. *The Last Years of Apartheid: Civil Liberties in South Africa.* New York: Ford Foundation & Foreign Policy Association.

Duncan, Jane, and Mandla Seleoane, eds. *Media & Democracy in South Africa.* Pretoria: HSRC & FXI, 1998.

Du Preez, Max. *Of Warriors, Lovers and Prophets.* Cape Town: Zebra Press, 2004.

Du Toit, André, ed. *Towards Democracy: Building a Culture of Accountability in South Africa.* Cape Town: Idasa, 1991.

Du Toit, Betty. *Ukubamba Amadolo—Workers' Struggles in the South African Textile Industry.* London: Onyx Press. 1978.

Ebrahim, Hassen. *The Soul of a Nation.* Cape Town: Oxford University Press, 1998.

Ebrahim, Noor. *Noor's Story.* Cape Town: District Six Museum, 1999.

Ebr.-Vally, Rehana. *Kala Pani: Caste and Colour in South Africa.* Cape Town: Kwela, 2001.

Eldredge, Elizabeth A., and Fred Morton. *Slavery in South Africa.* Pietermaritzburg: University of Natal Press, 1994.

Elliott, Aubrey. *Zulu: Heritage of a Nation.* Cape Town: Struik, 1991.

Ellis, Stephen, and Tsepo Sechaba. *Comrades Against Apartheid: The ANC and the South African Party in Exile.* London: James Currey; Bloomington: Indiana University Press, 1992.

Elphick, Richard. *Kraal and Castle: Khoikhoi and the Founding of White South Africa.* New Haven: Yale University Press, 1977.

———, and Hermann B. Giliomee, eds. *The Shaping of South African Society, 1652–1840.* Middletown, CT: Wesleyan University Press, 1989.

Emmett, Tony, and Alex Butchart, eds. *Behind the Mask.* Pretoria: HSRC, 2000.

Emmett, Tony, ed. *Squatting in the Hottentots Holland Basin: Perspectives on a South African Social Issue.* Pretoria: HSRC, 1992.

Engberg-Pedersen, Poul, et al. *Limits of Adjustment in Africa.* Copenhagen: Centre for Development Research, 1996.

Engelbrecht, Bushie, and Micel Schnehage. *A Christmas to Remember.* Johannesburg: Maskew Miller Longman, 1999.

Engels, Dagmar, and Shula Marks, eds. *Contesting Colonial Hegemony: State and Society in Africa and India.* New York: Tauris, 1994.

Erasmus, Zimitri, ed. *Coloured by History, Shaped by Place.* Cape Town: Kwela Books, 2001.

Erkens, Rainer, and John Kane-Berman. *Political Correctness in South Africa.* Johannesburg: South African Institute of Race Relations, 2000.

Esterhuyse, Willie, and Pierre du Toit, eds. *The Myth Makers.* Johannesburg: Southern Book Publishers, 1990.

Evans, Nicholas, and Monica Seeber. *The Politics of Publishing in South Africa.* London: Holger Ehling, 2000.

Fage, John D., and Roland Oliver, eds. *The Cambridge History of Africa,* 8 vols. New York: Cambridge University Press, 1975–1986.

Fakier, Yazeed. *Grappling with Change.* Cape Town: Idasa, 1998.

Fanon, Frantz. *Black Skin, White Masks.* New York: Grove Press, 1967.

Fatton, Robert. *Black Consciousness in South Africa: The Dialectics of Ideological Resistance to White Supremacy.* Albany: SUNY Press Press, 1986.

February, Vernon. *The Afrikaners of South Africa.* New York: Paul International, 1991.

Federal Council of the National Party. *Constitutional Rule in a Participatory Democracy: The National Party's Framework for a New Democratic South Africa.* Pretoria: Federal Council of the National Party, 1991.

Feit, Edward. *Urban Revolt in South Africa 1960–1964: A Case Study.* Evanston: Northwestern University Press, 1971.

Fieldhouse, Roger. *Anti-Apartheid: A History of the Movement in Britain.* London: The Merlin Press, 2005.

Fine, Ben, and Zavareh Rustomjee. *The Political Economy of South Africa.* London: C. Hurst, 1996.

Finnegan, William. *Crossing the Line: A Year in the Land of Apartheid.* New York: Harper and Row, 1986.

———. *Dateline Soweto.* New York: Harper and Row, 1988.

First, Ruth. *117 Days.* New York: Monthly Review Press, 1989.

Foster, Don, with Dennis Davis and Diane Sandler. *Detention and Torture in South Africa.* Cape Town: David Philip, 1987.

———, Paul Haupt, and Marésa de Beer. *The Theatre of Violence: Narratives of the Protagonists in the South African Conflict.* Cape Town: HSRC Press, 2005.

Frankel, Glenn. *Rivonia's Children.* London: Weidenfield & Nicolson, 1999.

Frankel, Philip. *An Ordinary Atrocity: Sharpeville and Its Aftermath.* Johannesburg: Witwatersrand University Press.

———. *Pretoria's Praetorians: Civil-Military Relations in South Africa.* Cambridge: Cambridge University Press, 1984.

Frederikse, Julie. *South Africa: A Different Kind of War: From Soweto to Pretoria.* Boston: Beacon Press, 1987.

Fredrickson, George M. *White Supremacy.* London: Oxford University Press, 1981.

Freund, Bill. *Insiders and Outsiders: The Indian Working Class of Durban 1910–1990.* Pietermaritzburg: University of Natal Press, 1995.

Friedman, Steven, and Richard Humphries, eds. *Federalism and Its Foes.* Johannesburg: Centre for Policy Studies, 1993.

———. *Reform Revisited.* Johannesburg: South African Institute of Race Relations, 1988.

———, ed. *The Long Journey: South Africa's Quest for a Negotiated Settlement.* Johannesburg: Ravan Press, 1993.

———, and Doreen Atkinson, eds. "The Small Miracle: South Africa's Negotiated Settlement," *South African Review 7.* Johannesburg: Ravan Press, 1993.

Fuze, Magema M. *The Black People.* Scottsville: University of Natal Press, 1979.

Gandhi, M.K. *An Autobiography.* London: Penguin, 2001.

Gelb, Stephen, ed. *South Africa's Economic Crisis.* Cape Town: David Philip, 1991.

Geldenhuys, Jannie. *A General's Story.* Johannesburg: Jonathan Ball, 1995.

Gerhart, Gail M. *Black Power in South Africa: The Evolution of an Ideology.* Berkeley: University of California Press, 1978.

Gibson, James L., and Amanda Gouws. *Overcoming Intolerance in South Africa.* Cambridge: Cambridge University Press, 2003.

———. *Overcoming Apartheid.* Cape Town: HSRC Press, 2004.

Giliomee, Hermann, and Richard Elphick. *The Shaping of South African Society, 1652–1820.* Cape Town: Longman, 1979.

Giliomee, Hermann, and Charles Simkins, eds. *The Awkward Embrace: One Party Domination and Democracy.* Cape Town: Tafelberg, 1999.

Giliomee, Hermann, and Jannie Gagiano, eds. *The Elusive Search for Peace: South Africa, Israel and Northern Ireland.* Cape Town: Oxford University Press, 1990.

Giliomee, Hermann, and Lawrence Schlemmer, eds. *Up Against the Fences: Poverty, Passes, and Privilege in South Africa.* Cape Town: David Philip, 1985.

Giliomee, Hermann, and Lawrence Schlemmer. *From Apartheid to Nation Building—Contemporary South African Debates.* Cape Town: Oxford University Press, 1989.

Giliomee, Hermann. *The Afrikaners: Biography of a People.* Cape Town: Tafelberg, 2003.

Ginsberg, Anthony. *South Africa's Future.* London: Macmillan, 1998.

Glanz, Lorraine, ed. *Managing Crime in the New South Africa: Selected Readings.* Pretoria: Proceedings of "Managing Crime in the New South Africa," Human Sciences Research Council, August, 1992.

Godsell, Bobby, et al, *Economic Alternatives*. Cape Town: Juta, 1990.

Golan, Daphna. *Inventing Shaka: Using History in the Construction of Zulu Nationalism*. Boulder, CO: Lynne Rienner, 1994.

Goldstone, Richard J. *For Humanity*. Johannesburg: Witwatersrand University Press, 2000.

Goodman, David. *Fault Lines*. Berkeley: University of California Press, 1999.

Goodwin-Gill, Guy S. *Free and Fair Elections: International Law and Practice*. Geneva: Inter-Parliamentary Union, 1994.

Gordimer, Nadine. *Living in Hope and History: Notes from Our Century*. Cape Town: David Philip, 2000.

Gromyko, Anatoly, and John Kane-Berman. *The Moscow Papers: The USSR and South Africa*. Johannesburg: SAIRR, 1991.

Grundy, Kenneth W. *The Militarization of South African Politics*. Bloomington: Indiana University Press, 1986.

Guelke, Adrian. *South Africa in Transition*. London: I. B. Tauris, 1999.

Gumede, William Mervin. *Thabo Mbeki and the Battle for the Soul of the ANC*. Cape Town: Zebra Press, 2005.

Gutteridge, William F., ed., with contributions by Deon Geldenhuys and David Simon. *South Africa: From Apartheid to National Unity, 1981–1994*. Brookfield, VT: Dartmouth, 1995.

Guy, Jeffrey. *The Destruction of the Zulu Kingdom: The Civil War in Zululand, 1879–1884*. London: Longman, 1979.

Hadland, Adrian, and Jovial Rantao. *The Life and Times of Thabo Mbeki*. Johannesburg: Zebra Press, 1999.

Hagemann, Albrecht. *Nelson Mandela*. Johannesburg: Fontein Books, 1996.

Halisi, C.R.D. *Black Political Thought in the Making of South African Democracy*. Bloomington: Indiana University Press, 1999.

Hamann, Hilton. *Days of the Generals*. Cape Town: Zebra Press, 2001.

Hamilton, C., ed. *The Mfecane Aftermath: Reconstructive Debates in Southern African History*. Johannesburg: Witwatersrand University Press, 1995.

Hamilton, Carolyn, et al., eds. *Refiguring the Archive*. Cape Town: David Philip, 2002.

———. *A Prisoner in the Garden*. Johannesburg: Penguin, 2005.

Hampshire, Stuart. *Morality and Conflict*. Oxford: Basil Blackwell, 1983.

Hanlon, Joseph. *Apartheid's Second Front: South Africa's War Against Its Neighbors*. New York: Penguin, 1986.

———. *Beggar Your Neighbours: Apartheid Power in Southern Africa*. Bloomington: Indiana University Press, 1986.

Hare, A. Paul, Gerd Wiendieck, and Max H. Von Broembsen, eds. *South Africa: Sociological Analyses*. New York: Oxford University Press, 1979.

Hare, A. Paul, ed. *The Struggle for Democracy in South Africa: Conflict and Conflict Resolution*. Cape Town: Centre for Intergroup Studies, 1983.

Harrison, David. *The White Tribe of Africa*. Berkeley: University of California Press, 1982.

Harvey, Robert. *The Fall of Apartheid—The Inside Story from Smuts to Mbeki*. New York: Palgrave Macmillan, 2003.

Hay, Mark, O.M.I. *Ukubuyisana: Reconciliation in South Africa*. Pietermaritzburg: Cluster Publications, 1998.

Hayner, Priscilla B. *Unspeakable Truths*. New York: Routledge, 2001.

Haysom, Nicholas. *Mabangalala: The Rise of Right-Wing Vigilantes in South Africa*. Johannesburg: Centre for Applied Legal Studies, University of the Witwatersrand, 1986.

Hellman, Ellen, and Henry Lever, eds. *Conflict and Progress: Fifty Years of Race Relations in South Africa*. Johannesburg: Macmillan, 1979.

Hill, Iris Tillman, and Alex Harris, eds. *Beyond the Barricades: Popular Resistance in South Africa*. New York: Aperture, 1989.

Hill, Romaine, Marie Muller and Martin Trump, eds. *African Studies Forum*. Pretoria: HSRC, 1991.

Hirsch, Alan. *Season of Hope: Economic Reform Under Mandela and Mbeki*. Scottsville: University of KwaZulu-Natal Press, 2005.

Hirson, Baruch. *Revolutions in My Life*. Johannesburg: Witwatersrand University Press, 1995.

———. *The Cape Town Intellectuals: The Story of Ruth Schecter*. Johannesburg: Witwatersrand University Press, 2001.

Hoagland, Jim. *South Africa: Civilizations in Conflict*. Boston: Houghton Mifflin, 1972.

Hochschild, Adam. The *Mirror at Midnight: A South African Journey*. New York: Viking Penguin, 1990.

Horrell, Muriel. *The African Homelands of South Africa*. Johannesburg: SAIRR, 1973.

Howe, Graham, and Peter le Roux, eds. *Transforming the Economy: Policy Options for South Africa*. Durban: Centre for Social and Development Studies, and Cape Town: Institute for Social Development, University of the Western Cape.

Huddlestone, Trevor. *Naught for Your Comfort*. New York: Doubleday, 1956.

Hugo, Pierre. *Redistribution and Affirmative Action*. Johannesburg: Southern Book Publishers, 1992.

Innes, Duncan. *Anglo: Anglo American and the Rise of Modern South Africa*. Johannesburg: Ravan Press, 1984.

Jacobs, Sean, and Richard Calland. *Thabo Mbeki's World*. Pietermaritzburg: University of Natal Press, 2002.

James, Wilmot. *The State of Apartheid*. Boulder: L. Rienner, 1987.

James, Wilmot, and Moira Levy, eds. *Pulse: Assessing South Africa's Transition*. Cape Town: Idasa, 1998.

James, Wilmot, and Linda van de Vijver, eds. *After the TRC: Reflections on Truth and Reconciliation in South Africa*. Cape Town: David Philip, 2000.

Jeffery, Anthea. *The Natal Story: 16 Years of Conflict*. Johannesburg: South African Institute of Race Relations, 1997.

———. *Bill of Rights Report 1996/97*. Johannesburg: South African Institute of Race Relations, 1997.

Jenkin, Tim. *Escape from Pretoria*. London: Kliptown Books, 1987.

Joffe, Joel. *The Rivonia Story*. Cape Town: Mayibuye Books, UWC, 1995.

Johns, Sheridan, and R. Hunt Davis Jr., eds. *Mandela, Tambo and the African National Congress—The Struggle Against Apartheid, 1948–1990, a Documentary Survey*. New York: Oxford University Press, 1991.

Johnston, Alexander, "South Africa: The Election and the Transition Process: Five Contradictions in Search of a Resolution," *Third World Quarterly* [London], 15, No. 2, June 1994, pp. 187–204.

Johnson, R.W., and Lawrence Schlemmer, eds. *Launching Democracy in South Africa*. New Haven and London: Yale University Press, 1996.

Johnson, R.W. and David Welsh, eds,. *Ironic Victory: Liberalism in Post Liberation South Africa*. Cape Town: Oxford University Press, 1998

Johnson, R.W. *How Long Will South Africa Survive?* New York: Oxford University Press, 1977.

———. *South Africa—The First Man, the Last Nation*. Johannesburg: Jonathan Ball, 2004.

Johnson, Shaun. *Strange Days Indeed*. Johannesburg: Bantam Books, 1993.

Joseph, Helen. *Side by Side: The Autobiography of Helen Joseph*. Johannesburg: A. D. Donker Publishers, 1993.

———. *If This Be Treason*. Johannesburg: Contra Press, 1998.

Joyce, Peter. *A Concise Dictionary of South African Biography*. Cape Town: Francolin Publishers, 1999.

Jukes, Tim J. *Opposition in South Africa: The Leadership of Z. K. Matthews, Nelson Mandela, and Stephen Biko*. Westport, CT: Praeger, 1995.

Kane-Berman, John. *Political Violence in South Africa*. Johannesburg: South African Institute of Race Relations, 1993.

———. *South Africa's Silent Revolution*. Johannesburg: Southern Book Publishers, 1990.

Karis, Thomas. "South African Liberation: The Communist Factor," *Foreign Affairs*, Winter 1986/87, pp. 267–88.

Karis, Thomas G, and Gail M. Gerhart. *From Protest to Challenge*. Bloomington: Indiana University Press, 1997, Vol. 1: *Protest and Hope, 1882–1934*; Vol. 2: *Hope and Challenge, 1935–1952*; Vol. 3: *Challenge and Violence, 1953–1964*; Vol. 4: *Nadir and Resurgence, 1964–1979*.

Kasrils, Ronnie. *Armed and Dangerous*. Johannesburg: Jonathan Ball, 1993.

Kathrada, Ahmed. *Letters from Robben Island*. Cape Town: Mayibuye Books, 1999.

———. *Memoirs*. Cape Town: Zebra Press, 2004.

Keegan, Timothy. *Colonial South Africa and the Origins of the Racial Order*. Cape Town: David Philip, 1996.

Kenney, Henry. *Power, Pride & Prejudice: The Years of Afrikaner Nationalist Rule in South Africa*. Johannesburg: Jonathan Ball, 1991.

Khoisan, Zenzile. *Jakaranda Time: An Investigator's View of South Africa's Truth and Reconciliation Commission*. Cape Town: Garib Communications, 2001.

Kitchen, Helen, and J. Coleman Kitchen, eds. *South Africa: Twelve Perspectives on the Transition*. Westport: Praeger, 1994.

Kok, Pieter, et al., *Post-Apartheid Patterns of Internal Migration in South Africa*. Cape Town: HSRC, 2003.

Kotzé, Hennie, ed. *A Negotiated Democracy in South Africa? A Survey of Attitudes Towards Political, Economic and Social Transformation*. Stellenbosch: Research Report No. 2 of 1993 Centre for International and Comparative Politics, University of Stellenbosch, 1993.

Kretzschmar, Louise. *The Voice of Black Theology in South Africa*. Johannesburg: Ravan Press, 1986.

Kriger, Robert, and Abebe Zegeye. *Culture in the New South Africa*. Cape Town: Kwela Books, 2001.

Krikler, Jeremy. *The Rand Revolt: The 1922 Insurrection and Racial Killing in South Africa*. Cape Town: Jonathan Ball, 2006.

Krog, Antjie. *Country of My Skull*. Johannesburg: Random House, 1998.

Kruger, Daniel Wilhelmus. *The Making of a Nation: A History of the Union of South Africa*. Johannesburg: Macmillan, 1969.

Kuper, Leo. *An African Bourgeoisie: Race, Class, and Politics in South Africa*. New Haven: Yale University Press, 1965.

Labuschagne, Riaan. *On South Africa's Secret Service*. Alberton: Galago, 2002.

La Guma, Alex. *Apartheid: A Collection of Writings on South African Racism by South Africans*. London: Lawrence and Wishart, 1972.

Landsberg, Christopher. *The Quiet Diplomacy of Liberation*. Johannesburg: Jacana, 2004.

L'Ange, Gerald. *The White Africans: From Colonialisation to Liberation*. Johannesburg: Jonathan Ball, 2005.

Lapping, Brian. *Apartheid—a History*. London: Grafton, 1986.

Leach, Graham. *South Africa*. London: Methuen, 1986.

———. *South Africa: No Easy Path to Peace*. London: Routledge & Kegan, 1986.

———. *The Afrikaners*. Johannesburg: Southern Book Publishers, 1989.

Leape, Jonathan, Bo Baskin and Stefan Underhill. *Business in the Shadow of Apartheid: U.S. Firms in South Africa*. Lexington: Lexington Books, 1985.

Leatt, James, Theo Kneifel, and Klaus Nurnberger, eds. *Contending Ideologies in South Africa*. Cape Town: David Philip, 1986.

Lee, Robin and Lawrence Schlemmer, eds. *Transition to Democracy*. Cape Town: Oxford University Press, 1991.

Lelyveld, Joseph. *Move Your Shadow: South Africa, Black and White*. New York: Random House, 1985.

Le May, G. *The Afrikaners, a Historical Interpretation*. Oxford: Blackwell, 1995.

Lemon, Anthony. *Apartheid in Transition*. Boulder: Westview Press, 1987.

Leonard, Richard. *South Africa at War: White Power and the Crisis in Southern Africa*. Chicago: Chicago Review, 1983.

Levy, Norman, ed. *Balancing Secrecy and Transparency in a Democracy: The Hefer Commission—the Case Study*. Johannesburg: South African National Academy of Intelligence, 2004.

——— and Chris Tapscott, eds. *Intergovernmental Relations in South Africa*. Cape Town: Idasa, 2001.

Lewin, Hugh. *Bandiet: Out of Jail*. Johannesburg: Random House, 2002.

Licht, Robert A. and Bertus de Villiers. *South Africa's Crisis of Constitutional Democracy: Can the U.S. Constitution Help?* Washington: The AEI Press, 1994.

Lipton, Merle. *Capitalism and Apartheid, South Africa 1910–84.* Totowa, NJ: Rowman & Allanheld, 1983.

Lodge, Tom. *Black Politics in South Africa Since 1945.* New York: Longman, 1983.

———. *Consolidating Democracy: South Africa's Second Popular Election.* Johannesburg: Witwatersrand University Press, 1999.

———. *Politics in South Africa: From Mandela to Mbeki.* Cape Town: David Philip, 2002.

———. *Mandela—a Critical Life.* Cape Town: Oxford University Press, 2006.

———, et al. *All, Here, and Now: Black Politics in South Africa in the 1980s.* Cape Town: David Philip, 1991.

Louw, P. Eric. *The Rise, Fall, and Legacy of Apartheid.* Westport: Praeger, 2004.

Luthuli, Albert. *Let My People Go: An Autobiography.* London: Fount Paperbacks, 1962.

McKendrick, Brian, and Wilma Hoffmann, eds. *People and Violence in South Africa.* Cape Town: Oxford University Press, 1990.

McKinley, Dale T. *The ANC and the Liberation Struggle.* London: Pluto Press, 1997.

Magubane, Bernard Makhosezwe. *The Political Economy of Race and Class in South Africa.* New York: Monthly Review Press, 1979.

———. *African Sociology—Towards a Critical Perspective.* Trenton: Africa World Press, 2000.

Magubane, Bernard, and Ibbo Mandaza. *Whither South Africa?* Trenton: Africa World Press, 1988.

Maharaj, Gitanjali, ed. *Between Unity and Diversity.* Cape Town: Idasa and David Philip, 1999.

Maharaj, Mac, ed. *Reflections in Prison.* Cape Town: Zebra Press, 2001.

Maharaj, Zarina. *Dancing to a Different Rhythm.* Cape Town: Zebra Press, 2006.

Makgoba, Malegapuru William, ed. *African Renaissance.* Johannesburg: Mafube, 1999.

———. *Mokoko: The Makgoba Affair.* Johannesburg: Vivlia, 1997.

Malan, Rian. *My Traitor's Heart.* New York: Atlantic Monthly Press, 1990.

Malan, Robin, ed. *The Essential Nelson Mandela.* Cape Town: David Philip, 1997.

Mallaby, Sebastian. *After Apartheid.* New York: Times Books, 1992.

Maloka, Eddy. *The South African Communist in Exile.* Pretoria: Africa Institute of South Africa, 2002.

Mandela, Nelson. *No Easy Walk to Freedom.* London: Heinemann Educational Books Ltd., 1965.

———.*The Struggle Is My Life.* London: International Defence and Aid Fund for Southern Africa, 1986.

———. *Long Walk to Freedom.* Boston: Little, Brown, 1994.

———, et al. *Voices from Robben Island.* Jurgen Schadeberg, comp. Randburg: Ravan Press, 1994.

Mandela, Zindzi. *Black as I Am.* Durban: Sereti sa Sechaba and Madiba, 1978.

Manganyi, N. Chabani, and André du Toit, eds. *Political Violence and the Struggle in South Africa.* London: Macmillan Academic and Professional Ltd., 1990.

Manning, Tony, ed. *Trends Transforming South Africa.* Cape Town: Juta, 1991.

Marais, H.C., ed. *South Africa: Perspectives of the Future.* Pinetown: Owen Burgess Publishers, 1988.

Marais, Hein. *South Africa Limits to Change.* Cape Town: University of Cape Town Press, 1998.

Mare, Gerhard, and Georgina Hamilton. *An Appetite for Power: Buthelezi's Inkatha and South Africa.* Johannesburg: Ravan Press, 1987.

Marinovich, Greg, and Joao Silva. *The Bang-Bang Club.* London: William Heinemann, 2000.

Marks, Monique. *Young Warriors.* Johannesburg: Witwatersrand University Press, 2001.

Marks, Shula. *The Ambiguities of Dependence in South Africa: Class, Nationalism, and the State in Twentieth-Century Natal.* Johannesburg: Ravan Press, 1986.

———, and Stanley Trapido, eds. *The Politics of Race, Class, and Nationalism in Twentieth-Century South Africa.* New York: Longman, 1982.

Marks, Shula, and Richard Rathbone. *Industrialization and Social Change in South Africa: African Class, Culture, and Consciousness.* New York: Longman, 1982.

Marks, Susan Collin. *Watching the Wind—Conflict Resolution During South Africa's Transition to Democracy.* Washington, D.C.: United States Institute of Peace Press, 2000.

Marx, Anthony. *Lessons of Struggle: South African Internal Opposition, 1960–1990.* New York: Oxford University Press, 1992.

Mashinini, Emma. *Strikes Have Followed Me All My Life*. New York: Routledge, 1989.

Massie, Robert Kinloch. *Loosing the Bonds: The United States and South Africa in the Apartheid Years*. New York: Doubleday, 1997.

Mathabane, Mark. *Kaffir Boy*. New York: Macmillan, 1986.

Matshikiza, Todd, and John Matshikiza. *With the Lid Off*. Johannesburg: M&G Books, 2000.

Matshoba, Mtutuzeli. *Call Me Not a Man*. Johannesburg: Ravan Press, 1979.

Mattes, Robert. *The Election Book: Judgment and Choice in South Africa's 1994 Election*. Cape Town: Idasa Public Information Centre, 1995.

Matthews, Z.K. *Freedom for My People*. Cape Town: David Philip, 1981.

Mayekiso, Mzwanele. *Township Politics: Civic Struggles in a New South Africa*. New York: Monthly Review Press, 1986.

Maylam, Paul. *A History of the African People of South Africa: From the Early Iron Age to the 1970s*. New York: St. Martin's Press, 1986.

Mbeki, Govan Archibald Mvunyelwa. *South Africa—the Peasants' Revolt*. Baltimore: Penguin, 1964.

———. *Sunset at Midday*. Johannesburg: Nolwazi Educational Publishers, 1996.

———. *Learning from Robben Island*. Cape Town: David Philip,1991.

Mbeki, Thabo. *Africa Define Yourself*. Cape Town: Tafelberg, 2002.

Meer, Fatima. *Portrait of Indian South Africans*. Durban: Avon House, 1969.

———. *Higher Than Hope*. Johannesburg: Skotaville, 1988.

———, ed. *Treason Trial—1985*. Durban: Madiba Publications, 1989.

Meer, Ismail. *A Fortunate Man*. Cape Town: Zebra Press, 2002.

Meiring, Piet. *Chronicle of the Truth Commission*. Johannesburg: Carpe Diem Books, 1999.

Meli, Francis. *A History of the ANC: South Africa Belongs to Us*. Harare: Zimbabwean Publishing House, 1986.

Melville, Neville. *From Apartheid to Zaamheid—Breaking Down Walls and Building Bridges in South African Society*. Valyland: Aardvark Press, 2004.

Meredith, Martin. *Fischer's Choice: A Life of Bram Fischer*. Johannesburg: Jonathan Ball, 2002.

———. *In the Name of Apartheid*. New York: Harper and Row, 1988.

———. *Coming to Terms: South Africa's Search for Truth*. New York: Public Affairs, 1999.

———. *The State of Africa*. Johannesburg: Jonathan Ball, 2005.

Miles, John. *Deafening Silence*. Cape Town: Human & Rousseau, 1997.

Minnaar, Anthony, and Mike Hough, eds. *Conflict, Violence and Conflict Resolution: Where Is South Africa Heading?* Pretoria: HSRC Press, 1997.

Modisane, Bloke. *Blame Me on History*. New York: Simon & Schuster/Touchstone, 1986.

Moleah, Alfred Tokollo. *South Africa: Colonialism, Apartheid, and African Dispossession*. Wilmington, DE: Disa Press, 1993.

Moll, Peter, Nicoli Nattrass, and Lieb Loots, eds. *Redistribution: How Can It Work in South Africa?* Cape Town: David Philip, 1991.

Moodie, T. Dunbar. *The Rise of Afrikanerdom: Power, Apartheid, and the Afrikaner Civil Religion*. Berkeley: University of California Press, 1975.

Morris, Alan. *Bleakness and Light: Inner City Transitions in Hillbrow, Johannesburg*. Johannesburg: Witwatersrand University Press, 1999.

Morris, Donald R. *The Washing of the Spears: A History of the Rise of the Zulu Nation Under Shaka and Its Fall in the Zulu War of 1879*. New York: Simon & Schuster, 1965.

Moss, Glenn, and Ingrid Obrey, eds., "From Red Friday to CODESA," *South African Review 6*, Johannesburg: Ravan Press,1992.

———. *South African Review 5*, Johannesburg: Ravan Press, 1989.

Moss, Rose. *Shouting at the Crocodile*. Boston: Beacon Press, 1990.

Mostert, Noël. *Frontiers: The Epic of South Africa's Creation and the Tragedy of the Xhosa People*. New York: Alfred A. Knopf, 1992.

Motlhabi, Mokgethi. *The Theory and Practice of Black Resistance to Apartheid*. Johannesburg: Skotaville, 1984.

Mufamadi, Thembeka. *Raymond Mhlaba's Personal Memoirs*. Pretoria: HSRC, 2001.

Mufson, Steven. *Fighting Years*. Boston: Beacon Press, 1990.

Mulemfo, Mukanda M. *Thabo Mbeki and the African Renaissance.* Pretoria: Actua Press, 2000.

Muller, A. *Minority Interests: The Political Economy of the Coloured and Indian Communities in South Africa.* Johannesburg: SAIRR, 1968.

Murray, Christina, and Catherine O'Regan, eds. *No Place to Rest: Forced Removals and the Law in South Africa.* Cape Town: Oxford University Press, 1990.

Mutwa, Vusamazulu Credo. *Indaba, My Children.* Edinburgh: Payback Press, 1998.

Naidoo, Indres. "Prisoner 885/63," *Island in Chains.* London: Penguin, 1982.

Naipaul, Shiva. *North of South.* London: Penguin, 1978.

Nattrass, Nicoli. *Macro Economics: Theory and Practice in South Africa.* Cape Town: David Philip, 1997.

Ndlovu, Sifiso Mxolisi. *The Soweto Uprisings: Counter-Memories of June 1976.* Johannesburg: Ravan Press, 1998.

Nicholas, Lionel J. and Saths Cooper, eds. *Psychology and Apartheid.* Johannesburg: Vision Publications, 1990.

Nicol, Mike. *The Waiting Country.* London: Victor Gollancz, 1995.

Nieumeijer, Louise, and Renée du Toit, eds. *Multicultural Conflict Management in Changing Societies.* Pretoria: HSRC, 1994.

———and Fanie Cloete, eds. *The Dynamics of Negotiation in South Africa.* Pretoria: HSRC, 1991.

Nolan, Albert. *God in South Africa.* Cape Town: David Philip, 1988.

Noonan, Patrick. *They're Burning the Churches.* Johannesburg: Jacana, 2003.

North, James. *Freedom Rising.* New York: Macmillan, 1985.

Ntloedibe, Elias. *Here Is a Tree: Political Biography of Robert Mangaliso Sobukwe.* Mogoditshane, Botswana: Century Turn, 1995.

Nuttall, Sarah, and Carli Coetzee, eds. *Negotiating the Past: The Making of Memory in South Africa.* Oxford: Oxford University Press, 1998.

———and Cheryl-Ann Michael, eds. *Senses of Culture.* London: Oxford University Press, 2000.

Nyatsumba, Kaizer. *All Sides of the Story.* Johannesburg: Jonathan Ball, 1997.

O'Meara, Dan. *Volkskapitalisme: Class, Capital, and Ideology in the Development of Afrikaner Nationalism, 1934–1948.* New York: Cambridge University Press, 1983.

———. *Forty Lost Years: The Apartheid State and the Politics of the National Party, 1948–1994.* Johannesburg: Ravan Press, 1996.

Orkin, Mark, ed. *Disinvestment, the Struggle, and the Future.* Johannesburg: Ravan Press, 1986.

———. *Sanctions Against Apartheid.* Cape Town: David Philip, 1989.

Orr, Wendy. *From Biko to Basson.* Johannesburg: Contra Press, 2000.

Ottaway, David. *Chained Together: Mandela, De Klerk and the Struggle to Remake South Africa.* New York: Random House, 1993.

Ottaway, Marina. *South Africa: The Struggle for a New Order.* Washington, D.C.: Brookings Institution, 1993.

Owomoyela, Oyekan. *The African Difference.* Johannesburg: Witwatersrand University Press, 1996.

Pakenham, Thomas. *The Boer War.* London: Futura Publications, 1982.

———. *The Scramble for Africa.* New York: Random House, 1991.

Parsons, Raymond. *The Mbeki Inheritance.* Johannesburg: Ravan Press, 1999.

———, et al., eds. *Manuel, Markets and Money.* Cape Town: Double Storey Books, 2004.

Pascoe, Elaine. *South Africa, Troubled Land.* New York: Franklin Watts, 1987.

Pauw, Jacques. *In the Heart of the Whore: The Story of Apartheid's Death Squads.* Johannesburg: Southern Book Publishers, 1991.

———. *Into the Heart of Darkness: Confessions of Apartheid's Assassins.* Johannesburg: Jonathan Ball, 1997.

Peires, Jeffrey B. *The House of Phalo: A History of the Xhosa People in the Days of Their Independence,* Perspectives on Southern Africa, No. 32. Berkeley: University of California Press, 1982.

———. *The Dead Will Arise: Nongqawuse and the Great Xhosa Cattle-Killing Movement of 1856–7.* Johannesburg: Ravan Press, 1989.

Picard, John, ed. *The State of the State.* Johannesburg: Witwatersrand University Press, 2006.

Picard, Louis A. *The State of the State: Institutional Transformation, Capacity and Political Change in South Africa.* Johannesburg: Wits University Press, 2005.

Pilger, John. *Freedom Next Time.* London: Bantam Books, 2006.

Pillay, Udesh, Benjamin Roberts, and Stephen Rule, eds. *South African Social Studies: Changing Times, Diverse Voices.* Cape Town: HSRC Press, 2006.

Plaatje, Sol. *Native Life in South Africa.* Johannesburg: Ravan Press, 1982.

———. *Selected Writings.* Johannesburg: Witwatersrand University Press, 1996.

Platzky, Laurine, and Cherryl Walker. *The Surplus People.* Johannesburg: Ravan Press, 1985.

Pogrund, Benjamin. *How Can Man Die Better: The Life of Robert Sobukwe.* Johannesburg: Jonathan Ball, 1990.

———. *War of Words.* New York: Seven Stories Press, 2000.

Pollak, Richard. *Up Against Apartheid: The Role and Plight of the Press in South Africa.* Carbondale: Southern Illinois University Press, 1981.

Posel, Deborah, and Graeme Simpson, eds. *Commissioning the Past: Understanding South Africa's Truth and Reconciliation Commission.* Johannesburg: Witwatersrand University Press, 2002.

———. *The Making of Apartheid 1948–1961.* Oxford: Clarendon Press, 1991.

Price, Robert. *The Apartheid State in Crisis: Political Transformation in South Africa 1975–1990.* New York: Oxford University Press, 1991.

Ramphele, Mamphela. *Steering by the Stars: Being Young in South Africa.* Cape Town: Tafelberg, 2002.

———. *A Bed Called Home.* Cape Town: David Philip, 1993.

Rantete, Johannes. *The African National Congress and the Negotiated Settlement in South Africa.* Pretoria: J. L. van Schaik, 1998.

Razis, Vic. *The American Connection: The Influence of United States Business on South Africa.* London: Pinter, 1986.

Reader's Digest Association. *Illustrated History of South Africa: The Real Story.* Pleasantville, NY: 1989.

Rembe, Nasila, ed. *Reflections on Democracy and Human Rights: A Decade of the South African Constitution.* Johannesburg: Human Rights Commission, 2006.

Reynolds, Andrew. *Election '94 South Africa.* New York: St. Martin's Press, 1994.

———. *Election '99 South Africa.* Cape Town: David Philip, 1999.

Rich, Paul B. *White Power and the Liberal Conscience.* Johannesburg: Ravan Press, 1984.

Roberts, Jack. *Nelson Mandela: Determined to Be Free.* Brookfield, CT: Millbrook Press, 1995.

Robertson, Ian, and Phillip Whitten. *Race and Politics in South Africa.* New Brunswick: Transaction Books, 1978.

Robins, Steven L. *Limits to Liberation After Apartheid.* Oxford: James Currey, 2005.

Rogers, Barbara. *Divide and Rule.* London: International Defence & Aid Fund, 1980.

Rosenthal, Richard. *Mission Improbable.* Cape Town: David Philip, 1998.

Ross, Robert. *A Concise History of South Africa.* Cambridge: Cambridge University Press, 1999.

Roux, Edward. *Time Longer Than Rope.* Madison: University of Wisconsin Press, 1964.

Sachs, Albie. *The Jail Diaries of Albie Sachs.* London: Paladin Grafton Books, 1990.

———. *Advancing Human Rights in South Africa.* Cape Town: Oxford University Press, 1992.

Sampson, Anthony. *Black and Gold.* London: Hodder & Stoughton, 1987.

———. *Mandela: The Authorized Biography.* New York: Alfred A. Knopf, 1999.

Sanders, Mark. *Complicities: The Intellectual and Apartheid (Philosophy and Postcoloniality).* Pietermaritzburg: University of Natal Press, 2002.

Saul, John S., and Stephen Gelb. *Crisis in South Africa.* New York: Monthly Review Press, 1986.

Saunders, Christopher C. *Historical Dictionary of South Africa.* New Jersey: Scarecrow Press, 1983.

———. *The Making of the South African Past: Major Historians on Race and Class.* Cape Town: David Philip, 1998.

———, and Nicholas Southey. *A Dictionary of South African History.* Cape Town: David Philip, 1998.

Scadeberg, Jurgen, ed. *Nelson Mandela and the Rise of the ANC.* Parklands: Jonathan Ball and A. D. Donker, 1990.

———. *Voices from Robben Island*. Johannesburg: Ravan Press, 1994.

Schipper, Mineke. *Imagining Insiders: Africa and the Question of Belonging*. London: Cassell, 1999.

Schneidman, Witney W. *Postapartheid South Africa: Steps Taken, the Path Ahead*. CSIS Africa Notes, No. 156. Washington, D.C.: Center for Strategic and International Studies, January 1994.

Schönteich, Martin. *Unshackling the Crime Fighters*. Johannesburg: South African Institute of Race Relations, 1999.

Schrire, Robert. *Critical Choices for South Africa*. Cape Town: Oxford University Press, 1990.

———. *Leadership in the Apartheid State*. Cape Town: Oxford University Press, 1994.

Schutte, Charl, Ian Liebenberg, and Anthony Minnaar, eds. *The Hidden Hand: Covert Operations in South Africa*. Pretoria: HSRC, 1998.

Seekings, Jeremy. *The UDF: A History of the United Democratic Front in South Africa 1983–1991*. Cape Town: David Philip, 2000.

Serote, Mongane Wally. *Hyenas*. Johannesburg: Vivlia Publishers and Booksellers, 2000.

Serfontein, J. *Brotherhood of Power: An Exposé of the Secret Afrikaner Broederbond*. London: Rex Collings, 1979.

Sethi, S. Prakash. *The South African Quagmire*. Cambridge: Ballinger, 1987.

Shain, Milton, ed. *Opposing Voices: Liberalism and Opposition in South Africa Today*. Johannesburg: Jonathan Ball, 2006.

Shaw, Mark. *Crime and Policing in Post-Apartheid South Africa*. Cape Town: David Philip, 2002.

Shubin, Vladimir. *ANC: A View from Moscow*. Cape Town: Mayibuye Books, 1999.

Simon, David. *South Africa in Southern Africa*. Oxford: James Currey, 1998.

Simons, Harold Jack, and Ray Alexander. *Class and Colour in South Africa*. Harmondsworth: Penguin, 1969.

Sipho, Seepe. *Truth to Power: Reflections on Post-1994 South Africa*. Pretoria: Vista University and Skotaville Media 2005.

Sisulu, Elinor. *Walter & Albertina Sisulu: In Our Lifetime*. Cape Town: David Philip, 2002.

Slabbert, Frederik van Zyl. *South Africa's Options: Strategies for Sharing Power*. London: Palgrave Macmillan, 1979.

———, and Jeff Opland. *South Africa: Dilemmas of Evolutionary Change*. Grahamstown: Institute of Social and Economic Research, Rhodes University, 1980.

Slabbert, Frederik van Zyl, et al., eds. *Youth in the New South Africa: Towards Policy Formulation*. Pretoria: HSRC, 1994.

Slabbert, Frederik van Zyl. *Tough Choices*. Cape Town: Tafelberg, 2000.

———. *The Other Side of History*. Cape Town: Jonathan Ball, 2006.

Slovo, Joe. "South Africa—No Middle Road" in Basil Davidson, Joe, Slovo, and Anthony R. Wilkinson, eds. *Southern Africa: The New Politics of Revolution*. Harmondsworth: Penguin, 1976.

———. *The Unfinished Autobiography*. Johannesburg: Ravan Press, 1995.

Smith, Charlene. *Robben Island*. Cape Town: Struik, 1997.

Smith, David M. *The Apartheid City and Beyond*. London: Routledge, 1992.

Smith, I. *The Origins of the South African War*. London: Longman, 1996.

South African Communist Party. *The African Communist: Viva Socialism! Learning from the Crisis*. Johannesburg: Inkululeko Publications, 1991.

South Africa Democracy Trust. *The Road to Democracy in South Africa*, Vol. 1 (1960–1970). Cape Town: Zebra Press, 2004.

South African Institute of Race Relations (SAIRR). *Survey of Race Relations*. Johannesburg: SAIRR, annual.

———. *South Africa in Travail: The Disturbances of 1973/77*. Johannesburg: SAIRR, 1978.

Sono, Themba. *Reflections on the Origins of Black Consciousness in South Africa*. Pretoria: HSRC, 1993.

Sparks, Allister. *Beyond the Miracle: Inside the New South Africa*. Johannesburg: Jonathan Ball, 2003.

———. *Tomorrow Is Another Country*. Chicago: University of Chicago Press, 1995.

———. *The Mind of South Africa: The Story of the Rise and Fall of Apartheid*. New York: Alfred A. Knopf, 1990.

Spitz, Richard, and Matthew Chaskalson. *The Politics of Transition*. Johannesburg: Witwatersrand University Press, 2000.

Stadler, Alfred William. *The Political Economy of Modern South Africa.* Cape Town: David Philip, 1987.

Steinberg, Jonny, ed. *Crime Wave: The South African Underworld and Its Foes.* Johannesburg: Witwatersrand University Press, 2001.

———. *Midlands.* Johannesburg: Jonathan Ball, 2002.

Steyn, Jan. *Managing Change in South Africa.* Cape Town: Human and Rousseau and Tafelberg, 1990.

Steyn, Melissa E., and Khanya B. Motshabi, eds. *Cultural Synergy in South Africa.* Johannesburg: Knowledge Resources, 1996.

Stiff, Peter. *The Silent War.* Alberton: Galago,1999.

———. *Warfare by Other Means* Alberton: Galago, 2001.

Strachan, Beth. *South Africa's Second Democratic Election 1999.* Johannesburg: Electoral Institute of Southern Africa, 2001.

Straker, Gill, with Fathima Moosa, Rise Becker, and Madiyoyo Nkwale. *Faces in the Revolution: The Psychological Effects of Violence on Township Youth in South Africa.* Cape Town: David Philip, 1992.

Suckling, John, and Landeg White. *After Apartheid: Renewal of the South African Economy.* Heslington: Centre for Southern African Studies, 1988.

Sunter, Clem. *The High Road: Where Are We Now?* Cape Town: Human & Rousseau and Tafelberg, 1996.

———. *Never Mind the Millennium. What About the Next 24 Hours?* Cape Town: Human & Rousseau and Tafelberg, 1999.

Suzman, Helen. *In No Uncertain Terms.* New York: Alfred A. Knopf, 1993.

Swilling, Mark. *Views on the South African State.* Pretoria: HSRC, 1990.

Switzer, L. *Power and Resistance in an African Society: The Ciskei Xhosa and the Making of South Africa.* Madison: University of Wisconsin, 1993.

Tambo, Adelaide. *Preparing for Power: Oliver Tambo Speaks.* London: Heinemann Educational Books, 1987.

Temkin, Ben. *Buthelezi: A Biography.* London: Frank Cass, 2003.

Terreblanche, Sampie. *A History of Inequality in South Africa 1652–2002.* Pietermaritzburg: University of Natal Press and KMM Review Publishing, 2002.

Thompson, Leonard, and Jeffrey Butler. *Change in Contemporary South Africa.* Berkeley: University of California Press, 1975.

Thompson, Leonard, and Andrew Prior. *South African Politics.* New Haven: Yale University Press, 1982.

Thompson, Leonard. *A History of South Africa.* New Haven: Yale University Press, 2001.

———. *The Political Mythology of Apartheid.* New Haven: Yale University Press, 1985.

Truth and Reconciliation Commission. *Report of the Truth and Reconciliation Commission, Vols. 1–5.* Cape Town: Juta, 1998.

Turner, Barry. *Southern Africa Profiled.* London: Macmillan, 2000.

Turok, Ben. *Nothing but the Truth.* Johannesburg: Jonathan Ball, 2003.

———. *Beyond the Miracle: Development and Economy in South Africa: A Reader.* Cape Town: Fair Share, 1999.

———, et al. *Development and Reconstruction in South Africa.* Johannesburg: Institute for African Alternatives, 1993.

Tutu, Desmond. *Crying in the Wilderness.* Grand Rapids, MI: Wm. B. Eerdmans, 1982.

———. *No Future Without Forgiveness.* London: Rider, 1999.

Twala, Mwezi, and Ed Benard. *Mbokodo: Inside MK: Mwezi Twala—A Soldier's Story.* Johannesburg: Jonathan Ball, 1994.

Uhlig, Mark A. *Apartheid in Crisis.* New York: Random House, 1986.

Vadi, Ismail. *The Congress of the People and Freedom Charter Campaign.* New Delhi: Sterling Publishers, 1995.

Van den Berghe, Pierre L. *South Africa, a Study in Conflict.* Middletown: Wesleyan University Press, 1965.

————. *The Liberal Dilemma in South Africa*. New York: St Martin's Press, 1979.

Van der Merwe, Hendrik W. *Pursuing Justice and Peace in South Africa*. London: Routledge, 1989.

————. *Peacemaking in South Africa*. Cape Town: Tafelberg, 2000.

Van Kessel, Ineke. *Beyond Our Wildest Dreams: The United Democratic Front and the Transformation of South Africa*. Charlottesville: University of Virginia Press, 2000.

Van Rooyen, Johann. *Hard Right: The New White Power in South Africa*. London: I. B. Tauris, 1994.

Van Schalkwyk, Rex. *One Miracle Is Not Enough*. Johannesburg: Bellwether, 1998.

Van Vuuren, D. J., et al., eds. *South Africa: A Plural Society in Transition*. Durban: Butterworths, 1985.

Van Vuuren, D. J., et al., eds. *South Africa in the Nineties*. Pretoria: HSRC, 1991.

Venter, Albert. *Government & Politics in the New South Africa*. Pretoria: J. L. van Schaik, 1998.

Venter, Lester. *In the Shadow of the Rainbow*. Johannesburg: Heinemann, 2001.

————. *When Mandela Goes*. Johannesburg: Doubleday, 1997.

Villa-Vicencio, Charles, and Erik Doxtader, eds. *The Provocations of Amnesty: Memory, Justice and Impunity*. Cape Town: David Philip, 2003.

Villa-Vicencio, Charles, and Carl Niehaus, eds. *Many Cultures, One Nation*. Cape Town: Human and Rousseau, 1995.

Villa-Vicencio, Charles. *A Theology of Reconstruction*. Cape Town: David Philip, 1992.

————, and Wilhelm Verwoerd, eds. *Looking Back Reaching Forward: Reflections on the Truth and Reconciliation Commission of South Africa*. Cape Town: University of Cape Town Press, 2000.

Waldmeir, Patti. *Anatomy of a Miracle: The End of Apartheid and the Birth of the New South Africa*. New York: Norton, 1997.

Walker, Eric Anderson. *The Great Trek*. London: Murray, 1972.

Walshe, Peter. *The Rise of African Nationalism in South Africa*. Berkeley: University of California Press, 1971.

Warwick, Peter. *Black People and the South African War*. Cambridge: Cambridge University Press, 1983.

Welsh, Frank. *A History of South Africa*. London: HarperCollins, 1998.

Wentzel, Jill. *The Liberal Slideaway*. Johannesburg: SAIRR, 1995.

Werbner, Richard, and Terence Ranger. *Postcolonial Identities in Africa*. London: Zed Books, 1996.

Willan, Brian, ed. *Sol Plaatje: Selected Writings*. Johannesburg: Witwatersrand University Press, 1996.

Wilson, Francis. *South Africa: The Cordoned Heart*. New York: Norton, 1986.

————, and Mamphela Ramphele. *Uprooting Poverty*. Cape Town: David Philip, 1989.

Wilson, Monica, and Leonard Thompson, eds. *The Oxford History of South Africa,* Vols. I and II. Oxford: Clarendon Press, 1978.

Wilson, Richard A. *The Politics of Truth and Reconciliation in South Africa*. Cambridge: Cambridge University Press, 2001.

Wilson, William. *Power, Racism, and Privilege: Race Relations in Theoretical and Socio-Historical Perspectives*. New York: Macmillan, 1973.

Wolpe, Harold. *Race, Class and the Apartheid State*. London: James Currey, 1988.

Wolpert, Stanley. *Gandhi's Passion: The Life and Legacy of Mahatma Gandhi*. New York: Oxford University Press, 2001.

Wolvaardt, Pieter. *A Diplomat's Story: Apartheid and Beyond 1969–1998*. Alberton: Galago, 2005.

Woods, Donald. *Biko*. New York: Henry Holt, 1987.

————. *Rainbow Nation Revisited*. London: André Deutsch, 2000.

Worden, Nigel. *The Making of Modern South Africa*. Oxford: Blackwell, 1994.

Zegeye, Abebe, ed. *Social Identities in the New South Africa*. Cape Town: Kwela Books, 2001.

————, and Robert Kriger, eds. *Culture in the New South Africa*. Cape Town: Kwela Books, 2001.

Zwelonke, D. M. *Robben Island*. London: Heinemann, 1973.

INDEX

Abrahams, Archie, 223
Africa
  decolonization of, 76–77, 82–83
  liberation movements (1970s), 198
  See also South Africa
African Communist, The, 85
African National Congress (ANC)
  Afrikaners, meetings with, 261
  apartheid ends. *See* Apartheid
    abolished; South Africa,
    restructuring
  armed struggle. *See* Armed anti-
    apartheid movement; Umkhonto
    we Sizwe (MK) (Spear of the
    Nation)
  ban lifted, 21, 335, 337
  core of five, 339*n*–41
  Defiance Campaign (1952), 32,
    54–55, 63
  Department of National Security
    (NAT), 220*n*
  exile of, 32–33, 77–79, 88, 95, 204
  first conference (1962), 94–95
  first legal meetings (1990), 341–44
  founding/development, 31–32
  Freedom Charter (1955), 63–64, 71
  Freedom Day strike (1950), 54*n*
  Geneva Protocol, 228–29
  government opens talks (1987), 243
  Green Book, 206–7, 222–23
  Hani memorandum, 186–88
  Harare Declaration, 265–66, 317–20
  Indian membership, 38, 43, 165, 215,
    483
  informant problem, 219–20*n*
  Kabwe conference, 233–38
  leadership roles (1991), 391, 396, 405
  legitimacy/effectiveness of, 203
  and Mac. *See* Maharaj,
    Sathyandranath Ragunanan (Mac)
  and Mandela. *See* Mandela, Nelson
  after Mandela release, issues of,
    339–44, 347–57, 363
  mass movements, 207–8, 225–26,
    232–33, 247
  Mbeki as president. *See* Mbeki, Thabo
  and MK, 95, 99–100
  Morogoro conference (1969), 204–5
  Ngcuka investigation, 23, 417,
    419–34, 443–46
  Nzo as acting president. *See* Nzo,
    Alfred
  "people's war" position, 207–8,
    225–26, 232–33
  political evolution (1912–1959),
    61–64
  Politico-Military Council (PMC),
    234–36
  power position (2006), 471–73,
    491–92
  racial attitudes/practices (2006),
    473–75
  Revolutionary Council (RC), 203,
    205–6, 218, 220–21

African National Congress *(cont.)*
  Robben Island operation, 153–57,
    161–62
  and South African Communist Party,
    62–63, 71, 95
  Strategy and Tactics policy, 204
  Tambo as president. *See* Tambo,
    Oliver
  Treason Trial (1956), 64, 74
  tribalism, view of, 61
  underground. *See* Operation Vula
  and Vula trial, 383–89
African National Congress Youth
    League (ANCYL)
  formation of, 32
  ideology of, Manifesto (1944), 62
  leaders of, 62
African Peer Review Mechanism
    (APRM), 450*n*
African people
  death penalty, 138
  -Indian relationship, 38, 53, 483
  indigenous of South Africa, 25–28
  racial discrimination. *See* Apartheid
  Robben Island conditions for,
    148–49
  slavery, beginning of, 25–26
African Union (AU), formation of, 316*n*
Afrikaner Resistance Movement
    (AWB), 395–96
Afrikaners
  Afrikaans language, 26, 30
  ANC meetings with, 261, 325
  and basis of apartheid, 28
  Boers, control of Cape, 26–29
  Broederbond, 30
  chosen people myth, 28
  national identity, 30
  origin of, 25–26
  political parties of, 29–30
  and South African republic
    referendum (1960), 77–78
Afrikaner Volksfront (AVF), 394
Ainslie, Ros, 84
Alexander, Ray, 215
All-In Africa Conference (1961), 78

Anglo-Boer South African War
    (1899–1902), 29
Angola, liberation movement, 198
Anti-apartheid. *See* Apartheid abolition
    movement
Anti-Apartheid Movement (AAM)
  formation of, 80, 84
  Robben Island prisoners as cause, 152
Apartheid
  educational discrimination, 65, 69–70
  end of. *See* Apartheid abolished;
    South Africa, restructuring
  Grand Apartheid, 93–94
  historical basis, 25–29
  independent homelands plan, 93–94
  Indians, restrictions on, 40–42, 48,
    53, 65, 67–68
  initial laws (1948–58), 31
  institutionalization of, 29–31
  land ownership limits, 29, 41–42,
    93–94
  mixed marriage prohibition, 31
  pass book policy, 26, 27*n*, 29, 31,
    41–43
  population registration, 31
  repeal of, 339
  at Robben Island, 148
  separate amenities, 31, 67–68
  and tricameral constitution, 200
  Verwoerd plan, 77–78, 93–94, 232
  voting rights discrimination, 30
Apartheid abolished, 314–39
  ANC ban lifted, 21, 335, 337
  ANC first meetings (1990), 341–44
  ANC first national conference
    (1991), 391
  armed struggle suspended, 12–13,
    365–67, 371, 390
  and De Klerk, 21, 305, 324–27,
    337–39
  D. F. Malan Accord, 390
  end of apartheid, 324, 339
  government restructured. *See* South
    Africa, restructuring
  Groote Schuur Minute, 12, 343, 356
  immunity to NEC members, 343

Mac and negotiations, 315–20, 323, 328–32, 334–35

Mandela and negotiations, 243, 253, 261, 266, 301–3, 337–38

Apartheid abolition movement

armed methods. *See* Armed anti-apartheid movement; Umkhonto we Sizwe (MK) (Spear of the Nation)

communist association. *See* Communism; South African Communist Party (SACP)

Defiance Campaign (1952), 32

East German/Soviet support, 87–88

government security against, 118*n*, 190, 199–201

Mac in. *See* Maharaj, Sathyandranath Ragunanan (Mac)

Mandela/ANC actions. *See* African National Congress (ANC); Mandela, Nelson

mass demonstrations. *See* Mass movements

political groups, early, 32–33, 62–64, 78, 80, 84–85

post-cold war factors, 21, 33

Sharpeville massacre (1960), 77–78, 86*n*

and Soweto uprising, 189–90

state support, 137*n*

and trade unions, 241–42

tricameral constitution protest, 200–201

Vaal uprising, 201

Area Political Committees (APC), 225

Arkatias (Indian immigrant recruiters), 39*n*

Armed anti-apartheid movement

and ANC, 88, 94–96, 99–101

arms smuggling, 262, 265, 283

end of, 12–13, 365–67, 371, 390

first steps (1961), 86*n*, 88

guerrilla warfare, 96, 99–100, 187

gunpowder production, 116

inadequacy of, 98–100, 202*n*–3, 270

indigenous methods, 99

Mac participation. *See* Umkhonto we Sizwe (MK) (Spear of the Nation)

Mandela on, 79, 204

MK. *See* Umkhonto we Sizwe (MK) (Spear of the Nation)

Operation Mayibuye, 95–97, 99–100

pipe bombs, 111, 115–16

sabotage, 88, 90, 93, 95, 100

self-defense units (SDUs), 390

soft targets, 236–38

South African Communist Party sabotage, 88, 90, 100

Soviet/East German support, 88

Strategy and Tactics document, 187–88, 204

training, 90, 98*n*, 99–100, 115, 251–52

Vula. *See* Operation Vula

Asiatic Land Tenure and Indian Representation Act (Ghetto Act), 42

Asmal, Kader, 80, 82

Ayob, Ismail

and Mandela sell-out rumor, 302–3, 306–8

and Mandela-Tambo communication, 261, 280, 304, 311–12

Badenhorst, Piet, 148

Bantu people, 28

Bantustans

ANC position on, 155–56, 223

defined, 94

Bardien, Tofi, 167

Barnard, Niel

government restructuring, 401

meetings with Mandela, 243, 300, 301, 305, 324

Batane, Baba, 179–81

Bengu, Siegfried, 299

Berlin Wall, 87, 92

Bernal, J.D., 83

Bernstein, Hilda

escapes South Africa, 130, 131

propaganda committee, 108, 113–14

BARKEU . 553,554, 579, 614 [BIb.]

Bernstein, Rusty
  arrest (1963), 95n, 108, 113–14
  escapes South Africa, 114, 130
  and MK, 103
Beyleveld, Piet
  arrest (1963), 117
  on Central Committee, 106, 108,
    113
  interrogation of, 123
  state's evidence by, 145–46
Bhagwandeen, Rubbi, 192
Biko, Steve, 188
Bisho Stadium massacre, 393
Bizos, George, Little Rivonia Trial, 140,
  142–141, 145–46, 453
Black Authorities Act, 200
Black Consciousness
  Black Consciousness Movement
    (BCM), 188
  elements of, 188–89, 188n
Black Local Authorities (BLAs),
    200–201
Black Sash, 137n
Blomkamp, Peter, 382, 386
Blood River, Battle of (1838), 28
Bobat, Sabera, 282
Boers
  Anglo-Boer South African War, 29
  control of Cape, 26
  Voortrekker Great Trek, 27–28
  See also Afrikaners
Boipatong massacre, 392
Bophuthatswana (Bop)
  homeland plan, 94n
  succession threat, 394–95
Bose, Subhash Chandra, 54, 56
Boshoff, W.G., 143
BOSS (Bureau of State Security), 190
Botha, Major Hentjie, 290
Botha, Louis, 29
Botha, P.W.
  on apartheid, 199
  Mandela communication with, 302,
    314
  Nkomati Accord, 201
  reforms, 198–201, 239–40

  resignation of, 320
  Rubicon speech, 239–40
Boycott Movement (1960), 80, 84
Braam, Connie, 256–57
Breytenbach, Breyten, 257
Brill brothers, 106
British Communist Party (BCP)
  on African independence, 83
  Mac contact with, 79–80
British South Africa Company, 29
Brockway, Fenner, 83, 84
Broederbond, 30
Brown, Mannie, 105
Brutus, Dennis, 105
Bukharia, Essopbhai, 107
Bunting, Brian, 70
Bush, George H.W., 316, 339, 344
Buthelezi, Mangosuthu
  ANC position on, 295–96, 338
  anti-ANC position, 286, 293–94, 299,
    338–39
  and KwaZulu independence, 94n
  See also Inkatha

Cajee, Ameen, 108. See also Doha
Cape of Good Hope
  Boer control of, 26–29
  British control of, 26–29
  Dutch control of, 26
  slavery, origin of, 25–26
  white immigration to, 25–26
Capital punishment, in South Africa,
    138
Carim, Zarina. See Maharaj, Zarina
    (wife)
Carter, Jimmy, 193–94
Caste system, 41
Castro, Fidel, 96, 251
Central Committee of the Communist
  Party of South Africa (CPSA),
    62–63   CHASKALSON 453
Chetty, Manna, 80
Chiba, Chips, 226, 254
Chiba, Laloo
  arrest, 100–101
  on guerrilla training, 100

on Little Rivonia Trial, 138
at Robben Island, 8, 178–79
on Robben Island imprisonment, 153
trial of, 137–46
Chikane, Frank, 281–82
Ciliza, Henry, 197
Ciskei, homeland plan, 94n
Coetsee, Kobie
and Interim Constitution, 401–2
Mandela meetings, 243, 301–2
Cold war, end of and South Africa, 21,
33, 326
Colonialism of a Special Type (CST), 94
Coloured people
defined, 43
political parties of, 64
Robben Island conditions for, 148–49
voting discrimination, 30
Coloured People's Congress, 32n
Committee of Ten, 232–33
Communism
and ANC, 62–63, 71
appeal to colonized people, 79
East Germany. See German
Democratic Republic (GDR)
Freedom Charter arrests, 64
ideological position, 63
Mac, early association with, 65,
68–75, 79–80, 82–85, 103–17
Robben Island prisoners, 164–65
South Africa. 62–63. See also South
African Communist Party (SACP)
Soviet era, end of, 21, 314
Concentration camps, 91
Congress Alliance
formation of, 32n, 63
Freedom Charter (1955), 63–64, 71
Congress of Democrats
in Congress Alliance, 64
formation of, 32n
Congress Movement, 68
Congress of South African Trade
Unions (COSATU)
attacks on ANC, 469–70
formation of, 33
power of, 241–42, 263

Conservative Party
formation of, 200
growth of, 242
Constitutional Court, 452–53   **471**
Convention for a Democratic South
Africa (CODESA), 391–402
formation of, 391–92n
Mac negotiations, 391–96, 401–2
Convention for Free Speech, 54n
Cornforth, Maurice, 83
Cox, Idris, 83
Cronin, Jeremy, 357
Cross-situation, 471–72
Cuba
guerrilla warfare, 96, 99
Mac training, 251–52
Curtis, Jenny, 221

Dadoo, Dr. Yusuf
and Mandela autobiography, 213–14
passive resistance movement, 42–43,
54
Daniels, Eddie, 179
Danziger, Dr. Kurt
in London, 82
and New Age, 72
professional life, 72n
Davidson, Christo, 382
Death squads, 243, 276
Declaration of Intent (1991), 391
Defiance Campaign (1952), 32, 54–55,
63
De Klerk, F.W.
ANC ban lifted, 21, 335
apartheid, end of, 324, 339
apartheid repeal negotiation, 21, 305,
324–27, 337–39
government restructuring, 390–93,
398–400
popularity of, 390–92
releases Mandela, 21, 337–38
replaces Botha, 320
visits United States, 339
and Vula arrests/trial, 366–67,
371–72, 381n–82n, 386
De Lange, Damian, 254

De Lange, Pieter, 252
Democratic Alliance (DA), 473
Department of National Security
    (NAT), 220n
De Villiers, H.H.W., 137
D. F. Malan Accord (1991), 390
Dikeledi, Paul, 218, 223
Dingake, Michael
    propaganda committee, 108
    on Robben Island imprisonment,
        153–54
Dlamini, Chris, 281, 308
Dobb, Maurice, 83
Doha. See also Cajee, Ameen
    arrest, 126–29
    explosion injury, 116–17
Douglas, Bob, 255–56
Douglas, Helen, 255–56
Durban riots (1949), 44
Dutch East India Company, 25–26
Dutch Reformed Church, 242n
Dutt, Palme, 83

East Germany. See German Democratic
    Republic (GDR)
Ebrahim, Ebrahim, 223, 257
Educational discrimination, University
    of Natal, 65, 69–70
Eminent Persons Group (EPG), 301n
End Conscription Campaign (ECC),
    229
Ennals, Martin, 84
Erasmus, Gerrit, 122, 133
Esakjee, Solly, 104, 111
Esterhuyse, Willie, 261

Federation of South African Women
    (FSAW), in Congress Alliance, 64
First, Ruth
    leaves South Africa, 113
    on Mandela autobiography, 214
    and New Age, 70
    propaganda committee, 108–10
    on Swanepoel, 121
FirstRand, 397, 415–16, 438, 440
Fisher, Bram, 96, 108, 112–13

arrest (1963), 117
    and Little Rivonia Trial, 146
    Mac smuggled notes to, 127, 132
    Wilton testimony, 146
Fisher, Ilse, 142
Freedom Charter (1955), 63–64, 71, 241
Freedom Day strike (1950), 54n
Free State Republic, 47
Frontline states, 203n

Gandhi, Mohandas Karamchand
    Natal Indian Congress (NIC), 37–38,
        41–42
    passive resistance movement, 42–43,
        61
Gay, Lionel
    escape from South Africa, 145
    MK activities, 109, 111, 114, 139–40
    state's evidence by, 138–41, 144–45
Gebuza. See Nyanda, Siphiwe
Geneva Convention, 138
Geneva Protocol, ANC association
    with, 228–29
German Democratic Republic (GDR)
    African liberation, involvement in,
        87–88
    Berlin Wall, 92
    Mac in, 87–92
    political climate, 87–88, 91–92
Goldberg, Denis, arrest (1963), 95n
Goldreich, Arthur
    arrest (1963), 95n
    escape of, 134
    at Lilliesleaf Farm, 139
    and Mayibuye Operation, 96
    violence, training in, 98n
Goldstone Commission, 402–3
Gordhan, Ketso
    boycotts, 193
    on Mac, 396
    and restructured government, 407,
        409, 411–12
Gordhan, Pravin
    arrest/trial (1990), 383, 385–88
    in MDM, 298
    and Vula, 277, 282

Gqabi, Joe
    arrest (1976), 219n
    in Botswana, 221
    Mandela on, 155n
    murder of, 228
    at Robben Island, 155–56
Grabeck, Susan, 255–56
Great Britain
    communist party, 79–80, 83
    control of Cape, 26–29
    and decolonialization, 77, 82–83
    London, Mac early years, 79–86
    South African republic versus
        Commonwealth, 77–78
Great Trek, 27–28
Green Book (1979–80), 206–7, 222–23
Griqualand West, British annexation, 28
Groote Schuur Minute, 12, 343, 356
Group Areas Act (1950), 31, 46, 339
Growth, Employment, and
        Redistribution (GEAR), 410n
Guardian, The, 104
Guerrilla warfare
    Cuba, 96, 99
    Operation Mayibuye, 96
    Strategy and Tactics statement,
        187–88
Gwala, Harry
    arrest (1976), 219
    as danger to Vula, 266, 285–86, 361
    Mandela clash, 266
    at Robben Island, 155, 164–65, 285
    SACP interim leadership, 361–62
    scorched-earth policy, 264

Hani, Chris
    ANC memorandum, 186–88
    and MK, 235, 291
    Moloi, conflict with, 206
Harare Declaration, 262, 265–66, 313
    development of, 317–19, 330
Harmel, Michael, 85
Hefer Commission Inquiry, 421–33,
        445–46
Heilscher, Almut, 217
Hepple, Bob, arrest (1963), 95n

Hervormde National Party (HNP), 30
Hinduism, 41, 52–53
Hintze, Henning, 217
Hitler, Adolf, 91
HIV/AIDS, 449, 486–87, 490
Hobsbawm, Eric, 83
Hodgon, Jack, 98n
Homelands policy
    Bantustan, 94
    historical basis, 29
    See also Land ownership
Huddleston, Father Trevor, 84
Hunger strikes, Robben Island, 149,
        160, 175

Imber, Michael, 381
Indentured laborers, Indians as, 39–40,
        47
Independent Broadcasting Commission
        (IBC), 394
Independent Electoral Commission
        (IEC), 393
Independent Media Commission
        (IMC), 394
Indians
    -African relationship, 38, 53, 483
    ANC membership, 38, 43, 165, 215,
        483
    caste system, 41
    discrimination/restrictions against,
        40–42, 48, 53, 65, 67–68
    Gandhi campaign, 37–38, 42–43
    and Hinduism, 41, 52–53
    as indentured laborers, 39–40, 47
    Natal community, 39–41
    passenger Indians, 40–41
    passive resistance movement, 42–43,
        54
    political parties/organizations of, 32,
        37–38, 41–42, 56, 64, 73–74
    Robben Island conditions for, 148–49
    settlement restrictions, 41
Indian Youth Congress, 56, 74
Indigenous
    mass movements, 33
    of South Africa, 25–28

Influx control, abolition of, 31
Inkatha, 292–99
    anti-ANC position, 286, 293–94, 299,
        338–39
    formation of, 201–2
    Inkathagate, 408–9n
    Mandela on, 13–14
    postapartheid power play, 390–95
    and Vaal Triangle violence, 366–67
Inkululeko, 211
Interim Constitution (1993), 393,
    400–402
Internal Political Committee (IPC),
    354n
Internal Political and Reconstruction
    Department (IPRD)
    formation of, 203
    ineffectiveness of, 217–18
    Mac as secretary, 205–6, 215–16, 222
    rebuilding of, 222
International Bulletin, 85
Ismail, Aboobaker (Rashid), 230n–31n

Jassat, Abdulhay, 134
Jassat, Dr. Essop
    arrest (1963), 134
    treats Doha, 116
Jele, Josiah, 235
Jenkin, Tim, Vula communications
    system, 246, 254–55, 279, 280, 284
Joffe, Joel
    as ANC donor, 250
    on Little Rivonia Trial, 139, 146
Joffe, Dr. Max, 84
Joffe, Saura, 84
Jones, Cyril, 167
Jordan, Pallo, 220n, 325
Joseph, Dasu
    on guerrilla training, 100
    as London liaison, 154
    and MK, 105–6
    political activism, 97
Joseph, Paul
    on guerrilla training, 100
    and MK, 105
    political activism, 97

Joseph, Peter
    and MK, 105
    political activism, 97

Kabwe conference, 233–38
Kajee, A.I., 54
Kasrils, Ronnie
    indemnity for, 359–60
    and MK, 139, 223, 235, 254
    and SACP reorganization, 361–62
    and Vula, 278, 297, 331–32, 365
Kathrada, Ahmed
    arrest (1963), 95n, 112
    banning of, 102
    Communist Party, unit leader, 103–4
    and Doha, 116n
    political activism, 97
    at Robben Island, 147, 177–79
Kaunda, Kenneth, 216n
Khoikhoi people, 25, 26
Khrushchev, Nikita, 89
Kikia, Yusuf, 66
Kitson, Dave
    arrest (1963), 117
    MK activities, 108, 139, 141
    trial of, 137–46
Kodesh, Wolfie, 70
Kreuss, Anita, 255–56
Kriel, Hernus, 399
Kroonstad prison, 182–83
Kruger, Jimmy, 152, 189, 192
Kuluma, John (Mac pseudonym), 82
Kunene, Mazizi, 67
Kuzwayo, Judson, 194
KwaZulu
    homeland plan, 94n
    Inkatha, 201–2, 292–99

Labour Party, 30, 77
Lala, Raymond
    arrest/trial (1990), 383, 385–88
    and Vula, 278
Land Act 1913, 29
    1936, 93
Land ownership
    independent homeland plan, 93–94n

limits for Africans, 29
limits for Indians, 41–42
Lebowa, homeland plan, 94n
Lekota, Mosius Patrick "Terror," 345
Leo, Maud, 276–77, 289
Lessing, Doris, 84
Lewis, John, 83
Liberation Front of Mozambique
    (FRELIMO), 198
Lilliesleaf, 95–96, 139
Little Rivonia Trial, 137–46
    Beyleveld's state's evidence, 145–46
    Gay's state's evidence, 138–41,
        144–45
    judge, 143–44n
    lawyers/advocates, 138, 141
    Mac testimony, 142, 145–46
    sentencing, 146
    statements of accused, 146
Lobatse Conference (1962), 94–95n
Lodge, Tom, 187n
London School of Economics, Mac at,
    82, 86
Long Walk to Freedom (Mandela)
    Mac smuggling off Robben Island, 3,
        8, 177–79
    on Mandela sell-out, 328n
    transcription of, 8, 211, 213–14
Louw, Mike, 324
Love, Janet
    on Mac, 420
    and Vula, 278, 280, 369
Lusaka Manifesto, 216n

Mabhida, Moses, 73, 223
Mabizela, Stanley, 218
McBride, Robert, 208n, 398–400
Machel, Samora, 201
Macmillan, Harold, 77
Magoo's bar bombing, 207–8
Maharaj, Amilcar (son)
    birth of, 227–28
    and family life, 459–64
Maharaj, Sathyandranath Ragunanan
    (Mac)
    ANC minister of transport

(1994–1999), 3–4, 23, 396–97,
    405–13
apartheid repeal negotiations,
    315–20, 323, 328–32, 334–35
armed struggle. See Umkhonto we
    Sizwe (MK) (Spear of the Nation)
arrest (1964), 101, 117. See also Little
    Rivonia Trial (1964)
arrest/interrogation/trial (1990), 22,
    365, 370–80, 385–88
authority, attitude toward, 45–46,
    50–51, 57–58, 65
car bomb planted for, 388–89
children of. See Maharaj, Amilcar
    (son); Maharaj, Sekai (daughter)
CODESA negotiations, 391–96,
    401–2
communist association, 65, 68–75,
    79–80, 82–85, 103–117. See also
    South African Communist Party
    (SACP)
in Cuba, 251–52
escapes to Lusaka (1977), 194–97,
    210
eye, loss of, 66n
family/early years, 43–60, 64–74
family/fatherhood, 227–28, 458–66
at FirstRand, 397, 415–16, 438, 440
in GDR, 87–92
imprisonment. See Robben Island
indemnity granted, 11, 359–60
interrogation/torture of, 14–16,
    122–36, 372–74
as IPRD secretary, 205–6, 215–16,
    222
in London, early years, 75, 79–86
Mandela on, 1–20
on Mandela/ANC after release,
    346–64
and Mandela autobiography, 3, 8,
    177–79
-Mandela relationship, 4–9, 80,
    162–64, 341–42, 352–53, 372,
    377–80
Mandela sell-out rumor intervention,
    302–3, 306–9

Maharaj, Sathyandranath Ragunanan
     (cont.)
  and Marxism, 65, 69, 73, 90, 467–68
  and *New Age,* 68, 70–74, 80
  Ngcuka as spy investigation, 23, 417,
     419–34, 443–46
  and NIC, 73
  Operation Green Vegetables, 228–31
  personality descriptions, 4–6, 18–19,
     24, 33–37, 65–66, 101, 209–10,
     270–71, 420, 475–78
  postimprisonment activities, 190–97
  pseudonyms, 82, 106, 121–22, 127, 328
  retirement, 2–3, 341–42, 345–46,
     350–53, 362–63, 388, 397
  Scorpion investigation (2001–2005),
     36, 414–17, 438–46
  on South Africa (2006), 447–57
  South Africa, return to (1962–1964),
     101–17
  in Soviet Union, 272, 321, 323, 328
  suicide attempts, 126, 131–33, 135
  tax fraud investigation (2005), 446
  and Treason Trial (1956), 74
  underground propaganda campaign,
     103–17
  in United States (1986), 252–53
  at University of Natal, 65–75
  and Vula, 10–12, 244–59
  wives. *See* Maharaj, Tim (wife);
     Maharaj, Zarina (wife)
Maharaj, Sekai (daughter)
  birth of, 228
  father's absence, reaction to, 460,
     462–63, 466
Maharaj, Shanthee (sister), 45, 321
Maharaj, Tim (wife)
  as activist, 73–74, 88, 209
  arrest (1964), 101, 117, 121–22
  divorces Mac, 209–10, 212–13
  in London, 85–86, 209
  during Mac's trial, 142, 143
  marries Mac, 85–86
  nurse, work as, 109, 209, 212
  in prison, 133–34, 141

  Robben Island years, 173–74, 183,
     208–9
Maharaj, Zarina (wife)
  as activist, 227
  background information, 226–28
  Brighton residence, 330, 332, 335–36
  car accident/recovery, 280–81,
     321–23, 327, 329–30
  children of, 227–28, 230–31
  as columnist, 397
  intelligence agent accusation, 268
  on life with Mac, 458–66
  on Mac's unpopularity, 479–80
  and Scorpion investigation, 440–41,
     445
  Vula communications system, 10–11,
     246, 249, 254–55, 279
Makatini, Johnny, 215
Make, Cassius, 235, 237
Makgothi, Henry, 215, 221, 222
Malan, Magnus, 11, 408
Malherbe, Dr. E. G., 67
Mandela, Nelson
  on ANC Indian membership, 38, 165
  as ANC president, 23, 32*n*, 156–57,
     391
  as ANCYL leader, 62
  apartheid repeal negotiation, 243,
     253, 261, 266, 301–3, 337–38
  on armed conflict, 79, 204
  arrest/trial (1963–64), 95–97, 111–14
  autobiography, 3, 177–79, 211,
     213–14
  communist association, 63
  imprisonment. *See* Robben Island
  on Mac, 1–20
  -Mac relationship, 4–9, 80, 162–64,
     341–42, 352–53, 372, 377–80
  -Mbeki clash, 154–57, 266, 303, 326
  and MK, 32, 88, 95*n*, 114
  and NAC, 78–79, 95*n*
  personality descriptions, 156, 162–63
  policy, attitude toward, 156
  at Pollsmoor Prison, 301–2
  release from prison, 21, 337–38

MANDANI-481

sell-out rumor, 216–17, 262–63, 268, 300–303, 320
and South Africa restructuring, 391–93, 397–402
as Transvaal president, 32*n*
Treason Trial, 64, 74, 78
at Victor Verster Prison, 10, 302–5, 310–13
and Vula, 9–14, 262, 304–5, 309–13
and Vula arrests, 368–69, 371–72, 377–80
Mandela, Winnie, child activist death, 263
Mandla Judson Kuzwayo (MJK), 267*n*, 270
Mangope, Lucas, 394–95
Manning, Claudia, 282, 365
Manye, Christopher, 250
Mao Tse-tung (Mao Zedong), 69
Maphosho, Florence, 215
Mapumulo, Shadrack, 195–96
Mapungubwe people, 28
Maputo development corridor (MDC), 397*n*
Maree, Willie, National Party leader, 46, 55
Marks, J.B., 114
Marriage, mixed, prohibition of, 31
Marxism, and Mac, 65, 69, 73, 90, 467–68
Masemola, Jafta, 176
Maseru massacres, 235*n*
Masethla, Billy, 219*n*
Masondo, Andrew, at Robben Island, 155–56
Mass Democratic Movement (MDM)
ANC connection with, 247–48, 262–66, 281–82
component groups, 263
formation of, 242
and Harare Declaration, 317–20
and Mbeki, 264, 288
Mass movements
ANC "people's war" position, 207–8, 225–26, 232–33

increase in, 281
MDM. *See* Mass Democratic Movement (MDM)
message to whites, 33, 242
and trade unions, 241–42
See also Strikes
Matthews, John, trial of, 137–46
Matthews, Joe, on armed struggle, 86*n*
Matthews, Solly (Mac pseudonym), 106, 121–22, 127, 134
May Day strike (1950), 54
Mayibuye, 281
Mbeki, Govan
Afrikaner/ANC meetings, 261, 325
ANC member, 154*n*
arrest (1963), 32, 95*n*, 96
as danger to Vula, 266, 287–90, 303
in London, 80
in Lusaka, 215
-Mandela clash, 154–57, 266, 303, 326
and MDM, 264, 288
New Age, 70
and Operation Mayibuye, 96–97
at Robben Island, 147, 154–57, 175, 285
son. *See* Mbeki, Thabo
Mbeki, Thabo
ANC president, 23, 397, 470–73, 482
core of five nominees, 339*n*–41
and HIV/AIDS problem, 486–87, 490
and Ngcuka spy investigation, 417, 421–22, 443–45
"Path to Power," 261–62
and PMSC, 223
racial attitude, 473–74
Meer, Ismail, 54
Meli, Francis, 268
Memela, Totsie, 273
Memoirs (Kathrada), 156
Meyer, Roelf, 391, 392, 399, 401–2
Mfecane, 27
Mhlaba, Raymond
MK leader, 114
at Robben Island, 147, 155–57

CP IN HAVANA
271, 602
470

Middleton, Jean, 80
Minty, Abdul, 84
Mistry, Teeruth, 277
Mji, Diliza, 281, 288
MK. *See* Umkhonto we Sizwe (MK)
    (Spear of the Nation)
Mkhatshwa, Smangaliso, 281–82
Mkwayi, Wilton
    and armed movement, 110–11
    life sentence, 146
    on Little Rivonia Trial, 138
    MK leader, 99, 108–9, 112, 114–15
    trial of, 137–46
Mlangeni, Andrew, at Robben Island,
    147
Modise, Joe
    anti-Republic Day campaign, 224
    MK leader, 204, 218, 235
Mohamed, Yunus, 386
Mohamed, Yusuf
    arrest (1990), 374–75
    and intelligence gathering, 276–77,
        289
    and Maharaj house raid, 403
Mokgatle, Naboth, 84
Mokoape, Keith, 218
Mokoba, Peter, 268
Molefe, Jacqueline, 235, 254
Moloi, Lehlohonolo, 206*n*
Moloi, Super, 219*n*
Momoniat, Ismail, and Vula, 274–75,
    281, 302, 306
Monomotapa people, 28
Moola, Ibrahim, 104
Moola, Mosie, 134
Moosa, Valli
    and Mandela sell-out rumor, 306–9
    and Vula, 12, 262, 281, 302
Morobe, Murphy, 219*n*, 262, 281
Morogoro conference (1969), 204–5
Motlana, Dr. Nthato, 223
Motlanthe, Kgalema, 281, 288
Motsabi, John, 215, 216, 223
Motsoaledi, Elias, at Robben Island, 147
Movement for Colonial Freedom,
    82–83

Mozambique
    liberation movement, 198
    and Nkomati Accord, 201
Mozambique Resistance Movement,
    198
Mpabanga "we the poor," 164
Mposho, Florence, 216
Msimang, Mendi, 385, 488–89
Mufumadi, Sydney
    and MDM, 262, 281–82, 288
    on negotiation with government, 319
Multiparty Negotiating Process
    (MPNP), 393
Mvelase, Catherine (also known as
        Mvelase, Dipuo)
    arrest/trial (1990), 383, 385–88
    and Vula, 278
Mvulane, Baba, 179–81
Mxenge, Griffith, murder of, 228*n*–29
Mxenge, Victoria, murder of, 228*n*
Mzi, Dr. Diliza, 288

Naicker, George, 174
Naicker, Dr. G.M. "Monty"
    New Age, 72
    passive resistance movement, 42–43,
        54
Naicker, M.P., 70
Naidoo, Amah, 103
Naidoo, Indres
    on IPRD political committee, 223
    political activism, 97, 102–3
    retirement of, 101
Naidoo, Jayendra
    and Mandela sell-out rumor, 302,
        306
    and Mandla Judson Kuzwayo, 267*n*
    and MDM, 281
Naidoo, M.D.
    High Organ position, 157
    political activism, 73–74
Naidoo, M.J., 73
Naidoo, Phyllis, 196
Naidoo, Shanthie, 103, 107
Naidoo, "Steve" Nandha"
    arrest (1963), 134

as fellow student, 65
in London, 80, 82
training, in China, 108
in underground operations, 109
Naidoo, Tim. *See* Maharaj, Tim (wife)
Nair, Billy
  heart attack, 377
  meets Mac, 71, 73
  at Robben Island, 162
  and Vula, 258, 275, 281, 297, 303
Namibia, independence of, 314–15
Natal
  British annexation, 28
  Indian community, origins of, 39–41
Natal Indian Congress (NIC)
  formation of, 37–38, 41–42
  Mac membership, 73
  printing operation, 106–7
National Action Council (NAC),
  Mandela leadership, 78, 95*n*
National Executive Committee (NEC),
  return to South Africa, 244–45, 248
National Party (NP)
  bans ANC, 88
  Conservative Party faction, 200, 242
  and De Klerk presidency, 324
  established, 30–31
  party platform (1987), 242–43
National Security Management System
  (NSMS), 199, 241
National stay-at-home (1958), 84*n*
National Union of Metalworkers of
  South Africa (NUMSA), 317*n*
National Union of Mineworkers
  (NUM), 241, 263
National Union of South African
  Students (NUSAS), 71
National Union of Teachers, 82
National Union for Total Independence
  of Angola (UNITA), 198
Native Labour Regulation Act (1911), 29
Nazism, concentration camps, 91
Ndaba, Charles
  arrest (1990), 267–368
  and Vula, 277
Ndebele, 27

Necklacings, 233*n*
New Age
  banned, 104, 114
  Mac participation, 68, 70–74, 80
Newcastle
  coal miners strike, 42
  Maharaj family in, 43–60, 64–65
Ngcuka, Bulelani
  ANC activities, 417–18
  as spy investigation, 268, 417,
    419–34, 443–46
Nguni people, 27
Nhlanhla, Joe, 234, 275
Nicholls, Edward, 67
Nieuwoudt, Gideon, 373–74
Nkadimeng, John
  and IPRD, 219–22
  and NEC, 215, 294
Nkobi, Thomas
  ANC treasurer, 343
  as communist, 63
Nkomati Accord, 201, 231, 235
Nkrumah, Dr. Kwame, 76
Nokwe, Duma, propaganda committee,
  108, 112
Non-European Unity Movement
  (NEUM), 72
Nqakula, Charles, 250, 278
Nyanda, Siphiwe
  arrest/trial (1990), 12, 365, 368,
    378–83, 385–88
  after Mandela release, 352
  and MK, 223, 250
  self-defense units (SDUs) leader,
    379–80
  and Vula, 244, 250, 260, 272–74,
    277–78, 281–83, 285, 296–97
Nzima, 195, 197
Nzo, Alfred
  ANC acting president, 323–24,
    331–34
  ANC secretary-general, 215
  as communist, 63
  interim leaders announcement,
    350–51
  and Vula trial, 381*n*

Okhela, 257*n*
Omar, Dullah, 288, 308
Operation Bible
  on Ngcuka as spy, 417, 420, 424, 427
  and Vula, 267–70, 275–76
Operation Eagle, 357–59
Operation Green Vegetables, 228–31
Operation Mayibuye
  and ANC member arrests, 95–97
  ANC member disagreements, 154–55
  overthrow plans, 99–100
Operation Vula, 244–91
  ANC members against, 285–90
  arms smuggling, 262, 265, 283
  arrests/trial (1990), 365–89
  chronicle of, 265, 269, 302–3
  communications system, 10–11, 246,
    249, 254–55, 279–80
  effectiveness of, 262–72
  funding of, 249–50, 269–70, 355
  goals of, 244, 248, 260–61
  leadership quest, 248–49
  legal ANC participation issue, 353–56
  Mac arrest/interrogation (1990), 12,
    22, 365, 367–80
  and Mandela, 262, 304–5, 309–13
  Mandela on, 9–14
  and MDM, 247–48, 262–66, 281–82
  military operations, 282–83
  and Operation Bible, 267–70, 275–76
  South Africa, Mac return to, 245–46,
    250–59, 270–80
  structures of, 277–78
  underground activities, 244, 246,
    250–52, 255–59, 265, 269, 272–84
  Western Cape operation, 278, 291
Orange Free State, founding of, 28
Organization of African States (OAS),
  316*n*
Organization of African Unity (OAU),
  215
Ossewa Brandwag, 143
Ozinsky, Max, 278

Padmore, George, 69
Pahad, Aziz, 80, 335

Pahad, Essop, 80
Pan-Africanist Congress (PAC)
  armed section, 147
  exiled, 77
  formation of, 64   PARLIAMENT 470→
Pass books
  beginning of, 26, 27*n*, 29, 31
  for Indians, 41–43
Passenger Indians, goals in South
  Africa, 40–41
Passive resistance movement
  formation of, 42–43
  and Gandhi, 42–43, 61
  imprisonment of activists, 43, 53–54
Patel, Dipak
  arrest/trial (1990), 383, 385–88
  and Vula, 277
Pather, P.R., 54
"Path to Power," 261–62, 271
"People's war," ANC position, 207–8,
  225–26, 232–33
Phatudi, Cedric, 94*n*
Pieterson, Hector, 189
Piet Retief, 375
Pillay, Ivan
  Mandla Judson Kuzwayo (MJK), 267*n*
  and military operations, 223
  and Vula, 246–47, 279–80
Pillay, Krishna, 389
Pillay, Patsy, in London, 82, 84, 172
Pillay, Selina, 282
Pillay, Vella
  Anti-Apartheid Movement president,
    80
  letter from Robben Island, 172–73
  in London, 80, 82, 84, 86
Pipe bombs, 111, 115–16
Political parties
  of Afrikaners, 29–30
  of Coloureds, 64
  Communist, 62–63
  early parties, 29–31
  of Indians, 32, 37–38, 41–42, 56, 64,
    73–74
Politico-Military Council (PMC),
  234–36

Politico-Military Strategy Commission (PMSC), 206, 223
Pollitt, Harry, 79–80
Pollsmoor Prison, Mandela at, 301–2
Poll tax, for Indians, 41–42
Popular Movement for the Liberation of Angola (MPLA), 198
Population Registration Act (1950), 31, 339
Poqo, 147
Press, Ronnie, 246, 254–55
Pretoria Minute, 366–67, 371
Pretoria 12, 219n
Prohibition of Mixed Marriages Act (1949), 31
Project Avani, 436

Raadschelders, Lucia, 279
Rabkin, Sue, 213–14, 223
Ramaphosa, Cyril
    ANC negotiator, 392, 401
    ANC secretary-general, 391
    on Mac, 22, 396, 477
    and MDM, 262, 281–82, 288
    NUM leader, 242, 268
Reconstruction and Development Program, 405n
Record of Understanding (1992), 392–93, 397–400
Reddy, Dr. Freddy, 66n
Reflections in Prison, 7, 397
Release Mandela campaign, 211–12
Republic (South Africa)
    antirepublic campaign, 78–79, 224–25
    rationale for republic, 77–78
Reservation of Separate Amenities Act (1953), 31, 339
Revolutionary Council (RC)
    functions of, 203, 218
    inadequacy of, 205–6, 221
    and IPRD, 203, 220–22
Rhodes, Cecil John, 29
Rivonia
    Little Rivonia. See Little Rivonia Trial
    Rivonia Trial, 111–14

Road to South African Freedom, 94
Robben Island, 147–84
    ANC Communications Committee, 153, 155, 171–72
    ANC member discord, 154–57n
    ANC member rule breaking, 174–77
    ANC members study sessions, 6, 161, 165–66, 170–71, 178
    ANC operation in, 153–57, 161–62
    apartheid at, 148
    Communist Party operation in, 164–65
    hunger strikes, 149, 160, 175
    improved conditions at, 168–73
    international attention, 152, 169–70
    letter-writing method, 172–73
    living conditions, 148–52, 159–60, 165–66
    Mac communication system, 153–54
    Mac escape plan, 166–68
    Mac and Mandela autobiography, 3, 8, 177–79
    Mac-Mandela relationship, 4–8, 80, 162–64
    Mac release, 181–83
    Mac sentence, 146
    Mac-Sisulu relationship, 163
    Mac as teacher, 179–81
    Mandela leadership issue, 156–57n
    Mandela as prisoner representative, 152, 161
    Mandela release, 21, 337–38
    and political prisoners, 148
    visitation/mail restrictions, 150–51, 171, 173–74
Robeson, Paul, 83n
Rooi gevaar (red danger), 203
Roussos, Mike, 281
Routh, Guy, 84
Routh, Thelma, 84
Rubicon speech, 239–40

Sabotage
    Mac training in, 90
    by MK, 88, 93, 95
    and Republic Day, 224

Sabotage *(cont.)*
  by South African Communist Party, 88, 90, 100
  state security measures, 95, 118–19
Sabotage Act (1961), 95
Sachs, Albie, 84*n*
Sachs, Solly, 84
St. Aidan's Hospital, 377–78
Saloojee, Babla, murder of, 134–35
Sankar, Anesh, arrest/trial (1990), 378, 383, 385–88
San people, 25–26
Saponet, 280
Satyagraha (firmness in truth), 42
Savimbi, Jonas, 198
Schoon, Marius, 221, 222
Scorpions investigation (2001–2005), 36, 414–17, 438–46
Scott, Mpho, 277, 297, 298
Searchlight, The, 104
Sechaba, 207, 281
Security Branch
  functions of, 118*n*, 190
  informant for ANC, 267
  Shaik, torture of, 267
  surveillance of ANC/Mac, 191–92, 260
  Vula arrests, 365–80
Seedat, Dawood, 65–66, 68–69
Seedat, Hassim, 81–82
Seedat, Tony, 81–82
Self-defense units (SDUs), 390
  Nyanda as leader, 379–80
Selebi, Jackie, 326
Sexwale, Mathabatha Peter, 206*n*
Sexwale, Tokyo, 219*n*
Shaik, Moe
  corruption indictment (2005), 434–35
  government positions, 416
  and Maharaj house raid, 403
  and Mandla Judson Kuzwayo, 267*n*, 275
  and Ngcuka spy accusation, 420, 422, 424, 426–27, 430, 442

Shaik, Schabir
  arrest, 368
  Scorpions investigation, 414–15, 439–42
  and Vula, 270
Shaik, Soraya, 289
Shaik, Yunus, and Mandla Judson Kuzwayo, 267*n*
Sharpeville massacre (1960), 77–78, 86*n*
Shope, Gertrude, 215
Shubin, Vladimir, 251, 272
Singh, Debi, 54
Singh, J. Kissoon, 68, 195
Singh, J.N., 53–54, 75
Singh, Vish, 73
Sisulu, Albertina, 222
Sisulu, Walter
  ANC deputy president, 391*n*
  ANCYL leader, 62
  on armed struggle, 221
  arrest/trial (1963–64), 32, 95*n*, 96, 111–14
  as communist, 63 ,543-4
  -Mac relationship, 163
  and MK, 88, 114
  and Operation Mayibuye, 96–97
  personality descriptions, 163
  radio broadcast of, 139
  release from prison, 325, 331, 334
  at Robben Island, 147, 154–55, 157
Sithole, Jabu, 277, 297, 298
Slavery, beginning of, 25–26
Slovo, Joe
  ANC negotiator, 400–401
  exile from South Africa, 114
  Green Book, 222–23
  on Harare Declaration, 318–19
  Mac conflict with, 345, 350, 356–57
  on Mandela autobiography, 214
  and MK, 88, 103, 114, 235–36
  and Operation Mayibuye, 96
  in Special Operations, 218
  and termination of armed struggle, 365
  on violent practices, 98*n*

and Vula, 244–45, 249–51, 258–59
and Vula arrests, 371, 385
Smit, Basie, 371–73, 389
Smuts, Jan, 299
Sobukwe, Robert, 64
Socialism
and GDR, 87
phases in process, 83
South Africa
apartheid ends. *See* Apartheid abolished; South Africa, restructuring
arms deal (1998), 414*n*–15
Botha leadership. *See* Botha, P.W.
brutality of society, 135–36
chronology (1806–2006), xiii–xix
conditions in (2006), 447–57, 484–88
constructive engagement and U.S., 21
death penalty, 138
De Klerk leadership. *See* De Klerk, F.W.
early colonialism. *See* Cape of Good Hope
economic conditions (1960s–70s), 185–86
and Geneva Convention, 138
human rights abuses, 488
military training, 190
national identity issues, 481–82
people of. *See* African people; Afrikaners; Coloured people; Indians; whites
police/security agencies, 118*n*, 190, 199, 241, 243
political parties, early, 29–31
racial discrimination. *See* Apartheid
republic, referendum for (1960), 77–78
Soweto uprising, 188–90
states of emergency (1960, 1986, 1987), 21, 77–78, 241
trade sanctions, 88
tricameral constitution, 200
unemployment (2006), 447*n*–48
Union of South Africa, 29–31

Verwoerd leadership, 77–78, 93–94, 232
Vorster leadership, 95, 118, 189–90
South Africa, restructuring, 390–413
Convention for a Democratic South Africa (CODESA), 391–402
and De Klerk, 390–93, 398–400
government oversight commissions, 393–94
Growth, Employment, and Redistribution (GEAR), 410*n*
Interim Constitution, 393, 400–402
judiciary restructuring (2005), 453*n*–54*n*
Mac role in, 391–96, 401–2
Mandela/ANC role in, 391–93, 397–402
Reconstruction and Development Program, 405*n*, 410*n*
Record of Understanding (1992), 392–93, 397–400
Truth and Reconciliation Commission, 393
violence/unrest, 13, 367, 392–96
South African Coloured Organization, 64
South African Communist Party (SACP)
and ANC, 62–63, 71, 95
armed movement, support of, 100
ban lifted, 335
East German support of, 87–88
formation of, 62–63
Mac as member, 82
Mac breaks with, 359–63
Mac and reorganization (1990), 357–63
publications of, 85
Road to South African Freedom, 94
sabotage by, 88, 90, 100
South African Congress of Trade Unions (SACTU)
in Congress Alliance, 64
formation of, 32*n*
and IPRD, 216

South African Council of Churches (SACC), 137n
South African Defense Force (SADF), 190, 198
South African Freedom Association, 80, 84
South African Indian Congress
  in Congress Alliance, 64
  formation of, 32
South African Institute of Race Relations (SAIRR), 137n
South African Police (SAP)
  increase in force, 190
  See also Security Branch
South Africa Party (SAP), 30
Southwest Africa People's Organization (SWAPO), 121, 198, 315
Soviet Union
  communism, end of, 21, 314
  Mac in, 272, 321, 323, 328
  MK, support of, 88
Soweto Council, 64n
Soweto uprising, 188–90
Spaarwater, Maritz, 324
Spear of the Nation. *See* Umkhonto we Sizwe (MK) (Spear of the Nation)
Sports Parade, 105, 109, 111, 114
Stand by Our Leaders campaign, 74
State Security Council (SSC)
  death squads, 243, 276
  growth of power, 199
Stay-at-homes
  national (1958), 84n
  See also Strikes
Stein, Sylvester, 84
Strachan, Harold
  in London, 80
  violence, training in, 98n
Strategy and Tactics document, 187–88, 204
Strikes
  African mineworkers (1946), 62
  antirepublic campaign (1960), 78–79
  Indian coal miners (1913), 42
  mass workday loss (1987), 241
  May Day (1950), 54

mineworkers (1918, 1987), 32, 241
national stay-at-home (1958), 84n
success of, 191n
and trade union emergence, 191n
Suez Canal crisis, 87
Suppression of Communism Act (1950), 62
Swanepoel, T.J. "Rooi Rus," Mac interrogation/torture, 14–16, 118, 120–26
Swart gevaar (black threat), 29, 203

Tambo, Oliver
  ANC leader, 93, 201, 202, 333
  ANCYL leader, 62
  effectiveness of, 333
  holistic approach of, 261
  Mac escape plan, 194
  Mac briefing to (1977), 211–12
  Mandela communication with, 261, 280, 304–5, 311–14
  on Mandela sell-out rumor, 216–17, 320
  and negotiation with apartheid regime, 314–20
  stroke, 323, 330
  on tricameral constitution, 201
  in United States, 253
  and Vula, 244–45, 249–51, 260–61, 263
Tausand, 179–81
Thatcher, Margaret, 266, 296, 315
Tloome, Dan, propaganda committee, 108, 112, 127
Torture
  forms of, 119–25
  legal support of, 119
  of Mac, 14–16, 122–36, 372–74
  Mandela on, 14–16
  Truth and Reconciliation Commission, 120
Trade sanctions, 88
Trade unions
  COSATU, 33, 241–42
  emergence of, 31, 191n
  NUMSA, 317n

power of, 241–42
See also Strikes
Transitional Executive Council (TEC),
    393
Transkei, homeland plan, 94*n*
Transvaal
    founding of, 28
    provinces established (1994), 28*n*
Transvaal Asiatic Ordinance (1906),
    42–43
Transvaal British Indian Association, 42
Treason Trial (1956)
    Mac support, 74
    Mandela apartheid statement, 78
    outcome of, 64
Treatment Action Campaign (TAC),
    449*n*
Treaty of Amiens (1803), 26
Tricameral constitution
    operation of, 200
    opposition to, 200–201
Truth and Reconciliation Commission
    (TRC)
    judiciary, findings on, 137
    mandate for, 393
    torture victims statements, 120
Tshabalala, Henry, 64*n*
Tshabalala-Msimang, Manto, 486–87
Tshabalala, Mbuso
    arrest (1990), 367–68
    and Vula, 277
Tshabalala, Siphiwe, 64*n*
Tshabalala, Susan
    arrest/trial (1990), 383, 385–88
    and Vula, 278
Tshabalala, Vusi, 277
Tshwete, Steve
    and MK, 235, 356
    and NEC, 363, 490

Umkhonto we Sizwe (MK) (Spear of
    the Nation), 87–88
    and ANC, 95, 99–100
    attacks by (1980s), 207–8
    ban lifted, 335
    East German/Soviet support of, 87–88

formation of, 32, 88
goals of, 88
leadership, 88, 114
Mac activities, 90, 97–98, 103–8,
    110–11
Mac bomb making, 114–17
Mac as commissar, 114–15
Mac printing operation, 103–8, 111,
    115
and Mandela, 32, 88, 114
Mandela on ANC link, 95*n*
Mandla Judson Kuzwayo (MJK), 267*n*
and Operation Mayibuye, 95–97,
    99–100
sabotage by, 88, 93, 95
training of members, 90, 98*n*,
    99–100, 115
See also Armed anti-apartheid
    movement
Umsebenzi, 281
Underground. *See* Operation Vula
Union of South Africa
    apartheid, institutionalization of,
        29–31
    political parties, early, 29–31
    racial discrimination, 29
Unions, labor. *See* Strikes; Trade unions
United Democratic Front (UDF)
    component groups, 263
    formation of, 33, 200–201, 232
    Inkatha conflict, 243, 292–99
United Party (UP), 30
United South African National Party, 30
United States
    ANC meeting, 252–53
    constructive engagement, 21
    De Klerk visit, 339
    Mac visit (1986), 252–53
University of Natal
    Mac at, 65–75
    racial discrimination, 65, 69–70

Vaal Triangle violence (1990), 13, 367
Vaal uprising (1984–85), 201
Van der Merwe, Fanie, CODESA
    negotiations, 391–96, 401

Van der Merwe, Willem, 118, 122
Van Rensburg, Nic, 130–31
Van Zyl Slabbert, Frederick, meets with
    ANC, 243
Vawda, Yusuf, 258
Venda, homeland plan, 94n
Venter, Frik, 374–75, 377
Verwoerd, Hendrik, apartheid policy,
    77, 93–94, 232
Victor Verster Prison, Mandela at, 10,
    302–5, 310–13
Viktor, Johannes Jacobus, 122
Viljoen, Constand, 394
Vlok, Adriaan, 377
Voegelsang, Antoinette, 278–79
Voortrekkers, Great Trek, 27–28
Vorster, John, 95, 118
    and Soweto uprising, 189–90
Voting rights
    limits for Africans/Coloureds, 30
    oversight commission, 393
Vula. See Operation Vula

Wankie campaign, 186–87
Wemme, Walter, 89
Wessels, Elsabe, 370
Wessels, Leon, 399, 401
Western Cape Operation, 278, 291
Whites
    Afrikaners, 26, 29–30
    Boers, 26–28
    British, 26–29
    Cape of Good Hope settlers, 25–26
Wiehahn Commission, 191n
Willemse, W.H., 301
Williamson, Craig, 135n
Wills, Ashley, 193n–94n, 252n

Wimpy Bar bombing, 207n–8n,
    236–37
Wolpe, Harold, 104, 134
Woodis, Jack, 83
World Conference for Action Against
    Apartheid, 214–15
World War I era, 30
World War II era, 30, 53, 76, 80

Xhosa people, 27
Xundu, Reverend M., 287–88, 340

Yacoob, Zak, 192, 386

Zukas, Cynthia, 84
Zukas, Simon, 84
Zulu, Joshua, 299
Zulu, Maxwell, 268, 428
Zulu people, 27–28
    Inkatha, 201–2, 292–99
Zulu, Thami, 428
Zuma, Jacob
    ANC leadership positions, 417,
        469–70
    corruption accusation (2006), 435,
        488–91
    escapes South Africa, 219, 221–22
    and Mandla Judson Kuzwayo, 267n
    and Ngcuka spy accusation, 420–23,
        426, 433
    and Operation Bible, 267, 275, 288
    rape charge, 436–38
    Scorpions investigation, 414–17
    and Vula, 366
    Zulu image, 470
Zwangendaba, 311
Zwelithini, Goodwill, 201